Second Edition

deutsch aktuell 2

Teacher's Edition

Wolfgang S. Kraft

EMC Publishing, Saint Paul, Minnesota

ABOUT THE AUTHOR

Wolfgang S. Kraft, a native of Germany, is Director of Foreign Languages of EMC Publishing. He graduated from the University of Minnesota with a B.A., B.S., and M.A. degrees, and has taught German at University High School, Minneapolis, Minnesota; White Bear Senior High School, White Bear Lake, Minnesota; Bethel College, St. Paul, Minnesota, as well as in several adult education programs.

Mr. Kraft also has been a Native Informant at NDEA Foreign Language Institutes, has participated on various foreign language panels, and conducted many foreign language workshops.

Besides writing and taking most of the pictures for *Deutsch: Aktuell*, Mr. Kraft has authored several other German programs among them *So sind die Deutschen* and *Passport to Germany*.

Mr. Kraft has traveled extensively throughout German-speaking countries to accumulate vital and up-to-date information indispensable in the development of *Deutsch: Aktuell*.

ISBN 0-8219-0083-8

Published by EMC Publishing
300 York Avenue
St. Paul, Minnesota 55101

Printed in the United States of America
0 9 8 7 6 5 4 3 2

CONTENTS

SCOPE AND SEQUENCE CHART

LEKTION	DIALOG	ERGÄNZUNG	ÜBUNGEN	LESESTÜCK 1
11	*Auf dem Flughafen* (München)	luggage & other bags; airport personnel & facilities; parts of the body	word order of dative & accusative pronouns; reflexive verbs & pronouns suffixes *-ig*, *-lich* & *-isch*	*Eine Reise nach Deutschland* (USA — Frankfurt)
12	*Gehen wir surfen!* (Schluchsee/ Schwarzwald)	holidays & holiday greetings	past tense — narrative past tense (regular & irregular verbs); *gern-lieber*; infinitives used as nouns	*Eine Hochzeit in Neubrandenburg*
13	*In einem Wiener Café* (Wien)	professions	genitive; verbs with prepositions	*Ein Besuch in Bremen*
14	*Der Briefträger kommt* (Lienz)	writing a letter; mail items; addressing mail; post office facilities	demonstrative pronouns; adjectives after *der-* words	*Auf der Post* (Essen-Werden)
15	*Im Zoo* (Heidelberg)	animals; rooms of a house	adjectives after *ein-* words; adjectives used as nouns; adjectives not preceded by articles	*Das Leben in einer Kleinstadt in der DDR* (Ostrau)
C			*Flughafen, Hafen oder Bahnhof?;* essay; questions; identification of sights; abbreviations; present tense; word description; adjectives	*Beim Karneval oder Fasching*

ERWEITERUNG	RÜCKBLICK	LESESTÜCK 2	SPRACHSPIEGEL	KULTURECKE
questions; compound nouns; *Wie heißt das . . .?*; word definition; responses; identification	possessive adjectives; present, future & present perfect tense; sentence completion	*Wien — die Hauptstadt Österreichs*	dialog construction; essay; *Du bist dran!*	*Means of Transportation*
questions; *Wie heißt das . . .?*; sentence completion, word definition; responses	reflexive verbs; dative & accusative pronouns (word order); past & present perfect tense; dative & accusative prepositions	*Bern — die Hauptstadt der Schweiz*	essay; holidays; *Du bist dran!*	*Holidays & Festivals in Germany*
Wie heißt das . . .?; *Wer bin ich?*; responses; word description; questions	parts of the body; past tense; holidays	*Das Fürstentum Liechtenstein*	essay; dialog construction; *Du bist dran!*	*Bavaria*
questions; *Wie heißt das . . .?*; word description; matching words; responses	genitive; sentence completion; prepositions, past tense	*Fußball ist König* (Frankfurt)	dialog construction; writing a letter; *Du bist dran!*	*Youth Activities in the DDR*
questions; *Wie heißt das . . .?*; sentence completion; word definition; responses	questions; adjectives; sentence completion	*Das Studentenleben in der DDR*	essay; description; *Du bist dran!*	*Life in the DDR*
		Ein Ausflug zum Zoo		Cultural Notes: postal service

LEKTION	DIALOG	ERGÄNZUNG	ÜBUNGEN	LESESTÜCK 1
16	*Im Restaurant* (Düsseldorf)	dishes & silverware; menu	prepositions with dative or accusative; *da/dahin — dort/dorthin*; *da-* & *wo-* compounds; verbs with dative	*Wandern an der Ahr*
17	*Im Geschäft* (München)	store departments; fruits & vegetables	modal auxiliaries (past & present perfect); past perfect tense; question words	*Frau Nobel kauft ein* (Essen-Werden)
18	*In der Apotheke* (Altenmarkt)	ailments; medicine	relative pronouns; conjunctions	*Beim Arzt* (Düsseldorf)
19	*Beim Fahrunterricht* (Deggendorf)	parts of a car; traffic signs	passive voice; infinitive construction with *zu* & *um . . . zu*	*In der Werkstatt* (Landshut)
20	*Im Büro* (Stuttgart)	office equipment; letter format; letter	subjunctive	*Singers sind im Urlaub* (Müritz See)
D			word categories; questions; past & present perfect tense; sentence completion; active/passive; relative pronouns	*Hoffmanns fahren in die Ferien*

ERWEITERUNG	RÜCKBLICK	LESESTÜCK 2	SPRACHSPIEGEL	KULTURECKE
questions; sentence completion; *Wie heißt das . . .?*; word definition	adjectives; sentence completion; *Wie heißt das . . .?*	*Wie und wo essen die Deutschen?*	dialog construction; word definition; *Du bist dran!*	*Foods*
questions; word description, *Wie heißt das . . .?*, word categories; questions; matching words	past, present perfect & past perfect tense; sentence construction; articles & adjectives; verb forms	*Auf dem Markt*	essay; questions; *Du bist dran!*	*A Tour through a Department Store*
compound nouns; *Wie heißt das . . .?*; word definition; word description; questions	past, present perfect & past perfect tense; question words; word recognition	*Wo kann man übernachten?*	dialog construction; *Du bist dran!*	*Housing*
questions; sentence formation; *Wie heißt das . . .?*; compound nouns; word description	relative pronouns; sentence construction; sentence completion; articles & adjectives; matching words	*Die Deutsche Lufthansa*	essay; situational description; *Du bist dran!*	*Measure for Measure*
sentence completion; *Wie heißt das . . .?*; questions; word description	passive; question formation; articles & adjectives	*Weinbau an der Deutschen Weinstraße*	essay; situational dialog; *Du bist dran!*	*Famous Castles in Germany*
		In der Tankstelle	Interview: *Freizeitgestaltung der Deutschen*	Cultural Notes: dialects; eating manners; visiting Germans

INTRODUCTION

This new edition of *Deutsch: Aktuell* is the result of extensive research involving hundreds of teachers who have used the previous edition, numerous discussions at professional workshops and application of the state-of-the-art in the field of foreign language instruction.

The strength of *Deutsch: Aktuell* becomes apparent in the variety of exercises presented, as well as in the cultural coverage of all German-speaking countries (West Germany, East Germany, Switzerland, Austria and even Liechtenstein).

Recent trends in both foreign language methods and technology have made it possible to add microcomputer software to this basal textbook program. *Deutsch: Aktuell* is perhaps the most comprehensive German textbook series today. Each level of *Deutsch: Aktuell* now includes these components: *textbook*, *teacher's edition*, *workbook*, *test booklet*, *sound-filmstrips*, *tape program* and *microcomputer software*.

Deutsch: Aktuell is not just a reworked textbook, but a completely rewritten and redesigned textbook. The major improvements are the use of full-color photos and illustrations throughout, addition of creative and communication activities, more up-to-date situations showing everyday German life, the listing of both German-English and English-German vocabulary sections, easy chapter identification and, finally, a more systematic introduction of the grammar.

Extensive research and a survey revealed that more than 75% of the students who had used the first edition textbooks were able to finish each book in one year. For that reason, the level of difficulty has been maintained. Furthermore, the number of lessons in the textbook is still twelve (ten regular and two review). Based on an average school year, it is estimated that each lesson will take about three weeks to complete.

In summary, *Deutsch: Aktuell* teaches the language and culture of today. The material has been reviewed by many young adults in Germany and the various situations and themes were judged by them to be realistic and true to life.

A WORD ABOUT THIS TEACHER'S EDITION

The purpose of this section of the teacher's edition is to provide a complete overview of *Deutsch: Aktuell 2* (Scope and Sequence Chart), outline the components of the program, suggest a step-by-step approach to teaching a lesson, and give a detailed description of each lesson — including objectives and recommended games and activities, as well as background notes on the cultural material presented.

This teacher's edition contains an annotated version of the student textbook. Marginal notes, printed in red, include numerous comments and suggestions expanding the material to provide additional information that may be useful to the teacher. Furthermore, the teacher will find the answers to the oral exercises included in this teacher's edition.

COMPONENTS

Deutsch: Aktuell is a two-level German language program designed to meet the needs of today's language students. Each level includes the following components:

- textbook
- teacher's edition
- workbook
- test booklet (end-of-unit *written* and *listening comprehension* tests)
- sound-filmstrips
- tape program (exercises and tests)
- microcomputer software

TEXTBOOK

Similar to the first-level textbook, this textbook contains twelve lessons (ten regular and two review lessons), a grammar summary, a vocabulary summary (German/English *and* English/German) and an index. The grammar and vocabulary summaries, as well as the index, combine grammar and vocabulary introduced in both books. As an additional feature, reading selections have been included in this second-level textbook.

Lesson Format

Dialog — Each dialog dramatizes a situation typical of everyday life in German-speaking countries. The speakers in the dialogs represent a cross-section of age groups from different parts of German-speaking countries.

Most dialogs have been divided into several sections so that each section can be treated as a mini-dialog to facilitate the learning process. The dialogs are presented visually on the accompanying filmstrips. These on-location, full-color photos reenact the printed and audio material, thus providing a more meaningful situation. Each dialog exemplifies grammatical structures to be learned as well as those previously introduced. Its vocabulary is limited to words already presented, with the exception of new words to be learned within the context of the conversations. Following the dialog are questions carefully structured to review the content of the dialog. Finally, there is the English version of the dialog that will assist the student in clarifying the meaning. This version is not a literal translation. Consequently, the student should be cautioned not to compare individual words.

Nützliche Ausdrücke — This section extracts useful and idiomatic expressions from the *Dialog* and *Lesestück 1*.

Sprichwort — Each lesson includes a well-known proverb, which students should be encouraged to memorize. To facilitate understanding of the meaning, a literal translation as well as the equivalent English proverb are presented.

Ergänzung — This section expands the topic of the lesson theme and provides additional language and cultural information.

Übungen — A grammar explanation leads off each exercise section. After the grammatical structure has been explained, several oral and written exercises illustrating the grammar point are introduced. For easy identification, the oral exercises have been marked with the symbol 🎤 and the written exercises with the symbol ✏ . Of course, many of the oral exercises can be changed to written ones and vice versa. The *du* form has been used in most exercises. The teacher may wish to change the instructions and/or question-answer exercises using *Sie*, depending on the circumstances.

Lesestück 1 — This reading selection introduces additional cultural situations that occur in everyday German life. This is another section where the student can see the visual sequence in the filmstrip. The new vocabulary is presented in the margin for easy reference. New words and phrases are indicated by the symbol°. Questions follow the reading selection to help the teacher measure the student's comprehension of this material.

Erweiterung — Additional exercise material is presented in this section. A wide variety of communication exercises are provided to challenge the student's understanding of the grammatical and cultural content of the lesson.

Rückblick — The review section reenters the various grammatical structures learned in previous lessons. Continuous review of this type, along with that in the two review units, insures retention and reinforcement of previously learned material.

Lesestück 2 — This reading selection familiarizes the student with geographical and cultural features of all German-speaking countries (West and East Germany, Austria, Switzerland and even Liechtenstein). This section is also supported by the accompanying filmstrip section.

Sprachspiegel — This section provides numerous opportunities for the student to become involved creatively in language expression, such as writing short essays and constructing dialogs based on information provided. Whereas the first-level book presented mini-situations in the *Wie sagt man's* section, this textbook includes a section called *Du*

bist dran! Students are given the opportunity to complete short situations, thus becoming more involved in the creative process.

Kulturecke — This section presents, in a mini-social studies format, a cross-cultural approach. The text is presented in English so that students, from the very beginning, can be exposed to important cultural information. In the filmstrips, on-location photography reinforces each cultural topic.

Vokabeln — The vocabulary section gives the student an easy reference source to the new words introduced in each lesson. Nouns are listed with their plural forms and verbs include stem vowel changes where appropriate. The past and present perfect tense of strong (irregular) verbs are also provided. The vocabulary meaning is confined strictly to those words introduced in the particular lesson. In cases where the meaning of the same German word changes, the word is listed again in subsequent lessons.

Selected Readings — A number of readings have been selected from EMC's *Easy Readers*, a series of shortened and simplified texts adapted from the works of well-known German authors. The individual excerpts appear in sequential order in terms of vocabulary and grammar difficulty. The vocabulary words not included in the vocabularies at the end of the book are explained in the margin of the line in which the word or phrase appears.

Grammary Summary — The grammar introduced in *Deutsch: Aktuell* has been summarized in this section for convenient reference.

Vocabulary — The total vocabulary from both levels has been listed here for easy reference. Each word or phrase is followed by a number indicating the lesson in which it appears for the first time. For convenient and flexible use, both German-English and English-German vocabularies have been provided.

Index — A complete index of all the grammar and cultural material presented in both levels is provided at the end of the book for easy reference and location.

TEACHER'S EDITION

This teacher's edition contains the following sections:

- scope and sequence chart
- components
- teaching approaches (model unit)
- an introduction to each of the *Lektionen*
  1. instructional objectives
  2. *Allerlei* — suggestions on teaching the cultural material (activities, games, class or individual projects)
  3. background information for the *Dialog*, *Lesestück 1*, *Lesestück 2* and *Kulturecke*
- annotated version of the student textbook

WORKBOOK

The workbook expands the material introduced in the textbook. It includes numerous written exercises that reinforce the language skills and the culture covered in the textbook. Various exercises, including practical paraphernalia of German life, allow the student to get the gist of the original material. An answer key for all exercises contained in the workbook is also available.

TEST BOOKLET

The test booklet includes two sections: (1) the student answer sheets for the *listening comprehension tests* for each lesson and (2) the *written tests* for each lesson.
Listening Comprehension Tests have been recorded and are part of the tape program. The tests provide various ways of checking how well students have learned the material of each lesson. A typical test includes a listening comprehension section (short conversations or narratives) and tests on *Lesestück 1* and 2 as well as the *Kulturecke*. The recorded material (with an answer key) for all of the listening comprehension tests is printed in the teacher's edition of the test booklet.
Written Tests have been prepared for each lesson. These tests are intended to be given to the students after each lesson has been completed. An answer key to the written tests also has been included in the teacher's edition of the test booklet.

SOUND-FILMSTRIPS

A total of ten full-color filmstrips and ten cassettes (one for each regular lesson) and a transcript are part of this level. Each filmstrip contains an average of about 100 on-location photos, carefully coordinated with the printed and recorded sections of the *Dialog*, *Lesestück 1*, *Lesestück 2* and *Kulturecke*.

It should be stressed here that the photography scenes in the filmstrips were taken in many different parts of German-speaking countries. An attempt has been made to familiarize students with various aspects of German culture in different regions. Furthermore, the emphasis in the scenes has been placed on situations depicting everyday life.

Different voices from many different parts of Germany have been recorded on the cassettes so that students will hear a variety of native speakers. Whenever appropriate, sound effects have been added, particularly in the *Dialoge*, in order to provide a more authentic and meaningful situation. The *Kulturecke* has been recorded both in English (for beginning students) and in German (for more advanced students). Teachers wishing to present the German version of the *Kulturecke* should begin the visual presentation with the title frame for this section and advance the cassette sound track to the beginning of the German material that follows the English equivalent.

The manual accompanying the sound-filmstrips includes the complete text of each lesson with indication of frame numbers for easy identification.

TAPE PROGRAM

The tape program is an integral part of *Deutsch: Aktuell 2*. The following material has been recorded on cassettes or reel-to-reel tapes:

Lektionen 11–20 (Cassettes/Tapes 1–10)

Dialog — introduced first as a listening experience and then broken into manageable phrases for student repetition.
Nützliche Ausdrücke — for student repetition.
Ergänzung — for student repetition.
Übungen — a variety of exercises such as substitution, transformation and communication. The specific exercises recorded have been marked in the textbook with the symbol ▨ .
Erweiterung — additional exercises to reinforce and expand the lesson content.
Lektionen C-D (Cassette/Tape 11) — A review lesson follows each fifth lesson and includes short reading selections, dialogs, useful expressions, exercises summarizing and reinforcing previously learned material, and cultural information.
Tests (Cassettes/Tapes 12–14) — A test that measures comprehension of the material covered is included for each of the ten regular lessons. Special emphasis has been placed on the listening skill and understanding of the readings and cultural material introduced in each lesson.

MICROCOMPUTER SOFTWARE

A set of ten diskettes (one per lesson) is available. The purpose is to review, reinforce and expand the grammatical and cultural material of each lesson. It is also an excellent device to give students who need help a source for independent study.

TEACHING APPROACHES

Model Unit (Lektion 12)

Instructional approaches vary considerably among teachers. Furthermore, the length of each class period often differs from one school to the next. Consequently, it is impossible to provide a detailed plan for each individual lesson that would apply to all students using this material.

We have, however, selected one lesson from *Deutsch: Aktuell 2* to provide some guidelines for using the content successfully. Needless to say, teachers will find some useful information here but may not want to follow each individual suggestion as presented. We have chosen *Lektion 12* as our model unit.

Because class periods vary in length, we have arbitrarily chosen a 50-minute period and planned the learning activities accordingly. On the basis of a 50-minute period and a schedule of 170 to 180 school days, it is estimated that *Deutsch: Aktuell 2* can be covered in its entirety (ten regular lessons and two review lessons) in one year at the high school level.

DAY 1

1. Review
— Go over sections from *Lektion 11* that you feel students had difficulties with, after checking their unit tests.
— You may want to use some of the exercises from the *Rückblick* section of *Lektion 12*. Be sure to personalize the material as much as possible.
2. Introduce *Lektion 12* by going over the main objectives of the lesson. You may wish to refer to the "Instructional Objectives" listed in this teacher's edition (at the beginning of *Lektion 12*).
3. Introduce the dialog, *Gehen wir surfen!* (p. 27)
— Play the recorded material so that students can become familiar with the content as well as the different native speakers. If possible, show the accompanying filmstrip sequence of the dialog portion while your students listen to the recorded section.
— Ask questions or have students ask each other questions about this particular situation. For example: *Wie ist das Wetter?*, *Wie kommen die Jungen zum See?*, *Wie heißt der See?*, *Wo ist Matthias' Surfbrett?*, *Was tragen sie alle zum Strand?*, *Wer geht zuerst surfen?*, etc.
— Show and/or play the first third of the dialog section once more.
— Practice pronunciation of the first section. Have students repeat individual sentences that you may want to break down into parts. Students should follow along in their textbooks for better understanding.
— Ask simple, but detailed questions about the first section. Find out if your students noticed the past tense of *haben* in the sentence *Das letzte Mal hatten wir Pech*. See if they can tell you what the meaning is and then go on to the next point.
4. Introduce the past tense (p. 31).
— Explain the use of the past tense (often used in story telling) versus the present perfect tense (mostly used in conversation).
— Discuss the formation of regular verb forms in the past tense.
— Go over *Übungen 1–4* (p. 33).
Assignment
1. Review the first third of the dialog (p. 27).
2. Review *Übungen 1–4* (p. 33).

DAY 2

1. Review

— Play the first third of the dialog (p. 27). Ask questions.
— Have students role-play parts of the dialog and ask each other questions.
— Spot-check *Übungen 1–4* (p. 33) to make sure that your students understand the material.
2. Introduce the past tense forms of irregular verbs. Have students look at the list of all irregular verb forms (p. 32). This list offers a good opportunity to review the meaning of all these verbs. Also, tell your students that each irregular verb form has its past and present perfect tense form listed in the lesson and end vocabulary.
— Pick some of the verbs and provide some sample sentences for better understanding. Find out if your students can come up with the proper forms.
— Go over *Übungen 5–7* (pp. 33–34).
3. Introduce the second third of the dialog. You may wish to play this section on the tape. Ask questions to assure complete understanding.
4. Introduce the names of the holidays and expressions for special occasions in the *Ergänzung* (p. 30). If you have a calendar you can expand this section by reviewing the days and the months. Discuss the similarities and differences of holidays in the U.S. and in Germany. You may want to use the detailed description on pages TE15-16 of this front section.
5. Begin reading *Lesestück I* (p. 290), *Es klingelt an der Tür*.
— Have students read through the introduction to the *Selected Readings* to familiarize them with the symbols and general marginal notes.
— Have students read aloud as pronunciation practice.
— Ask questions about each section or have students ask each other.
Assignment
1. Study the first two sections of the dialog (p. 27).
2. Review *Übungen 1–7* (pp. 33–34).

DAY 3

1. Review
— Go over *Übungen 1–7*, picking some material that you feel students need to practice.
— Ask questions about the first two sections of the dialog.
2. Complete *Übungen 8–9* (p. 34). For additional practice you may want to go back to *Lesestück I* of *Lektion 11* (pp. 12-14) and ask students to put the sentences into the past tense.
3. Finish reading *Lesestück I* (p. 290). Ask questions as you read through the material.
4. Go over the last part of the dialog (p. 27). You may want to play this section on tape. Ask questions and have students read individual parts.
5. Introduce the game *Ratet mal!* described on page TE15 of this front section.

Assignment
1. Do workbook exercise 1.
2. Review *Lesestück I* (p. 290).

DAY 4

1. Review
— Go over the complete dialog. Ask detailed questions.
— Go over workbook exercise 1.
— Review Lesestück I.
2. Have students complete *Übung 10* (p. 34).
3. Introduce *Lesestück 1* (p. 37). Have students read individual paragraphs or play the sound track version (without the visual section on the filmstrip). Ask questions about the content.
4. Go over exercise I of the *Rückblick* section (p. 41).
Assignment
1. Study the complete dialog very thoroughly.

DAY 5

1. Review
— Go over the complete dialog. Ask questions. Have students take parts.
— If available, show the sound-filmstrip section of the dialog and play the recorded version once more.
— Show the visual section of the filmstrip and have students supply the descriptive material. Encourage creativity on the part of your students and see how much they can deviate from the exact text.
2. Finish reading *Lesestück 1* (p. 37) and then show the filmstrip of this section, if available, and play the coordinated sound track. Stop the individual picture frames and have students discuss each picture and its content.
3. Have students cover the German expressions in the *Nützliche Ausdrücke* section (p. 29) and see how well they remember them from the *Dialog* and *Lesestück 1*.
4. Do workbook exercises 2–3. Go over them in class.
5. Go over exercise II of *Rückblick* (p. 41).
Assignment
1. Complete workbook exercises 4–5.
2. Study the list of verbs including past and present perfect tense forms (p. 32).

DAY 6

1. Review
— Go over workbook exercises 4–5.
— Go over various irregular verb forms (p. 32) and find out if your students can give you the past and present perfect tense forms without difficulties.
2. Do *Übungen 11–12* (p. 35).
3. Introduce *gern* and *lieber* (p. 35).
4. Complete *Übungen 13–14*. Personalize these questions further.
5. Have students finish workbook exercise 6. See if

they can fill in the blanks without looking at the text of *Lesestück 1*.
Assignment
1. Have students read the *Kulturecke* (p. 46).

DAY 7

1. Review
— Ask questions, using *gern* and *lieber*.
2. Complete *Übung 15*.
3. Discuss the *Kulturecke* (p. 46). Which of the holidays and festivals are similar to and which are different from those in the U.S.?
4. If available, show the sound-filmstrip section of the *Kulturecke*. It will enhance the students' understanding of the cultural content. As an option, you may want to play the German version of the sound track that follows the English recorded text and ask simple questions in German: *Wer ist Sankt Nikolaus und wann kommt er?*, *Wo befindet sich der Christkindlesmarkt?*, *Wo feiert man den Karneval?*, *Wann ist Silvester?*, *Was ist die Landshuter Hochzeit?*, *Was ist die Kinderzeche?*, etc.
5. Have students do workbook exercise 10. Go over it in class.
Assignment
1. Have students review all the verb forms listed on p. 32.

DAY 8

1. Review
— Select verbs from the list (p. 32) and have students supply the past and present perfect tense forms.
— Use sections from *Übungen 1–9* to review past tense.
2. Introduce "Infinitives Used as Nouns" (p. 37).
3. Go over *Übungen 16–18* (p. 37).
4. Do workbook exercise 7. Go over it in class. Have students be as creative as possible. Have students read their material in class.
5. Complete *Übung 19*. You may want to have the students do this exercise orally or in writing.
Assignment
1. Do workbook exercise 8.
2. Do *Übung 20* (p. 40).

DAY 9

1. Review
— Go over workbook exercise 8 and *Übung 20* (p. 40).
— Select additional parts from *Übungen 16–18* (p. 37).
— Review special occasions, *Sprachspiegel*, *Übung II* (p. 44).
2. Start reading *Lesestück 2* (p. 42). You may want to use a map to illustrate the location of Bern. Have students read sentences. You can also use the recorded section on tape (accompanying the

filmstrip). Furthermore, you may wish to show the accompanying filmstrip to assure a better understanding of the content. Ask questions about the reading selection.

3. Select some of the mini-situations from the *Du bist dran!* section (*Sprachspiegel*, p. 45) and find out the different responses and replies your students can create.

4. Go over *Rückblick*, *Übung III* (p. 42).

Assignment

1. Finish reading *Lesestück 2*.
2. Complete workbook exercise 9.

DAY 10

1. Review
— Go over workbook exercise 9.
— Ask additional questions, following *Lesestück 2* (p. 44).

2. If available, show the filmstrip section of *Lesestück 2* to make the content more meaningful. Ask additional questions while showing the individual filmstrip frames.

3. Go over the remaining mini-situations in the *Du bist dran!* section (*Sprachspiegel*, p. 45). Encourage different responses.

4. Have students do workbook exercise 11.

Assignment

1. Complete *Übung I* of *Sprachspiegel* (p. 44).

DAY 11

1. Review
— Have students read their material from *Übung I* of *Sprachspiegel* (p. 44). Have students ask each other questions about the material read in class.

2. Go over *Übung 24* (p. 41). Personalize these questions as much as possible.

3. Do workbook exercise 13.

4. Go over *Übung III* in *Rückblick* (p. 42).

5. Introduce *Sprichwort* (p. 29).

Assignment

1. Do *Übungen 22–23* (pp. 40–41).

DAY 12

1. Review
— Go over *Übungen 22–23* (pp. 40–41). Find out from students how many different answers they came up with.

2. Have students do *Übung 21* (p. 40).

3. Complete the *Kreuzworträtsel*, workbook exercise 12.

Assignment

1. Go over *Lektion 12*. Jot down questions about any material that is not clear.

DAY 13

1. Review *Lektion 12*. Be sure that your students understand the material. Clarify questions.

DAY 14

Hand out the test section for *Lektion 12* (answer sheet for listening comprehension test and the written test pages).

1. Play the recorded test material as your students mark their answer sheets. You may decide to play the German material twice to give your students an opportunity to understand each item thoroughly before completing it.

2. After your students have completed the listening comprehension test, they are now ready to begin the written test.

IMPORTANT! You may decide to give two tests (listening comprehension and written) on separate days, depending on the time available during one class period.

TEACHING SUGGESTIONS

LEKTION 11

A. Instructional Objectives

After completing all the material in *Lektion 11*, the student should be able to:

1. describe an imaginary trip to Germany
2. identify various travel items
3. describe facilities at the airport
4. identify parts of the body
5. discuss the city of Vienna
6. name the various means of transportation
7. use dative and accusative nouns and pronouns in the proper word order
8. use reflexive verbs
9. understand the meaning of noun suffixes *-ig*, *-lich* and *-isch*

B. Allerlei

1. Game — *Was nimmst du mit?*

If you have a large class, you might want to divide your class into several sections. The first student will ask the question "*Ich mache eine Reise. Ich nehme einen Koffer mit.*" The second student might say, "*Ich mache eine Reise. Ich nehme einen Koffer und eine Tasche mit.*" The third student will repeat what the second student said and add another item. The game continues until a student makes a mistake, such as not remembering all the words, the right sequence or giving the wrong article. The student who makes a mistake is out and the next person attempts to say the correct sequence. Since it's easier to be at the beginning of the sequence, you may want to switch students around (starting from the end) to give others a chance to be challenged. You could play the same game, using the question "*Was für Körperteile hat ein Mensch? Ein Mensch hat …*"

2. Class activity — *Wir fahren nach Deutschland.*

After learning the material in the *Dialog* and *Lesestück 1,* have students prepare their own trip to Germany. Their description should include all the details (planning, papers needed, day of departure, flight, arrival, etc.). The presentation could be done orally, in writing, or both. This activity lends itself quite well to being acted out in class, using a dialog format.

3. Class project — A trip to Germany

If you are interested, you might want to sponsor a trip to Germany. Start a year ahead so that students have an opportunity to come up with most, if not all, of the money. Find out how many of your students are interested at the beginning by having them fill out a tentative questionnaire. This will give you a rough idea whether or not a trip is feasible. Various fund-raising activities will have to be sponsored throughout the year to make this trip become a reality. If you are not familiar with travel arrangements, be sure to talk to someone who has taken students on a trip so that you can find out firsthand what details are involved.

C. Background Information

page 1 — This dialog sequence was photographed at the Munich Airport (*Flughagen Riem*). Whereas most American airports display their arrival/departure times on TV screens, travelers in Germany find these times displayed on boards attached to the wall or suspended from the ceiling. The flight from München to Köln/Bonn is about one hour. Not all the flights within Germany require a boarding pass; many have open seating.

page 12 — To travel to Germany, the traveler will need a passport. To get a passport, the traveler has to fill out an application form, bring along two color photos, a birth certificate and a check for the application.

The plane in which Kathy flies is a Boeing 747. It is over 230 ft. long and 190 ft. wide and has a seating capacity of 361. Upon arrival in Germany, passengers must first show their passport and then proceed to customs. There are usually several green lanes and one red lane. If the traveler has nothing to declare s/he can follow the green lane; otherwise s/he has to stop at the red lane and declare duty items.

page 18 — Vienna is the capital and federal province of Austria, with an area of 414 sq. km and over 1.6 million inhabitants. The area around Vienna was the site of the Roman fortification of Vindobona 2,000 years ago. Vienna became a city, the character of which was increasingly shaped by its geographical location. It is not only today that this city has been a symbolic crossroad between West and East. Vienna lies not only at the end of the Alps, which terminate in the gentle hills of the Vienna Woods; it is also situated at the edge of the lowlands of the East. The Crusaders passed through Vienna on the way to free the Holy Land. Here it was that the merchants who plied the Danube used to meet. Here it was that the Turks finally gave up their conquest of Central Europe in 1683. And it was from Vienna that an empire embracing many people and countries was ruled.

"Vienna gloriosa" — that was the name given Vienna in the 18th century when a baroque building boom swept the city. It was during this time that *Schönbrunn* and *Belvedere*, Vienna's most beautiful palaces, were built; as were the *Karlskirche*, the celebrated great hall of the National Library, and almost all the major palaces of the nobility (called "palais"). It was only in 1857 that the city walls that still surrounded the ancient core of the city came to be considered as unnecessary, and work was begun on pulling them down. At this time the *Ringstraße* around the inner city was built. The *Ringstraße* is Vienna's only real boulevard — and an exceptionally impressive one. Over the centuries very little thought was given to radical demolition, and as a result, the city has retained many of its ancient, narrow streets.

A walk around the *Ring* — as the Viennese call it — will take you past many magnificent buildings and gardens: past the State Opera, which critics described as a "sunken box" as a result of subsequent road-surfacing work; past the *Stadtpark*, with the world-famous Johann Strauss Monument; past the unfinished "Kaiser forum" with its great museums, the Hofburg and the Winter Residence; past the neo-classical Parliament Building; past the neo-gothic town hall, sometimes mistaken for a church because of its very high spire; past the *Burgtheater*, founded 200 years ago as the German National Theater; and past the *Votivkirche*, the style of which is so beautiful that it could never be mistaken for genuine Gothic (built 1853). For a long time the *Ring* has been considered a hodgepodge of styles, and valued all the more for it today. Tickets for performance at the *Burgtheater* or the *Staatsoper* are often sold out months ahead. When ordering tickets, write to the *Bundestheaterverband, Goethegasse 1, A-1010 Vienna.* The final program and order forms will automatically be sent to you about two months before the date of the performance you request. Belvedere was the summer residence of Prince Eugene of Savoy, a famous general and conqueror of the Turks. It is one of the most beautiful baroque buildings in the world, built between 1721 and 1723.

Schönbrunn was the summer residence of the Hapsburgs. The original building was completed in 1698. It was extensively modified between 1744 and 1749. There are magnificent rooms of state with exquisite works of art. There are also a famous baroque garden and a rococo palace theater.

Performances of the Spanish Riding School normally take place on Sunday mornings, except during the months of January, February, July and August. Advance reservations are absolutely essential. Training sessions can be visited between 10 A.M. and 12 noon every day except Monday.

page 22 — Drivers are not allowed to pass on the right. The right lane is always reserved for slower-moving vehicles, whereas the left lane is strictly for passing cars. German law requires drivers to put on their seat belts. It is quite expensive to get a driver's license in Germany. It is not uncommon for a person to pay DM 1,000 (including driver's training and test) to receive his/her license. The German road system is excellent. There are basically three types of roads — *Autobahnen* (super highways, freeways or turnpikes), *Bundesstraßen* or *Schnellstraßen* (two or four-lane highways) and *Landstraßen* (country roads).

Most service stations have a sign indicating either *Selbstbedienung* (self service) or the letters for it, *SB*. When the driver is finished filling the car with gas, a white slip of paper is generated on the side of the fuel pump. This paper indicates the exact amount of fuel and money to be paid. The driver takes this piece of paper inside the service station to pay. A visitor, coming to Germany and using the subway, may be wondering what the German system is like when s/he sees that some people apparently buy a ticket while others simply walk through the open gate. The explanation is *Zeitkarten* (subscription tickets valid for a week, a month, etc.), which are used by those regularly taking subways or trains. Never enter a subway without holding a ticket — you may have to pay a fine. There are checks either in the trains themselves or at the exit gates. *Zeitkarten* also are used for streetcars and buses. In Hamburg and Munich, a practical system has been introduced that allows the same ticket to be used for all means of public transportation — the subway, the city train (S-Bahn), streetcars, buses, and even (in Hamburg) river boats and ferries.

LEKTION 12

A. Instructional Objectives
After completing all the material in *Lektion 12*, the student should be able to:
1. describe the major parts of a surfboard
2. name the major holidays and festivals in Germany
3. be able to congratulate others for special occasions
4. discuss a wedding in East Germany
5. describe in general terms the city of Bern
6. use the past tense (including irregular verbs)

7. use *gern* and *lieber* in meaningful sentences
8. form nouns from infinitives

B. Allerlei
1. Game — *Ratet mal!*
Write a jumbled German word referring to a holiday and/or festival on the board. Example: T E O S N R = *OSTERN*. You may want to divide the class into teams. Furthermore, you may also want to have the person or team member indicate what the holiday or festival is in English. In case of a festival, have your students describe it with one or two sentences.

2. Class activity — Celebrate a special occasion
To make the meaning of a well-known German holiday (*Weihnachten*, *Ostern*, etc.) or festival (*Karneval*, *Oktoberfest*, etc.) more meaningful for the students, you may want to have them make the necessary preparations and get the whole school involved. For example, you could have the theme, *Weihnachten in Deutschland*. Have students decorate the room with appropriate ornaments, collect articles and other interesting items for the bulletin board (or perhaps the showcase in the hallway) and bake Christmas cookies and breads (*Lebkuchen*, *Stollen*, etc.), which can be offered for sale as a fund-raiser. Learn a few songs appropriate to the festivity. If you prepare this event early enough, you can contact some of the German organizations for brochures and posters (See *Deutsch: Aktuell 1* Teacher's Edition, page TE16).

3. Class project — Invite a guest from Germany
Ask your students if they know someone from Germany. Find out if this person is willing to come to your school and talk about a particular festival in Germany. If such a meeting can be arranged, you may want to ask your students to prepare questions beforehand to make the guest's visit more interesting. Of course, a talk about a particular holiday season or festival might be a springboard to other topics of interest.

C. Background Information
page 27 — In recent years, surfing has become one of the most popular sports activities on lakes and rivers during the summer. Most of the surfing is done in the southern part of Germany, where there are many lakes (*Schluchsee*, *Titisee*, *Starnberger See*, *Ammersee*, etc.).

page 30 — The legal holidays in the Federal Republic of Germany are as follows:
Neujahr (New Year's Day), January 1, a legal holiday in all states. Note: *Silvester* (New Year's Eve) is not a public holiday, but shops and offices close in the early afternoon on December 31.
Heilige Drei Könige (Feast of the Three Kings, Day of the Magi), January 6, a legal holiday in the states of Baden-Württenberg and Bavaria. Note: The Roman Catholic Church celebrates the feast of Epiphany on this day.

Rosenmontag, 42 days before Easter, not a legal holiday, but an unofficial one in the areas where carnival is celebrated. Note: *Rosenmontag* is the highlight of the carnival season.

Karfreitag (Good Friday), the Friday before Easter, a legal holiday in all states. Note: The week before Easter is called *Karwoche* in Germany.

Ostern (Easter), the first Sunday and Monday after the first full moon in spring, i.e. following the vernal equinox (March 21). Thus Easter cannot come earlier than March 22 or later than April 25. Easter Monday is a legal holiday in all states. Note: The dates of all movable Church celebrations depend on that of Easter.

Tag der Arbeit (Labor Day), May 1, a legal holiday in all states. Note: In contrast to the U.S., Labor Day is celebrated on May 1 in all European countries.

Himmelfahrt (Ascension Day), 40 days after Easter and ten days before Pentecost, always on a Thursday, a legal holiday in all states.

Pfingsten (Pentecost), the seventh Sunday and Monday after Easter, i.e. between May 9 and June 13. Pentecost Monday is a legal holiday in all states.

Fronleichnam (Corpus Christi Day), the Thursday after Trinity Sunday (Sunday after Pentecost), i.e. in May or June, a legal holiday in Baden-Württemberg, Bavaria (in communities with predominantly Catholic population), Hessen, Nordrhein-Westfalen, Rheinland-Pfalz and Saarland.

Tag der Einheit (Day of Unity), June 17, a legal holiday in all states. Note: In recent years there has been much controversy as to whether this day should remain a legal holiday. It may be abolished some day.

Mariä Himmelfahrt (Mary's Assumption), August 15, a legal holiday only in Saarland and in those communities in Bavaria that have a predominantly Catholic population. Note: This is a Roman Catholic Church celebration that has been celebrated since Pope Pius XII announced the dogma of Mary's Assumption in 1950.

Allerheiligen (All Saints Day), November 1, a legal holiday in Baden-Württemberg, Bavaria (with special regulations in communities with a predominantly Protestant population), Nordrhein-Westfalen, Rheinland-Pfalz, and Saarland. Note: Halloween on October 31 is not celebrated in Germany. Catholics used to visit the cemeteries on All Saints Day to put flowers and candles on the graves.

Volkstrauertag (National Day of Mourning), the Sunday before *Totensonntag* in November. *Totensonntag* is the Protestant population's special day of remembering the dead and is celebrated on the last Sunday of the church year, on the last Sunday before Advent. It is celebrated in all states.

Buß- und Bettag (Repentance Day), the Wednesday before the last Sunday of the church year, i.e. mostly between November 18 and 22, a legal holiday in all states except for Bavaria, where it is only observed in communities that have a predominatly Protestant population.

Weihnachten (Christmas), December 24, 25, 26; December 25 and 26 are legal holidays in all states. Note: December 24 is not a legal holiday, but shops and offices close in the early afternoon.

page 37 — Most of the weddings in East Germany are strictly civil weddings and are not part of church ceremonies. The wedding described in the *Lesestück* is quite typical for larger cities. The months of May through August are the most popular. The bride and groom often contact the local marriage bureau (*Standesamt*) several months in advance to be assured of a specific time and day. Weddings are performed every 20 minutes to half an hour throughout the day. Couples to be married come by car, horse and carriage, taxi, or even walk. Any celebration before or after the wedding ceremony is strictly up to the wedding party. However, the procedure at the marriage bureau is clearly prescribed. The bride and groom briefly meet with the official in a separate room and turn over the rings (if they are desired) and sign some legal documents. Then they join the wedding party in the hallway and wait until the previous wedding guests come out of another room in which the civil wedding will be performed. The official precedes the wedding party and turns on the music, which has been selected by the bride and groom before. By the way, the selection is from about ten to twenty furnished by the marriage bureau, not by the couple. As soon as the music plays, the bride and groom enter followed by the guests.

As soon as the music stops, the official greets the party and says a few words concerning the couple's responsibility to each other as well as to the State. After the rings have been exchanged and the family book returned, the wedding party leaves, usually going to a restaurant for dinner or to the bride's home where a meal is served.

page 42 — Bern is an ancient city, built between the 12th and 18th centuries. The city is located on the Aare River, which embraces the city in a great natural loop. It has molded and protected Bern over the years. The cathedral (*Münster*) has undergone many changes over its lifetime. The main portal was restored after 1970. The Clock Tower (*Zeitglockenturm*) is right on top of the first west gate of the city, erected about 1191. Today it is considered the symbol of Bern. The clock has performing figures that start at three minutes to the hour. The Bear Pit (*Bärengraben*) was originally part of the city moat and enclosed in its present form in 1857. The market (*Markt*) is open Tuesdays and Saturdays in the morning.

page 46 — Those who contend that a candle-lighted Christmas tree is not safe will often meet with opposition in Germany. Many Germans still prefer a tree with real candles to one electrically illuminated. To be on the safe side those who use real candles usually keep a bucket of water in the room — just in case. Christmas Eve (*Heiliger Abend*) is the main event in Germany, and both the 25th and 26th of December are national holidays.

The origin of *Karneval* or *Fasching* goes back to pre-Christian time when people had superstitious fears about the change of seasons, when demons who might win power over man had to be exorcized by noise, lights and conjurings. It was believed that men dressed up as demons and witches, animals or spirits were better able to take up the battle with supernatural powers, to help the spring season overcome the demons of winter. In time the Church condoned the ancient pagan practice by regarding them as a legitimate period of healthy release of merriment before Lent.

Official preparations for the carnival start punctually at 11 minutes after 11 on the 11th day of the 11th month of the preceding year, but the first preparations take place as early as late summer. Köln (*Karneval*), Mainz (*Fassenacht*) and München (*Fasching*), are regarded as the three major carnival cities of Germany.

The climax of the carnival is *Rosenmontag*. On that day, a parade and the people of the city virtually take over. Rich and poor, simple and educated people — they all are just one big, crazy family. The city is turned upside down, and normal business is practically at a standstill.

Next to Christmas, Easter is the most celebrated event on the German calendar of festivals. The most common symbol of this festivity are the Easter eggs, pagan in origin. Eggs frequently appeared in the ancient rites of spring as an image of fertility and renewal of life. Very soon this custom, like many others, was assimilated into Christianity, and until the 17th century Easter eggs were blessed in church. On the other hand, the origin of the Easter Bunny (*Osterhase*) has remained a matter of speculation. Most schools close their doors for two weeks of vacation during Eastertime. Pentecost (*Pfingsten*) is another event when students get several days off. During this time various festivities take place that signify the beginning of the spring and summer season.

The *Landshuter Hochzeit* is the biggest historical event in Europe. The whole town participates in this well-known event, which takes place every three years.

The Thirty Years' War was one of the darkest periods in German history and it is, therefore, not surprising that many historical festival plays and processions still commemorate the end of those dreadful sufferings — especially in Franconia, which was particularly devastated at that time. Rothenburg ob der Tauber, for instance, has its *Meistertrunk,* a historical play performed every year on Pentecost Day. The play is preceded by a procession of people in historical costumes and followed by activities in which the entire population participates. The *Kinderzeche* too dates back to that period of time. The children of Dinkelsbühl begged the Swedish soldiers to leave the citizens unharmed. Moved by the children's plea, the Swedes decided not to harm the town.

The Pied Piper of Hamelin (*Rattenfänger von Hameln*) has been immortalized by the Brothers Grimm. On June 26, 1284, the Pied Piper is said to have led 130 children from Hamelin out of town, never to be seen again, in revenge for the city fathers' refusal to pay him for freeing the town from a plague of rats. The tale has been included in nearly every collection of fairy tales since the Brothers Grimm as a parable of the consequences of human evil and greed.

The *Oktoberfest* had its origin a little over 150 years ago, when the Princess Therese of Saxe-Hildburghausen was married to Bavaria's Crown Prince, Ludwig, who later became King Ludwig I. To celebrate the wedding, it was suggested that a horse race be held. This met with the king's approval and horsemen from the whole of Bavaria came to take part, with 40,000 visitors looking on. The celebration following the race on the next day was such a great success that it was decided to call the place *Theresienwiese* in honor of the Princess and that the festival be repeated each year. Thus the *Oktoberfest* has become what it is today — Europe's biggest folk festival.

LEKTION 13

A. Instructional Objectives

After completing all the material in *Lektion 13*, the students should be able to:
1. act out a scene similar to the one presented in the dialog
2. identify various professions
3. describe a harbor trip
4. talk and/or write about Liechtenstein
5. discuss the most familiar landmarks of Bavaria
6. use the genitive case
7. use verbs with prepositions

B. Allerlei

1. Game — *Was bin ich von Beruf?*

Divide the class into two or more groups. Have each team member think of a profession. The object of the game is for the other team(s) to guess that profession by asking questions that can be answered only with *ja* or *nein*.

2. Class activity — *Gehen wir ins Café!*

Have students set up a scene in a café, preferably with a table, plates, silverware, etc. Have students select roles (customer, waiter/waitress, cashier). Students should be encouraged to be as creative as possible. It can be lots of fun and, above all, an excellent learning experience.

3. Class activity — *Was willst du werden?*

Ask students to select jobs they would like to do or careers they would like to pursue. The various jobs/professions listed in the *Ergänzung* probably are not enough for students to select from. Expand this list by having students look up other possible career opportunities in dictionaries. Once students have selected his/her future job/profession, ask them to write a short description about how they envision their career.

4. Class project — *Bayern heute*

Many Americans today think that people in Bavaria still wear only *Dirndlkleider* or *Lederhosen*, drink only beer and dance mostly polkas. However, visitors are often surprised how modern Bavaria is, particularly the city of München. In order for students to become more familiar with today's Bavaria, you may ask them to write a letter to various organizations, some of which have been mentioned before (*Deutsch: Aktuell 1*, Teacher's Edition, p. 16). The following are some other more local organizations to contact:

Fremdenverkehrsverband
  München-Oberbayern e.V.
Sonnenstr. 10
8000 München 2

Landeshauptstadt München
Fremdenverkehrsamt
Rindermarkt 5
8000 München 5

Fremdenverkehrsverband Franken e.V.
Am Plärrer 14
8500 Nürnberg 18

Fremdenverkehrsverband Ostbayern e.V.
Richard-Wagner-Straße 10
8400 Regensburg

C. Background Information

page 51 — The *Café* or *Kaffeehaus* is a well-known institution in Austrian social life. It is not uncommon to find cafés full from mid-morning through late afternoon. You can order a cup of coffee (it's usually quite strong!) and sit there for an hour without being rushed. Don't expect to get a refill, unless you are willing to pay for another cup. A waitress will bring cake or torte to you upon request. You can preview the fantastic selection of pastries right at the counter as you enter the café. You can order your selection as you enter and your waitress will bring it to you after you have been seated.

Many people who come to these cafés sit there for a long time, write letters, read papers, discuss politics and, most important of all, relax. The tip and value-added tax usually are included so that you need only to round off your check to the nearest full amount. If the service was especially good, customers normally give a little extra.

page 61 — Bremen, deep in the interior, is the southernmost German seaport. It is located on the Weser River, which runs north into the North Sea. The harbor cities of Bremen and Bremerhaven (only 40 miles away) complement each other and have all the advantages that can be offered to large overseas ships (cargo or passenger). These two ports serve annually some 12,000 ships, flying the flags of over 70 countries.

A town like Bremen, covering a small area and with such an eventful history, is able to provide the visitor with much that is worth seeing: from the Roman nave to the Expressionist architecture of the famous Böttcherstraße, from the words of Tilman Riemenschneider to those of Paula Becker-Modersohn, from the narrow streets in the old town to the modern and futuristic buildings ranging from the City Parliament building to the university.

Anyone standing in Bremen's market place will certainly realize right away that s/he is surrounded by a city whose development and history stretch far into the past. A great number of the cultural monuments that have been preserved or restored testify above all to the significance of the economic role of this Hanseatic city, which even in the Middle Ages was a thriving center of commerce.

page 66 — The population of Liechtenstein is about 20,000, of which one third are foreigners. The people are almost exclusively Roman Catholic and are under the auspices of the Bishop of Chur. Since 1912 Liechtenstein has had its own stamps, which have become extremely popular and are valued throughout the world. The revenue from the sale of these stamps is an important part of the country's annual income.

Liechtenstein is a constitutional monarchy that is hereditary in the male line. Prince Franz Josef II is the twelfth governing prince. He came to power in 1938. Legislative power is exercised by a 15-member Diet (*Landtag*) elected for a four-year term. Since 1924, Switzerland has taken care of Liechtenstein's diplomatic affairs and consular representation abroad. These two countries share customs, postal and monetary systems.

The history of Liechtenstein goes back to the Roman period. In the year 15 B.C., Liechtenstein was part of the ancient Roman province of Rheathia. During the Middle Ages, Liechtenstein became an autonomous feudal state. In 1342 the Counts of Werdenberg-Sargans established the capital at Vaduz. Hartmann I resided as its first Count of Vaduz in the castle, which is still in existence today. The founder of today's principality, Prince Hans Adam of Liechtenstein, bought Vaduz in 1699 and the principality in 1712. In 1719, he obtained the title of Prince from Emperor Charles VI and ruled as vassal of the Holy Roman Empire.

After the dissolution of the Holy Roman Empire in 1806, Liechtenstein joined the German

Confederation in 1815 and was part of it until its dissolution in 1866. Since 1868 Liechtenstein has not maintained any military force.

page 69 — Munich owes its foundation to a strategic coup of the Guelfian Duke Henry the Lion. He destroyed the Bishop of Freising's Isar bridge and diverted the salt trade to his own bridge *"bei den Munichen"* (at the home of the monks; hence the monk in the coat of arms). From then on, Henry levied the bridge toll. In 1158, Emperor Barbarossa granted "Munichen" market and coinage rights. In 1180, the Duchy of Bavaria fell to the Wittelsbachs. After its partition, Munich became the royal residence in 1255 and was closely linked with the destiny of the royal family up to 1918. Emperor Louis the Bavarian laid out the old city in the early 14th century, including the fortifications, of which the *Karlstor, Sendlinger Tor* and *Isartor* gates still remain. The citizens wanted the city to have a central church and so the *Frauenkirche* was built, 1468–88. That the royal Wittelsbachs appreciated art was apparent back in the 16th century when they laid the foundations for the city's finest collections (*Alte Pinakothek, Schatzkammer, Staatsbibliothek*). Over the centuries they were patrons of famous composers such as Orlando di Lasso (1556) and Richard Wagner (1813–1883). They sponsored the visual arts by commissioning works such as Altdorfer's Battle of Alexander. Above all, the Wittelsbachs were industrious builders. A good example of this legacy is the *Residenz*, on which work continued for five centuries. The Wittelsbachs also built the *Michaelskirche*, the *Münzamt* (Mint), *Schloß Nymphenburg*, the *Theatinerkirche* and *Schloß Schleißheim*.

In 1806 Bavaria became a kingdom under Maximilian I. It was he who gave the city its *Nationaltheater*. But it was the artistic taste of King Ludwig I that did most to mold the face of the city. Ludwig said: "I will make of Munich a city that so resounds to the honor of Germany that none shall know Germany unless he has seen Munich." He created the magnificent *Ludwigstraße, Brienner Straße*, with the *Karolinen-Platz*, and the delightful *Königsplatz*. He had the *Alte Pinakothek* and the former *Neue Pinakothek* (art galleries) built and completed the extension of the *Residenz* on a grand scale. Under his successor, the *Maximilianstraße* and the *Prinzregentenstraße* were constructed. Then, in the Second World War, Munich was ravaged by 66 air raids. They brought severe destruction, especially in the center of the city. But during reconstruction, the historical flavor of the old city was recaptured. Much that was believed lost was restored, thanks to the inhabitants' zeal and love of art.

Munich's *Deutsche Museum* is the biggest technological museum of its kind in the world. Thousands of original devices, models and copies, exhibited on a floor space of 40,000 sq. m. (430,500 sq. ft.), demonstrate the history of science and technology. Many of the working models can be operated by the visitors themselves.

Schloß Nymphenburg with its 495 acres of park is one of the most impressive palaces in Europe. The main area features sumptuous decorations and the Gallery of Beauties of King Ludwig I. In the south wing of the palace is the *Marstallmuseum*, housing many state carriages and sleighs. Exhibition rooms of the Nymphenburg China Factory are located on the northern crescent of the grounds.

The *Frauenkirche* (Cathedral of Our Lady) is late Gothic. It is Munich's most distinctive landmark and a rich depository of works of art.

LEKTION 14

A. Instructional Objectives

After completing all the material in *Lektion 14*, the student should be able to:

1. write a short letter in German to a friend and address the envelope properly
2. identify and name various postal items
3. describe a German post office
4. talk about and describe a big league soccer game
5. be familiar with the basic rules of soccer
6. talk about youth in East Germany
7. use demonstrative pronouns
8. understand and be able to form adjectives with proper endings

B. Allerlei

1. Game — Password

Divide the class into teams. Each team makes up a set of cards, possibly limiting these cards to one category. One team gives the other team one card. A person from the other team then gives a partner a one word clue, which could be an antonym or a synonym. The partner gets one guess. If s/he doesn't guess the word, the opposing team takes over. If a word is guessed on the first try, the team gets ten points; on the second try, nine points, etc.

2. Class activity — *Wir gehen zur Post.*

Have students act out a scene at the post office. Students should prepare for this scene beforehand. The post office scene should include such facilities as a counter, mailbox or telephone booth. Furthermore, have students prepare some forms, such as a *Paketkarte* and a *Telegramm*. After the initial preparations, students may want to write out a creative dialog and learn it before acting out this whole situation. The scene can be very straightforward or funny (a lost letter/telegram, wrong phone connection, too big a package to send, etc.), depending on the students' imagination.

3. Class activity — *Wir spielen Fußball.*

If your students are not familiar with the rules of soccer, you may want to invite someone who will demonstrate some of the basic rules and skills. Ask students (through the German Club or in class) to select the best players (including substitutes) and challenge another school club (French, Spanish, etc.) to a game. This activity might get the whole school involved and draw some interest.

4. Class project — *Schreibt einen Brief!*

Write a letter to a friend, to someone who knows some German, or to an organization in a German-speaking country (*Auf deutsch, bitte!*). Your students may also want to find a pen pal and begin writing letters that way. The purpose is to develop writing skill and practice communicating with others who know German.

C. Background Information

page 75 — This particular scene takes place in Austria, although the postal service is quite similar to that in Germany. In smaller cities and towns, the mail carrier is well known and, quite often, stops to chat with people he knows. Usually, letter carriers start delivering mail early in the morning and are done with their delivery route by noon.

page 87 — Each city, town and village in the Federal Republic of Germany possessing a post office — there are 24,000 of them altogether — has its own zip code number (*Postleitzahl*). This number is written in front of the town's name.

This is how the number system works: the territory of the Federal Republic of Germany and West Berlin has been divided into eight main postal districts, each with one major city. Frankfurt, for instance, has been given the postal number 6000. Wiesbaden, which is smaller, is located in the Frankfurt postal district. It is number 6200. Idstein in the Taunus belongs to the Wiesbaden sub-district and has number 6270. Wörsdorf, which is near Idstein, has the number 6271.

Until recently, it was also possible to use the small numbers without the zeros (6 Frankfurt), but because automatic machines now read the figures and distribute mail, all postal numbers must have four digits now.

The German Federal Postal System (*Bundespost*) not only collects and delivers mail, but is involved in numerous other aspects. It also:
— owns and operates West Germany's telephone and telegraph systems (facilities for both are available at local post offices)
— owns or controls the equipment for West Germany's radio and television networks
— licenses and collects fees for radios and TV sets (a German pays the post office a monthly fee for the use of the radio and TV)
— offers banking services, both savings and checking accounts (through local post offices)
— pays out Social Security money and certain Federal pensions (through local post offices)
— offers subscriptions to newspapers and magazines
Following are some tips on how to use the local German post office.

Telegram — Except for the fact that you send telegrams from the post office rather than Western Union, the system is much the same as it is in the U.S. You merely put your message on a form, available at the post office, and take it to the counter. You can also phone in a telegram.

Telephone — Telephone calls to any place in the world can be made at a German post office. Simply go to the counter marked "*Telefon*" or "*Fernsprecher*" and give the operator the number you want. Each country has a different prefix (before the area code and local number). For instance, if you call someone in the U.S., the first three digits are "001" (then the area code and local number). Of course, the operator will assist you if you don't know what to do. S/he will direct you to a booth where you can dial direct. You may be asked to pay a deposit before the call; you pay the final bill after you have completed the call. Usually, the cost for making long-distance calls from a post office or a public telephone booth is less than half of that paid in a hotel.

Buying Stamps — As a rule, stamps can be bought in a post office. Sometimes shops selling picture postcards also have stamps available.

Letter and Card Service — Letter and card service is comparable to the American system. There is a standard rate for letters (up to 20 grams — 0.7 oz.) sent anywhere in Germany. To send mail to other countries, Germans usually take their letters and cards to the post office and have it weighed to be sure that the right postage is paid.

Parcels — There are two types of parcels, the *Paket* and the *Päckchen*. The *Paket* is a normal package sent by parcel post, and the postage depends on the weight and the distance sent. In addition to the address on the package itself, a separate card (*Paketkarte*) must be filled out. If you indicate on this card the value of its contents, you will get up to DM 500 worth of free insurance. Additional insurance can be purchased; it's called *Wertgebühr*.

If your package is small, ask if it can go as a *Päckchen*. A *Päckchen* goes first class, but at a much cheaper rate. No *Paketkarte* is required for it. Standard, pre-printed boxes of various sizes are available at many post offices for a nominal fee. This method makes it possible, especially for tourists, to send presents directly without having to worry about packaging.

Money Orders — There are two main kinds of German postal money orders, the *Zahlkarte* and the *Postanweisung*. The *Zahlkarte* is designed for paying money into a postal checking account. Most firms and businesses have such an account (individuals have them too), and they provide a convenient instrument for transferring money. The system works like this.

Let's say you get a bill from a German business — your insurance company. Chances are it will show a *Konto* (account) number at the bank. There may be two — one for a private bank and another for the postal checking account (*Postscheckamt*). If you don't have a checking account, and if your debtor has a postal checking account, just fill out a *Zahlkarte* (pale-blue form) to his/her *Konto* number, at the proper *Postscheckamt*. The post office will credit the money to his/her account and s/he will be notified of the action. S/he is thus relieved of all bookkeeping on the transaction. Businesses naturally prefer that you pay bills owed them into their bank accounts, either postal or private, rather than to the business itself.

page 92 — *Fußball* (soccer) is by far the most popular sport in the world and in Germany as well. The soccer season in Germany begins in late August and ends sometime in May. Each of the 18 teams in the national league (*Bundesliga*) play a total of 34 games (17 at home and 17 away). A team winning the game, regardless of the score, receives 2 points. When a game ends in a tie, each team receives 1 point. The team with the most points at the end of the season is the national champion or *Deutscher Fußballmeister*. Each goal consists of two goal posts 8 feet high and 8 yards apart, connected by a crossbar at the top, with goal nets attached to the rear. The playing area has a maximum length of 120 yards and a minimum length of 100 yards. The width ranges from 55 to 75 yards. The area is outlined by a white line, and flags are placed in each corner; the sidelines are known as touch lines and the end lines as the goal lines.

The halfway line goes from one touch line to the other and runs through the center of the field parallel with the goal lines. In the center of the field is a circle that the ball is placed in at the beginning of the game or after a goal has been scored. Near each goal are two rectangular areas. The one nearest the goal is the goal area; the other is called the penalty-kick area. Also, at each corner there is a small marked area to be used for a corner kick.

The soccer ball has a circumference of about 27 inches and has a weight of between 14 and 16 ounces with an inflation pressure of about 12 pounds. Shoes are the most important part of the player's equipment. Regulation shoes are laced shoes with leather or rubber cleats.

There are eleven players on a soccer team. Most professional teams today use various formations. The objective is to put the ball through the opponents' goal. When the ball has been kicked into the goal, the scoring team gets one point. A regulation game lasts 90 minutes (two periods of 45 minutes each) with a half time of ten minutes.

page 96 — As early as kindergarten, sports are an integral part of the school curriculum in the *DDR*. Almost all the boys and girls learn to swim by the age of ten. School sports clubs offer a wide choice of extracurricular sporting activities and opportunities.

Every year thousands of youngsters participate in the *Jugend-Spartakiade*. Only the best athletes, who have qualified after having participated in their specialty, compete in this national event. Among the best of these athletes are usually the future Olympic medal winners.

About two million children are sent annually to the various youth camps during the summer. Each day at camp is planned with a number of activities, including excursions and participation in sports and other activities.

Youngsters between six and sixteen years of age come to the *Pionierpalast* to participate in the various activities that take place there throughout the year. This building was constructed from 1976 to 1979. It is 700 ft. long and almost 400 ft. wide. There is a large auditorium, several lecture rooms and many rooms for various hobbies and activities — including history, natural science, engineering, art and hiking. Furthermore, there are special rooms for handicrafts, a stage for fairy tales, a disco and a room for special guests. The sports facilities include a swimming pool and a gymnasium. They are intended for all kinds of recreational group sports and games. The *Pionierpalast* can provide instruction and entertainment to a maximum of 2,000 children every day.

LEKTION 15

A. Instructional Objectives

After completing all the material in *Lektion 15*, the student should be able to:

1. name common animals
2. describe the various rooms and facilities in a German home
3. describe a small town in East Germany
4. summarize the reading selection on student life in East Germany
5. discuss life in East Germany and compare it to his/her own
6. use the proper adjective endings after *ein*-words
7. form adjectives used as nouns
8. understand adjectives not preceded by articles
9. use adjectives after *nichts*, *etwas*, *viel* and the quantity words *viele*, *wenige*, *einige*, *andere* and *ein paar*

B. Allerlei

1. Game — *Wie heißt dieses Tier?*

To make this game more challenging, you may want to have students include other animals besides those listed in this lesson. Each of the two teams makes up a list of animals. One team starts to ask questions in German, which the other team answers with either "*ja*" or "*nein*." This game is very similar to "Password" (see *Lektion 14*). You may want to choose other categories as well, such as items to be found in a room, at school, sports, etc.

2. Class activity — *Was für Tiere gibt's im Zoo?*

Have students go through magazines (German or American) and cut out all the animals they can find. Each student is responsible for finding at least 10 different animals. Have students prepare a bulletin board with pictures of the various animals as well as their names in German, including the article and plural form. Your students will need a dictionary for this activity because some of the animals picked by the students may not be introduced in this book.

3. Individual project — *Mein Traumhaus*

Have each student write a short essay about their dream house. Students should be as creative and imaginative as possible to describe the kind of house in which they would like to live.

C. Background Information

page 101 — The scene takes place at the zoo in Heidelberg. Most major German cities have a zoo. The Heidelberg Zoo opened in 1934 and was completely destroyed during World War II. The few remaining animals were cared for by a handful of the Heidelberg citizens. A major construction program to expand the facilities was started in 1972. Five years later, the *Afrika-Anlage* was opened and several African animals are housed here. A number of other facilities to accommodate many different types of animals have been built during the past few years.

page 114 — Ostrau is a typical town in East Germany. Farms are not owned by individuals but belong to so-called *Genossenschaften*. The workers all share in the profits after the grain, potatoes and sugar beets have been harvested. Furthermore, the equipment and machinery between smaller towns are often shared to be more productive and cost effective. There are no construction workers available to build residences in East Germany because these workers are needed to construct buildings needed by the state. Citizens interested in building a house must apply to the local authority in Ostrau to receive a plot of land. Once such a plot has been allocated, usually only six to eight a year, the future home owners can build their own house, provided their friends and neighbors help them. The monthly payment for such a house is about 80 marks per month or approximately 5% to 8% of the family's monthly income.

page 120 — The city of Freiberg in East Germany, built in 1210, was enclosed by a city wall. In 1670, the wall was reinforced and made higher. Today, there are only a few remains and one of the five towers left that remind visitors of the past. Several mines were built here during the 18th century. The only remaining mine is now used for teaching purposes. Students come here periodically to study the mining system and get some practical experience.

The mining college has one of the most impressive rock collections of it kind.

Students usually spend four years at this college. A year before graduation students are quaranteed a job from their future employer. There is no tuition for students. Besides having free tuition, students also receive some spending money plus some additional financial recognition (*Leistungsgeld*), depending primarily on their university record. Not all students find accommodations at the college dormitory (*Studentenheim* or *Studentenwohnheim*). Students pay a nominal amount of 10 marks a month for accommodations at a dormitory. All medical and hospital expenses are paid by the government.

page 124 — Of the total population of 16.85 million, 4.14 million live in rural areas and 12.71 million live in urban areas. Foreigners traveling in East Germany have to buy *Mark*, the official monetary currency of the country. The official exchange rate of the *Deutsche Mark* (West Germany) and the *Mark* (East Germany) is 1:1.

The following forms of retail and service trade exist in East Germany: (1) the nationally owned sector (state trading organizations called *HO — Handelsorganisation*) (2) the cooperative sector (*Konsum*) with approximately 33,000 outlets and (3) the private sector with some 33,000 shops and restaurants.

Alongside the *HO*, which accounts for the largest proportion of the country's retail business, a major role is played by consumer cooperative societies. These cooperative groups own a great number of retail outlets and department stores, a mail order service (catering primarily to the rural population) and approximately 1,500 production firms. Anyone can become a member of this type of cooperative undertaking and receive dividends on the commodities purchased.

The state trading organizations and the consumer cooperative societies operate a complete range of service establishments (laundries, dry-cleaners, repair shops, etc.) as well as restaurants and hotels. All shops have voluntary councils and committees that consist of trade employees and shoppers and are elected by the customers. These elected bodies check on complaints and rejects, look after customer interests, and hold discussions with the public and the staff.

All employees are entitled to annual paid vacation of 18 days. Extra vacation can be granted, depending on the responsibilities and qualifications of the people involved. The Confederation of Free German Trade Unions is responsible for arranging about 1.5 million package tours annually. The price charged for a trade union vacation package varies, according to the kind of accommodations and other circumstances. It is slightly higher during the peak season, but in the final analysis it depends on the income of the persons concerned. A mere 30 marks is charged for children. An employee with a monthly income of up to 750 marks will pay 52.50 marks for a 13-day stay (full board and lodging) in a trade union home during the peak season. If s/he earns more than 1,250 marks s/he will be charged 84 marks. These low prices are due to the heavy subsidies paid by the trade unions. The railway grants a 33⅓% reduction in fares for the annual vacation. Package vacations are awarded by trade union committees, with consideration being given to personal circumstances and record of service. Apart from homes maintained or used on a contractual basis by the trade union confederation (the latter being former boarding houses and hotels), there are some 1,000 vacation homes run by nationally-owned enterprises, social organizations and other establishments. There are used by approximately 1.5 million vacationers. Over and above this, the *Reisebüro der DDR* (the national travel agency) arranges 200,000 two-week stays in hotels and boarding houses each year.

The most popular vacation spots in East Germany are the Baltic coast (attracting 2.5 million each year), the *Thüringer Wald*, the *Harz* mountains, the lake district in the north of the country, the *Erzgebirge*, the *Sächsische Schweiz* and the *Zittauer Gebirge*. The most popular sports in East Germany are soccer, fishing, gymnastics, track and field, and bowling. Leisure sports for the mass of the people are no less promoted than competitive sports aiming at high performance. Hundreds of thousands make use of the wide opportunities available for maintaining physical fitness and participating in sports clubs, factory and neighborhood contests open to everyone.

LEKTION C

A. Instructional Objectives

After completing all the material in *Lektion C*, students should be able to:
1. describe the festivals of *Karneval* and *Fasching*, based on *Lesestück 1*
2. understand *Lesestück 2*
3. discuss the German postal system
4. complete all the exercises (grammar has been covered before)

B. Allerlei

1. Game — *Wer weiß das?*
Find out if your students remember the proverbs introduced in *Lektionen 11–15*. You may want to ask students to challenge each other. In order to expand this game, you may want to review the *Zungenbrecher* (Book 1) or the *Nützliche Ausdrücke* from *Lektionen 11–15*.

2. Class activity — *Wie heißt dieses Fest oder dieser Feiertag?*
Have students make a list of German festivals and holidays (see *Lektion 12*). You may want to add some others that you have run across and students have heard about. Put all the names on the board or on a sheet of paper. Go over this list and have students describe each one in German.

LEKTION 16

A. Instructional Objectives

After completing all the material in *Lektion 16*, students should be able to:
1. act out a restaurant scene
2. be familiar with various items found on a table (table setting)
3. read a German menu
4. describe a hiking trip (imaginary or real)
5. discuss (in German) how and where Germans eat
6. talk about the most common German foods and compare them to American foods
7. make up a short German menu
8. use prepositions with the dative or accusative case
9. understand the difference between *da/dort* vs. *dahin/dorthin*
10. use *da-* and *wo-*compounds
11. use verbs with the dative case

B. Allerlei

1. Game — Charades
Each team prepares a list of proverbs, tongue twisters, dialogue sentences or idiomatic expressions. The list (prepared on slips of paper) is then put into a container for the other team from which a student will draw the paper. S/he will then look at this slip and act out the item to his/her teammates who will have to guess the content in the shortest time possible.

2. Class activity project — *Wir kochen*...
With the help of the home economics department you may want to have your students cook a German meal or bake some pastries or cookies. This is an excellent fund-raising activity. Of course, such a project depends to a large extent on the facilities available. If such a project cannot be done in school, you may want to have students bake some goodies at home and bring them to school, to a German Club meeting or for a bake sale.

page 139 and page 142 — Ordering a dinner à la carte may be difficult for those who don't know any German. If you want to play it safe, you may be better off to order a *Tagesgericht*, a *Gedeck* or *Menü* — several of which are offered on most menus — which is a complete dinner with soup (*die Suppe*) and dessert (*der Nachtisch*). Bread and rolls are rarely served with hot meals in Germany. If you order them, there will be a small charge. There is also a charge for butter, which must be ordered.

When asking for the menu, just say *"Die Speisekarte, bitte!"*, or more politely, *"Ich hätte gern die Speisekarte, bitte!"* The waiter (*der Kellner*) is addressed as *"Herr Ober,"* the waitress as *"Fräulein."*

When asking for the check, you simply say, *"Herr Ober (Fräulein), ich möchte zahlen!"* or *"Meine Rechnung, bitte!"* or very briefly, *"Zahlen, bitte!"* Normally you pay your waiter at your table, rarely at the counter or cash register. The prices include 10 to 15% for service (*Bedienung*) and 14% for value-added tax (*Mehrwertsteuer*). Although the extra tip is not necessary, most people do round the bill off to the nearest fifty *Pfennige* or *Mark*, according to the amount to be paid and the service rendered. For instance, if the check amounts to DM 17,80 you may say *"Neunzehn Mark, bitte!"* to the waiter, thus indicating that you expect change only for twenty marks and that the rest is for him. Usually, the tip is given directly to the waiter or waitress when paying the check and is not left on the table when leaving, as is done in the U.S.

The custom of serving ice water as a matter of course in restaurants is not known in Germany. You will rarely see a German drink plain water with meals; beer or wine is more common. A waiter asked to bring a glass of water (he'll bring a small lukewarm one, in most cases) probably thinks that you want to swallow a pill!

Germans often drink beer with their meals. They like their beer cool, but not ice-cold. Most are horrified at the American habit of putting beer into the refrigerator, because this kills the foam in German beer — and the taste to boot! If you wish to stay away from wine or beer, you may drink mineral water (*Mineralwasser*), fruit juice (*Saft* — like *Apfelsaft*, apple juice), or a soft drink (usually called *Limonade*).

The following is a handy reference table to help you make the right selection in a restaurant:

The Menu Language

Vorspeisen	Hors d'Oeuvres
Austern	Oysters
Gänseleberpastete	Paté de foie Gras
Krebsschwanzsalat	Crayfish salad
Blätterteigpastete	Puff paste patty
Räucheraal	Smoked eel
Räucherlachs	Smoked salmon
Russische Eier	Russian eggs
Weinbergschnecken	Snails

Salate	Salads
Endiviensalat	Endive salad
Gurkensalat	Cucumber salad
Gemischter Salat	Mixed salad
Kopfsalat	Lettuce salad
Rohkostplatte	Vegetarian salad
Selleriesalat	Celery salad
Tomatensalat	Tomato salad

Suppen	Soups
Erbsensuppe	Pea soup
Gulaschsuppe	Hungarian soup
Hühnerbrühe	Chicken broth
Königinsuppe	Cream of chicken
Kraftbrühe	Clear soup
Linsensuppe	Lentil soup
Nudelsuppe	Noodle soup
Ochsenschwanzsuppe	Oxtail soup
Schildkrötensuppe	Turtle soup
Tomatensuppe	Tomato soup

Fische	Fish
Aal	Eel
Bodensee-felchen	Snipe (from Lake Constance)
Forelle	Trout
Hecht	Pike
Karpfen	Carp
Makrele	Mackerel
Rheinsalm	Rhine salmon
Schellfisch	Fresh Haddock
Scholle	Plaice
Seezunge	Sole
Steinbutt	Turbot
Zander	Pike-perch Jack salmon

Fleisch	Meat
Hammel	Mutton
Kalb	Veal
Lamm	Lamb
Rind/Ochsen-	Beef
Schweine-	Pork
Braten	Roast
Filet	Fillet
Frikassee	Fricassee
Haxe	Knuckle
Hirn	Brains
Leber	Liver
Nieren	Kidneys
Ragout	Ragout/Stew
Steak	Beefsteak
Bratwurst	Fried sausage
Eisbein	Pickled pork
Filetsteak	Fillet steak
Rumpsteak	Rumpsteak
Schnitzel à la Holstein	Fillets of veal à la Holstein
Wiener Schnitzel	Fillets of veal à la Viennoise (Breaded veal cutlet)
Schinken	Ham

Geflügel	Poultry
Ente	Duck
Gans (Gänsebraten)	Goose
Hähnchen	Spring chicken
Huhn	Chicken
Küken	Squab chicken
Taube	Pigeon
Truthahn/Puter	Turkey

Wild/Wildgeflügel	Game/Venison
Hase	Hare/Rabbit
Hirsch	Venison
Reh	Roebuck
Wildschwein	Wild Boar
Keule	Saddle
Rücken	Haunch

Eierspeisen
Pfannkuchen
Rührei
Spiegeleier
Verlorene Eier

Egg Dishes
German pancake
Scrambled eggs
Fried eggs
Poached eggs

Beilagen
Bratkartoffeln
Kartoffelbrei (Püree)
Pommes Frites
Reis
Salzkartoffeln
Spätzle
Knödel
Leberknödel

Served With
Fried potatoes
Mashed potatoes
French fries
Rice
Boiled potatoes
Spätzle (dumplings)
Dumplings
Liver dumplings

Gemüse
Blumenkohl
Champignons
Grüne Bohnen
Grüne Erbsen
Gurken
Karotten (Möhren)
Morcheln
Rosenkohl
Rotkraut
Spargel
Weißkraut

Vegetables
Cauliflower
Mushrooms
String beans
Green peas
Cucumbers
Carrots
Turnips
Brussel Sprouts
Red cabbage
Asparagus
White cabbage/Kale

Zubereitungsarten
Blau (Fisch)
Gebacken
Gebraten
Gefüllt
Gekocht
Geschmort
in Backteig
mit Butter
Paniert
mit Remouladen-
   sauce
vom Rost/grilliert
mit Schlagsahne

Preparation
Blue (fish boiled)
Baked/fried
Roasted/fried
Stuffed
Boiled
Braised/stewed
in batter
with butter
with breadcrumbs
with remoulade sauce

Grilled
with whipped cream

Kalte Speisen
Aufschnitt
Kaltes Geflügel
Käseplatte
Schinken
   (roh/gekocht)
Wurst

Cold Dishes
Cold cuts
Cold poultry
Assorted cheeses
Ham
   (smoked/boiled)
Sausage

Gebäck
Berliner Pfannkuchen

Blätterteiggebäck

Obstkuchen
Teegebäck
Torte

Amerikaner

Keks
Zwieback
Sandkuchen

Pastry
Berlin doughnuts
   (Bismarcks)
Puff pastry (turnovers,
   tarts)
Fruit cake
Tea cakes
Cake with icing
   (very sweet)
Special chocolate or
   sugar-covered cookie
   (named after Americans)
Cookies
Hard toast
Coffee cake (dry, less
   sweet)

Nachtisch
Gefrorenes/Eis
Kompott
Obstsalat
Obst, frisches

Dessert
Ice cream
Stewed fruit
Fruit salad
Fresh fruit

Alkoholische Getränke
Bier (hell/dunkel)
Bowle
Liköre/Spirituosen
Rotwein
Schaumwein

Süßwein
Weinbrand
Weißwein

Alcoholic Beverages
Beer (pale/dark)
Wine cup
Liqueurs/spirits
Red wine
Champagne/Sparkling
   Hock
Dessert wine
Brandy
White wine

In smaller towns the best places to eat are usually the hotels. Restaurants are known by different names such as *Gasthöfe, Gasthäuser, Gaststuben* and *Gastwirtschaften*. In many regions the most authentic and typical German food and atmosphere is found in the less pretentious hotels and *Gasthaus* restaurant. *Weinstuben* (inns specializing in wines) often do not serve complete lunches and dinners, but they provide you with substantial snacks and, of course, wine.

Bräus (inns specializing in their own beer) and *Bierkeller* (beer cellars) usually have plenty of food on hand as well as beer. Cafés sometimes offer hot meals, but most specialize in snacks and beverages exclusively.

A *Ratskeller*, located in the basement of the *Rathaus*, was once the meeting place of the city fathers who gathered here to make the town's decisions. Wherever a *Ratskeller* is still in existence today, chances are that the steaks and beer are likely to be better than anywhere else in town.

A *Schnellimbiß, Schnellgaststätte* or *Imbißstube* is strictly a German snack bar. The quality of food in these places is usually not the highest, but they are cheap and practical, particularly for those who are in a hurry.

In many German *Gasthäuser* and small-town hotels you will find one special table reserved for the local people who come here regularly, usually in the evening, to have a beer, argue politics and perhaps play a game of *Skat*. This table quite often bears the sign *Stammtisch* (reserved table) or a little banner. So when looking for a table, don't be surprised if the management suggests you choose a table other than this one.

The practice of sharing tables in a restaurant is quite common in Germany. In Southern Germany, especially, it is the most natural thing in the world to sit together at a table, if there is no other table available. Of course, one must ask permission before sitting down, "*Gestatten Sie?*" or, less formally, "*Entschuldigen Sie, ist hier noch frei?*" The answer is mostly, "*Ja, bitte sehr!*" When starting to eat, many people often wish each other "*Guten*

Appetit!" to which the answer is "*Danke, gleich-falls*" (the same to you).

page 150 — The Ahr River, a tributary of the Rhine, is located south of Bonn. Although most wines in Germany are white, this area (around Bad Neuenahr) produces red wines. It's quite common for families and friends to get together on a weekend during the warm season and go on short trips, which are usually coupled with hiking. Many of these families prefer to take a picnic lunch along rather than eating at restaurants.

page 160 — The following represents a variety of recipes for various German foods related to those or presented in the *Kulturecke*.

Kartoffelpuffer mit Zwiebel

1½ kg	large potatoes
4	Tbsp. flour
1	large onion
100 g	lean smoked pork
1	level tsp. salt
½	level tsp. black pepper
2	eggs
2	Tbsp. chopped green onion or chives
	oil for frying

Peel potatoes and grate into cold water. Put grated potatoes on a cloth and squeeze out moisture. Put into a bowl and dust immediately with flour so that the potatoes won't brown. Pour off the water in which the potatoes had been grated saving the potato starch which has been deposited at the bottom of the bowl. (If you want to spare a lot of work, use packaged potato pancakes.) Grate the onions and dice the pork, add to the potatoes with the salt, pepper, eggs, potato starch and chopped green onion (or chives). Fry the potato pancakes individually in heated oil. Serve with green salads, applesauce and beer.

Rheinischer Sauerbraten

¼ liter of wine vinegar
½ liter water
2 Tbsp. oil
1 medium-sized carrot
1 medium-sized leek
1 medium-sized onion
½ parsley root
½ tsp. salt
6 black peppercorns
1 tsp. mustard seed
2 juniper berries
2 cloves
2 bay leaves
1 kg beef roast
¼ liter marinade
¼ liter white wine
1 Tbsp. tomato (pulp) puree
3 Tbsp. raisins

4 Tbsp. (grated) almonds
4 Tbsp. cream

Mix vinegar, water, and oil. Add cut-up vegetables and spices. Chill. Put the meat into a pot and pour chilled marinade over it. Cover and refrigerate for 3–4 days. Turn occassionally. Take the meat out and wipe dry. Brown meat in hot oil. Slowly pour over ¼ liter strained hot marinade and ¼ liter wine. Spice with tomato puree and simmer for 90 minutes, covered. Remove meat from liquid and keep it warm. Put raisins and almonds into the sauce, thicken with cream; taste for seasonings, and cook, covered, for 10 minutes. Slice the roast and spoon some sauce over the meat on a preheated platter. Pour the remaining sauce into a bowl. With it serve raw potato dumplings.

Wiener Schnitzel

Pound 4 veal cutlets (5 oz. each) lightly until ⅛-inch thick. Salt both sides and coat with flour. Mix 1 egg with 1 Tbsp. milk and 1 tsp. oil. Dip floured cutlet into egg mixture. Let dry somewhat. Then coat with bread crumbs. Fry in hot fat until crispy on both sides. Drain on paper towels and garnish with parsley and a lemon wedge. Serve with a cucumber salad and french fried potatoes.

Schwarzwälder Kirschtorte (mit Buttercreme)

½ c. butter or margarine
¾ c. sugar
1 tsp. vanilla
½ tsp. almond extract
5 eggs
2½ oz. pkg. slivered almonds, ground
4 oz. bar German sweet chocolate, grated
½ c. flour (sifted)
½ c. cornstarch (sifted)
2 tsp. baking powder

Cream the butter with the flavorings and sugar. Add the eggs one at a time and mix until sugar has dissolved. Add almonds and grated chocolate (save a little to decorate top). Mix in cornstarch, sifted flour and baking powder. Beat well. Bake in 2 greased and floured round cake tins at 350° for 20–25 min. After cooking, divide one layer in half.

Buttercreme: Heat 1 c. milk and 1 c. sugar to boiling. Combine 1 pkg. vanilla pudding powder with the 4 Tbsp. milk and 2 egg yolks. Gradually pour into hot milk. Cook until thick, stirring. Let cool, stirring occasionally. Cream 1 c. butter and 1½ c. powdered sugar and slowly add cooled pudding mixture. Add 1 Tbsp. Kirsch.

To assemble: Using Redi-Whip or similar product, make a ring around the outside and the inside of the bottom (uncut) layer. Fill the inside ring with cherries (may be canned and drained). Cover the next layer with Buttercreme. Put on the last layer and cover the entire torte with Buttercreme. Using a decorating tube, make flowers around outside edge and stud with maraschino cherries. Shave chocolate pieces in the center. Refrigerate.

LEKTION 17

A. Instructional Objectives

After completing all the material in *Lektion 17*, the student should be able to:

1. make up a situation relating to a shopping scene
2. name some of the facilities found in a German department store
3. name common fruits and vegetables
4. describe a trip to a store (grocery, bakery, butcher, etc.)
5. discuss and describe a typical German market
6. talk about the differences and similarities between a German and an American department store
7. make up his/her own shopping list in German (using metric measurements)
8. understand the past and present perfect tense of modal auxiliaries
9. use the past perfect tense
10. become familiar with additional question words

B. Allerlei

1. Game — *Was kaufen wir ein?*

If you have a large class, divide students into several groups. The first person in each group begins with the question, *Was kaufen wir ein?*, and answers the question including one shopping item, for example, *Äpfel*. S/he gives this answer: *Wir kaufen Äpfel.* The next student repeats the questions and the complete previous answer and adds another item. The object of the game is to see how many items can be named in sequence (with correct pronunciation) until the first student makes a mistake. That student is then eliminated from the game. The game lasts until there is only one student left — he or she being the winner. If the game seems to be too easy, have students add some metric units (*ein Pfund Äpfel, 200 Gramm Wurst*, etc.).

2. Class activity — *Einkaufen macht Spaß!*

When students are familiar with the vocabulary relating to shopping, have them take different roles in a shopping spree. You may want to have students work in groups and prepare such a scene beforehand to make it more effective and meaningful. As soon as students are ready, have them act out the scene. Let them be as creative as possible.

3. Class project — Shopping items

Have students go through German magazines and/or newspapers and see how many shopping items they can find and identify. If German newspapers or magazines are not available, have students go through U.S. magazines and ask them to prepare a list of shopping items. For some words, a dictionary may be necessary.

C. Background Information

page 165 — The small store portrayed in this scene is typical of what Germans call *Tante Emma-Laden.* Such stores, however, are gradually disappearing. Only 14% of grocery stores today are not affiliated with chains, but this group is responsible for only 2.3% of the grocery retail business. Nevertheless, these family-owned stores are particularly popular in smaller towns. Needless to say, the owner knows all of his/her customers well and a rather social atmosphere prevails between customer and the shopkeeper.

page 176 — Americans intending to buy in German stores are often confused and irritated by the early hours at which German shops close their doors. The shop owners are required by law to close from 6:30 P.M. until 7 A.M. the following day, Monday through Friday, and at 2 P.M. Saturday. On every first Saturday in the month and on the four Saturdays before Christmas, shops can be kept open until 6 P.M. Within these limits, shop owners can fix their individual opening and closing hours. In smaller towns, as well as in the suburbs of larger cities, most stores close for a couple of hours around noontime.

Stands selling fruit, candy, newspapers and similar articles at German railroad stations can be kept open all day and throughout the night. Other exceptions are tourist spots during the season, when shops may be open all day on Saturday and also on Sunday afternoon.

Although the U.S. type of supermarket is becoming increasingly popular in Germany, the old-fashioned specialized store is still popular. Quite often, a sign outside these stores indicates what kind of commodity they sell. Grocery stores often can be recognized by signs of certain cooperative associations or chains they belong to. Examples for such names are: Konsum, Edeka, Spar, Ve-Ge, VIVO, Rewe, etc.

page 181 — Regularly on market days (once or twice a week), summer and winter, open-air markets are still held all over Germany, in small towns as well as in big cities. In the parking lots, you can see the heavily laden counters of eggs, salami and cheese, the tables piled high with fruit and vegetables, the stands selling fish and meat, flowers and household utensils, inexpensive books, and clothes. There is always a bustling, lively atmosphere about these markets, with dealers enticing the potential buyers to buy their goods and not those of their neighbor.

The *Markt* in modern Europe today is practically as it was many centuries ago. Probably because of their personalized atmosphere, the open markets are growing in popularity in Germany, especially if they are held in the center of the shopping districts and near modern supermarkets. In Hamburg, for example, there are 36 open-air markets held every week. Two-thirds of all German housewives like to buy at these markets if they have the opportunity.

LEKTION 18

A. Instructional Objectives

After completing all the material in *Lektion 18*, the student should be able to:

1. name the ailments and related items presented
2. describe a scene at the doctor's office
3. describe the various overnight accommodations found in German-speaking countries
4. list similarities and differences of German and U.S. accommodations
5. discuss housing in Germany and relate it to that found in the U.S.
6. understand relative pronouns
7. use coordinating and subordinating conjunctions

B. Allerlei

1. Game — *Was ist denn passiert?*

Ask students to make up a fictitious situation (sudden ailment, accident, etc.). Have others ask individual students questions to which the student being asked will answer with either *ja* or *nein*. The object of this game or activity is to find out what tricky situation each student can create and how fast the others can guess what happened.

2. Class activity — Housing

Have students write a short essay (in German) describing the differences and similarities between housing in Germany and the U.S.

C. Background Information

page 189 — An *Apotheke* is strictly a pharmacy and sells medicine with and without prescription and also some toilet articles. Most pharmacies, particularly in cities, use computers to determine their inventory of medicines.

page 200 — Most Germans have an excellent medical plan that assures them that all doctor's and hospital expenses are covered, regardless how minor the sickness may be. Health protection is better today than ever before. Doctors and hospitals have the most modern technical facilities at their disposal. The costs of health care are rising at an accelerated pace — a serious threat to the economy as about 15% of the national income is spent on health care. Many Germans take advantage of their medical system in that they go to the doctor even for minor treatments that often do not require medical attention. Consequently, doctors' offices and hospitals often are full of patients. If the present trend of medical coverage were to continue, experts estimate that health costs could rise to 60% of the national income by the year 2000.

page 205 — The *Zimmernachweis* or *Tourist Information* is usually located downtown, close to the railroad station. As the tourist offices close around 6 P.M., many cities have installed a board listing the hotels (including information on prices and facilities) in the area. The tourist can select a hotel and make a phone call to be sure that rooms are still available.

If you intend to stay in a moderately priced hotel, bring soap and wash cloths along. All hotels supply towels, but only the more expensive ones supply soap. If you wish to have a room with private bath and toilet, both must be specifically ordered but are not always available. Usually, there is at least one bathroom with shower at the disposal for all hotel guests. However, you should announce your intention to use the shower or bathtub before actually using it, as there may be other hotel guests who have made time reservations to use it. There is usually a charge for using the shower or the bathtub.

Americans sometimes resent all the additional charges for small extra services in German hotels, but Germans, as a rule, prefer to know precisely what they're paying for, instead of having all the extras added at the end. Some Americans may also be irked by the necessity to fill out intricate forms when registering in a hotel. Many German states have drastically shortened these forms in recent years, and several have abolished them altogether. In all German hotels, pensions, etc. you pay when you check out. Service charges, taxes, etc. will be included in the bill. The final amount is always what was quoted when you inquired. Therefore, there should be no surprise.

The continental breakfast is another feature that may surprise Americans in German hotels. It consists of *Kaffee*, *Tee*, *Kakao* or *Milch* (usually hot), *Brötchen* (Mondays through Saturdays) or *Brot* (Sundays — since bakeries are closed), *Butter Marmelade* and, sometimes, a boiled egg (*ein gekochtes Ei*).

In recent years, even the smaller hotels are beginning to serve assorted cold cuts and cheese. Sometimes hotels offer their guests assorted cheeses and spreads in small packages. A plastic bucket normally stands on the table to be used for the leftover wrappers. German hotels and pensions expect their guests to eat their breakfast there. It does make sense, because most hotels include the breakfast in their room charge and will deduct very little if you decide to have your breakfast elsewhere. Of course, you won't find American-style breakfast places.

Camping has been popular in Germany for many years. Millions of people spend their vacation in tents and campers in the many camping grounds found throughout Europe. The *Campingführer* is the official guide of the Deutscher Camping Club, listing some 3,000 selected camping sites in Germany and 20 other countries. Especially recommended German camping sites are marked with the symbol of the Deutscher Camping Club, a tent (resembling an Indian tepee) enclosed in a big "C." A map of all German sites is attached to the booklet.

The guide furnishes a wealth of information that a camper may wish to know, such as fees, sanitary facilities, food service, swimming and fishing possibilities, special sights and possibilities of car service or repair. Although the text is in German, the symbols used in describing every site are explained in English and French. Besides many pictures, there are tips of general interest (in German) regarding campers, tent equipment, insurance needs, winter camping, special regulations to be observed in the different countries, and — in order to avoid overcrowded sites — a list of the school holidays in the various German states.

The Deutscher Camping Club recommends traveling out of the season. For a vacation in July or August, one should look for the lesser-known places, away from big cities and popular tourist sights, The *Campingführer* is available in bookstores and sporting goods stores. It also can be ordered directly from: Deutscher Camping Club e.V., Mandlstraße 28, 8000 München 23.

page 209 — Since 1949 some fifteen million dwellings have been built, more than six million of them state-subsidized. These dwellings or apartments are rented to low-income tenants, large families, handicapped and old people. Their owners are permitted to charge at most the so-called "cost-rent," which is clearly below that for new apartments on the open market.

In the immediate postwar years the main need was for housing of any kind and its facilities were less important. With growing income and rapid economic advancement, demands for quality also rose. Thus, there is hardly any new apartment that does not have a bath and central heating. The owners of older buildings have also done a lot of modernizing. Almost all buildings are connected to public electricity and water supplies. The rising standard of living is also reflected by the increasing size of apartments. In 1960 new apartments averaged 70 square meters of living space, and in 1984, 102 square meters.

The readiness of West Germans to spend money on outfitting their homes is due partially to the climate. Germans have to spend more time indoors than people in warmer climates. In nine out of ten households there are TV's and radios. More than half have telephones. Appliances that ease housework are particularly popular among Germans. Refrigerators, vacuum cleaners, electric washing machines and sewing machines are taken for granted in almost all homes.

Germans who earn too little to pay for adequate accommodations are helped by housing subsidies from the state. The amount depends on size of income, size of family and total outlay for accommodations.

It is the dream of most Germans to own a house or an apartment. There is a variety of state programs making it possible to build their own homes for those who wish to do so.

LEKTION 19

A. Instructional Objectives

After completing all the material in *Lektion 19*, the student should be able to:
1. describe some general rules and procedures in driving a car
2. name the most important parts of a car
3. identify some of the more important traffic signs
4. describe and discuss facilities and repair procedures at an automobile repair shop
5. summarize the history of flying in Germany
6. understand metric measurements
7. use the passive voice
8. use infinitive construction with *zu* and *um . . . zu*

B. Allerlei

1. Game — *Wer bin ich?*

Have a student think of a profession or a well-known person (entertainer, athlete, politician, etc.). A panel of several students will ask him/her about the identity of the person or profession. The student will answer only with *ja* or *nein*. You may decide on a time limit for this game.

2. Class activity — *Welches Auto möchtest du kaufen?*

Have students go through newspapers and magazines (if German ones are available, all the better) and clip ads for automobiles. Ask them to prepare a short essay about why they want to buy a particular automobile. Students should use the facts and figures usually provided in these ads for their argument.

C. Background Information

page 213 — There is no driver's training provided by public schools in Germany as there is in many U.S. public school systems. Anyone who wishes to obtain a driver's license (*Führerschein*) will have to take about 10 to 12 lessons offered by any driving school (*Fahrschule*) found throughout Germany. These schools offer theoretical as well as practical training in operating an automobile or other motorized vehicle. Each lesson is fairly expensive, but the driver is taught not only how to drive an automobile but also receives instruction in basic repair and maintenance procedures. A driver's license in Germany does not have to be renewed every few years; it is good for a lifetime.

page 225 — Each German car is equipped with a triangular sign (short vertical line on white with red trim). In case of an emergency on secondary roads, drivers are required to put this sign about 30 yards away from their car to alert other drivers to drive cautiously. In case of a breakdown on the *Auto-*

bahn, drivers usually look for the little arrows near the top of the white posts lining the road. These lead to the nearest emergency call box. These call boxes are located every 1½ to 3 kilometers along the *Autobahn*. To use them, merely lift the handle; the *Autobahn* superintendent's office will answer. Most of the operators speak English, and if they don't they will connect you with someone who does. Describe your problem, and help will be on the way in minutes.

page 230 — Otto Lilienthal was the first German who glided from a hill in Berlin-Lichterfelde (about 1894). Siegfried Hoffmann on a "Harlan"-monoplane (about 1910) followed. The first official mail-flight was introduced in 1912, from Frankfurt to Darmstadt with an Euler biplane called "Yellow Dog." Ernst Henkel flew over the *Cannstatter Wasen* near Stuttgart in his self-made "Farman"-biplane in 1911.

The Deutsche Lufthansa AG, inaugurated regular passenger service when the Dornier Komet III first flew the Berlin-Halle-Erfurt-Stuttgart-Zurich route on April 6, 1926.

The world's first strut-free, all-metal, low-wing monoplane with a closed cabin, the Junkers F 13, was the workhorse of the Lufthansa fleet between 1926 and 1932. More than forty of them operated as landplanes when equipped with wheels or skis, or seaplanes when fitted with pontoons. The heated cabin provided four passenger seats equipped with safety belts.

In the early days of air travel, passengers had to sit outside and wait for their plane to depart. Due to a small payload capacity of early commercial airplanes, all Lufthansa passengers and freight had to be weighed. Lufthansa's "airboy" (*Luftjunge*) carried luggage to the aircraft and lent a helping hand to passengers. Shuttle-buses carried passengers from Berlin-Tempelhof to the city (around 1928).

The airship LZ 127 "Count Zeppelin" first crossed the South Atlantic non-stop on May 18, 1930, from Seville, Spain to Recife, Brazil. On March 20, 1932, the Zeppelin was put into regular service between Friedrichshafen and Recife. Lufthansa planes made airmail feeder flights to the Zeppelin to shorten airmail delivery times. The four-engine Junkers G 38 was the biggest landplane of its time. It had a twin fuselage and seats in the wings giving a unique forward view. Lufthansa put the first Junkers G 38 into regular service in 1931.

An aircraft renowned for its safety and economy. the tri-engine Junkers Ju 52, nicknamed "*Tante Ju*," was put into service in 1933. Initially it flew on routes within Europe, later to East Asia and across South America to Santiago de Chile.

When Lufthansa began its regular airmail service between Germany and South America on February 3, 1934, the world's first transocean airline

route was opened. From Germany, a Heinkel He 70 flew to Seville or Larache, North Africa, where a Junkers Ju 52 took over and transported the mail to a waiting Dornier-Wal seaplane in Bathurst, West Africa. It carried the mail, with one stopover at the base-ship, to Natal, Brazil, where an airplane of "Syndicato Condor Ltd." took it finally to Rio de Janeiro. On August 10/11, 1938, Lufthansa flew the Berlin-New York route non-stop for the first time with a four-engine Focke-Wulf Fw 200 "Condor." Flying time: 24 hours 57 minutes.

Lufthansa began scheduled flying operations (after World War II) on April 1, 1955, after extensive test flights. During the first months, Lufthansa planes flew with British and American flight captains. For the first time a Super-Constellation with an all-German crew took off for New York on March 22, 1956.

page 233 — If you want to think metrically, you'll have to start with two basic facts. First, remember that measurements are based on 100, not all kinds of odd numbers such as 16 ounces to a pound, or 5,280 feet to a mile. Second, the prefix "centi" means hundred; "kilo" means thousand.

For practical purposes, you don't have to be so exact. Suppose you want to buy some fabric for a dress. Since a meter is slightly more than a yard, you know you'll have some material left over if you order four meters when the pattern calls for four yards. Or say you need 10 gallons of gas. Since there are about four liters in a gallon, you'll buy 40 liters.

Shopping for food, you have another help, because Germans commonly measure by the *Pfund*, or pound. A *Pfund* is half kilo, or 500 grams. This makes it slightly more than our pound (454 grams), but for most recipes the difference is unimportant.

Shopping for clothes is probably the least complicated. If the purchase is for you, the salesperson can easily estimate your size. Many large department stores have conversion tables of American and German sizes.

The way German figures are written is often confusing for new-comers to Germany. To Americans, the German numeral "one" may look like an American "seven" and the "seven" has a slight resemblance to the capital "F," as it has its stem crossed. Another difference when reading German figures: the period separates billions, millions, thousands and hundreds, while the comma sets off the decimal fraction. For example: American amount — $10,000.50; German amount — DM 10.000,50.

LEKTION 20

A. Instructional Objectives

After completing all the material in *Lektion 20*, the student should be able to:

1. make up and/or act out an office scene

2. describe the facilities of an office
3. know how to address an envelope and start a German letter, as well as end it
4. write a personal or business letter in German
5. describe last year's vacation or the one coming up
6. talk about wine-growing in Germany
7. discuss famous castles in Germany
8. use the various forms of the subjunctive

B. Allerlei

1. Game — *Wie geht's weiter?*

The class is divided into two teams. A student from the first team says a sentence. The first player from the second team has to start his/her sentence with the last letter of the last word in the previous sentence. For each sentence that the team says, they get a point. Example: Team 1 says, "*Wir gehen in die Schule.*" The other team might say, "*Ein Zug kommt an.*" The first team continues with "*Nach dem Essen spielen wir Fußball.*", etc.

2. Class activity — *Ich wünschte, ich hätte (wäre)* . . .

Have students prepare (orally or in writing) a wish list. Assuming that they could have anything they wanted to do, what would they like to do, in what kind of dream world would they like to live, etc. This activity lends itself quite well to being creative and, of course, the subjunctive forms will have to be used to express an imaginary world.

C. Background Information

page 237 — Many German offices today resemble those found in American firms. However, the smaller German companies show quite a variance, ranging from daily procedures to office furniture and equipment.

page 252 — The vacation resort (*FDGB-Erholungsheim* "Herbert Warnke", *FDGB = Freier Deutscher Gewerkschaftsbund*) was built in 1974. It has 412 rooms with 1,190 including 100 beds for children. Over 600 people can be seated at any one time in the main restaurant. The vacation resort offers also several smaller restaurants, a bank, pharmacy, beauty salon, a disco, Olympic-size indoor pool and shopping facilities. Each family is assigned a particular mealtime. During each of the three daily meals, there are three seating times in order to accommodate all the guests.

Usually, the vacationers stay here for 13 days at a maximum cost of 210 marks per family. This amount includes the room and all meals. The amount to be paid depends on the family income and the number of children. The additional expenses are absorbed by the *FDGB* (a union organization in the DDR). During the two-week vacation, the resort offers a total of 30 different cultural events such as theater plays, dances, movies, art projects and more.

page 258 — Here is a summary of the most important wine categories found in Germany:

Deutscher Tafelwein (German Table or Dinner Wine)

This group includes all so-called consumer wines, i.e. the lower price ranges. These wines can be a mixture of several wines harvested in different locations of one larger wine-growing area. A name designating the special location of the vineyard (*Lage*) is not permitted on the label. However, details like the region, place-name, kind of grapes and vintage year may be indicated if they apply to at least 75% of the bottle content. Certain officially defined improvements of the grape juice are permitted.

Qualitätswein bestimmter Anbaugebiete (Quality Wines from Certain Regions)

These are good wines of the medium price ranges. Quality wines must have been produced in one special wine-growing region. Labels must show an official control number. The kind of grapes used (Riesling, Sylvaner, Müller-Thurgau, Gewürztraminer, Burgunder, etc.) must be indicated. Minor improvements of the grape juice officially defined, are permitted. The prescribed minimum specific gravity of the grape juice lies higher than with table wines. If a special location of vineyard is indicated, this must apply to at least 75% of the bottle content.

Qualitätswein mit Prädikat (Quality Wines with Distinction)

This is the top group of the quality wines. The wine must come from vineyards of equal quality (condition of soil, etc.) within one special location, yielding grapes of the same quality and kind. No improvements allowed. Higher minimum specific gravity of the grape juice. Distinctions: *Kabinett*, *Spätlese* (late harvested wine), *Auslese* (selected late harvested wine), *Beerenauslese* and *Trockenbeerenauslese* (raisin wines).

page 262 — King Ludwig II of Bavaria who succeeded to the throne at the age of 18 (in 1864) withdrew more and more from the world following disappointments suffered during the first years of his reign. Much of his later life he lived in a dream world that is reflected in his dream castles, Neuschwanstein, Linderhof and Herrenchiemsee. The king died a tragic death, having drowned in the Starnberger See in 1886.

LEKTION D

A. Instructional Objectives

After completing all the material in *Lektion D*, the student should be able to:
1. understand and discuss *Lesestück 1*
2. talk about the content of *Lesestück 2* and relate it to his/her own experience going to a filling station in the U.S.

3. understand and discuss the general content of the interview presented
4. talk about the differences and similarities of the various topics presented in "Cultural Notes"
5. complete all the exercises without any difficulty

B. Allerlei

1. Game — *Wer kann sich daran noch erinnern?*

Have students challenge each other by making a list of the *Sprichwörter, Nützliche Austrücke*, parts from dialogs, and other sections. These items can be presented in English. The object is for the other team to come up with the correct expression or word presented.

2. Class activity — *An wen schreiben wir einen Brief?*

Ask students to compose a letter in German (to a real or ficticious friend or business in Germany). If the possibility and a reason exists, have students send their letter to that person or organization. This activity is an excellent opportunity to start the channel of communication with Germans.

Second Edition

deutsch aktuell 2

Wolfgang S. Kraft

Consultants

Chief Consultant
Hans J. König
The Blake Schools
Hopkins, Minnesota

Karl-Heinz Gabbey
Buffalo Grove High School
Buffalo Grove, Illinois

Richard C. Helt
University of Arizona, Tucson

Anthony Jung
University of Nebraska at Omaha

Peter Klose
Grand Blanc High School
Grand Blanc, Michigan

Roland Specht
Ruhr-Universität Bochum
Bochum, Germany

EMC Publishing, Saint Paul, Minnesota

ISBN 0-8219-0079-X

Published by EMC Publishing
300 York Avenue
St. Paul, Minnesota 55101

Printed in the United States of America
0 9 8 7 6 5 4 3 2

A Word to the Student

Now that you have completed *Deutsch: Aktuell 1,* you are well on your way to using the basic language skills — listening, speaking, reading and writing. In addition, the cultural topics in *Deutsch: Aktuell 1* gave you insight into the way of life among people in different regions of all the German-speaking countries (West and East Germany, Austria and Switzerland).

Deutsch: Aktuell 2, the second-level textbook, will expand your knowledge of the language and understanding of the culture. Great emphasis is placed on communication, and the necessary tools, namely the grammar, are provided to help you learn to use the language. A variety of everyday situations let you practice these new skills. You will continue to explore life styles and regional differences in German-speaking countries (even the principality of Liechtenstein is included).

The general format of this book is similar to Book 1. You will, however, notice a few changes. First of all, each lesson introduces a proverb that will be fun to learn. Secondly, the *Du bist dran!* section located in the *Sprachspiegel* of each lesson gives you an opportunity to become involved and create your own responses. Finally, there is a special section called "Selected Readings," which follows *Lektion D.* These readings are shortened and simplified texts adapted from works of well-known German authors. Through these readings you will gain a deeper insight into German literature of the past and present.

Alles Gute und viel Glück!

Wolfgang Kraft

Lektion 14

Lektion 15

Lektion D

Map

Grammar Summary

Selected Readings

Table of Contents

Land und Leute

Schilder

Größtes Trachtenangebot in Füssen! für Damen, Herren u. Kinder Verkauf ges. 1. Stock

Frühling bei Ihrem Bäcker – oh wie lecker!

Neu bei uns:

Geöffnet:

Täglich auch Sonn. und Feiertags

von 7⁰⁰h - 12⁰⁰h und 13⁰⁰h - 18⁰⁰h

Lieferverkehr frei 6-10 u. 18-22

RATHAUS INFORMATION

HOTEL ALTE POST

Flughafenstraße

Einbahnstraße

Dialog

Instructional Objectives for each *Lektion* appear in the front section of this teacher's edition. Suggestions on ways to present the various sections in this and subsequent lessons appear in the "Teaching Approaches" section in the front of this teacher's edition.

Auf dem Flughafen

FRAU SEHLERS: Ich freue mich schon sehr auf diesen Flug.

HERR SEHLERS: Ich auch. Hoffentlich benimmt sich Heiko, besonders im Flugzeug.

FRAU SEHLERS: Das wird er bestimmt. Wann fliegen wir denn genau ab? Wir wollen doch unser Flugzeug nicht verpassen.

HERR SEHLERS: Erst in einer halben Stunde.

FRAU SEHLERS: Ach ja, du hast recht. Hier steht's…ll Uhr 20.

HERR SEHLERS: Gehen wir erst einmal zum Schalter.

ANGESTELLTE: Guten Tag! Wohin wollen Sie fliegen?

HERR SEHLERS: Nach Bonn.

ANGESTELLTE: Darf ich Ihre Flugscheine sehen?

FRAU SEHLERS: Bitte sehr. Wir möchten gern vorne sitzen…

HERR SEHLERS: …und wenn möglich einen Platz am Fenster.

ANGESTELLTE: Ja, einen Moment, bitte. Ich will mal sehen, ob noch Plätze frei sind…Ja, das geht, zwei Erwachsene und ein Kind…alles klar.

ANGESTELLTE: Haben Sie Gepäck?

HERR SEHLERS: Ja, aber nur einen Koffer.

ANGESTELLTE: Sicherlich bleiben Sie dann nicht lange in Bonn.

FRAU SEHLERS: Wir besuchen meine Eltern für ein paar Tage.

ANGESTELLTE: Hier sind Ihre Flugscheine und Bordkarten. Gehen Sie gleich zum Flugsteig 3. Guten Flug und viel Spaß in Bonn!

HERR SEHLERS: Danke schön.

Most German airports display their arrival and departure times on electronic blackboards that are updated every few minutes.

This family is leaving from München. The flying time to Köln/Bonn Airport is about one hour.

On many flights within Germany boarding passes are eliminated and seats are on a first-come basis.

Fragen über den Dialog

1. Wer fliegt alles nach Bonn?
2. Um wieviel Uhr fliegen Sehlers ab?
3. Was geben Sehlers der Angestellten am Schalter?
4. Wo möchten Sehlers im Flugzeug sitzen?
5. Gibt es noch Plätze?
6. Wieviel Gepäck haben Herr und Frau Sehlers?
7. Warum fliegen sie nach Bonn?
8. Was gibt ihnen die Angestellte?
9. Von wo fliegt das Flugzeug ab?

At the Airport

MRS. SEHLERS: I'm looking forward to this flight.

MR. SEHLERS: I am too. I hope Heiko is going to behave, especially in the plane.

MRS. SEHLERS: I'm sure he will. When are we taking off exactly? We don't want to miss our plane.

MR. SEHLERS: Half an hour from now.

MRS. SEHLERS: Oh yes, you're right. Here it is…11:20.

MR. SEHLERS: Let's go to the counter first.

CLERK: Hello! Where are you going today?

MR. SEHLERS: To Bonn.

CLERK: May I see your tickets?

MRS. SEHLERS: Here you are. We would like to sit up front…

MR. SEHLERS: …and, if possible, we'd like a seat at the window.

CLERK: Yes, just a moment, please. I'll see if there are still seats available…Yes, that's possible, two adults and one child…everything is O.K.

CLERK: Do you have luggage?

MR. SEHLERS: Yes, but only one suitcase.

CLERK: You're probably not staying long in Bonn.

MRS. SEHLERS: We're visiting my parents for a few days.

CLERK: Here are your tickets and boarding passes. Go to gate 3 right away. Enjoy your flight and have lots of fun in Bonn!

MR. SEHLERS: Thank you.

Die Angestellte sieht sich die Flugscheine an.

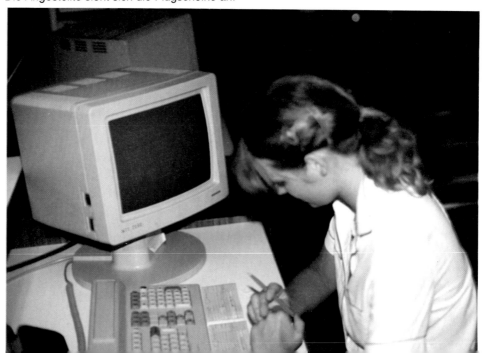

Nützliche Ausdrücke

Practice these expressions that students have learned in the *Dialog* and *Lesestück 1*.

Ich freue mich auf diesen Flug.	I'm looking forward to this flight.
Er benimmt sich nicht.	He isn't behaving.
Wir fliegen bald ab.	We're taking off soon.
Wohin geht's denn?	Where are you going?
Wir möchten am Fenster sitzen.	We would like to sit at the window.
Alles klar.	Everything is O.K.
Gehen Sie zum Flugsteig!	Go to the gate.
Hört bitte zu!	Listen, please.
Ich übersetze es ins Englische.	I'm translating it into English.
Wir sind begeistert.	We're enthusiastic.
Ich habe es ihm zum Geburtstag geschenkt.	I gave it to him for his birthday.
Gibst du deinen Koffer auf?	Are you checking your suitcase?
Verabschiede dich von ihm!	Say good-bye to him.
Ich wünsche dir eine gute Reise.	I hope you have a good trip.
Ich suche mir einen Sitzplatz aus.	I'm selecting a seat.
Er gibt den Abflug bekannt.	He's announcing the departure (of the plane).
Ich mache es mir gemütlich.	I'm going to get comfortable.
Wo befindet sich die Gepäckausgabe?	Where is the baggage claim?

Sprichwort

Morgenstund hat Gold im Mund.
(Morning hour has gold in its mouth.)

The early bird catches the worm.

3

Ergänzung

Ask various questions: Was für Gepäck nimmst du auf deine Reise mit?, Was trägst du zur Schule?, Was brauchst du zum Einkaufen?, Was schickst du deinen Verwandten (Bekannten) zu Weihnachten?, etc.

1. Gepäck und andere Sachen zum Tragen

Was möchten Sie aufgeben?

Meinen Koffer. (die Tasche, das Paket, der Karton, die Kiste)

Was tragen Sie?

Meine Aktentasche. (die Handtasche, die Einkaufstasche, die Schultasche, der Rucksack)

der Rucksack   die Aktentasche   die Handtasche   die Einkaufstasche

das Paket   der Koffer   die Tasche   der Karton   die Kiste

2. Im Flughafen

Was braucht man vor dem Flug?

Einen Flugschein.

Was bekommt man am Schalter?

Eine Bordkarte.

Wer bedient Sie am Schalter?

Der/Die (Schalter) Angestellte.

Was muß man vor dem Flug machen?

Man muß durch eine Personenkontrolle gehen.

Was gibt es auf jedem Flughafen?

Es gibt eine Sicherheitsüberprüfung.

Wo steht das Flugzeug?

Am Flugsteig.

Wer fliegt mit dem Flugzeug?

Die Fluggäste.

Wer fliegt das Flugzeug?

Der/Die Pilot(in).

Was erklären die Flugbegleiter vor dem Abflug?

Sie erklären die Sicherheitsmaßnahmen.

Was muß man gleich nach der Ankunft in einem anderen Land machen?

Man muß durch die Paßkontrolle und den Zoll gehen.

Wo bekommt man das Gepäck?

Bei der Gepäckausgabe.

3. Körperteile

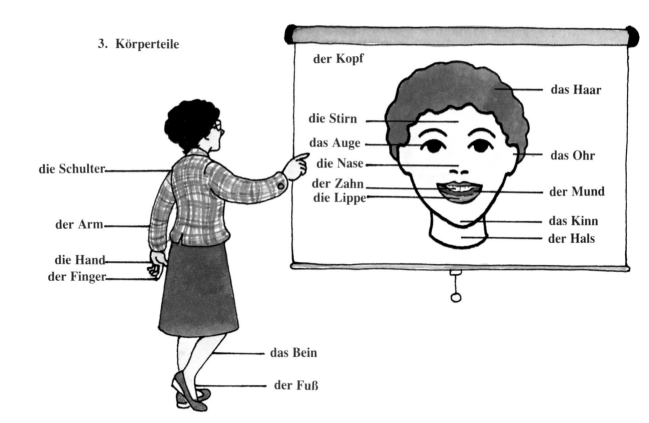

der Kopf
das Haar
die Stirn
das Auge
die Nase
der Zahn
die Lippe
das Ohr
der Mund
das Kinn
der Hals

die Schulter
der Arm
die Hand
der Finger
das Bein
der Fuß

Ask students how they get ready for school: *Beschreibt, was ihr am Morgen vor der Schule macht?*

sich bürsten **sich rasieren** **sich duschen**

sich putzen **sich waschen** **sich kämmen**

Übungen

Word Order of Dative and Accusative Cases

In a sentence containing both an indirect object noun (dative) and a direct object noun (accusative), the indirect object noun usually precedes the direct object noun.

	indirect object noun (dative)	direct object noun (accusative)
Er gibt	*dem Fluggast*	*eine Bordkarte.*

When the indirect object noun or the direct object noun appears as a pronoun, the pronoun precedes the noun object.

	indirect object pronoun (dative)	direct object noun (accusative)
Er gibt	*ihm*	*eine Bordkarte.*

	direct object pronoun (accusative)	indirect object noun (dative)
Er gibt	*sie*	*dem Fluggast.*

If a sentence contains both an indirect object pronoun and a direct object pronoun, then the direct object pronoun precedes the indirect object pronoun.

	direct object pronoun (accusative)	indirect object pronoun (dative)
Er gibt	*sie*	*ihm.*

As a general rule, you should remember that a direct object pronoun (accusative) always precedes an indirect noun object or an indirect pronoun object.

Folgt den Beispielen!

Ask questions. (Wer gibt der Dame die Flugscheine?, Wem gibt Frau Sehlers die Flugscheine?, Was gibt Frau Sehlers der Dame?)

1. Frau Sehlers gibt der Dame die Flugscheine.

   Er zeigt dem Touristen den Weg.
   Ich sage meiner Freundin kein Wort.
   Wir kaufen unserer Mutter eine Tasche.
   Geben Sie dem Herrn die Bordkarte.
   Bringst du deinem Freund die Schultasche?

   Frau Sehlers gibt ihr die Flugscheine.

   Er zeigt ihm den Weg.
   Ich sage ihr kein Wort.
   Wir kaufen ihr eine Tasche.
   Geben Sie ihm die Bordkarte.
   Bringst du ihm die Schultasche?

2. Wem kauft sie die Karte?   Sie kauft sie der Tante.
    (die Tante)

Wem zeigt er den Weg?   Er zeigt ihn dem Besucher.
    (der Besucher)

Wem bringt er die Tasse Kaffee?   Er bringt sie der Dame.
    (die Dame)

Wem gibt sie die Bordkarte?   Sie gibt sie dem Studenten.
    (der Student)

Wem sagt er die Zeit?   Er sagt sie der Amerikanerin.
    (die Amerikanerin)

Wem kauft sie die Bluse?   Sie kauft sie der Freundin.
    (die Freundin)

3. Ich bringe meinem Freund die Kassette.   Ich bringe sie ihm.
Ich bringe ihrem Vater das Buch.   Ich bringe es ihm.
Ich bringe deinem Lehrer das Geld.   Ich bringe es ihm.
Ich bringe unserem Besucher den Flugschein.   Ich bringe ihn ihm.
Ich bringe meiner Schwester die Tasche.   Ich bringe sie ihr.
Ich bringe meiner Großmutter das Geschenk.   Ich bringe es ihr.

4. Sie hat ihm den Flugschein gegeben.   Sie hat ihn ihm gegeben.
Warum hast du ihnen nicht das Fahrrad gezeigt?   Warum hast du es ihnen nicht gezeigt?
Ich habe ihr das Wort gesagt.   Ich habe es ihr gesagt.
Kaufen Sie ihm die Schallplatte?   Kaufen Sie sie ihm?
Er bringt dir den Koffer.   Er bringt ihn dir.
Muß sie euch den Ausdruck erklären?   Muß sie ihn euch erklären?

5. Substitute pronouns for the italicized words. Change the word order where necessary.

1. Der Angestellte zeigt *den Fluggästen den Flugsteig.*
2. Wann kannst du *meiner Freundin einen Brief* schreiben?
3. Warum bringst du *deinem Onkel ein Geschenk?*
4. Wir kaufen *unseren Eltern zwei Flugscheine.*
5. Gib *dem Touristen den Prospekt!*
6. Sag *deinem Freund das Wort!*
7. Buchen *deine Lehrer eine Reise?*
8. Kannst du *deiner Schwester die Frage* beantworten?
9. Der Pilot erklärt *den Fluggästen den Flug.*
10. Der Herr zeigt *der Dame den Reisepaß* vor.

6. **Form a complete sentence using the information given. Then substitute pronouns for the indirect and direct object nouns.**

Beispiel: *ich / zeigen / meine Freundin / Geschenk*
Ich zeige meiner Freundin das Geschenk.
Ich zeige es ihr.

1. Mädchen / schreiben / ihr Lehrer / Brief
2. Vater / kaufen / sein Sohn / Fahrrad
3. Wir / wollen / Dame / ihre Tasche / bringen
4. Angestellte / geben / Ausländer / Prospekt
5. Ich / werden / meine Mutter / Tasse Kaffee / kochen
6. Flugbegleiter / zeigen / Fluggäste / Schalter

Reflexive Verbs

Accusative

In German, reflexive verbs are usually identified (in a vocabulary section) by the reflexive pronoun *sich* preceding the infinitive form. The reflexive pronoun *sich,* similar to the English word *oneself,* is always used in the third person singular and plural. All other reflexive pronouns are the same as the regular accusative pronouns.

The accusative reflexive pronoun refers to a person who is both the subject and the object of the sentence. When a reflexive pronoun is used as a direct object, it appears in the accusative case.

	sich kämmen	**sich waschen**
ich	kämme mich	wasche mich
du	kämmst dich	wäschst dich
er sie es	kämmt sich	wäscht sich
wir	kämmen uns	waschen uns
ihr	kämmt euch	wascht euch
sie	kämmen sich	waschen sich
Sie	kämmen sich	waschen sich

Contrary to English verbs, many German verbs always have a reflexive pronoun and, therefore, are called *reflexive verbs.*

Beispiele: *sich freuen, sich beeilen, sich anziehen*

Dative

The reflexive pronoun appears in the dative case when it functions as an indirect object. The dative reflexive pronouns in the first and second person singular and plural are the same as the regular dative pronouns. The dative reflexive pronoun refers to both the subject and the indirect object of the sentence.

Beispiele: *Ich kämme mir die Haare.*
Er putzt sich die Zähne.
Seht ihr euch das Schloß an?

Command Forms

Command forms are constructed in the same way that you learned before, except that the reflexive pronoun is now part of the sentence.

Beispiele: *Setz dich!*
Zieht euch den Mantel an!
Hören Sie sich die Musik an!

	Reflexive Pronouns	
	accusative	*dative*
ich	mich	mir
du	dich	dir
er **sie** **es**	sich	sich
wir	uns	uns
ihr	euch	euch
sie	sich	sich
Sie	sich	sich

Folgt den Beispielen!

7. Freust du dich auf die Reise? — Ja, ich freue mich auf die Reise.

Variation: Have students change answers to the negative.

Setzt du dich? — Ja, ich setze mich.
Strengst du dich sehr an? — Ja, ich strenge mich sehr an.
Kämmst du dich? — Ja, ich kämme mich.
Interessierst du dich dafür? — Ja, ich interessiere mich dafür.
Wäschst du dich? — Ja, ich wasche mich.
Kühlst du dich ab? — Ja, ich kühle mich ab.
Duschst du dich? — Ja, ich dusche mich.

8. Freut ihr euch auf die Reise? — Nein, wir freuen uns nicht auf die Reise.

Variation: Change answers to the positive.

Setzt ihr euch? — Nein, wir setzen uns nicht.
Strengt ihr euch an? — Nein, wir strengen uns nicht an.
Kämmt ihr euch? — Nein, wir kämmen uns nicht.
Interessiert ihr euch dafür? — Nein, wir interessieren uns nicht dafür.
Wascht ihr euch? — Nein, wir waschen uns nicht.
Kühlt ihr euch ab? — Nein, wir kühlen uns nicht ab.
Duscht ihr euch? — Nein, wir duschen uns nicht.

9. Ich habe mich beeilt. Und du? — Ich habe mich auch beeilt.
Wir freuen uns auf die Reise. Und ihr? — Wir freuen uns auch auf die Reise.

Ich habe mich gekämmt. Und du?   Ich habe mich auch gekämmt.

Wir verabschieden uns. Und ihr?   Wir verabschieden uns auch.

Sie ziehen sich an. Und du?   Ich ziehe mich auch an.

Wir werden uns setzen. Und ihr?   Wir werden uns auch setzen.

Variation: Use sentences to form different commands. (Wasch dich!, Beeilt euch! Freuen Sie sich!, etc.)

10. wir / sich waschen   **Wir waschen uns.**

    die Angestellte / sich beeilen   Die Angestellte beeilt sich.

    die Touristen / sich freuen   Die Touristen freuen sich.

    der Sportler / sich anstrengen   Der Sportler strengt sich an.

    du / sich setzen   Du setzt dich.

    ich / sich anziehen   Ich ziehe mich an.

    ihr / sich duschen   Ihr duscht euch.

Ask students each question and have them supply different answers. (Was siehst du dir an? Ich sehe mir das Geschäft / das Museum / die Stadt / den Reisepaß an.)

11. Was siehst du dir an?   **Ich sehe mir das Schloß an.**
    (das Schloß)

    Was wünschst du dir?   Ich wünsche mir ein Auto.
    (ein Auto)

    Was ziehst du dir an?   Ich ziehe mir einen Mantel an.
    (ein Mantel)

    Was hörst du dir an?   Ich höre mir die Musik an.
    (die Musik)

    Was wäschst du dir?   Ich wasche mir die Hände.
    (die Hände)

Personalize this exercise with a question such as: Was hast du dir heute angezogen?

12. Er zieht sich den Anzug an.   **Er zieht sich den Anzug an.**

    die Dame / das Kleid   Die Dame zieht sich das Kleid an.

    das Mädchen / die Bluse   Das Mädchen zieht sich die Bluse an.

    die Kinder / die Schuhe   Die Kinder ziehen sich die Schuhe an.

    ich / das Hemd   Ich ziehe mir das Hemd an.

    wir / die Strümpfe   Wir ziehen uns die Strümpfe an.

13. Seht ihr euch die Stadt an?   **Ja, wir sehen uns die Stadt an.**

    Kämmt ihr euch die Haare?   Ja, wir kämmen uns die Haare.

    Bürstet ihr euch den Mantel?   Ja, wir bürsten uns den Mantel.

    Putzt ihr euch die Zähne?   Ja, wir putzen uns die Zähne.

    Kauft ihr euch die Kassetten?   Ja, wir kaufen uns die Kassetten.

Variation: Answer each question. (Wäschst du dir Füße? Ja,…Nein,…)

14. Wäschst du dir die Füße?   **Wasch dir die Füße!**

    Putzt du dir die Zähne?

    Kämmst du dir die Haare?   Kämm dir die Haare!

    Setzt du dich?   Setz dich!

    Ziehst du dir die Hose an?   Zieh dir die Hose an!

    Strengst du dich an?   Streng dich an!

Variation: Ask questions. (Siehst du dir das Haus an? or Was siehst du dir an?)

15. Sehen Sie sich bitte das Haus an!   **Sehen Sie sich bitte das Haus an!**

    Flughafen   **Sehen Sie sich bitte den Flughafen an!**

    Stadtmauer   Sehen Sie sich bitte die Stadtmauer an!

    Museum   Sehen Sie sich bitte das Museum an!

Rathaus   Sehen Sie sich bitte das Rathaus an!
Zimmer   Sehen Sie sich bitte das Zimmer an!

16. Insert the proper reflexive pronoun.

1. Hast du _____ heute morgen die Zähne geputzt?
2. Setz _____ !
3. Die Läufer haben _____ etwas abgekühlt.
4. Könnt ihr _____ die Hausaufgaben ansehen?
5. Ich will _____ diese Musik nicht anhören.
6. Wasch _____ die Hände!
7. Wir haben _____ die Flugscheine gekauft.
8. Freust du _____ sehr?
9. Was haben Sie _____ gewünscht?
10. Habt ihr _____ nicht verabschiedet?

17. Form complete sentences using the information given.

1. Ich / sich waschen / und / sich kämmen / die Haare
2. Jungen / und / Mädchen / sich anhören / Schallplatten
3. Ihr / sollen / sich beeilen
4. Müssen / du / die Zähne / sich putzen
5. Wir / sich ansehen / Film
6. Du / sollen / warm / sich anziehen
7. Können / ihr / nicht mehr / sich anstrengen
8. Ich / sich vorstellen / die Reise

Suffixes *-ig, -lich* and *-isch*

Many German adjectives or adverbs end in *-ig, -lich* or *-isch*. You may be able to identify the meaning of some of these words by simply knowing the nouns from which they are derived.

The ending *-ig* is similar to the English "-y."

hungr*ig*	— hungr*y*
lust*ig*	— funn*y*

The ending *-lich* is similar to the English "-ly."

freund*lich*	— friend*ly*
hoffent*lich*	— hopeful*ly*
natür*lich*	— natural*ly*

The ending *-isch* is similar to the English "-al."

polit*isch*	— politic*al*
typ*isch*	— typic*al*
elektr*isch*	— electric*al*

18. Add the suffix -ig, -isch or -lich and indicate the meaning of the word.

Find out if students know other words with these endings.

1. französ_____
2. gründ_____
3. richt_____
4. ruh_____
5. wirk_____
6. europä_____
7. deut_____
8. typ_____
9. wen_____
10. polit_____
11. wicht_____
12. herz_____
13. plötz_____
14. ungeduld_____
15. einschließ_____
16. hungr_____
17. end_____
18. histor_____
19. hoffent_____
20. wässer_____
21. prakt_____
22. natür_____
23. günst_____
24. phantast_____
25. pünkt_____
26. auswend_____
27. fert_____
28. mög_____
29. engl_____
30. gemüt_____

Lesestück 1

You may want to use additional information provided for *Lesestück 1* (also in subsequent lessons) in the "Background Information" section located in the front part of this teacher's edition. The new words are listed in the margin for easy reference. They are also listed at the end of each lesson *(Vokabeln)* and summarized at the end of the book.

Eine Reise nach Deutschland

Kathy Jordan hat gerade den Briefkasten° aufgemacht° und einen Brief° von ihrer Brieffreundin° aus Deutschland gefunden. Schon seit einem Jahr schreiben Kathy und Martina sich Briefe, aber heute ist der Brief für sie besonders wichtig. Kathys Eltern hören zu°, wie sie den Brief so gut wie möglich ins Englische übersetzt. Alle sind begeistert. Martina hat Kathy nach Deutschland eingeladen°. Sie soll im Juli zu Martina kommen und vier Wochen bei ihr wohnen.

Kathy lernt Deutsch in der Schule. Sie hat schon fast drei Jahre Deutsch gehabt. Natürlich will sie jetzt besonders viel lernen. In ein paar Monaten geht's schon los°. Kathy erzählt° ihrer Freundin Diana von ihrer Reise. In einem Buch — Martina hat es ihr zum Geburtstag geschenkt — zeigt sie ihrer Freundin Bilder° von einigen Städten in Deutschland.

Vor der Abreise° bekommt Kathy ihren Reisepaß°. Bei der Bank kauft sie Reiseschecks und Deutsche Mark. Das Reisebüro schickt ihr die Flugscheine zu. Endlich ist der Tag der Abreise da. Kathy freut sich sehr auf die Reise. Schon am Morgen packt sie den Koffer und die Tasche. Ihre Eltern werden sie zum Flughafen fahren. Kathys Vater legt ihr Gepäck ins Auto. Dann fahren sie los°.

Im Flughafen geht Kathy direkt zum Schalter. Dort gibt sie ihren Koffer auf. Sie wird ihn erst in Frankfurt wiedersehen. Auf

mailbox/opened
letter/pen pal

listen

invited

she'll take off/tells

pictures

departure/passport

fahren...los drive off

Was zeigt Kathy
ihrer Freundin?

Kathy steigt ins Flugzeug ein.

Was macht Kathy
am Flugschalter?

Was braucht man alles
auf der Reise?

Was macht Kathy
im Flugzeug?

Der Zollbeamte sieht
in der Tasche nach.

dem Weg zum Flugsteig muß sie durch eine Personenkontrolle gehen. Ihre Eltern verabschieden sich von Kathy und wünschen ihr eine gute Reise. Dann fliegt° sie nach Chicago.

Gleich nach der Ankunft in Chicago geht Kathy zum internationalen Flughafengebäude°. Am Flugschalter muß sie ihre Flugscheine und ihren Reisepaß vorzeigen°. Sie kann sich auch gleich einen Sitzplatz im Flugzeug aussuchen. Die Dame am Schalter gibt Kathy eine Bordkarte und sagt ihr, sie soll eine halbe Stunde vor dem Abflug zum Flugzeug gehen. Kathy hat fast zwei Stunden Zeit. Sie setzt sich° auf einen Sitzplatz und liest eine Zeitschrift°.

Ein Ansager gibt den Abflug nach Frankfurt eine halbe Stunde vorher bekannt. Alle Fluggäste gehen jetzt zum Flugzeug. Auch Kathy steigt ein. Vor dem Start erklären° die Flugbegleiter die Sicherheitsmaßnahmen. Dann fliegt das Flugzeug von Chicago ab.

Kathy macht es sich gemütlich. Sie hört sich Musik an° und liest eine deutsche Zeitung. Sie versucht alles so gut wie möglich zu verstehen. Eine Stunde nach dem Abflug bekommen die Fluggäste das Abendessen°. Es schmeckt Kathy sehr gut. Der Flug nach Frankfurt dauert ungefähr acht Stunden. Während dieser Zeit sieht° Kathy einen Film, schläft° ein wenig und bekommt noch Frühstück°.

Am Morgen informiert der Pilot die Fluggäste, daß sie bald landen° werden. Aus dem Fenster kann Kathy zum ersten Mal wieder Land sehen. Eine Weile bestaunt° sie die vielen Felder und Städte. Endlich landet das Flugzeug auf dem Flughafen in Frankfurt.

Mit allen Fluggästen verläßt Kathy das Flugzeug. Zuerst geht sie durch die Paßkontrolle. Dort muß sie einem Beamten ihren Reisepaß zeigen. Ein paar Schritte° weiter befindet sich die Gepäckausgabe. Kathy muß nicht lange warten, bis ihr Koffer kommt. Sie setzt° ihr Gepäck auf einen Koffer-Kuli und rollt° ihn direkt durch den Zoll. Gleich beim Ausgang° stehen Martina und ihre Eltern. Martina und Kathy haben Fotos ausgetauscht° und erkennen sich sofort. Alle freuen sich sehr. Nach einem Jahr haben sie sich endlich persönlich° kennengelernt.

flies

airport building
show

sits down/magazine

explain

hört sich an…
listens to

supper

watches
sleeps
breakfast

land

marvels at

steps

puts/rolls
exit
exchanged

in person

Fragen über das Lesestück

1. Von wem hat Kathy einen Brief bekommen?
2. Wem übersetzt sie den Brief?
3. Warum sind alle begeistert?
4. Wie lange hat Kathy schon Deutsch gelernt?
5. Mit wem spricht Kathy noch über die Reise?
6. Was braucht Kathy alles noch vor der Reise?
7. Wie kommt sie zum Flughafen?
8. Was macht Kathy zuerst auf dem Flughafen?

9. Was muß sie am Flugschalter in Chicago vorzeigen? Warum?
10. Was soll Kathy eine halbe Stunde vor dem Abflug tun?
11. Was erklären die Flugbegleiter vor dem Abflug?
12. Was macht Kathy im Flugzeug?
13. Wie lange dauert der Flug?
14. Was machen die Fluggäste im Flugzeug?
15. Wie weiß Kathy, daß das Flugzeug bald landen wird?
16. Was sieht sie aus dem Fenster?
17. Was müssen die Fluggäste einem Beamten zeigen?
18. Trägt Kathy ihren Koffer und ihre Tasche?
19. Wo wartet Kathys Brieffreundin?
20. Warum erkennen sich die beiden Mädchen?

Erweiterung

19. Beantwortet diese Fragen!

Have students ask each other questions dealing with the topic *Eine Reise.*

1. Wohin möchtest du fliegen? Warum?
2. Was nimmst du mit auf die Reise?
3. Was für Gepäck nimmst du mit?
4. Was brauchst du alles für eine Reise?
5. Was bekommt man in einem Reisebüro?
6. Wie lange möchtest du in Europa bleiben?
7. Welche Länder möchtest du besuchen?

20. Combine each word listed on the right side with the proper word on the left. Indicate the English meaning of each new word.

1. Sitz_____	-haus
2. Ruck_____	-teil
3. Hand_____	-platz
4. Körper_____	-essen
5. Bord_____	-karte
6. Aus_____	-paß
7. Früh_____	-sack
8. Gast_____	-stück
9. Reise_____	-gang
10. Abend_____	-tasche

21. Wie heißt das auf deutsch?

1. I'll translate it into German.
2. You'll need a passport and some traveler's checks.

3. The flight takes four hours.
4. I hope you have a good trip.
5. Would you like to check your luggage?
6. The tourists need their boarding passes.
7. I'll have to brush my teeth.
8. Are you taking a shower?

22. Define each of the following words, using one complete German sentence.

1. der Flughafen
2. der Schalter
3. der Reisepaß
4. die Brieffreundin
5. die Bordkarte
6. der Flugschein

23. Provide an appropriate response in German. Be sure that the whole conversation ties together and becomes meaningful.

1. Grüß Gott! Wohin fliegen Sie denn?
2. Wie schön! Sie fliegen also zur Hauptstadt Österreichs.
3. Wie viele Personen fliegen denn dorthin?
4. Und wo möchten Sie sitzen?
5. Ja, das geht.

24. Identify the part of the body described. Name the word in German.

1. Mit meinem _____ kann ich sprechen.
2. Meine _____ sehen sehr weiß aus. Ich putze sie mir oft.
3. Mit meinen zwei _____ kann ich gut hören.
4. Ich kämme mir die _____ .
5. Ich kann mit meinen beiden _____ gut sehen.
6. Meine Hand hat fünf _____ .
7. Dein _____ ist zu groß. Nein, der Schuh ist zu klein.
8. Oh, es gibt heute ein tolles Abendessen. Wie weißt du das? Ich habe eine gute _____ .

25. Beantwortet die Fragen!

1. Was braucht man alles vor einem Abflug?
2. Was kann man aus einem Flugzeug sehen?
3. Was findet man alles in einem Flughafen?
4. Was gibst du im Flughafen auf?
5. Nenne sechs Körperteile!

Was geben
die Leute auf?

Rückblick

If students have difficulties completing any of these exercises, you may want to go back to the particular lesson (Book 1) in which the grammar points were covered.

I. Provide the proper possessive adjective with its noun for those listed in parentheses.

1. Wo ist (our car, her present, my boarding pass)?
2. Suchst du (her coat, your briefcase, his house)?
3. Daniela kommt mit (her boyfriend, my brother, his sister).
4. Sie brauchen (their tickets, his money, your passport).
5. Dieter spricht mit (his girlfriend, our uncle, my teacher).
6. Fahren wir ohne (his mother, their aunt, her sister)?

II. Change each of the following sentences to the present perfect tense.

1. Warum fragen Sie nicht die Angestellte?
2. Gehst du um drei Uhr ins Kino?
3. Petra gibt mir ihr Buch.
4. Habt ihr keine Zeit?
5. Auf dem Weg nach München sehen wir uns Rothenburg an.
6. Sven ruft mich spät am Abend an.
7. Was lesen Sie denn da?
8. Warum sagst du das nicht gleich?

III. Form complete sentences using the future tense.

1. Wann / Flugzeug / abfliegen / Deutschland
2. Ausländer / besichtigen / Museum / München
3. Jungen / Mädchen / spielen / morgen / Tennis
4. Ich / kaufen / Hose / Hemd
5. Flugbegleiter / bringen / Abendessen
6. Sprechen / Touristen / Deutsch

IV. Supply the proper forms for the present, future or present perfect tense. Use the verbs provided in parentheses. Make sure that the whole sentence is meaningful.

1. (gehen) Die Jungen _____ letzten Sonntag ins Theater _____ .
2. (sehen) Wir _____ diesen Film nächste Woche _____ .
3. (kommen) Wann _____ du zu uns?
4. (bekommen) Maria _____ morgen viele Geschenke zum Geburtstag _____ .
5. (abfahren) Es ist drei Uhr. Der Zug _____ pünktlich um zwei Uhr _____ .
6. (kosten) Diese Bluse _____ 40 DM.
7. (abfliegen) Heute ist der 15. Juni. Schneiders _____ am 5. Juli nach Europa _____ .

Die beiden fahren gern mit ihren Fahrrädern. (Ravensburg)

Lektion 11

17

Lesestück 2

For additional details about *Lesestück 2*, refer to "Background Information" (in this and subsequent lessons) in the front section of this teacher's edition. The new words in this and the subsequent material from *Lesestück 2* are listed in the margin as well as in the end volcabulary of the book, but not in the *Vokabeln* section at the end of each lesson.

Wien — die Hauptstadt Österreichs

Jedes Jahr besuchen Touristen aus der ganzen Welt Österreich. Nicht alle Besucher kommen bis nach Wien. Diese Stadt liegt weit im Osten. Manche Leute fahren mit dem Zug oder mit dem Auto. Eine Autobahn führt° direkt von Deutschland über Salzburg und Linz nach Wien. Von Linz aus fließt die Donau immer ganz in der Nähe der Autobahn bis nach Wien. Kurz vor Wien ist das Land ziemlich° flach. Das ist besonders günstig für die Landwirtschaft°. Nördlich von Wien gibt es kleine Berge, wie zum Beispiel den Leopoldsberg und den Kahlenberg. Von dort oben hat man meistens einen schönen Blick auf die Stadt und die Donau. Wien — die Hauptstadt Österreichs — ist eine politische und wirtschaftliche° Verbindung° zwischen dem Osten und dem Westen.

leads

quite

agriculture

economic/link

Der Stefansdom, mit seinem über 130 Meter hohen Turm, überragt° die Stadt Wien. Man hat an diesem Dom° fast 350 Jahre lang gebaut° (1263-1611). Viele Besucher machen eine Stadtrundfahrt° mit einer Kutsche°. Die Kutschen stehen gleich bei der Hofburg, in der Innenstadt. In der Hofburg haben früher Kaiser° gewohnt. Heute gibt es dort viele Kunstschätze, ein Museum und die berühmte Spanische Reitschule°.

towers above/ cathedral built city tour/carriage

emperors

Spanish Riding School

Zahlreiche° Geschäfte bieten Möglichkeiten zum Einkaufen. Sehr beliebt und bekannt ist die Kärntner Straße. Diese Straße führt vom Stephansdom direkt zur „Ringstraße". Die Ringstraße ist die Hauptstraße° um die Innenstadt herum°. Auf dieser Straße findet man einige der bekanntesten historischen Gebäude Österreichs. Das Parlament, zum Beispiel, ist das größte Regierungsgebäude in der Hauptstadt. Das Burgtheater ist in der ganzen Welt bekannt. Es ist mehr als 200 Jahre alt. Natürlich darf man die berühmte Staatsoper nicht vergessen°. Auch sie steht direkt an der Ringstraße. Die Theater- und Musiksaison dauert jedes Jahr von September bis Juni. Während der Sommermonate sind die meisten Theater geschlossen°.

numerous

main street/ um…herum around

forget

closed

In Wien gibt es viele Gebäude im Barockstil. Schloß Belvedere zum Beispiel ist 250 Jahre alt und gehört zu den schönsten Schlössern der Welt. Schloß Schönbrunn liegt außerhalb der Stadt. Dieses Schloß ist fast 300 Jahre alt und hat mehr als 1 400 Zimmer. Davon° können die Besucher aber nur 43 besichtigen. Schloß Schönbrunn ist früher die Sommerresidenz der Habsburger gewesen.

of those

Jung und alt, Österreicher und Ausländer, besuchen gern den Prater, den größten Vergnügungspark° in Österreich. Vom Riesenrad° aus (65 m hoch) kann man die ganze Stadt überblicken. Manche Besucher möchten auch gern die Umgebung Wiens kennenlernen.

amusement park

Ferris wheel

Kahlenberg

die Donau

Zahlreiche Geschäfte bieten
Möglichkeiten zum Einkaufen.

Musiker sorgen für Stimmung.

Stephansdom

Schloß Schönbrunn

Im Norden, zum Beispiel, liegt der beliebte Ort Grinzing. Die Österreicher kommen oft hierher und treffen sich° in den Gasthäusern°. Da sitzen dann die Leute beisammen° und kosten° das gute Essen und vor allem den Heurigen°, den jungen Wein. Musiker sorgen für° Stimmung°. Tanzgruppen führen den Gästen verschiedene Volkstänze vor°. Auch Volkslieder hört man. Für Besucher ist das alles ein richtiges Erlebnis°, das sie so leicht nicht vergessen werden.

meet
inns/together/taste
wine
provide for/ atmosphere
führen...vor perform
experience

Fragen über das Lesestück

1. In welchem Teil von Österreich liegt Wien?
2. Wie ist das Land in der Nähe von Wien?
3. Was liegt nördlich von Wien? Warum fahren viele Leute gern dorthin?
4. Wie heißt das größte Gebäude in Wien und wie alt ist es?
5. Was kann man alles in der Hofburg besichtigen?
6. Wo kaufen die Österreicher und die Besucher gern ein?
7. Was für bekannte Gebäude findet man auf der Ringstraße?
8. Wie lange dauert die Theater- und Musiksaison?
9. Liegt Schloß Schönbrunn in der Innenstadt? Wer hat dort früher gewohnt?
10. Warum ist der Prater so berühmt und beliebt?
11. Warum kommen viele Besucher gern nach Grinzing?
12. Was ist der Heurige?

Sprachspiegel

Have students present their dialog to the class. They may want to read their version with others to make it more realistic.

I. **Construct a short dialog based on the information given.**

You and your friend are at the airport to pick up your uncle. You inquire whether the plane will be on time, and you are told that it will be fifteen minutes late. You suggest to your friend that the two of you go to the giftshop while you wait. S/he goes along with your idea. Your friend inquires how long it has been since you have seen your uncle, and you tell him/her that it has been about five years.

When your uncle arrives, you tell him that you will help him with his luggage. He asks you whether the bus still runs directly past your house. You say that it still does, but that you won't have to take the bus. You tell him that you have a driver's license now and that your car is parked right at the airport. He is quite surprised.

Ask students to read some of their material to the class. Have students ask questions about the material read.

II. *Schreibe einen kurzen Aufsatz!* **Write a short essay in German on the topic,** *"Ich mache eine Reise nach Deutschland."* **Use your imagination and include details about preparation (going to a travel agency, asking for information, etc.) and the flight itself (day of departure, airport, flight details and arrival).**

Du bist dran! (It's your turn.)

In this section your students should be encouraged to come up with various responses to complete each mini-dialog. Have students take parts, one reading the printed material and another responding to it.

Fliegen Sie nach Kassel?

. . . .

Dort ist es auch viel schöner.

. . . .

Wieviel Gepäck haben Sie denn?

. . . .

Na, dann bleiben Sie bestimmt ein paar Wochen.

. . . .

. . . .

Haben Sie auch Ihren Flugschein?

. . . .

Ich sitze gerne in der Mitte vom Flugzeug.

Können Sie mir sagen, von welchem Flugsteig die Amerikaner abfliegen?

. . . .

Und wo ist der?

. . . .

. . . .

Was hat der Pilot denn gesagt?

. . . .

Das ist ja schon in einer halben Stunde.

Darf ich Ihren Reisepaß sehen, bitte?

. . . .

Wohin geht's denn?

. . . .

Warum bist du so begeistert?

. . . .

Wer hat es dir geschenkt?

. . . .

Da freue ich mich aber.

. . . .

Wieviel Gepäck haben Sie denn?

. . . .

Warum nimmst du deine Einkaufstasche mit?

. . . .

Hast du so viel Geld zum Einkaufen?

. . . .

Ich komme gern mit. Vielleicht kaufst du mir auch etwas.

. . . .

Kulturecke

Refer to "Background Information" of *Lektion 11* (see front section of this teacher's edition) for additional information. Additional background notes will be provided in the front section for subsequent *Kulturecken*.

Means of Transportation

Driving in Germany is much more hazardous than it is in the U.S. because of the great density of traffic. There are many more cars for every mile of road than in this country. Foreigners are advised, therefore, to study driving rules and the traffic signs. The number of bicycles is also much greater in Germany than in the U.S. You will find people of all ages riding their bikes on pedestrian sidewalks, special bicycle paths or in urban or rural streets.

The smallest and most economical motor-driven vehicle is the *Mofa,* which stands for *Motorfahrrad,* or the somewhat larger model, the *Moped,* which is basically a bicycle with an auxiliary motor attached. You must observe the same traffic regulations when driving a moped as when operating any other means of transportation. Because of their limited speed, mopeds cannot be driven on the *Autobahn* or other expressways. Those who intend to use Germany's freeways must drive a vehicle at least the size of a motorcycle *(Motorrad).*

Germans who intend to drive a motorized vehicle must get a driver's license *(Führerschein).* The potential driver, who is at least eighteen years old, must attend an authorized driver's school *(Fahrschule).* After taking at least ten to twelve hours of private lessons, he or she must pass both written and behind-the-wheel driving tests. By the way, a German driver's license is good for a lifetime and doesn't need to be renewed periodically.

Secondary roads in Germany are narrow; some have high curbs, dangerous curves and cobblestone pavement, which is treacherous when wet. However, the highways *(Bundesstraßen)* are excellent and are welcomed especially by drivers who want to avoid the super expressways or freeways *(Autobahnen).* When driving on the *Autobahn,* you must adhere to strict rules. Passing on the right side is absolutely forbidden unless cars have slowed to a near standstill and are moving in two lanes. Passing is allowed only in the left lane. The suggested speed limit is 130 kilometers per hour (approximately 80 miles per hour), but many Germans drive much faster. In case of a breakdown on the *Autobahn,* there are emergency phones located every 1½ to 3 kilometers. Lift the receiver and then explain your problem. A car called *Straßenwacht* will be on the way within minutes.

A car in Germany keeps the same license plate as long as it is registered with the local traffic authority. If the owner moves to another district, the car will get another license plate. The letters on the license plate indicate the town or district where the car is registered. The letters *"GL,"* for example, stand for the town of *Gladbach.*

If your car is low on gas, you will look for a *Tankstelle* (service station). These are located throughout the cities and along the highways. Prices for diesel, regular and super gasoline usually are posted. To figure out the cost of gas, you must not only convert liters into gallons but also marks into dollars. Just as in the U.S., you will find the cost per liter, number of liters and the final amount indicated on the gas pump.

Of course, there are other means of transportation. You may decide to leave the driving to others. Some of the cities, particularly those that attract tourists, provide transportation in horse-drawn carriages for sightseers. In a few smaller towns, horses still are used to transport goods. If you are in a hurry, you should look for a *Taxi.* Don't be surprised to see a Mercedes car or other automobile of equal quality picking you up. Germans take special pride in buying good dependable cars that will last for many years.

Cars or vans of the German Federal Post Office *(Deutsche Bundespost)* are easily recognized by their yellow color and the black postal horn printed on the side. Police cars, marked *Polizei,* are usually white and green. In case of an accident, you will notice an ambulance *(Unfall-Rettung)* or the Red Cross *(Rote Kreuz)* rushing to the scene. Trucks *(Lastwagen)* crowd the city streets and major highways throughout the country. Most German companies have their

Womit fahren die Jugendlichen?

Wie heißt dieses
Verkehrsmittel?

die
Autobahn
(Köln)

eine Straßenbahn
in Würzburg

Woher kommt das Auto?

Wo fährt dieser Doppeldecker?

eine Fähre auf dem Bodensee

own trucks for their deliveries. The train is not used to transport goods as commonly as it is in the U.S.

Public transportation in Germany is excellent. In many German cities, the streetcar *(Straßenbahn)* is still the most important local public transportation. Some of the streetcars have been painted with flashy colors and advertising slogans. You must buy your ticket in advance because there is no conductor on the streetcar itself. Most stops have free-standing ticket automats marked *Fahrscheine,* where tickets can be purchased. To reduce the heavy demand on streetcars, and in some instances to phase them out, city buses have been introduced. These modern buses are often very long. They usually provide transportation between the city center and the suburbs. Double-decker buses *(Doppeldecker)* are still the trademark of bus service in West-Berlin. They are especially popular with tourists on sightseeing tours. Long-distance tour buses *(Reisebusse)* are even better equipped, with air conditioning, comfortable seats and huge windows to view the scenery.

Major cities such as Berlin, Hamburg and Munich have subways *(U-Bahnen)* and city trains *(S-Bahnen).* You can find these by locating signs at the entrances marked with a big "U" or "S." As with the streetcar system, you must purchase your tickets from the automat or directly at a ticket counter. When you buy a ticket from an automat, you should study carefully the zone to which you are going. The price of your ticket depends on the number of zones or the distance of your ride. The *S-Bahn,* an elevated city train, is faster because it can move freely in comparison to the city streetcars or buses. The *U-Bahn* runs underground except in such areas as Hamburg, where it must run overland due to the harbor. To eliminate the heavy traffic congestion, the city of Wuppertal introduced an elevated train, called *Schwebebahn,* which literally is attached to the tracks above. Several other cities, such as Hamburg, are now experimenting with similar transportation systems.

Many Germans ride the comfortable trains of the *Bundesbahn* (Federal Railroads). When you get to a railroad crossing in Germany, don't be surprised if suddenly a bell sounds and red-and-white gates are lowered to close the streets off from an approaching train.

There are other means of transportation that are intended to attract tourists to certain areas. In Rüdesheim on the Rhine, for example, you can ride a small open-air gondola *(Gondel)* for two to the top of the hill while enjoying the view of the vineyards around you. In the Bavarian Alps, on the other hand, cable cars *(Seilbahnen)* take you through treacherous heights to the mountain top. If you don't want to take a cable car, you could go up using the slower mountain trains *(Bergbahnen).*

The beautiful scenery surrounding Germany's lakes and rivers is enjoyed by visitors who use various kinds of boats to explore them. If you would like to have scenes from the Middle Ages recreated right in front of your eyes, you may want to take a boat ride on the Rhine. You will pass numerous castles and old towns, the sites of many unforgettable legends, on the most memorable stretch of the Rhine between Koblenz and Mainz. Many Germans enjoy taking pleasure boats and yachts to the islands in the North Sea. The most international means of transportation linking continents within hours is, of course, the airplane. Modern technology has made it possible to accommodate between 300 to 400 people in a jumbo jet, flying from New York to Frankfurt in about eight hours.

Was macht das Flugzeug?

eine Seilbahn (Zugspitze)

Vokabeln

The vocabulary section of each unit includes the forms of verbs with stem vowel change and past and present perfect tense of irregular verbs.

das **Abendessen** supper, dinner

abfliegen (*flog ab, ist abgeflogen*) to take off (plane)

der **Abflug,-̈e** departure (flight)

die **Abreise** departure

die **Aktentasche,-n** briefcase

sich **anhören** to listen to

der **Arm,-e** arm

aufgeben (*gibt auf, gab auf, aufgegeben*) to check (luggage)

aufmachen to open

das **Auge,-n** eye

der **Ausgang,-̈e** exit

aussuchen to select

austauschen to exchange

bedienen to help, wait on

sich **befinden** (*befand, befunden*) to be located, be

begeistert enthusiastic

das **Bein,-e** leg

sich **benehmen** (*benimmt, benahm, benommen*) to behave

bestaunen to marvel at

das **Bild,-er** picture

die **Bordkarte,-n** boarding pass

der **Brief,-e** letter

die **Brieffreundin,-nen** pen pal

sich **bürsten** to brush one's hair

sich **duschen** to shower, take a shower

die **Einkaufstasche,-n** shopping bag

einladen (*lädt ein, lud ein, eingeladen*) to invite

sich **erkennen** (*erkannte, erkannt*) to recognize each other

erklären to explain

erst not until, only

der **Erwachsene,-n** adult

erzählen to tell

der **Finger,-** finger

fliegen (*flog, ist geflogen*) to fly

der **Flugbegleiter,-** flight attendant

der **Fluggast,-̈e** flight passenger

der **Flughafen,-̈** airport

das **Flughafengebäude,-** airport building

der **Flugschein,-e** flight ticket

der **Flugsteig,-e** gate (flight)

das **Foto,-s** photo

sich **freuen auf** to look forward to

das **Frühstück** breakfast

gemütlich comfortable, cozy

es sich gemütlich machen to get comfortable

die **Gepäckausgabe,-n** baggage claim

das **Haar,-e** hair

der **Hals,-̈e** neck

die **Hand,-̈e** hand

international international

sich **kämmen** to comb one's hair

der **Karton,-s** carton, cardboard box

das **Kind,-er** child

das **Kinn,-e** chin

die **Kiste,-n** box, trunk

der **Kopf,-̈e** head

der **Körperteil,-e** part of the body

korrespondieren to correspond

landen to land

legen to place, put

die **Lippe,-n** lip

losfahren (*fährt los, fuhr los, ist losgefahren*) to drive off

losgehen (*ging los, ist losgegangen*) to start, take off

die **Nase,-n** nose

das **Ohr,-en** ear

packen to pack

das **Paket,-e** package

die **Paßkontrolle,-n** passport inspection

die **Personenkontrolle,-n** bodily search, security check

persönlich in person

der **Pilot,-en** pilot

sich **putzen** to clean oneself

sich die Zähne putzen to brush one's teeth

sich **rasieren** to shave oneself

der **Reisepaß,-̈sse** passport

rollen to roll

der **Rucksack,-̈e** knapsack

schenken to give (as a gift)

schlafen (*schläft, schlief, geschlafen*) to sleep

sich **schreiben** (*schrieb, geschrieben*) to correspond

der **Schritt,-e** step

die **Schulter,-n** shoulder

setzen to set, put, place

sich **setzen** to sit down

die **Sicherheitsüberprüfung,-en** security check

sicherlich surely, certainly

der **Start,-s** take-off, start

die **Stirn,-en** forehead

übersetzen to translate

sich **verabschieden** to say good-bye

verpassen to miss

vorne in front

vorzeigen to show

sich **waschen** (*wäscht, wusch, gewaschen*) to wash oneself

wiedersehen (*sieht wieder, sah wieder, wiedergesehen*) to see again

der **Zahn,-̈e** tooth

die **Zeitschrift,-en** magazine

der **Zoll** customs

zuhören to listen

Dialog

It is quite common and fashionable today to turn English words into German and simply add the appropriate German verb ending. (*surfen*, *campen*, *joggen*, *trampen*, etc.)

Gehen wir surfen!

MATTHIAS:	Was? Ihr seid schon da?
JOCHEN:	Bei dem schönen Wetter wollen wir früher surfen gehen.
KARSTEN:	Das letzte Mal hatten wir Pech. Dieser blöde Wind und der Regen auch noch.
MATTHIAS:	Na, dann mal los! Mein Wagen ist schon startbereit.
JOCHEN:	Hier ist die Tasche mit allen Badesachen.
KARSTEN:	Wo ist dein Surfbrett, Matthias?
MATTHIAS:	Ich hab's am Schluchsee gelassen.
MATTHIAS:	Kommt, Jungs! Wir nehmen alles mit zum Strand. Ich schleppe das Surfbrett; ihr bringt den Rest.
JOCHEN:	Erklär' uns mal, wie du alles zusammensetzt.
MATTHIAS:	Das ist ganz einfach. Zuerst nimmt man den Gabelbaum und spannt das Segel. Jochen, halte bitte den Mast!
KARSTEN:	Warte, die Leine ist noch etwas locker…so jetzt ist sie straff.
MATTHIAS:	Ich werde das Segel tragen. Zieht euch lieber um, ihr werdet nämlich naß.
MATTHIAS:	Paßt genau auf. Wer surfen will, muß es das nächste Mal selbst machen.
JOCHEN:	Ich halte das Surfbrett. Du kannst den Mast festmachen.
MATTHIAS:	Leider ist das Wasser für mich etwas zu ruhig, aber es ist gut zum Lernen. So, jetzt den Mast hochziehen und das Gleichgewicht behalten. Seht ihr, ganz einfach! Ich surfe eine Weile, dann kommt ihr dran.
KARSTEN:	Willst du's zuerst probieren?
JOCHEN:	Warum nicht?

The *Schluchsee* is located about 30 miles southeast of Freiburg *(Schwarzwald)*. In conversational language, Germans often contract words such as *hab's (habe es)*.

Fragen über den Dialog

1. Warum wollen Jochen und Karsten schon früher zum Schluchsee fahren?
2. Wie war das Wetter das letzte Mal?
3. Wo ist Matthias' Surfbrett?
4. Wer trägt das Surfbrett zum Strand?
5. Welche Teile braucht man, um surfen zu gehen?
6. Wer soll den Mast halten?
7. Wie ist das Wasser?
8. Was muß man beim Surfen tun?
9. Wer wird nach Matthias surfen gehen?

Let's Go Surfing!

MATTHIAS: What? You're here already?

JOCHEN: We want to go surfing earlier in this nice weather.

KARSTEN: We had bad luck last time. There was a strong wind and rain too.

MATTHIAS: O.K. Let's get going. My car is ready to go.

JOCHEN: Here is the bag with all the swimming stuff.

KARSTEN: Where is your surfboard, Matthias?

MATTHIAS: I've left it at the *Schluchsee*.

MATTHIAS: Come on, boys! We'll take everything to the beach. I'll haul the surfboard; you'll bring the rest.

JOCHEN: Explain to us how you'll put everything together.

MATTHIAS: That's quite simple. First you'll take the boom and tighten the sail. Jochen, hold the pole.

KARSTEN: Wait, the rope is still a little loose…there, now it's tight.

MATTHIAS: I'll carry the sail. You'd better change because you'll get wet.

MATTHIAS: Watch closely. Whoever wants to surf will have to do it himself next time.

JOCHEN: I'll hold the surfboard. You can fasten the pole.

MATTHIAS: Unfortunately the water is a bit too calm for me, but it's good for learning. So, now I'll pull up the pole and keep my balance. Look, it's easy. I'll surf a while, then it's your turn.

KARTSEN: Do you want to try it first?

JOCHEN: Why not?

Nützliche Ausdrücke

Review these expressions with your students after they have learned them in the *Dialog* and *Lesestück 1*.

Bei dem schönen Wetter…	In this nice weather…
Ich hatte Pech.	I had bad luck.
Dann mal los!	Let's get going.
Ich hab's dort gelassen.	I left it there.
Schleppst du das Surfbrett?	Are you hauling the surfboard?
Die Schnur ist straff.	The rope (string) is tight.
Zieht euch lieber um!	You'd better change (clothes).
Mach es selbst!	Do it yourself.
Es ist gut zum Lernen.	It's good for learning.
Behalte das Gleichgewicht!	Keep your balance.
Ihr kommt dann dran.	Then it will be your turn.
Es stellt sich heraus, daß…	It turns out that…
Ich mache Aufnahmen.	I'm taking pictures.
Das Paar ist schon verheiratet.	The couple is already married.
Was passiert später?	What will happen later?
Sie warten auf dem Korridor.	They are waiting in the hallway.
Eine Tür öffnet sich.	A door opens.
Sie stehen auf.	They get up.
Ich bin mit dir einverstanden.	I agree with you.
Hast du uns zum Essen eingeladen?	Did you invite us for a meal?

Sprichwort

Kleider machen Leute.	Clothes make the person.
(Clothes make people.)	

Ergänzung
Ask questions: *Wann ist Ostern? Muttertag? Weihnachten?…*

Feiertage in der BRD:

Neujahr	— 1. Januar
Karfreitag	— Freitag vor Ostern
Ostern	— zwischen dem 22. März und dem 25. April
Tag der Arbeit	— 1. Mai
Himmelfahrt	— 40 Tage nach Ostern
Pfingsten	— sieben Wochen nach Ostern
Tag der Einheit	— 17. Juni
Volkstrauertag	— im November
Weihnachten	— 25. und 26. Dezember

Andere besondere Tage:

Geburtstag
Muttertag
Vatertag

Wie sagt man…?

Merry Christmas!	Fröhliche Weihnachten! (oder: Ein frohes Weihnachtsfest!)
Happy New Year!	Ein glückliches Neues Jahr! (oder: Viel Glück im Neuen Jahr!)
Happy Birthday!	Herzlichen Glückwunsch zum Geburtstag!
Happy Easter!	Frohe Ostern! (oder: Ein frohes Osterfest!)

Übungen

Past Tense (Narrative Past Tense)

The past tense is frequently used in narratives and stories.

Regular verbs

The past tense has the following endings added to the stem of the verb:

ich	sag-te
du	sag-test
er **sie** **es**	sag-te
wir	sag-ten
ihr	sag-tet
sie	sag-ten
Sie	sag-ten

Beispiel: *Sie wohnte in Deutschland.*
(She lived in Germany.)

When the stem of the verb ends in -*t* or -*d*, an -*e*- is inserted between the stem and the ending.

Beispiel: *ich arbeit-e-te* (I worked)
er bad-e-te (he bathed)

Irregular verbs

The irregular verbs do not follow the pattern above but must be learned individually. To learn to use these verbs more easily you should study the first or the third person singular of the past tense. This will give you the base form to which endings are added in all other persons. Here are these endings:

	kommen	**gehen**	**fahren**
ich	kam	ging	fuhr
du	kam-st	ging-st	fuhr-st
er **sie** **es**	kam	ging	fuhr
wir	kam-en	ging-en	fuhr-en
ihr	kam-t	ging-t	fuhr-t
sie	kam-en	ging-en	fuhr-en
Sie	kam-en	ging-en	fuhr-en

Beispiele: *Sie fuhren in die Stadt.*   *Das Kleid gefiel mir nicht.*
              (They drove downtown.)   (I didn't like the dress.)

To facilitate learning the correct use of the irregular verbs, you should always remember three forms: the infinitive, the past and the past participle. These forms are also called the "principal parts" of a verb. The most frequently used irregular verbs, which you already know, are listed below. You will find the complete list of all irregular verbs in the *Grammar Summary* at the end of this book. Only the basic forms (without prefixes) are listed here.

Infinitive	Past	Past Participle	Meaning
beginnen	begann	begonnen	to begin
bieten	bot	geboten	to offer
bitten	bat	gebeten	to ask
bleiben	blieb	ist geblieben	to stay
denken	dachte	gedacht	to think
essen	aß	gegessen	to eat
fahren	fuhr	ist gefahren	to drive
finden	fand	gefunden	to find
fliegen	flog	ist geflogen	to fly
geben	gab	gegeben	to give
gefallen	gefiel	gefallen	to like
gehen	ging	ist gegangen	to go
gewinnen	gewann	gewonnen	to win
haben	hatte	gehabt	to have
halten	hielt	gehalten	to stop, hold
helfen	half	geholfen	to help
kennen	kannte	gekannt	to know
klingen	klang	geklungen	to sound
kommen	kam	ist gekommen	to come
lassen	ließ	gelassen	to leave
laufen	lief	ist gelaufen	to run
lesen	las	gelesen	to read
liegen	lag	gelegen	to lie, be located
nehmen	nahm	genommen	to take
rufen	rief	gerufen	to call
schlafen	schlief	geschlafen	to sleep
schlagen	schlug	geschlagen	to beat
schreiben	schrieb	geschrieben	to write
schwimmen	schwamm	ist geschwommen	to swim
sehen	sah	gesehen	to see
sein	war	ist gewesen	to be
singen	sang	gesungen	to sing
sitzen	saß	gesessen	to sit
sprechen	sprach	gesprochen	to speak
springen	sprang	ist gesprungen	to jump
stehen	stand	gestanden	to stand
steigen	stieg	ist gestiegen	to climb
tragen	trug	getragen	to carry
treffen	traf	getroffen	to meet
trinken	trank	getrunken	to drink
tun	tat	getan	to do
waschen	wusch	gewaschen	to wash
wissen	wußte	gewußt	to know

Folgt den Beispielen!

1. Was machten die Schüler gestern?   Sie spielten Fußball.

Variation: Change sentences to the present perfect tense. (Sie haben Fußball gespielt.)

    Fußball spielen

    die Aufgaben üben   Sie übten die Aufgaben.

    Musik hören   Sie hörten Musik.

    ein paar Hefte kaufen   Sie kauften ein paar Hefte.

    sehr oft tanzen   Sie tanzten sehr oft.

    Deutsch lernen   Sie lernten Deutsch.

2. Wer brauchte das Surfbrett?   Angelika brauchte es.

    (Angelika)

Variation: Have students answer each question differently (without using the cues).

Wer kochte das Essen?   Mein Vater kochte es.

    (mein Vater)

Wer stempelte den Ausweis?   Der Polizist stempelte ihn.

    (der Polizist)

Wer fragte den Lehrer?   Susanne fragte ihn.

    (Susanne)

Wer parkte den Wagen?   Peter parkte ihn.

    (Peter)

3. Hörtest du etwas?   Nein, ich hörte nichts.

Variation: Have students answer in the positive.

    Sagtest du etwas?   Nein, ich sagte nichts.

    Machtest du etwas?   Nein, ich machte nichts.

    Kauftest du etwas?   Nein, ich kaufte nichts.

    Glaubtest du etwas?   Nein, ich glaubte nichts.

    Suchtest du etwas?   Nein, ich suchte nichts.

4. Die Reise dauert lange.   Die Reise dauerte lange.

    Regnet es?   Regnete es?

    Die Hose paßt gut.   Die Hose paßte gut.

    Die Jungen fragen ihren Lehrer.   Die Jungen fragten ihren Lehrer.

    Sie spielen Schach.   Sie spielten Schach.

    Wartest du beim Eingang?   Wartetest du beim Eingang?

5. Hattest du viel Zeit?   Nein, ich hatte nicht viel Zeit.

Variation: Have students ask each other the questions, using the ihr and/or Sie forms and answer them accordingly.

Warst du in der Schule?   Nein, ich war nicht in der Schule.

Kamst du spät nach Hause?   Nein, ich kam nicht spät nach Hause.

Wußtest du das?   Nein, ich wußte das nicht.

Sprachst du mit ihm?   Nein, ich sprach nicht mit ihm.

Bliebst du lange da?   Nein, ich blieb nicht lange da.

6. der Pilot / abfliegen   Der Pilot flog ab.

Variation: Ask students to change sentences to the present perfect tense. (Der Pilot ist abgeflogen.)

    der Herr / anhalten   Der Herr hielt an.

    die Mädchen / aussteigen   Die Mädchen stiegen aus.

die Besucher / hierherkommen   Die Besucher kamen hierher.

mein Freund / anrufen   Mein Freund rief an.

der Zug / ankommen   Der Zug kam an.

Variation: Encourage students to answer each question with an appropriate response.

7. Wohin läufst du?   Wohin liefst du?

Wo steht es?   Wo stand es?

Wer schreibt denn?   Wer schrieb denn?

Warum rufst du an?   Warum riefst du an?

Wen kennen Sie?   Wen kannten Sie?

Was trinken wir?   Was tranken wir?

8. Wo seid ihr?   Wo wart ihr?

Ich bin verärgert.   Ich war verärgert.

Sie sind an der Reihe.   Sie waren an der Reihe.

Der Mann ist beliebt.   Der Mann war beliebt.

Bist du zu Hause?   Warst du zu Hause?

Das Wetter ist sehr schön.   Das Wetter war sehr schön.

9. Wir sind lange gelaufen.   Wir liefen lange.

Ich habe ihn getroffen.   Ich traf ihn.

Hast du keine Zeit gehabt?   Hattest du keine Zeit?

Wann seid ihr gekommen?   Wann kamt ihr?

Haben Sie ihm geholfen?   Halfen Sie ihm?

Sie hat viel gegessen.   Sie aß viel.

Ich bin in der Schule geblieben.   Ich blieb in der Schule.

10. Change the following sentences from the present to the past tense.

You may also want to have students change sentences to the future and present perfect tense for additional review.

Beispiel: *Ich trage das Segel.*
Ich trug das Segel.

1. Wohin fährst du dieses Jahr?
2. Wir sprechen immer Deutsch.
3. Im Januar schneit es bei uns.
4. Verstehen Sie den Ausländer gut?
5. Wie schmeckt das Essen?
6. Wir trinken Limonade und essen Brot und Wurst.
7. Ich kaufe keinen Mantel.
8. Matthias bekommt das Surfbrett zum Geburtstag.
9. Die Besucher warten schon lange.
10. Gibt er dir sein Fahrrad?
11. Die Touristen tragen ihre Koffer.
12. Er fragt seinen Lehrer.

11. **Rewrite the following short paragraph, changing the verbs to the past tense where necessary.**

Werner und Peter wohnen nicht weit von der Stadt. Am Sonnabend gehen sie zum Kaufhaus. Werner fragt die Verkäuferin: „Wieviel kostet die Gitarre?" Sie sagt: „Sie kostet 80 DM." Die Jungen sagen, daß das nicht zu teuer ist. Leider haben sie nur 60 DM. Deshalb gehen sie schnell nach Hause zurück. Werners Vater gibt ihnen 20 DM. Dann fahren sie schnell mit ihren Fahrrädern zum Kaufhaus und kaufen die Gitarre.

12. **Complete each sentence by selecting one of the verbs from the list below. Change this verb to the past tense, making sure that each sentence is meaningful. You will not use all the verbs.**

beginnen	warten
essen	lesen
bleiben	haben
fliegen	kommen
gehen	stehen
sein	dauern
geben	spielen
schmecken	steigen

1. Die Dame _____ um drei Uhr zu uns.
2. Das Essen _____ sehr gut.
3. Die Touristen _____ wenig Zeit.
4. Herr Held _____ beim Eingang.
5. Der Film _____ pünktlich.
6. Am Abend _____ wir sehr hungrig.
7. Sein Onkel _____ nicht lange bei uns.
8. Die Jugendlichen _____ viele Bücher.
9. Die Mädchen _____ Gitarre.
10. Die Reise _____ drei Stunden.
11. Die Amerikaner _____ von New York direkt nach Köln.
12. Mein Vater _____ mir etwas Geld.

gern and lieber

As you have learned before (*Deutsch: Aktuell 1,* Unit 4), the word *gern* indicates liking something or someone. The comparative form of *gern* is *lieber,* which is primarily used in expressing comparisons.

Beispiele: *Ich spiele gern Klavier.*
(I like to play piano.)

Ich spiele lieber Gitarre.
(I prefer to play guitar.)

Was fährst du lieber, Fahrrad oder Auto?
(What do you prefer to drive, a bicycle or a car?)

Ich fahre lieber Auto.
(I prefer to drive a car.)

Folgt den Beispielen!

13. Spielst du gern Klavier? — Ja, ich spiele gern Klavier.

Variation: Personalize
questions. (*Was spielst du
gern?, Welche Musik hörst
du gern?, Welches/Was für
ein Buch liest du gern?*, etc.)

Singst du gern? — Ja, ich singe gern.

Hörst du gern Musik? — Ja, ich höre gern Musik.

Liest du gern? — Ja, ich lese gern.

Schreibst du gern einen Brief? — Ja, ich schreibe gern einen Brief.

Ißt du gern Käse? — Ja, ich esse gern Käse.

Fährst du gern Fahrrad? — Ja, ich fahre gern Fahrrad.

14. Was spielst du lieber, Fußball oder Tennis? (Tennis) — Ich spiele lieber Tennis.

Variation: Have students ask
each other additional
questions using *lieber.*

Wohin fährst du lieber, nach Mainz oder Wiesbaden? (Mainz) — Ich fahre lieber nach Mainz.

Was hast du lieber, Mathe oder Chemie? (Mathe) — Ich habe lieber Mathe.

Wo wohnst du lieber, in der Stadt oder im Vorort? (im Vorort) — Ich wohne lieber im Vorort.

Wann ißt du lieber, um sieben oder um acht? (um acht) — Ich esse lieber um acht.

Was trinkst du lieber, Milch oder Limonade? (Limonade) — Ich trinke lieber Limonade.

15. **Write answers to the following questions. Use *gern* when the answer begins with "Ja..." and *nicht gern* plus *lieber* when the answer begins with "Nein..."**

Beispiel: *Spielst du gern Tischtennis? Ja...*
Ja, ich spiele gern Tischtennis.

Fährst du gern Fahrrad? Nein... (Motorrad)
Nein, ich fahre nicht gern Fahrrad. Ich fahre lieber Motorrad.

1. Lesen Sie gern? Ja,...
2. Sprechen Sie gern Deutsch? Nein...(Englisch)
3. Spielst du gern Fußball? Nein...(Golf)
4. Singen Sie gern? Ja ..
5. Ißt du gern Käse? Nein...(Wurst)
6. Lernst du gern Biologie? Nein...(Physik)
7. Hörst du gern Musik? Ja...
8. Trägst du gern den Koffer? Nein...(Tasche)

Infinitives Used as Nouns

An infinitive of a verb becomes a noun when it is preceded by the prepositions *beim (bei dem)*, *zum (zu dem)* or *mit (mit dem)*.

Examples: *Beim Spielen haben wir viel Spaß.*
(While playing we have a lot of fun.)

Das Wetter ist gut zum Surfen.
(The weather is good for surfing.)

Bist du mit dem Fotografieren fertig?
(Are you done taking pictures?)

Folgt den Beispielen!

16. Beim Sprechen geht es besser.
     spielen
     lesen
     schreiben
     fahren

Beim Sprechen geht es besser.
Beim Spielen geht es besser.
Beim Lesen geht es besser.
Beim Schreiben geht es besser.
Beim Fahren geht es besser.

17. Auto / fahren
     Tisch / schreiben
     Bett / schlafen
     Mund / sprechen
     Ohren / hören
     Beine / laufen

Er braucht das Auto zum Fahren.
Er braucht den Tisch zum Schreiben.
Er braucht das Bett zum Schlafen.
Er braucht den Mund zum Sprechen.
Er braucht die Ohren zum Hören.
Er braucht die Beine zum Laufen.

18. Beantwortet diese Fragen!

1. Was braucht man zum Surfen?
2. Was braucht man zum Schreiben?
3. Was braucht man zum Lesen?
4. Was braucht man zum Fahren?

Lesestück 1

Eine Hochzeit in Neubrandenburg

Das Standesamt° in Neubrandenburg ist jeden Freitag, besonders im Frühling und im Sommer, der Mittelpunkt der Stadt. Verschiedene Gruppen von Verwandten° und Bekannten° versammeln sich alle zwanzig Minuten vor dem Standesamt. Warum sind die Leute so

marriage bureau

relatives/friends

Die Braut und der Bräutigam kommen in einer Hochzeitskutsche.

An welchen Tagen finden hier Hochzeiten statt?

Das Hochzeitspaar kommt in ein Zimmer herein.

Die Standesbeamtin fragt Volker und Giesela, ob sie mit der Heirat einverstanden sind.

Herr und Frau Hesse

Das Ehepaar und die Hochzeitsgäste kommen aus dem Standesamt heraus.

elegant angezogen°? Auf wen° warten sie denn? Es stellt sich bald *dressed/for whom*
heraus, daß hier ein besonderes Ereignis stattfindet — eine
Hochzeit.

Eine Hochzeitskutsche° kommt langsam näher. Endlich hält *wedding carriage*
sie an. Braut° und Bräutigam° steigen aus. Die Leute sehen interes- *bride/groom*
siert zu°. Manche machen Aufnahmen. Geduldig° warten die Braut *sehen…zu watch/ patiently*
und der Bräutigam, bis man mit dem Fotografieren° fertig ist. Wäh- *taking pictures*
rend alle ins Standesamt gehen, kommt ein anderes Paar heraus.
Dieses Paar ist nun schon verheiratet.

In einem Büro spricht gerade die Standesbeamtin° mit einer *registrar*
Braut und einem Bräutigam — Giesela Mendel und Volker Hesse.
Die Beamtin erklärt beiden noch einmal kurz, was in ein paar Minu-
ten passiert. Sie gibt Volker die Geburtsurkunden° und die Ausweise *birth certificates*
zurück°. Er muß noch schnell etwas unterschreiben°. Auf dem Tisch *gibt…zurück returns/sign*
liegt das „Buch der Familie". In diesem Buch stehen wichtige Da-
ten von Volkers und Gieselas Eltern und Großeltern.

Volker, Giesela und die Hochzeitsgäste° warten eine Weile auf *wedding guests*
dem Korridor. Plötzlich hört man Musik. Eine Tür öffnet sich und
alle gehen in ein Zimmer — an der Spitze die Braut und der Bräutigam. Volker und Giesela setzen sich ganz vorne auf zwei Stühle°. *chairs*
Die Hochzeitsgäste sitzen hinter ihnen. Alle sitzen ganz ruhig und
hören klassische Musik. Volker und Giesela haben vorher auf einer
Kassette Musik ausgewählt. Die Stimmung ist sehr feierlich°. *solemn*

Die Standesbeamtin spricht ungefähr fünf Minuten. Dann ste-
hen alle auf. Sie fragt Volker und Giesela, ob sie mit der Heirat° *marriage*
einverstanden sind. Nach dem „ja" von beiden, bittet° sie Volker *asks*
zuerst, die Heiratsurkunde° zu unterschreiben. Dann unterschreibt *marriage certificate*
Giesela auch. Der Höhepunkt° kommt, als Volker und Giesela die *highlight*
Trauringe° austauschen°. Jetzt sind beide Ehemann° und Ehefrau°. *wedding rings/ exchange/husband/ wife*
Die Beamtin wünscht ihnen Glück und gibt ihnen das „Buch der
Familie".

Volker und Giesela kommen glücklich° als Herr und Frau Hes- *happy*
se aus dem Standesamt heraus°. Ihre Verwandten und Bekannten *kommen…heraus come out*
folgen ihnen. Sie gehen nur ein paar Schritte auf der Straße. Ihr
Wagen ist gleich vor dem Eingang. Volker öffnet die Tür und Giesela steigt ein. Dann fahren sie Richtung Innenstadt. Ihre Eltern
haben alle Hochzeitsgäste zum Essen eingeladen.

Fragen über das Lesestück

1. Wo versammeln sich die Leute?
2. Warum warten sie dort?
3. Was machen die Leute, als die Braut und der Bräutigam aus der Kutsche
   aussteigen?
4. Warum spricht die Standesbeamtin mit Volker und Giesela?
5. Wie heißt das Buch auf dem Tisch. Warum ist es so wichtig?

6. Was hört man plötzlich? Was machen die Hochzeitsgäste dann?
7. Wo sitzen Volker und Giesela? Und die Hochzeitsgäste?
8. Was macht die Beamtin?
9. Was müssen Volker und Giesela unterschreiben?
10. Wann ist der Höhepunkt?
11. Was gibt die Standesbeamtin Volker und Giesela?
12. Wohin fahren dann alle? Warum?

Erweiterung

Expand these questions by finding out more about your students. (*Was für ein Hobby hast du?*, *Was hast du in den Ferien vor?*, etc.)

19. Beantwortet diese Fragen mit einem ganzen Satz!

1. Fotografierst du gern? Was für Aufnahmen machst du?
2. Wo kann man in deiner Gegend surfen gehen?
3. Was machst du an deinem Geburtstag?
4. An welchem Tag ist Weihnachten?
5. Wie ist das Wetter zu Ostern meistens in deiner Gegend?

20. Wie heißt das auf deutsch?

1. Is he taking pictures?
2. We have no luck.
3. I'm hauling the sail.
4. Who is married?
5. Are you getting up, Dieter?
6. Why are they waiting in the hallway?
7. We'll swim in this nice weather.
8. I have invited my friend.

21. Complete each sentence. Be sure that each sentence is meaningful.

1. Eine Hochzeitskutsche _____ .
2. Die Leute warten _____ .
3. Die Beamtin erklärt _____ .
4. Warum hast du denn _____ .
5. Um wieviel Uhr _____ .
6. Sie unterschreiben _____ .

22. Define each word with one complete German sentence.

1. Trauringe
2. Braut
3. Geburtsurkunde
4. Hochzeit
5. Standesamt
6. Hochzeitsgäste

Variation: Ask your students to write a paragraph using all of the six words in their story.

23. Provide an appropriate response in German for each statement or question.

Have pairs of students participate in this activity, one reading the sentences and the other responding with original statements or questions.

1. Das letzte Mal war das Wetter nicht so schön.
2. Bringst du dein Surfbrett mit?
3. Soll ich mich umziehen?
4. Ich will den Mast noch festmachen.
5. Der See ist nicht weit entfernt.

24. Beantwortet die Fragen!

1. Wie ist das Wetter heute?
2. Was nimmst du alles zum Strand mit?
3. Warum brauchst du eine Schnur?
4. Was willst du denn tragen?
5. Wer kommt zu Weihnachten zu euch?
6. Wen möchtest du zu deiner Party einladen?
7. Was steht auf einer Geburtsurkunde?

Rückblick

Should your students have some problems in completing these exercises, you may want to review the specific grammar point that was covered in previous lessons.

I. Complete each sentence by supplying the appropriate reflexive pronoun.

1. Hast du _____ die Zähne geputzt?
2. Die Studenten freuen _____ sehr auf die Reise.
3. Habt ihr _____ bei der Arbeit angestrengt?
4. Ich ziehe _____ den Mantel an.
5. Setzen Sie _____ bitte!
6. Volker muß _____ noch schnell rasieren.
7. Bürste _____ die Haare!
8. Wir müssen _____ etwas beeilen.
9. Die Touristen sehen _____ die Stadtmauer an.
10. Ich werde _____ verabschieden.

II. Change the direct and indirect objects to pronouns. Change the word order, where necessary.

> **Beispiel:** *Ich gebe **meinem Freund das Surfbrett**.*
> *Ich gebe **es ihm**.*

1. Kannst du *deiner Schwester den Computer* zeigen?
2. Geben Sie *der Dame die Bordkarte!*
3. Hilfst du *deinem Freund?*
4. Suchen Sie *einen Sitzplatz?*
5. Wir kaufen *unseren Eltern ein Geschenk.*
6. Sag *deiner Freundin das Wort!*
7. Der Herr erklärt *den Besuchern die Geschichte.*

8. Ich glaube *dieser Angestellten* nicht.

9. Sie gibt *den Leuten die Prospekte*.

10. Das Museum gefällt *meinem Onkel* gar nicht.

III. Retell the following story in the past and then in the present perfect tense.

Ursula und Claudia haben Lust, ins Kino zu gehen. Sie treffen sich um dreiviertel drei bei Ursula. Sie verlassen sofort Ursulas Wohnung. Zum Kino sind es nur zehn Minuten zu Fuß.

Im Kino läuft ein Film aus Frankreich. Vor dem Kino stehen ihre zwei Freunde, Rainer und Walter. Die beiden gehen auch ins Kino, aber erst um fünf Uhr. Sie laden Ursula und Claudia ein, mit ihnen um fünf Uhr ins Kino zu gehen. Jetzt haben die Vier noch zwei Stunden Zeit. Eine Eisdiele ist gleich in der Nähe. Dort schmeckt das Eis immer besonders gut.

IV. Complete the sentences, using the words provided in parentheses. Contract the prepositions where possible.

       Beispiele: *Er kommt aus* _____ *(Kino, Schule)*
                Er kommt aus dem Kino.
                Er kommt aus der Schule.

1. Treffen wir uns doch bei _____ ! (Flughafen, Schalter, Eisdiele)

2. Habt ihr Lust, um _____ zu laufen? (Rathaus, die Universität, Marktplatz)

3. Ich fahre ohne _____ . (mein Bruder, er, Sie)

4. Haben Sie mit _____ gesprochen? (Pilot, Dame, Touristen)

5. Wer kommt außer _____ noch zum Tanz? (mein Freund, seine Schwester, du)

6. Die Haltestelle ist zwei Ecken von _____ entfernt. (unser Haus, Sie, meine Wohnung)

7. Morgen werden wir gegen _____ spielen. (ihr, deine Mannschaft, du)

8. Geht nicht durch _____ ! (Zimmer, Bahnhof, Geschäft)

9. Um wieviel Uhr kommst du aus _____ ? (Theater, Reisebüro, Jugendherberge)

10. Wir müssen schnell zu _____ gehen. (Hotel, Fenster, Wagen)

Lesestück 2

Bern — die Hauptstadt der Schweiz

Die Stadt Bern liegt im Nordwesten der Schweiz. Die meisten Touristen besuchen Bern mit dem Auto oder mit dem Bus. Manche kommen mit dem Zug auf dem modernen Bahnhof in der Hauptstadt an.

Das Münster überragt die ganze Stadt. Man hat mit dem Bau° *structure* schon im Jahre 1421 begonnen. Der Turm ist ungefähr 100 Meter hoch. Die Aare, der drittlängste Fluß der Schweiz (nach dem Rhein und der Rhone), fließt direkt durch die Stadt. Die Regierungsgebäude überblicken den Fluß. Die Hauptstadt hat natürlich Botschaften° aus verschiedenen Ländern. Bern hat auch einige Museen. Das *embassies* bekannteste ist das Historische Museum. Hier kann man über die Geschichte der Schweiz viel lesen und lernen.

Für Touristen ist die Altstadt von besonderem Interesse. Die Häuser sind in diesem Stadtteil° sehr alt. In der Altstadt befindet sich der Zeitglockenturm°. Diese astronomische Uhr ist mehr als 400 Jahre alt; das Stadttor neben der Uhr ist sogar fast 800 Jahre alt. Das Stadtwappen° ist ein Bär°. Man sieht ihn auf vielen Fahnen°. Deshalb gibt es in der Stadt den sogenannten° „Bärengraben"°. Dort kann man junge und alte Bären bewundern°.

In der Stadt ist meistens viel Verkehr. Die Berner fahren mit Straßenbahnen und Bussen oder mit Autos und Fahrrädern durch die Stadt. Auf dem Markt ist viel los°. Die Einwohner kommen hierher und kaufen ihr frisches° Obst° und Gemüse°. Für Unterhaltung° hat man auch gesorgt. Eine Musikgruppe oder eine Kapelle° spielt oft auf dem Markt. Das bringt die Berner richtig in Stimmung. In der Nähe vom Markt sind Geschäfte für jeden Geschmack. Wer nichts° auf dem Markt findet, hat hier in den zahlreichen Geschäften eine große Auswahl.

district
Clock Tower

city coat of arms/ bear/flags so-called/Bear Pit admire

a lot is going on
fresh/fruit/ vegetables/ entertainment band

nothing

der Zeitglockenturm

Die Aare fließt durch Bern.

Die Regierungsgebäude überblicken den Fluß.

Die Einwohner der Stadt sind auf ihre Parks sehr stolz°. Der Rosengarten ist bei den Bernern besonders beliebt. Da kann man überall° spazierengehen°. Für Kinder gibt es im Rosengarten Spielplätze° und für Erwachsene zahlreiche Bänke. Nur ein paar Minuten von Bern entfernt liegen schöne Ausflugsorte, viele Seen und Berge. Wenn man nicht mit dem Auto fahren will, hat man die Möglichkeit mit der Bergbahn° hoch auf die Berge zu fahren. Von dort oben sieht alles so märchenhaft aus und ist für Besucher ein unvergeßliches° Erlebnis.

proud

all over/stroll
playgrounds

mountain train

unforgettable

Fragen über das Lesestück

1. Wie kommen die meisten Besucher nach Bern?
2. Wie heißt das größte Gebäude und wie hoch ist es?
3. Wie heißt der längste Fluß in der Schweiz?
4. Welches Museum ist das bekannteste? Was kann man dort tun?
5. Was befindet sich alles in der Altstadt?
6. Was sieht man auf den Fahnen?
7. Warum ist der Markt so beliebt?
8. Was bringt die Berner oft in Stimmung?
9. Wo können die Berner einkaufen gehen?
10. Welcher Park ist in Bern sehr bekannt? Was gibt es dort alles?
11. Wohin fahren viele Touristen sehr gern?

Sprachspiegel

I. *Schreibe einen kurzen Aufsatz!* **Include some or all of the following details, and any other items you can think of.**

You may want to have students read their short essays. Have others ask questions about what was read.

Your class is going on a three-day trip. You and your classmates meet in front of the school. A bus takes you to a small town located at a lake, about 100 miles away. Your teacher has made reservations at a small hotel. From there you are within walking distance of the beach. There is plenty to do — swimming, boating, surfing, etc. You also go on short hiking and sightseeing trips in the surrounding area. After three days you return home by train.

II. Weißt du, an welchen Tagen diese Feiertage sind?

1. Ostern
2. Weihnachtsabend und Weihnachtstag
3. Muttertag
4. Pfingsten
5. Vatertag
6. Neujahr
7. dein Geburtstag

Du bist dran!

Encourage your students to be as creative as possible in completing each mini-dialog. Have pairs of students present their material to the rest of the class.

Wo ist dein Surfbrett?

. . . .

Dann bringe ich lieber meins.

. . . .

Mein Schwester heiratet am Samstag?

. . . .

Nein, sie hat ihn schon drei Jahre gekannt.

. . . .

. . . .

Gut, ich nehme meine Badesachen mit.

. . . .

Hast du denn deinen Führerschein?

Fotografierst du gern?

. . . .

Ich eigentlich auch.

Warum brauchst du deine Geburtsurkunde?

. . . .

Wann fährst du denn nach Europa?

. . . .

Oh, wie schön!

. . . .

Nein, heute nicht. Es ist zu windig.

. . . .

Das ist eine gute Idee.

Kannst du mir das noch einmal erklären?

. . . .

Das sagst du jedes Mal.

. . . .

So ein Pech! Ich habe mein Geld verloren.

. . . .

Nein, in der Schule habe ich es noch gehabt.

. . . .

. . . .

Aber wir haben doch noch viel Zeit.

. . . .

Na, dann komme ich gern mit.

> **Fotografierst du gern?**

Kulturecke

Holidays and Festivals in Germany

The German calendar is filled with religious and secular holidays, as well as numerous local and regional festivals. The four Sundays of Advent mark the beginning of the Christian celebration and with it the beginning of the Christian church year. On each Sunday, many families gather around the Advent wreath and light one candle until all four are burning together. *Sankt Nikolaus,* the German Santa Claus, does not come — as might be assumed — on Christmas Eve, but on December 6. Sometimes he shows up in person, to the delight of the children, but in most cases *Sankt Nikolaus* visits during the night. When the children get up the next morning, they find their shoes — which they had put outside the door the night before — filled with all kinds of goodies.

During the Christmas season, the stores are packed with an abundance of items. Many stores specialize in selling woodcarvings that can be displayed throughout the home. Christmas markets with their colorful displays offer shoppers and curiosity seekers many opportunities to absorb the beautiful surroundings. Famous among the Christmas markets is the *Christkindlesmarkt* in Nürnberg. Most children don't see the fully decorated tree until Christmas Eve *(Heiliger Abend)*. Many German homes still use traditional wax candles on their trees. Christmas Eve is the focal point of the celebration in Germany, and both the 25th and 26th of December are national holidays.

The German New Year's Eve, called *Silvester,* is usually celebrated with close friends and relatives. Smaller towns, like Schiltach in the Black Forest, have a special celebration. There, the townspeople gather in front of the local church from which they parade with torchlights to the market square. Before midnight, various groups sing and then the mayor talks to the townspeople about the past and the future.

One of the most famous German festivals is the *Karneval* in Cologne. Although the carnival season lasts several weeks, the climax is reached on *Rosenmontag,* the Monday before Ash Wednesday. On Rose Monday, a five-mile parade winds in slow procession through the city with floats, horses and bands. In their traditional picturesque uniforms, the Fools' Guilds are one of the many highlights of this event. Prince Carnival *(Prinz Karneval)* reigns over the city. Cologne does not name a princess as other cities do, but names instead the Cologne Peasant *(Kölnischer Bauer)* and the Cologne Virgin *(Kölnische Jungfrau).* The Cologne Virgin is a man — a relic of ancient times when women were excluded from the carnival celebration. Many groups of clowns contribute to the enjoyment and laughter of the tens of thousands of spectators lining the streets. Although Cologne's celebration is known as *Karneval,* this celebration is called *Fassenacht* in Mainz and *Fasching* in Munich. As in Cologne, Munich also has a spectacular, colorful parade.

During the Lenten season there are almost no celebrations in Germany. One week before Palm Sunday, however, the *Sommertagszug* takes place in Heidelberg. Many people parade through the city, dressed as white and green straw figures decorated with colorful ribbons. These traditional figures suggest that winter is over and spring and summer are not far away.

Easter activities center around the decoration of traditional Easter eggs *(Ostereier).* It is quite common for families to spend many hours decorating the eggs, using elaborate techniques. Occasionally these decorated Easter eggs are hung on the Easter Tree *(Osterbaum),* a tradition brought into Germany by settlers from eastern countries. Children anxiously look forward to hunting for the Easter eggs. These colorful eggs, together with egg-shaped candies, usually are placed in a small basket and hidden inside or outside the home.

Pentecost is celebrated between May 9 and June 13 (the seventh Sunday and Monday after Easter). A variety of celebrations take place at that time. The *Siedertanz* in Schwäbisch

Der Weihnachtsbaum steht auf dem Tisch.

Karneval in Köln

Alles sieht so bunt aus.

Rattenfänger von Hameln

Ostereier

ein Fest aus dem Mittelalter (Schwäbisch Hall)

Sommertagszug in Heidelberg

die Geißbock-versteigerung (Deidesheim)

Eine Kapelle spielt. (Schwäbisch Hall)

Hall reminds everyone in the town that it was saved from a disastrous fire over 600 years ago. Besides this dance, the main event of this celebration, there are several other activities scheduled during Pentecost. Religious processions, particularly in Southern Germany, illustrate the meaning of Pentecost, which according to belief also marks the beginning of summer.

The many festivals scheduled during the summer months allow participants and spectators to enjoy the outdoors. Among the summer festivals is the *Uracher Schäferlauf* (Shepherds' Run of Urach), a tradition that dates back several hundred years. At that time, the shepherds of Urach completed their work and then competed in various games, including a 300-meter run. The winner received a sheep. Another local event is the *Ravensburger Rutenfest*. Hundreds of elementary school students participate in this celebration, which dates back to the 15th century, when students had to cut sticks *(Ruten)* for the teachers who used them for keeping strict discipline.

One of the oldest festivals is the *Ulmer Fischerstechen,* which comes from the tournaments that were popular during the Middle Ages. Groups of two men try to push each other into the water, using a pole. Thousands of spectators watch from the shore of the Danube River. Every three years the famous *Landshuter Hochzeit* is celebrated. Hundreds of the townspeople participate in this spectacular event that recreates the legendary wedding of George, the son of Duke Ludwig, and Hedwige, the daughter of the Polish King Kasimir in the year 1475. It is said that 10,000 people, mostly friends and relatives of the royal families, had to be fed and housed for a whole week, thus creating an event discussed throughout Europe.

Every ten years, the Bavarian town of Oberammergau stages the world-famous passion plays *(Passionsspiele),* which portray the last days of Christ's suffering and death. Hundreds of the townspeople participate in various capacities, ranging from acting to making costumes and designing the stage sets.

Many of the festivals date back to the Middle Ages. The *Meistertrunk* in Rothenburg ob der Tauber had its origin during the Thirty Years' War. At that time, the Swedish army, headed by General Tilly, intended to destroy the town unless someone could be found to drink a huge jug of wine. Mayor Nusch agreed and accomplished this feat, thus saving the town from certain destruction. A similar festival, called the *Kinderzeche,* takes place in Dinkelsbühl, near Rothenburg. In Dinkelsbühl, the children saved the town from destruction during the Thirty Years' War, and the annual children's parade commemorates this event. Another well-known festival is in Hameln. Twice a year, in May and in September, the legend of the Pied Piper of Hamelin *(Rattenfänger von Hameln)* is recreated. This legend dates back to the year 1284.

The fall season is known for the numerous festivals that take place along the wine-growing areas of the Rhine and Moselle Rivers. Each town schedules its own festival during which a queen *(Weinkönigin)* is elected. In Southern Germany, particularly in Bavaria, towns such as Fürstenfeldbruck have parades in which the townspeople participate. Various bands march down the main street to the delight of the local audience and the many tourists.

The largest German festival is the annual *Oktoberfest,* celebrated in Munich. Although this famous festival is called the *Oktoberfest,* it actually begins during September and ends on the first Sunday in October after sixteen days. A big parade kicks off the festive activities, as it winds through the center of the city, ending up on the *Theresienwiese,* called simply "Wies'n." Over a million people, both Germans and foreigners, visit the *Oktoberfest* every year and enjoy not only the many opportunities but also the abundance of food and beer. Especially popular are the big pretzels that often are sold in front of the beer tents. These beer tents are constructed to accommodate the thousands of people who congregate here on long benches at wooden tables, socializing with friends and even strangers, singing songs and consuming beer while brass bands provide the musical atmosphere.

Vokabeln

sich **anziehen** *(zog an, angezogen)* to get dressed
Er ist angezogen. He is dressed.
die **Aufnahme,-n** picture, photo
Aufnahmen machen to take pictures
die **Badesachen** (pl.) swimming stuff
behalten *(behält, behielt, behalten)* to keep
der **Bekannte,-n** friend, acquaintance
bitten *(bat, gebeten)* to ask
blöd dumb, stupid
die **Braut,-̈e** bride
der **Bräutigam,-e** groom
die **Ehefrau,-en** wife
der **Ehemann,-̈er** husband
die **Einheit** unity
Tag der Einheit Day of Unity
einverstanden sein to agree
feierlich solemn, festive
der **Feiertag,-e** holiday
festmachen to attach, fasten
der **Gabelbaum,-̈e** boom (surfing)
die **Geburtsurkunde,-n** birth certificate
geduldig patient(ly)
genau closely
das **Gleichgewicht** balance
das Gleichgewicht behalten to keep one's balance
glücklich happy
halten *(hält, hielt, gehalten)* to hold
die **Heirat,-en** marriage
die **Heiratsurkunde,-n** marriage certificate
herauskommen *(kam heraus, ist herausgekommen)* to come out (of)
sich **herausstellen** to turn out, prove
der **Himmelfahrtstag** Ascension Day

die **Hochzeit,-en** wedding
der **Hochzeitsgast,-̈e** wedding guest
die **Hochzeitskutsche,-n** wedding carriage
hochziehen *(zog hoch, hochgezogen)* to pull up
der **Höhepunkt,-e** highlight
der **Karfreitag** Good Friday
klassisch classical
der **Korridor,-e** corridor, hallway
lassen *(läßt, ließ, gelassen)* to leave
die **Leine,-n** rope
locker loose
der **Mann,-̈er** husband
der **Mast,-en** pole
der **Muttertag** Mother's Day
naß wet
das **Neujahr** New Year's Day
sich **öffnen** to open
Ostern Easter
Frohe Ostern! Happy Easter!
das **Paar,-e** couple, pair
passieren to happen
das **Pech** bad luck
Pfingsten Pentecost
probieren to try
der **Regen** rain
der **Rest,-e** rest
schleppen to haul, drag
die **Schnur,-̈e** rope, string
das **Segel,-** sail
selbst in person
Mach es selbst! Do it yourself.
das **Standesamt,-̈er** marriage (license) bureau
die **Standesbeamtin,-nen** registrar, official at marriage bureau
startbereit ready to take off
spannen to tighten, stretch
straff tight
der **Strand,-̈e** beach

der **Stuhl,-̈e** chair
das **Surfbrett,-er** surfboard (for windsurfing)
surfen to (wind) surf
surfen gehen to go (wind) surfing
der **Trauring,-e** wedding ring
sich **umziehen** *(zog um, umgezogen)* to change (clothes)
unterschreiben *(unterschrieb, unterschrieben)* to sign
der **Vatertag** Father's Day
verheiratet married
der **Verwandte,-n** relative
Volkstrauertag Day of National Mourning
das **Wasser** water
Weihnachten Christmas
Fröhliche Weihnachten! Merry Christmas!
der **Wind,-e** wind
zusehen *(sieht zu, sah zu, zugesehen)* to watch
zurückgeben *(gibt zurück, gab zurück, zurückgegeben)* to return, give back
zusammensetzen to put together

Dialog

In einem Wiener Café

The word *schauen* is used more often than *sehen* in Southern Germany and Austria. In these regions, people will also say *Auf Wiederschauen!* instead of *Auf Wiedersehen!*

FRAU STAINER: Was meinst du? Sollen wir hier reingehen?

HERR STAINER: Die Auswahl ist heute gar nicht so groß.

FRAU STAINER: Schau mal! Die haben noch Obstschnitten.

HERR STAINER: Aber keine Sachertorte.

FRAU STAINER: Gehen wir doch am besten zum Wiener Café.

HERR STAINER: Hier gibt es immer alles.

FRAU STAINER: Stimmt, mein Lieber! Deshalb mag ich dieses Café so.

HERR STAINER: Na, da habe ich zu früh geurteilt. Die meisten Kuchen und Torten sind auch hier schon weg.

FRAU STAINER: Aber deinen Lieblingskuchen haben sie wenigstens.

KELLNERIN: Grüß Gott! Haben Sie sich schon etwas ausgesucht?

HERR STAINER: Ein Stück Sachertorte für mich, bitte.

FRAU STAINER: Und mir bringen Sie eine Obstschnitte…Ach ja, und dann noch zwei Melangen.

HERR STAINER: Du bestellst immer dasselbe.

FRAU STAINER: Die Obstschnitte schmeckt eben so gut.

HERR STAINER: Eine Wiener Spezialität für eine spezielle Wienerin.

FRAU STAINER: Du machst mir mal wieder richtig Komplimente.

KELLNERIN: So, bitte schön, die Dame, der Herr.

FRAU STAINER: Mmmh…einfach köstlich.

HERR STAINER: Über mein Stück Torte kann ich mich auch nicht beklagen.

FRAU STAINER: Ich nehme etwas von deiner Schlagsahne. So macht man einen guten Kaffee noch etwas besser.

HERR STAINER: Davon kannst du ruhig mehr haben. Die Schlagsahne macht einen sowieso viel zu dick.

FRAU STAINER: Mußt du noch ins Büro?

HERR STAINER: Nein, ich habe mir für heute nachmittag freigenommen.

FRAU STAINER: Oh, wie herrlich. Dann laß uns gleich zur Kärntner Straße gehen. Ich möchte ein Geschenk für Rudi kaufen.

HERR STAINER: Stimmt. Dein Bruder hat ja am Freitag Geburtstag.

FRAU STAINER: Fräulein, die Rechnung bitte.

KELLNERIN: Das macht 126 Schillinge. Ich hoffe, es hat Ihnen geschmeckt.

he *Sachertorte* is perhaps e most well-known torte in of Austria. It is named er the Sacher family who troduced it.

elange is coffee mixed with am. In Germany, it is of rse *Kaffee mit Sahne*.

e *Kärntner Straße* is a ry popular shopping street Vienna.

int out to your students t the currency used in stria is the schilling.

Fragen über den Dialog

1. Zu welchem Café gehen Stainers?
2. Gibt es dort heute eine gute Auswahl?
3. Welche Torte ißt Herr Stainer gern? Und Frau Stainer?
4. Was bestellen Stainers noch?
5. Ißt Frau Stainer die Obstschnitte oft?
6. Was macht Frau Stainer mit der Schlagsahne?
7. Muß Herr Stainer heute noch arbeiten?
8. Wohin wollen Stainers später gehen? Warum?
9. Wieviel kostet alles zusammen?

At a Viennese Café

MRS. STAINER:	What do you think? Should we go inside here?
MR. STAINER:	The selection isn't so great today.
MRS. STAINER:	Look! They still have fruit pie.
MR. STAINER:	But no Sacher torte.
MRS. STAINER:	Why don't we go to the *Wiener Café*.
MR. STAINER:	They always have everything here.
MRS. STAINER:	That's true, dear. That's why I like this café so much.
MR. STAINER:	Well, I judged too soon. Most of the cakes and tortes are already gone here too.
MRS. STAINER:	But at least they have your favorite cake.
WAITRESS:	Hello! Did you select something already?
MR. STAINER:	A piece of the Sacher torte for me, please.
MRS. STAINER:	And bring me a piece of the fruit pie...Oh yes, and two coffees.
MR. STAINER:	You always order the same thing.
MRS. STAINER:	The fruit pie is so good.
MR. STAINER:	A Viennese specialty for a special Viennese.
MRS. STAINER:	You're paying me compliments again.
WAITRESS:	Here you are, Madam, Sir.
MRS. STAINER:	Mmmm...simply delicious.
MR. STAINER:	I can't complain about my piece of torte.
MRS. STAINER:	I'll take some of your whipped cream. That's how you make good coffee a bit better.
MR. STAINER:	You can have more of that. The whipped cream makes one much too fat anyway.

MRS. STAINER:	Do you still have to go to the office?
MR. STAINER:	No, I took this afternoon off.
MRS. STAINER:	Oh, great. Then let's go right away to the *Kärntner Straße*. I would like to buy a present for Rudi.
MR. STAINER:	That's right. Your brother's birthday is on Friday.
MRS. STAINER:	Waitress, the check please.
WAITRESS:	That comes to 126 schillings. I hope you liked it.

Nützliche Ausdrücke

Review these expressions after students have thoroughly covered the *Dialog* and *Lesestück 1*.

Was meinst du?	What do you think? What's your opinion?
Schau mal!	Look!
Ich habe zu früh geurteilt.	I judged too soon.
Sie sind schon weg.	They are gone already.
Ich mache dir Komplimente.	I'm paying you compliments.
Er kann sich nicht darüber beklagen.	He can't complain about that.
Hast du dir freigenommen?	Did you take time off?
Das macht…	That comes to…
Was haben Sie vor?	What are you planning?
Die Straßen sind gut markiert.	The streets are well marked.
Sie bezahlen zwölf Mark pro Karte.	They pay twelve marks per ticket.
Er zeigt auf ein Haus.	He points to a house.
Bist du startbereit?	Are you ready to take off?
Er spritzt es mit Farbe.	He is spraying it with paint.
Kennst du dieses bekannte Märchen?	Do you know this well-known fairy tale?
Sammelst du sie?	Do you collect them?

Sprichwort

Erst wägen, dann wagen! (First weigh, then dare.)	Look before you leap!

Ergänzung

You may wish to expand this section by adding other careers. Besides asking the questions, *Was willst du werden?*, you may also ask, *Warum willst du...werden?*, *Wie kannst du dich auf diesen Beruf vorbereiten?*, *Welche Möglichkeiten gibt es für diesen Beruf?*, etc.

If you have access to a German newspaper, you could use the section in the want ads *(Stellenangebote)* to further illustrate this topic.

Was willst du werden?

Berufe für Jungen	Berufe für Mädchen
Apotheker	Apothekerin
Arzt	Ärztin
Bäcker	Bäckerin
Elektriker	Elektrikerin
Fleischer (Metzger)	Fleischerin (Metzgerin)
Flugbegleiter	Flugbegleiterin
Friseur	Friseuse
Ingenieur	Ingenieurin
Krankenpfleger	Krankenschwester
Landwirt	Landwirtin
Lehrer	Lehrerin
Mechaniker	Mechanikerin
Musiker	Musikerin
Pilot	Pilotin
Polizist	Polizistin
Rechtsanwalt	Rechtsanwältin
Schauspieler	Schauspielerin
Sekretär	Sekretärin
Verkäufer	Verkäuferin
Zahnarzt	Zahnärztin

ein Bäcker

eine Zahnärztin

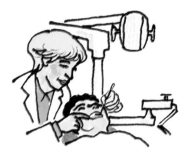

ein Musiker

eine Friseuse

Übungen

Genitive

The definite and indefinite article and possessive adjectives

Up to now you have been acquainted with three cases in German: the nominative (subject case), the accusative (direct object case) and the dative (indirect object case). Besides these three cases, there is a fourth case: the *genitive*.

The genitive shows possession or relationship. The genitive forms of the definite and indefinite article and the possessive adjectives are as follows:

	Singular		Plural
masculine	*feminine*	*neuter*	
des	der	des	der
eines	einer	eines	—
meines	meiner	meines	meiner
deines	deiner	deines	deiner
seines	seiner	seines	seiner
ihres	ihrer	ihres	ihrer
seines	seiner	seines	seiner
unseres	unserer	unseres	unserer
eueres	euerer	eueres	euerer
ihres	ihrer	ihres	ihrer
Ihres	Ihrer	Ihres	Ihrer

An -*es* is added to one-syllable masculine and neuter nouns, whereas an -*s* is added to masculine and neuter nouns with two or more syllables.

Beispiele: *des Mannes   eines Verkäufers*   Emphasize that feminine nouns do not have any noun
des Kindes   seines Tellers   endings. *(der Hut der Frau, die Häuser dieser Straße)*
ihres Buches   dieses Anzugs

NOTE: There are several nouns ending in -*en* in the genitive such as *Pilot, Junge, Beamter, Tourist, Student, Nachbar* and *Herr*.

Folgt den Beispielen!

Variation: *Wer hat einen Reisepaß?, Was hat der Ausländer?* or: Change sentences on the right side to the plural.

1. Der Ausländer hat einen Reisepaß.

Das ist der Reisepaß des Ausländers.

Das Mädchen hat einen Freund.

Das ist der Freund des Mädchens.

Die Lehrerin hat einen Kuli.

Das ist der Kuli der Lehrerin.

Der Student hat einen Wagen.

Das ist der Wagen des Studenten.

Die Dame hat einen Fahrplan.

Das ist der Fahrplan der Dame.

Der Mann hat ein Geschäft.

Das ist das Geschäft des Mannes.

2. Wo ist das Haus seiner Mutter?

    Vater / dein
    Bruder / ihr
    Tante / sein
    Onkel / unser
    Schwester / mein

Wo ist das Haus seiner Mutter?

Wo ist das Haus deines Vaters?
Wo ist das Haus ihres Bruders?
Wo ist das Haus seiner Tante?
Wo ist das Haus unseres Onkels?
Wo ist das Haus meiner Schwester?

3. Das Auto meines Bruders ist rot.

    meine Freundin
    der Ausländer
    euer Lehrer
    die Amerikanerin
    sein Freund
    dieser Mann

Das Auto meines Bruders ist rot.

Das Auto meiner Freundin ist rot.
Das Auto des Ausländers ist rot.
Das Auto eueres Lehrers ist rot.
Das Auto der Amerikanerin ist rot.
Das Auto seines Freundes ist rot.
Das Auto dieses Mannes ist rot.

4. Das Kleid ist teuer.
    (die Dame)

   Das Geschenk ist preiswert.
    (mein Freund)

   Die Farbe ist braun.
    (die Krawatte)

   Das Telefon ist neu.
    (sein Vater)

   Das Buch ist interessant.
    (ihr Onkel)

   Die Reise ist lang.
    (meine Mutter)

Das Kleid der Dame ist teuer.

Das Geschenk meines Freundes ist preiswert.

Die Farbe der Krawatte ist braun.

Das Telefon seines Vaters ist neu.

Das Buch ihres Onkels ist interessant.

Die Reise meiner Mutter ist lang.

Variation: Wessen Kleid ist teuer? If you use wessen, you may want to have students look at the examples on page 57.

5. die Reise / Tourist

    der Brief / Schüler
    die Frage / Lehrer
    die Bluse / Mädchen
    der Preis / Karte
    die Arbeit / Student
    das Büro / Beamter

die Reisen der Touristen

die Briefe der Schüler
die Fragen der Lehrer
die Blusen der Mädchen
die Preise der Karten
die Arbeiten der Studenten
die Büros der Beamten

6. Form a complete phrase, incorporating the words in parentheses. Use the genitive case.

    Beispiel: *die Gitarre (mein Freund)*
              die Gitarre meines Freundes

   1. das Tor (die Stadtmauer)
   2. die Farbe (dieser Anzug)

3. die Schultasche (die Jungen)
4. der Mantel (die Dame)
5. das Buch (das Mädchen)
6. die Tür (mein Wohnzimmer)
7. die Frage (ein Tourist)
8. der Name (die Ausländer)
9. das Spiel (die Mannschaft)
10. der Flug (der Pilot)
11. das Fahrrad (seine Freundin)
12. die Wohnung (ihre Großmutter)

7. Provide the proper form of the genitive case for the words in parentheses.

1. Kennst du den Sohn (of the saleslady, of the American, of the teacher)?
2. Gefällt Ihnen die Tür (of my car, of the building, of her room)?
3. Die Farbe (of his coat, of their house, of the bicycles, of these suits) ist sehr schön.
4. Wir besuchen den Bruder (of his sister, of my aunt, of her father).
5. Möchtest du die Spezialität (of this café, of my mother, of the house)?
6. Sie hören die Musik (of the boys, of their daughter, of this girl).
7. Haben Sie die Karten (of my wife, of these students, of the tourists) gesehen?

Prepositions
The following prepositions require the genitive case:

anstatt	instead of
trotz	in spite of
während	during
wegen	because of

Examples: *Während meines Besuchs lernte ich viele Leute kennen.*
Er kam trotz des Regens zu uns.

Interrogative pronoun: *wessen?*
The interrogative pronoun in the genitive is *wessen,* which is used in asking for persons in the singular as well as in the plural.

Beispiele: *Wessen Fahrrad ist das?*   *Das ist das Fahrrad meines Freundes.*
Wessen Fahrräder sind das?   *Das sind die Fahrräder unserer Freunde.*

Names
The genitive case of proper names is usually formed by adding -*s*. Contrary to English, there is no apostrophe added.

Beispiele: *Walters Freundin*
Herrn Schmidts Auto
Giselas Buch
Deutschlands Flüsse

Folgt den Beispielen!

Variation: Have students vary their answers to each question, using the genitive case.

8. Wann arbeitet ihr schwer?
   (Winter)

   Wann spielt ihr Fußball?
   (Woche)

   Wann gehen wir in die Stadt?
   (Tag)

   Wann fliegen Sie nach Deutschland?
   (Sommer)

   Wann wird er essen?
   (Arbeit)

   Wann lesen Sie die Zeitung?
   (Reise)

Während des Winters.

Während der Woche.

Während des Tages.

Während des Sommers.

Während der Arbeit.

Während der Reise.

9. die Zeit / wegen

   der Film / anstatt

   die Hochzeit / während

   das Wetter / trotz

   das Geld / wegen

   die Klasse / während

   der Tanz / trotz

wegen der Zeit

anstatt des Filmes

während der Hochzeit

trotz des Wetters

wegen des Geldes

während der Klasse

trotz des Tanzes

Variation: Change sentences on the right and left to the singular.

10. Die Koffer gehören den Touristen.

    Die Fahrpläne gehören den Beamten.

    Die Hefte gehören den Schülern.

    Die Kassetten gehören den Studenten.

    Die Surfbretter gehören den Mädchen.

    Die Bücher gehören den Lehrern.

Das sind die Koffer der Touristen.

Das sind die Fahrpläne der Beamten.

Das sind die Hefte der Schüler.

Das sind die Kassetten der Studenten.

Das sind die Surfbretter der Mädchen.

Das sind die Bücher der Lehrer.

Personalize questions: *Wessen Kuli ist das?, Wessen Mathebuch ist das?, Wessen Pullover ist das?*

11. Wessen Gepäck ist das?
    (mein Freund)

    Wessen Zimmer ist das?
    (ihre Tante)

    Wessen Haus ist das?
    (dieser Junge)

    Wessen Fahrrad ist das?
    (sein Bruder)

    Wessen Geschäft ist das?
    (unser Onkel)

    Wessen Auto ist das?
    (meine Lehrerin)

Das ist das Gepäck meines Freundes.

Das ist das Zimmer ihrer Tante.

Das ist das Haus dieses Jungen.

Das ist das Fahrrad seines Bruders.

Das ist das Geschäft unseres Onkels.

das ist das Auto meiner Lehrerin.

12. während dieses Tages

    wegen meines Bruders

    anstatt seiner Großmutter

während dieser Tage

wegen meiner Brüder

anstatt seiner Großmütter

58

trotz des Mädchens	trotz der Mädchen
anstatt ihres Buches	anstatt ihrer Bücher
während dieser Woche	während dieser Wochen
wegen unseres Autos	wegen unserer Autos

13. Complete each of these sentences with genitive forms using the words in parentheses.

1. Hast du das Rathaus (die Stadt) _____ gesehen?
2. Während (der Abend) _____ hat er keine Zeit.
3. Was macht die Schwester (dein Freund) _____ ?
4. Kennst du den Mann (die Verkäuferin) _____ ?
5. Ich besuche den Bekannten (mein Vater) _____ .
6. Wir hören die Musik (die Gäste) _____ .
7. Hier ist ein Fotoalbum (seine Familie) _____ .
8. Gehen Sie nicht wegen (die Jungen) _____ !
9. Sie fahren trotz (das Wetter) _____ .
10. Anstatt (meine Tante) _____ ist mein Onkel gekommen.

14. Form questions asking for the italicized words.

> **Beispiel:** *Rolands* Freund kommt zu Besuch.
> *Wessen* Freund kommt zu Besuch?

1. Ich habe *Petras* Buch gelesen.
2. Webers haben *Frau Bäckers* Haus gekauft.
3. Peter ißt *Angelikas* Kuchen gern.
4. Der Herr hat das Geld *der Dame* gefunden.
5. Wir haben den Platz *der Touristen* bekommen.
6. Sie haben die Schallplatte *meines Bruders* gehört.
7. Er wird mir die Fahrkarte *seines Freundes* geben.

15. Wie heißt das auf deutsch?

1. I'll buy a shirt instead of a tie.
2. Are you going to your uncle's house?
3. Did you buy the girls' tickets?
4. Do you have your boyfriend's book?
5. Where do you have your sister's letter?
6. We've seen the tourists' bus.
7. During the night it's very cold.
8. Because of the weather I can't drive.

Der Kaffee schmeckt gut.

Verbs with Prepositions

As in the English language, a number of German verbs are used with certain prepositions. In English, for example, there are verbs (including prepositions) such as: to depend *on*, to talk *about*, to ask *for*. In German, these prepositions that follow certain verbs require either the dative or the accusative case. Below you will find a list of those verbs with their corresponding prepositions that you have learned up to now.

Point out to your students that verbs with prepositions should be treated like idioms and memorized.

These verbs and prepositions are followed by the *accusative* case:

sich beklagen über	to complain about
sich erinnern an	to remember
sich freuen auf	to look forward to
grenzen an	to border on
sich interessieren für	to be interested in
schreiben über	to write about
sehen auf	to look at
sprechen über	to talk about
warten auf	to wait for
zeigen auf	to point to

Beispiele: *Ich denke oft an unsere Reise.*
(I think often of our trip.)
Warten Sie auf den Zug?
(Are you waiting for the train?)

These verbs and prepositions are followed by the *dative* case:

bestehen aus	to consist of
erzählen von	to tell about
gehören zu	to belong to
übereinstimmen mit	to agree with
sich verabschieden von	to say good-bye to

16. Form complete sentences using the cue words given.

1. Leute / zeigen auf / Berge
2. Herr Meier / sprechen über / Reise
3. Erzählen von / Sie / Stadt
4. Müssen / Studenten / warten auf / Bus
5. Ich / sich freuen auf / Flug / Deutschland
6. Lehrer / sich beklagen über / Klasse
7. Wir / schreiben über / unser / Hochzeit
8. Jungen / gehören zu / diese Mannschaft

17. Provide the proper preposition that accompanies each verb.

1. Die Jugendlichen verabschieden sich _____ dem Herbergsvater.
2. Die Lehrerin zeigt _____ die Tafel.
3. Freut ihr euch schon _____ die Musik?
4. Vor der Reise sehen wir noch _____ die Karte.
5. Haben Sie _____ ihr Erlebnis geschrieben?
6. Ich stimme _____ dir überein.
7. Ich interessiere mich nicht _____ diese Arbeit.
8. Erzähl doch _____ der Hochzeit.

Lesestück 1

Ein Besuch in Bremen

Familie Tauber hat schon lange vorgehabt, die Stadt Bremen zu besuchen. Taubers wohnen in Osnabrück. Diese Stadt liegt ungefähr 150 Kilometer von Bremen entfernt. Um acht Uhr am Samstag verlassen sie ihr Haus und fahren auf einer Bundesstraße° nördlich nach Bremen. — *highway*

In der Gegend von Bremen folgen Taubers den Schildern zum Hafen°. Alles ist gut markiert. Sie parken ihren Wagen nicht weit vom Hafen und gehen dann fünf Minuten zu Fuß. An der Kasse kauft Frau Tauber vier Karten. Die Karten kosten 30 Mark. Herr und Frau Tauber und Beate — sie ist fünfzehn — müssen DM 8,50 pro Karte bezahlen, aber Ullis Karte kostet nur DM 4,50. Er ist erst vierzehn Jahre alt. Taubers haben Glück. Eine Barkasse° fährt um zehn Uhr ab. Viele Besucher gehen schon zur Barkasse. Deshalb beeilen sich Taubers. Hoffentlich bekommen sie noch einen guten Platz. Die meisten Leute sitzen draußen°, ganz oben auf der Barkasse. Von dort kann man besser sehen. — *harbor* / *large motor boat* / *outside*

Herr Tauber erklärt seiner Familie, was sie auf dieser Hafenrundfahrt° sehen werden. Er hat einen Prospekt über Bremen. Es dauert nicht lange, bis die Barkasse losfährt. Frau Tauber fotografiert gern. Sie macht Aufnahmen von den verschiedenen Sehenswürdigkeiten. Ulli zeigt plötzlich auf ein Motorboot. Es ist grün und weiß. Was ist denn so besonders an diesem Boot? Oh, es ist die Hafenpolizei. Herr Tauber deutet° in eine andere Richtung. Da liegen viele Schiffe am Kai°. Sie kommen aus der ganzen Welt. — *trip around harbor* / *points* / *wharf*

der Marktplatz
in Bremen

Taubers stehen vor einem Schaufenster.

Herr Tauber liest
einen Prospekt.

Jetzt kommen sie an einem Dock° vorbei. Dort baut man Schiffe. Ein Schiff ist riesengroß°. Die Schraube° selbst ist vier bis fünf Meter hoch. Gleich daneben° ist ein anderes Schiff. Es ist schon fast startbereit. Ein Mann spritzt° dieses Schiff gerade mit Farbe°. Nach einer Stunde und fünfzehn Minuten kommt die Barkasse wieder am Landungssteg° an. Alle müssen aussteigen.

Taubers gehen zu Fuß zur Innenstadt. Der Marktplatz ist sehr bekannt. Das Rathaus ist schon mehr als 360 Jahre alt. Neben dem Rathaus stehen alte Häuser aus dem 16. Jahrhundert. Auf dem Marktplatz befindet sich das Denkmal° der Bremer Stadtmusikanten°. Taubers bewundern die vier Tiere° — einen Esel°, einen Hund°, eine Katze° und einen Hahn°. Jedes Kind in Deutschland kennt dieses berühmte Märchen der Gebrüder Grimm°. In der Nähe vom Marktplatz sehen Taubers viele Tauben°. Sie füttern° sie mit Brotkrumen°.

Der älteste Teil Bremens heißt „der Schnoor". Die Straßen hier sind sehr eng°. Sie sind nur für Fußgänger. Autos dürfen nicht durchfahren. Manche Häuser sind schon 400 Jahre alt. Man hat sie

dockyard

gigantic/propeller

next to it

sprays/paint

gangway

monument

*Bremen Town
Musicians/animals/
donkey
dog/cat/rooster
Brothers Grimm
pigeons/feed
bread crumbs*

narrow

aber unterdessen renoviert. Auf Schildern lesen Taubers die Geschichte dieser Häuser. Ulli und Beate kaufen ein paar Ansichtskarten°. Ulli will sie sammeln, aber Beate wird zwei oder drei Karten an ihre Verwandten schicken°.

picture postcards
send

Nach dem Mittagessen gehen Taubers wieder zu ihrem Wagen zurück. Beate und Ulli schlagen vor°, auf einem anderen Weg nach Hause zu fahren. Herr Tauber holt° seine Karte aus dem Auto und studiert sie. Er weiß nun genau, wie er nach Osnabrück zurückfahren kann.

suggest
fetches

Fragen über das Lesestück

1. In welcher Stadt wohnen Taubers? Wie weit ist diese Stadt von Bremen entfernt?
2. Wie wissen Taubers, wo der Hafen ist?
3. Wie viele Karten kaufen Taubers? Wie teuer sind sie?
4. Wo sitzen Taubers in der Barkasse?
5. Warum kann Herr Tauber seiner Familie etwas von Bremen erklären?
6. Was macht Frau Tauber gern?
7. Woher kommen die Schiffe im Hafen?
8. Was machen die Leute im Dock?
9. Um wieviel Uhr kommt die Barkasse wieder am Landungssteg an?
10. Wohin gehen Taubers zuerst?
11. Was sind die Bremer Stadtmusikanten?
12. Was füttern Taubers?
13. Beschreibe den ältesten Stadtteil Bremens!
14. Warum kauft Beate Ansichtskarten? Was macht Ulli mit den Ansichtskarten?
15. Warum studiert Herr Tauber seine Karte?

Erweiterung

18. Wie heißt das auf deutsch?

1. Don't judge too soon.
2. That comes to 120 marks.
3. I'm collecting stamps.
4. When does he take time off?
5. Who knows this fairy tale?
6. The cities are well marked.
7. Are you paying her compliments?
8. I don't want to complain.

19. ***Wer bin ich? Wer spricht hier?*** **Select the appropriate profession from the list below and match each with the following description. You will not need all the professions listed.**

Have individual students read a sentence and ask the question, *Wer bin ich?* Be sure that students answering the question indicate the proper noun for a male or female career. *(Du bist/Sie sind Lehrer/Lehrerin.)* Also point out that no article is necessary in front of the name of a career or profession.

Friseur	Rechtsanwalt
Pilot	Bäcker
Schauspieler	Polizist
Sekretär	Musiker
Verkäufer	Lehrer
Mechaniker	Flugbegleiter
Fleischer	Arzt

1. Ich habe schon in vielen Filmen gespielt.
2. Sie sind viel zu schnell gefahren.
3. Wir werden in einer halben Stunde landen.
4. Bei mir können Sie Brote, Brötchen und Kuchen kaufen.
5. Heute schreiben wir eine Arbeit.
6. Ihr Haar ist etwas zu lang.
7. Ihr Wagen fährt zu langsam? Da muß ich mal nachsehen.
8. Ich habe schon viele Jahre Klavier gespielt.
9. Trinken Sie drei Gläser pro Tag. Dann geht es Ihnen bestimmt bald besser.
10. Das Hemd kostet 40 Mark. Dafür können Sie gleich bei mir an der Kasse bezahlen.
11. Wir haben noch viel Schinken und auch noch etwas Wurst.
12. Zuerst werde ich Ihnen die Sicherheitsmaßnahmen erklären. Dann bringe ich Ihnen das Essen.

20. **Provide an appropriate response in German. Be sure that the whole conversation ties together and becomes meaningful.**

1. Warum haben Sie heute keine Auswahl?
2. Aber sonst haben Sie doch immer noch viele Kuchen und Torten.
3. Das ist schade.
4. Das tue ich.
5. Bis morgen dann.

21. **Beschreibt jedes Wort mit einem ganzen Satz!**

1. Lieblingskuchen
2. Café
3. Kellnerin
4. Barkasse
5. Sehenswürdigkeit
6. Märchen

22. **Beantwortet die Fragen!**

1. Welchen Kuchen ißt du am liebsten?
2. Was willst du später einmal werden?

3. Was macht eine Kellnerin?

4. Welche Stadt möchtest du besuchen und warum?

5. Hast du einen Hund oder eine Katze?

6. Warum kauft man Ansichtskarten?

Warum
kaufen sie
Ansichtskarten?

Rückblick

I. Wie heißt dieser Körperteil?

1. Ich spreche mit dem _____ .

2. Ich zeige mit dem _____ auf die Tafel.

3. Man hört mit den _____ .

4. Seine _____ sind blond und ziemlich kurz.

5. Ich kann mit meinen _____ weit sehen.

6. Dein Schuh paßt nicht auf meinen _____ .

7. Man braucht Handschuhe für die _____ .

8. Hast du dir die _____ geputzt?

II. Change the following short paragraphs from the present perfect to the past tense.

Vor einem Jahr sind Neumanns in Deutschland gewesen. Dort haben sie einen Wagen gekauft und sind dann durch Deutschland gefahren. In Stuttgart haben sie ihre Freunde besucht. Ihre Freunde haben gut Englisch verstanden. Deshalb haben sie alle meistens Englisch gesprochen. Neumanns haben Glück gehabt.

Auf ihrer Reise sind sie durch viele Städte gekommen. München hat ihnen besonders gut gefallen. Sie sind in dieser Stadt zwei Wochen geblieben und haben während dieser Zeit viele Sehenswürdigkeiten gesehen.

III. Fill in the proper past tense forms of the verbs provided in parentheses.

Beispiel: *(sprechen) _____ du nicht zu viel?*
Sprachst du nicht zu viel?

1. (geben) _____ er dir sein Fahrrad?

2. (lesen) _____ Katrin einen Brief?

3. (helfen) Wir _____ ihm gestern bei der Arbeit.

4. (sprechen) Die Touristen _____ kein Deutsch.

5. (verlassen) Um drei Uhr _____ die Schüler das Gebäude.

6. (fahren) _____ Herr und Frau Sieder in die DDR?

7. (sehen) Ich _____ das Flugzeug.

8. (kommen) Die Kinder _____ mit ihren Eltern.

9. (trinken) Was _____ du denn?

10. (gefallen) Das Auto _____ mir nicht.

IV. Beantwortet diese Frage: „An welchem Tag ist…?"

> **Beispiel:** *dein Geburtstag*
> *Am 16. September.*

1. Weihnachtsabend (Heiliger Abend)
2. Ostersonntag
3. dein Geburtstag
4. Muttertag
5. Neujahr
6. Pfingsten

Lesestück 2

Das Fürstentum Liechtenstein

Das Fürstentum° Liechtenstein gehört zu den kleinsten Ländern der Welt. Liechtenstein ist ungefähr so groß wie Washington, D.C. Das Land grenzt im Osten und Norden an Österreich, im Süden und Westen an die Schweiz. *(principality)*

Liechtenstein ist sehr gebirgig°. Die Berge erreichen eine Höhe von 2 600 m. Liechtenstein liegt auf der rechten Seite des Rheins. Das Land hat heute eine Bevölkerung von 22 000 Einwohnern und ist schon seit 1719 ein Fürstentum. *(mountainous)*

Tausende von Touristen besuchen jedes Jahr das Fürstentum Liechtenstein. Es gibt nur einen Grenzübergang° zwischen Österreich und Liechtenstein, aber keinen zwischen der Schweiz und Liechtenstein. In diesem Land gibt es keinen Flughafen und keinen Bahnhof. Die meisten Touristen kommen mit dem Auto oder mit dem Bus. Mit dem Auto kann man nur auf einer Straße in die Hauptstadt fahren, entweder von Osten oder° von Westen. *(border crossing)* *(entweder…oder either…or)*

Die Hauptstadt Liechtensteins ist Vaduz. Gleich bei der Einfahrt° in Vaduz sieht man das Schloß ganz oben auf dem Berg. Das Schloß ist das Wahrzeichen° der Hauptstadt. Es ist schon 700 Jahre alt. Heute wohnen dort der Fürst und seine Familie. Vom Schloß hat man einen schönen Blick auf die Hauptstadt. Ungefähr 4 000 Einwohner, ein Fünftel der Bevölkerung Liechtensteins, wohnen in Vaduz. Die Stadt bietet den Besuchern ein paar gute Hotels und Restaurants. *(entrance)* *(landmark)*

Genaue Information bekommt man im Verkehrsbüro° im Zentrum der Stadt. In diesem Gebäude befindet sich auch die weltberühmte Gemäldesammlung° des Fürsten von Liechtenstein und das Briefmarkenmuseum°. Seit 1912 hat Liechtenstein seine eigenen° *(tourist office)* *(collection of paintings)* *(Museum of Stamps/own)* *(artistic/valuable)*

das Schloß

Liechtenstein ist ein Fürstentum.

Vaduz, die Hauptstadt Liechtensteins

Briefmarken. Diese schönen und künstlerisch° wertvollen° Briefmarken sind in der ganzen Welt bekannt. Es gibt einige Spezialgeschäfte für Briefmarken und Münzen°. Natürlich kann man die Briefmarken auch beim Postamt° bekommen. Das Rathaus ist der Mittelpunkt der Hauptstadt. Dort sind die Büros der Stadtverwaltung°. Die offizielle Währung° des Landes ist der Schweizer Franken°.

      Von der Hauptstadt aus gibt es mehrere° Möglichkeiten, in die Berge zu fahren. Eine Karte vor dem Verkehrsbüro gibt den Besuchern Auskunft°, wohin die Straßen führen. Ein Besuch in Liechtenstein dauert für die meisten nicht sehr lange. Trotzdem° ist es für jeden ein besonderes Erlebnis.

coins
post office

city administration/ currency monetary unit several

information nevertheless

Fragen über das Lesestück

1. Wie groß ist Liechtenstein?
2. Welche Länder grenzen an dieses Land?
3. Wie alt ist Liechtenstein?
4. Wie kommen die meisten Touristen nach Liechtenstein?
5. Wie heißt die Hauptstadt und wie viele Leute wohnen dort?
6. Wer wohnt im Schloß?
7. Was gibt es alles im Verkehrsbüro?
8. Wie lange hat Liechtenstein schon seine eigenen Briefmarken?
9. Wo kann man diese Briefmarken bekommen?
10. Wie heißt die Währung Liechtensteins?

Sprachspiegel

I. Schreibe ganz kurz über das Thema „Was willst du werden?"! Beantworte solche Fragen wie „Welche Fächer (Wie lange) mußt du studieren? Warum willst du diesen Beruf haben?"!

II. Create your own dialog centering around the topic of *Im Café*. Be as creative as possible.

Du bist dran!

. . . .
Nein, dieses Café gefällt mir nicht.

. . . .
Das ist eine gute Idee.

Was ist die Spezialität des Hauses?

. . . .
Hm, das klingt ja ganz gut.

. . . .
Das ist nett von Ihnen.

Du willst Pilot werden?

. . . .
Wie viele Jahre dauert es denn, bis du selbst fliegen kannst?

. . . .
Das dauert mir zu lange.

. . . .
Wir fahren lieber zum Hafen.

. . . .
Nein, nach Hamburg.

. . . .
Erst am Dienstag.

. . . .
Warum denn? Wir haben doch noch viel Zeit?

. . . .
Schon so früh?

. . . .
Na, dann mal los.

Die Stadt ist schon mehr als 500 Jahre alt.

. . . .
Nein, ich bin noch nie dort gewesen.

. . . .
Das möchte ich schon, aber es kostet zu viel Geld.

. . . .

Kulturecke

Bavaria

To many foreigners, Bavaria represents Germany. The Bavarians themselves would rather be taken as they really are — the most independent German ethnic group and one with a very strongly developed sense of pride. In both the small and large cities, Bavarians still wear their traditional costumes on occasion. Children, to the delight of their parents, often are dressed in *Lederhosen* (leather shorts) and *Dirndls* (dirndl dresses). Visiting Bavaria, the largest German *Land,* can be a unique experience on any travel itinerary.

No traveler can claim to have seen or experienced Bavaria without having visited the capital, the city of *München*. The main shopping area, extending from the *Karlstor* to the *Marienplatz*, is closed to traffic. The *Karlstor* is one of the remaining sections from the fortifications built in the early 14th century. Walking through the *Karlstor,* you'll walk past countless shops and eventually come to the *Marienplatz,* the heart of the city. The big square is the site of the *Neues Rathaus*. Almost immediately to the left of the *Rathaus,* you'll see another landmark of München, the *Frauenkirche*, built about 500 years ago. At 11:00 A.M. you'll join hundreds or even thousands of spectators standing in the square or sitting in outside cafés to witness the famous *Glockenspiel*, the recreation of a royal Bavarian wedding. Within two minutes of the *Marienplatz,* you'll find the *Viktualienmarkt*, a huge market square where casual shopping is at its best. Numerous stands offer the shopper selections ranging from fruits and vegetables to sausages, dairy products and flowers. Those who need a rest have opportunities to relax in the open-air beer gardens or cafés, located right at the market.

There is no denying it — München is a theater-loving city, and has been for centuries. As an example, the first operas were performed here about 1650. Notable names like Wagner, Strauss, Orff and Egk are closely linked with München. The Bavarian State Opera, one of Europe's leading opera houses, presents world famous singers in the *Nationaltheater.* München has more museums and art collections than any other German city. The *Deutsches Museum* is the largest technological museum of its kind in the world. Thousands of original devices, models and copies illustrate the history of science and technology.

The world-famous *Hofbräuhaus* lures many visitors and local people to its huge indoor and outdoor beer halls. No other German city has as many festivities as München. The most well-known festival is the annual *Oktoberfest*, which runs for sixteen days beginning in late September. Large quantities of food and beer are consumed in the various beer tents, located on the *Theresienwiese*. The second largest annual celebration is *Fasching*, which reaches its climax with a city-wide parade on the Monday preceding Ash Wednesday. Opposite the *Theresienwiese* in the northeastern corner of the city is the *Englischer Garten*, a huge park enjoyed by citizens and visitors throughout the year.

A portrait of München would be incomplete without mentioning the *Olympiapark*, located in the northwestern part of the city. It was here that the 1972 Olympic Games were held. In the western section on the edge of the city, you'll find one of the most impressive palaces in Europe, *Schloß Nymphenburg*. This castle, built by King Ludwig I, is located on 495 acres of park land.

When you leave the city of München, you may travel through many small Bavarian towns located in the hilly countryside. Although there are several major cities north of München, many tourists are attracted by the smaller towns that have not changed much in their appearance during the past few hundred years. *Rothenburg*, for example, has maintained its medieval character in every respect. The town of *Dinkelsbühl*, near Rothenburg, with its cobblestone streets and half-timbered houses, also appeals to the numerous visitors who come here every year.

die Universität in München

Viele Leute sitzen in einem Biergarten.

München, die Hauptstadt Bayerns

Leopoldstraße in München

das Hofbräuhaus

Neues Rathaus mit Frauenkirche

70

Was haben die Kinder an?
(Garmisch-Partenkirchen)

Deutsche und
Ausländer fahren
gern in den Urlaub
nach Bayern.

Oftmals sorgt eine Kapelle
für Stimmung.

ein typisches Haus im Süden Bayerns (Grainau)

Die Alpen liegen im Süden Bayerns.

Was steht alles
auf den
Schildern?

Einkaufszentrum,
vom Karlstor zum
Marienplatz

Lektion 13

South of München you'll drive through hilly and mountainous terrain. Undoubtedly, you'll pass through many towns and villages that will capture your attention with their picturesque houses. Because Germans love flowers, it is not surprising to see them displayed in windows, window boxes and on balconies. In some of these towns it seems as if time has been standing still. Don't be alarmed if you're confronted by cows being herded across the street. It's just a daily occurrence.

Southeast of München, located in the Alps next to Germany's second largest mountain *(Watzmann)*, you'll come to *St. Bartholomä* at the *Königsee*. The famous little church, in its uniquely interesting setting at the edge of the lake, has been immortalized by painters and other artists. South of München you may pass through the town of *Oberammergau*, where every ten years the world-famous Passion Play takes place. Close by is the ornate castle *Schloß Linderhof*, built in the 19th century by the eccentric King Ludwig II of Bavaria. Another castle built by Ludwig II is *Schloß Neuschwanstein*, a fairy tale-like castle that has been immortalized in books and movies.

Garmisch-Partenkirchen is surrounded by majestic mountain peaks. The *Zugspitze*, Germany's highest peak, overlooks the town. With their breathtaking scenery, the Bavarian Alps attract people from all over the world throughout the year. Garmisch-Partenkirchen was the site of the Winter Olympics at one time and, because of its beauty and location, attracts sports enthusiasts during the winter months. Here they can enjoy the refreshing outdoors and test their skill on the mountain slopes.

in einer Kleinstadt (Grainau)

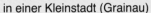

Tegernsee

Maria Gern in Ramsau,
in der Nähe von Berchtesgaden

Vokabeln

die **Ansichtskarte,-n** picture postcard
der **Apotheker,-** pharmacist
der **Arzt,⁖e** doctor
der **Bäcker,-** baker
die **Barkasse,-n** large motor boat, launch
sich **beklagen über** to complain about
der **Besuch,-e** visit
  bitte schön here you are
die **Bremer Stadtmusikanten** Bremen Town Musicians
die **Brotkrume,-n** bread crumb
  daneben next to it
das **Denkmal,⁖er** monument, memorial
  deuten to point
  dick thick, fat
das **Dock,-s** dock, dockyard
  draußen outside
  durchfahren *(fährt durch, fuhr durch, ist durchgefahren)* to drive through
  eng narrow
der **Elektriker,-** electrician
der **Esel,-** donkey
die **Farbe,-n** paint
der **Fleischer,-** butcher
  freinehmen *(nimmt frei, nahm frei, freigenommen)* to take (time) off
der **Friseur,-e** barber, hair stylist
die **Friseuse,-n** ladies' hair stylist, beautician
  füttern to feed
die **Gebrüder Grimm** Brothers Grimm
der **Hafen,⁖** harbor
die **Hafenpolizei** harbor police
die **Hafenrundfahrt,-en** boat trip around harbor
der **Hahn,⁖e** rooster
  herrlich great, splendid
  holen to get, fetch
der **Hund,-e** dog
der **Ingenieur,-e** engineer
das **Jahrhundert,-e** century
der **Kai,-s** wharf

die **Katze,-n** cat
das **Kompliment,-e** compliment
  Komplimente machen to pay compliments
  köstlich delicious
der **Krankenpfleger,-** nurse (male)
die **Krankenschwester,-n** nurse
der **Kuchen,-** cake
der **Landungssteg,-e** gangway
der **Landwirt,-e** farmer
  lassen *(läßt, ließ, gelassen)* to let
die **Lehrerin,-nen** (female) teacher
der **Lieblingskuchen,-** favorite cake
  losfahren *(fährt los, fuhr los, ist losgefahren)* to depart, drive off
das **Märchen,-** fairy tale
  markieren to mark
  gut markiert well marked
der **Mechaniker,-** mechanic
  meinen to mean, think
die **Melange,-n** Austrian coffee (mixed with cream)
der **Metzger,-** butcher
das **Motorboot,-e** motor boat
der **Musiker,-** musician
  nehmen *(nimmt, nahm, genommen)* to take
die **Obstschnitte,-n** piece of fruit cake
der **Polizist,-en** police office (male)
die **Rechnung,-en** bill, check
der **Rechtsanwalt,⁖e** lawyer
  reingehen *(ging rein, ist reingegangen)* to go inside
  riesengroß gigantic
die **Sachertorte** Sacher torte (famous Viennese torte)
  sammeln to collect
  schauen to look
  schicken to send
die **Schlagsahne** whipped cream
der **Schauspieler,-** actor
die **Schraube,-n** propeller (ship)
der **Sekretär,-e** secretary (male)
  selbst itself

die **Spezialität,-en** specialty
  speziell special
  spritzen to spray
das **Stück,-e** piece
die **Taube,-n** pigeon
das **Tier,-e** animal
die **Torte,-n** torte, type of cake
  urteilen to judge
der **Verkäufer,-** sales clerk
  vorschlagen *(schlägt vor, schlug vor, vorgeschlagen)* to suggest
  weg sein to be gone
der **Wiener,-** Viennese
der **Zahnarzt,⁖e** dentist

Dialog

This scene takes place in Lienz, Austria. The uniforms of mail carriers look slightly different than those usually seen in Germany.

Der Briefträger kommt

BRIEFTRÄGER: Grüß Gott, Frau Löffler!

FRAU LÖFFLER: Grüß Gott! Oh, wie schön…ein Päckchen. Es ist von meiner Tante aus Amerika. Sie denkt immer an meinen Geburtstag.

BRIEFTRÄGER: Bitte unterschreiben Sie die Quittung. Ich habe übrigens auch Verwandte drüben. Die sind schon vor dreißig Jahren ausgewandert.

e sentence Die (Verwandten) sind schon… the noun andten can be left out as it refers to the same word in revious sentence. Germans make frequent use of this rn when they refer to objects or persons just ioned and it's clear who they are referring to. Also see 80.

BRIEFTRÄGER: Hier ist noch mehr Post…ein paar Briefe und eine Karte.

FRAU LÖFFLER: Der erste Brief ist keine Überraschung. Das ist eine Rechnung. Die anderen Briefe sind von Bekannten.

BRIEFTRÄGER: So viel Post bekomme ich das ganze Jahr über sonst nicht. Sie müssen ja einen großen Bekanntenkreis haben.

he Wörthersee is a well-nown resort area in Austria.

FRAU LÖFFLER: Sehen Sie!…eine Ansichtskarte von meinen Eltern. Sie sind auf einer Ferienreise am Wörthersee.

BRIEFTRÄGER: Da bin ich schon oft mit meiner Frau gewesen. Ja, wissen Sie, mein Bruder wohnt sogar in Pörtschach. Es ist dort so schön und wirklich ideal zum Ausruhen.

FRAU LÖFFLER: Wir fahren nächstes Jahr dorthin, nach Velden. Ich freue mich schon jetzt auf den Urlaub.

BRIEFTRÄGER: Für heute habe ich leider nichts mehr.

FRAU LÖFFLER: Ich bedanke mich sehr für die guten Nachrichten.

BRIEFTRÄGER: Keine Ursache. Ich bereite anderen gern Freude.

Fragen über den Dialog

1. Wer hat Frau Löffler ein Päckchen geschickt und warum?
2. Wo wohnen jetzt einige Verwandte des Briefträgers?
3. Warum ist der erste Brief keine Überraschung für Frau Löffler?
4. Wo sind Frau Löfflers Eltern? Was machen sie da?
5. Was machen Löfflers nächstes Jahr?
6. Wer wohnt in Pörtschach?

The Mail Carrier Is Coming

MAIL CARRIER: Hello, Mrs. Löffler.

MRS. LÖFFLER: Hello. Oh, how nice…a package. It's from my aunt in America. She always remembers my birthday.

MAIL CARRIER: Sign this receipt, please. By the way, I have relatives over there, too. They emigrated thirty years ago.

MAIL CARRIER: Here is some more mail…a few letters and a card.

MRS. LÖFFLER: The first letter is no surprise. That's a bill. The other letters are from friends.

MAIL CARRIER: I don't get that much mail all year. You must have a lot of friends.

MRS. LÖFFLER: Look!…a picture postcard from my parents. They are on a vacation trip at the *Wörthersee*.

MAIL CARRIER: I've been there quite often with my wife. You know, my brother even lives in Pörtschach. It's so beautiful there and really ideal for relaxing.

MRS. LÖFFLER: We're going there next year, to Velden. I'm already looking forward to our vacation.

MAIL CARRIER: Unfortunately, I don't have anything else for today.

MRS. LÖFFLER: I thank you very much for the nice news.

MAIL CARRIER: Don't mention it. I like to please others.

Nützliche Ausdrücke   Review the expressions that students have learned in the *Dialog* and *Lesestück 1*.

Ich denke an seinen Geburtstag.	I remember (think of) his birthday.
Wann sind Sie ausgewandert?	When did you emigrate?
Bekommst du viel Post?	Do you get a lot of mail?
Das ist eine Überraschung.	That's a surprise.
Wir haben einen großen Bekanntenkreis.	We have lots of friends.
Sie sind auf einer Ferienreise.	They are on a vacation trip.
Ich freue mich auf meinen Urlaub.	I'm looking forward to my vacation.
Ich bedanke mich für…	I thank you for…
Keine Ursache.	Don't mention it.
Sie bereitet ihm gern Freude.	She likes to please him.

Was machen diese Leute? (Hamburg)

Ich mache verschiedene Besorgungen.	I'll do some shopping.
Er steckt den Brief in den Briefkasten.	He puts the letter into the mailbox.
Was ist Ihr Vor- und Nachname?	What is your first and last name?
Ich möchte ein Ferngespräch führen.	I would like to make a long-distance call.
Wissen Sie die Vorwahlnummer?	Do you know the area code?
Die Bücher sind alphabetisch angeordnet.	The books are arranged alphabetically.
Heben Sie den Hörer ab!	Lift the receiver.

Was kann man hier kaufen?

Sprichwort

Ein wahrer Freund bleibt auch in der Not treu.
(A true friend remains true in an emergency too.)

A friend in need is a friend indeed.

Ergänzung

Have students practice writing a letter to a friend or relative.

Ein Brief

Osterhofen, den 14. Februar

Liebe Petra,

vielen Dank für Deinen Brief mit den beiden Fotos. Das eine Foto an der Nordsee hat mir besonders gut gefallen. Ihr habt da letzten Sommer bestimmt viel Spaß gehabt. Das Wetter war ja sicherlich sehr schön. Wer ist denn das andere Mädchen? Deine Schwester? Was macht Dein Hobby? Sammelst Du immer noch fleißig Briefmarken? Ich habe beim Postamt besondere Briefmarken für Dich gekauft. Vielleicht hast Du die noch nicht in Deiner Sammlung.

Bei uns liegt jetzt viel Schnee. Am Wochenende fahren wir -- meine Eltern und mein Bruder-- oft in die Berge. Klaus und ich haben zu Weihnachten Skier bekommen. Die sind toll! Bei Euch in Hamburg gibt es wahrscheinlich wenig Schnee. Schreib doch bald wieder. Ich freue mich immer, von Dir wieder einmal zu hören. Ich muß jetzt den Brief beenden. Meine Mutter braucht mich in der Küche.

Herzliche Grüße
Deine Karin

1. Was steht alles auf einem Briefumschlag oder auf einer Postkarte?

Besondere Angaben: zum Beispiel *Drucksache, Luftpost, Einschreiben.*

Explain to students the German zip code system. (See front section of this teacher's edition.)

Briefmarke (rechts oben).

Absender (links oben).

Karin Becker
Dü555tr. 15
8353 Osterhofen

Name des Empfängers, Straße, Hausnummer oder Postfach.

Petra Hocker
Hallesstr. 7
2000 Hamburg

Postleitzahl, Ort und Nummer des Postamts.

2. Was schickt man mit der Post?

Ein Telegramm.

Ein Paket (Päckchen).

Einen Brief.

Eine Karte (Ansichtskarte, Postkarte).

3. Was kann man alles auf einem Postamt machen? Man kann…

Telefongespräche führen

Briefe/Karten in den Briefkasten einwerfen

ein Paket oder Päckchen aufgeben

ein Sparkonto führen

Briefmarken kaufen

ein Telegramm schicken

Begin a discussion by asking the question, Welche Unterschiede gibt es zwischen einem amerikanischen und einem deutschen Postamt?

Übungen

Demonstrative Pronouns

Demonstrative pronouns refer to a person or thing just mentioned that needs to be referred to in more detail. In English the demonstrative pronouns are "this (one)," "that (one)," "these" and "those." The most common demonstrative pronouns in German are the forms of *der, die* and *das*. You will notice that the forms are the same as the definite article, except for the dative plural, which adds an *-en* to *den*, thus becoming *denen*.

Beispiele: *Sehen Sie dort den Wagen?*
***Den** möchte ich gern haben.*
Kennst du diese Leute?
*Ja, **die** kenne ich gut.*

The demonstrative pronouns are used especially in conversation. They should always be emphasized because they refer to a previously discussed person or thing.

	Singular			Plural
	masculine	*feminine*	*neuter*	
nominative	der	die	das	die
accusative	den	die	das	die
dative	dem	der	dem	den*en*

Folgt den Beispielen!

1. Verstehst du den Ansager?

   Nein, *den* verstehe ich nicht.

   Variation: Answer the questions in the positive.

   Verstehst du die Dame?

   Nein, *die* verstehe ich nicht.

   Verstehst du das Wort?

   Nein, *das* verstehe ich nicht.

   Verstehst du die Bedeutung?

   Nein, *die* verstehe ich nicht.

   Verstehst du den Amerikaner?

   Nein, *den* verstehe ich nicht.

   Verstehst du die Kellnerin?

   Nein, *die* verstehe ich nicht.

2. Kennen Sie diese Leute?

   Ja, *die* kenne ich gut.

   Variation: Answer the questions in the negative.

   Kennen Sie diesen Sportler?

   Ja, *den* kenne ich gut.

   Kennen Sie diese Mädchen?

   Ja, *die* kenne ich gut.

   Kennen Sie diesen Briefträger?

   Ja, *den* kenne ich gut.

   Kennen Sie diese Schauspieler?

   Ja, *die* kenne ich gut.

   Kennen Sie diese Lehrerin?

   Ja, *die* kenne ich gut.

3. Hat dir Angelika geschrieben?

   Nein, von *der* habe ich nichts gehört.

   Variation: Ask and answer the questions, using the present tense.

   Haben dir Peter und Günter geschrieben?

   Nein, von *denen* habe ich nichts gehört.

   Hat dir deine Mutter geschrieben?

   Nein, von *der* habe ich nichts gehört.

   Hat dir dein Freund geschrieben?

   Nein, von *dem* habe ich nichts gehört.

| Haben dir deine Verwandten geschrieben? | Nein, von *denen* habe ich nichts gehört. |
| Hat dir Wolfgang geschrieben? | Nein, von *dem* habe ich nichts gehört. |

4. Mit den Mädchen tanze ich gern.　　　Mit *denen* tanze ich gern.

ariation: Ask questions so
at the left side sentences
ecome answers. *(Mit wem
nzt du gern? Mit den
ädchen tanze ich gern.)*

Bei meiner Tante wohne ich gern.	Bei *der* wohne ich gern.
Auf den Bäcker warte ich gern.	Auf *den* warte ich gern.
In die Tanzschule gehe ich gern.	In *die* gehe ich gern.
Zu den Bekannten fahre ich gern.	Zu *denen* fahre ich gern.
Von der Reise erzähle ich gern.	Von *der* erzähle ich gern.

5. Hast du schon viel mit Christine gesprochen?　　Ja, mit *der* habe ich schon viel gesprochen.

Bist du zu der Tankstelle gefahren?	Ja, zu·*der* bin ich gefahren.
Bist du manchmal mit Rainer gegangen?	Ja, mit *dem* bin ich gegangen.
Hast du letztes Jahr bei deinen Großeltern gewohnt?	Ja, bei *denen* habe ich gewohnt.
Hast du von der Verkäuferin die Quittung bekommen?	Ja, von *der* habe ich die Quittung bekommen.
Hast du für deine Freunde etwas gekauft?	Ja, für *die* habe ich etwas gekauft.

Was kann man hier alles kaufen?

Was machen diese Leute?

6. **Answer the following questions in the affirmative or negative, using the proper demonstrative pronoun.**

　　　Beispiele: *Kennst du den Briefträger? Nein,…*
　　　　　　　Nein, den kenne ich nicht.

　　　　　　　Suchst du die Karte? Ja,…
　　　　　　　Ja, die suche ich.

1. Ist der Kunde bald dran? Ja,…
2. Verstehen die Touristen das auf deutsch? Nein,…
3. Kennst du die Jungen? Nein,…
4. Läuft der Fußballspieler schnell? Ja,…
5. Ist das Schloß sehr bekannt? Ja,…
6. Hast du die Musik schon gehört? Nein,…
7. Glaubst du deiner Freundin? Ja,…
8. Kaufst du deinen Bekannten ein paar Ansichtskarten? Ja,…
9. Fährst du ohne deine Eltern an den See? Nein,…
10. Hast du das Wörterbuch gefunden? Ja,…

Adjectives after *der*-words

The endings of adjectives in the singular following *der*-words are *-en* except in the nominative (all genders) and in the accusative (feminine and neuter) where they are *-e*. In the plural all adjective endings are *-en*.

		masculine	feminine	neuter
Singular	nominative	-e	-e	-e
	accusative	-en	-e	-e
	dative	-en	-en	-en
	genitive	-en	-en	-en
Plural	nominative	-en	-en	-en
	accusative	-en	-en	-en
	dative	-en	-en	-en
	genitive	-en	-en	-en

In order for you to understand the adjective endings more clearly, look carefully at the chart below. It incorporates the adjective endings above as well as articles and corresponding nouns.

		masculine	feminine	neuter
Singular	nominative	der alt-e Film	die jung-e Dame	das neu-e Haus
	accusative	den alt-en Film	die jung-e Dame	das neu-e Haus
	dative	dem alt-en Film	der jung-en Dame	dem neu-en Haus
	genitive	des alt-en Films	der jung-en Dame	des neu-en Hauses
Plural	nominative	die alt-en Filme	die nett-en Damen	die neu-en Häuser
	accusative	die alt-en Filme	die nett-en Damen	die neu-en Häuser
	dative	den alt-en Filmen	den nett-en Damen	den neu-en Häusern
	genitive	der alt-en Filme	der jung-en Damen	der neu-en Häuser

The adjective endings listed above follow these *der*-words: *dieser, jeder, welcher, mancher, solcher.*

Alle and *beide* can only be used in the plural with their corresponding adjective endings for *der*-words.

Beispiele (singular):

nominative: *Wo ist der neue Schüler?*
Die junge Verkäuferin ist dort.
Welches rote Fahrrad gefällt dir?

accusative: *Er sieht jeden interessanten Film.*
Kaufst du diese teu(e)re Gitarre?
Geht ihr durch das berühmte Museum?

<table>
<tr><td>dative:</td><td>*Ich spreche mit dem bekannten Amerikaner.*
Aus welcher großen Stadt kommen Sie?
Sie gibt jedem kleinen Kind ein Geschenk.</td></tr>
<tr><td>genitive:</td><td>*Wir besuchen euch während des schönen Sommers.*
Das ist der Wagen der deutschen Frau.
Trotz dieses schlechten Wetters fahren wir in die Stadt.</td></tr>
</table>

Beispiele (plural):

nominative:	*Die guten Restaurants sind nicht immer teuer.*
accusative:	*Habt ihr diese deutschen Filme gesehen?*
dative:	*Wir wohnen bei den netten Amerikanern.*
genitive:	*Während der regnerischen Tage spielen wir nicht.*

NOTE: In an adjective ending in -*el*, the "e" is omitted if an added ending begins with the letter *e*.

dunkel: das dunkle Zimmer

The same is true for adjectives with an -*er* ending whereby the -*e* of the last syllable can be omitted.

teuer: der teuere Wagen
der teure Wagen

The adjective *hoch* loses its -*c* when the ending begins with an -*e*.

Das Haus ist hoch.
Das hohe Haus steht dort drüben.

Folgt den Beispielen!

7. Museum / bekannt   Wo ist das bekannte Museum?

    Schloß / berühmt   Wo ist das berühmte Schloß?

    Student / deutsch   Wo ist der deutsche Student?

    Lehrerin / neu   Wo ist die neue Lehrerin?

    Prospekt / interessant   Wo ist der interessante Prospekt?

    Straße / alt   Wo ist die alte Straße?

8. Der schwarze Mantel ist teuer.   Welchen schwarzen Mantel meinst du?

    Die bunte Bluse ist preiswert.   Welche bunte Bluse meinst du?

    Das rote Kleid ist schön.   Welches rote Kleid meinst du?

    Die alte Stadtmauer ist dort drüben.   Welche alte Stadtmauer meinst du?

    Der bekannte Ansager ist nicht da.   Welchen bekannten Ansager meinst du?

    Das neue Rathaus ist in der Stadt.   Welches neue Rathaus meinst du?

9. Flug / lang   der lange Flug

    Übung / einfach   die einfache Übung

    Kaffee / heiß   der heiße Kaffee

    Zug / schnell   der schnelle Zug

    Café / alt   das alte Café

Ansichtskarte / schön   die schöne Ansichtskarte

Film / toll   der tolle Film

Zeitung / deutsch   die deutsche Zeitung

Tag / kalt   der kalte Tag

10. Was möchtest du sehen?   **Den großen See.**

    See / groß

Variation: Have students answer each question with a different noun and adjective.

Was möchtest du besuchen?   Das bekannte Museum.

    Museum / bekannt

Wen willst du kennenlernen?   Die neue Schülerin.

    Schülerin / neu

Wen wirst du fragen?   Den jungen Arzt.

    Arzt / jung

Wem glaubst du das nicht?   Dem kleinen Mädchen.

    Mädchen / klein

Wer hat dir das gesagt?   Die alte Verkäuferin.

    Verkäuferin / alt

11. Welche kleine Stadt verlassen sie?   Welche kleine Stadt verlassen sie?

    Land / groß   Welches große Land verlassen sie?

    Bahnhof / alt   Welchen alten Bahnhof verlassen sie?

    Geschäft / teuer   Welches teuere Geschäft verlassen sie?

    Flughafen / neu   Welchen neuen Flughafen verlassen sie?

    Jugendherberge / schön   Welche schöne Jugendherberge verlassen sie?

    Schiff / lang   Welches lange Schiff verlassen sie?

12. Wir haben diesen deutschen Film gesehen.   Wir haben diesen deutschen Film gesehen.

    interessant   Wir haben diesen interessanten Film gesehen.

    Kaufhaus   Wir haben dieses interessante Kaufhaus gesehen.

    neu   Wir haben dieses neue Kaufhaus gesehen.

    Schauspielerin   Wir haben diese neue Schauspielerin gesehen.

    berühmt   Wir haben diese berühmte Schauspielerin gesehen.

    Schloß   Wir haben dieses berühmte Schloß gesehen.

    alt   Wir haben dieses alte Schloß gesehen.

    Brücke   Wir haben diese alte Brücke gesehen.

    lang   Wir haben diese lange Brücke gesehen.

13. Wo hast du denn gewohnt?   **Bei dem neuen Bahnhof.**

    Bahnhof / neu

Variation: Have students answer each question with a different noun and adjective.

Wo hast du denn gewartet?   Bei dem teueren Geschäft.

    Geschäft / teuer

Wo bist du denn gewesen?   Bei der alten Dame.

    Dame / alt

Wo hast du denn geparkt?   Bei der grauen Parkuhr.

    Parkuhr / grau

Wo hast du das denn gesehen?   Bei dem schönen Rathaus.
   Rathaus / schön

14. Die Besucher kommen aus dem modernen   Die Besucher kommen aus dem
    Kino.   modernen Kino.
    beliebt   Die Besucher kommen aus dem
                                beliebten Kino.

    Theater   Die Besucher kommen aus dem beliebten Theater.
    deutsch   Die Besucher kommen aus dem deutschen Theater.
    Schule   Die Besucher kommen aus der deutschen Schule.
    groß   Die Besucher kommen aus der großen Schule.
    Kaufhaus   Die Besucher kommen aus dem großen Kaufhaus.
    elegant   Die Besucher kommen aus dem eleganten Kaufhaus.
    Bank   Die Besucher kommen aus der eleganten Bank.

Variation: Use singular forms in the sentences on the right.

15. Die alten Städte gefallen uns.   Die alten Städte gefallen uns.
    Flugzeug / modern   Die modernen Flugzeuge gefallen
                                uns.

    Auto / klein   Die kleinen Autos gefallen uns.
    Buch / deutsch   Die deutschen Bücher gefallen uns.
    Ansichtskarte / schön   Die schönen Ansichtskarten gefallen uns.
    Zimmer / groß   Die großen Zimmer gefallen uns.
    Hemd / bunt   Die bunten Hemden gefallen uns.

16. Was habt ihr besucht?   Diese bekannten Theater.
    Theater / bekannt
  Was habt ihr gesehen?   Diese interessanten Länder.
    Land / interessant
  Was habt ihr gelesen?   Diese politischen Zeitungen.
    Zeitung / politisch
  Was habt ihr gehört?   Diese deutschen Schallplatten.
    Schallplatte / deutsch
  Was habt ihr verstanden?   Diese neuen Wörter.
    Wort / neu
  Was habt ihr gekauft?   Diese schwarzen Koffer.
    Koffer / schwarz

Variation: Have students form complete sentences, using the answers on the right side.

17. das Buch des deutschen Studenten   die Bücher der deutschen Studenten
    der Preis der blauen Fahrkarte   die Preise der blauen Fahrkarten
    die Tochter des neuen Lehrers   die Töchter der neuen Lehrer
    das Paket meiner netten Tante   die Pakete meiner netten Tanten
    das Auto seines großen Bruders   die Autos seiner großen Brüder
    die Rechnung des jungen Verkäufers die Rechnungen der jungen Verkäufer
    der Brief meiner alten Freundin   die Briefe meiner alten Freundinnen

18. **Supply the proper adjective endings.**

1. Fahren Sie doch lieber mit dem schnell_____ Zug.
2. Wann wirst du diese neu_____ Bücher lesen?
3. Die bekannt_____ deutsch_____ Mannschaft kommt bald nach Amerika.
4. Haben Sie diese alt_____ Städte besucht?
5. Was wollen wir nach dem toll_____ Film machen?
6. Die Ausländer machen eine Reise durch das schön_____ Land.
7. Zu welchem gemütlich_____ Restaurant gehen wir?
8. Bringen Sie mir bitte die grün_____ Krawatte.
9. Während des schlecht_____ Wetters können wir leider nicht spielen.
10. Hast du mit der jung_____ Dame gesprochen?
11. Trotz der lang_____ Fahrt bin ich nicht müde.
12. Was ist die genau_____ Zeit?
13. Diese klein_____ Torten schmecken sehr gut.
14. Wir haben die interessant_____ Zeitungen geholt.
15. Warten Sie doch bei dem mittelalterlich_____ Tor.

19. **Complete each sentence, using the words in parentheses.**

   Beispiel: *Wo ist _____? (Buch, toll)*
   Wo ist das tolle Buch?

1. Hast du _____ gesehen? (Film, neu)
2. Welches _____ möchtest du kaufen? (Fahrrad, preiswert)
3. Die Ausländer kommen aus _____ . (Stadt, groß)
4. Der Herr sucht _____ . (Rathaus, alt)
5. Ich muß _____ besuchen. (Kirche, historisch)
6. Der Bruder meines _____ wohnt in Süddeutschland. (Freund, alt)
7. Wir gehen zu _____ . (Restaurant, teuer)
8. _____ gefällt mir nicht. (Kleid, rot)
9. Was macht ihr nach _____? (Spiel, lang)
10. Während _____ sitzen wir gern draußen. (Tag, schön)
11. Möchten Sie lieber _____? (Mantel, braun)
12. Habt ihr _____ geschrieben? (Aufsatz, kurz)

20. **Form complete sentences using the information given.**

1. Können / du / tragen / groß / Koffer
2. Deutsch / Flugzeug / acht Uhr / abfliegen
3. Lesen / dein / Mutter / lang / Brief
4. Morgen / wir / interessant / Film / sehen
5. Fluggast / bekommen / gut / Abendessen / nach / Abflug
6. Herr und Frau Köhler / haben / neu / Reisepaß
7. Wie / gefallen / du / gemütlich / Platz
8. Jungen / nicht surfen / während / windig / Tag

9. Verstehen / ihr / einfach / Aufgabe
10. Wollen / du / halb / Stück Kuchen / essen

21. **Complete each sentence by providing the German equivalents for the words in parentheses.**

1. Haben Sie _____ besucht? (the large cities)
2. _____ hat mir gut gefallen. (the German restaurant)
3. Herr Schulz hat letzte Woche _____ gekauft. (this red car)
4. Hast du _____ gesehen? (the excellent soccer game)
5. _____ soll ich denn anprobieren? (which blue shirt)
6. Anstatt _____ kaufe ich lieber etwas anderes. (the red flowers)
7. Ich habe mit _____ gesprochen. (the new doctor)
8. Wir sind durch _____ gegangen. (this famous castle)
9. Gehen Sie gern zu _____? (this modern store)
10. Nach _____ kann ich wirklich nichts mehr essen. (this good meal)
11. _____ möchtest du zuerst lesen? (which long letter)
12. Von _____ habe ich schon lange nichts gehört. (this old gentleman)
13. Zeig mir doch _____ ! (these beautiful picture postcards)
14. Seit _____ hat er uns nicht geschrieben. (the first of March)
15. Während _____ machen wir eine Ferienreise. (the warm weather)

Lesestück 1

Auf der Post

Herr Hofer muß heute noch verschiedene Besorgungen in der Stadt machen. Mit schnellen Schritten geht er Richtung Innenstadt. Auf dem Weg fragt ihn ein Autofahrer nach° einer Straße. Herr Hofer gibt ihm genaue Auskunft. Vor der Post steckt er einen Brief in den Briefkasten. Hier leert° man den Briefkasten alle zwei Stunden. Dann geht Herr Hofer in die Post hinein.

    An einem Schalter füllt er eine Paketkarte aus. Er will das Paket an seinen Onkel in Oldenburg schicken. Auf die Paketkarte schreibt er die folgende° Information: Vor- und Nachname seines Onkels und seine Anschrift°, einschließlich Straße, Hausnummer, Postleitzahl und Bestimmungsort°. Natürlich muß er seinen Absender auch noch genau aufschreiben°. Am Paketschalter gibt Herr Hofer einem Beamten sein Paket. Der Beamte legt es auf eine Waage°, wiegt° es genau und schreibt das Porto° auf das Paket. Dann sagt er Herrn Hofer, wieviel die Sendung° kostet.

    An einem anderen Schalter möchte Herr Hofer ein paar Briefmarken kaufen. Dort stehen schon einige Leute. Herr Hofer wartet eine Weile, bis er an die Reihe kommt. An diesem Schalter kauft er Briefmarken für Briefe und Postkarten.

fragt...nach asks for

empty

following
address
destination
write down

scale/weigh/postage
parcel

Herr Hofer sieht
im Telefonbuch nach.

Was steckt Herr Hofer
in den Briefkasten?

Herr Hofer gibt dem Beamten eine Telefonnummer.

Dann sagt er dem Beamten, daß er ein Ferngespräch führen möchte. Leider weiß Herr Hofer die Vorwahlnummer nicht. Deshalb bittet der Beamte ihn, die genaue Telefonnummer im Telefonbuch nachzusehen. Die Telefonbücher von den größeren Städten sind alle alphabetisch an einem Tisch angeordnet. Herr Hofer findet seine Nummer auch gleich und geht zum Schalter zurück. Er gibt dem Beamten seine Telefonnummer auf einem Zettel°. Der Beamte deutet auf° die Telefonzelle in der Ecke. Herr Hofer wartet dort ganz kurz, bis die Zelle° frei ist. Dann geht er hinein, setzt sich, hebt den Hörer ab und führt sein Gespräch°.

piece of paper
points to
booth
makes his call

Fragen über das Lesestück

1. Warum muß Herr Hofer in die Stadt gehen?
2. Was macht er mit seinem Brief?
3. Warum muß Herr Hofer eine Paketkarte ausfüllen?
4. Was macht der Beamte am Schalter mit seinem Paket?
5. Warum wiegt der Beamte das Paket?
6. Was kauft Herr Hofer an einem anderen Schalter?
7. Was braucht Herr Hofer für sein Ferngespräch?
8. Warum muß Herr Hofer bei der Telefonzelle warten?

Erweiterung

22. Beantwortet diese Fragen mit einem ganzen Satz!

1. Wie heißt deine Anschrift?
2. Was braucht man für einen Brief?
3. Schickst du lieber einen Brief oder eine Karte? Warum?
4. Was ist deine Telefonnummer, einschließlich Vorwahlnummer?
5. Gibt es in deiner Nähe einen Briefkasten? Wie oft leert man ihn?

23. Wie heißt das auf deutsch?

1. I thank you for your letter.
2. Do you know his address?
3. I didn't get much mail.
4. Would you like to make a long-distance call?
5. My grandparents emigrated to America.
6. I'm thinking about her party.
7. Were you on a vacation trip?
8. Are you looking forward to your birthday?
9. That's no surprise.
10. Put the card into the mailbox.

24. Beschreibt jedes Wort mit einem ganzen Satz!

As an additional activity, have students write a short paragraph, using all of these seven words.

1. Briefträger
2. Paketkarte
3. Briefmarken
4. Rechnung
5. Post
6. Telefonbuch
7. Ferngespräch

25. Match each word on the left side with its counterpart on the right. Indicate also the meaning for each word pair.

1. Briefträger: _____	Wurst
2. Lehrer: _____	Haare
3. Schiedsrichter: _____	Flugzeug
4. Fürst: _____	Schloß
5. Einwohner: _____	Post
6. Pilot: _____	Klavier
7. Kellnerin: _____	Café
8. Braut: _____	Schule
9. Schauspielerin: _____	Fußballspiel
10. Sekretärin: _____	Kuchen

11. Fleischer: _____
12. Bäcker: _____
13. Friseuse: _____
14. Musiker: _____

Hochzeit
Land
Büro
Theater

26. Provide an appropriate response in German. Be sure that the whole conversation ties together and becomes meaningful.

1. Was bringen Sie mir denn heute?
2. Ich glaube, es ist von meiner Schwester. Sie hat mir bestimmt ein Geburtstagsgeschenk geschickt.
3. Die ist von meiner Freundin. Sie ist jetzt für zwei Wochen auf der Insel Fehmarn.
4. Wann sind Sie denn dort gewesen?
5. Hat es Ihnen denn dort gefallen?
6. Vielleicht fahren wir nächstes Jahr auch dorthin.

Encourage varied responses.
The students' answers will
most likely lead to a short
discussion.

27. Beantwortet diese Fragen!

1. Schreibst du gern einen Brief?
2. Von wem bekommst du manchmal Post?
3. Was ist dein Vor- und Nachname?
4. Wo kann man Briefmarken kaufen?
5. Wo kann man Telefonnummern finden?

Rückblick

If your students have any difficulties with these exercises, you may wish to review the grammar point and some of the related exercises in the particular lesson in which these were covered.

I. Form a phrase, using the words below.

Beispiel: *das Buch / meine Schwester*
das Buch meiner Schwester

1. das Geschäft / mein Onkel
2. die Farbe / sein Motorrad
3. das Kleid / unsere Freundin
4. die Reise / die Bekannte
5. die Ankunft / die Fluggäste
6. der Reisepaß / der Tourist
7. die Rechnung / dieser Kunde
8. die Ansichtskarte / meine Eltern
9. der Fahrplan / der Beamte
10. das Haus / jeder Einwohner

II. Complete the following sentences.

1. Während des Tages _____ .
2. Trotz des schlechten Wetters _____ .
3. Ich besuche _____ .
4. Die Fahrkarten der Besucher _____ .

90

5. Wessen Brief _____?

6. Werners Telefongespräch _____ .

7. Wegen deiner Eltern _____ .

8. Anstatt der Jungen _____ .

III. Provide one of the following prepositions for each sentence: *an, auf, aus, für, mit, über, von.*

1. Kannst du dich noch _____ die Reise erinnern?

2. Sie verabschieden sich _____ ihren Verwandten.

3. Interessierst du dich _____ diese Briefmarken?

4. Mein Freund schreibt viel _____ seinen Urlaub.

5. Die Leute warten _____ den Zug.

6. Erzähl mir doch _____ deinem Flug nach Europa!

7. Die Eltern beklagen sich _____ ihre Kinder.

8. Das Buch besteht _____ fünf Teilen.

9. Die Schweiz grenzt _____ Österreich.

10. Die Touristen zeigen _____ das alte Rathaus.

11. Ich freue mich _____ meinen Geburtstag.

12. Warum beklagst du dich _____ deine Noten?

IV. Change the following sentences to the past tense.

> **Beispiel:** *Wohin geht er?*
> *Wohin ging er?*

1. Der Briefträger kommt um neun Uhr.

2. Sagst du das nicht?

3. Sie wandern nach Amerika aus.

4. Meine Freundin ist auf einer Ferienreise.

5. Wann fährst du dorthin?

6. Wißt ihr die Vorwahlnummer?

7. Der Beamte legt das Paket auf die Waage.

8. Die Spieler laufen auf den Fußballplatz.

9. Wir sehen dem Spiel gespannt zu.

10. Er hat keine Chance.

Der Beamte
legt das Paket
auf die Waage.

Lesestück 2

Fußball ist König

Es gibt keinen Zweifel°, welcher Sport in Deutschland an der Spitze steht. Jeder Deutsche wird ganz klar sagen: „Fußball ist König." Die achtzehn besten Mannschaften spielen in der Bundesliga°. Zwei dieser Mannschaften sind Eintracht Frankfurt und Arminia Bielefeld. Wie alle anderen Mannschaften spielen auch diese beiden am Samstag. Gewöhnlich° ist das Stadion° ziemlich voll, aber an diesem Samstag ist das Wetter trübe° und regnerisch. Deshalb bleiben viele Zuschauer heute zu Hause. Manche Frankfurter Fußballanhänger° kommen schon eine halbe Stunde vor dem Spiel. Die meisten Leute parken ihre Fahrzeuge° auf den Straßen in der Nähe des Stadions und gehen dann zehn oder fünfzehn Minuten zu Fuß. Am Stadion gibt es fast keine Parkplätze.

Die Preise der Plätze sind verschieden. Ein paar Zuschauer stehen an der Kasse und kaufen Stehplätze. Die sind am billigsten. Andere ziehen Sitzplätze vor. Natürlich kosten die mehr. Manche Leute stehen vor dem Stadion und warten bis kurz vor dem Spiel. Erst dann gehen sie ins Stadion hinein. Wer Durst und Hunger hat°, kann an den kleinen Kiosken Bier oder Cola trinken und Würstchen° essen. Einzelne° Gruppen von Fußballfans versammeln sich vor dem Stadion. Die meisten sind Jugendliche. Sie haben sich alle bunt angezogen.

Das Fernsehen ist schon da. Ein Techniker° stellt alles genau ein°. Heute abend wird man in der Sportschau Auszüge° dieses Spiels im Fernsehen zeigen. Auf einer großen Tafel — sie ist beleuchtet° — gibt man die wichtigen Einzelheiten° bekannt. Eine Viertelstunde vor dem Spiel laufen die Spieler von beiden Mannschaften auf den Fußballplatz. Sie laufen sich warm°, spielen mit dem Ball und machen ihre Leibesübungen°. Kurz vor dem Spiel versammeln sich die Spieler und laufen zusammen mit dem Schiedsrichter° und den beiden Linienrichtern° auf das Feld.

Endlich geht's los. Das Tempo ist am Anfang° etwas langsam. In einem Fußballspiel versuchen die Spieler, den Ball ins Tor° des Gegners° zu schießen°. Die Spieler spielen hauptsächlich° mit dem Fuß. Wenn der Ball zu hoch kommt, köpfen° sie ihn. Die Frankfurter versuchen immer wieder anzugreifen°, aber die Bielefelder verteidigen° heute sehr gut. In der Halbzeit steht es 0:0. Die Halbzeit dauert zehn Minuten.

Gleich nach der Halbzeit steigern° die Frankfurter ihr Tempo. Plötzlich passiert es. Der Bielefelder Torwart° kann den Ball nicht halten° und Nummer 7 schießt das erste Tor für die Frankfurter. Die Frankfurter Spieler jubeln°. Die Zuschauer jubeln auch und schwingen° ihre Fahnen. Auf der großen Tafel blinkt° das Wort „Tor". Da

doubt

Federal League

usually/stadium
cloudy

soccer fans
vehicles

Whoever is thirsty and hungry
hot dogs
individual

technician
stellt...ein adjusts/ excerpts
lit up/details

warm up
(physical) exercises

referee/linesmen

beginning
goal
opponent/shoot/ mainly
to head
attack
defend

increase
goalie
stop
cheer
wave/flashes

Ist das
Stadion voll?

Welche Mannschaft hat gerade
ein Tor geschossen?

Die Spieler spielen hauptsächlich mit dem Fuß.

Die Zuschauer sehen gespannt zu.

stehen jetzt auch das Ergebnis° und andere wichtige Informationen. *score*
Es dauert aber nicht lange und ein Bielefelder schießt den Ball rechts
ins Tor. Jetzt ist das Spiel unentschieden°. *tied*

    Die Zuschauer sehen dem Spiel gespannt zu. Wird ihre
Mannschaft noch gewinnen? Beide Mannschaften spielen sehr
aggressiv. Ein Bielefelder fällt plötzlich hin°, denn ein Frankfurter   *fällt...hin falls*
Spieler hat ihn gefoult°. Der Schiedsrichter verwarnt° den Spieler   *down*
und das Spiel geht weiter. Der Bielefelder Torwart ist in den letzten   *fouled/cautions*
Minuten sehr gut. Er muß viele Bälle halten. Aber in der letzten
Minute des Spiels passiert es. Nummer vier schießt den Ball rechts
in die Ecke. Der Bielefelder hat keine Chance, diesen Schuß zu
halten. Die Frankfurter sind begeistert. Am Ende haben sie das Spiel
doch noch gewonnen. Diesmal° haben sie wirklich Glück gehabt.   *this time*
Die Tafel zeigt das Endergebnis° deutlich: *final score*

EINTRACHT — BIELEFELD
2 : 1

Fragen über das Lesestück

1. Wie viele Mannschaften spielen in der Bundesliga? Was ist die Bundesliga?
2. Warum kommen nicht viele Zuschauer zu diesem Spiel?
3. Warum müssen die Zuschauer ihre Wagen in der Nähe des Stadions parken?
4. Was für Karten kann man bei einem Fußballspiel kaufen?
5. Wo kann man etwas zu essen und trinken bekommen?
6. Was macht der Fernsehtechniker und warum?
7. Was steht alles auf der großen Tafel?
8. Was machen die Spieler vor dem Spiel?
9. Was machen die Spieler mit dem Ball?
10. Wie steht das Spiel in der Halbzeit?
11. Wer schießt das erste Tor?
12. Was tun die Zuschauer?
13. Was muß der Schiedsrichter während des Spiels tun?
14. Was passiert in der letzten Minute?
15. Welche Mannschaft hat das Fußballspiel gewonnen?

Sprachspiegel
You may want to have students work in groups to develop this conversation. Have them read their dialogs and others ask questions.

I. **Schreibe einen Dialog über das Thema (topic) „Der Briefträger kommt."! (Was bringt er? Was besprecht ihr? usw.)**

II. **Schreibe einen Brief an deinen Freund oder deine Freundin — auf deutsch natürlich!**

Du bist dran!

Have students respond to the various questions and statements to complete each mini-situation. Encourage as much creative effort as possible.

Was füllen Sie denn aus?
. . . .
Warum müssen Sie das tun?
. . . .

Von wem hast du dieses
    Päckchen bekommen?
. . . .
Ich wußte gar nicht, daß sie
    nicht mehr hier wohnt.
. . . .

. . . .
Wissen Sie die Vorwahlnummer?
. . . .
Dann sehen Sie bitte im
    Telefonbuch nach.
. . . .

. . . .
Wahrscheinlich zum Fußballspiel.
. . . .
Hamburg gegen Stuttgart.
. . . .
Das glaube ich auch.

Die Spitzplätze sind zu teuer.
. . . .
Du hast recht, wir haben ja junge Beine.
. . . .
Dann haben wir noch etwas Zeit.

. . . .
Nein, ich habe aber Hunger.
. . . .
Vielleicht ein Brötchen und ein Würstchen.
. . . .

Haben Sie Post für uns?
. . . .
Da bin ich gespannt, was sie uns schreiben.
. . . .
Ja, sie haben recht.

Was essen und
trinken sie?

Kulturecke

Youth Activities in the DDR

Leisure-time activities are as important to the young people in the German Democratic Republic as they are in any other country. A favorite place, particularly on weekends, is the local movie theater. Most of the movies shown are produced either in the *DDR* or in other Eastern countries. However, Western influence is apparent in the numerous discos. Here the young people dance to rock music that has been brought in from the West. Another popular place to go after school or on weekends is the local ice cream parlor.

Besides the family, the school and its related activities have the greatest impact on the life of the young people. Tremendous emphasis is placed on sports activities of all kinds. Those students with natural ability are particularly encouraged to compete in the sport of their choice. Several times a year, students go on field trips. Most of these school-sponsored trips last only one day, although it is not uncommon for a whole class to go on a week-long trip.

During the summer months, many children spend two or three weeks in youth camps *(Pionierlager),* which are scattered all over the country. Various activities are scheduled here throughout the day. Most children do not have to pay a fee, although some do pay a very nominal one. The older teenagers prefer to go camping. Most of the camp grounds are located in the northern regions along the Baltic Sea *(Ostsee).* Those who don't like to go camping can stay at youth hostels. As with the youth camps, the youth hostels offer various activities throughout the day, ranging from outdoor bowling to table tennis.

Although students can do what they want to do after school, the state, the youth organizations and other organizations offer a variety of activities that focus on education as it relates to the interest of the country. Many children between the ages of 6 and 14 belong to the Young Pioneers *(JP or Junge Pioniere),* whereas those between 14 and 25 belong to the Free German Youth *(FDJ or Freie Deutsche Jugend).* There are 6,400 youth clubs *(Jugendklubs)* scattered throughout the country. These clubs are managed totally by the young adults who participate there in such daily activities as projects or discussions on art, science, sports and language. On the other hand, the *Junge Pioniere,* the younger group, has more guided activities, especially designed by educational organizations with direct support by the state.

Let's visit the *Pionierpalast — Ernst Thälmann* in East Berlin. This immense building is a good example of the state's strong support for education of young people. The Pioneer Palace provides instruction and entertainment for about 2,000 children every day. Youngsters come here after school to participate in many daily activities. Upon entering the building, you'll be confronted with a detailed map of the building that shows all the facilities. Next to it is a schedule of daily and weekly events as well as other important announcements. In the lobby, a group of boys and girls practice singing folk songs that they will sing in front of an audience when they have perfected their performance.

Sports receive a great deal of attention and emphasis. An Olympic-size indoor pool, for example, provides fun and enjoyment for many children. But even here, the skill-building for swimming is supervised and guided by knowledgeable adults. In the gym, one group of boys practices judo while another group plays badminton. Adjacent to the gym, a group of girls is just getting ready to start their daily ballet lesson.

Various posters around the building exemplify the purpose and duty of these Young Pioneers. Some of the posters and banners are made by the children to explain the activities in which they participate. Whatever activity a Young Pioneer takes part in, careful guidance by a teacher is available. The teacher of an art group, for example, is able to demonstrate a skill to a few children at a time. In another room, some boys are quite involved in a woodwork project.

Wohin gehen die Jugendlichen? (Leipzig)

Zu welchen Organisationen gehören
diese Jugendlichen? (Leipzig)

Was spielen sie? (Rügen)

Was machen diese Jugendlichen?
(Pionierpalast – Berlin/Ost)

auf einem Campingplatz (Rügen)

an der Ostsee

Was ist sein Hobby?

im Kosmonautenzentrum
(Pionierpalast – Berlin/Ost)

Another group next door is completing some paintings. The goal of all these children is to demonstrate their best ability. Those whose work is considered among the best can display their drawings in the hallways. Throughout the building there are many items displayed by the children who have spent many hours perfecting them. These activities are not part of the school curriculum and are strictly on a voluntary basis; but they do emphasize the creative aspects and combine the knowledge that these children have gained in school and at home.

Some of the youngsters go to the Pioneer Palace strictly with the intention of playing. Several rooms provide an abundance of toys that all have been tested for their educational value as prescribed by the State. Other young adults are testing their skill in playing chess. The handicapped participate in those activities that they choose. In an isolated room, a group of boys and girls are getting instruction in target shooting. Marksmanship is practiced by children who must be at least twelve years of age.

The pride and joy of the Pioneer Palace is the space center called *Kosmonautenzentrum*. Children, under the supervision of adults, come to this room to investigate and ride in the miniature-style spaceship of the type that was launched by the Soviet Union. The three cosmonauts, two Soviets and one East German, signed their names on this model of their spaceship. A control panel gives these children an opportunity to use their imagination as they participate in an imaginary trip into outer space.

Vokabeln

abheben *(hob ab, abgehoben)* to lift, take off
den Hörer abheben to lift the receiver
der **Absender,-** sender
alphabetisch alphabetical
die **Angabe,-n** description, statement
anordnen to arrange, group
die **Ansichtskarte,-n** picture postcard
aufgeben *(gibt auf, gab auf, aufgegeben)* to send, dispatch
aufschreiben *(schrieb auf, aufgeschrieben)* to write down
ausruhen to rest, relax
zum Ausruhen for relaxing
auswandern to emigrate
der **Autofahrer,-** (car) driver
sich **bedanken** to thank
der **Bekanntenkreis,-e** (circle of) friends
bereiten to prepare
anderen Freude bereiten to please others
die **Besorgung,-en** errand
Besorgungen machen to do some shopping, run errands
der **Bestimmungsort,-e** destination
der **Briefträger,-** mail carrier (male)
der **Briefumschlag,-e** envelope
denken an *(dachte an, gedacht an)* to remember, think about
drüben over there
die **Drucksache,-n** printed matter
das **Einschreiben** registered (letter)
einwerfen *(wirft ein, warf ein, eingeworfen)* to mail (letter)
der **Empfänger,-** receiver, addressee
die **Ferienreise,-n** vacation trip
auf einer Ferienreise sein to be on a vacation trip
das **Ferngespräch,-e** long-distance call
ein Ferngespräch führen to make a long-distance call
folgend following
fragen nach to ask for

das **Gespräch,-e** conversation, talk
ein Gespräch führen to make a call
die **Hausnummer,-n** street number
herzlich sincere, cordial
herzliche Grüße kind regards, (intimately) love
das **Hobby,-s** hobby
der **Hörer,-** receiver (phone)
ideal ideal
leeren to empty
die **Luftpost** airmail
der **Nachname,-n** family name
das **Päckchen,-** parcel
das **Paket,-e** package
die **Paketkarte,-n** package card (form to be filled out when sending a package)
der **Paketschalter,-** package counter
das **Porto,-s** postage
die **Post** mail, post office
das **Postamt,-er** post office
das **Postfach,-er** post office box
die **Postkarte,-n** postcard
die **Postleitzahl,-en** zip code
die **Quittung,-en** receipt
rufen *(rief, gerufen)* to call
der **Schnee** snow
schön nice
die **Sendung,-en** parcel, shipment
der **Ski,-er** ski
das **Sparkonto,-ten** savings account
ein Sparkonto führen to keep a savings account
stecken to put
einen Brief in den Briefkasten stecken to put a letter into the mailbox
das **Telefonbuch,-er** phone book
das **Telefongespräch,-e** phone call
ein Telefongespräch führen to make a phone call
das **Telegramm,-e** telegram
die **Überraschung,-en** surprise

übrigens by the way
der **Urlaub,-e** vacation
die **Ursache,-n** cause, reason
Keine Ursache. Don't mention it.
der **Vorname,-n** first name
die **Vorwahlnummer,-n** area code
die **Waage,-n** scale
wiegen *(wog, gewogen)* to weigh
das **Wochenende,-n** weekend
die **Zelle,-n** booth
der **Zettel,-** piece of paper

ZOO

TIERGARTEN
HEIDELBERG

GEMEINNÜTZIGE GESELLSCHAFT MBH HEIDELBERG

Im Tiergarten
allgemeines Füttern

...gszeiten
...– 19 Uhr

Dialog

Im Zoo

...dents with a
...ülerausweis can often buy
...ets at a reduced price.
...ngsters under 14 or 15
...rs of age afe usually
...sidered *Kinder*. Their
...ets are reduced even
...her.

KATRIN:	Hier sind die Eintrittspreise angeschlagen.
TINA:	Meine Karte ist sogar billiger als deine.
KATRIN:	Eine Karte zu vier Mark und eine zu drei Mark, bitte.
DAME:	Hast du einen Ausweis?
KATRIN:	Ja, den habe ich.
DAME:	In Ordnung. Viel Spaß!

TINA:	Wo fangen wir denn an?
KATRIN:	Wir folgen einfach den Schildern.
TINA:	Schau mal, die vielen Zebras!
KATRIN:	Die will ich gleich mal knipsen.
TINA:	Was bin ich froh. Ich habe meine Kamera auch mitgebracht.
KATRIN:	Bei dem schönen Wetter werden die Fotos sicher gut.
TINA:	Schade! Die Elefanten sind zu weit weg.

e word *knipsen* is used
stly in colloquial
guage. Of course, the
mal word is *fotografieren*.

KATRIN:	Geh näher an den Zaun ran! Der Adler fliegt bestimmt nicht in deinen Apparat.
TINA:	Der sitzt so schön brav da, wie ein Modell.
KATRIN:	Die Esel mag jeder.
TINA:	Die kann man wenigstens anfassen. Ich streichle sie auch gern.
KATRIN:	Aber nicht die Robben, es sei denn, du springst mit ins Wasser.
TINA:	Nur noch eine Aufnahme und der Film ist schon voll.

conversation, people often
'was for *etwas*.

KATRIN:	Es ist schon drei. Ich habe großen Durst.
TINA:	Willst du 'was dazu essen?
KATRIN:	Nein, kauf nur eine Cola.
TINA:	Hier, für die durstige Dame.
KATRIN:	Du hast ja auch großen Durst.
TINA:	Da kann ich nicht mithalten. Du trinkst ja schon dein zweites Glas.
KATRIN:	Ich will noch die Bären, Löwen und Tiger sehen.
TINA:	Prima, ich auch.

Fragen über den Dialog

1. Wieviel bezahlt Katrin für ihre Karte?
2. Was muß Katrin der Dame zeigen?
3. Wie wissen Katrin und Tina, wo alle Tiere sind?
4. Welche Tiere sehen sie zuerst?
5. Warum glaubt Katrin, daß die Fotos gut ausfallen werden?
6. Warum können die Mädchen keine guten Aufnahmen von den Elefanten machen?
7. Was kann man mit dem Esel machen?
8. Kann Tina noch viele Aufnahmen machen?
9. Hat Katrin Hunger? Was will sie tun?
10. Welche Tiere wollen die beiden Mädchen noch sehen?

At the Zoo

KATRIN:	The prices for admission are posted here.
TINA:	My ticket is even cheaper than yours.
KATRIN:	One ticket for four marks and one for three marks, please.
LADY:	Do you have identification?
KATRIN:	Yes, I've got it.
LADY:	O.K. Have fun.

TINA:	So, where do we start?
KATRIN:	We'll simply follow the signs.
TINA:	Look at all of the zebras!
KATRIN:	I'll have to take pictures of them right away.
TINA:	Am I glad I brought my camera along, too.
KATRIN:	The pictures will be good in this beautiful weather.
TINA:	Too bad! The elephants are too far away.

KATRIN:	Move closer to the fence. The eagle certainly won't fly into your camera.
TINA:	He is sitting there so well-behaved, like a model.
KATRIN:	Everybody likes the donkeys.
TINA:	At least you can touch them. I also like to pet them.
KATRIN:	But not the seals, unless you jump into the water.
TINA:	Only one more photo and I've used up the film.

KATRIN:	It's already three. I'm really thirsty.
TINA:	Do you want to eat something, too.
KATRIN:	No, just buy a cola.
TINA:	Here, for the thirsty lady.
KATRIN:	You are thirsty, too.
TINA:	I can't keep up with you. You're drinking the second glass already.
KATRIN:	I still want to see the bears, lions and tigers.
TINA:	Great! Me too.

Nützliche Ausdrücke

Review these expressions with your students after they have learned them in the *Dialog* and *Lesestück 1*.

Die Preise sind da angeschlagen.	The prices are posted there.
Ich knipse die Tiere.	I'll take a picture of the animals.
Geh näher ran!	Move closer.
Ich komme, es sei denn, du hast keine Zeit.	I'm coming unless you don't have any time.
Hast du Durst?	Are you thirsty?
Sie züchten Kühe für ihren eigenen Bedarf.	They are raising cows for their own use.
Sie pflanzen verschiedenes an.	They are growing various things.
Was haben Sie renoviert?	What did you renovate?
Wir wohnen in einem Einfamilienhaus.	We live in a single family home.
Habt ihr genug Platz?	Do you have enough room?
Welche möglichen Berufe gibt es dort?	Which possible jobs do they have there?
Wir plaudern gern mit unseren Freunden.	We like to chat with our friends.
Die Dörfer haben sich zusammengeschlossen.	The towns merged.
Wir tauschen unsere Erfahrungen aus.	We are exchanging our ideas.

Sprichwort

Du machst aus einer Mücke einen Elefanten.
 (You make an elephant out of a mosquito.)

You are making a mountain out of a molehill.

Ergänzung

You may wish to expand the list of animals provided. Ask personalized questions, *Hast du ein Tier/Tiere zu Hause?*, *Wa... ein Tier/Tiere hast du?*, *Welche Tiere hast du gern? Warum? Gibt es in deiner Gegend einen Zoo?*, *Welche Tiere kann ma... da sehen?*

1. Einige Tiere

der Affe · das Zebra · der Elefant · die Robbe · der Fisch · die Schlange · der Löwe · der Wolf · der Bär · der Tiger

die Ziege · das Schaf · die Kuh · das Schwein · das Pferd · der Esel · das Huhn · der Vogel · die Ente · der Hund · die Katze

2. In einem Haus

Ask students such questions as *Kannst du dein Zimmer beschreiben?*, *Was befindet sich alles in deinem Wohnzimmer?*

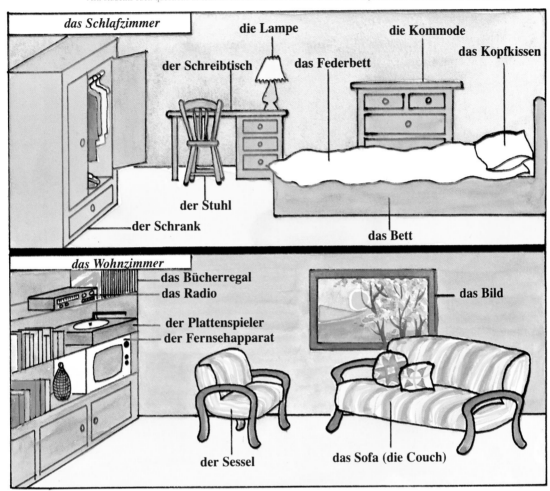

das Schlafzimmer

die Lampe — der Schreibtisch — das Federbett — die Kommode — das Kopfkissen — der Stuhl — der Schrank — das Bett

das Wohnzimmer

das Bücherregal — das Radio — der Plattenspieler — der Fernsehapparat — das Bild — der Sessel — das Sofa (die Couch)

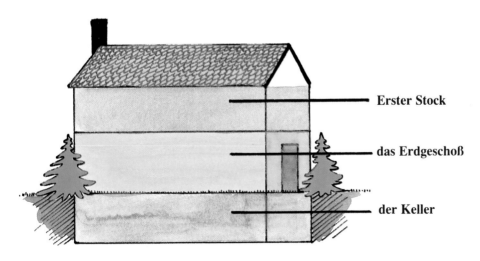

Erster Stock

das Erdgeschoß

der Keller

Übungen

Adjectives after *ein*-words*

The endings of adjectives following *ein*-words differ in only three places from those following *der*-words. In the nominative singular (masculine) the ending is *-er* and in the nominative and accusative singular (neuter) the endings are *-es* in both cases. *Ein-* words are *ein*, *kein* and all possessive adjectives *(mein, dein, sein, ihr, sein, unser, euer, ihr, Ihr)*.

		masculine	*feminine*	*neuter*
Singular	nominative	-er	-e	-es
	accusative	-en	-e	-es
	dative	-en	-en	-en
	genitive	-en	-en	-en
Plural	nominative	-en	-en	-en
	accusative	-en	-en	-en
	dative	-en	-en	-en
	genitive	-en	-en	-en

The charts below further illustrate these endings, together with corresponding nouns.

		masculine		
Singular	nominative	ein	alt-er	Film
	accusative	einen	alt-en	Film
	dative	einem	alt-en	Film
	genitive	eines	alt-en	Films
Plural	nominative	keine	alt-en	Filme
	accusative	keine	alt-en	Filme
	dative	keinen	alt-en	Filmen
	genitive	keiner	alt-en	Filme

		feminine		
Singular	nominative	eine	nett-e	Dame
	accusative	eine	nett-e	Dame
	dative	einer	nett-en	Dame
	genitive	einer	nett-en	Dame
Plural	nominative	keine	nett-en	Damen
	accusative	keine	nett-en	Damen
	dative	keinen	nett-en	Damen
	genitive	keiner	nett-en	Damen

Die Dame kauft ein belegtes Brötchen.

Sie warten eine ganze Weile, bis sie an der Reihe sind.

		neuter		
Singular	nominative	ein	neu-es	Haus
	accusative	ein	neu-es	Haus
	dative	einem	neu-en	Haus
	genitive	eines	neu-en	Hauses
Plural	nominative	keine	neu-en	Häuser
	accusative	keine	neu-en	Häuser
	dative	keinen	neu-en	Häusern
	genitive	keiner	neu-en	Häuser

Beispiele (singular):

nominative: *Ein kleiner Junge steht dort.*
Meine große Schwester ist siebzehn Jahre alt.
Sein neues Auto fährt sehr gut.

accusative: *Er will keinen alten Film sehen.*
Siehst du meine braune Krawatte?
Sie gehen durch ein amerikanisches Museum.

dative: *Gib deinem Freund ein Geschenk!*
Wir sprechen mit unserer netten Tante.
Maria kommt mit ihrem roten Fahrrad.

genitive: *Anstatt eines billigen Mantels kaufe ich mir lieber einen Anzug.*
Die Tochter meiner alten Tante besucht uns.
Ist die Tür Ihres großen Zimmers geöffnet?

Beispiele (plural):

nominative: *Meine neuen Schuhe gefallen mir sehr gut.*

accusative: *Habt ihr keine interessanten Bücher gelesen?*

dative: *Er hat von seinen alten Freunden lange nichts gehört.*

genitive: *Die Preise seiner neuen Kassetten sind toll.*

Folgt den Beispielen!

1. Was für ein Tag ist heute? (schön)   Heute ist ein schöner Tag.

Variation: *Was für ein Tag war gestern?*, *Was für ein Tag soll morgen sein?*

    kalt   Heute ist ein kalter Tag.
    ruhig   Heute ist ein ruhiger Tag.
    schlecht   Heute ist ein schlechter Tag.
    warm   Heute ist ein warmer Tag.
    regnerisch   Heute ist ein regnerischer Tag.

2. Ist das eine gute Schülerin?   Nein, das ist keine gute Schülerin.
    Ist das ein guter Bäcker?   Nein, das ist kein guter Bäcker.
    Ist das ein guter Pilot?   Nein, das ist kein guter Pilot.
    Ist das eine gute Lehrerin?   Nein, das ist keine gute Lehrerin.

Ist das eine gute Friseuse?   Nein, das ist keine gute Friseuse.

Ist das ein guter Verkäufer?   Nein, das ist kein guter Verkäufer.

Variation: Ask students the question, *Was gefällt dir?*, and have them use different adjectives (after *ein-words*) and nouns in their answers.

3. Gefällt dir mein neues Fahrrad?   Ja, mir gefällt dein neues Fahrrad.

Gefällt dir mein brauner Anzug?   Ja, mir gefällt dein brauner Anzug.

Gefällt dir meine bunte Krawatte?   Ja, mir gefällt deine bunte Krawatte.

Gefällt dir mein altes Haus?   Ja, mir gefällt dein altes Haus.

Gefällt dir mein kleiner Fernsehapparat?   Ja, mir gefällt dein kleiner Fernsehapparat.

Gefällt dir mein bequemer Sessel?   Ja, mir gefällt dein bequemer Sessel.

4. Ist diese Jugendherberge neu?   Ja, das ist eine neue Jugendherberge.

Ist dieser Brief lang?   Ja, das ist ein langer Brief.

Ist diese Karte schön?   Ja, das ist eine schöne Karte.

Ist diese Telefonnummer bekannt?   Ja, das ist eine bekannte Telefonnummer.

Ist dieser Zettel wichtig?   Ja, das ist ein wichtiger Zettel.

Ist dieses Dorf bekannt?   Ja, das ist ein bekanntes Dorf.

5. Wie gefällt dir das alte Motorrad?   Nicht gut. Ich möchte lieber ein neues Motorrad.

Wie gefällt dir die alte Schultasche?   Nicht gut. Ich möchte lieber eine neue Schultasche.

Wie gefällt dir der alte Wagen?   Nicht gut. Ich möchte lieber einen neuen Wagen.

Wie gefällt dir die alte Kamera?   Nicht gut. Ich möchte lieber eine neue Kamera.

Wie gefällt dir das alte Radio?   Nicht gut. Ich möchte lieber ein neues Radio.

Wie gefällt dir der alte Koffer?   Nicht gut. Ich möchte lieber einen neuen Koffer.

6. Film / toll   ein toller Film

    kein   kein toller Film

    Flug / lang   kein langer Flug

    ein   ein langer Flug

    Restaurant / gemütlich   ein gemütliches Restaurant

    sein   sein gemütliches Restaurant

    Tag / wichtig   sein wichtiger Tag

    unser   unser wichtiger Tag

    Stadt / deutsch   unsere deutsche Stadt

    kein   keine deutsche Stadt

    Anzug / preiswert   kein preiswerter Anzug

    Ihr   Ihr preiswerter Anzug

    Ausweis / neu   Ihr neuer Ausweis

    mein   mein neuer Ausweis

Variation: Have students come up with different answers rather than using the cue words.

7. Was hast du denn gelesen?   Ich habe eine deutsche Zeitung gelesen.

    Zeitung / deutsch

Was hast du denn gesehen?   Ich habe ein interessantes Spiel gesehen.

    Spiel / interessant

Was hast du denn gekauft?	Ich habe einen kleinen Ball gekauft.
Ball / klein	
Was hast du denn geschrieben?	Ich habe einen langen Brief geschrieben.
Brief / lang	
Was hast du denn gestreichelt?	Ich habe eine graue Katze gestreichelt.
Katze / grau	
Was hast du denn gehört?	Ich habe eine deutsche Kassette gehört.
Kassette / deutsch	

Variation: Substitute different personal pronouns or subjects to ask each question. Have students use different modal auxiliaries in their answers. *(Sucht Peter ein Program? Nein, er will kein gutes Programm finden.)*

8. Suchst du ein Programm?　　　　Ich kann kein gutes Programm finden.

Suchst du eine Ansichtskarte?	Ich kann keine gute Ansichtskarte finden.
Suchst du ein Bild?	Ich kann kein gutes Bild finden.
Suchst du ein Fahrrad?	Ich kann kein gutes Fahrrad finden.
Suchst du einen Wagen?	Ich kann keinen guten Wagen finden.
Suchst du eine Zeitung?	Ich kann keine gute Zeitung finden.

9. Wir haben deinen alten Freund gesehen.　　Wir haben deinen alten Freund gesehen.

Gitarre / sein	Wir haben seine alte Gitarre gesehen.
Lehrer / unser	Wir haben unseren alten Lehrer gesehen.
Bordkarte / eure	Wir haben eure alte Bordkarte gesehen.
Ausweis / dein	Wir haben deinen alten Ausweis gesehen.
Buch / ihr	Wir haben ihr altes Buch gesehen.

10. Wo haben Sie gewohnt?　　　　Beim alten Rathaus.

Rathaus / alt	
Zoo / modern	Beim modernen Zoo.
Schule / neu	Bei der neuen Schule.
Café / bekannt	Beim bekannten Café.
Bahnhof / groß	Beim großen Bahnhof.
Stadtmauer / historisch	Bei der historischen Stadtmauer.

11. Provide the necessary endings. Not all blanks require an ending.

1. Meine Eltern kaufen ein_____ klein_____ Haus.
2. Wo sind euer_____ deutsch_____ Bücher?
3. Er fährt mit sein_____ neu_____ Auto durch Europa.
4. Hast du mein_____ alt_____ Kamera gesehen?
5. Heute ist kein_____ schön_____ Tag.
6. Sie fahren durch kein_____ groß_____ Städte.
7. Er gibt sein_____ gut_____ Freundin ein_____ klein_____ Geschenk.
8. Die Touristen besuchen ein_____ international_____ Museum.
9. Sie gehen zu ein_____ interessant_____ Film.
10. Mein deutsch_____ Freund kommt zu Besuch.

11. Wir machen Aufnahmen von unser_____ gut_____ Mannschaft.

12. Sein_____ braun_____ Schuhe gefallen ihm sehr gut.

12. Complete each sentence providing the given nouns with their respective adjectives. Use the possessive adjective that corresponds to the subject of the sentence.

Beispiel: *Hast du _____ gesehen? (Schwester, klein)*
Hast du deine kleine Schwester gesehen?

1. Er liest _____ . (Buch, neu)
2. Wir besuchen _____ . (Schloß, berühmt)
3. Ich habe _____ gesucht. (Krawatte, blau)
4. Frau Schulz kauft _____ . (Zeitschrift, interessant)
5. Gibst du _____ ein Geschenk? (Bruder, groß)
6. Haben Sie _____ mitgebracht? (Kamera, teuer)
7. Was macht ihr mit _____? (Apparat, alt)
8. Ich kann _____ nicht finden. (Ansichtskarte, schön)

Folgt dem Beispiel!

Variation: After learning the grammar point on page 112, have your students change this exercise as follows: *Hast du schöne (bunte, interessante) Ansichtskarten? Nein, ich habe keine schönen (bunten, interessanten) Ansichtskarten.*

13. Ich habe eine schöne Ansichtskarte. Und du?

    Ich habe keine schönen Ansichtskarten.

Ich kaufe ein bekanntes Buch. Und du?

    Ich kaufe keine bekannten Bücher.

Ich kenne ein deutsches Mädchen. Und du?

    Ich kenne keine deutschen Mädchen.

Ich fotografiere einen jungen Elefanten. Und du?

    Ich fotografiere keine jungen Elefanten.

Ich streichele eine weiße Katze. Und du?

    Ich streichele keine weißen Katzen.

Ich lese ein interessantes Buch. Und du?

    Ich lese keine interessanten Bücher.

14. Complete each sentence by using an *ein*-word with an adjective and a noun. Use a different adjective in each sentence.

1. Kaufst du _____?
2. Habt ihr _____ gesehen?
3. Ich brauche _____ .
4. Er wohnt bei _____ .
5. Die Touristen fahren durch _____ .
6. Haben Sie _____?
7. Wo bekommen wir _____?
8. Hast du _____ geknipst?
9. Wann haben Sie _____ verloren?
10. Seht ihr euch _____ an?

Der Herr fotografiert die Leute.

15. Form a new sentence by using the adjective provided in parentheses.

> **Beispiel:** *Wann lesen Sie ein Buch? (deutsch)*
> *Wann lesen Sie ein deutsches Buch?*

1. Wir sind durch sein Haus gegangen. (groß)
2. Meine Reise hat mir gut gefallen. (lang)
3. Eine Verkäuferin steht an der Kasse. (neu)
4. Habt ihr einen Film gesehen? (interessant)
5. Er hat von seiner Freundin einen Brief bekommen. (alt)
6. Die Studenten besichtigen unser Geschäft. (elegant)
7. Hast du deinen Mantel gefunden? (grau)
8. Ich füttere meinen Hund. (klein)
9. Wir haben eine Torte gekauft. (lecker)
10. Während meines Flugs habe ich nichts gegessen. (kurz)

Adjectives Used as Nouns

Some adjectives appear as nouns. Although these adjectives are capitalized, they still have the same endings as if they were to appear with nouns.

Beispiele: *Suchst du den Kleinen?*
(Are you looking for the little one?)
Ich kenne die Kluge.
(I know the smart one.)

Folgt den Beispielen!

16. Mit wem spielst du gern?   Mit dem Kleinen.
     (klein - der)
    Wen kennst du?   Die Große.
     (groß - die)
    Wer ist das denn?   Der Kluge.
     (klug - der)
    Mit wem tanzt er?   Mit der Neuen.
     (neu - die)
    Wem hast du geschrieben?   Dem Bekannten.
     (bekannt - der)

17. Wo ist er? (deutsch)   Meinst du den Deutschen?
    Wo ist sie? (klein)   Meinst du die Kleine?
    Wo ist er? (klug)   Meinst du den Klugen?
    Wo ist sie? (groß)   Meinst du die Große?
    Wo ist er? (langsam)   Meinst du den Langsamen?
    Wo ist sie? (ruhig)   Meinst du die Ruhige?

Adjectives Not Preceded by Articles

Whenever an adjective is not preceded by an article, the adjective ending itself is identical to the ending of the article as if it had appeared. This is true for all four cases you have learned so far (nominative, accusative, dative and genitive). Note the variations in the neuter (nominative and accusative), where the ending actually is *-es* instead of *-as* as it appears in the article *das*, and in the masculine and neuter (genitive), where the ending is *-en*.

	Singular			Plural
	Masculine	*Feminine*	*Neuter*	
Nominative	alt*er* Freund	rot*e* Bluse	neu*es* Auto	klein*e* Kinder
Accusative	alt*en* Freund	rot*e* Bluse	neu*es* Auto	klein*e* Kinder
Dative	alt*em* Freund	rot*er* Bluse	neu*em* Auto	klein*en* Kinder*n*
Genitive	alt*en* Freundes	rot*er* Bluse	neu*en* Autos	klein*en* Kinder

Beispiele: *Die Kapelle spielt die moderne Musik.*
Die Kapelle spielt moderne Musik.

Das braune Haar gefällt mir gut.
Braunes Haar gefällt mir gut.

Adjectives after *nichts, etwas* and *viel*

Adjectives following the words *nichts, etwas* or *viel* and appearing without a noun are always in the singular and are capitalized. Adjective nouns always end in *-es*.

Beispiele: *Ich habe viel Gutes über ihn gehört.*
(I have heard a lot of good things about him.)
Wir lesen nichts Wichtiges.
(We are reading nothing important.)

Adjectives Following Quantity Words *viele, wenige, einige, andere* and *ein paar.*

There are a number of quantity words such as *viele, wenige, einige, andere* and *ein paar*. If these quantity words are followed by adjectives, then the adjective endings are the same as those in *dieser*.

Beispiele: *Wo sind diese schönen Briefmarken.*
Viele schöne Briefmarken sind hier.

Bring mir diese neuen Bälle.
Bring mir ein paar neue Bälle.

Er erklärt diesen deutschen Schülern den Satz.
Er erklärt einigen deutschen Schülern den Satz.

NOTE: Whenever these quantity words are followed by adjectives, the adjective endings are either *-e* (nominative and accusative) or *-en* (dative).

Folgt den Beispielen!

18. Das rote Kleid gefällt mir.

Variation: *Was gefällt dir?* or *Was gefällt dir nicht?* Have students use adjectives and nouns in their answers.

Der teure Mantel gefällt mir.
Die enge Straße gefällt mir.
Die schwarze Katze gefällt mir.
Das alte Pferd gefällt mir.
Der ruhige Platz gefällt mir

Rote Kleider gefallen mir.

Teure Mäntel gefallen mir.
Enge Straßen gefallen mir.
Schwarze Katzen gefallen mir.
Alte Pferde gefallen mir.
Ruhige Plätze gefallen mir.

19. Hast du etwas gekauft?
    (schön)

Variation: *Was hast du gekauft? Ich habe etwas Schönes gekauft.*

Wir haben viel gehört. (interessant)
Ich habe nichts gelesen. (wichtig)
Sagt ihr ihm etwas? (toll)
Ich werde nichts essen. (gut)
Sie möchte etwas bekommen. (preiswert)

Hast du etwas Schönes gekauft?

Wir haben viel Interessantes gehört.
Ich habe nichts Wichtiges gelesen.
Sagt ihr ihm etwas Tolles?
Ich werde nichts Gutes essen.
Sie möchte etwas Preiswertes bekommen.

20. Er kauft die schönen Karten. Du auch?

Variation: *Kaufst du die schönen Karten? Ich kaufe nur eine schöne Karte.*

Er kauft die klassischen Schallplatten. Du auch?
Er kauft die neuen Bücher. Du auch?
Er kauft die praktischen Hosen. Du auch?
Er kauft die deutschen Zeitungen. Du auch?

Ich habe schon ein paar schöne Karten.

Ich habe schon ein paar k lassische Schallplatten.
Ich habe schon ein paar neue Bücher.
Ich habe schon ein paar praktische Hosen.
Ich habe schon ein paar deutsche Zeitungen.

21. **Restate the following sentences.**

> **Beispiel:** *Das Brot schmeckt gut. (deutsch)*
> *Deutsches Brot schmeckt gut.*

1. Ich esse die Torten sehr gern. (frisch)
2. Wir sehen nicht sehr oft Fußballspiele. (toll)
3. Das Haar gefällt mir nicht. (braun)
4. Das Wetter habe ich gern. (sonnig)
5. Lesen Sie die Zeitschriften gern? (international)
6. Das Essen schmeckt mir nicht. (kalt)
7. Ich kann den Kaffee nicht trinken. (heiß)
8. Hörst du die Musik? (klassisch)

22. **Form complete sentences using the information given.**

1. Liechtenstein / sein / ein / märchenhaft / Land
2. Sein / klein / Bruder / gern spielen / Tennis
3. Ich / können / du / nicht / interessant / sagen
4. Werden / die Mädchen / ein / teuer / Surfbrett / kaufen
5. Haben / Sie / kein / praktisch / Mantel
6. Mein / Onkel / kaufen / er / kein / neu / Gitarre

7. Aussuchen / wir / sonnig / Platz
8. Wollen / du / nicht / ein paar / klein / Tiere / fotografieren
9. Haben / Sie / ein / gut / und / preiswert / Karte
10. Ich / schreiben / er / nichts / schön

Lesestück 1

Das Leben in einer Kleinstadt in der DDR

Zwischen Leipzig und Dresden liegt die Kleinstadt oder das Dorf° Ostrau. Das Dorf selbst hat nur 2 500 Einwohner. Ostrau ist allerdings° das Zentrum von zehn kleineren Dörfern in der Gegend. Im Gemeindeverband° Ostrau, einschließlich aller zehn Dörfer, wohnen ungefähr 10 000 Einwohner. Ostrau liegt im Kreis° Döbeln und im Bezirk° Leipzig. Herr Fankhähnel ist der Bürgermeister° des Dorfes.

In Ostrau gibt es hauptsächlich Tier- und Pflanzenproduktion°. Wer will, kann neben seiner Arbeit noch eine oder zwei Kühe für den eigenen Bedarf züchten. Auf den Feldern pflanzt man verschiedenes an: Getreide°, Kartoffeln und Zuckerrüben°. Im Einkaufszentrum können die Einwohner alles kaufen, was sie für das tägliche° Leben brauchen. Die Ostrauer kommen ein paar Mal die Woche zum Einkaufszentrum. Gleich daneben gibt es ein Blumengeschäft°. Hier kaufen die Einwohner Blumen für besondere Festlichkeiten°. Die Blumen sind sehr preiswert.

Die meisten Ostrauer wohnen in Wohnungen. In den letzten Jahren hat man aber viele alte Häuser renoviert. Zum Beispiel steht im Dorf eine alte Scheune°. Anstatt die Scheune abzureißen°, haben die Ostrauer angefangen, das Gebäude zu renovieren. Die eine Seite ist schon fertig. Es wird noch ein oder zwei Jahre dauern bis die andere Seite auch fertig ist.

Manche Ostrauer wohnen in Einfamilienhäusern. Jedes Jahr bauen einige Familien neue Häuser. Ihre Bekannten und Verwandten helfen ihnen oft beim Bau des Hauses. Die Ostrauer zahlen nur 80 bis 100 Mark im Monat für ihr Haus. Im Haus gibt es genug Platz für die Familie. Das Haus ist nicht groß aber sehr gemütlich. Natürlich haben alle Federbetten. Die sind besonders warm.

Das Dorf hat zwei Schulen. Kinder bis zum 6. Jahr gehen in den Kindergarten. Danach° kommen sie in die Ernst Thälmann Oberschule°. Gleich am Eingang steht eine Tafel mit der Überschrift „Betriebe° in unserem Schulbereich°". Auf dieser Tafel beschreiben die Schüler mit Hilfe° von Fotos, welche Betriebe es in Ostrau gibt und was man da produziert. Eine andere Tafel beschreibt die großen Erforscher° von gestern und heute. Auf einer dritten Tafel erzählen sie von den möglichen Berufen in der Ostrauer Gegend.

town

though

community association

district

large district/mayor

plant production

grain/sugar beets

daily

flower shop

festivities

barn/tear down

after that

high school

title/businesses/ school area

help

explorer

Herr Fankhähnel, der
Bürgermeister von Ostrau.

die Ostrauer Gegend

Was pflanzt
man in
Ostrau an?

eine alte Scheune

Jedes Jahr bauen einige Familien neue Häuser.

Die Ostrauer renovieren viele alte Gebäude.

Lektion 15

Wo kaufen die Ostrauer ein?

Im Wohnzimmer ist es sehr gemütlich.

Die Blumen sind sehr preiswert.

Nach der Schule treffen sich viele Schüler in der Turnhalle°. Dort spielen sie gern Tischtennis. Viele Erwachsene° kommen nach der Arbeit in der Gaststätte° im Dorf zusammen. Dort trinken sie gern ein Bier und plaudern mit ihren Kollegen° und Bekannten.

    Ist Ostrau eine typische Kleinstadt in der DDR? Die Antwort ist „ja". Viele Dörfer wie Ostrau haben sich mit anderen kleineren Dörfern zusammengeschlossen und einen Gemeindeverband gegründet°. Auf diese Weise° können sie gemeinsam° ihre Erfahrungen austauschen und in vielen Angelegenheiten° zusammenarbeiten.

gym
adults
restaurant
colleagues

set up/this way/ together matters

116

Fragen über das Lesestück

1. Wie groß ist Ostrau und wo liegt diese Kleinstadt?
2. Wie viele Dörfer gehören zum Gemeindeverband Ostrau?
3. Was können die Ostrauer noch neben ihrer Arbeit züchten?
4. Was pflanzen die Ostrauer auf den Feldern an?
5. Wo gehen die Einwohner einkaufen?
6. Welches andere Geschäft gibt es da noch? Was kann man dort kaufen?
7. Was hat man mit der alten Scheune gemacht?
8. Was für Häuser bauen manche Ostrauer?
9. Wie sind die Häuser?
10. Welche zwei Schulen gibt es im Dorf?
11. Was beschreiben die Schüler auf der Tafel gleich beim Eingang?
12. Was machen viele Schüler nach der Schule?
13. Wohin gehen die Erwachsenen gern und was machen sie dort?
14. Warum ist es für Ostrau günstig, daß die Einwohner einen Gemeindeverband gegründet haben?

Erweiterung

23. Beantwortet diese Fragen mit einem ganzen Satz!

1. Bist du schon einmal in einem Zoo gewesen? Welche Tiere hast du dort gesehen?
2. Hast du einen Ausweis? Was für einen hast du?
3. Hast du eine Kamera? Was fotografierst du gern?
4. Hast du ein Tier zu Hause? Was für ein Tier hast du?
5. Was steht alles auf deinem Bücherregal?
6. Hast du ein Radio? Was für Musik hörst du gern?
7. Gibt es in der Nähe, wo du wohnst, ein Einkaufszentrum? Gehst du oft dorthin?
8. Was machst du gern an einem sonnigen Tag?

24. Wie heißt das auf deutsch?

1. What are you growing there?
2. We would like to chat with them.
3. Why don't you move closer?
4. Do you live in an apartment or a single family home?
5. I'll take a snapshot of my friends.
6. They have many jobs there.
7. I'm not thirsty.
8. Are the scores posted?

9. They are renovating many buildings.

10. We aren't raising horses.

25. Complete each sentence. Incorporate a different adjective and make sure that each sentence is meaningful. Encourage students to come up with different adjectives and nouns.

1. Hast du _____ gesehen?

2. Ich möchte lieber ein paar _____ fotografieren.

3. Wir haben ihm _____ geschrieben.

4. Wollt ihr euch _____ noch einmal ansehen?

5. _____ habe ich noch nicht gelesen.

6. Die deutschen Touristen besuchen _____ .

7. Hamburg ist _____ .

8. Die Studenten besprechen _____ .

9. Man hat viele _____ gebaut.

10. Haben Sie seinen _____ gekauft?

26. Erkläre die folgenden Wörter mit einem ganzen Satz!

1. Kamera

2. Tier

3. Ausweis

4. Einfamilienhaus

5. Beruf

6. Radio

7. Bett

8. Zoo

27. Provide an appropriate response in German. Be sure that the whole conversation ties together and becomes meaningful.

1. Ist das ein neuer Apparat?

2. Hast du schon viele Aufnahmen gemacht?

3. Ich auch.

4. Mein Film ist leider schon voll.

5. Vielen Dank.

6. Das tue ich gern.

28. Beantwortet die Fragen!

1. Machst du gern Aufnahmen?

2. Hast du einen Hund oder eine Katze?

3. Was siehst du gern im Fernsehen?

4. Hast du dein eigenes Zimmer?

5. Gibt es in deiner Schule einen Speisesaal?

6. Wo kannst du ruhig deine Bücher lesen?

Rückblick

If your students have some problems completing these exercises, you may want to review the particular grammar point or topic that was covered in earlier units.

I. *Beantwortet die folgenden Fragen!* **Answer them first in the affirmative and then in the negative, using the proper demonstrative pronoun.**

> **Beispiel:** *Suchst du die Kamera?*
> *Ja, die suche ich.*
> *Nein, die suche ich nicht.*

1. Glauben Sie dem Jungen?
2. Fragen Sie die Verkäuferin?
3. Beschreibst du das Studentenleben?
4. Hilfst du deinen Freunden?
5. Hast du den Bürgermeister gesehen?
6. Füttert er seine Tiere?
7. Verstehen die Ausländer das?
8. Ist der Student sehr klug?

II. **Change the indefinite to the definite article. Be sure to change the adjective endings where necessary.**

> **Beispiel:** *Holen Sie einen neuen Fahrplan!*
> *Holen Sie den neuen Fahrplan!*

1. Fragen Sie doch eine deutsche Lehrerin!
2. Sie fahren zu einem beliebten Wintersportplatz.
3. Da steht ein langer Satz.
4. Wir helfen einem französischen Studenten.
5. Wo ist eine bunte Krawatte?
6. Hast du eine alte Schultasche?
7. Ich kaufe eine internationale Zeitung.
8. Kennst du ein berühmtes Museum?

III. **Supply the proper endings for the articles and the adjectives.**

> **Beispiel:** *d_____ weiß_____ Strand*
> *der weiße Strand*

1. d_____ kalt_____ Wasser
2. d_____ grau_____ Esel
3. d_____ teur_____ Rechnung
4. d_____ lang_____ Brief
5. d_____ interessant_____ Bücher
6. d_____ schlecht_____ Wetter
7. d_____ gut_____ Noten
8. d_____ schön_____ Reise
9. d_____ bequem_____ Sofa
10. d_____ hungrig_____ Elefanten

IV. Complete each sentence by using one of the words from the list below.

Kamera   Scheune
Kartoffeln   Wahrzeichen
Turnhalle   Mark
Platz   Brücke
Surfbrett   Kasse

1. Der Landwirt pflanzt _____ an.
2. Eine _____ geht über den Fluß.
3. Nehmen Sie _____ , bitte!
4. Die Jungen und Mädchen spielen in der _____ .
5. Was ist das _____ von Ost-Berlin?
6. Mit dieser _____ kann ich gute Aufnahmen machen.
7. Bezahlen Sie an der _____ , bitte!
8. Die Tiere sind in der _____ .
9. Das macht neun _____ .
10. Hast du dein _____ zum Strand mitgebracht?

Lesestück 2

Das Studentenleben in der DDR

Fast 100 000 Studenten studieren jedes Jahr auf den Hochschulen in der DDR. Das Studentenleben ist auf den verschiedenen Hochschulen° sehr ähnlich°. Als Beispiel dient° uns die Bergakademie° Freiberg. Diese Stadt liegt zwischen Dresden und Karl-Marx-Stadt. Die Bergakademie ist schon mehr als 200 Jahre alt und ist die älteste montanwissenschaftliche° Hochschule der Welt. Die Mineralsammlung ist sehr bekannt. Die Studenten besuchen oft die Räume° und lernen dort viel über die einzelnen Sammlungen.

 *colleges/similar/
serves/mining
college*

 science of mining

 rooms

Die Bibliothek° der Hochschule besitzt° 370 000 Bücher und Zeitschriften. Wer Bücher und Zeitschriften ausleihen° will, geht direkt zur Kartei°. Alles ist alphabetisch angeordnet. Man braucht nur den Titel, den Autor oder das Fachgebiet° zu kennen. Die Studenten finden die Bücher auf den Regalen. Manche Studenten leihen sich die Bücher aus und lesen sie in ihrem Wohnheim°. Andere gehen lieber zum Lesesaal. Dort stört° sie niemand und sie können ruhig studieren.

 library/owns

 check out

 card-index

 subject

 dormitory

 disturbs

Die Mensa°, das ist der Speisesaal für die Studenten, liegt direkt gegenüber von der Bibliothek. Die Mensa ist oft der Treffpunkt° der Studenten. Die wichtigsten Veranstaltungen° der Woche stehen gleich am Eingang auf einer „Kultur-Säule°". Andere Bekanntmachungen° sind auf einer großen Tafel angeschlagen.

 cafeteria

 meeting place

 events

 post

 announcements

Was können die Studenten heute essen? An jedem Tag der Woche gibt es eine Auswahl von zwei Speisen. Heute gibt es entweder Schweinebraten° oder Wurstschaschlik°. Schweinebraten

 *roast pork/sausage
kebab*

Wo wohnen die Studenten?

Die Zimmer der Studenten
sind klein aber bequem.

die Mensa

Was macht
diese
Studentin?

Flurreinigen

in dieser Woche:

WE 110

Was steht auf der Tafel?

die Bibliothek der Hochschule

bekommt man am ersten Schalter, Wurstschaschlik am zweiten. Am
Schalter muß man nicht warten. Das Essen bekommt man gleich.
Im Speisesaal stehen viele Tische und Stühle. Die Studenten sitzen
meistens mit ihren Bekannten zusammen und plaudern mitein-
ander°.

with each other

    Die meisten Studenten wohnen in der Nähe der Akademie. Sie
brauchen nur ein paar Minuten zu Fuß zu gehen. Manche Studenten
fahren die kurze Strecke mit dem Fahrrad. Die Studenten wohnen in
großen und modernen Wohnheimen. Diese Wohnheime sind ziem-

lich neu. Man hat sie erst in den letzten zehn Jahren gebaut. Am Eingang vom Wohnheim sitzt ein Student und gibt den Bewohnern° ihren Schlüssel°. Gleich um die Ecke sind die Brieffächer° für die einzelnen Zimmer. Die Post kommt meistens nach dem Mittagessen. Wird heute Post in dem Brieffach liegen?

residents
key/postal boxes

Die Zimmer sind klein aber bequem. In jedem Zimmer gibt es drei oder vier Betten. In manchen Zimmern schlafen die Studenten sogar in Schlafkojen°. Jeder Student hat einen kleinen Tisch. Hier können sie studieren und ihre schriftlichen° Arbeiten machen. Wer nicht im eigenen Zimmer studieren will, kann in die kleine Bibliothek gehen. Da gibt es genug Platz und es ist auch immer ruhig. In den einzelnen Zimmern sind keine Toiletten. Auf jedem Stock gibt es ein gemeinsames Badezimmer° und Toiletten. Auf einem Regal stehen Toilettenartikel°, wie zum Beispiel Zahnbürsten°, Zahnpasta° und Seife°.

bunkbeds
written

bathroom
toiletries/
toothbrushes
toothpaste/soap

Alle Studenten in dem Wohnheim sorgen selbst für Ordnung und Sauberkeit°. Auf einer kleinen Tafel steht, wer diese Woche den Flur° reinigen° muß.

cleanliness
hallway/clean

Fragen über das Lesestück

1. Ist das Studentenleben auf den Hochschulen in der DDR sehr verschieden?
2. Was für eine Hochschule findet man in Freiberg?
3. Warum ist diese Hochschule so bekannt?
4. Warum gehen die Studenten zur Kartei in der Bibliothek?
5. Was machen die Studenten mit den Büchern?
6. Was ist eine Mensa?
7. Wie wissen die Studenten, welche Veranstaltungen während der Woche stattfinden?
8. Was gibt es heute zu essen und wo bekommt man das Essen?
9. Was machen die Studenten während des Essens?
10. Wie kommen die Studenten von ihren Wohnheimen zur Hochschule?
11. Was macht der Student am Eingang des Wohnheims?
12. Wo bekommen die Studenten ihre Post?
13. Beschreibe ein Zimmer, wo die Studenten wohnen!
14. Studieren alle Studenten in ihren Zimmern?
15. Was findet man auf jedem Stock?
16. Wie wissen die Studenten, wer den Flur reinigen soll?

Sprachspiegel

You may want to have students work in groups. One person in the group could be the interviewer, the other could describe his/her city or town.

I. Schreibe einen kurzen Aufsatz über das Thema „Wir gehen zum Zoo"!

II. Beschreibe kurz die Stadt oder das Dorf, wo du wohnst!

Du bist dran! Have students read their mini-dialogs in pairs to be more realistic. Others can ask questions about each situation.

Hast du deinen Ausweis mitgebracht?

. . . .

Wie können sie denn wissen, wie alt du bist?

. . . .

. . . .

Nein, die habe ich noch nicht geknipst.

. . . .

Mein Film ist schon ganz voll.

. . . .

Ja, die sehe ich mir gern an.

. . . .

Vielleicht in einer halben Stunde.

Hast du großen Hunger?

. . . .

Was möchtest du essen?

. . . .

Das schmeckt mir nicht.

Was für Tiere züchtet denn dein Vater?

. . . .

Hat er viele?

. . . .

. . . .

Habt ihr einen Fernsehapparat?

. . . .

Wann habt ihr den denn gekauft?

. . . .

. . . .

Nein, wir haben eine Wohnung.

. . . .

Erst seit einem Jahr.

Was machen Sie nach der Arbeit?

. . . .

Gehen Sie oft dorthin?

. . . .

Ja, ich komme gern mit.

> Was für Tiere züchtet denn dein Vater?

Kulturecke

Life in the *DDR*

The German Democratic Republic has a population of almost 17 million people. The population density is the lowest in the northern part, where the land is used primarily for agriculture, and highest in the southern part, where most of the major cities are located. There are more than 1,000 small or medium-size towns. Of the country's territory, 27 percent is wooded, and many of the smaller towns are located in the wooded areas. Only one-fourth of the population lives in rural areas. Three-fourths live in towns with a population of more than 2,000 inhabitants.

One of the major objectives of the *DDR* is to meet the growing demand for better housing conditions. Town planning concentrates on the construction of new apartment buildings, primarily in major cities. Natural, economic and historical conditions are taken into account in building and reconstructing communities. Planning concentrates on making the best possible use of existing buildings. Many apartment buildings that were not harmed or only slightly damaged during World War II have been totally renovated or reconstructed.

The economic recovery immediately following World War II was quite slow in comparison to that of Western countries. However, since the early 1960's the *DDR* has seen tremendous growth. The economic improvements are seen most readily in the cities, which are becoming more and more congested. Although two different makes of automobiles are manufactured in the *DDR,* many others are imported to meet the growing demand. Since the purchase of automobiles can involve a lengthy waiting period, sometimes up to ten years, many people make use of motorcycles or bicycles, particularly in smaller towns. Public transportation has become very important, especially in the cities.

The monetary unit in the *DDR* is the *Mark,* issued in five different denominations — 5 marks, 10 marks, 20 marks, 50 marks and 100 marks. Most city dwellers do their main shopping in big department stores. In these department stores, people can take care of most of their shopping needs. Western currency, such as the *Deutsche Mark* (the currency of the Federal Republic) and the dollar, is in high demand and is accepted only at Inter-Shops, which are usually linked with the Inter-Hotels where the clientele consists mainly of foreigners.

Communities in the *DDR* have several kinds of stores. Grocery stores with the letters *"HO" (Handelsorganisation)* indicate that they are nationalized and operated by the State. Those grocery stores marked with the letter *"K" (Konsum)* are operated by a cooperative association *(Konsumgenossenschaft).* However, many of the smaller stores are privately owned. At these stores, the shopkeeper pays closer attention to the shoppers' needs. At a fruit and vegetable store *(Obst und Gemüse),* the shopkeeper displays the fresh goods that have been brought in from the market. A bakery, specializing in rolls, breads and pastries *(Feinbäckerei),* is usually crowded during the morning hours when the baked goods are fresh from the oven.

Germans who don't want to prepare their own meals have a wide selection of reasonably priced restaurants. In the big cities are the outdoor cafés, which are very popular during the summer months. Some are specialized and serve only coffee and ice cream. People will gather here, sit down and enjoy the environment for an hour or so.

One of the main goals of the German Democratic Republic is to provide recreational opportunities and facilities for its citizens. Every school plans short or long field trips to different parts of the town, city or country. During the summer months people enjoy the sunshine in the beautiful outdoor surroundings right in the heart of the city.

On weekends, many families escape the city and drive to areas where they can do some sightseeing. The city of Eisenach with its Wartburg has become a particularly popular place to visit. This city has received international attention because of its celebration commemorating 500 years since Luther's birth. Another popular place is Wernigerode, a spa and resort town

ein Haus in Norden

Greifswald, eine Stadt im Norden

neue Wohngebäude in Erfurt

Im Norden ist das Land flach.

Im Sommer sitzen die Leute gern im Freien.

ein Konsum (Sellin/Ostsee)

ein HO-Geschäft

ein großes Kaufhaus in Leipzig

Viele wohnen in Städten.

often called *"bunte Stadt im Harz"* (colorful city in the Harz mountains). To this day, Werniger-ode still displays its medieval character, half-timbered houses *(Fachwerkhäuser)* surrounding the market square. Many people also enjoy hiking. Therefore, the area of the *Sächsische Schweiz* with its hills and small mountains is the delight of hikers.

What do people do in their spare time? The big cities such as Ost-Berlin, Leipzig and Dresden offer numerous opportunities to go to operas, plays, movies and other entertainment. The concert hall in Leipzig *(Gewandhaus),* for example, has been completely rebuilt and just celebrated its 200-year anniversary. Many internationally-known conductors have performed here. People enjoy going to the various theaters that stage performances on a continuous basis. The local movie theater is also a favorite place. The *Capitol* in Leipzig has a seating capacity of over 1,000. On weekends many people go to the *Tanzbar* (dancing bar), where they can dance to local as well as Western-style music.

In every community there is a *Jugendklub* (Youth Club) for the youngsters in the neigh-borhood. Here they hold frequent meetings, play cards or other games and have discussions. The country has also made provisions to take care of its senior citizens. Newly constructed apartment buildings for the elderly have been carefully integrated into the total community.

Where do people vacation in the German Democratic Republic? The most popular area is the shore along the *Ostsee* (Baltic Sea). Vacation time for working families is approved by the companies for which they work. Vacation expenses are absorbed to a large extent by the com-panies, depending on income, time of vacation and type of accommodations. Those families who don't want to stay in hotels or vacation homes go to specially designed camping grounds.

Numerous youth camps are found throughout the country. More than two million school age children take advantage of these facilities every year. For their child's three-week stay at one of these camps, parents pay a total amount of only 12 marks. The actual costs are absorbed by the State, the companies and the unions.

The German Democratic Republic puts strong emphasis on the positive development of its citizens. Banners and posters throughout the country are a constant reminder of the obliga-tions and responsibilities the people must meet to further the goals of the country. The citizens are expected to follow the path of communism as it was defined by its founder Karl Marx.

in den Ferien (Oberhof)

Jugendliche und Erwachsene gehen gern ins Kino. (Leipzig)

die Ostsee, eine beliebte Gegend im Sommer

Vokabeln

abreißen (*riß ab, abgerissen*) to tear down

der **Adler,-** eagle

der **Affe,-n** ape, monkey

allerdings at any rate, though

anfangen (*fängt an, fing an, angefangen*) to begin, start

anfassen (*faßt*) to touch

die **Angelegenheit,-en** matter, affair

anpflanzen to grow, plant

anschlagen (*schlägt an, schlug an, angeschlagen*) to post, put up

die **Antwort,-en** answer

der **Apparat,-e** camera

ausfallen (*fällt aus, fiel aus, ist ausgefallen*) to turn out

der **Bär,-en** bear

der **Bedarf** need, demand, use

der **Beruf,-e** job, profession

der **Betrieb,-e** business, firm

der **Bezirk,-e** (large) district

billig cheap

das **Blumengeschäft,-e** flower shop

brav well-behaved

das **Bücherregal,-e** bookshelf

der **Bürgermeister,-** mayor

danach after that

dienen to serve

das **Dorf,-er** town, village

durstig thirsty

das **Einfamilienhaus,-er** single family home

das **Einkaufszentrum,-tren** shopping center

der **Eintrittspreis,-e** admission price

der **Elefant,-en** elephant

die **Ente,-n** duck

das **Erdgeschoß,-sse** ground floor, first floor (in America)

die **Erfahrung,-en** experience, idea

der **Erforscher,-** explorer

das **Federbett,-en** feather-bed

die **Festlichkeit,-en** festivity

der **Fisch,-e** fish

die **Gaststätte,-n** restaurant, inn

der **Gemeindeverband,-e** community association

genug enough

das **Getreide** grain

gründen to set up, organize

das **Huhn,-er** chicken

die **Kamera,-s** camera

der **Keller-** basement, cellar

knipsen to take a picture

der **Kollege,-n** colleague

die **Kommode,-n** (chest of) drawers

das **Kopfkissen,-** pillow

der **Kreis,-e** district

die **Kuh,-e** cow

die **Lampe,-n** lamp

das **Leben** life

der **Löwe,-n** lion

mithalten (*hält mit, hielt, mit, mitgehalten*) to keep up

das **Modell,-e** model

die **Oberschule,-n** high school

der **Plattenspieler,-** record player

plaudern to chat

produzieren to produce

das **Radio,-s** radio

rangehen (*ging ran, ist rangegangen*) to go up

Geh näher ran! Move closer!

die **Robbe,-n** seal

das **Schaf,-e** sheep

die **Scheune,-n** barn

die **Schlange,-n** snake

der **Schrank,-e** closet, wardrobe

der **Schreibtisch,-e** desk

der **Schulbereich,-e** school district

das **Schwein,-e** pig

der **Sessel,-** armchair

das **Sofa,-s** sofa

der **Stock,-e** floor

Erster Stock first floor (America: second floor)

streicheln to stroke, pet

täglich daily

die **Tier- und Pflanzenproduktion** animal and plant production

der **Tiger,-** tiger

die **Turnhalle,-n** gymnasium

die **Überschrift,-en** title

verschiedenes different items

der **Vogel,-** bird

die **Weise,-n** manner, way

auf diese Weise in this way

der **Wolf,-e** wolf

zahlen to pay

der **Zaun,-e** fence

das **Zebra,-s** zebra

die **Ziege,-n** goat

der **Zoo,-s** zoo

die **Zuckerrübe,-n** sugar beet

züchten to raise (animals)

zusammenarbeiten to work together

zusammenkommen (*kam zusammen, ist zusammengekommen*) to come together

sich **zusammenschließen** (*schloß zusammen, zusammengeschlossen*) to merge

zusammensitzen (*saß zusammen, zusammengesessen*) to sit together

Lesestück 1

You may want to select only particular sections of this unit for review. The only new words introduced are listed in the margin of the line in which they appear. If your students have some difficulties in completing the exercises, you may want to go back to the lesson in which the particular grammar point or topic was discussed.

Beim Karneval oder Fasching

Karneval° ist ein sehr bekanntes Fest° in Deutschland. Der Kölner Karneval erreicht seinen Höhepunkt am Rosenmontag°. An diesem Tag ist in allen großen und kleinen Städten am Rhein sowie in Süddeutschland sehr viel los. Der Rosenmontag ist sogar ein Feiertag. Alle Geschäfte sind geschlossen und niemand arbeitet. Schon früh am Morgen gehen Tausende von Menschen in die Innenstadt. Die meisten müssen ihre Autos weit von der Innenstadt entfernt parken, denn es gibt in der Stadtmitte einfach keine Parkplätze an diesem Tag.

carnival/festival
Monday before Lent

Die Leute suchen sich schon früh die besten Plätze aus. Sie müssen lange warten, bevor der Zug° beginnt. Die Polizei ist auch schon sehr beschäftigt°. Sie sorgt überall für Ordnung. Manche Zuschauer haben sogar Kostüme° an. Man sieht besonders viele Clowns. Langsam vergeht° die Zeit. Viele Menschen laufen die Straßen auf und ab°, um noch einen guten Platz zu bekommen. Die besten Plätze sind aber schon besetzt°. Die meisten Leute müssen stehen, aber einige haben sich Sitzplätze auf der Tribüne° gekauft. Dort hat man einen besonders guten Blick auf den Zug.

parade
busy
costumes
passes
up and down
occupied
grandstand

Endlich geht es los. Viele Kapellen kommen vorbei. Es ist nicht nur auf den Straßen viel zu sehen, sondern auch in der Luft°. Dort fliegen Flugzeuge und machen Reklame°. Die Zuschauer sind von den Festwagen° begeistert. Der Höhepunkt beim Karnevalszug° ist der Prinzenwagen°. Die Kölner begrüßen ihn mit dem Ruf° „Alaaf".

air
advertise
floats/carnival parade
prince's float/cheer

Während in Köln der Karneval stattfindet, feiern° die Münchner den sogenannten „Fasching"°. Genauso wie in Köln stehen auch in München Tausende von Menschen im Zentrum der Stadt und sehen dem Faschingszug zu. Nicht nur die Erwachsenen machen mit; auch die Jugend° hat beim Fasching viel Spaß. Oftmals haben sogar kleine Kinder Kostüme an. Im Faschingszug spielen die Kapellen eine wichtige Rolle°. Sie bringen die Zuschauer in die richtige Stimmung.

celebrate
carnival
young people
role

Fragen über das Lesestück

1. An welchem Tag erreicht der Kölner Karneval seinen Höhepunkt?
2. Sind die Geschäfte an diesem Tag geöffnet?
3. Wo parken die meisten Leute ihre Wagen? Warum?
4. Was macht die Polizei?
5. Wo findet man die besten Plätze?
6. Was ist der Höhepunkt beim Karnevalszug?
7. Wie heißt dieses Fest in München?
8. Machen nur die Erwachsenen mit?
9. Wer bringt die Zuschauer in die richtige Stimmung?

Übungen

I. *Flughafen, Hafen oder Bahnhof?* **Determine where you would most likely find each of the following:**

1.	Dock	9.	Gleis
2.	Pilot	10.	Bordkarte
3.	Reisezugauskunft	11.	Fahrkarte
4.	TEE	12.	D-Zug
5.	Landungssteg	13.	Zoll
6.	Barkassen	14.	Schiffe
7.	Schlafwagen	15.	Paßkontrolle
8.	Personenkontrolle	16.	Bahnsteig

II. **Schreibt einen kurzen Aufsatz oder Dialog!**

Pretend you are living in the city of Munich. A pen pal from the U.S. is visiting you during the summer. Of course, you want to show him/her the sights of the city as well as the surrounding area. Be as creative as possible.

III. **Beantwortet die folgenden Sätze!**

1. Was machen die Leute beim Karneval?
2. Was gibt es alles in einem Wohnheim für Studenten?
3. Was hast du in deinem Koffer oder in deiner Schultasche?
4. Was möchtest du gern in einem Café bestellen? Warum?
5. Was kann man alles im Hafen sehen?
6. Warum gehen die Leute zur Post?
7. Was können die Fluggäste in einem Flugzeug machen?
8. Bekommst du manchmal Post? Von wem?

IV. Wo findet man die folgenden Sehenswürdigkeiten? In München, Wien, Bern oder Liechtenstein?

1. Spanische Reitschule
2. Fürstentum
3. Viktualienmarkt
4. Olympiapark
5. Zeitglockenturm
6. Deutsches Museum
7. Schloß Schönbrunn
8. Glockenspiel
9. Marienplatz
10. Ringstraße
11. Burgtheater
12. Vaduz
13. Bärengraben
14. Briefmarkenmuseum
15. Prater
16. Rosengarten
17. Englischer Garten
18. Stefansdom
19. Frauenkirche
20. Schloß Nymphenburg

V. Write out the word(s) for these abbreviations:

1. DDR
2. km
3. TEE
4. DM
5. BRD
6. m
7. HO
8. FDJ
9. cm
10. JP

VI. Provide the proper present tense form of the verbs in parentheses.

1. (sprechen) _____ Renate Deutsch?
2. (geben) _____ er dir ein Fahrrad?
3. (lesen) _____ Sie die tägliche Zeitung?
4. (tragen) Peter _____ sein Surfbrett zum Strand.
5. (verlassen) Um drei Uhr _____ die Klasse die Schule.
6. (fahren) Herr und Frau Meier _____ nach Österreich.
7. (sehen) _____ du das Flugzeug?
8. (mitnehmen) Frau Lesemann _____ ihren Hund in die Stadt _____ .
9. (essen) Was _____ du denn zum Mittagessen?
10. (gefallen) Das Auto _____ mir nicht.

VII. Beschreibt jedes der folgenden Wörter mit zwei oder drei Sätzen!

1. der Zoo
2. dein Wohnzimmer
3. der Brief
4. Weihnachten
5. eine Hochzeit
6. der Flughafen

Supply the necessary endings of the articles as well as the adjectives. Some blanks may not require an ending.

1. Er kommt mit schnell_____ Schritten zur Tür.
2. Meine Tante hat ein_____ elegant_____ Hochzeit gehabt.
3. Hast du d_____ viel_____ Tiere im Zoo gesehen?
4. Kannst du d_____ deutsch_____ Lehrer nicht antworten?
5. Wir werden ein paar märchenhaft_____ Schlösser besichtigen.
6. Während d_____ warm_____ Tages brauche ich mein_____ schwarz_____ Mantel nicht.
7. Ich möchte mein_____ gut_____ Freundin ein_____ lang_____ Brief schreiben.
8. Er braucht sein_____ neu_____ Reisepaß.
9. Wo ist dein_____ alt_____ Radio?
10. Dies_____ klug_____ Schüler wissen immer alles.
11. Ich suche mir gern ein_____ ruhig_____ Platz aus.
12. Unser_____ klein_____ Paket ist ein_____ groß_____ Überraschung.
13. Dies_____ bunt_____ Kleider gefallen uns sehr.
14. D_____ amerikanisch_____ Touristen fliegen nach München.
15. Mit mein_____ neu_____ Kamera habe ich schon viele Aufnahmen gemacht.

Lesestück 2

Ein Ausflug zum Zoo

Einmal im Jahr fahren Thielmanns mit der ganzen Familie zum Zoo. Besonders freuen sich ihre beiden Kinder, Gudrun und Klaus, auf diesen Ausflug°. An einem schönen Sonntag im Juli entschließen sie sich°, wieder einmal einen Besuch im Zoo zu machen. Thielmanns wohnen ungefähr 30 Kilometer vom Zoo entfernt. Sie fahren mit dem Wagen dorthin. Den größten Teil der Strecke fahren sie auf der Autobahn, dann geht's weiter durch die Stadt, und schließlich° folgen sie den Schildern bis sie an ihrem Ziel° ankommen.

outing
entschließen...sich decide

finally
destination

Sie parken ihren Wagen auf einem Parkplatz und gehen zum Eingang. Herr Thielmann kauft zwei Karten für Erwachsene und zwei für Kinder. Die Karten für ihre Kinder sind viel billiger. Gudrun ist erst vier Jahre alt. Sie interessiert sich besonders für die Affen und Bären. Ihr Bruder Klaus, er ist zehn Jahre alt, sieht sich lieber die Löwen, Tiger und Schlangen an. Die sind für ihn viel interessanter. Während die beiden Kinder die Tiere bestaunen, macht Herr Thielmann viele Aufnahmen. Die kommen später ins Fotoalbum.

Endlich kommen sie bei den Elefanten vorbei. Die sind ja wirklich riesengroß. Viele Besucher füttern die Elefanten. Gudrun tut das auch, aber eigentlich hat sie ein wenig Angst. In einem Kä-

Hagenbeck's Tierpark ist in Hamburg.

Was steht alles auf diesem Schild?

Die Elefanten sind riesengroß.

Viele Besucher interessieren sich besonders für die Bären.

ein Park im Hamburger Zoo

Was sehen sich manche Leute gern an?

fig° sehen sie viele Vögel aus verschiedenen Ländern. Es gibt auch   *cage*
zwei Adler. Die sind ziemlich groß.

Auf dem Weg durch den Zoo kommen sie bei den Eseln vor-
bei, und die Kinder dürfen reiten°. Frau Thielmann bezahlt für jede   *ride*
Karte zwei Mark. Während Klaus und Gudrun auf den Eseln reiten,
fotografiert Herr Thielmann seinen Sohn und seine Tochter. Das
Reiten hat viel Spaß gemacht.

Im Zoo gibt es ein kleines Café. Dort macht Familie Thiel-
mann noch kurz eine Pause. Klaus und Gudrun möchten gern Eis
essen. Das Schokoladen- und Erdbeereis° schmeckt besonders gut.   *strawberry ice*
Frau Thielmann bestellt sich eine Tasse Kaffee und ihr Mann ißt ein   *cream*
Stück Torte°. Nach einer Weile gehen sie langsam zum Ausgang.   *torte*
Der Besuch im Zoo war für alle ein schönes Erlebnis.

Fragen über das Lesestück

1. Während welcher Jahreszeit fahren Thielmanns zum Zoo?
2. Wie kommen sie dorthin?
3. Was kauft Herr Thielmann am Eingang?
4. Wie alt sind die beiden Kinder und wie heißen sie?
5. Was macht Herr Thielmann während seine Kinder die Tiere bestaunen?
6. Was machen die Besucher bei den Elefanten?
7. Was sehen Thielmanns in einem Käfig?
8. Was hat bei den Eseln viel Spaß gemacht?
9. Was essen Gudrun und Klaus in dem Café?
10. Was bestellen sich Herr und Frau Thielmann?

Nützliche Ausdrücke

Here are some phrases that are particularly helpful when congratulating people on special occasions:

Herzlichen Glückwunsch zum Geburtstag!	Happy Birthday!
Herzliche Glückwünsche!	Best wishes!
Mit allen guten Wünschen!	With all best wishes!
Alles Gute (für die Zukunft)!	Best wishes (for the future)!
Fröhliche Weihnachten und ein glückliches Neues Jahr!	Merry Christmas and a Happy New Year!
Fröhliche Ostern!	Happy Easter!
Gute Besserung!	Get well soon.

Cultural Notes

The German Postal System *(Die Deutsche Bundespost)*

The German Postal System is easily recognized by its bright yellow mailboxes and trucks with their distinctive post horn symbols. There are even yellow buses, which carry both mail and passengers. The German Postal System constitutes Europe's largest enterprise. Besides performing what Americans think of as normal postal services, the *Bundespost* also:
— owns and operates the telephone and teletype systems and handles telegrams.
— owns or controls the equipment for the radio and TV networks.
— licenses and collects fees for radios and TV sets. (Every German owning a radio and/or TV set pays a monthly fee, which is collected by the postal service.)
— offers banking services (both savings and checking accounts can be handled through local post offices).
— pays out Social Security money and certain Federal pensions (through local post offices).
— offers subscriptions to newspapers and magazines.
How do you use the local German post office? Here are some tips.

das Postamt (Steingaden)

Was macht dieser Briefträger?

Was kann man auf der Post kaufen?

Stamps

As a rule, stamps can be purchased only in a post office. Sometimes, shops selling picture postcards also have stamps available. If bought from machines, you get stamps worth the full amount you deposit.

Telegrams

Except for the fact that you send them from the post office rather than Western Union, the system is much the same as in the States. You merely put your message on a form, available at the post office, and take it to the counter. You can also phone in a telegram from your own telephone.

Telephone

Telephone calls to anywhere in the world can be placed at a German post office. Simply go to the counter marked *"Telefon"* or *"Fernsprecher"* and give the clerk the number you want. He/She will place the call and direct you to a booth to take it. You may be asked to pay a deposit before the call; you'll pay the final bill after your call.

Letter and Card Service

Letter and card service is pretty much like in the U.S. Normal letters to German cities go by airmail *(Luftpost)*. Airmail letters to foreign countries like the U.S. are weighted in units of 5 grams (0.175 oz.) Of course, you can send a letter or postcard by registered mail *(per Einschreiben)*, or you can have a letter or postcard sent by special delivery *(per Eilboten)*.

Postleitzahlen

Germany has zip-code numbers *(Postleitzahlen)*. In an address the zip code is written *before* the name of the city. If the number of the delivery post office (used in large cities only) is known, the number appears *after* the name of the city.

Here's the proper way to address a letter or package to someone in Germany:

Frau	Herrn
Katrin Hoffmann	Peter Fischer
Hermannstr. 33	Bahnhofstraße 127
5882 Meinerzhagen	3100 Celle 1

The *Bundespost* prefers that you put the return address, in the same format, at the upper-left corner, preceded by the word *"Absender"* (sender). Mail sent abroad has a letter preceding the zip-code that identifies the country ("D" for Germany, "F" for France, etc.).

Parcels

There are two classes of packages, the *"Paket"* and the *"Päckchen."* The *Paket* is a normal package sent by parcel post, the rate depending on the weight and the distance to the destination. In addition to the address on the package itself, a separate card *(Paketkarte)* must be filled out. If a package is small, it will go as a *Päckchen*. A *Päckchen* goes first class, but at a much cheaper rate in comparison to the letter weight. No *Paketkarte* is required when sending a *Päckchen*.

Warum warten die Leute vor
der Telefonzelle? (München)

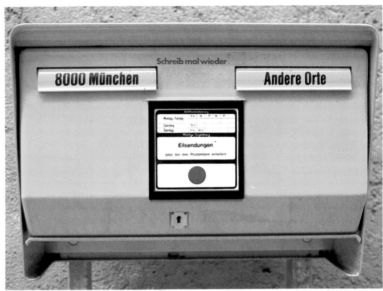

Wo befindet sich
dieser Briefkasten?

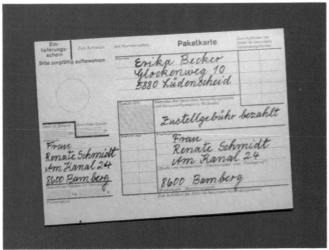

eine Paketkarte

Dialog

Im Restaurant German restaurants post their daily menu outside, next to the entrance.

ny German restaurants
er one or two meals called
esgericht or *Menü*. These
cials often include soup
dessert and are more
sonable than the other
ctions offered.

HERR:	Die Auswahl ist hier immer gut.
DAME:	Du hast recht. Der Preis für das Tagesgericht ist auch nicht schlecht.
HERR:	Na, dann mal los! Ich bin nämlich sehr hungrig.
KELLNERIN:	Bitte sehr?
HERR:	Zwei Helle, und bringen Sie uns bitte die Speisekarte.
KELLNERIN:	Selbstverständlich.
DAME:	Da haben wir uns wieder mal die richtige Gaststätte ausgesucht.
HERR:	Ja, ich kenne Herrn Pröhl, den Besitzer. Er weiß, worauf seine Kunden Appetit haben.
KELLNERIN:	Bitte schön, zwei Bier. Zum Wohl!...und hier ist die Speisekarte. Unsere Spezialität heute ist Schweinefilet mit Kartoffeln und Salat.
HERR:	Ich glaube, da brauche ich gar nicht weiter zu lesen.
DAME:	Hm, wer die Wahl hat, hat die Qual.
HERR:	Wie wär's mit dem Rinderfilet?
DAME:	Dazu lasse ich mich gern überreden.
KELLNERIN:	Also, dann ein Schweinefilet und ein Rinderfilet.
HERR:	Gehört der Salatteller dazu?
KELLNERIN:	Ja, den bekommen Sie sowieso.
KELLNERIN:	So, einmal Rinderfilet für Sie. Ihr Schweinefilet serviere ich gleich selbst. Ich wünsche Ihnen einen guten Appetit!
DAME:	Das schmeckt ganz ausgezeichnet.
HERR:	Damit werde ich wohl kaum fertig. Es ist einfach zu viel.
DAME:	Wir haben es ja nicht eilig. Nimm dir nur Zeit. Iß mit Ruhe und Genuß!
KELLNERIN:	Hat's geschmeckt?
HERR:	Danke, sehr gut.
DAME:	Das Essen war wirklich reichlich.
HERR:	Ich möchte gleich zahlen.
KELLNERIN:	Schweinefilet...Rinderfilet...und zwei Bier. Das macht DM 46,10.
HERR:	48 Mark, stimmt so.
KELLNERIN:	Besten Dank.

he printed price of meals
sted on the menu include a
rvice charge *(Trinkgeld)*
d a value-added-tax
Mehrwertsteuer). Germans
ill usually add a small
nount to their bill for an
dditional tip.

Fragen über den Dialog

1. Warum gehen der Herr und die Dame in dieses Restaurant?
2. Was bestellt der Herr zu trinken?
3. Warum weiß der Herr, daß das ein gutes Restaurant ist?
4. Was ist die Spezialität des Restaurants?
5. Was bestellt die Dame?
6. Glaubt der Herr, daß er alles essen kann?
7. Was kostet die Mahlzeit für beide?

In the Restaurant

GENTLEMAN:	The selection here is always good.
LADY:	You're right. The price for the daily menu isn't bad either.
GENTLEMAN:	O.K., then let's go in. I'm really quite hungry.
WAITRESS:	May I help you?
GENTLEMAN:	Two (light) beers and bring us the menu, please.
WAITRESS:	Of course.
LADY:	We've selected the right restaurant once again.
GENTLEMAN:	Yes, I know Mr. Pröhl, the owner. He knows his customers' appetites.
WAITRESS:	Here you are, two beers. Cheers!…and here is the menu. Our special today is filet of pork with potatoes and a salad.
GENTLEMAN:	I think I won't need to look any further.
LADY:	Hm, it's hard to make a choice.
GENTLEMAN:	How about the filet of beef?
LADY:	I'd like to be talked into that.
WAITRESS:	O.K. then, a filet of pork and a filet of beef.
GENTLEMAN:	Does the salad plate go with it?
WAITRESS:	Yes, you'll get that anyway.
WAITRESS:	So, here's your filet of beef. I'll serve the filet of pork for you myself. Enjoy your meal!
LADY:	That tastes excellent.
GENTLEMAN:	I can hardly finish this. It's simply too much.
LADY:	Well, we don't have to rush. Take your time. Eat in peace and with pleasure.
WAITRESS:	Did you like it?
GENTLEMAN:	Thank you very much.
LADY:	The portions were really generous.

GENTLEMAN:	I would like to pay right away.
WAITRESS:	Filet of pork…filet of beef…and two beers. That comes to 46 marks and 10 pfennigs.
GENTLEMAN:	48 marks, that's O.K.
WAITRESS:	Thank you very much.

Nützliche Ausdrücke

Review tnese expressions with your students. They have been covered in the *Dialog* and *Lesestück 1*.

Bringen Sie uns die Speisekarte, bitte.	Bring us the menu, please.
Zum Wohl!	Cheers!
Wer die Wahl hat, hat die Qual.	It's hard to make a choice.
Wie wär's mit…?	How about…?
Ich überrede ihn dazu.	I'm talking him into that.
Guten Appetit!	Enjoy your meal!
Hat's geschmeckt?	How was it? Did you like it?
Sie machen einen Tagesausflug.	They are going on a one-day excursion.
Er begrüßt sie.	He greets her.
Sie wandern gemeinsam.	They are hiking together.
Ich nehme mir etwas mehr Zeit.	I'm taking some more time.
Sie setzen sich hin.	They are sitting down.
Wir essen belegte Brote.	We are eating sandwiches.
Die Eltern unterhalten sich.	The parents are talking.
Sie ist guter Laune.	She is in a good mood.

Sprichwort

Ein Spatz in der Hand ist besser als eine Taube auf dem Dach.
(A sparrow in the hand is better than a dove on the roof.)

A bird in the hand is worth two in the bush.

Ergänzung

Have students ask each other questions such as *Was steht gewöhnlich auf deinem Frühstückstisch?*, *Wozu braucht man eine Schüssel? (…einen Löffel?,…ein Glas?)*

1. Was liegt oder steht auf dem Tisch?

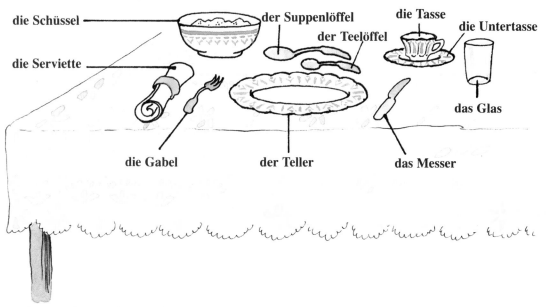

die Schüssel — der Suppenlöffel — die Tasse — die Untertasse

der Teelöffel

die Serviette

das Glas

die Gabel — der Teller — das Messer

Ask such questions as *Welche Speisen ißt du gern?*, *Welchen Nachtisch hast du am liebsten?*

2. Was gibt's zu essen?

SUPPEN
Tagessuppe
Gulaschsuppe
Gemüsesuppe
Tomatensuppe

FLEISCH
Wiener Schnitzel
Schweinebraten
Rinderbraten
Sauerbraten
Bratwurst
Würstchen

FISCH
Forelle
Karpfen

GEMÜSE
und **SALAT**
Bohnen
Erbsen
Karotten (Möhren)
Spargel
Spinat
Champignons
Gemischter Salat
Tomatensalat
Gurkensalat

BEILAGEN
Pommes frites
Bratkartoffeln
Salzkartoffeln
Knödel

NACHTISCH
Eis
Kompott
Pudding
Obst
Apfelkuchen

GETRÄNKE
Bier
Wein
Kaffee
Tee
Kakao
Apfelsaft
Cola
Mineralwasser
Limonade

Übungen

Prepositions with Dative or Accusative

There are a number of prepositions requiring the dative or the accusative case, depending on the particular situation. These prepositions are as follows:

an	on, at, to
auf	on
hinter	behind
in	in, into
neben	beside, next to
über	above, over, across
unter	under, below
vor	before, in front of
zwischen	between

Any of the prepositions above requires the dative case when used with a verb that does not indicate motion. The dative case can be determined by asking the question: where? *(wo?)*

Any of the prepositions above requires the accusative case when used with a verb that indicates motion toward a specific point or direction. The accusative case can be determined by asking the question: where to? *or* in which direction? *(wohin?)*

Beispiele:

dative (wo?)	*accusative (wohin?)*
Er wohnt an der Ecke.	*Er geht an die Ecke.*
Der Teller steht auf dem Tisch.	*Sie stellt den Teller auf den Tisch.*
Der Wagen ist hinter dem Haus.	*Er fährt den Wagen hinter das Haus.*
Wohnst du in der Stadt?	*Gehst du in die Stadt?*
Sie treffen ihn neben der Schule.	*Sie laufen neben die Schule.*
Das Flugzeug ist über dem Flughafen.	*Das Flugzeug fliegt über den Flughafen.*
Er steht unter der Brücke.	*Er geht unter die Brücke.*
Die Klasse wartet vor dem Bus.	*Der Lehrer bringt die Klasse vor den Bus.*
Das Fahrrad steht zwischen dem Tor und dem Haus.	*Er stellt das Fahrrad zwischen das Tor und das Haus.*

NOTE: A sentence expressing motion within a given area or in general terms, without indicating a specific destination, requires the dative case.

Beispiele: *Er fährt in der Stadt herum.*   *Schwimmst du im See?*
Bist du am Kino vorbeigegangen?   *Was machst du im Sommer?*

Some of the prepositions can be contracted with articles. These contractions are used more frequently in spoken German.

Dative Contractions	Accusative Contractions
an dem = am	an das = ans
in dem = im	in das = ins

The contractions *hinterm (hinters), überm (übers), unterm (unters), vorm (vors)* occur primarily in colloquial German.

Folgt den Beispielen!

1. Wo wohnt Herr Schröder?
   die Stadt / in

   Wo wohnt Frau Mahler?
   diese Schule / hinter

   Wo wohnt Erika?
   ein Flughafen / an

   Wo wohnt Rainer?
   das Rathaus / neben

   Wo wohnt Familie Weber?
   dieses Gebäude / in

   Wo wohnen die Studenten?
   unser Geschäft / über

   Herr Schröder wohnt in der Stadt.

   Frau Mahler wohnt hinter dieser Schule.

   Erika wohnt an einem Flughafen.

   Rainer wohnt neben dem Rathaus.

   Familie Weber wohnt in diesem Gebäude.

   Die Studenten wohnen über unserem Geschäft.

Variation: Ask questions and provide answers in the present perfect tense.

2. Setzen Sie sich auf meinen Stuhl!
   sein Tisch / an

   Ihr Platz / auf

   das Wohnzimmer / in

   meine Freundin / neben

   dieses Haus / vor

   die Küche / in

   Setzen Sie sich auf meinen Stuhl!
   Setzen Sie sich an seinen Tisch!

   Setzen Sie sich auf Ihren Platz!

   Setzen Sie sich ins Wohnzimmer!

   Setzen Sie sich neben meine Freundin!

   Setzen Sie sich vor dieses Haus!

   Setzen Sie sich in die Küche!

3. Wo hängt das Bild?
   das Sofa / über

   Wo steht dein Stuhl?
   das Wohnzimmer / in

   Wo ist sein Auto?
   die Gaststätte / vor

   Wo sitzt ihr Bruder?
   die Bank / auf

   Wo wartet Herr Schmidt?
   der Bahnhof / an

   Wo liegt die Speisekarte?
   die Zeitung / neben

   Überm Sofa.

   Im Wohnzimmer.

   Vor der Gaststätte.

   Auf der Bank.

   Am Bahnhof.

   Neben der Zeitung.

Germans often answer with an incomplete sentence. For the purpose of practicing complete sentences you may want to have students give complete sentences. (Wo hängt das Bild? Es hängt überm Sofa.)

4. Gehst du in die Stadt? (das Kino)
   Gehst du ins Wohnzimmer? (die Küche)
   Gehst du in dieses Restaurant? (dieses Café)
   Gehst du in die Bank? (das Geschäft)
   Gehst du in die Schule? (das Haus)

   Nein, ich gehe ins Kino.

   Nein, ich gehe in die Küche.

   Nein, ich gehe in dieses Café.

   Nein, ich gehe ins Geschäft.

   Nein, ich gehe ins Haus.

Variation: Practice the infinitive clause by having students answer as follows: Nein, ich habe keine Lust, ins Kino zu gehen.

5. Liegt die Schultasche auf dem Stuhl?

Variation: *Wo liegt die Schultasche? (Stuhl/auf) Sie liegt auf dem Stuhl.*

   Liegt die Karte auf dem Tisch?
   Liegen die Kassetten auf dem Regal?
   Liegen die Messer auf dem Platz?
   Liegt der Rucksack auf dem Bett?

Nein, ich werde sie auf den Stuhl legen.

Nein, ich werde sie auf den Tisch legen.

Nein, ich werde sie aufs Regal legen.

Nein, ich werde sie auf den Platz legen.

Nein, ich werde ihn aufs Bett legen.

6. Wir gehen in den Wald.
   Stadt
   Haus
   vor
   Hotel
   Bahnhof
   hinter
   Schule
   Wagen

Wir gehen in den Wald.

Wir gehen in die Stadt.

Wir gehen ins Haus.

Wir gehen vors Haus.

Wir gehen vors Hotel.

Wir gehen vor den Bahnhof.

Wir gehen hinter den Bahnhof.

Wir gehen hinter die Schule.

Wir gehen hinter den Wagen.

7. Wo ist dein Fahrrad?

Variation: *Wohin stellst du dein Fahrrad? Ich stelle es hinter das alte Haus.*

   das alte Haus / hinter
   das große Rathaus / vor
   die enge Straße / in
   das weiße Gebäude / neben
   das kleine Geschäft / vor
   der blaue Wagen / .hinter

Hinter dem alten Haus.

Vor dem großen Rathaus.

In der engen Straße.

Neben dem weißen Gebäude.

Vor dem kleinen Geschäft.

Hinter dem blauen Wagen.

8. Wohin hast du mein Buch gelegt?

Variation: *Wo liegt mein Buch? das große Zimmer/in) Es liegt in meinem großen Zimmer.*

   das große Zimmer / in
   der kleine Tisch / auf
   die braune Schultasche / hinter
   der grüne Stuhl / auf
   die alte Zeitung / unter
   das bunte Kopfkissen / neben

Ins große Zimmer.

Auf den kleinen Tisch.

Hinter die braune Schultasche.

Auf den grünen Stuhl.

Unter die alte Zeitung.

Neben das bunte Kopfkissen.

9. Ich lege die Hose auf den Stuhl. Wo liegt die Hose?

Variation: *Wohin hast du die Hose gelegt? Ich habe sie auf den Stuhl gelegt.*

   Sie legen die Hefte neben die Tasche. Wo liegen die Hefte?
   Er stellt den Koffer an den Schalter. Wo steht der Koffer?
   Die Besucher setzen sich in den Speisesaal. Wo sitzen die Besucher?
   Wir stellen uns vor das Haus. Wo stehen wir?
   Ihr setzt euch auf das Fahrrad. Wo sitzt ihr?

Die Hose liegt auf dem Stuhl.

Die Hefte liegen neben der Tasche.

Der Koffer steht am Schalter.

Die Besucher sitzen im Speisesaal.

Wir stehen vorm Haus.

Wir sitzen auf dem Fahrrad.

10. Provide the proper dative or accusative form of the definite article.

1. Warum hast du dein Auto nicht vor _____ Haus geparkt?
2. Der Bus hält direkt hinter _____ Schule an.
3. Er stellt sein Fahrrad zwischen _____ Wagen und _____ Motorrad.
4. Seid ihr über _____ Fluß geschwommen?
5. Sie fährt an _____ Ecke vorbei.
6. Hast du Lust, auf _____ Fußballplatz zu gehen?
7. Die Gäste sitzen sehr lange an _____ Tisch.
8. Bleibt ihr bis drei Uhr in _____ Schule?
9. Die Zeitung liegt unter _____ Stuhl.
10. Die Touristen treffen sich vor _____ Flughafen.
11. Um wieviel Uhr gehen Sie in _____ Theater?
12. Das schöne Bild hängt über _____ Klavier.

11. Change the nouns after the prepositions to the plural.

> **Beispiel:** *Er geht ins Zimmer.*
> *Er geht in die Zimmer.*

1. Viele Kinder spielen vor dem Haus.
2. Mußt du in die Stadt fahren?
3. Setzt euch unter die Brücke!
4. Er steht zwischen dem Stuhl und dem Tisch.
5. Der Lehrer hat die Klasse an den Zug gebracht.
6. Hast du das Buch auf die Zeitung gelegt?
7. Das Flugzeug fliegt über das Land.
8. Kannst du hinter dem Gebäude warten?
9. Sie sind in die Straßenbahn eingestiegen.
10. Die Boote fahren auf dem See.

12. Change the following sentences by replacing *Sie ist* with *Sie geht.*

> **Beispiel:** *Sie ist im großen Zimmer.*
> *Sie geht ins große Zimmer.*

1. Sie ist unter der hohen Brücke.
2. Sie ist am langen Tisch.
3. Sie ist auf der kleinen Straße.
4. Sie ist hinter der historischen Stadtmauer.
5. Sie ist im neuen Theater.
6. Sie ist vor dem eleganten Geschäft.
7. Sie ist neben der großen Tür.

13. *Wie heißen die englischen Wörter auf deutsch?* Complete each sentence by changing the words in parentheses into German.

  1. Das Gebäude (between this bank and this hotel) _____ ist sehr alt.
  2. Meine Mutter bringt das Essen (into the room) _____ .
  3. Hast du dein Motorrad (next to the new car) _____ gestellt?
  4. Das Hemd liegt (under my blue tie) _____ .
  5. Die Jungen schießen den Ball (across the street) _____ .
  6. Herr Schmidt wohnt (behind the old church) _____ .
  7. Haben Sie lange (in front of the airport) _____ gewartet?
  8. Im Sommer fahren wir (to the lake) _____ .
  9. Die Kellnerin legt die Speisekarte (on the brown table) _____ .
  10. Die Leute warten (at the entrance) _____ .

da vs. dahin and dort vs. dorthin

The words *da* (there) and *dort* (there) indicate that there is no motion. The person or object referred to stays in a predetermined area. Therefore, the question word *wo?* is used to ask for the location of the person or object.

Beispiel: *Wo ist das Geschäft?*
Das Geschäft ist da (dort).

The words *dahin* (there, to that place) and *dorthin* (there, to that place) indicate motion to a specific place. Therefore, the question word *wohin?* is used to ask for the direction.

Beispiel: *Wohin stellen Sie Ihr Fahrrad?*
Ich stelle es dahin (dorthin).

Folgt den Beispielen!

14. Wo steht das Flugzeug?   Es steht da.
    Wohin stellt er das Fahrrad?   Er stellt es dahin.
    Wo steht der Zug?   Er steht da.
    Wohin setzt sie sich?   Sie setzt sich dahin.
    Wohin legt sie die Zeitung?   Sie legt sie dahin.
    Wo sitzt der Mann?   Er sitzt da.
    Wo liegt das Kleid?   Es liegt da.
    Wohin gehen sie?   Sie gehen dahin.
    Wohin fährt er?   Er fährt dahin.

15. Der Koffer steht dort.   Wir stellen den Koffer dorthin.
    Die Schultasche steht dort.   Wir stellen die Schultasche dorthin.
    Der Koffer-Kuli steht dort.   Wir stellen den Koffer-Kuli dorthin.
    Die Gitarre steht dort.   Wir stellen die Gitarre dorthin.
    Der Wagen steht dort.   Wir stellen den Wagen dorthin.
    Das Glas steht dort.   Wir stellen das Glas dorthin.

16. Ergänzt *dort* oder *dorthin*!

1. Mein Freund fährt gern _____ .
2. Wann fliegt das Flugzeug _____?
3. Warum sitzt ihr _____?
4. Der Teller steht _____ .
5. Stellen wir den Rucksack _____ !
6. Was machen die Jugendlichen _____?
7. Setzen Sie sich doch _____ !
8. Wie viele Jahre haben Sie _____ gewohnt?
9. Mein Boot steht _____ .
10. Diese Stadt liegt _____ .

da– and *wo*– Compounds

Da– is combined with a preposition in place of a prepositional phrase that refers to an inanimate object. If the preposition begins with a vowel, an –*r*– is added to *da*– (darüber. darunter, daran, etc.).

Beispiele: Ich schreibe *mit dem Kuli*.   Ich schreibe *damit*.
              Denkst du *an die schönen Ferien?*   Denkst du *daran?*
              Die Mutter stellt den Teller *auf den*   Die Mutter stellt den Teller *darauf*.
                  Tisch.

Wo– compounds are used in questions in which they replace a prepositional phrase. An –*r*– is also added to *wo*– if the preposition begins with a vowel.

Beispiele: Er wartet *auf die Straßenbahn*.   *Worauf* wartet er?
              Sie erzählen *von den alten Schlössern*.   *Wovon* erzählen sie?
              Ich bezahle viel Geld *für diese Reise*.   *Wofür* bezahle ich viel Geld?

Folgt den Beispielen!

17. Die Tasse steht auf dem Tisch.   Die Tasse steht darauf.

Variation: Have students ask questions for the sentences on the left. *(Worauf steht die Tasse? Die Tasse steht auf dem Tisch.)*

    Er schreibt mit dem Bleistift.   Er schreibt damit.

    Denkst du an die Reise?   Denkst du daran?

    Wir fragen nach dem Restaurant.   Wir fragen danach.

    Sie stehen neben dem Bus.   Sie stehen daneben.

    Die Kinder laufen über die Straße.   Die Kinder laufen darüber.

    Das Heft liegt zwischen dem Buch und der   Das Heft liegt dazwischen.
        Zeitschrift.

    Der Wagen steht vor der Tür.   Der Wagen steht davor.

18. Günter ging mit seinen Kassetten ins   Womit ging er ins Sprachlabor?
      Sprachlabor.

Variation: *Günter ging damit ins Sprachlabor.*

    Der Lehrer spricht viel über Österreich.   Worüber spricht der Lehrer viel?

148

Die Schüler warten auf den Zug.   Worauf warten die Schüler?
Ich denke gern an unsere Reise.   Woran denke ich gern?
Walter hat zehn Mark für eine Kinokarte Wofür hat Walter zehn Mark bezahlt?
  bezahlt.
Die Ausländer erzählen von dem langen Flug.   Wovon erzählen die Ausländer?
Das Motorrad ist gegen die Brücke gefahren.   Wogegen ist das Motorrad gefahren?

19. Replace the italicized phrase with a *da*-compound.

1. Warum interessierst du dich nicht *für diesen französischen Film?*
2. Die Schüler fragen *nach den neuen Büchern.*
3. Haben Sie sich *über Ihr Geschenk* gefreut?
4. *Zwischen dem Berg und dem Dorf* fließt ein Fluß.
5. Was hast du *in dem Koffer?*
6. Ich habe schon lange *auf diesen Brief* gewartet.
7. Dein Kuli liegt *unter deinem Heft.*
8. Ich möchte gern *von deiner interessanten Reise* hören.
9. Vor neun Uhr stehen schon viele Leute *vor dem Geschäft.*
10. Das bunte Bild hängt *über dem Schrank.*

20. Construct a question asking for the italicized phrase using a *wo*-compound.

1. Wir haben viel *über unseren Flug* gesprochen.
2. Paul freut sich schon sehr *auf den Sommer.*
3. Ich schreibe meine Ansichtskarte *mit einem Kuli.*
4. Die Touristen erzählen *von den alten Städten.*
5. Die Gäste setzen sich *an einen großen Tisch.*
6. Die Eltern bezahlen viel Geld *für die neue Flöte.*
7. Sie holen das Surfbrett *aus dem See.*
8. Die Studenten verstehen etwas *von diesem Fach.*

Verbs with Dative

There are several verbs in German that take the dative case. The following verbs that you have learned already fall into this category:

danken	to thank
folgen	to follow
geben	to give
gefallen	to like, please
gehören	to belong
gratulieren	to congratulate
helfen	to help
passen	to fit
schmecken	to taste

Folgt den Beispielen!

Variation: Personalize questions. *Wem gehört dieses Buch (dieser Kuli, diese Schultasche)? (Es gehört ihm/ihr).*

21. Wem gehört das Auto?   Es gehört meinem Freund.
    (mein Freund)

Wem gehört die Schultasche?   Sie gehört meiner Schwester.
    (meine Schwester)

Wem gehört der Ball?   Er gehört dem Kind.
    (das Kind)

Wem gehört das Geschenk?   Es gehört deinem Lehrer.
    (dein Lehrer)

Wem gehört die Karte?   Sie gehört seiner Mutter.
    (seine Mutter)

Wem gehört der Reisepaß?   Er gehört dem Ausländer.
    (der Ausländer)

Variation: *Wem willst du helfen? Ich will der Frau helfen.*

22. Was soll ich tun?   Du sollst der Frau helfen.
    die Frau / helfen

    der Herr / antworten   Du sollst dem Herrn antworten.

    mein Onkel / gratulieren   Du sollst meinem Onkel gratulieren.

    seine Tante / danken   Du sollst seiner Tante danken.

    der Bus / folgen   Du sollst dem Bus folgen.

23. Wie heißt das auf deutsch?

1. Did you thank the waiter for the meal?
2. Did you help him?
3. To whom does this ball belong?
4. The boys and girls follow their teacher.
5. I don't like this movie.
6. These shoes don't fit me.
7. Did you congratulate her?

Lesestück 1

Wandern an der Ahr

Verschiedene Familien aus der Nachbarschaft° in einem Kölner Vor-   *neighborhood*
ort haben sich entschlossen, an einem Sonntag einen Tagesausflug
an die Ahr zu machen. Schon am Morgen treffen sich Herr und Frau
Bauer, die Organisatoren, mit den meisten der Wanderer an der Haltestelle. Wie verabredet°, sind sie kurz vor neun Uhr da. Die Er-   *as agreed*
wachsenen und die Kinder steigen in die Straßenbahn ein.

Sie sehen sich den Wanderweg auf einer Tafel an.

Da oben sind viele Weinberge.

Am Nachmittag machen alle eine Rast.

Wandern macht viel Spaß.

Am Bahnhof treffen sie noch einige andere Familien. Sie sind direkt in die Innenstadt nach Köln gefahren und haben dort ihre Wagen geparkt. Herr Bauer begrüßt Herrn Vogel. Jetzt sind alle da. Die Familien fahren mit dem Zug an die Ahr°. Bis zur Ahr sind es 65 km. Nach einer Fahrt von einer Stunde und zehn Minuten kommen sie an ihrem Ziel an. *name of river*

Herr Bauer sieht sich den Wanderweg° auf einer Tafel an. *hiking path*
Dann zeigt er allen, wo sie auf dem Weg zwischen den Weinbergen° *vineyards*
entlanggehen° werden. Gemeinsam wandern sie nun auf dem *walk along*
„Rotweinwanderweg" an der Ahr. Bald bilden sich° kleinere Grup- *form*
pen. Einige wandern etwas schneller, andere nehmen sich etwas
mehr Zeit. Alle freuen sich über° das schöne Wetter. Die Sonne *are happy about*
scheint, und es wird bald sehr warm.

Am Mittag machen sie eine Rast. Herr Karl öffnet° eine Wein- *opens*
flasche°, natürlich Rotwein, denn in dieser Gegend wächst° fast nur *wine bottle/*
roter Wein. Herr Bauer setzt sich auch hin und trinkt den Rotwein *grows*
von Herrn Karl. Die meisten Familien sitzen im Gras, essen ihre
belegten Brote und trinken etwas dazu.

Lektion 16   151

Was macht
Herr Bauer?

Dann geht es weiter. Links oben° sind die meisten Weinberge, *above*
rechts unten liegen die Weindörfer im Tal. An diesem schönen Tag
macht das Wandern zwischen den Weinstöcken° besonders viel *vine stakes*
Spaß. Nach einer Weile finden sie einen idealen Platz mit Tischen,
Bänken und einer herrlichen Aussicht° ins Ahrtal. „Hier machen *view*
wir noch eine Rast!" sagt Herr Bauer. Sie öffnen die Rucksäcke und
wieder gibt es etwas zu essen und zu trinken. Während sich die
Eltern unterhalten, klettern° ein paar Jungen auf einen großen *climb*
Stein°. Alle sind guter Laune, besonders an einem so schönen Tag. *rock*
Herr Vogel lobt° Herrn Bauer für die gute Organisation dieser *praises*
Wanderung°. *hike*

Nach einer Wanderung von etwa fünf Stunden kommen sie
wieder auf einem Bahnhof im Ahrtal an. Sie sehen noch einmal
zurück auf den Rotweinwanderweg und sind ganz erstaunt°, was für *amazed*
eine lange Strecke sie gewandert sind. Endlich kommt der Zug. Sie
sind jetzt alle ein wenig müde. Sie steigen in den Zug ein. Sie haben
Glück. Der Zug ist ziemlich leer und alle finden einen bequemen
Sitzplatz.

Fragen über das Lesestück

1. Aus welcher Gegend kommen diese Familien?
2. Treffen sie sich alle an der Haltestelle?
3. Wer hat diese Wanderung geplant?
4. Wohin fahren sie und wie lange dauert die Fahrt?
5. Wie weiß Herr Bauer, wohin sie wandern?
6. Auf welchem Weg wandern sie? Wie heißt er?
7. Wandern die Familien zusammen?
8. Was machen sie alles während der ersten Rast?
9. Warum macht das Wandern an diesem Tag besonders viel Spaß?
10. Warum ist der Platz während der zweiten Rast so ideal?
11. Was machen die Erwachsenen und die Kinder während der Rast?
12. Warum lobt Herr Vogel Herrn Bauer?
13. Wie viele Stunden sind sie gewandert?
14. Warum haben sie Glück?

Erweiterung

24. Beantwortet diese Fragen mit einem ganzen Satz!

1. Was steht auf deinem Tisch?
2. Was liegt auf einem Regal?
3. Wo stehen viele Autos?
4. Worüber schreibst du gern?
5. Worauf freust du dich?
6. Wovon sprichst du viel?
7. Wofür interessierst du dich am meisten?

25. Form complete sentences by using the cues given.

1. Wir / Appetit haben auf / Spezialität / Restaurant
2. Welche / Speisen / stehen / auf / Speisekarte
3. Denken an / Sie / oft / Ihr / schön / Ferien
4. Er / sprechen über / interessant / Reise
5. Touristen / stehen / schon / fünf Uhr / vor / deutsch / Restaurant
6. Jugendlichen / vorbeifahren / an / groß / See
7. Was / machen / du / in / Winter
8. Dorf / liegen / in / Berge
9. Können / du / deine Schwester / nicht / antworten
10. Meine / Bekannten / schreiben über / lang / Wanderung

26. Complete the following sentences.

1. Was liegt _____?
2. _____ im Wasser.
3. Stell dein Auto _____ !
4. Ich habe Appetit auf _____ .
5. Zum Nachtisch möchte ich _____ .
6. Bringen Sie uns _____ .
7. Wie wär's mit _____?
8. Zum Frühstück essen wir _____ .

27. Wie heißt das auf deutsch?

1. Are you in a good mood?
2. When did they hike?
3. Sit down here.
4. He is taking very little time.
5. Do these sandwiches taste good?
6. Don't talk her into that.
7. We like to talk (converse).

28. Erkläre die folgenden Wörter mit einem ganzen Satz!

1. Restaurant
2. Speisekarte
3. Getränk
4. Tagesausflug
5. Rucksack
6. Mittagessen

You may want to have students write a paragraph or two in which they develop a story and use these six words.

29. Beantwortet die Fragen!

1. Was ißt du gern zum Nachtisch?
2. Was möchtest du trinken?
3. Was braucht man zum Essen?
4. Was steht auf dem Tisch?
5. Zu welchem Restaurant gehst du gern?
6. Wo kann man in deiner Gegend wandern?

Rückblick

If your students have some difficulties completing these exercises, you may wish to go back to the particular lesson in which the grammar point or topic was covered.

I. Supply the necessary nominative endings.

1. ein_____ klein_____ Stadt
2. sein_____ neu_____ Freundin
3. ihr_____ beid_____ Töchter
4. kein_____ interessant_____ Film
5. unser_____ schön_____ Zimmer
6. dein_____ bunt_____ Hemd
7. ein_____ deutsch_____ Student
8. euer_____ alt_____ Schultasche

II. Form complete sentences, using the information given.

1. ich / sehen / dein / groß / Bruder
2. wo / sein / euer / schwarz / Hund
3. wir / werden / mein / alt / Freund / Sonntag / besuchen
4. mein / englisch / Bücher / gefallen / ich
5. fahren / er / mit / sein / neu / Fahrrad / in / Stadt
6. warum / schreiben / du / dein / Eltern / kein / Brief
7. mein / preiswert / Karte / geben / ich / mein / klein / Schwester

III. Wie heißt das auf deutsch?

1. Have you seen our new house?
2. This German restaurant is very popular.
3. His older brother will take a long trip to Europe.
4. When will these American students visit us?
5. Did you get a good seat?
6. The tourists are driving through these small towns.
7. I'll talk with the young waitress.

IV. Provide the necessary endings.

Heute ist ein_____ schön_____ Tag. Willi trinkt ein_____ Tasse Kaffee und ißt
ein_____ Stück frisch_____ Brot dazu. Er muß sich beeilen. In ein paar Minuten
kommt sein_____ gut_____ Freund Hans, und beide werden dann zusammen mit
ihr_____ Fahrrädern zur Schule fahren.

Willi holt schnell sein_____ interessant_____ Bücher und verläßt das Haus. Auf der
Straße ist viel Verkehr. Beide Jungen sehen, wie viele alt_____ und neu_____ Autos
und Motorräder vorbeifahren. Alle wollen pünktlich zu ihr_____ täglich_____
Arbeit kommen. Seit einigen Wochen gehen Willi und Hans auf ein_____
modern_____ Schule. Diese neu_____ und groß_____ Schule gefällt ihnen sehr
gut.

Nach der englisch_____ Klasse haben sie ein_____ kurz_____ Pause. Dann kommt
ihr Deutschlehrer, Herr Uhland. Er ist ein_____ älter_____ Lehrer. Willi hat die
deutsch_____ Stunde gern. Er bekommt in Deutsch ein_____ besser_____ Note als
in Englisch.

Am Nachmittag fahren Willi und Hans um ein_____ klein_____ See herum, nicht
weit von ihr_____ Haus. Sie sitzen dort oft an dem schön_____ See und sprechen
über die Schule.

Was für ein Tag
ist heute?
(Schwäbisch Hall)

Lesestück 2

Wie und wo essen die Deutschen?

Wenn man nach Deutschland kommt, merkt° man sofort den Unter-   *notices*
schied° zwischen deutschen und amerikanischen Mahlzeiten. Schon   *difference*
das Frühstück ist sehr verschieden. In den meisten Hotels bekom-
men die Gäste° zum Frühstück Brötchen°, Butter, Marmelade und   *guests/hard rolls*
Kaffee. Manchmal gibt es auch ein gekochtes Ei° und eine Auswahl   *boiled egg*
von Käse und Wurst. Bei den Hauptmahlzeiten°, zum Mittag- und   *main meals*
Abendessen, trinken viele Deutsche ein Bier. Man stellt kein Wasser
auf den Tisch wie es in Amerika üblich° ist. Deutsche halten wäh-   *customary*
rend der Mahlzeit die Gabel in der linken Hand und das Messer in
der rechten. Beim Bezahlen nach der Mahlzeit gibt man dem
Kellner oder der Kellnerin kein großes Trinkgeld°. Die Rechnung   *tip*

Was kauft man hier?

eine Imbißstube (Heidelberg)

ein Café

Was verkauft dieser Stand? (Wiesbaden)

Was für ein Restaurant ist dieses? (Bad Nauheim)

Die Deutschen gehen gern in eine Konditorei.

ein gemütliches
deutsches
Restaurant

Was gibt es hier
zu essen und
zu trinken?

Das Gasthaus ist für
viele Deutsche das
beliebteste Restaurant.

enthält° schon 10% oder 15% Trinkgeld. Das steht auch auf der Speisekarte. — *contains*

Wo essen die Deutschen, wenn sie nicht zu Hause sind? Es gibt viele Möglichkeiten. Es kommt natürlich darauf an°, ob man viel oder wenig Geld ausgeben° will und wieviel Zeit man hat. Viele Restaurants machen Reklame und versuchen, neue Gäste zu gewinnen. Wenn man es eilig hat und sich nicht hinsetzen will, dann bieten die kleinen Imbißstuben ein schnelles und billiges Essen. Manchmal hängt ein Schild aus° mit dem Wort „Straßenverkauf". Das bedeutet, daß die Kunden ihr Essen dort kaufen und mitnehmen müssen, denn es gibt da keine Sitzplätze. Manche Stände, besonders im Verkaufszentrum°, verkaufen nur Brezeln°.

kommt...darauf an depends on
spend

hängt...aus is displayed

shopping center/ pretzels

Während der Sommermonate gehen die Deutschen gern in ein Gartenlokal°. Dort sitzen sie im Freien, essen und trinken, unterhalten sich und beobachten° den Straßenverkehr. In den letzten paar Jahren hat man verschiedene Hamburger-Restaurants eingeführt°. Viele dieser Restaurants, wie zum Beispiel McDonald's, zeigen den starken° amerikanischen Einfluß°.

outside restaurant
watch
introduced

strong/influence

Die Gaststätte oder das Gasthaus° ist für die meisten Deutschen das beliebteste Restaurant. Vor dem Gasthaus am Eingang hängt in einem kleinen Schaufenster die tägliche Speisekarte aus. Manche Restaurants schreiben die Speisekarte auf eine Tafel und stellen sie neben den Eingang. Ein Ratskeller ist ein Keller-Restaurant im Rathaus. Dort bekommt man immer ein gutes Essen. Im Ratskeller ist es aber oft auch sehr teuer. Wer nicht in der Stadt essen will, hat eine gute Auswahl außerhalb der Stadt. Auf dem Lande° gibt es Restaurants mit lokalen Spezialitäten. Manche Restaurants sind direkt am See oder am Fluß mit einem schönen Ausblick aufs Wasser. Meistens kosten die Mahlzeiten dort etwas mehr. In den Großstädten kann man heute auch viele Spezialitäten aus dem Ausland° kosten. Besonders beliebt sind Speisen aus Italien und China.

type of restaurant

in the country

foreign countries

Für Deutsche ist es eine Tradition, ab und zu° in eine Kondi- *once in a while*
torei° zu gehen. An warmen Tagen kann man sogar im Freien sitzen, *café*
Kaffee trinken und ein Stück Torte oder Eis essen. Die Auswahl an
Kuchen und Torten in einer Konditorei ist phantastisch.

Fragen über das Lesestück

1. Was essen die Deutschen zum Frühstück?
2. Was trinken viele Deutsche zum Mittagessen?
3. Wie essen die Deutschen? Was machen sie mit dem Messer und der Gabel?
4. Wieviel Trinkgeld muß man dem Kellner oder der Kellnerin geben?
5. Was ist ein Imbiß?
6. Wo können die Gäste die Speisekarte lesen?
7. Wo sitzen die Deutschen gern im Sommer?
8. Wie heißt das beliebteste Restaurant?
9. Was ist ein Ratskeller und wo findet man ihn?
10. Welche Speisen sind bei den Deutschen heute beliebt?
11. Was ist eine Konditorei?

Sprachspiegel Have students write about their own experience going to a restaurant.

I. *Schreibe einen Dialog über das Thema „Wir gehen ins Restaurant"!* **Include some or all of the following details and any other items you can think of.**

You have decided to go to a special restaurant where you've always wanted to eat. You suggest to your friend that s/he comes along. You explain to him/her some of the special features of this restaurant. Your friend agrees to join you. In front of the restaurant you study the menu and discuss it with your friend, and then you go inside. Soon after you've found a table, the waitress comes and you order something to drink first while both of you continue looking at and talking about the menu and the restaurant's specialties. When the waitress returns, you ask her about today's specialty which she explains. Both of you order different meals. While you're waiting for your meal, you talk about things of interest to both of you. When the waitress brings your meals, you compliment her on the delicious appearance of the food. Later you order some dessert, ask for the check, pay and leave the restaurant.

II. Besprich den Unterschied zwischen den verschiedenen Restaurants!

1. das Café
2. der Ratskeller
3. die Konditorei
4. die Imbißstube
5. die Gaststätte
6. das Hamburger-Restaurant

Du bist dran! Ask students to write out logical response to the statements and questions presented.

Bringen Sie die Speisekarte, bitte.

. . . .

Eine Limonade.

. . . .

. . . .

Bitte sehr?

. . . .

Sonst noch etwas?

. . . .

Das bringe ich Ihnen sofort.

Fräulein, ich möchte zahlen.

. . . .

Das ist ja sehr preiswert.

. . . .

. . . .

Ich muß noch den Tisch decken.

. . . .

Es dauert nur ein paar Minuten.

Wie schmeckt Ihnen der Nachtisch?

Steht alles schon da?

. . . .

Trinken wir denn etwas zum Essen?

. . . .

Wie schmeckt Ihnen der Nachtisch?

. . . .

Möchten Sie noch etwas anderes?

. . . .

Dann bringe ich Ihnen gleich die Rechnung.

. . . .

Ja, dieses Restaurant hat viele deutsche Spezialitäten.

. . . .

Das ist mir recht.

Wohin gehst du nach der Schule?

. . . .

Gut, ich komme mit.

. . . .

Kulturecke

Foods

Thousands of restaurants of varying kinds are scattered throughout Germany. Almost all German restaurants clearly display their daily menu outside, next to the entrance. People who plan to eat in a specific restaurant can decide what they will eat and how much they will pay before entering. The menu lists the prices including the value-added tax and the tip.

The evening meal, appropriately call *Abendbrot*, is quite standard in German homes. Households and restaurants alike offer cold plates *(Kalte Platten)* consisting of various cold cuts and breads. There are many different kinds of breads and rolls from which to choose. And the variety of cheeses and sausages is unbelievable too. Some of the cold plates, as for example in Northern Germany, consist of various kinds of herring.

Most Germans eat their warm meal for lunch. An important part of most warm meals is the potato. Germans make numerous dishes with potatoes, ranging from potato pancakes with a green salad *(Kartoffelpuffer mit Salat)* to sauerbrauten with potato dumplings *(Sauerbraten mit Kartoffelklößen)*. Sauerbraten is beef marinated in vinegar and spices.

Germans usually prefer fresh vegetables to canned. Therefore, it is not surprising that the cook in the family spends a great deal of time in preparing a warm meal. Germans eat a variety of vegetables — peas, beets, tomatoes, carrots, red cabbage, cauliflower, sauerkraut and, probably the greatest delicacy of all vegetables, asparagus. Unlike the green American asparagus, the German asparagus is white.

A very popular German dish is *Schnitzel*. It can be prepared in many different ways, depending on one's preference. For example, veal cutlet with mushrooms *(Kalbsschnitzel mit Champignons)*, a dish that can be found on almost all German menus, is quite well known. What are some other common meals? Certainly one such dish is fried chicken *(Gebratenes Huhn)* or roulade with mashed potatoes *(Rouladen mit Kartoffelbrei)*. Pig's knuckles with cabbage salad *(Schweinehaxen mit Krautsalat)*, however, is not every gourmet's delight as a main dish.

Was ist alles auf dieser Platte?

Kartoffelpuffer mit Salat

eine Kalte Platte

verschiedene Arten
von Broten und Brötchen

eine gute Auswahl an
verschiedenen Lebensmitteln

Die Deutschen essen Würstchen gern.

Kalbsschnitzel
mit Champignons

Spargel

Germans love venison, a rather expensive dish. In all first-rate and most good restaurants you will find at least one venison dish, such as saddle of venison *(Rehrücken)*. More frequently hunted, and therefore less expensive, is the rabbit. There are many kinds of rabbit dishes, ranging from the popular *Hasenpfeffer* (spiced rabbit) to a lesser known dish called *Hase im Topf* (Rabbit in the pot).

The inner parts of animals, such as liver, are very much appreciated in Germany. The *Berliner Leber* is a favorite that is flavored with onions and slices of apples. At Christmastime, a dish that has long been a specialty is roasted goose *(Gebratene Gans)* with all its trimmings. In some parts of the country, carp *(Karpfen)* is still a traditional meal during the Christmas season.

Desserts, or *Nachspeisen,* are also listed on many menus. Selections differ according to individual tastes. Almost all restaurants serve some kind of ice cream. A favorite dessert during the warm season is vanilla ice cream and strawberries *(Vanilleeis und Erdbeeren)*. During the colder season, a dessert such as roasted apples topped with a specially concocted whipped cream *(Bratäpfel mit Baiserhaube)* is one of many popular dishes.

A discussion of German foods is not complete without mentioning the tremendous variety of cakes and pastries found throughout the country. A very common cake in all parts of Germany is the apple cake *(Apfelkuchen)*. Related to this cake is the *Apfelstreuselkuchen,* an apple cake with lots of streusel on top. Many cafés and pastry shops offer one or two kinds of cheese cake, such as the *Käsecremetorte*. But the most sought-after cake or pastry is the Black Forest Cherry Torte *(Schwarzwälder Kirschtorte)*.

Perhaps the largest selection of baked goods in a typical German household can be found during the Christmas season. The eyes of children light up when the Christmas cookies *(Weihnachtsgebäck)* are displayed. Many cookies for the festive occasion are baked in special forms, adding to the spirit of the Christmas season. Besides the many beautifully decorated cookies, Germans also bake various kinds of breads during Christmas such as *Kletzenbrot,* which is a sweet bread containing figs, raisins, dried pears, chopped walnuts, hazelnuts and various spices. But the most popular German Christmas cake is the *Stollen* filled with raisins, orange and lemon peels, almonds and then covered with powdered sugar — a tradition in most German households during the Christmas season.

Schwarzwälder Kirschtörte

Weihnachtsgebäck

Torten sind bei den Deutschen immer beliebt.

Vokabeln

der **Appetit** appetite
    Appetit haben auf to have appetite for
    Guten Appetit! Enjoy your meal!
der **Apfelkuchen,-** apple cake
der **Apfelsaft,-̈e** apple juice
die **Aussicht,-en** view
die **Beilage,-n** addition
    Beilagen served with, side dish
    belegt covered
    belegte Brote sandwiches
sich **bilden** to form
die **Bohne,-n** bean
die **Bratkartoffel,-n** fried potato
der **Champignon,-s** mushroom
    eilig speedy, urgent
    es eilig haben to be in a hurry
das **Eis** ice, ice cream
    entlanggehen to walk along
    erstaunt astonished, amazed
das **Fleisch** meat
die **Forelle,-n** trout
sich **freuen über** to be happy about
die **Gabel,-n** fork
die **Gaststätte,-n** restaurant
die **Gemüsesuppe,-n** vegetable soup
der **Genuß,-̈sse** pleasure
das **Gras,-̈er** grass
die **Gulaschsuppe,-n** goulash soup
der **Gurkensalat,-e** cucumber salad
    hell light
    ein Helles a light beer
sich **hinsetzen** to sit down
die **Karotte,-n** carrot
der **Karpfen,-** carp
    klettern to climb
der **Knödel,-** dumpling
das **Kompott,-e** stewed fruit
die **Laune,-n** mood
    loben to praise
das **Messer,-** knife

das **Mineralwasser** mineral water
die **Möhre,-n** carrot
die **Nachbarschaft,-en** neighborhood
    oben on top, above
    öffnen to open
die **Organisation,-en** organization
der **Organisator,-en** organizer
die **Pommes frites** (pl.) French fries
der **Pudding,-e** pudding
    reichlich generous, plentiful
der **Rinderbraten,-** beef roast
das **Rinderfilet,-s** beef tenderloin
der **Rotwein,-e** red wine
der **Rotweinwanderweg** Red Wine Hiking Path (name)
der **Salat,-e** salad
der **Salatteller,-** salad plate
die **Salzkartoffel,-n** boiled potato
der **Sauerbraten,-** sauerbraten (marinated beef)
das **Schnitzel,-** cutlet
    Wiener Schnitzel breaded veal cutlet
die **Schüssel,-n** bowl
das **Schweinefilet,-s** pork tenderloin
    selbst in person, self
    selbstverständlich of course
    servieren to serve
die **Serviette,-n** napkin
der **Spargel,-** asparagus
die **Speisekarte,-n** menu
der **Spinat** spinach
der **Stein,-e** stone, rock
die **Suppe,-n** soup
der **Suppenlöffel,-** soupspoon
der **Tagesausflug,-̈e** day's excursion
das **Tagesgericht,-e** daily menu
die **Tagessuppe,-n** soup of the day
der **Teelöffel,-** teaspoon
der **Teller,-** plate
der **Tomatensalat,-e** tomato salad

die **Tomatensuppe,-n** tomato soup
    überreden to persuade, talk into
    sich überreden lassen to be talked into
sich **unterhalten** (*unterhält, unterhielt, unterhalten*) to converse, talk
die **Untertasse,-n** saucer
sich **verabreden** to make an appointment
    wie verabredet as agreed
    wachsen (*wächst, wuchs, ist gewachsen*) to grow
die **Wahl,-en** choice, selection
    Wer die Wahl hat, hat die Qual. It's hard to make a choice.
der **Wanderer,-** hiker
die **Wanderung,-en** hike
der **Wanderweg,-e** hiking path
der **Weinberg,-e** vineyard
das **Weindorf,-̈er** wine-growing village
die **Weinflasche,-n** wine bottle
der **Weinstock,-̈e** grape vine
    wohl indeed, well (used for emphasis)
    Wohl: Zum Wohl! Cheers! To your health!
das **Ziel,-e** destination
    zurücksehen (*sieht zurück, sah zurück, zurückgesehen*) to look back

Dialog

The small stores, called *Tante Emma Laden*, are slowly disappearing in Germany. However, in small towns they still can be seen. The service in these small, privately owned stores is quite personal.

Im Geschäft

FRAU REUTER: Guten Tag!

VERKÄUFERIN: Ach, guten Tag, Frau Reuter! Es freut uns, Sie wiederzusehen. Haben Sie schöne Tage im Urlaub verbracht?

FRAU REUTER: Einfach herrlich. Geben Sie mir doch bitte ein Dutzend Eier.

VERKÄUFERIN: Bitte schön. Sonst noch etwas?

FRAU REUTER: Ja, einmal sauren Rahm und die Blaubeermarmelade hier. Haben Sie übrigens Schreibpapier?

VERKÄUFERIN: Große oder kleine Bogen?

FRAU REUTER: Große, bitte. Da kann ich wenigstens meinen Verwandten viel über unsere Reise schreiben.

VERKÄUFERIN: Sind die Ihnen recht?

FRAU REUTER: Ja, das ist die richtige Größe.

FRAU REUTER: Haben Sie noch das gute Poliermittel?

VERKÄUFERIN: Nein, das habe ich leider nicht mehr.

FRAU REUTER: Oh, wie schade! Geben Sie mir doch eine Dose Erdnüsse. Die stehen gleich auf dem Regal darunter.

VERKÄUFERIN: Da haben Sie gerade noch die letzte Dose erwischt.

FRAU REUTER: Die roten Äpfel sehen ganz frisch aus. Geben Sie mir doch zwei Kilo davon. Das ist dann alles.

VERKÄUFERIN: Es ist etwas mehr als zwei Kilo.

FRAU REUTER: Das macht nichts. Wir essen Äpfel sehr gern.

VERKÄUFERIN: So, jetzt alles schnell zusammenzählen…Das macht dann 25 Mark 60.

FRAU REUTER: Hier sind zwei Zwanzig-Markscheine. Leider habe ich es nicht passend.

VERKÄUFERIN: Das geht schon…Auf Wiedersehen, Frau Reuter. Kommen Sie bald wieder

Fragen über den Dialog

1. Warum hat die Verkäuferin Frau Reuter in letzter Zeit nicht gesehen?
2. Wie viele Eier kauft Frau Reuter?
3. Was will sie mit dem Schreibpapier tun?
4. Wo befinden sich die Erdnüsse? Stehen da noch viele Dosen?
5. Was für Obst kauft Frau Reuter?
6. Wieviel Geld gibt sie der Verkäuferin und wieviel bekommt sie zurück?

In the Store

MRS. REUTER: Hello!

SALESLADY: Oh, hello, Mrs. Reuter! We're glad to see you again. Did you have a nice vacation?

MRS. REUTER: Just great. Would you give me a dozen eggs, please.

SALESLADY: Here you are. Anything else?

MRS. REUTER: Yes, sour cream and the blueberry jam here. By the way, do you have writing paper?

SALESLADY: Large or small sheets?

MRS. REUTER: Large, please. Then I can write a lot to my relatives about our trip.

SALESLADY: Are these O.K. with you?

MRS. REUTER: Yes, that's the right size.

MRS. REUTER: Do you still have the good polish?

SALESLADY: No, I don't have any more left.

MRS. REUTER: Oh, too bad. Why don't you give me a can of peanuts. They are on the shelf below.

SALESLADY: Well, you just got the last can.

MRS. REUTER: The red apples look quite fresh. Why don't you give me two kilos of those. That's all then.

SALESLADY: It's a bit more than two kilos.

MRS. REUTER: That doesn't matter. We like apples very much.

SALESLADY: So, let's add everything now…That comes to 25 marks and 60 pfennigs.

MRS. REUTER: Here are two twenty-mark bills. Unfortunately, I don't have the right change.

SALESLADY: That's O.K… Good-bye, Mrs. Reuter. Come again soon.

ein kleines Lebensmittelgeschäft

eine Bäckerei

ein Fleischer

Nützliche Ausdrücke

Review these expressions with your students. They have been covered in the *Dialog* and *Lesestück 1*.

Es freut mich, Sie wiederzusehen.	I'm glad to see you again.
Wir haben einen schönen Urlaub verbracht.	We had a nice vacation.
Geben Sie mir doch…!	Why don't you give me…
Das ist aber schade.	That's too bad.
Ich habe gerade noch die letzte Karte erwischt.	I just got the last ticket.
Das macht nichts.	That doesn't matter.
Haben Sie passendes Geld?	Do you have the right change?
Wie ist die Bedienung?	How is the service?
Sie machen ihre eigene Wurst.	They make their own sausage.
Sie schneidet es in Scheiben.	She is slicing it.
Ich bediene mich selbst.	I'm helping myself.
Der Laden macht bald zu.	The store is closing soon.
Ich biete dir etwas Leckeres an.	I'm offering you something delicious.
Nebenan ist ein Lebensmittelgeschäft.	Next door is a grocery store.

Sprichwort

Der Apfel fällt nicht weit vom Stamm.   A chip off the old block.
(The apple does not fall far from the tree.)

Ergänzung

Personalize this section asking such questions as *Gibt es in deiner Gegend ein Kaufhaus? Kannst du es beschreiben?*

1. Im Kaufhaus

Wie kommen Sie von einem Stock zum anderen?

Mit dem Fahrstuhl.
Mit der Rolltreppe.
Zu Fuß.

Wo kauft man das Obst und Gemüse?
Wo ist die Sportabteilung?

Im Erdgeschoß.
Im dritten Stock.

Herren(abteilung)
Damen(abteilung)
Kinder(abteilung)
Schreibwaren(abteilung)
Spielwaren(abteilung)
Lebensmittel(abteilung)
Bücher(abteilung)

Reine Wolle

2. Obst und Gemüse

Students should learn the singular as well as the plural noun forms.
Have students ask each other questions. *(Was für Obst/Gemüse ißt du gern?)*

Übungen

Model Auxiliaries

Past tense

The past tense of modal auxiliaries is formed like the past tense of regular verbs. You add -*t*- and the endings to the stem. Also, there is no umlaut.

dürfen:	ich *durfte*	I was permitted to, allowed to
können:	ich *konnte*	I was able to
mögen:	ich *mochte*	I liked to
müssen:	ich *mußte*	I had to
sollen:	ich *sollte*	I was supposed to
wollen:	ich *wollte*	I wanted to

Present perfect tense

The present perfect tense of modal auxiliaries is formed with the infinitive. However, this construction is usually avoided in colloquial usage. All six modal auxiliaries use *haben* in the present perfect form.

Beispiele:

Hast du ins Kino *gehen dürfen?*

Have you been allowed to go to the movie theater?

Der Junge hat nicht *lesen können.*

The boy hasn't been able to read.

Ich habe das nicht *essen mögen.*

I haven't liked to eat that.

Sie haben viel *arbeiten müssen.*

They have had to work a lot.

Die Jungen haben nach Hause *kommen sollen.*

The boys were supposed to have come home.

Er hat mit ihm *sprechen wollen.*

He has wanted to talk with him.

Folgt den Beispielen!

1. Wohin mußtest du gehen?
   (ins Geschäft)

   Ich mußte ins Geschäft gehen.

   Was mußtest du machen?
   (die Arbeit)

   Ich mußte die Arbeit machen.

   Wo mußtest du warten?
   (an der Haltestelle)

   Ich mußte an der Haltestelle warten.

   Wen mußtest du besuchen?
   (meinen Onkel)

   Ich mußte meinen Onkel besuchen.

   Wohin mußtest laufen?
   (zur Uni)

   Ich mußte zur Uni laufen.

2. Ich will das nicht. Was sagte er?

   Er wollte das nicht.

   Ich muß einen Brief schreiben. Was sagte sie?

   Sie mußte einen Brief schreiben.

   Ich kann nicht kommen. Was sagte er?

   Er konnte nicht kommen.

Point out that the main verb often can be dropped. (Wohin mußtest du?)

Variation: Use the present perfect tense. (Ich will das nicht? Was hat er gesagt? Er hat es nicht gewollt.)

Ich will in den Urlaub fahren. Was sagte sie? Sie wollte in den Urlaub fahren.

Ich darf mitmachen. Was sagte er? Er durfte mitmachen.

Ich soll den Reisescheck einlösen. Was sagte sie? Sie sollte den Reisescheck einlösen.

3. Können Sie einen Brief schreiben? Konnten Sie einen Brief schreiben?

Er kann die Straße nicht finden. Er konnte die Straße nicht finden.

Warum könnt ihr nicht kommen? Warum konntet ihr nicht kommen?

Der Verkäufer kann ihr das Kleid sofort geben. Der Verkäufer konnte ihr das Kleid sofort geben.

Wann können sie Karten spielen? Wann konnten sie Karten spielen?

Ich kann die Kellnerin fragen. Ich konnte die Kellnerin fragen.

4. Darf er Auto fahren? Durfte er Auto fahren?

Ich will meine Freundin besuchen. Ich wollte meine Freundin besuchen.

Die Touristen müssen auf den Bus warten. Die Touristen mußten auf den Bus warten.

Sie soll es nicht sagen. Sie sollte es nicht sagen.

Könnt ihr den Zug sehen? Konntet ihr den Zug sehen?

Magst du das nicht? Mochtest du das nicht?

Variation: Use the present tense. *(Warum liest du das Buch nicht? Ich will das Buch einfach nicht lesen.)*

5. Warum hast du das Buch nicht gelesen? Ich habe das Buch einfach nicht lesen wollen.

Warum hast du mit ihr nicht gesprochen? Ich habe mit ihr einfach nicht sprechen wollen.

Warum hast du Peter die Karte nicht gegeben? Ich habe Peter die Karte einfach nicht geben wollen.

Warum hast du ihm das nicht gesagt? Ich habe ihm das einfach nicht sagen wollen.

Warum hast du den Lehrer nicht besucht? Ich habe den Lehrer einfach nicht besuchen wollen.

Warum bist du nicht nach Europa gefahren? Ich habe einfach nicht nach Europa fahren wollen.

6. Monika kann das Essen bezahlen. Monika hat das Essen bezahlen können.

Ich muß schnell spielen. Ich habe schnell spielen müssen.

Ihr sollt das Fahrrad mitbringen. Ihr habt das Fahrrad mitbringen sollen.

Warum möchtest du nichts trinken? Warum hast du nichts trinken mögen?

Er will den Karneval sehen. Er hat den Karneval sehen wollen.

Dürfen sie auf den Sportplatz gehen? Haben sie auf den Sportplatz gehen dürfen?

7. Paul wollte das Telegramm schicken. Paul hat das Telegramm schicken wollen.

Warum mochte sie den Kuchen nicht essen? Warum hat sie den Kuchen nicht essen mögen?

Das konnten sie nicht machen. Das haben sie nicht machen können.

Wir durften die Stadt verlassen. Wir haben die Stadt verlassen dürfen.

Ihr mußtet vor der Tür warten. Ihr habt vor der Tür warten müssen.

Die Studenten sollten Deutsch lernen. Die Studenten haben Deutsch lernen sollen.

8. Supply the correct past tense form of the modal auxiliary indicated in parentheses.

1. (wollen) _____ ihr das Schweinefilet essen?
2. (dürfen) Die Kinder _____ nicht auf der Straße spielen.
3. (müssen) Die Touristen _____ zuerst in Hamburg landen.
4. (können) Er _____ nicht schnell fahren.
5. (müssen) _____ Herr und Frau Meier lange warten?
6. (können) Das _____ die Schüler nicht glauben.
7. (mögen) Wir _____ das nicht trinken.
8. (wollen) Viele Ausländer _____ die deutsche Sprache lernen.

9. Change the following sentences to the past tense and then to the present perfect.

      Beispiel: *Ich will mit ihm sprechen.*
                    Ich wollte mit ihm sprechen.
                    Ich habe mit ihm sprechen wollen.

1. Können Sie ihr bei der Arbeit helfen?
2. Nach der Schule muß er seine Hausaufgaben machen.
3. Wir sollen pünktlich sein.
4. Wollen Sie sich den Film ansehen?
5. Kannst du die Kapelle hören?
6. Karin muß lange auf ihn warten.
7. Dürft ihr nicht ins Kino gehen?
8. Müßt ihr nicht ein Dutzend Eier kaufen?
9. Was wollt ihr später machen?
10. Ihr sollt die Milch trinken.

10. Complete the following sentences using either the past or the present perfect tense of a modal auxiliary. Be sure that each sentence is meaningful.

1. Frau Reuter _____ zwei Kilo Äpfel kaufen.
2. Er _____ das neue Auto fahren _____ .
3. Welche Mahlzeit _____ Sie essen _____?
4. Ich _____ die Arbeit nicht schaffen.
5. _____ ihr den Schildern folgen?
6. Die Kinder _____ die Tiere streicheln _____ .
7. Wir _____ die Ausweise vorzeigen _____ .
8. Tina _____ die moderne Musik gern hören.
9. Die Touristen _____ diese Sehenswürdigkeit fotografieren _____ .
10. Am Sonntag _____ die Nachbarn einen Ausflug machen.

Omission of Infinitive

The infinitive of a verb may be omitted if the meaning of the sentence is clear without it.

Beispiele:

> *Müssen Sie in die Stadt?* Do you have to go downtown?
> *Ich darf das nicht.* I'm not allowed to do that.

If the modal auxiliary is not accompanied by a verb, the present perfect tense is formed by converting the modal auxiliary to the past participle.

Beispiele:

> *Sie hat es nicht gemußt.* She hasn't had to.
> *Hast du es nicht gekonnt?* Haven't you been able to?

Folgt dem Beispiel!

Variation: Change from present to future tense.

11. Kann sie das? — Hat sie das gekonnt?

    Sie wollen nicht. — Sie haben nicht gewollt.

    Mögen Sie das Essen? — Haben Sie das Essen gemocht.

    Mußt du in die Stadt? — Hast du in die Stadt gemußt?

    Ihr sollt nach Hause. — Ihr habt nach Hause gesollt.

    Wir dürfen ins Kino. — Wir haben ins Kino gedurft.

Past Perfect Tense

The formation of the past perfect tense in German is quite simple. All you have to do is to use the past tense of *haben* or *sein* and add the past participle.

Past Perfect	
ich *hatte* gelesen	ich *war* gegangen
du *hattest* gefragt	du *warst* geschwommen
er, sie, es *hatte* gehabt	er, sie, es *war* gewesen
wir *hatten* geschrieben	wir *waren* geflogen
ihr *hattet* gesprochen	ihr *wart* gelaufen
sie, Sie *hatten* geholt	sie, Sie *waren* geblieben

The past perfect tense is considerably different from the other past tenses. It expresses an event or action that has taken place prior to an event or action that occurred in the past.

Beispiele:

> *Wir fuhren in die Ferien. Vor unserer Abreise hatten wir natürlich die Koffer gepackt.*
> *Mein Freund hat mich gefragt. Leider hatte ich ihn nicht verstanden.*

Folgt den Beispielen!

12. Wir lesen sehr gern. — Wir hatten sehr gern gelesen.

    Ich schreibe ihr oft. — Ich hatte ihr oft geschrieben.

    Was fragst du? — Was hattest du gefragt?

    Er freut sich. — Er hatte sich gefreut.

Die Touristen machen eine lange Reise.   Die Touristen hatten eine lange Reise gemacht.

Wer wartet auf mich?   Wer hatte auf mich gewartet?

Sie sehen viele Schiffe.   Sie hatten viele Schiffe gesehen.

Variation: Change the sentences on the right side to the present perfect tense.

13. Geht ihr ins Restaurant?   **Wart ihr ins Restaurant gegangen?**

    Wann fliegen wir nach Europa?   Wann waren wir nach Europa geflogen?

    Bleibt Monika zu Hause?   War Monika zu Hause geblieben?

    Um wieviel Uhr kommst du?   Um wieviel warst du gekommen?

    Mein Onkel ist zu Besuch.   Mein Onkel war zu Besuch gewesen.

    Sie fahren zum Schloß.   Sie waren zum Schloß gefahren.

14. Wo warst du denn?   **Wo warst du denn gewesen?**

    Hatte er keine Zeit?   Hatte er keine Zeit gehabt?

    Wir gingen später ins Kino.   Wir waren später ins Kino gegangen.

    Ich fragte sie nach der Straße.   Ich hatte sie nach der Straße gefragt.

    Frau Hebel sprach mit dem Kellner.   Frau Hebel hatte mit dem Kellner gesprochen.

    Was holten sie aus dem Haus?   Was hatten sie aus dem Haus geholt?

    Wohin lieft ihr nach der Schule?   Wohin wart ihr nach der Schule gelaufen?

15. Sabine hatte ihn nicht gesehen.   **Sabine sieht ihn nicht.**

    Die Kinder hatten dort immer gespielt.   Die Kinder spielen dort immer.

    Wir hatten das Fahrrad ans Haus gestellt   Wir stellen das Fahrrad ans Haus.

    Wart ihr ins Theater gegangen?   Geht ihr ins Theater?

    Was hattet ihr vorgehabt?   Was habt ihr vor?

    Du warst in der Schule gewesen.   Du bist in der Schule.

    Die Dame hatte keine Zeit gehabt.   Die Dame hat keine Zeit.

16. Provide the proper form of the past perfect tense.

     Beispiel: *essen / ihr*

               Hattet ihr gegessen?

   1. du / sein / Hause

   2. wir / lesen

   3. Herr Reuter / fliegen

   4. warten / ihr

   5. die Gäste / bleiben

   6. Renate und Ingrid / fragen

   7. kommen / sein Bruder

   8. fahren / ihr

   9. die Jugendlichen / spielen

  10. trinken / Sie

Question Words

As you have learned in previous lessons, the question word *wer* asks for persons and *was* asks for objects or for an action. After prepositions you must use *wen* or *wem* if the question refers to persons.

Beispiele:

    Bei wem wohnen Sie?   *Bei meinem Freund.*
    Neben wen stellst du dich?   *Neben meine Schwester.*

The expression *was für ein…?* asks for an indefinite person or object from a known group of persons or objects.

Beispiele:

    Ich möchte ein rotes Hemd kaufen. *Was für ein Hemd möchten Sie kaufen?*
    Er liest eine deutsche Zeitung.   *Was für eine Zeitung liest er?*
    Das sind Touristen aus Amerika.   *Was für Leute sind das?*

17. Form questions asking for the italicized words.

    Beispiele: Er hat *mit seinem Vater* gesprochen.
                  Mit wem hat er gesprochen?
                  Wir haben *ein leckeres* Essen bestellt.
                  Was für ein Essen haben wir bestellt?

1. Katrin sitzt *neben Werners Schwester.*
2. Frau Reuter kauft *große* Bogen Papier.
3. Meine Mutter ißt gern *frische* Erdbeeren.
4. Wir haben *die Angestellte* kennengelernt.
5. Die Schüler haben *ihrem Lehrer* geantwortet.
6. Heute ist ein *schöner* Tag.
7. Unsere Nachbarn haben einen *herrlichen* Urlaub verbracht.
8. Die Ausländer haben das *historische* Gebäude besucht.
9. Die Verkäuferin hat *neues* Poliermittel.
10. Außer *Petra* sind alle da gewesen.

Gibt es hier eine gute Auswahl?

Lesestück 1

Frau Nobel kauft ein

Zwei- oder dreimal die Woche geht Frau Nobel einkaufen. Wie immer beginnt sie ihren Einkauf beim Fleischer Hubert, gleich in der Nähe ihres Hauses. Frau Nobel geht sehr gern zu diesem Fleischer, denn die Auswahl von Fleisch- und Wurstwaren° ist dort immer gut. Außerdem ist die Bedienung besonders freundlich° und hilfsbereit°. *meats and sausages / friendly / helpful*

Huberts haben ihre eigene Schlachterei°. In einem Kühlraum° hängen° verschiedene große Stücke Fleisch. In einem anderen Raum arbeitet der Fleischer und schneidet° das Fleisch in kleinere Stücke. Huberts machen ihre eigene Wurst. Die schmeckt besonders gut. *butcher shop / cooler / hang / cuts*

Frau Nobel kauft heute gekochten° Schinken, Gehacktes° und Salami. Eine Angestellte schneidet die Salami in Scheiben. Sie wiegt° die Fleischwaren, wickelt sie ein°, schreibt die Preise auf die Packungen° und legt sie in Frau Nobels Einkaufskorb°. An einer anderen Theke bedient sich Frau Nobel selbst. Dort kauft sie Schlagsahne und Margarine. Dann bezahlt sie an der Kasse und steckt alles in ihre Einkaufstasche. *cooked / ground meat / weighs / wraps them up / packages / shopping basket*

Frau Nobel geht einkaufen.

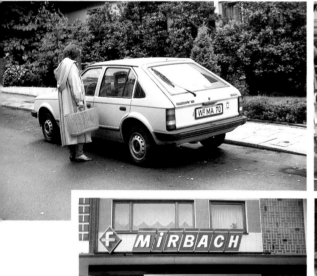

Das Obst und Gemüse ist immer frisch.

Aus welchem Geschäft kommt Frau Nobel?

Warum geht Frau Nobel gern zum Fleischer Huber?

Es ist schon sechs Uhr und die Läden machen um halb sieben zu. Mit schnellen Schritten geht sie zum Zentrum. Sie muß noch einige Sachen° im Delikatessengeschäft kaufen, denn heute abend kommen ihre Bekannten zu Besuch. Sie möchte ihnen etwas Leckeres anbieten.

things

Gleich nebenan ist ein großes Lebensmittelgeschäft. Die Preise sind hier immer günstig. Frau Nobel nimmt einen Wagen° und geht zuerst zur Obst- und Gemüseabteilung. Sie kauft ein paar Bananen; sie sind heute sehr preiswert. Dann kauft sie noch einige von den frischen Äpfeln. Die Verkäuferin wiegt die Früchte°, packt sie in Tüten° und schreibt die Preise darauf.

cart

fruits
bags

In einer anderen Abteilung kauft Frau Nobel ein Pfund Schweizer Käse. Sie beendet ihren Einkauf mit einer Packung Kaffee und geht dann direkt zur Kasse. Während Frau Nobel die einzelnen Waren° auf den Ladentisch° legt, registriert die Kassiererin° die Preise. Frau Nobel steckt alle Lebensmittel° in ihre Einkaufstasche und gibt der Kassiererin das passende Geld. Jetzt muß Frau Nobel aber schnell nach Hause; die Gäste kommen schon um halb acht und sie hat noch viel zu tun.

articles/counter/
cashier
groceries

Fragen über das Lesestück

1. Wie oft kauft Frau Nobel ein?
2. Warum geht sie gern zu Huberts?
3. Was befindet sich in dem Kühlraum?
4. Was kauft Frau Nobel beim Fleischer?
5. Wo bekommt sie Schlagsahne?
6. Warum muß sich Frau Nobel beeilen?
7. Was kauft Frau Nobel in der Obst- und Gemüseabteilung?
8. Was kauft sie noch im Lebensmittelgeschäft?
9. Was macht Frau Nobel alles an der Kasse?

Erweiterung

18. Construct a question asking for the italicized words.

Change these sentences to
the past perfect tense.

1. Der Zug fährt *in einer halben Stunde* ab.
2. *Die Kellnerin* bringt uns die Speisekarte.
3. Mein Freund hat *für dich* bezahlt.
4. Seine Verwandten wohnen *in der Nähe*.
5. Das Flugzeug fliegt *über der Stadt* herum.

6. Herr Braun geht *zu seiner Tante*.

7. Die Dame kauft *ein elegantes Kleid*.

8. Meine Schwester sitzt *neben mir*.

9. Sie fahren *in den Wald*.

10. Ich treffe *sie* beim Reisebüro.

11. Wir besuchen *ein bekanntes Restaurant*.

12. Der Ball gehört *uns*.

13. Werner spielt gern *Klavier*.

14. Das Geschäft ist schon *um acht Uhr* geöffnet.

19. Beschreibt die folgenden Wörter mit einem ganzen Satz!

1. das Obst   Develop a dialog situation in which you use all these ten words.

2. die Verkäuferin

3. der Fahrstuhl

4. der Fleischer

5. die Einkaufstasche

6. das Lebensmittelgeschäft

7. das Gemüse

8. die Kassiererin

9. das Poliermittel

10. der Urlaub

20. Wie heißt das auf deutsch?

1. I don't have the right change.

2. The store closed already.

3. The butcher is next door.

4. The service is excellent.

5. Why don't you give me a dozen peaches.

6. Please slice the cheese.

7. We are glad to see you again.

8. Help yourself, please.

9. When is this store closing?

10. He just got hold of the last newspaper.

21. *Obst, Gemüse oder andere Lebensmittel?* **Determine if the items below fall into the category of (1)** *Obst*, **(2)** *Gemüse* **or (3)** *andere Lebensmittel*.

1. Käse

2. Erdbeeren

3. Karotten

4. Eier

5. Butter

6. Zwiebeln

7. Wurst

8. Kirschen

9. Bohnen

10. Schlagsahne

11. Spargel
12. Birnen

22. Beantwortet diese Fragen mit einem ganzen Satz!

1. Gehst du manchmal einkaufen? Was kaufst du dann?
2. Wo hast du deinen letzten Urlaub verbracht? Was hast du da gemacht?
3. Gibt es in deiner Nähe ein Kaufhaus? Was kann man dort alles kaufen?
4. Zu welcher Abteilung gehst du am liebsten und warum?
5. Was kann man alles beim Fleischer kaufen?
6. Was macht man an der Kasse?
7. Warum braucht man oft einen Einkaufskorb oder einen Wagen beim Einkaufen?
8. Warum gehen viele Leute auf dem Markt einkaufen?

23. Welche der Wörter (rechts und links) passen am besten zusammen?

1. Kaufhaus: _____	Torte
2. Fleischer: _____	Bordkarte
3. Gaststätte: _____	Tiere
4. Flughafen: _____	Reiseschecks
5. Bank: _____	Bücherabteilung
6. Surfbrett: _____	Barkasse
7. Feiertag: _____	Schinken
8. Hochzeit: _____	Zug
9. Café: _____	Ostern
10. Hafen: _____	Stadt
11. Briefträger: _____	Speisekarte
12. Zoo: _____	Segel
13. Bürgermeister: _____	Ansichtskarte
14. Bahnhof: _____	Braut

24. Beantwortet diese Fragen!

1. Was kaufst du im Kaufhaus?
2. Was brauchst du zum Schreiben?
3. Was ißt du gern?
4. Wo kaufst du Obst und Gemüse?
5. Was für Obst schmeckt dir am besten?
6. Was kann man im Lebensmittelgeschäft kaufen?

Was kann man in diesem Lebensmittelgeschäft kaufen?

Rückblick

If your students have difficulties completing any of these exercises, you may want to go back to the lesson in which the particular grammar point was covered.

I. Supply the past, present perfect and past perfect tense for each of the following sentences.

Beispiel: *Er schreibt einen Brief.*
Er schrieb einen Brief.
Er hat einen Brief geschrieben.
Er hatte einen Brief geschrieben.

1. Fährst du nach Hause?
2. Ich spreche kein Wort.
3. Haben Sie keine Zeit?
4. Wir fragen ihn.
5. Was macht ihr denn?
6. Kaufst du dir ein Auto?

II. Change the following sentences from the present to the present perfect tense.

1. Ich habe keine Lust, das Buch zu lesen.
2. Leider besuche ich ihn nicht.
3. Warum kauft ihr diese teuren Karten?
4. Manchmal regnet es und ich kann dort nicht spielen.
5. Freust du dich auf deinen Urlaub?
6. Wir erzählen viel vom Rhein.
7. Die Verkäuferin gibt ihrem Kunden ein paar Äpfel.
8. Die Auswahl ist dort leider nicht gut.
9. Sie steckt alles in ihre Einkaufstasche.
10. Meine Freundin fliegt am Montag nach Österreich.

III. Construct meaningful sentences from the information given. Use the present perfect tense only.

1. die Ausländer / verbringen / ihr / Urlaub / Schweiz
2. schneien / gestern
3. Studenten / lernen / viel / von / Bücher
4. Deutschland / sprechen / wir / viel / Deutsch
5. Günter / mit / S-Bahn / fahren
6. wohin / ihr / so schnell / laufen
7. wir / warten / vor / Geschäft
8. Frau Nobel / bezahlen / Kasse

IV. Supply the endings.

Am früh_____ Morgen packen Roland und Peter ihr_____ Rucksäcke und fahren mit ihr_____ neu_____ Fahrrädern in Richtung Rothenburg. Sie fahren schon um sechs Uhr weg. Zu dies_____ Zeit sehen sie auf den klein_____ Landstraßen noch kein_____ Autos. Nach zwei Stunden halten sie an, setzen sich auf ein_____ groß_____ Bank und essen ihr_____ belegt_____ Brote. Dann geht's weiter.

Sie haben nur noch ein_____ kurz_____ Strecke zu fahren, bis sie in der klein_____ alt_____ Stadt ankommen. In Rothenburg bestaunen sie die eng_____ Straßen dies_____ mittelalterlich_____ Stadt. In der Nähe der Stadt übernachten sie in ein_____ beliebt_____ Jugendherberge.

V. Complete each sentence by using the noun and adjective provided.

1. Trinken Sie diesen (Kaffee, heiß) _____?
2. Hat Ihnen unser (Restaurant, neu) _____ gefallen?
3. Wir freuen uns, daß der (Student, deutsch) _____ zu Besuch kommt.
4. Frau Nobel wohnt in einem (Haus, alt) _____ .
5. Können wir durch die (Zimmer, groß) _____ gehen?
6. Mit welchem (Kleid, bunt) _____ kommst du zum Tanzunterricht?
7. Leider kenne ich dieses (Museum, historisch) _____ nicht.
8. Wir steigen in die (U-Bahn, voll) _____ ein.
9. Stell den Teller auf den (Tisch, braun) _____ !
10. Er kommt heute ohne seinen (Freund, gut) _____ in die Schule.

VI. Supply the proper verb form.

1. Gestern hatte ich keine Hausaufgaben (machen) _____ .
2. Wann werdet ihr wieder (zurückkommen) _____?
3. Hast du denn von den Gästen noch nichts (hören) _____?
4. Die Kellnerin hat uns die Speisekarte (bringen) _____ .
5. Hatten Sie für die Karten schon (bezahlen) _____?
6. Die Klasse wird zu Ostern einen Ausflug (machen) _____ .
7. Petra und Renate haben das Spiel (sehen) _____ .
8. Meine Freundinnen hatten diese Stadt schon (besuchen) _____ .
9. Ich bin um den Flughafen (fahren) _____ .
10. Zu Mittag haben wir (essen) _____ und (trinken) _____ .

Lesestück 2

Auf dem Markt

Einen offenen° Markt gibt es fast überall° in Deutschland. In den Großstädten findet man nicht nur einen Markt in der Innenstadt, sondern auch in den verschiedenen Vororten. In Hamburg gibt es sogar einen besonderen Markt, den Fischmarkt. Schon früh am Morgen kommen die Leute hierher und kaufen frischen Fisch. *open-air/all over*

Für Ausländer ist es ein interessantes Erlebnis, einmal einen Markt zu besuchen. Dort herrscht° immer eine persönliche Atmosphäre, und die Auswahl an verschiedenen Waren ist auch meistens gut. Der größte Betrieb° ist am Morgen. *is*

traffic

ein offener Markt
(Esslingen)

Der Markt ist meistens in der
Innenstadt. (Schwäbisch Hall)

Was verkauft man an
diesem Stand?

Die Dame kauft
Karotten. (Esslingen)

Was gibt es an diesem Stand
zu kaufen? (Tübingen)

Die Äpfel sehen aber
gut aus. (Esslingen)

Was machen die Kunden
und Verkäufer? (München)

frischer Spargel (München)

Wieviel kosten die Trauben?

An den Fruchtständen muß man eine erste Entscheidung tref-
fen°. Hier findet man eine große Auswahl an Früchten wie zum   *make…decision*
Beispiel Bananen, Pfirsiche, Erdbeeren und Kirschen. Manche
Stände verkaufen nur eine Fruchtart°. Dort kann man vielleicht saf-   *kind of fruit*
tige° Äpfel kaufen oder auch reife° Erdbeeren, besonders im Juli.   *juicy/ripe*
Wenn man damit nicht zufrieden ist, kann man weitergehen°. Die   *keep going*
Verkäufer lassen ihre Kunden auch gerne kosten. Sie wollen sicher°   *sure*
sein, daß ihre Kunden zufrieden° sind und wiederkommen.   *satisfied*

Während sich einige Stände auf Obst spezialisieren, bieten
andere hauptsächlich Gemüse an. Hier findet man zum Beispiel
Karotten, Zwiebeln, Tomaten und viele andere Gemüsearten. Die
Preise sind gut markiert. Jeder Stand hat eine Waage. Sobald man
sich entschieden° hat, etwas zu kaufen, wiegt die Verkäuferin das   *decided*
Obst oder Gemüse, und packt es in eine Tüte. Sollte man eine eigene
Einkaufstasche oder einen Korb° mitbringen, dann wird die Ver-   *basket*
käuferin das Obst oder Gemüse direkt in den Behälter° legen.   *container*

Außer den Obst- und Gemüseständen gibt es auch noch andere
Stände. Deutsche essen sehr gern Brot. Es ist deshalb nicht erstaun-
lich°, daß man auf dem Markt einen Brotstand findet. Die Brote,   *amazing*
Brötchen und anderen Backwaren° sind frisch und knusprig°, denn   *baked goods/crispy*
sie kommen am Morgen direkt von den Bäckereien°. Möchten Sie   *bakeries*
Fleisch- oder Wurstwaren kosten? Das kann man auch auf vielen
Märkten. Wenn man Käse gern ißt, findet man auch davon eine gute
Auswahl. An den Käseständen kann man oft verschiedene Käsesor-
ten° kosten, bevor man sich entscheiden muß. Manche Stände bie-   *kinds of cheese*
ten nur Eier an. Die Eier sind natürlich ganz frisch, denn sie
kommen direkt von den Bauernhöfen.

Die Deutschen lieben° Blumen und schenken sie gern ihren   *love*
Verwandten und Bekannten. Deshalb ist ein Markt ohne einen Blumenstand undenkbar°. Die Auswahl ist auch hier gut. Manchmal   *unthinkable*
gibt es auf einem Markt einen Stand mit Holzschnitzereien° oder   *woodcarvings*
sogar mit Gemälden. Auf jeden Fall° ist ein Besuch auf einem deut-   *in any case*
schen Markt für jeden zu empfehlen°.   *ist…zu empfehlen is to be recommended*

Fragen über den Dialog

1. Was für einen Markt gibt es in Hamburg und was kann man dort kaufen?
2. Zu welcher Zeit gehen die meisten Leute auf den Markt?
3. Was für Früchte kann man an einem Fruchtstand kaufen?
4. Warum lassen die Verkäufer die Kunden kosten?
5. Wie wissen die Leute, wieviel alles kostet?
6. Was machen die Verkäufer am Stand?
7. Warum ist ein Brotstand so beliebt?
8. Von wem kaufen die Verkäufer ihre Eier?

Sprachspiegel

Have students read portions of their essays. Others should ask questions about the material read.

I. Schreibe einen kurzen Aufsatz über das Thema „Ich gehe einkaufen"!

II. Beantworte diese Fragen so gut wie möglich!

1. Wozu braucht man Geld?
2. Was ißt du meistens zum Frühstück?
3. Wie kommst du am Morgen zur Schule?
4. Was machst du manchmal mit deinem Freund oder mit deiner Freundin?
5. Was hast du am letzten Wochenende gemacht?

Du bist dran!

Ask students to act out their mini-dialogs in pairs.

. . . .
Geben Sie mir ein Päckchen Kaffee.
. . . .
Ja, vielleicht noch die Erdbeermarmelade da.
. . . .

Wir sind im Juli an der Nordsee gewesen.
. . . .
Einfach herrlich.
. . . .
Leider nur zwei Wochen.

. . . .
Die sind aber nicht mehr sehr frisch.
. . . .
Dann nehme ich lieber zwei Pfund Birnen.

Können Sie die Salami in Scheiben schneiden?
. . . .
Ein halbes Pfund, bitte.
. . . .

Wie schmeckt Ihnen denn diese Wurst?
. . . .
Das freut uns. Die kommt ganz frisch aus unserer Schlachterei.
. . . .
Bitte schön.

. . . .
Direkt am Marktplatz.
. . . .
Das kann ich Ihnen leider nicht sagen.
. . . .

Können Sie die Salami in Scheiben schneiden?

Kulturecke

A Tour through a Department Store

German cities have many stores, ranging from small shops to large department stores. People who want to complete all of their shopping quickly should go to the large department store. As you enter most department stores on the ground floor *(Erdgeschoß)*, you will see a list of the departments posted at the entrance and again at the escalator. Let's take a tour through a department store, starting downstairs *(Untergeschoß)*. What will you find?

In most major department stores, you'll find a supermarket downstairs. Notice that Germans take a shopping cart and then select their groceries. At counters such as those with sausages and cold meats *(Wurst)*, you'll find sales personnel to assist you. If you want to buy pre-packed cold cuts and spreads, you can go directly to the packaged meat display and help yourself.

Besides sausages, Germans love to eat cheese *(Käse)*. A combination of these two is usually the main part of the cold evening meal called *Abendbrot*. Most Germans have their warm meal at noon. Germans prefer fresh fish to frozen fish. Therefore, it's not surprising to find a special section where fresh water and salt water fish are offered for sale.

The fruit counter closely resembles one in the U.S.; however, the unit of measurement is different. The metric pound used in Germany *(Pfund)* weighs about 10 percent more than our pound. You'll also find a bread counter with a variety of differently sized and shaped loaves. Germans are great bread eaters and can choose from 200 different kinds of bread and 30 kinds of rolls — not in the same store, of course!

Although some Germans believe that frozen foods are *ungesund* (unhealthy), you will nevertheless find a large selection in the frozen food section. Prices are clearly marked and

in der Sportabteilung

Was möchte die Dame kaufen?

Die Backwaren sind jeden Tag frisch.

verschiedene Größen

Wofür interessiert sich diese Person?

shouldn't cause any problems. If you need assistance, look for sales personnel dressed in white smocks. An unusual sight for many Americans is liquor being sold at the supermarket. After you have finished shopping, you can go directly to any of the cash registers. If you haven't brought your own shopping bag, the clerk will provide you with a plastic bag and expect you to bag your own groceries while he or she is ringing up the various items.

You'll find the greatest selection of goods on the ground floor. Shoppers usually will spend more time here than on any other floor. Cookies *(Kekse)* and candies *(Bonbons)* are enjoyed by Germans just as in our country. In many department stores you'll be asked to select your own candies and put them in a bag, which a salesperson will weigh. If you're looking for pastries, you've come to the right country. There are 1,200 different kinds to be found. With such great variety you won't have any trouble finding baked goods to suit your taste.

Standing in the record department, you may have the feeling you're back in the U.S. Most of the music on records and cassettes *(Schallplatten und Kassetten)* comes from the U.S. You'll find many well-known recordings of popular American singers, although in recent years more and more German rock groups have become popular both in Germany and on the international scene.

More than 50,000 titles are published in Germany every year. Therefore, it isn't surprising to find a fantastic selection of books displayed in the book department *(Bücherabteilung)*. Greeting cards are nearby for those who are looking for a card for a special occasion. And, of course, the section displaying gifts *(Geschenkartikel)* is usually popular with shoppers. Bargain hunters can purchase items that have been reduced considerably for quick sale. These are always well advertised. Most department stores make travel arrangements for those who are planning to go on vacation trips. A travel agency *(Reisebüro)* is quite often located on the ground floor as well.

Although small clothing items, such as socks, stockings, ties, scarfs and other special accessories, are found on the ground floor, major items of clothing for children, women and men are normally located on the first upper floor *(Erstes Obergeschoß)*. In case, you're interested in buying a pair of slacks, you should have a general idea of what size you wear. There are charts that tell you the sizes in metric measures. However, many department stores list clothing sizes also in inches to avoid confusion and disappointment later. When buying shirts, you'll have to know your size (actually the size of your neck). Shirt size 15, for instance, is actually size 38 in Germany (15 inches = 38 cm). However, shoe size 38 is equivalent to U.S. size 7. Confused? Be sure to learn the measurement system or ask a salesperson for assistance. Jeans are just as popular in Germany as they are here. American brands are prominently displayed.

Continuing your tour through the department store, you'll go to the second upper floor *(Zweites Obergeschoß)*. Here you'll find all the typical small household articles *(Haushaltsartikel)*, such as electric coffee pots and cooking utensils. The excellent quality of German porcelain and china is recognized widely throughout the world. You'll see a noticeable difference between German and American washers, dryers and refrigerators. These German appliances are quite a bit smaller than ours. This is partially due to the fact that many Germans don't have enough space in their apartments to accommodate American-sized appliances.

Television is just as popular in Germany as it is in our country. Several brands of TV sets are displayed. Many shoppers stop in the radio and television department *(Rundfunk- und Fernsehabteilung)* to watch well-known programs. In recent years, videocassette recorders have become tremendously popular with Germans.

If you're interested in furniture *(Möbel)*, you may want to go up to the third upper floor *(Drittes Obergeschoß)* and have a look. You'll notice that Germans like to buy modern sectional furniture and that they love bookshelf units, which are often prominently displayed in their living rooms.

Vokabeln

die **Abteilung,-en** department
anbieten *(bot an, angeboten)* to offer
der **Apfel,-̈** apple
die **Apfelsine,-n** orange
die **Banane,-n** banana
sich **bedienen** to help oneself
die **Bedienung** service
die **Birne,-n** pear
die **Blaubeermarmelade,-n** blueberry jam
der **Bogen,-** sheet
die **Bohne,-n** bean
die **Brombeere,-n** blackberry
das **Delikatessengeschäft,-e** delicatessen (store)
die **Dose,-n** can
das **Dutzend,-e** dozen
der **Einkauf,-̈e** purchase
der **Einkaufskorb,-̈e** shopping basket
einwickeln to wrap (up)
die **Erdbeere,-n** strawberry
das **Erdgeschoß,-sse** ground floor, main floor
die **Erdnuß,-̈sse** peanut
erwischen to get (hold of)
die **Fleischwaren** (pl.) meats
Fleisch- und Wurstwaren meats and sausages
freundlich friendly
die **Frucht,-̈e** fruit
das **Gehackte** ground meat
gekocht cooked, boiled
die **Gemüseabteilung,-en** vegetable department
die **Größe,-n** size

hängen *(hing, gehangen)* to hang
hilfsbereit helpful
die **Kassiererin,-nen** cashier
das **Kilo,-s** kilogram
die **Kirsche,-n** cherry
der **Kühlraum,-̈e** cooler
der **Laden,-̈** store
der **Ladentisch,-e** counter
die **Lebensmittel** (pl.) groceries
das **Lebensmittelgeschäft,-e** grocery store
die **Margarine** margarine
die **Obstabteilung,-en** fruit department
die Obst- und Gemüse- abteilung the fruit and vegetable department
die **Packung,-en** package
passend suitable, right
das passende Geld the right change
der **Pfirsich,-e** peach
die **Pflaume,-n** plum
das **Poliermittel,-** polish
der **Rahm** cream
saurer Rahm sour cream
registrieren to register
die **Rolltreppe,-n** escalator
die **Sache,-n** thing, item
die **Salami,-** salami
sauer sour
die **Scheibe,-n** slice
der **Schein,-e** bill, note
die **Schlachterei,-en** butcher shop
schneiden *(schnitt, geschnitten)* to cut
das **Schreibpapier** writing paper

die **Schreibwaren** (pl.) stationery
sonst otherwise
der **Spargel,-** asparagus
die **Spielwaren** (pl.) toys
der **Spinat** spinach
die **Sportabteilung,-en** sports department
die **Tüte,-n** bag
der **Urlaub,-e** vacation
den Urlaub verbringen to spend the vacation
der **Wagen,-** cart
die **Ware,-n** ware, article, product
die **Weintraube,-n** bunch of grapes, grapes
wiederkommen *(kam wieder, ist wiedergekommen)* to come again
zusammenzählen to add
die **Zwiebel,-n** onion

In welcher Abteilung
befindet sich
dieser Herr?

187

Dialog

Non-prescription medicine is sold by pharmacists. In Germany, non-prescription medicine is always kept behind the counter and cannot be picked from a shelf as in most U.S. drugstores.

In der Apotheke

JUNGE DAME: Hier, bitte schön, ein Rezept von meinem Arzt.

APOTHEKER: Ja, gut. Sie können die Medizin gleich mitnehmen. Da haben wir sie schon; genau das, was der Arzt verschrieben hat.

JUNGE DAME: Ich habe außerdem furchtbare Halsschmerzen. Haben Sie dafür etwas?

APOTHEKER: Mal nachsehen, was wir alles in der Computerliste haben. Ach ja, am besten gebe ich Ihnen diese Tabletten hier. Nehmen Sie eine davon nach jeder Mahlzeit.

JUNGE DAME: Hoffentlich werde ich diese Grippe bald los.

APOTHEKER: Bestimmt, denn diese Tabletten wirken Wunder. So, das macht 17 Mark 50 zusammen.

JUNGE DAME: Hier sind 20 Mark.

APOTHEKER: Und 2 Mark 50 zurück. Ich stemple noch Ihr Rezept. Damit ist dann alles in Ordnung.

JUNGE DAME: Haben Sie vielen Dank für Ihre Bemühung.

APOTHEKER: Gern geschehen. Und gute Besserung!

doctor's prescription is mped as evidence that the icine has been bought. y Germans get all or ions of their medical ds reimbursed through r medical insurance erage.

Fragen über den Dialog

1. Von wem hat die junge Dame ein Rezept bekommen?
2. Wie lange muß sie warten, bis der Apotheker die Medizin fertig hat?
3. Wofür soll der Apotheker einen Vorschlag machen?
4. Wie oft soll die junge Dame Tabletten nehmen?
5. Wieviel muß die junge Dame für alles bezahlen?
6. Was wünscht ihr der Apotheker?

At the Pharmacy

YOUNG LADY: Here you are, a prescription from my doctor.

PHARMACIST: O.K. You can take the medicine along right away. Here it is, exactly what the doctor prescribed.

YOUNG LADY: I have a terrible sore throat besides. Do you have something for that?

PHARMACIST: Let's see what we have on the computer list. Oh yes, the best thing for you will be these tablets. Take one of these after every meal.

YOUNG LADY: I hope I'll get rid of this flu soon.

PHARMACIST: I'm sure you will because these tablets work wonders. So, that's 17 marks and 50 pfennigs all together.

YOUNG LADY: Here are 20 marks.

PHARMACIST: And 2 marks 50 pfennigs back. I'll stamp your prescription. Then everything is in order.

YOUNG LADY: Thank you very much for your help.

PHARMACIST: You're welcome. And get well.

Nützliche Ausdrücke

Review these expressions after students have thoroughly covered the *Dialog* and *Lesestück 1*.

Ich habe Halsschmerzen.	I have a sore throat.
Haben Sie dafür etwas?	Do you have something for that?
Hoffentlich werde ich es bald los.	I hope I'll get rid of it soon.
Die Tabletten wirken Wunder.	The tablets work wonders.
Vielen Dank für Ihre Bemühung.	Thank you very much for your help.
Gern geschehen.	You're welcome. Don't mention it.
Gute Besserung!	Get well.
Was für Beschwerden hast du?	What's the trouble?
Das ist sehr vernünftig.	That's quite wise.
Er mißt den Puls.	He measures the pulse (rate).
Ich habe starke Kopfschmerzen.	I have a severe headache.
Es gibt ihm etwas zu bedenken.	It makes him think a little.
Es ist entzündet.	It's infected.
Der Arzt mißt meinen Blutdruck.	The doctor measures my blood pressure.

Sprichwort

Wer andern eine Grube gräbt, fällt selbst hinein.
(He who digs a trap for others will fall into it himself.)

He that mischief hatcheth, mischief catcheth.

Ergänzung

Personalize these questions: *Bist du schon einmal krank gewesen? Was hat dir gefehlt? Bist du zum Arzt/zur Ärztin gegangen? Was hat er/sie dir gesagt? Hat er/sie dir Medizin verschrieben?*

1. Bist du krank?
   Was fehlt dir denn?
   Wo tut's denn weh?
   Hast du Fieber?
   Fühlst du dich nicht wohl?

   Nein, ich bin ganz gesund.
   Ich habe Kopfschmerzen.
   Im Kopf. (Hals, Bauch, Fuß)
   Ja, ich habe hohes Fieber.
   Nicht besonders.
   Nein, mir ist schwindlig.
   Nein, ich habe mich erkältet.

2. Was brauchst du vielleicht, wenn du krank bist?

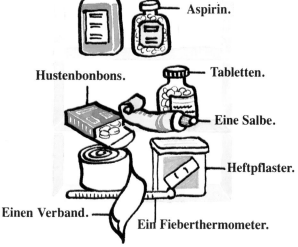

Hustensaft.
Aspirin.
Hustenbonbons.
Tabletten.
Eine Salbe.
Heftpflaster.
Einen Verband.
Ein Fieberthermometer.

Lektion 18

191

3. Warum geht Gisela heute nicht in die Schule?

den 1.3.

Lieber Herr Wehner!
Leider kann Gisela heute nicht
die Schule besuchen. Sie hat hohes
Fieber und außerdem noch eine Mandel-
entzündung. Unser Arzt hat geraten,
daß sie zwei oder drei Tage zu Hause
bleiben soll. Mit freundlichen Grüßen
Erika Bauer

Übungen

Relative Pronouns

The relative pronoun relates to the noun in the main clause (the antecedent), reflecting the case, gender and number. The relative pronouns in German are *der* and *welcher*.* The relative pronouns correspond to *who*, *which*, and *that* in English. The emphasis in this unit has been placed on the various forms of the relative pronoun, *der*.

	Singular			Plural
	masculine	*feminine*	*neuter*	
nominative	der	die	das	die
accusative	den	die	das	die
dative	dem	der	dem	denen
genitive	dessen	deren	dessen	deren

NOTE: Except for the genitive (singular and plural) and the dative plural relative pronoun, all other relative pronouns are identical to the forms of the definite article.

*The form of *welcher* is not used in the genitive case.

The relative pronoun follows its antecedent as soon as possible. It may follow the main clause or be positioned within the main clause. The verb appears at the end of a relative clause.

Beispiele:

Nominative
Der Mann, der ins Auto einsteigt, ist mein Vater.
Kennst du die Verkäuferin, die so freundlich ist?
Wo ist das Buch, das so interessant sein soll?
Die Touristen, die nach Europa fliegen, kommen aus New York.

Accusative
Wer ist der Herr, den du getroffen hast?
Wo ist die Zeitung, die du vorhin gelesen hast?
Das neue Buch, das ich gekauft habe, gefällt mir sehr.
Gibt es deutsche Städte, durch die du gefahren bist?

Dative
Der Ausländer, dem ich geholfen habe, war mir sehr dankbar.
Wo wohnt die Dame, von der du mir erzählt hast?
Das Mädchen, mit dem ich ins Kino ging, ist meine Freundin.
Das sind unsere Verwandten, denen wir ab und zu ein Geschenk schicken.

Genitive
Wo wohnt der Arzt, dessen Tochter in unsere Schule geht?
Dort ist die Angestellte, deren Haus wir gekauft haben.
Ich kenne das Mädchen, dessen Bruder Deutsch studiert.
Wer sind die Jungen, deren Motorräder so toll sind?

Folgt den Beispielen!

1. Wen kennst du?

       Ich kenne den Herrn, der hier wohnt.

Variation: Answer the question in the plural. (Ich kenne die Herren, die hier wohnen.)

   Herr / hier wohnen
   Dame / dort einkaufen
   Arzt / da drüben gehen
   Apotheker / den Kunden bedienen
   Lehrerin / diesen Wagen fahren
   Mädchen / das Rezept haben

Ich kenne die Dame, die dort einkauft.
Ich kenne den Arzt, der da drüben geht.
Ich kenne den Apotheker, der den Kunden bedient.
Ich kenne die Lehrerin, die diesen Wagen fährt.
Ich kenne das Mädchen, das das Rezept hat.

2. Die Verkäuferin, die dort steht, ist sehr freundlich.

   Frau
   Kellner
   Bäcker
   Ausländerin
   Kassiererin

Die Verkäuferin, die dort steht, ist sehr freundlich.

Die Frau, die dort steht, ist sehr freundlich.
Der Kellner, der dort steht, ist sehr freundlich.
Der Bäcker, der dort steht, ist sehr freundlich.
Die Ausländerin, die dort steht, ist sehr freundlich.
Die Kassiererin, die dort steht, ist sehr freundlich.

3. Was steht denn da?
   Kuchen
   Torte
   Wurst

Das ist der Kuchen, der so gut schmeckt.

Das ist die Torte, die so gut schmeckt.
Das ist die Wurst, die so gut schmeckt.

Variation: Ask questions about sentences on the left. *Wo wohnt mein Onkel?, Wer ist sehr jung?, Was ist so interessant?*

Kalte Platte

Wiener Schnitzel

Brot

Das ist die Kalte Platte, die so gut schmeckt.

Das ist das Wiener Schnitzel, das so gut schmeckt.

Das ist das Brot, das so gut schmeckt.

4. Da ist mein Onkel. Er wohnt in Hamburg.

Da ist mein Onkel, der in Hamburg wohnt.

Dort sitzt seine Schwester. Sie ist sehr jung.

Dort sitzt seine Schwester, die sehr jung ist.

Liest du die Zeitung? Sie ist so interessant.

Liest du die Zeitung, die so interessant ist?

Ich sehe das Kind. Es spielt auf der Straße.

Ich sehe das Kind, das auf der Straße spielt.

Er fragt den Beamten. Er kennt den Fahrplan.

Er fragt den Beamten, der den Fahrplan kennt.

Ich suche eine Verkäuferin. Sie weiß es.

Ich suche eine Verkäuferin, die es weiß.

5. Das ist eine Stadt, die ich sehen möchte.

Das ist eine Stadt, die ich sehen möchte.

ein Film

Das ist ein Film, den ich sehen möchte.

ein Museum

Das ist ein Museum, das ich sehen möchte.

eine Universität

Das ist eine Universität, die ich sehen möchte.

ein Zoo

Das ist ein Zoo, den ich sehen möchte.

eine Kapelle

Das ist eine Kapelle, die ich sehen möchte.

6. Der See, an den wir gefahren sind, ist groß.

Der See, an den wir gefahren sind, ist groß.

die Stadt / durch

Die Stadt, durch die wir gefahren sind, ist groß.

das Dorf / um

Das Dorf, um das wir gefahren sind, ist groß.

die Straße / über

Die Straße, über die wir gefahren sind, ist groß.

der Bahnhof / vor

Der Bahnhof, vor den wir gefahren sind, ist groß.

das Land / in

Das Land, in das wir gefahren sind, ist groß.

7. Dort ist die Dame. Ich kenne sie.

Dort ist die Dame, die ich kenne.

Student

Dort ist der Student, den ich kenne.

Apotheker

Dort ist der Apotheker, den ich kenne.

Kellnerin

Dort ist die Kellnerin, die ich kenne.

Kind

Dort ist das Kind, das ich kenne.

Lehrer

Dort ist der Lehrer, den ich kenne.

Variation: Ask questions about sentences on the left.

8. Der Wagen ist sehr teuer. Ich habe ihn gekauft.

Der Wagen, den ich gekauft habe, ist sehr teuer.

Das Kleid ist sehr billig. Ich habe es gesehen.

Das Kleid, das ich gesehen habe, ist sehr billig.

Das Buch ist sehr interessant. Ich habe es gelesen.

Das Buch, das ich gelesen habe, ist sehr interessant.

Die Musik ist ganz toll. Ich habe sie gehört.

Die Musik, die ich gehört habe, ist ganz toll.

Der Kuchen schmeckt gut. Ich habe ihn gegessen.

Der Kuchen, den ich gegessen habe, schmeckt gut.

9. Die Dame, der ich geholfen habe, ist meine Lehrerin.

    der Herr / sein Vater

    der Junge / ihr Bruder

    das Kind / ihre Tochter

    die Verkäuferin / seine Frau

    das Mädchen / deine Schwester

    die Friseuse / unsere Tante

Die Dame, der ich geholfen habe, ist meine Lehrerin.

Der Herr, dem ich geholfen habe, ist sein Vater.

Der Junge, dem ich geholfen habe, ist ihr Bruder.

Das Kind, dem ich geholfen habe, ist ihre Tochter.

Die Verkäuferin, der ich geholfen habe, ist seine Frau.

Das Mädchen, dem ich geholfen habe, ist deine Schwester.

Die Friseuse, der ich geholfen habe, ist unsere Tante.

Variation: Change sentences on the right to the present perfect tense. (Wo ist die Straßenbahn, mit der wir haben fahren wollen?)

10. Wo ist die Straßenbahn, mit der wir fahren sollen?

    der Zug

    die U-Bahn

    das Auto

    der Bus

    das Fahrrad

Wo ist die Straßenbahn, mit der wir fahren sollen?

Wo ist der Zug, mit dem wir fahren sollen?

Wo ist die U-Bahn, mit der wir fahren sollen?

Wo ist das Auto, mit dem wir fahren sollen?

Wo ist der Bus, mit dem wir fahren sollen?

Wo ist das Fahrrad, mit dem wir fahren sollen?

11. Das Restaurant, in dem ich arbeite, ist ganz in der Nähe.

    die Apotheke

    das Geschäft

    der Hafen

    das Café

    das Büro

Das Restaurant, in dem ich arbeite, ist ganz in der Nähe.

Die Apotheke, in der ich arbeite, ist ganz in der Nähe.

Das Geschäft, in dem ich arbeite, ist ganz in der Nähe.

Der Hafen, in dem ich arbeite, ist ganz in der Nähe.

Das Café, in dem ich arbeite, ist ganz in der Nähe.

Das Büro, in dem ich arbeite, ist ganz in der Nähe.

12. Der Mann ist alt. Ich helfe ihm.

    Die Dame hat es eilig. Ich folge ihr.

    Der Junge ist groß. Ich spreche mit ihm.

    Mein Freund wohnt um die Ecke. Ich gab ihm den Ball.

    Die Studentin ist Ausländerin. Ich habe von ihr gehört.

    Das Mädchen ist sechzehn. Ich frage nach ihr.

    Die Amerikanerin ist sehr freundlich. Ich habe ihr das Buch gegeben.

Der Mann, dem ich helfe, ist alt.

Die Dame, der ich folge, hat es eilig.

Der Junge, mit dem ich spreche, ist groß.

Mein Freund, dem ich den Ball gab, wohnt um die Ecke.

Die Studentin, von der ich gehört habe, ist Ausländerin.

Das Mädchen, nach dem ich frage, ist sechzehn.

Die Amerikanerin, der ich das Buch gegeben habe, ist sehr freundlich.

13. Kennst du sie?

    Tanten

    Onkel

    Freundinnen

Ja, das sind meine Tanten, die uns oft besuchen.

Ja, das sind meine Onkel, die uns oft besuchen.

Ja, das sind meine Freundinnen, die uns oft besuchen.

Verwandten	Ja, das sind meine Verwandten, die uns oft besuchen.
Lehrer	Ja, das sind meine Lehrer, die uns oft besuchen.

14. Wo wohnen die Ärzte? Ich habe sie gestern gesehen.

Wo wohnen die Ärzte, die ich gestern gesehen habe?

Ich schreibe meinen Freunden. Ich kenne sie gut.

Ich schreibe meinen Freunden, die ich gut kenne.

Das sind die Kinder. Wir bezahlen für sie.

Das sind die Kinder, für die wir bezahlen.

Dort drüben sind die Mädchen. Wir setzen uns neben sie.

Dort drüben sind die Mädchen, neben die wir uns setzen.

Hast du die Leute gefragt? Wir kennen sie so gut.

Hast du die Leute gefragt, die wir so gut kennen?

15. Die Ausländer arbeiten den ganzen Tag. Er wohnt bei ihnen.

Die Ausländer, bei denen er wohnt, arbeiten den ganzen Tag.

Die Touristen sprechen Deutsch. Ich gehe zu ihnen.

Die Touristen, zu denen ich gehe, sprechen Deutsch.

Die Kinder laufen sehr schnell. Du folgst ihnen.

Die Kinder, denen du folgst, laufen sehr schnell.

Die Mädchen sind seine Schwestern. Er glaubt ihnen.

Die Mädchen, denen er glaubt, sind seine Schwestern.

Kennst du die Österreicher? Du hast ihnen geholfen.

Kennst du die Österreicher, denen du geholfen hast?

16. Combine the following sentences by making a relative clause of the second sentence. Be sure to have the relative clause follow its reference word as closely as possible.

Variation: Have students follow this pattern in those sentences where it is appropriate: *Der Arzt, der es wissen wird, ist dort.*

Beispiel: *Dort ist der Arzt. Er wird es wissen.*
Dort ist der Arzt, der es wissen wird.

1. Da ist das Geschäft. Wir haben es schon lange gesucht.
2. Wann kommt die S-Bahn? Du mußt sie nehmen.
3. Wo sind die Mädchen? Sie wollen mit uns ins Theater gehen.
4. Kennst du meinen Freund? Sein Bruder ist ein guter Sportler.
5. Ich habe die Karten. Wir haben sie gestern gekauft.
6. Der Zug steht noch im Bahnhof. Ich muß in den Zug einsteigen.
7. Der Flughafen ist ganz in der Nähe. Auf dem Flughafen landen viele internationale Flugzeuge.
8. Die Touristen sprechen fast nur Englisch. Sie kommen aus Amerika.
9. Kennst du den Jungen? Er hat dir ein Geschenk mitgebracht.
10. Die Dame ist eine bekannte Ärztin. Ihr Mann ist Pilot.
11. Ihr Sohn ist vor Jahren nach Europa gegangen. Sie haben schon lange nichts von ihm gehört.
12. Meine Tante wohnt in München. Ich besuche sie oft.
13. Die Kunden studieren die Preise. Sie kommen oft hierher.
14. Der Junge ist erst acht Jahre alt. Seine Mutter gibt ihm Geld zum Einkaufen.
15. Der Beamte hat mir den Weg gezeigt. Ich habe ihn gefragt.

17. Supply the proper relative pronoun.

Variation: Have students practice the following pattern: *Den Studenten, dem du bei seiner Arbeit geholfen hast, kenne ich gut.*

1. Ich kenne den Studenten gut, _____ du bei seiner Arbeit geholfen hast.
2. Wo sind die Bücher, _____ ich Ihnen gegeben habe?
3. Hier ist der Lehrer, _____ mit dir sprechen will.
4. Besuchst du deinen Onkel, _____ Haus so riesengroß ist?
5. Warum liest du die Zeitung, _____ so sehr langweilig ist?
6. Frage doch die Kellnerin, _____ ich das Trinkgeld gegeben habe!
7. Zeigen Sie mir den Anzug, _____ ich kaufen möchte.
8. Wohnen die Jungen hier, _____ die Fahrräder gehören?
9. Das Mädchen, mit _____ ich gestern im Theater war, kommt aus Italien.
10. Gisela, _____ Eltern nach Köln geflogen sind, ist meine Freundin.
11. Die Ecke, an _____ ich gestern gewartet habe, ist gleich in der Nähe.
12. Die berühmte Stadt, durch _____ so viele Touristen fahren, liegt in Süddeutschland.
13. Viele Kunden, _____ mit der Verkäuferin zufrieden sind, kommen bestimmt wieder.
14. Da sind die amerikanischen Spieler, von _____ wir schon viel gehört haben.

Conjunctions

Coordinating

Coordinating conjunctions are used to connect two words, phrases or main clauses. The addition of a coordinating conjunction does not affect the word order of the two main clauses joined together. The most common coordinating conjunctions are:

aber	but
denn	for, because
oder	or
sondern	but (on the contrary)
und	and

Beispiele:
> *Ich möchte länger bleiben, aber ich habe keine Zeit.*
> *Er fährt nicht nach Köln, denn er hat die Stadt nicht gern.*
> *Fliegt ihr mit dem Flugzeug, oder fahrt ihr mit dem Schiff?*
> *Sie kommen nicht zu uns, sondern wir gehen zu ihnen.*
> *Werner bekommt eine Krawatte, und Paul bekommt ein Hemd.*

NOTE: After a preceding negation, use the conjunction *sondern* instead of *aber*.

Subordinating

Subordinating conjunctions are used to connect a main clause and a dependent clause. A subordinating conjunction does not affect the word order in English, but in German it does. In a sentence beginning with the main clause, the main verb of the dependent clause appears at the end of the dependent clause or the complete sentence.

Beispiele:
> *Wir gehen ins Restaurant, weil wir hungrig sind.*
> *Christa kauft ein Fahrrad, sobald sie genug Geld hat.*

In a sentence beginning with the dependent clause (the conjunction is at the beginning of the sentence), the main verb of the dependent clause appears at the end of the dependent clause (before the comma) and the main verb of the main clause is inverted.

Beispiele:

> *Weil wir hungrig sind, gehen wir ins Restaurant.*
> *Sobald sie genug Geld hat, kauft Christa ein Fahrrad.*

The most common subordinating conjunctions are:

als	when
bevor	before
bis	until
da	since (inasmuch as)
damit	so that, in order that
daß	that
ehe	before
nachdem	after (having)
ob	whether, if
obgleich, obwohl	although
seitdem	since
sobald	as soon as
solange	as long as
während	while
weil	because
wenn	when, if, whenever

NOTE: Although the two subordinating conjunctions *als* and *wenn* have similar meanings, *als* refers to a single event in the past and *wenn* refers to an action that is repeated in any tense. You can always say *immer wenn* in order to emphasize this habitual repetition.

Beispiele:

> *Als ich zehn Jahre alt war, schenkte mir mein Vater ein Fahrrad.*
> *Wenn ich nach Hause komme, muß ich meiner Mutter bei der Arbeit helfen.*

Folgt den Beispielen!

Variation: Ask questions.
Was macht sie? Wohin gehen wir? (Sie geht nach Hause. Wir gehen ins Theater.)

18. Sie geht nach Hause. Wir gehen ins Theater. (und)

> Sie geht nach Hause, und wir gehen ins Theater.

Er möchte Kaffee. Sie möchte Tee. (aber)

> Er möchte Kaffee, aber sie möchte Tee.

Der Junge schwimmt nicht. Er darf nicht. (denn)

> Der Junge schwimmt nicht, denn er darf nicht.

Die Touristen fahren zum Rathaus. Sie gehen zum Museum. (oder)

> Die Touristen fahren zum Rathaus, oder sie gehen zum Museum.

Wir essen Brot. Wir bestellen Kuchen. (oder)

> Wir essen Brot, oder wir bestellen Kuchen.

Meine Schwester fliegt nach Österreich. Ich
   fliege in die Schweiz. (aber)

Die eine Klasse fährt mit dem Zug. Die
   andere Klasse nimmt den Bus. (und)

Meine Schwester fliegt nach Österreich, aber
ich fliege in die Schweiz.

Die eine Klasse fährt mit dem Zug, und die
andere Klasse nimmt den Bus.

19. Form meaningful sentences by providing the proper coordinating conjunction.

   Beispiel: *Ich gehe auf den Fußballplatz, _____ Paul geht zu seinem Freund.*
   Ich gehe auf den Fußballplatz, und Paul geht zu seinem Freund.

1. Frau Müller kauft sich kein Kleid, _____ sie hat nicht genug Geld.
2. Peter hat Lust ins Theater zu gehen, _____ seine Freundin will lieber einen interessanten Film sehen.
3. Wir gehen heute morgen in die Stadt, _____ wir gehen später einkaufen.
4. Sie möchte kein Eis, _____ sie bestellt sich ein Stück Kuchen.
5. Susi wartet vor der Schule, _____ Renate steht an der Ecke.
6. Familie Meier fährt nicht nach Hamburg, _____ es ist zu weit.

20. Combine the following sentences using the conjunctions indicated.

Variation: Start each sentence with the conjunction. *(Wenn es warm ist, spiele ich gern Tennis.)*

   Beispiel: *Ich spiele gern Tennis. Es ist warm. (wenn)*
   Ich spiele gern Tennis, wenn es warm ist.

1. Katrin sieht fern. Helmut macht seine Hausaufgaben. (während)
2. Ich werde Fußball spielen. Es regnet. (obgleich)
3. Herr Hoffmann fährt mit dem Schiff. Herr Schulz fliegt. (aber)
4. Es ist nicht nur kalt. Es schneit auch. (sondern)
5. Sie schreibt. Walter will noch lange in Deutschland bleiben. (daß)
6. Sie sind nach Berlin gefahren. Sie haben schon viel von dieser Stadt gehört. (da)
7. Essen Sie Schweinebraten? Möchten Sie Sauerbraten? (oder)
8. Er sprach kein Deutsch. Er kam nach Deutschland. (als)
9. Was werden Sie denn machen? Sie haben das Buch gelesen. (nachdem)
10. Wir müssen uns beeilen. Wir haben keine Zeit. (denn)

21. Put the clause containing the conjunction at the beginning of the sentence. Make the necessary changes in word order.

Variation: Have students form pairs of sentences. *(Er war zu Hause. Seine Verwandten kamen zu Besuch.)*

   Beispiel: *Er war zu Hause, als seine Verwandten zu Besuch kamen.*
   Als seine Verwandten zu Besuch kamen, war er zu Hause.

1. Ich bin froh, wenn sie wieder zu uns kommen.
2. Er weiß nicht, ob er dorthin fahren soll.
3. Wir werden warten, bis sie kommt.
4. Ich kann keine Karten kaufen, solange ich kein Geld habe.
5. Das Restaurant hat gutes Essen, obgleich es nicht teuer ist.
6. Sie bekommt viel bessere Noten, seitdem sie ihre Hausaufgaben macht.
7. Er hat nicht gewußt, daß du Deutsch sprechen kannst.
8. Die Kinder spielen, während die Eltern miteinander sprechen.
9. Sie wollten schon früh in der Stadt sein, da heute die Geschäfte früh aufmachen.

Lesestück 1

Beim Arzt

Elke ist heute zur Untersuchung° ins Krankenhaus gekommen. Sie sitzt mit zwei anderen Patienten im Vorzimmer° und wartet ungeduldig, bis sie an die Reihe kommt. Endlich öffnet sich die Tür und eine Sprechstundenhilfe° bittet Elke, ins Arztzimmer zu kommen.

    Doktor Böhme begrüßt sie mit freundlichen Worten und fragt sie gleich: „Was für Beschwerden haben Sie denn?" „Furchtbare Halsschmerzen," erwidert° Elke und greift° automatisch an ihren Hals. Doktor Böhme hört sich Elkes Beschwerden mit Geduld° an. Sie sagt ihm, daß sie seit zwei Tagen fast gar nicht mehr schlucken° kann. Ihre Eltern hatten sich endlich entschlossen, sie ins Krankenhaus zu bringen. „Das war vernünftig von Ihren Eltern," meint Doktor Böhme.

    Zuerst mißt Doktor Böhme Elkes Puls. Der scheint° ganz normal zu sein. Elke erwähnt°, daß sie ab und zu starke Kopfschmerzen hat. Das gibt Doktor Böhme doch etwas zu bedenken. Zur weiteren Untersuchung bittet er Elke, ins Nebenzimmer zu kommen. Sie setzt sich auf einen Stuhl und macht den Mund auf°, damit sich Doktor Böhme ihre Mandeln° ansehen kann. Sie sind sehr entzündet°.

    Doktor Böhme will auch gleich feststellen°, ob Elke Fieber hat. Deshalb mißt er ihre Temperatur. Da Elke immer noch über Kopfschmerzen klagt°, will Doktor Böhme ihren Blutdruck messen. Der Blutdruck ist aber ganz normal.

    Schließlich stellt Doktor Böhme fest, daß Elke eine starke Erkältung° mit einer Mandelentzündung° hat. Er verschreibt ihr ein Rezept und bittet Elke, die Tabletten dreimal am Tag zu nehmen. Jetzt soll sie ein paar Tage zu Hause bleiben, bis sie wieder gesund° ist.

examination
outer office

receptionist

replies/touches
patience
swallow

seems to be
mentions

macht...auf opens
tonsils
infected

find out

complains

cold/tonsilitis

healthy

Elke sitzt im Vorzimmer.

Doktor Böhme

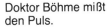
Doktor Böhme mißt
den Puls.

Der Arzt gibt
Elke ein
Fieberthermometer.

Elke hat furchtbare
Halsschmerzen.

Fragen über das Lesestück

1. Warum ist Elke im Krankenhaus?
2. Wie weiß sie, wann sie an die Reihe kommt?
3. Von welchen Schmerzen erzählt sie dem Arzt?
4. Wer hat Elke ins Krankenhaus gebracht?
5. Was macht Doktor Böhme zuerst?
6. Was gibt ihm etwas zu bedenken?
7. Was muß Elke im Nebenzimmer tun?
8. Worüber klagt Elke?
9. Hat Elke hohen Blutdruck?
10. Was stellt der Arzt fest?
11. Was soll Elke in den nächsten paar Tagen machen?
12. Was verschreibt ihr der Arzt?

Erweiterung

22. Form compound nouns by combining the appropriate words from the right side with those on the left. Indicate also the article and the meaning of each newly formed word.

1. Rinder-	platz
2. Delikatessen-	löffel
3. Bauch-	schmerzen
4. Roll-	braten
5. Suppen-	zimmer
6. Kranken-	wasser
7. Apfel-	thermometer
8. Camping-	saft
9. Laden-	entzündung
10. Arzt-	traube
11. Wein-	haus
12. Mineral-	treppe
13. Fieber-	geschäft
14. Mandel-	tisch
15. Wurst-	waren

23. Wie heißt das auf deutsch?

1. Do you have a headache?
2. What is the doctor measuring?
3. Your throat is infected.
4. Get well.
5. How is your blood pressure?
6. It makes me think somewhat.
7. I hope I get rid of my tonsilitis.
8. How many tablets should I take?

24. Beantwortet diese Frage mit einem ganzen Satz: „Wofür braucht man…?"

    Beispiel: *Aspirin*

        Aspirin braucht man für Kopfschmerzen.

1. Hustensaft
2. Verband
3. Fieberthermometer
4. Salbe
5. Tabletten

25. Beende die folgenden Sätze!

1. Wenn man einen Film sehen will, dann geht man ins _____ .
2. Wenn man krank ist, dann soll man zum _____ gehen.

3. Wenn man hungrig ist, dann kann man in einem _____ essen.

4. Wenn man nach Europa will, dann kann man mit einem _____ fliegen.

5. Wenn man studieren will, dann kann man zur _____ gehen.

6. Wenn man Medizin braucht, dann kann man sie in einer _____ bekommen.

7. Wenn man ein Zimmer sucht, dann kann man es in einem _____ finden.

8. Wenn man Geld braucht, dann kann man es in der _____ bekommen.

9. Wenn man Fleisch braucht, dann kann man es beim _____ kaufen.

10. Wenn man ein Paket schicken will, dann kann man zur _____ gehen.

26. Beschreibt die folgenden Wörter mit einem ganzen Satz!

1. Krankenhaus
2. Patient
3. Fieber
4. Apotheke
5. Arzt
6. Schmerzen
7. Rezept
8. Grippe

Ask students to write a short description, using all the eight words.

27. Beantwortet diese Fragen!

1. Bist du in letzter Zeit krank gewesen? Was hast du gehabt?
2. Zu welchem Arzt gehst du?
3. Wo kannst du deine Medizin kaufen?
4. Was soll man tun, wenn man krank ist?
5. Wo gibt es in deiner Gegend ein Krankenhaus?

Rückblick

If your students have some difficulties with these exercises, review the grammar point or topic in the lesson in which they were covered.

I. Supply first the past tense and then the present perfect tense for each of the following sentences.

1. Wir wollen nach Europa fahren.
2. Müßt ihr denn die Hausaufgaben machen?
3. Ich mag diesen Kuchen nicht.
4. Herr Hofer will früh am Morgen einkaufen.
5. Müssen Sie in die Stadt?
6. Ihr sollt die Einkaufstasche holen.
7. Können Sie bei dem Wetter fahren?
8. Er darf das nicht.
9. Willst du den Arzt besuchen?
10. Sie kann es nicht.

II. Change these sentences to the past perfect tense.

1. Wann brauchen Sie das Geld?
2. Wir waren gestern im neuen Theater.

3. Meine Freunde kommen aus dem Urlaub zurück.

4. Hast du dich gefreut?

5. Die Fluggäste steigen ein.

6. Fuhr der Herr langsam auf der Straße?

7. Wo habt ihr den Wagen geparkt?

8. Der Arzt hat alles auf dem Rezept aufgeschrieben.

9. Sahen Sie die mittelalterlichen Städte?

10. Die Dosen kosten viel.

11. Sie packt alles in die Tüte ein.

12. Endlich fanden sie den Zimmernachweis.

III. Provide an appropriate question word.

1. _____ machst du heute abend?

2. _____ hat er das Buch gegeben?

3. _____ kommen Sie zu Besuch?

4. _____ fährt die Familie denn?

5. _____ Freund hat er bei der Arbeit geholfen?

6. _____ bleibst du in der Stadt?

7. _____ wartet die Klasse auf den Bus?

8. _____ Motorrad wirst du kaufen?

9. _____ ist das Gasthaus?

10. _____ hast du auf der Straße getroffen?

11. _____ Hemd möchtest du kaufen?

12. _____ ist dieses Mädchen dort drüben?

IV. Supply the proper word for each sentence from the list below.

Apotheke	Markt
Fleischer	Einkaufstasche
Toilette	Krankenhaus
Rolltreppe	Brötchen
Gaststätte	Campingplatz
Trinkgeld	Café

1. Ein Zimmer in einem Gasthaus hat meistens keine _____ .

2. Auf dem _____ stehen viele Zelte.

3. Die Rechnung enthält 10 oder 15 Prozent _____ .

4. In vielen Hotels bekommen die Gäste zum Frühstück _____ .

5. Meine Tante ist in letzter Zeit nicht sehr gesund. Sie ist oft im _____ .

6. Die _____ ist für viele Deutsche ein beliebtes Restaurant.

7. Ich kaufe die Wurst beim _____ .

8. Obst und Gemüse kann man schon früh am Morgen auf dem _____ bekommen.

9. Viele Deutsche gehen gern in ein _____ und essen dort ein Stück Torte oder trinken ein Tasse Kaffee.

10. Mit dem Rezept gehen Sie am besten gleich zur _____ .

11. Die _____ geht bis zum vierten Stock.

12. Die Kundin steckt das Paket in ihre _____ .

Lesestück 2

Wo kann man übernachten?

Reisende°, die durch deutsche Städte fahren und Hotelzimmer suchen, brauchen nicht von einem Hotel zum anderen zu fahren. Sie fragen einfach nach dem *Zimmernachweis*° oder nach der *Tourist Information*. In diesen Büros wird man Ihnen Zimmer in verschiedenen Preisklassen° empfehlen. In manchen Städten, meistens im Zentrum gelegen°, gibt es eine *Hotelinformation*. Es ist gewöhnlich ein Stand, an dem die Namen der verschiedenen Hotels angeschlagen sind. Ein Stadtplan zeigt genau, wo die einzelnen Hotels liegen. Von diesem Stand kann man die Hotels direkt anrufen und sich dort nach den Einzelheiten erkundigen°.

    In kleineren Städten gibt es meistens keinen Zimmernachweis. Dort sieht man am Stadtrand° oft eine große Tafel mit den Schildern der einzelnen Hotels, Gasthäuser und Pensionen°. Die Besucher müssen dann selbst dort nach Zimmern fragen. Die Schilder geben den Gästen wichtige Hinweise°, wie zum Beispiel den Namen der Pension und andere Einzelheiten. Manche Schilder zeigen Reisenden sogar die Richtung und die genaue Entfernung zum Gasthaus.

    Ein Gasthaus ist ein typisches und preiswertes deutsches Hotel. Dort kann man auch immer gut essen. Nachdem Sie sich entschlossen haben, in einem Gasthaus zu übernachten, müssen Sie zuerst ein Formular° ausfüllen. Die wichtigsten Angaben sind der Name (Vor- und Nachname), die Anschrift, das Geburtsdatum, der Geburtsort und die Staatsangehörigkeit°. In den meisten Hotels (kleinen oder großen) schließt der Preis des Zimmers das Frühstück mit ein°. Um sicher zu sein, fragen Sie am besten gleich bei der Ankunft° danach. Die Zimmer in einem Gasthaus sind einfach und sauber°. Eine Toilette oder sogar ein Badezimmer gibt es dort nicht

travelers

hotel referral agency

price categories

located

sich nach… erkundigen inquire about

outskirts of city

type of inn

instructions

form

citizenship

schließt…ein includes
arrival
clean

eine Hotelinformation (Freiburg)

im Hotel

Was beschreibt das Schild?

Sind noch Zimmer
frei? (Füssen)

Es gibt Hotels in allen Preisklassen.

Die Zimmer in einem
Gasthaus sind einfach.

In vielen Hotelzimmern
gibt es Federbetten.

In den meisten Hotels schließt der
Preis das Frühstück mit ein.

Viele Hotels sind alt aber
gemütlich. (Rothenburg)

Pensionen sind sehr
beliebt.

Was steht auf diesem Schild?

Viele übernachten gern
auf Campingplätzen.

im Zimmer. Die finden Sie aber auf demselben° Stock. Seife müssen Sie meistens selbst mitbringen. *the same*

Manche kleine Hotels, besonders in Süddeutschland, sehen oft farbig° aus und laden die Reisenden freundlich ein. Hotels gibt es in allen Preisklassen. Es kommt nur darauf an, was Sie für ein Zimmer ausgeben wollen. Ein Hotel-Garni bedeutet°, daß es dort nur Frühstück gibt und kein Restaurant, wie es sonst in Hotels üblich ist. Viele deutsche Hotels sind alt aber gemütlich. In den Städten sowie in den bekannten Ferienorten° finden Sie erstklassige Hotels. Dort müssen Sie oft schon vorher Zimmer bestellen, besonders im Sommer. Sie können natürlich auch in den großen internationalen Hotels übernachten. Diese Hotels bieten Ihnen allen Luxus° und Komfort°. Selbstverständlich sind die Preise hoch. Die Gäste in diesen Hotels kommen nicht nur aus Deutschland, sondern auch aus dem Ausland. *colorful* *means* *vacation places* *luxury/comfort*

Wenn Sie eine preiswerte Übernachtung suchen, dann ist es ratsam°, in einer Pension zu übernachten. Die Besitzer wohnen in demselben Haus und vermieten° nur ein paar Zimmer. Die Atmosphäre in einer Pension ist immer sehr gemütlich und persönlich. Wenn Ihnen eine Pension nicht recht ist, haben Sie die Möglichkeit, in einer Jugendherberge zu übernachten. Die gibt es überall in Deutschland. Manche Jugendherbergen sehen moderner aus als viele Hotels. Allerdings übernachten mehrere Personen zusammen im Zimmer. Eine Jugendherberge ist natürlich sehr geeignet° für Jugendliche, die nicht viel Geld ausgeben möchten. Campingplätze sind noch preiswerter und beliebter als Jugendherbergen. In Deutschland haben Sie eine Auswahl von 3 000 Campingplätzen. Die Reisenden kommen mit Zelten° oder mit Wohnwagen° und verbringen manchmal eine oder zwei Wochen auf einem Campingplatz. *wise* *rent* *suitable* *tents/campers*

Fragen über das Lesestück

1. Wie können Reisende in Deutschland ein Hotel finden?
2. Was ist eine *Hotelinformation?* Wo findet man sie meistens?
3. Wie kann man in kleineren Städten ein Hotel finden?
4. Was steht alles auf den Schildern?
5. Wie sind die Mahlzeiten in einem Gasthaus?
6. Was muß man alles auf einem Anmeldeformular ausfüllen?
7. Wonach soll man gleich bei der Ankunft fragen?
8. Wo gibt es eine Toilette in einem Gasthaus?
9. Was ist ein Hotel-Garni?
10. Was ist für Reisende ratsam während der Sommermonate zu tun?
11. Was ist eine Pension?
12. Gibt es in Deutschland viele Campingplätze?
13. Womit kommen die Reisenden zu den Campingplätzen?

Sprachspiegel

After completion of this dialog, have students act them out in class.

I. Schreibe einen Dialog über das Thema „Ein Besuch beim Arzt"!

II. Pretend that you are living in Germany. While walking along, you are stopped by a tourist who has several questions that you'll answer.

Have students take parts of this dialog situation, one reading the questions and another responding accordingly.

1. Können Sie mir bitte sagen, wo die Hotelinformation ist?
2. Wie kommt man am besten dorthin?
3. Wissen Sie vielleicht, wo es hier in der Nähe ein gutes Hotel gibt?
4. Können Sie dieses Hotel beschreiben?
5. Was für Sehenswürdigkeiten gibt es in Ihrer Stadt?
6. Braucht man ein Auto, um das alles zu sehen?

Du bist dran!

Ask students to respond to the individual statements or questions.

Ich habe eine furchtbare Grippe.

. . . .

Der kann auch nichts dagegen tun.

. . . .

. . . .

Mein Arzt hat es verschrieben.

. . . .

Es ist sehr schwer zu lesen.

Seit wann hast du hohes Fieber?

. . . .

Hast du dich denn erkältet?

. . . .

Wie oft mußt du diese Tabletten nehmen?

. . . .

Schmecken sie wenigstens gut?

. . . .

. . . .

Schon seit drei Wochen.

. . . .

Ich werde morgen mit meinem Arzt sprechen.

. . . .

Hat das Zimmer eine Toilette?

. . . .

Nein, danke. Ich möchte lieber eine Toilette im Zimmer.

. . . .

Dafür bezahle ich gern etwas mehr.

Kulturecke

Housing

Housing conditions in Germany have changed dramatically during the past three to four decades. Completely new, modern cities have sprung up in places where pastures used to be. The improvement in the standard of living is strongly reflected in the increasing number of modern communities. Generally, these new communities can be found on the outskirts of major cities.

Nearly 60 percent of all Germans rent apartments. This is because land is scarce and costly. Houses cost considerably more than they do in the U.S. Therefore, the demand for new apartment buildings is quite heavy. Although living conditions have improved, not all the newer apartment complexes are luxurious by any means. Many provide adequate living space but have limited facilities such as playgrounds and parks. Most apartments are small. This is especially true of a typical apartment kitchen, which is small but extremely functional. Every appliance, gadget and piece of household equipment has its special place because Germans use every inch effectively. The family members usually gather in the living room. Here they can pursue their own interests, such as watching television, reading or knitting. The bedrooms in a German apartment are quite small too. Many families set up bunkbeds to accommodate their children.

Some older apartment buildings have been completely renovated and painted in bright colors to improve the neighborhood. Since most apartment dwellers do not have a yard of their own, there has been a demand for tiny cottages on small lots called *Kleingärten* or *Schrebergärten*. Usually there are hundreds of these lots at the edge of the city. Here Germans can relax in their spare time, plant vegetables, fruits and flowers and enjoy privacy away from their congested apartment buildings.

Fast 60% aller Deutschen mieten Wohnungen. (Hamburg)

In Wulfen hat man viele neue Wohnungen gebaut.

im Wohnzimmer

eine moderne neue Wohnung
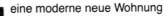

German families owning single family houses are in the minority. Many houses have been passed on from generation to generation. Germans love fences, which guarantee their privacy by carefully defining their property lines. Bigger houses or mansions, which before World War II were the property of the wealthy, are often divided up so that two or more families can afford them. Although many of these larger houses are still located in the city proper, there are also old, established and formerly wealthy residential areas in some suburban locations.

Most of the newly built houses are found outside the city. The land often costs as much as the house itself. Many Germans who have built their houses in recent years are fairly well-to-do. Because of the high cost of property, Germans who cannot afford a house may be able to buy a condominium. Here they will enjoy most of the conveniences of a house.

The small towns have not seen as rapid a growth as the cities. Only one-fifth of the total population lives in smaller towns. However, even here houses are built at an increasing rate. It's still customary to put up a small tree on top of a house after the basic frame has been constructed.

The interior as well as exterior of many farm houses has improved and kept pace with city homes, although the basic structure may be the same as it has been for a hundred years or more. Farms in the Black Forest area are quite isolated. Of all the German farm areas, the Black Forest has to cope most with the weather; it rains and snows here often. The roof line of Black Forest farm houses slopes quite steeply to protect the house against bad weather conditions. Typically, the living quarters are on one side of the house. On the other side of the house, under the same roof, are the animals.

Houses are markedly different in style from Bavaria to the North Sea. In North Germany most houses are built with brick and many have thatched roofs. In South Germany less brick but more wood is used in the construction of houses. Regardless of where they live, Germans always decorate their homes inside and outside with flowers and keep their front and backyards in impeccable shape.

ein neues Haus am Bodensee (Konstanz)

ein altes Haus im Schwarzwald (Gutach)

ein kleines Dorf (Bayern)

Nur ein Fünftel der Bevölkerung wohnt auf dem Lande. (Füssen)

Vokabeln

ach oh
die **Apotheke,-n** pharmacy
das **Arztzimmer,-** doctor's office
das **Aspirin** aspirin
außerdem besides
automatisch automatic(ally)
der **Bauch,-̈e** stomach
die **Bauchschmerzen** (pl.) stomachache
bedenken to think over, consider
Es gibt ihm zu bedenken. It makes him think.
die **Bemühung,-en** trouble, effort
die **Beschwerde,-n** complaint, trouble
Beschwerden haben to have trouble
die **Besserung,-en** improvement
Gute Besserung! Get well.
bestellen to reserve
der **Blutdruck** blood pressure
der **Campingplatz,-̈e** camping ground
damit so that, in order that
denn because, for
der **Doktor,-en** doctor
ehe before
entzündet infected
sich **erkälten** to catch a cold
die **Erkältung,-en** cold
sich **erkundigen nach** to inquire about, ask for/about
erwähnen to mention
erwidern to reply
fehlen to be missing
Was fehlt dir? What's wrong with you?
feststellen to determine, find out
das **Fieber** fever
das **Fieberthermometer,-** fever thermometer
freundlich friendly
mit freundlichen Grüßen sincerely
fühlen to feel
sich wohl fühlen to feel well
furchtbar terrible, awful
die **Geduld** patience
geschehen (geschieht, geschah, ist geschehen) to happen, occur
gern geschehen you're welcome, don't mention it

gesund healthy, well
greifen an (griff an, angegriffen) to touch
die **Grippe,-n** flu
der **Gruß,-̈e** greeting
mit freundlichen Grüßen sincerely
die **Halsschmerzen** (pl.) sore throat
das **Heftpflaster,-** adhesive tape, Band-Aid
der **Hustonbonbon,-s** (also: das Bonbon) cough drop
der **Hustensaft,-̈e** cough syrup
klagen to complain
die **Kopfschmerzen** (pl.) headache
krank sick, ill
das **Krankenhaus,-̈er** hospital
loswerden to get rid of
die **Mandel,-n** tonsil
die **Mandelentzündung** tonsilitis
die **Medizin** medicine
meinen to think, be of the opinion
messen (mißt, maß, gemessen) to measure
nachdem after (having)
das **Nebenzimmer,-** adjacent room
normal normal
obgleich although
obwohl although
das **Päckchen,-** packet
der **Patient,-en** patient
der **Puls,-e** pulse
raten (rät, riet, geraten) to advise, give advice
das **Rezept,-e** prescription
die **Rückenschmerzen** (pl.) backache
die **Salbe,-n** ointment
scheinen (schien, geschienen) to seem, appear
schlucken to swallow
der **Schmerz,-en** pain
schwindlig dizzy
Mir ist schwindlig. I'm dizzy.
seitdem since
solange wie as long as
die **Sprechstundenhilfe,-n** receptionist, (doctor's) assistant
stark severe
die **Tablette,-n** tablet, pill

die **Temperatur,-en** temperature
die **Untersuchung,-en** medical examination
der **Verband,-̈e** bandage
vernünftig sensible, wise
verschreiben (verschrieb, verschrieben) to write out (a prescription)
das **Vorzimmer,-** outer office
während while
weh: weh tun to hurt
Es tut mir weh. It hurts me.
weil because
wenn when, if, whenever
wirken to work, effect
Es wirkt Wunder. It works wonders.
wohl well
sich wohl fühlen to feel well
das **Wunder,-** wonder, miracle
die **Zahnschmerzen** (pl.) toothache
zurück back

Burkheim, ein Dorf in Süddeutschland

Dialog

Driver's instruction is quite expensive in Germany. To receive a driver's license, the driver must be 18 or older and have passed a driver's test after many hours of instruction that is given by private companies.

Beim Fahrunterricht

FAHRLEHRER: Heute fangen wir mit dem Fahren an. Bitte schön, hier sind die Schlüssel. Erklären Sie mir alle Einzelheiten!

CLAUDIA: Na, hoffentlich geht's gut...Da rechts ist das Gaspedal, in der Mitte die Bremse, und ganz links die Kupplung.

FAHRLEHRER: Und was haben wir hier?

CLAUDIA: Das ist die Schaltung. Damit werden die vier Gänge eingelegt. Vor dem Losfahren muß natürlich die Handbremse gelöst werden.

FAHRLEHRER: Sehr gut. Und wie geht's jetzt weiter?

CLAUDIA: Zunächst stelle ich den Innenspiegel ein. Dasselbe mache ich auch mit dem Außenspiegel.

FAHRLEHRER: Jetzt beschreiben Sie mir mal das Armaturenbrett.

FAHRLEHRER: Fahren Sie bitte langsam über den Parkplatz!

CLAUDIA: Wohin soll ich nun weiterfahren?

FAHRLEHRER: Auf die Straße, bitte. Versuchen Sie den Wagen an die Bordsteinkante zu fahren. Ja, aber der Abstand ist viel zu weit. Das muß nochmal geübt werden.

CLAUDIA: Ja, diesmal war es besser.

FAHRLEHRER: Nun parken Sie den Wagen, bitte...Das haben Sie gut gemacht.

CLAUDIA: Wofür wird denn das gebraucht?

FAHRLEHRER: Das ist der Wagenheber. Den brauchen Sie, wenn Sie die Reifen wechseln.

CLAUDIA: Unglaublich, was so alles unter der Motorhaube steckt.

FAHRLEHRER: Na, ich werde Ihnen die wichtigsten Motorteile jetzt ganz kurz erklären.

Fragen über den Dialog

1. Warum gibt der Fahrlehrer Claudia die Schlüssel?
2. Was befindet sich rechts und links von der Bremse?
3. Wozu braucht man eine Schaltung?
4. Warum stellt Claudia den Innen- und den Außenspiegel ein?
5. Was soll Claudia dem Fahrlehrer noch beschreiben?
6. Was muß Claudia noch einmal machen? Warum?
7. Was hat Claudia gut gemacht?
8. Wozu braucht man einen Wagenheber?
9. Was erklärt der Fahrlehrer Claudia zuletzt?

Driver's Training

DRIVING INSTRUCTOR: We'll start driving today. Here are the keys. Explain everything to me.

CLAUDIA: I hope everything will go well…There on the right is the gas pedal, in the middle the brake and, over on the left, the clutch.

DRIVING INSTRUCTOR: And what do we have here?

CLAUDIA: That's the shift. Any one of the four gears will be engaged with it. Of course, before driving off, you'll have to release the hand brake first.

DRIVING INSTRUCTOR: Very well. And how do we continue?

CLAUDIA: First, I'll adjust the inside mirror. I'll do the same with the outside mirror.

DRIVING INSTRUCTOR: Why don't you describe the dashboard to me.

DRIVING INSTRUCTOR: Please drive slowly across the parking lot.

CLAUDIA: Where should I drive now?

DRIVING INSTRUCTOR: Onto the street, please. Try to drive the car close to the curb. O.K., but you are too far away. You'll have to practice that again.

CLAUDIA: O.K., this time it was better.

DRIVING INSTRUCTOR: Now park the car, please…You did that well.

CLAUDIA: What's that used for?

DRIVING INSTRUCTOR: That's the jack. You need it to change the tires.

CLAUDIA: It's unbelievable what there is under the hood.

DRIVING INSTRUCTOR: Well, I'll explain to you now quickly the most important motor parts.

Claudia stellt den Innenspiegel ein.

Nützliche Ausdrücke

Practice these expressions, which students have learned in the *Dialog* and *Lesestück 1*.

Ich lege den Gang ein.	I'm putting the car into gear.
Lösen Sie die Handbremse!	Release the hand brake.
Er stellt den Spiegel ein.	He is adjusting the mirror.
Das muß nochmal geübt werden.	You'll have to practice that again.
Hast du das gut gemacht?	Did you do that well?
Müssen Sie die Reifen wechseln?	Do you have to change the tires?
Sein Wagen will einfach nicht weiter.	His car just won't go any further.
Wir suchen nach der Ursache.	We are looking for the cause.
Er hat eine Panne.	He has car trouble.
Der Wagen muß abgeschleppt werden.	The car has to be towed away.
Er untersucht den Wagen.	He checks the car.
Eine Zündkerze ist defekt.	A spark plug is defective.
Müssen die Scheibenbremsen repariert werden?	Do the disc brakes have to be repaired?
Mein Wagen wird inspiziert.	My car is being inspected.
Was muß installiert werden?	What has to be installed?

Sprichwort

Wo gehobelt wird, fallen Späne.
  (Where one planes, there will be shavings.)

You cannot make an omelette
  without breaking eggs.

Ergänzung

Ask such questions as *Wofür ist ein Nummernschild?*, *Wozu braucht man einen Sicherheitsgurt (ein Steuerrad, einen Kofferraum)?*, *Wie sieht dein Wagen (der Wagen deiner Eltern) aus?*

1. Die Teile eines Autos

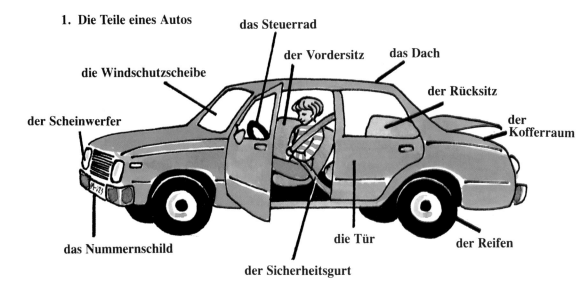

das Steuerrad

der Vordersitz

das Dach

die Windschutzscheibe

der Rücksitz

der Scheinwerfer

der Kofferraum

das Nummernschild

die Tür

der Reifen

der Sicherheitsgurt

2. Verkehrsschilder

Have students describe the meaning of these signs. *(Erkläre die einzelnen Schilder auf deutsch!)*

Nur für **Fußgänger**

Vorfahrtstraße
(Die anderen müssen warten)

Nur für **Radfahrer**
(Für Fußgänger nicht erlaubt)

Vorfahrt gewähren!
(Die anderen dürfen zuerst fahren)

Vorfahrt
nur an der nächsten Kreuzung
(Die anderen müssen warten)

Halt!
Vorfahrt gewähren!
(Die anderen dürfen zuerst fahren)

Gemeinsamer Weg für Radfahrer und Fußgänger

Hier helfen
Schülerlotsen
beim Überqueren
der Fahrbahn

Fußgängerunterführung

Kinder
(Fahrer aufpassen!)

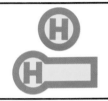

Fußgängerüberweg

Baustelle
(Fahrer und Fußgänger
aufpassen!)

Straßenbahnhaltestelle
und
Bushaltestelle

U-Bahn   S-Bahn   Straßenbahn   Bus

Übungen

Passive Voice

As in English, there is an active and a passive voice in German. A sentence like *Der Schüler fragt den Lehrer* is considered to be active, since the action is started by the subject, namely *der Schüler*. The same idea, however, can also be expressed as follows: *Der Lehrer wird von dem Schüler gefragt.* (The teacher is being asked by the student.) As you can readily see, the original subject of the active sentence is now passively involved. *Der Lehrer* is now the subject of the new sentence. Thus the previous active voice of *der Schüler* has changed to the so-called passive voice *von dem Schüler* (by the student).

Active:	Der Schüler	fragt	den Lehrer.	

Passive:	Der Lehrer	wird	von dem Schüler	gefragt.

From the illustration above you will notice that there are basically three changes that take place in converting an active sentence to the passive. These changes are as follows:

1. The subject becomes the dative case after the preposition *von*.
   (der Schüler   von dem Schüler)
2. The active verb form is changed to the passive verb form.
   (fragt   wird…gefragt)
   The auxiliary verb *werden* and the past participle of the main verb are used to form the passive voice.
3. The direct object (accusative) becomes the subject (nominative) of the new passive sentence.
   (den Lehrer   der Lehrer)

In the passive the focus is placed on the subject of the sentence. The originator of the action is given only secondary importance.

Unless you need to know where the action comes from, you can eliminate the original source of action. Thus, the sentence *Der Lehrer wird von dem Schüler gefragt* can be changed to *Der Lehrer wird gefragt.*

The most frequently used tenses in the passive are the present, the past and the present perfect. For the sake of completeness, the past perfect and the future tense have also been listed below.

NOTE: In situations in which no specific person is indicated, a passive construction can be replaced by an active construction.

Beispiele: *Man hat das Auto für viel Geld gekauft.*
(The car was bought for a lot of money.)
Man hat diese Geschichte ein paar Mal erzählt.
(This story was told several times.)

In an impersonal passive construction, the subject is the pronoun *es*.

Beispiele: *Es wird viel gelesen.*
(They read a lot.) or (A lot of reading is being done.)
Es wird gesagt, daß er gut Deutsch sprechen kann.
(They say he can speak German well.)

Passive verb forms

	Present *(is asked* or *is being asked)*		**Past** *(was asked)*	
ich	werde		wurde	
du	wirst		wurdest	
er, sie, es	wird	gefragt	wurde	gefragt
wir	werden		wurden	
ihr	werdet		wurdet	
sie, Sie	werden		wurden	

	Present Perfect *(have been asked)*		**Past Perfect** *(had been asked)*	
ich	bin		war	
du	bist		warst	
er, sie, es	ist	gefragt worden	war	gefragt worden
wir	sind		waren	
ihr	seid		wart	
sie, Sie	sind		waren	

	Future *(will be asked)*	
ich	werde	
du	wirst	
er, sie, es	wird	gefragt werden
wir	werden	
ihr	werdet	
sie, Sie	werden	

Folgt den Beispielen!

1. Wird das Haus gebaut?   Ja, es wird gebaut.

Variation: *Baut man das Haus? Ja, man baut es.*

   Wird der Student gefragt?   Ja, er wird gefragt.

   Wird das Buch gelesen?   Ja, es wird gelesen.

   Wird der Koffer getragen?   Ja, er wird getragen.

   Wird die Zeitung gekauft?   Ja, sie wird gekauft.

   Wird das Rathaus besucht?   Ja, es wird besucht.

2. Was wird gemacht?   Es wird Fußball gespielt.

   Fußball spielen

   Kuchen essen   Es wird Kuchen gegessen.

   Auto fahren   Es wird Auto gefahren.

   darüber sprechen   Es wird darüber gesprochen.

bei ihm anrufen | Es wird bei ihm angerufen.

eine Zeitung lesen | Es wird eine Zeitung gelesen.

3. Wir werden gefragt. | **Wir wurden gefragt.**

Ich werde angerufen. | Ich wurde angerufen.

Der Film wird gezeigt. | Der Film wurde gezeigt.

Gisela wird eingeladen. | Gisela wurde eingeladen.

Werden diese Bücher gelesen? | Wurden diese Bücher gelesen?

Wird viel Geld ausgegeben? | Wurde viel Geld ausgegeben':

Deutsch wird hier gesprochen. | Deutsch wurde hier gesprochen

Ihr werdet geholt. | Ihr wurdet geholt.

4. Wir werden gesucht. (er) | **Wir werden von ihm gesucht.**

Variation: Change the sentences on the right to the active voice. *(Er sucht uns.)*

Ich werde besucht. (mein Onkel) | Ich werde von meinem Onkel besucht.

Die Medizin wird verschrieben. (Ärztin) | Die Medizin wird von der Ärztin verschrieben.

Werden die Fahrräder gekauft? (ihr) | Werden die Fahrräder von euch gekauft?

Es wird alles erklärt. (der Lehrer) | Es wird alles von dem Lehrer erklärt.

Die Karten werden geholt. (wir) | Die Karten werden von uns geholt.

Die Einzelheiten werden beschrieben. (ich) | Die Einzelheiten werden von mir beschrieben.

5. Ich wurde eingeladen. | **Ich bin eingeladen worden.**

Variation: *Man lud mich ein. Man hat mich eingeladen.*

Es wurde viel darüber gesprochen. | Es ist viel darüber gesprochen worden.

Das Buch wurde schnell gelesen. | Das Buch ist schnell gelesen worden.

Die Schüler wurden gefragt. | Die Schüler sind gefragt worden.

Das Telegramm wurde geschickt. | Das Telegramm ist geschickt worden.

Das Haus wurde nicht gebaut. | Das Haus ist nicht gebaut worden.

Der Tanz wurde spät angefangen. | Der Tanz ist spät angefangen worden.

6. Die Karten sind gekauft worden. (meine Freundin) | **Die Karten sind von meiner Freundin gekauft worden.**

Variation: *Wer hat die Karten gekauft? Meine Freundin hat sie gekauft.*

Das Kind ist gesucht worden. (seine Eltern) | Das Kind ist von seinen Eltern gesucht worden.

Der Beamte ist gefragt worden. (ich) | Der Beamte ist von mir gefragt worden.

Die Kalte Platte ist gegessen worden. (wir) | Die Kalte Platte ist von uns gegessen worden.

Die Früchte sind getragen worden. (der Kunde) | Die Früchte sind von dem Kunden getragen worden.

Ich bin angerufen worden. (mein Freund) | Ich bin von meinem Freund angerufen worden.

---

7. Change the following sentences from the active to the passive. Do not change the tense.

Beispiel: *Wir sahen diesen Film gestern.*
Dieser Film wurde von uns gestern gesehen.

1. Hat der Schüler das Buch gelesen?
2. Unser Lehrer zeigt einen interessanten Film.
3. Meine Eltern bauten das Haus.
4. Die Touristen haben das Verkehrsbüro gesucht.
5. Deine Freunde laden uns ein.
6. Warum sagt ihr nichts?
7. Ich habe einen Brief geschrieben.
8. Haben Sie die Handbremse gelöst?
9. Frau Schulz kauft einen Mantel.
10. Wir haben das Theater besucht.

8. **Change the following sentences from the passive to the active. Do not change the tense.**

> **Beispiel:** *Er wird von der Polizei gesucht.*
> *Die Polizei sucht ihn.*

1. Das mittelalterliche Dorf ist von uns besucht worden.
2. Die neuen Autos werden von vielen Leuten schon jetzt gekauft.
3. Gisela wurde von ihrem Vater für ihre gute Arbeit bezahlt.
4. Bekannte Musik wird von der Kapelle gespielt.
5. Mein Bruder ist von Erika angerufen worden.
6. Wir wurden von unserem Onkel nach Hause gefahren.
7. Die amerikanische Zeitung ist von allen Studenten gelesen worden.
8. Das Mittagessen wird heute von meiner Schwester gekocht.
9. Das bekannte Museum wird von den Ausländern sehr bestaunt.
10. Das Geld ist schnell von mir ausgegeben worden.

Folgt den Beispielen!

9. Der Mann wird von den Leuten gesucht.

   Der Mann ist von den Leuten gesucht worden.

Die Schüler werden von dem Lehrer gefragt.

   Die Schüler sind von dem Lehrer gefragt worden.

Wird der Aufsatz von der Klasse geschrieben?

   Ist der Aufsatz von der Klasse geschrieben worden?

Das Buch wird schnell von ihm gelesen.

   Das Buch ist schnell von ihm gelesen worden.

Wann wird das Haus von ihnen gebaut?

   Wann ist das Haus von ihnen gebaut worden?

Wirst du früh von deinem Vater gerufen?

   Bist du früh von deinem Vater gerufen worden?

Die Reise wird von uns geplant.

   Die Reise ist von uns geplant worden.

10. Wir fragen ihn.

   Er wird von uns gefragt.

Variation: Change the sentences on the right as follows: *Wir fragen ihn.*

Die Klasse schreibt einen Aufsatz.

   Ein Aufsatz wird von der Klasse geschrieben.

Sie sprechen Deutsch.

   Deutsch wird von ihnen gesprochen.

Er holt die Zeitung.

   Die Zeitung wird von ihm geholt.

Kocht deine Mutter das Essen?

   Wird das Essen von deiner Mutter gekocht?

Ihr besucht das Museum.	Das Museum wird von euch besucht.
Paul bringt ein Geschenk.	Ein Geschenk wird von Paul gebracht.
Ich trinke ein Glas Milch.	Ein Glas Milch wird von mir getrunken.
Kauft Gabi eine Gitarre?	Wird eine Gitarre von Gabi gekauft?

11. Er sieht den Mann.

Variation: Change the sentences on the right to the active voice. (*Er hat den Mann gesehen.*)

Der Mann ist von ihm gesehen worden.

Zeigen Sie den Film?	Ist der Film von Ihnen gezeigt worden?
Wir lesen ein paar Bücher.	Ein paar Bücher sind von uns gelesen worden.
Die Lehrerin fragt die Klasse.	Die Klasse ist von der Lehrerin gefragt worden.
Suchst du den Wagen?	Ist der Wagen von dir gesucht worden?
Schreibt er eine Karte?	Ist eine Karte von ihm geschrieben worden?
Die Familie plant eine Reise.	Eine Reise ist von der Familie geplant worden.
Der Student beschreibt alle Einzelheiten.	Alle Einzelheiten sind von dem Studenten beschrieben worden.

12. Der Ball wird von ihr gesucht.

Sie sucht den Ball.

Die Hose wird von mir bezahlt.	Ich bezahle die Hose.
Zwei Karten werden von dem Mädchen bezahlt.	Das Mädchen bezahlt zwei Karten.
Englisch wird von uns nicht gesprochen.	Wir sprechen nicht Englisch.
Ein Film wird morgen von ihnen gezeigt.	Sie zeigen morgen einen Film.
Die Ausländer werden von uns gefragt.	Wir fragen die Ausländer.
Wirst du von deinen Freunden eingeladen?	Laden deine Freunde dich ein?

13. Deutsche Musik ist von der Kapelle gespielt worden.

Variation: Have students ask two questions for each of the sentences on the left. (*Was ist von der Kapelle gespielt worden? Von wem ist deutsche Musik gespielt worden?*)

Die Kapelle hat deutsche Musik gespielt.

Wir sind von meinem Onkel eingeladen worden.	Mein Onkel hat uns eingeladen.
Reiseschecks sind von den Touristen eingelöst worden.	Die Touristen haben Reiseschecks eingelöst.
Der Wagen ist von ihm geparkt worden.	Er hat den Wagen geparkt.
Das Geschenk ist von meiner Mutter gekauft worden.	Meine Mutter hat das Geschenk gekauft.
Sie ist von Joachim angerufen worden.	Joachim hat sie angerufen.
Ein Wagenheber ist von ihnen gebraucht worden.	Sie haben einen Wagenheber gebraucht.

14. Man besuchte viele Städte.

Variation: Have students answer each question. (*Von wem wurden viele Städte besucht? Viele Städte wurden von Ausländern besucht.*)

Viele Städte wurden besucht.

Man sprach Deutsch.	Deutsch wurde gesprochen.
Man besichtigte das Museum.	Das Museum wurde besichtigt.
Man kaufte Kleider.	Kleider wurden gekauft.
Man suchte den Flughafen.	Der Flughafen wurde gesucht.
Man trank Kaffee.	Kaffee wurde getrunken.
Man beschrieb die Reise.	Die Reise wurde beschrieben.

15. In der Englischstunde wird viel gesprochen.　Es wird viel in der Englischstunde gesprochen.

Um sieben wird gegessen.　Es wird um sieben gegessen.
Am Abend wird oft gespielt.　Es wird am Abend oft gespielt.
In der Schule wird gelernt.　Es wird in der Schule gelernt.
Während des Tages wird gearbeitet.　Es wird während des Tages gearbeitet.
Jeden Freitag wird eingekauft.　Es wird jeden Freitag eingekauft.
In der Tanzschule wird viel getanzt.　Es wird in der Tanzschule viel getanzt.

16. **Change the following sentences into the passive. Restate each sentence in the present, past, and present perfect tense.**

　　Beispiel: *Wir laden dich ein.*
　　　　　　Du wirst von uns eingeladen.
　　　　　　Du wurdest von uns eingeladen.
　　　　　　Du bist von uns eingeladen worden.

　1. Sie kauft Obst.
　2. Die Kinder suchen den Ball.
　3. Spricht er Deutsch?
　4. Ihr braucht kein Buch.
　5. Wir planen schon jetzt eine Reise.

17. **Complete each blank below. Use the verbs and the tense indicated in parentheses. Select either the active or passive voice to make each sentence meaningful.**

　　Beispiel: _____ ihr von ihnen _____? (*besuchen* – present)
　　　　　　Werdet ihr von ihnen besucht?

　1. Ich _____ von ihm _____ . (*fragen* – present perfect)
　2. _____ du das interessante Buch _____? (*lesen* – present perfect)
　3. Warum _____ es nicht von dir _____? (*kaufen* – past)
　4. Der Film _____ heute nicht _____ . (*zeigen* – present)
　5. Er _____ diesen neuen Wagen schon _____ . (*sehen* – present perfect)
　6. _____ du nur Deutsch? (*sprechen* – present)
　7. Der Brief _____ schnell _____ . (*schreiben* – present)
　8. Wir _____ viel Geld für die Karte _____ . (*ausgeben* – present perfect)
　9. Mein Bruder und ich _____ schon früh am Morgen _____ . (*anrufen* – past)
　10. Das Mittagessen _____ bald _____ . (*kochen* – present)

Infinitive Construction with *zu* and *um...zu*

Although an infinitive phrase in English uses the word *to*, the German infinitive phrase includes the word *zu*. An infinitive phrase including a modal auxiliary, however, does not make use of *zu*. Infinitive phrases with *zu* are usually followed by such expressions as *Ich habe Lust...*, *Ich habe vor...*, *Ich hoffe...*, *Ich versuche...* Note that a comma usually precedes the infinitive phrase if it contains additional words besides the *zu* and the infinitive.

Beispiele: *Ich habe Lust zu spielen.* but *Ich habe keine Lust, so spät am Abend ins Kino zu gehen.*

Wir hoffen, euch bald wieder zu besuchen. but *Wir hoffen, wir können euch bald wieder besuchen.*

If an infinitive has a separable prefix, the *zu* is placed between the prefix and the verb.

Beispiel: *Ich werde versuchen, ihn so bald wie möglich anzurufen.*

The German word for the English phrase "in order" is *um*.

Beispiele: *Ich beeile mich, um nicht zu spät nach Hause zu kommen.*
Wir hielten an, um uns die schöne Stadt anzusehen.

18. Rewrite each sentence based on the example provided.

    Beispiel: *Komm doch früh nach Hause!*
        Ich habe ihn gebeten, früh nach Hause zu kommen.

1. Such doch die beste Mahlzeit aus!
2. Mach doch das Zimmer sauber!
3. Park doch den Wagen vorsichtig!
4. Fahr doch etwas schneller zur Stadt!
5. Stell doch den Spiegel richtig ein!
6. Trag doch die Koffer direkt zum Zug!
7. Hilf doch der alten Dame über die Straße!

19. *Was hat Monika versucht?* Folge dem Beispiel!

    Beispiel: *bessere Noten bekommen*
        Sie hat versucht, bessere Noten zu bekommen.

1. ihren Führerschein machen
2. gleich zum Arzt gehen
3. mehr Deutsch sprechen
4. Heinz schon früher anrufen
5. erst am Montag zurückfahren
6. einen Autofahrer anhalten
7. mehrere Kleider anprobieren
8. einen langen Brief an ihren Freund schreiben

20. Complete each sentence using a different infinitive phrase with *um...zu.*

    Beispiel: *Ich gehe jetzt nach Hause,...*
        Ich gehe jetzt nach Hause, um meine Hausaufgaben zu machen.

1. Ich werde in die Stadt fahren,...
2. Wir sind in die Apotheke gegangen,...
3. Herr Meier hat dort schnell geparkt,...
4. Ich habe mich beeilt,...
5. Er ist zu seiner Tante gefahren,...
6. Sie sind schon früh losgegangen,...

Lesestück 1

In der Werkstatt

Herr Wenzel muß plötzlich seinen Wagen an der Landstraße anhalten, denn der Motor streikt° und will einfach nicht weiter. Er macht die Motorhaube auf und sucht nach der Ursache. Leider kann er nichts finden. Hinter dem Wagen, ungefähr 50 Meter entfernt, stellt er an der Straßenseite ein Warndreieck° auf. Andere Autofahrer sollen vorsichtig° an seinem Wagen vorbeifahren. Es ist zu weit, zum nächsten Ort zu Fuß zu gehen. Deshalb hält Herr Wenzel einen Wagen an. Er sagt dem Fahrer, daß er eine Panne hat. Der Fahrer verspricht° ihm, im nächsten Dorf Hilfe zu holen.

is stalling

warning sign
carefully

promises

Nach einer Weile kommt auch schon ein Mechaniker und sieht unter der Motorhaube nach. Aber auch er kann nichts feststellen. Der Mechaniker sagt Herrn Wenzel, daß sein Wagen ins nächste Dorf abgeschleppt werden muß. Er verbindet die beiden Wagen mit einer Stange° und schleppt Herrn Wenzel zur Werkstatt ab. Dort erklärt er dem Werkmeister°, was auf der Landstraße passiert war. Der Werkmeister hört sich alle Einzelheiten an. Dann öffnet er die Motorhaube und untersucht den Wagen. Er kann aber auch nichts

rod

supervisor

Herr Wenzels Wagen kommt in eine Werkstatt.

Der Werkmeister hört sich alle Einzelheiten an.

In dieser Werkstatt
werden Wagen inspiziert.

finden und deutet an°, daß der Wagen in die Werkstatt geschoben° *indicates/pushed*
werden soll.

Der Werkmeister versucht, mit verschiedenen Werkzeugen° *tools*
und Geräten°, die Ursache zu finden. Er überprüft° die Elektronik *equipment/checks*
des Wagens. Dabei stellt er fest, daß eine Zündkerze defekt ist.
Auch die übrigen° Zündkerzen sind nicht mehr in Ordnung. Deshalb *remaining*
holt er neue Zündkerzen vom Ersatzteillager°. *parts department*

Während sein Wagen repariert wird, sieht sich Herr Wenzel
ein wenig in der Werkstatt um°. Ein Lehrling° sucht die richtigen *sieht sich…um*
Werkzeuge, die er für seine Reparatur braucht. An dem Wagen, an *looks around/*
dem er arbeitet, müssen die Scheibenbremsen repariert werden. Ein *apprentice*
anderer Wagen wird gerade inspiziert. Man stellt fest, daß an diesem
Wagen ein neues Auspuffrohr° installiert werden muß. *exhaust pipe*

Innerhalb° einer halben Stunde ist Herr Wenzels Wagen fertig. *within*
Er geht an die Kasse und zahlt für die Reparatur. Er bedankt sich
beim Werkmeister und verläßt dann schnell die Werkstatt.

Fragen über das Lesestück

1. Warum hat Herr Wenzel angehalten?
2. Warum macht er die Motorhaube auf?
3. Was stellt er hinter seinem Wagen auf? Warum?
4. Warum hält Herr Wenzel einen Wagen an?
5. Was macht der Mechaniker mit Herrn Wenzels Wagen?
6. Was macht der Werkmeister zuerst, als der Wagen vor der Werkstatt steht?
7. Warum wird der Wagen in die Werkstatt geschoben?
8. Was überprüft der Werkmeister?
9. Was findet er dabei?
10. Was macht ein Lehrling in der Werkstatt?
11. Was installiert man an einem anderen Wagen?
12. Was macht Herr Wenzel, ehe er weiterfährt?

Erweiterung

21. Beantwortet diese Fragen mit einem ganzen Satz!

1. Hast du schon deinen Führerschein gemacht?
2. Fährst du ein Auto mit Kupplung oder mit automatischer Gangschaltung?
3. Hast du schon einmal eine Panne gehabt? Wo ist es gewesen?
4. Wo gibt es in deiner Gegend eine Werkstatt?
5. Wofür braucht man einen Sicherheitsgurt?
6. Was braucht man, um einen Reifen zu wechseln?
7. Was sind Schülerlotsen und was tun sie?
8. Was bedeutet „Vorfahrt gewähren!“?

22. **Form complete sentences by using the cues given.**

1. Ich / müssen / zuerst / Außenspiegel / einstellen
2. Die wichtigen Motorteile / werden erklärt / Fahrlehrer
3. Er / anhalten / Wagen / Landstraße
4. Warum / aufstellen / Warndreieck / hinter / Auto
5. Wagen / wird abgeschleppt / Werkstatt
6. Werkmeister / versuchen / Ursache finden
7. Er / feststellen / Zündkerze / defekt
8. Lehrling / müssen / Handbremse / reparieren

23. **Wie heißt das auf deutsch?**

1. The brakes are being repaired.
2. Try to drive a little slower.
3. I can't describe the dashboard.
4. You will have to release the hand brake.
5. Do you have car trouble?
6. My car has been inspected.
7. Who is checking the car?
8. I have to tow your car to the next repair shop.

24. **Form compound nouns by combining the words on the left with those on the right.** *Was bedeuten die neuen Wörter?*

Variation: Have students supply the article and plural forms.

1. das Land	das Rohr
2. die Hand	der Fahrer
3. der Auspuff	der Überweg
4. das Gas	die Bremse
5. das Auto	der Raum
6. der Schüler	der Werfer
7. das Steuer	der Lotse
8. der Fußgänger	das Rad
9. das Werk	der Heber
10. der Wagen	der Meister
11. der Schein	die Scheibe
12. die Nummer	das Schild
13. der Koffer	die Straße
14. das Ersatzteil	das Pedal
15. der Windschutz	das Lager

25. **Beschreibe die folgenden Wörter mit einem ganzen Satz!**

1. Werkmeister   Have students write a short paragraph using the eight words in their description.
2. Bremse
3. Reifen
4. Lehrling
5. Panne
6. Kofferraum

7. Nummernschild
8. Armaturenbrett

26. Beantworte diese Fragen so gut wie möglich!

1. Hast du Fahrunterricht gehabt?
2. Wo ist der Wagenheber?
3. Was muß man machen, wenn der Wagen nicht weiter fährt?
4. Was kann man in einer Werkstatt finden?
5. Wofür braucht man einen Außenspiegel?
6. Nenne drei Teile eines Autos!

Rückblick
If your students have problems completing any of these exercises, you may want to go back to the particular lesson in which the grammar or topic was discussed.

I. Complete each sentence with an appropriate relative pronoun.

1. Der Kellner, _____ uns das Essen bringt, wohnt in unserer Nachbarschaft.
2. Kennst du die Dame, _____ mit der Straßenbahn zum Büro fährt?
3. Mein Onkel, von _____ wir gestern einen Brief bekommen haben, wohnt in der Schweiz.
4. Wo sind die Kinder, _____ wir beim Lesen geholfen haben?
5. Ist das der Tisch, auf _____ du deine Schultasche gestellt hast?
6. Dort steht der Zug, mit _____ wir fahren können.
7. Warum fragst du nicht deine Freundin, _____ die Stadt so gut kennt?
8. Wir gehen zu unseren Verwandten, _____ ganz in der Nähe wohnen.
9. Das Museum, in _____ wir hineingehen, ist in der ganzen Welt bekannt.
10. Da läuft der Ausländer, für _____ ich die Karte gekauft habe.

II. Construct meaningful sentences using the information given.

1. Wir / fahren / mit / Schiff / oder / wir / fliegen / Flugzeug
2. Obgleich / Paul / keine Zeit / haben / besuchen / er / sein / Onkel / sein / Tante
3. Ich / müssen / Arbeit / machen / bevor / ich / zu / Tanzunterricht / gehen / können
4. Solange / wir / kein Geld / haben / können / wir / kein / Musikinstrumente / kaufen
5. Christa / Hausaufgaben machen / während / Gabi / sich anhören / Kassetten
6. Du / müssen / warten / bis / er / von / Theater / zurückkommen
7. Was / werden / wir / machen / wenn / dein / Freund / zu Besuch kommen

III. Complete each of the following sentences.

1. Ich möchte ins Kino gehen, aber _____ .
2. Herr Schmidt muß in die Stadt, weil _____ .
3. Da _____ , kann er keinen Anzug kaufen.
4. Frau Holzmann macht noch einige Einkäufe, bevor _____ .
5. Meine Verwandten kommen nicht zu uns, sondern _____ .
6. Nachdem _____ , lesen wir ein anderes Buch.

7. Peter bekommt ein Fahrrad, und _____ .

8. Ich weiß nicht, ob _____ .

9. Sie fliegen nach Europa, denn _____ .

10. Als _____ , sahen wir viele Städte.

IV. Provide the proper endings in the blanks.

Herr und Frau Schmidt haben Lust, zu d_____ neu_____ französisch_____
Restaurant in d_____ Stadt zu fahren. Ihre Bekannten haben ihnen in d_____
letzt_____ Tagen viel von dies_____ elegant_____ Restaurant erzählt. Am
spät_____ Nachmittag fahren sie mit d_____ Straßenbahn direkt zu_____ Bahnhof.
Von dort gehen sie bis zu_____ ersten_____ Hauptstraße und dann d_____
zweit_____ Nebenstraße nach rechts.

Im Restaurant herrscht ein_____ gemütlich_____ Atmosphäre. Schmidts bekommen
d_____ best_____ Platz am Fenster. Nach einer Weile bringt d_____
freundlich_____ Kellner d_____ groß_____ Speisekarte. Obwohl d_____
meist_____ Speisen französisch sind, bietet d_____ Restaurant auch ein paar
deutsch_____ Speisen an. Schmidts entschließen sich, d_____ französisch_____
Spezialität dies_____ Restaurants zu essen.

V. Find the matching word pairs. Each word on the right side has its corresponding counterpart on the left.

Have students provide the article as well.

1. Film – _____	Schiff
2. Essen – _____	Kuchen
3. Rinderfilet – _____	Kino
4. Bohnen – _____	Werkstatt
5. Torte – _____	Fuß
6. Fräulein – _____	Kellnerin
7. Hafen – _____	Obst
8. Gaststätte – _____	Auto
9. Kirschen – _____	Fleisch
10. Schuhe – _____	Speisekarte
11. Ersatzteillager – _____	Restaurant
12. Steuerrad – _____	Gemüse

Was für eine Torte wird hier verkauft?

Lesestück 2

Die Deutsche Lufthansa

Aller Anfang ist schwer. So war es auch am Anfang der Fliegerei. In den Jahren 1894 bis 1912 hatten eine Anzahl° von Deutschen versucht so weit wie möglich zu fliegen. Manche Strecken waren kurz (Berlin - Lichterfelde), andere etwas länger (Frankfurt - Darmstadt). Aber erst am 6. April 1926 eröffnete° die Deutsche Lufthansa einen planmäßigen° Flugverkehr auf der Strecke Berlin über Halle, Erfurt, Stuttgart nach Zürich. Vor dem Abflug wurde das Flugzeug noch schnell saubergemacht. Dann stiegen die Passagiere° ein. Nur vier Personen konnten in der Kabine untergebracht° werden. Die ersten Wartesäle° für die Fluggäste der Lufthansa waren im Freien. Die Flugzeuge konnten nicht viel Gewicht° mitnehmen. Deshalb mußte alles, was mitfliegen sollte, auf die Waage. Ein Junge trug das Gepäck zum Flugzeug und half den Passagieren beim Einsteigen.

Im Jahre 1928 warteten Busse auf die Ankunft der Flugzeuge und brachten die Fluggäste dann direkt in die Innenstadt. Das Luft-

°number

°started
°scheduled

°passengers
°accommodated
°waiting rooms
°weight

das größte Flugzeug im Jahr 1931

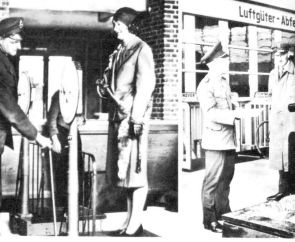

Alles mußte vor dem Abflug auf die Waage.

Was machte man noch vor dem Abflug?

schiff° „Graf Zeppelin" überquerte am 18. Mai 1930 zum ersten *blimp*
Mal den Südatlantik von Sevilla nach Recife, Brasilien. Ein Jahr
später flog die Lufthansa mit dem größten Landflugzeug der damali-
gen Zeit°. Die Junkers Ju 52 (auch „Tante Ju" genannt) wurde sehr *of that time*
bekannt. Wegen der Sicherheit° und Wirtschaftlichkeit° dieses Flug- *security/economy*
zeugs setzte man es auf Strecken innerhalb Europas und später auch
in Asien und Südamerika ein°. Im Jahre 1934 begann die Lufthansa *setzte…ein put into*
den ersten Luftpostdienst° der Welt (zwischen Deutschland und *service*
Südamerika). Auf dem Flughafen Berlin-Tempelhof konnte man *airmail service*
schon im Jahre 1936 viele Flugzeuge sehen. Am 10. August 1938
gelang° es der Lufthansa zum ersten Mal von Berlin direkt nach *succeeded*
New York zu fliegen. Der Flug dauerte 24 Stunden 57 Minuten. Der
2. Weltkrieg° unterbrach° dann die weitere Entwicklung° der Luft- *World War II/*
hansa. *interrupted/*
development

Am 1. April 1955 eröffnete die Deutsche Lufthansa ihren
Flugverkehr wieder und startete mit einer *Convair CV-340* von
Hamburg über Düsseldorf, Frankfurt nach München. Zwei Jahre
später wurde ein größeres Flugzeug auf Flügen über den Atlan-
tischen Ozean eingesetzt, die *Super Star*, die in Amerika gebaut
wurde. Aus England kam die *Vickers V-814 „Viscount"*.

Das Zeitalter° der Düsenflugzeuge° begann für die Lufthansa *age/jets*
am 2. März 1960. An diesem Tag bekam die Lufthansa ihren ersten
Jet. Zehn Jahre später startete die Lufthansa ihren ersten Großraum-
jet°, die *B-747*. Insgesamt° 361 Fluggäste können in einem dieser *jumbo jet/altogether*
großen Flugzeuge untergebracht werden. Wie andere Fluggesell-
schaften° fliegt heute auch die Lufthansa in alle Teile der Welt. Wäh- *airline companies*
rend der erste Flug von Deutschland nach Amerika ungefähr 25
Stunden dauerte, beträgt° die gesamte° Flugzeit in einer B-747 heute *amounts to/total*
nur noch acht Stunden. Mit Hilfe der Flugzeuge ist Europa heute
zeitlich° viel näher für uns als in früheren Jahren. *as to time*

Fragen über das Lesestück

1. Wie weit sind die Flugzeuge am Anfang der Fliegerei geflogen?
2. Wann begann der planmäßige Flugverkehr der Deutschen Lufthansa?
3. Zwischen welchen Städten flog man während dieser Zeit?
4. Was machte man, bevor die Passagiere einstiegen?
5. Warum mußte man alles wiegen?
6. Was passierte im Jahre 1930?
7. Warum war die Junkers Ju 52 so bekannt und beliebt?
8. In welchem Jahre flog man zum ersten Mal von Deutschland nach Amerika?
9. Was machte die Deutsche Lufthansa im Jahre 1955?
10. Wann hatte die Lufthansa zum ersten Mal einen Großraumjet eingesetzt? Wie groß ist dieses Flugzeug?
11. Wie lange dauert es heute, mit einem Flugzeug von Amerika nach Deutschland zu fliegen?

Sprachspiegel

You may also have students work in groups to develop a conversation on this topic. They need not follow the guided conversational cues provided.

I. *Schreibe einen kurzen Aufsatz über das Thema „Ich lerne Auto fahren"!* **If you have not had any driver's training, pretend you're going through the process and use your imagination as well as the information from this lesson.**

II. *Wir haben eine Panne. Beschreibe das folgende Erlebnis (mündlich oder schriftlich)!*

You and your friend are driving on the freeway. Suddenly you notice that there is something wrong. The car seems to pull to one side and you have trouble driving. You stop and check the problem. Your friend notices right away that you have a flat tire. You've never changed a tire, but your friend is an expert at it and does it for you. While s/he is changing the tire, s/he is explaining the process so that you'll know how to do it next time. After the job is done, you decide to drive to the nearest service station to have the flat tire repaired. Within another hour you're on your way again.

Encourage your students to be as creative as possible in completing each short situation. Have one student read the printed material and another his/her own version.

Du bist dran!

Fahr nicht so schnell auf dieser Straße!

. . . .

Ja, aber heute ist so viel Verkehr.

. . . .

. . . .

Nein, leider habe ich keinen Führerschein.

. . . .

Vielleicht im nächsten Jahr.

Wo haben Sie denn eine Panne gehabt?

. . . .

Sie haben wirklich kein Glück.

. . . .

Soll ich Ihren Wagen abschleppen?

. . . .

Das kann aber noch lange dauern.

. . . .

. . . .

Ich weiß nicht. Mein Motorrad will nicht mehr.

. . . .

Ich warte, bis mein Freund kommt.

Ist mein Wagen schon repariert?

. . . .

Aber ich habe ihn schon vor drei Tagen in Ihre Werkstatt gebracht.

. . . .

> Soll ich Ihren Wagen abschleppen?

Kulturecke

Measure for Measure

If you travel in Germany or any other European country, you'll have to learn the metric system. Remember first that all metric measurements are based on one hundred, and second, that the prefix *centi* means hundred and *kilo* means thousand. When you're given a distance in kilometers, you should be able to estimate the total distance initially by comparing it to miles.

Because Germans love to hike, particularly through forests, there are usually hiking maps available that show distances in kilometers. The numbers are usually followed by the letters *km*, an abbreviation for kilometers. You'll have to be aware especially of estimating distances or speed limits indicated in kilometers. A speed limit sign marked "50," for example, means that you must not travel faster than the equivalent of 30 miles per hour.

A unit of measurement smaller than the kilometer is the *Meter* (meter), usually abbreviated by the letter *m*, although sometimes the letters *mtr.* are used. Many signs, indicating hotels and other points of interest, inform the traveler about the various distances in meters. For instance, if you're standing in front of a sign pointing to a specific hotel 2,200 meters away, you should be able to estimate the distance to be less than 1.5 miles. There are 100 centimeters *(Zentimeter)*, abbreviated *cm*, in one meter. The centimeter is an important unit if you buy clothing items.

Wie weit ist das Freibad entfernt? (Füssen)

Wie schnell kann man auf dieser Strecke fahren?

Was kosten die verschiedenen Lebensmittel?

Wo gibt es hier eine Pension? (Füssen)

Was steht auf diesem Schild?

Wie viele Kilometer muß man bis Lindau fahren?

Wie warm
ist es heute?

Wie viele Liter Super
hat der Reisende getankt?

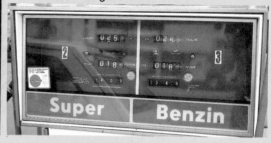

Super   Benzin

Was kann man hier alles kaufen?

Eier werden nach Stück verkauft. (Freiburg)

When buying groceries, it's important to know the metric weight units. Many groceries are packaged to make it convenient for the homemaker to follow recipes that have standard measures. Germans commonly measure by the *Pfund* (pound) or *Kilo*. A *Pfund* is half a kilo, or 500 *Gramm* (grams). This makes it slightly more than our pound (454 grams). A *Kilo* is two *Pfund* or 1,000 *Gramm*. When a package is marked *"50 Gramm,"* you should be able to estimate the contents to be one-tenth of a *Pfund* or slightly less than two ounces. When you buy a chicken advertised at 800 g in a department store, you should be able to come up with a rough estimate of slightly less than two U.S. pounds.

All liquids such as gasoline are measured by the *Liter* (liter), which is a little over a quart. German service stations always advertise the cost of gas by the liter. Some products, such as eggs, are sold by the *Stück* (piece). The same is true for fruit, such as apples, and the wide assortment of rolls and cookies sold in bakeries. This makes it easy to figure out the unit price.

Besides the metric measuring units, you should also be familiar with the way Germans write some letters, symbols and numbers. It can be a study in itself to decipher what the shopkeeper has to offer. The number "1" and "7" are the two numbers that are written quite differently from our way. The German number "1" looks like our number "7," and the German number "7" has a crossed stem, resembling our capital letter "F."

Finally, you may wonder why you aren't freezing when you see a thermometer reading of "24." However, the temperature is indicated in centigrade (Celsius). So relax — the temperature of 24°C is equivalent to 75°F.

Vokabeln

abschleppen to tow (away)
der **Abstand,-̈e** gap, distance
andeuten to indicate
das **Armaturenbrett** dashboard
aufstellen to put up
das **Auspuffrohr,-e** exhaust pipe
der **Außenspiegel,-** outside mirror
der **Autofahrer,-** driver
die **Baustelle,-n** construction site
die **Bordsteinkante,-n** curb
die **Bremse,-n** brake
die **Bushaltestelle,-n** bus stop
das **Dach,-̈er** roof
defekt defective
einlegen to put in
   den Gang einlegen to put into gear
einstellen to adjust
die **Elektronik** electronics
erlaubt allowed
das **Ersatzteillager,-** parts department
die **Fahrbahn,-en** road
der **Fahrer,-** driver
der **Fahrunterricht** driver's training, driving instruction
der **Fußgängerüberweg,-e** pedestrian crossing
die **Fußgängerunterführung,-en** pedestrian underpass
der **Gang,-̈e** gear
das **Gaspedal,-e** gas pedal
gemeinsam common, joint
das **Gerät,-e** piece of equipment, gadget, device
gewähren to yield, grant
   Vorfahrt gewähren! Yield the right of way!
die **Handbremse,-n** hand brake
der **Innenspiegel,-** inside mirror

innerhalb within
inspizieren to inspect
installieren to install
der **Kofferraum,-̈e** trunk
die **Kreuzung,-en** intersection
die **Kupplung,-en** clutch
der **Lehrling,-e** apprentice
lösen to loosen, release (brake)
der **Mechaniker,-** mechanic
die **Motorhaube,-n** hood
das **Nummernschild,-er** license plate
die **Panne,-n** car trouble, breakdown
der **Reifen,-** tire
die **Reparatur,-en** repair
reparieren to repair
der **Rücksitz,-e** back seat
die **Schaltung,-en** gearshift
die **Scheibenbremse,-n** disc brake
der **Scheinwerfer,-** headlight
schieben (*schob, geschoben*) to push
der **Schlüssel,-** key
der **Schülerlotse,-n** school patrol
der **Sicherheitsgurt,-e** safety belt
die **Stange,-n** rod
das **Steuerrad,-̈er** steering wheel
die **Straßenbahnhaltestelle,-n** streetcar stop
die **Straßenseite,-n** side of street
streiken to stall (motor)
die **U-Bahn,-en** subway
überprüfen to check, examine
überqueren to cross
übrig remaining
sich **umsehen** (*sieht um, sah um, umgesehen*) to look around
unglaublich unbelievable, incredible
untersuchen to examine, inspect

die **Ursache,-n** cause
versprechen (*verspricht, versprach, versprochen*) to promise
der **Vordersitz,-e** front seat
die **Vorfahrt** right of way
die **Vorfahrtsstraße,-n** main street
vorsichtig careful
der **Wagenheber,-** jack
das **Warndreieck,-e** warning sign
wechseln to change
der **Werkmeister,-** supervisor
die **Werkstatt,-̈en** repair shop, workshop
das **Werkzeug,-e** tool
die **Windschutzscheibe,-n** windshield
zuletzt finally, last of all
zunächst first
die **Zündkerze,-n** spark plug

Dialog

Im Büro

HERR GERBER:	Guten Morgen, Frau Nolde. Kommen Sie doch bitte in mein Büro. Und bringen Sie den Tagesplan mit.
FRAU NOLDE:	Guten Morgen, Herr Gerber. Hier ist die Post von heute. Übrigens kommt Herr Peters um zehn.
HERR GERBER:	Na, dann hat die Post noch Zeit. Hätte ich das gewußt, dann wäre ich etwas früher ins Büro gekommen. Ich muß noch diese wichtigen Briefe unterschreiben.
FRAU NOLDE:	Und vergessen Sie nicht die Briefe nach Berlin.
HERR GERBER:	Auch das noch. Ich wünschte, die Tage wären länger. Geben Sie bitte Fräulein Holz diese Dokumente zur Überprüfung. Ich brauche sie später, wenn Herr Peters hier ist.
FRAU NOLDE:	Soll ich jetzt das Diktat aufnehmen?
HERR GERBER:	Ach ja, stimmt…die Briefe nach Berlin. Zuerst schreiben wir an die Firma Braun…Sehr geehrte Damen und Herren…
FRAU NOLDE:	Der Chef ist heute morgen ganz nervös.
FRL. HOLZ:	Das ist doch nichts Neues.
FRAU NOLDE:	Aber heute hat er viel zu tun. Sie sollen sich noch vor zehn Uhr diese Dokumente durchlesen.
FRL. HOLZ:	Kein Problem. Das geht sehr schnell.
FRAU NOLDE:	Herr Gerber hat mir ein paar Briefe diktiert. Er hat mich gebeten, sie gleich zu tippen. Verflixt! Irgendetwas ist mit meiner Schreibmaschine los.
FRL. HOLZ:	Warten Sie, ich werde mal nachsehen…So, der Wagen war nur steckengeblieben.
FRAU NOLDE:	Sie sind ja ganz patent.
FRAU NOLDE:	Wann nehmen Sie dieses Jahr Ihren Urlaub?
FRL. HOLZ:	Ich glaube, im Juli oder August.
FRAU NOLDE:	Das klappt prima. Bernd und ich möchten unseren Urlaub im Februar oder März machen.
FRL. HOLZ:	Wohin geht's denn während der Wintermonate?
FRAU NOLDE:	Nach Garmisch, zum Ski laufen.

s quite common for
eagues in the same office
ddress each other with

Fragen über den Dialog

1. Was soll Frau Nolde tun?
2. Warum will Herr Gerber die Post jetzt nicht lesen?
3. Was soll Herr Gerber nicht vergessen?
4. Warum gibt Herr Gerber Frau Nolde ein paar Dokumente?
5. Wohin will Herr Gerber Briefe schicken?
6. Warum ist Herr Gerber heute so nervös?
7. Was soll Frau Nolde mit den Briefen machen, die Herr Gerber diktiert hat?
8. Was machte Frl. Holz, als etwas mit Frau Noldes Schreibmaschine nicht in Ordnung war?
9. Wann fährt Frl. Holz in den Urlaub?
10. Warum ist das für Frau Nolde sehr günstig?

In the Office

MR. GERBER:	Good morning, Mrs. Nolde. Would you come to my office, please? And bring the daily schedule along.
MRS. NOLDE:	Good morning, Mr. Gerber. Here is today's mail. By the way, Mr. Peters is coming at ten.
MR. GERBER:	Well, then the mail must wait. Had I known about Mr. Peters' visit, I would have come into the office a bit earlier. I'll have to sign these important documents now.
MRS. NOLDE:	And don't forget the letters to Berlin.
MR. GERBER:	That too. I wish the days were a little longer. Please give these documents to Miss Holz for her review. I'll need them later, when Mr. Peters is here.
MRS. NOLDE:	Should I take dictation now?
MR. GERBER:	Oh yes, that's right...the letters to Berlin. Let's write first the Braun Company...Ladies and Gentlemen...
MRS. NOLDE:	The boss is quite nervous today.
MISS HOLZ:	That's nothing new.
MRS. NOLDE:	But he has a lot to do today. You're supposed to read through these documents before ten o'clock.
MISS HOLZ:	No problem. That goes very fast.
MRS. NOLDE:	Mr. Gerber dictated a few letters. He asked me to type them right away. Darn it! Something is wrong with my typewriter.
MISS HOLZ:	Wait, I'll check it...Here you are, the carriage was only stuck.
MRS. NOLDE:	You are really clever.

MRS. NOLDE:	When are you going to take your vacation this year?
MISS HOLZ:	I think in July or August.
MRS. NOLDE:	That works out well. Bernd and I would like to go on vacation in February or March.
MISS HOLZ:	Where are you going during the winter months?
MRS. NOLDE:	To Garmisch, skiing.

Nützliche Ausdrücke

Review the expressions that students have learned in the *Dialog* and *Lesestück 1*.

Hätte ich das gewußt, dann…	If I had known that, then…
Auch das noch.	That too.
Ich nehme ein Diktat auf.	I'll take dictation.
Tippen Sie diese Briefe sofort!	Type these letters right away.
Verflixt!	Darn it!
Irgendetwas ist damit los.	Something is wrong with it.
Du bist ganz patent.	You're quite clever.
Wann nehmen Sie Ihren Urlaub?	When do you take your vacation?
Das klappt prima.	That works out well.
Wir verbringen eine Woche da.	We'll spend one week there.
Das ist Ihnen ganz und gar überlassen.	That's completely up to you.
Welches Programm hat man aufgestellt?	Which program did they plan?
Womit beschäftigt sie sich?	What is she busy with?
Sie vergnügt sich am Strand.	She is having fun at the beach.
Er hat sich einer Gruppe angeschlossen.	He joined a group.
Ich muß mich körperlich bewegen.	I have to exercise.
Hast du ihn herausgefordert?	Did you challenge him?
Das Spiel strengt sehr an.	The game is very strenuous.
Es macht viel Freude.	That's a lot of fun.
Ich muß meine Wahl treffen.	I have to make my choice.
Bist du satt?	Have you had enough (to eat)?
Sie machen ein Schläfchen.	They are taking a nap.

Sprichwort

Wenn man den Wolf nennt, kommt er gerennt.
(If you name the wolf, he comes running.)

Speak of the devil, and he is sure to appear.

Ergänzung

Ask questions such as *Wozu gebraucht man Akten?*, *Was macht man mit einer Schreibmaschine (einem Rechner, einem Diktiergerät)? Kannst du tippen? Wie viele Wörter pro Minute?*

1. das Büro

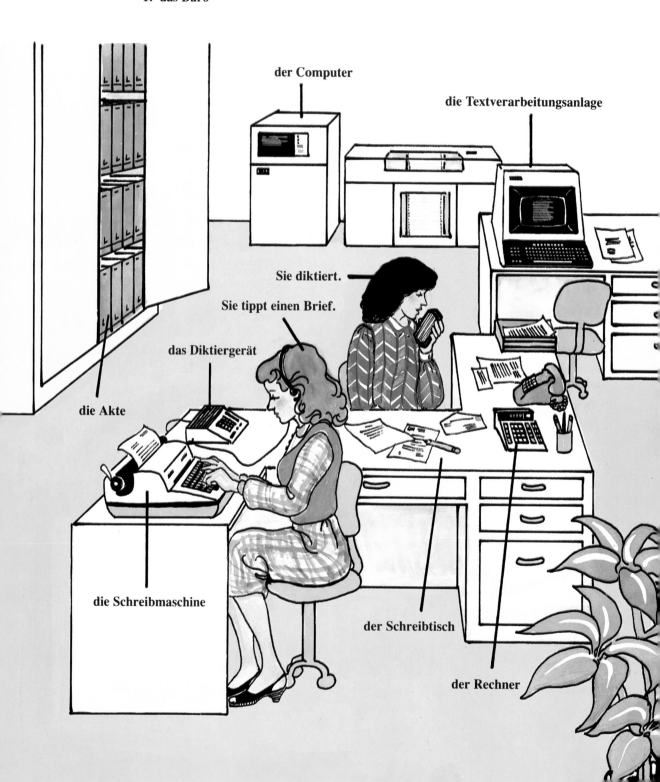

der Computer

die Textverarbeitungsanlage

Sie diktiert.

Sie tippt einen Brief.

das Diktiergerät

die Akte

die Schreibmaschine

der Schreibtisch

der Rechner

2. der Brief

Have students write a fictitious personal and/or business letter, using the information given.

Was steht alles im Brief?

Rechts oben: das Datum wie zum
Beispiel: Hamburg, den 10.7.85

Links oben der Absender (besonders
in einem Geschäftsbrief)

Wie fängt man einen persönlichen Brief an?

Lieber Michael!
Liebe Sabine!
Lieber Vati!
Liebe Mutti!

Wie fängt man einen Geschäftsbrief an?

Sehr geehrte Damen und Herren!
Lieber Herr Weber!
  (Sehr geehrter…!)
Liebe Frau Schell!
  (Sehr geehrte…!)

Wie beendet man einen persönlichen Brief?

Mit vielen herzlichen Grüßen! oder:
  Herzliche Grüße!
  Dein(e) oder: Euer(e)

Wie beendet man einen Geschäftsbrief?

Mit freundlichen Grüßen!

Was steht auf einem Briefumschlag?

Die Anschrift (der Vor- und
Nachname, die Straße und die
Hausnummer, die Postleitzahl,
der Ort) und der Absender

Was kommt noch auf den Briefumschlag?

Briefmarken.

Was bringt man zur Post?

Einen Brief, eine Postkarte, ein
Paket, ein Päckchen und ein
Telegramm.

---

den 24. August 1986

Firma
Max Heller GmbH
Rheinstraße 38
5000 Köln 80

Sehr geehrter Herr Steuber,

haben Sie vielen Dank für Ihr
Schreiben vom 10.8. Mittlerweile
ist unser neuer Katalog fertiggestellt
worden und wir lassen Ihnen diesen mit
getrennter Post zugehen.

Falls Sie noch andere Wünsche haben
sollten, zögern Sie bitte nicht, uns
davon zu unterrichten.

Mit freundlichen Grüßen

MUSIK VON HEUTE

Willi Bogner

Willi Bogner

MUSIK VON HEUTE
An der Alster 38
2000 Hamburg 1

Firma
Max Heller GmbH
Rheinstraße 38
5000 Köln 80

Übungen

Subjunctive

The subjunctive of a verb expresses a specific mood. It is used mostly to indicate actions that are unreal or not factual. Most English verbs do not have a special form for the subjunctive and, therefore, you use it often without realizing it. The subjunctive form is used frequently in German. It is used in *indirect discourse, expressions of politeness and wishes,* and in *contrary-to-fact statements.*

There are basically two tenses in the subjunctive: *present* (present subjunctive I and present subjunctive II) and *past* (past subjunctive I and past subjunctive II).

Subjunctive Tenses

Present subjunctive I

The present subjunctive I is formed by using the infinitive stem of the verb and adding the subjunctive endings that are identical for all verbs (regular and irregular) and all tenses.* These forms are used quite often in the media (TV and newspapers). In colloquial usage, the present subjunctive II forms are preferred.

		fragen	kommen	haben	sein
ich		frage	komme	habe	sei
du		fragest	kommest	habest	seiest
er sie es		frage	komme	habe	sei
wir		fragen	kommen	haben	seien
ihr		fraget	kommet	habet	seiet
sie Sie		fragen	kommen	haben	seien

*There is no ending in the first and third person singular of the verb *sein.*

Present subjunctive II

The present subjunctive II is formed by using the simple past stem of the verb and adding the subjunctive endings. The vowels *a, o* and *u* in the past stem of irregular verbs change to *ä, ö* and *ü.*

		fragen	kommen	haben	sein
ich		fragte	käme	hätte	wäre
du		fragtest	kämest	hättest	wärest
er sie es		fragte	käme	hätte	wäre
wir		fragten	kämen	hätten	wären
ihr		fragtet	kämet	hättet	wäret
sie Sie		fragten	kämen	hätten	wären

NOTE: The following modal auxiliaries have an umlaut in the present subjunctive II:

dürfen:	ich dürfte
mögen:	ich möchte
können:	ich könnte
müssen:	ich müßte

but

sollen:	ich sollte
wollen:	ich wollte

Past subjunctive I

The past subjunctive I is formed by using the present subjunctive I of *haben* or *sein* and adding the past participle.

ich	habe gesucht	ich	sei gegangen
du	habest gesucht	du	seiest gegangen
er	habe gesucht	er	sei gegangen
sie	habe gesucht	sie	sei gegangen
es	habe gesucht	es	sei gegangen
wir	haben gesucht	wir	seien gegangen
ihr	habet gesucht	ihr	seiet gegangen
sie	haben gesucht	sie	seien gegangen
Sie	haben gesucht	Sie	seien gegangen

Past subjunctive II

The past subjunctive II is formed by using the present subjunctive II of *haben* or *sein* and adding the past participle. This form is more widely used than the past subjunctive I.

ich	hätte gesucht	ich	wäre gegangen
du	hättest gesucht	du	wärest gegangen
er	hätte gesucht	er	wäre gegangen
sie	hätte gesucht	sie	wäre gegangen
es	hätte gesucht	es	wäre gegangen
wir	hätten gesucht	wir	wären gegangen
ihr	hättet gesucht	ihr	wäret gegangen
sie	hätten gesucht	sie	wären gegangen
Sie	hätten gesucht	Sie	wären gegangen

„Möchtest du sonst noch etwas?"

„Ich wünschte, ich hätte diese Briefe schon vorher gelesen."

Indirect Discourse

The indirect discourse is used in reporting rather than quoting a statement. In German the subjunctive is required in indirect discourse.

If the direct statement is in the present tense, use either the present subjunctive I or II.

Beispiele:
Er schrieb: „Ich komme am Dienstag an."
Er schrieb, er komme (käme) am Dienstag an.
Er schrieb, daß er am Dienstag ankomme (ankäme).

Der Polizist sagt: „Ich suche diesen Mann."
Der Polizist sagt, er suche diesen Mann.
Der Polizist sagt, daß er diesen Mann suche.

Should the verb form of the present subjunctive I be identical to the present tense of the direct statement, you should use the present subjunctive II form.

Beispiele:
Er sagte: „Die Touristen haben keine Zeit."
Er sagte, die Touristen hätten keine Zeit.
Er sagte, daß die Touristen keine Zeit hätten.

Use the past subjunctive I or II when the direct statement is in the simple past, present perfect, or past perfect.

Beispiele:
Er schrieb: „Ich bin am Dienstag angekommen."
Er schrieb, er wäre (sei) am Dienstag angekommen.

Der Polizist sagt: „Ich suchte diesen Mann."
Der Polizist sagt, er hätte (habe) diesen Mann gesucht.

Folgt den Beispielen!

1. Was sagt der Ansager?

   Das Spiel ist in München.

   Das Programm beginnt gleich.

   Die Polizei sucht einen Mann.

   Der Bundespräsident fliegt in die USA.

   Der Sportler läuft sehr schnell.

Er sagt, das Spiel sei in München.

Er sagt, das Programm beginne gleich.

Er sagt, die Polizei suche einen Mann.

Er sagt, der Bundespräsident fliege in die USA.

Er sagt, der Sportler laufe sehr schnell.

Variation: Have students provide sentences on the right with direct quotes. (Er sagt: „Das Spiel ist in München.")

2. Ich habe keine Zeit. Und was sagt sie dazu?

   Ich schreibe einen Brief. Und was sagt er dazu?

   Ich fahre in die Stadt. Und was sagt sie dazu?

   Ich gehe ins Kino. Und was sagt er dazu?

   Ich lese ein Buch. Und was sagt sie dazu?

Sie sagt, sie hätte auch keine Zeit.

Er sagt, er schriebe auch einen Brief.

Sie sagt, sie führe auch in die Stadt.

Er sagt, er ginge auch ins Kino.

Sie sagt, sie läse auch ein Buch.

Variation: Have students give the sentences on the right using daß. (Sie sagt, daß sie auch keine Zeit hätte.)

3. Er sagt: „Ich arbeite den ganzen Tag."

   Sie sagt: „Ich bin hungrig."

Er sagt, er arbeite den ganzen Tag.

Sie sagt, sie sei hungrig.

Er sagt: „Ich spiele Schach gern."

Sie sagt: „Ich sehe oft fern."

Er sagt: „Ich höre Musik gern."

Sie sagt: „Ich mache noch schnell die Arbeit."

Er sagt, er spiele Schach gern.

Sie sagt, sie sehe oft fern.

Er sagt, er höre Musik gern.

Sie sagt, sie mache noch schnell die Arbeit.

4. Die Lehrerin glaubt, daß die Schüler viel lesen sollten.

    wollen

    können

    dürfen

    müssen

    mögen

Die Lehrerin glaubt, daß die Schüler viel lesen sollten.

Die Lehrerin glaubt, daß die Schüler viel lesen wollten.

Die Lehrerin glaubt, daß die Schüler viel lesen könnten.

Die Lehrerin glaubt, daß die Schüler viel lesen dürften.

Die Lehrerin glaubt, daß die Schüler viel lesen müßten.

Die Lehrerin glaubt, daß die Schüler viel lesen möchten.

5. Sie fragte, ob er mitgefahren wäre.

    fliegen

    ankommen

    gehen

    laufen

    abfahren

Sie fragte, ob er mitgefahren wäre.

Sie fragte, ob er geflogen wäre.

Sie fragte, ob er angekommen wäre.

Sie fragte, ob er gegangen wäre.

Sie fragte, ob er gelaufen wäre.

Sie fragte, ob er abgefahren wäre.

6. Sie sagten: „Wir bekamen einen Brief."

Sie sagten: „Wir hatten ein Fahrrad."

Sie sagten: „Wir waren im Theater."

Sie sagten: „Wir hatten euch nicht gesehen."

Sie sagten: „Wir waren sehr weit gelaufen."

Sie sagten: „Wir sind ins Büro gegangen."

Sie sagten: „Wir kamen etwas spät."

Sie sagten, sie hätten einen Brief bekommen.

Sie sagten, sie hätten ein Fahrrad gehabt.

Sie sagten, sie wären im Theater gewesen.

Sie sagten, sie hätten euch nicht gesehen.

Sie sagten, sie wären sehr weit gelaufen.

Sie sagten, sie wären ins Büro gegangen.

Sie sagten, sie wären etwas spät gekommen.

Variation: Have students change sentences on the right eliminating daß. (Er meinte, er hätte den Film schon gesehen.)

7. Er meinte: „Ich habe den Film schon gesehen."

Sie sagte: „Ich habe im Restaurant gegessen."

Ich schrieb: „Ich komme bald zu euch."

Sie sagten ihm: „Wir sind nach Deutschland geflogen."

Er erzählte uns: „Ich bin im Museum gewesen."

Sie erklärte: „Ich habe das Geld nicht gefunden."

Sie schrieben: „Wir kommen am Montag an."

Er meinte, daß er den Film schon gesehen hätte.

Sie sagte, daß sie im Restaurant gegessen hätte.

Ich schrieb, daß ich bald zu euch käme.

Sie sagten ihm, daß sie nach Deutschland geflogen wären.

Er erzählte uns, daß er im Museum gewesen wäre.

Sie erklärte, daß sie das Geld nicht gefunden hätte.

Sie schrieben, daß sie am Montag ankämen.

8. Change the following quotations to indirect discourse.

> **Beispiel:** *Er sagt: „Ich komme heute spät nach Hause."*
> *Er sagt, er käme (komme) heute spät nach Hause.*

1. Der Amerikaner sagte: „Ich flog letztes Jahr nach Deutschland."
2. Meine Eltern schrieben: „Wir fahren morgen nach Hamburg."
3. Das Mädchen sagt: „Ich wußte das nicht."
4. Der Chef erklärte: „Ich habe den Brief gefunden."
5. Er sagt: „Die Spieler haben viel Glück."
6. Inge meinte: „Wir müssen zuerst die Arbeit machen."
7. Frau Schulz erzählte: „Wir sind durch den Schwarzwald gefahren."
8. Der Lehrer sagt: „Wir besprechen die neue Lektion."
9. Die Verkäuferin meint: „Ich habe leider diese Farbe nicht."
10. Wir sagten: „Wir haben das Museum besucht."
11. Der Ansager gab bekannt: „Nummer 12 hat gewonnen."
12. Die Zeitung schrieb: „Die Polizei sucht noch immer diese zwei Männer."

9. Change these statements to indirect discourse, using *daß*.

> **Beispiel:** *Sie erklärte: „Ich habe keine Zeit."*
> *Sie erklärte, daß sie keine Zeit hätte (habe).*

1. Sie hat ihm gesagt: „Ich bin noch nie in Frankfurt gewesen."
2. Der Herr sagte: „Ich bin darüber ganz erstaunt."
3. Mein Bruder meinte: „Ich kann dir dabei nicht helfen."
4. Der Student sagt: „Ich habe von diesem Aufsatz nichts gewußt."
5. Er wird sagen: „Ich habe schon davon gehört."
6. Ich sagte zu ihm: „Ich glaube dir nicht."
7. Er sagt: „Ich sprach kein Deutsch."

Expression of Politeness and Wish

You actually have used the subjunctive form before as for example in the phrase *ich möchte* (I would like), which is considered a polite expression. To emphasize politeness, Germans make use of the subjunctive quite often.

Beispiele:

Könnte ich noch ein Stück Kuchen haben?
(Could I have another piece of cake?)

Wir möchten ins Museum gehen.
(We would like to go to the museum.)

Das wäre mir recht.
(That would be all right with me.)

Ich möchte diesen Apfelstrudel.

246

The subjunctive is used quite often in expressing a wish that can or cannot be fulfilled.

Beispiele:

Wenn er nur hier wäre!
(If only he were here!)

Wenn ich doch etwas mehr Geld hätte!
(If only I had a little more money!)

Folgt den Beispielen!

10. Kann ich ein Stück Kuchen haben? — Könnte ich ein Stück Kuchen haben?
    Ich mag mit ihm nicht sprechen. — Ich möchte mit ihm nicht sprechen.
    Wir müssen jetzt nach Hause. — Wir müßten jetzt nach Hause.
    Das ist mir recht. — Das wäre mir recht.
    Darf ich mitkommen? — Dürfte ich mitkommen?
    Sie sollen bis neun Uhr schlafen. — Sie sollten bis neun Uhr schlafen.
    Kannst du ihm dabei helfen? — Könntest du ihm dabei helfen?
    Müssen Sie heute arbeiten? — Müßten Sie heute arbeiten?

11. Darf ich Ski laufen? — Dürfte ich Ski laufen?
    Kannst du mir das Buch geben? — Könntest du mir das Buch geben?
    Warum magst du das Essen nicht? — Warum möchtest du das Essen nicht?
    Sollen wir ihn besuchen? — Sollten wir ihn besuchen?
    Können Sie die Tür aufmachen? — Könnten Sie die Tür aufmachen?
    Darf ich noch eine Tasse Kaffee haben? — Dürfte ich noch eine Tasse Kaffee haben?
    Ich soll ihn fragen. — Ich sollte ihn fragen.
    Hast du das gern? — Hättest du das gern?

12. Wenn er doch gekommen wäre! — Wenn er doch gekommen wäre!
    lesen — Wenn er doch gelesen hätte!
    fliegen — Wenn er doch geflogen wäre!
    rufen — Wenn er doch gerufen hätte!
    gehen — Wenn er doch gegangen wäre!
    suchen — Wenn er doch gesucht hätte!
    schreiben — Wenn er doch geschrieben hätte!

13. Wenn ich nur das Buch gelesen hätte! — Wenn ich nur das Buch gelesen hätte!

    nach Europa fliegen — Wenn ich nur nach Europa geflogen wäre!

    den Platz finden — Wenn ich nur den Platz gefunden hätte!
    Gitarre spielen — Wenn ich nur Gitarre gespielt hätte!
    nach Hause gehen — Wenn ich nur nach Hause gegangen wäre!
    mit dem Zug fahren — Wenn ich nur mit dem Zug gefahren wäre!
    den Film sehen — Wenn ich nur den Film gesehen hätte!
    in der Schule sein — Wenn ich nur in der Schule gewesen wäre!

14. Wie heißt das auf deutsch?

1. If only we had more money.
2. If only I could drive.
3. If only I could come.
4. If only I were there.
5. If only we would play.
6. If only I could have gone.
7. If only we could have flown.
8. If only they had spoken.

Contrary-to-Fact Condition

Present time

The present subjunctive II is used to express a contrary-to-fact condition that exists at the present time. You may use either the subjunctive form or the auxiliary *würde* and the infinitive. The latter is more common in spoken German.

Beispiele:
Wenn ich Geld hätte, würde ich nach Deutschland fahren.
Wenn ich Geld hätte, führe ich nach Deutschland.
(If I had money, I would go to Germany.)

Wenn es warm wäre, würden wir ins Schwimmbad gehen.
Wenn es warm wäre, gingen wir ins Schwimmbad.
(If it were warm, we would go to the swimming pool.)

NOTE: The word *wenn* maybe omitted. However, if you do omit *wenn,* you must place the verb first in the clause. Also, in the conclusion the words *so* or *dann* are often introduced.

Beispiele:
Hätte ich Geld, so würde ich nach Deutschland fahren.
Wäre es warm, dann gingen wir ins Schwimmbad.

In making a contrary-to-fact statement, you should use the conjunction *als, als ob* or *als wenn.*

Beispiele:
Er sieht aus, als ob er müde wäre.
(He looks as if he were tired.)

Past time

The past subjunctive I or II is used to express a contrary-to-fact condition that existed at some time in the past. Generally, the past subjunctive is preferred to *würde* with the perfect infinitive.

Beispiele:
Wenn ich gestern gegangen wäre, hätte ich zuviel bezahlt.
Wenn ich gestern gegangen wäre, würde ich zuviel bezahlt haben.
(If I had gone yesterday, I would have paid too much.)

Folgt den Beispielen!

Variation: Have students eliminate *wenn*. (*Wäre ich zu Hause, dann könnte ich den Brief lesen.*)

15. Wenn ich zu Hause wäre, könnte ich den Brief lesen.

    meiner Mutter helfen

    ein Fernsehprogramm sehen

    meinen Aufsatz schreiben

    mit meinen Freunden spielen

    darüber sprechen

    meine neuen Kassetten hören

Wenn ich zu Hause wäre, könnte ich den Brief lesen.

Wenn ich zu Hause wäre, könnte ich meiner Mutter helfen.

Wenn ich zu Hause wäre, könnte ich ein Fernsehprogramm sehen.

Wenn ich zu Hause wäre, könnte ich meinen Aufsatz schreiben.

Wenn ich zu Hause wäre, könnte ich mit meinen Freunden spielen.

Wenn ich zu Hause wäre, könnte ich darüber sprechen.

Wenn ich zu Hause wäre, könnte ich meine neuen Kassetten hören.

16. Wenn ich viel Zeit hätte, würde ich mehr arbeiten.

    nach Österreich fliegen

    mit dir in die Diskothek gehen

    dich besuchen

    dir einen langen Brief schreiben

    die Zeitung lesen

    im Restaurant essen

    zu Hause bleiben

Wenn ich viel Zeit hätte, würde ich mehr arbeiten.

Wenn ich viel Zeit hätte, würde ich nach Österreich fliegen.

Wenn ich viel Zeit hätte, würde ich mit dir in die Diskothek gehen.

Wenn ich viel Zeit hätte, würde ich dich besuchen.

Wenn ich viel Zeit hätte, würde ich dir einen langen Brief schreiben.

Wenn ich viel Zeit hätte, würde ich die Zeitung lesen.

Wenn ich viel Zeit hätte, würde ich im Restaurant essen.

Wenn ich viel Zeit hätte, würde ich zu Hause bleiben.

Variation: Have students start with the main clause in the sentences on the right. (*Ich wäre zu euch gekommen, wenn ich Geld gehabt hätte.*)

17. Wenn ich Geld gehabt hätte, wäre ich zu euch gekommen.

    zur Tanzschule gehen

    einen Wagen kaufen

    mit dem Flugzeug fliegen

    meinen Führerschein machen

    länger am Telefon sprechen

    meine Freundin besuchen

    in den Urlaub fahren

Wenn ich Geld gehabt hätte, wäre ich zu euch gekommen.

Wenn ich Geld gehabt hätte, wäre ich zur Tanzschule gegangen.

Wenn ich Geld gehabt hätte, hätte ich einen Wagen gekauft.

Wenn ich Geld gehabt hätte, wäre ich mit dem Flugzeug geflogen.

Wenn ich Geld gehabt hätte, hätte ich meinen Führerschein gemacht.

Wenn ich Geld gehabt hätte, hätte ich länger am Telefon gesprochen.

Wenn ich Geld gehabt hätte, hätte ich meine Freundin besucht.

Wenn ich Geld gehabt hätte, wäre ich in den Urlaub gefahren.

18. Ich habe Zeit. Ich spreche mit ihm.

    Es ist Juni. Wir besuchen sie.
    Du weißt es. Du sagst es mir.
    Sie spricht langsamer. Ich verstehe sie.
    Es ist warm. Wir spielen im Freien.
    Es schneit. Ich laufe Ski.

Wenn ich Zeit hätte, würde ich mit
    ihm sprechen.

Wenn es Juni wäre, würden wir sie besuchen.

Wenn du es wüßtest, würdest du es mir sagen.

Wenn sie langsamer spräche, würde ich sie verstehen.

Wenn es warm wäre, würden wir im Freien spielen.

Wenn es schneite, würde ich Ski laufen.

19. Wenn es schöner wäre, würden wir an den
    Strand gehen.

Wenn du geschrieben hättest, würdest du es
    jetzt nicht zu tun brauchen.

Wenn du älter wärest, würest du das nicht
    machen.

Wenn du Deutsch könntest, würdest du ihn
    verstehen.

Wenn ich Geld hätte, würde ich das Fahrrad
    kaufen.

Wenn sie eine Gitarre hätte, würden wir
    besser singen.

Wäre es schöner, würden wir an den
    Strand gehen.

Hättest du geschrieben, würdest du es jetzt
    nicht zu tun brauchen.

Wärest du älter, würdes du das nicht machen.

Könntest du Deutsch, würdest du ihn
    verstehen.

Hätte ich Geld, würde ich das Fahrrad kaufen.

Hätte sie eine Gitarre, würden wir besser
    singen.

20. Warum würdest du froh sein?
    (zurückkommen)

    arbeiten

    zur Schule gehen

    den Mantel kaufen

    ein Buch lesen

    die Karten bestellen

    nicht so viel sprechen

    mich anrufen

Variation: Have students change sentences on the right to the present perfect tense. (Ich würde froh gewesen sein, wenn sie zurückgekommen wäre.)

Ich würde froh sein, wenn sie
    zurückkäme.

Ich würde froh sein, wenn sie arbeitete.

Ich würde froh sein, wenn sie zur Schule ginge.

Ich würde froh sein, wenn sie den Mantel kaufte.

Ich würde froh sein, wenn sie ein Buch läse.

Ich würde froh sein, wenn sie die Karten bestellte.

Ich würde froh sein, wenn sie nicht so viel spräche.

Ich würde froh sein, wenn sie mich anriefe.

21. Er sieht aus, als ob er fertig wäre.
    freundlich

    zufrieden

    erstaunt

    alt

    froh

    müde

Er sieht aus, als ob er fertig wäre.
Er sieht aus, als ob er freundlich
    wäre.

Er sieht aus, als ob er zufrieden wäre.

Er sieht aus, als ob er erstaunt wäre.

Er sieht aus, als ob er alt wäre.

Er sieht aus, als ob er froh wäre.

Er sieht aus, als ob er müde wäre.

Sie sehen aus, als
ob sie froh wären.

22. Construct contrary-to-fact statements, using the sentences given.

Variation: Have students use the present perfect tense. *(Wenn ich Geld gehabt hätte, hätte ich ein Auto gekauft.)*

Beispiel: *Wenn ich Geld habe, kaufe ich ein Auto.*
Wenn ich Geld hätte, würde ich ein Auto kaufen.

1. Wenn ich nach Hause komme, esse ich sofort.
2. Wenn wir dorthin fahren, übernachten wir in einer Jugendherberge.
3. Wenn er das hört, kommt er nicht nach Hause.
4. Wenn es kälter ist, können wir nicht schwimmen.
5. Wenn er lange wartet, bekommt er nichts zu essen.
6. Wenn es schneit, fahren wir in die Berge.
7. Wenn du willst, können wir es machen.
8. Wenn ich Lust habe, arbeite ich in einem Büro.
9. Wenn der Wagen streikt, lasse ich ihn abschleppen.
10. Wenn sie die Reise macht, komme ich gern mit.

23. Restate each sentence, omitting *wenn*.

Beispiel: *Wenn er das Buch gelesen hätte, hätten wir darüber sprechen können.*
Hätte er das Buch gelesen, hätten wir darüber sprechen können.

1. Wenn du mehr gearbeitet hättest, wärest du schneller fertig gewesen.
2. Wenn er das Geld bekommen hätte, wären wir ins Kino gegangen.
3. Wenn meine Freundin mir einen Brief geschrieben hätte, hätte ich mich sehr gefreut.
4. Wenn ich das gewußt hätte, wäre ich nicht gekommen.
5. Wenn sie mitgemacht hätte, wären wir bestimmt an erster Stelle gewesen.

24. Construct meaningful sentences, using the appropriate subjunctive form.

1. Wir / können / unser / Onkel / unser / Tante / bald / besuchen
2. Wenn / Frühling / sein / ich / auf / Sportplatz / sein
3. Wenn / du / Lust haben / können / wir / Reise / Europa / machen
4. Mögen / Sie / Sonntag / Zoo / gehen
5. Paul / sollen / sein / Hausaufgaben / machen
6. Haben / Monika / Auto / dürfen / wir / sofort / Stadt / fahren
7. Lehrling / sollen / bald / Werkstatt / zurückkommen

Wenn er nicht hier geparkt hätte, dann hätte man sein Auto nicht abgeschleppt. (Augsburg)

Lesestück 1

Singers sind im Urlaub

Familie Singer ist dieses Jahr an die Müritz in den Urlaub gefahren. Die Müritz ist der größte Binnensee° der DDR und eines der beliebtesten Urlaubsgebiete° des Landes. Singers haben vor, zwei Wochen lang im FDGB-Erholungsheim° „Herbert Warnke" zu verbringen. Es ist Singers ganz und gar überlassen, wie aktiv sie jeden Tag sein wollen. Langeweile° gibt es hier auf keinen Fall°. Das verspricht bereits eine große Tafel gleich am Eingang des Erholungsheimes. Auf der Tafel steht angeschlagen, welches Programm man für die Urlaubsgäste° aufgestellt hat. Es gibt nicht nur verschiedene kulturelle Veranstaltungen im Haus, sondern auch viele andere Möglichkeiten für Erholung° und Vergnügen° in der Gegend.

    Wie verbringen Singers also ihren Urlaub? Fast jeden Tag gehen sie in den kleinen Laden, direkt im Erholungsheim. Dort kann man Kleinigkeiten kaufen, wie zum Beispiel Ansichtskarten, Getränke, Süßigkeiten und verschiedene Sachen für den Strand. Heute kaufen Herr und Frau Singer einen Eimer° und eine Schaufel° für ihre fünfjährige Tochter Tanja. Damit wird Tanja sich bestimmt am Strand beschäftigen, denn sie spielt so gern im Sand.

    Während der Sommermonate ist das Wetter an der Müritz meistens sehr schön. Auch heute scheint die Sonne wieder und der Himmel ist nur leicht bewölkt°. Deshalb gehen Singers schon gegen halb zehn an den Strand. Später ist dort immer viel Betrieb. Sie brauchen nur einen halben Kilometer zu Fuß zu gehen, bis sie an den Strand kommen. Die meisten Urlauber haben sich für den ganzen Urlaub einen Strandkorb° gemietet°. Der ist sehr preiswert und garantiert ihnen einen bestimmten Platz am Strand. Das haben Singers auch getan.

    Kaum sind Herr und Frau Singer am Strand, da spielt Tanja schon mit ihrem neuen Eimer im Sand herum. Das macht ihr viel Spaß. Am Strand befinden sich Klettergeräte°. Da kann Tanja zeigen, was sie alles kann. Während Tanja sich am Strand vergnügt, sitzt Frau Singer im Strandkorb und schreibt ein paar Ansichtskarten an ihre Verwandten und Bekannten. Natürlich sollen die hören, wie es ihnen hier im Urlaub gefällt. Herr Singer dagegen° möchte etwas aktiver sein. Er hat sich einer Gruppe von Männern angeschlossen und spielt mit ihnen Volleyball. Er spielt Volleyball leidenschaftlich gern°, besonders da er sich körperlich bewegen muß und auch viel Spaß daran hat. Nach einer Weile wird er von einem der Volleyballspieler zum Schachspiel° herausgefordert. Dieses Spiel strengt natürlich mehr geistig° als körperlich° an. Auf einem Picknickplatz, ca. 200 Meter vom Strand entfernt, stehen die großen Schachfiguren auf Quadraten°, die ungefähr je einen halben Meter groß sind.

inland lake

vacation areas

resort

boredom/by no means

vacationers

relaxation/ enjoyment

pail/shovel

slightly overcast

beach chair/rented

climber

however

spielt…leidenschaftlich gern loves to play
game of chess
mental/physical

squares

das FDGB-Erholungsheim
„Herbert Warnke"

die Müritz

Was macht
Frau Singer?

Was kann man hier
alles bekommen?

Singers haben sich
ein Boot gemietet.

Das Zimmer
ist sehr bequem.

Was essen Singers
heute zum
Mittagessen?

Manche Urlaubsgäste
wohnen ganz in
der Nähe vom Strand.

Während sein Gegner eine Figur vorschiebt°, überblickt Herr Singer das ganze Feld, um seinen nächsten Zug° vorzubereiten°.

Um elf Uhr schlägt Herr Singer seiner Frau und Tochter vor, ein Boot zu mieten und auf dem Wasser herumzufahren. Das hat Tanja sehr gern. Sie ist auch die erste, die ins Boot springt. Herr Singer schiebt das Boot vorsichtig vom Landungssteg ab°, setzt sich hin, und rudert dann nicht weit vom Strand auf dem Wasser herum°. Die Schwäne und Enten sind gar nicht scheu° und kommen oft ziemlich nahe ans Boot heran. Tanja macht das besonders viel Freude. An manchen Tagen bringt sie sogar Brotkrumen mit, um die Tiere zu füttern.

Jetzt ist es bereits° nach zwölf Uhr. Singers müssen sich beeilen, denn um halb eins wird das Mittagessen serviert. Kaum sitzen sie an ihrem Tisch, da kommt auch schon die Kellnerin und bringt ihnen die Suppe. Heute gibt's Erbsensuppe°. Beim Tagesgericht haben Singers eine Auswahl von vier Speisen. Sie müssen ihre Wahl schon am vorhergehenden° Tag treffen. Für heute haben sie Kalbsfrikassee°, junge Erbsen und Reis bestellt. Herr und Frau Singer trinken dazu noch ein Bier. Tanja ißt nur ein paar Bissen°, dann ist sie schon satt.

Nach dem Essen gehen Frau Singer und Tanja auf ihr Zimmer im dritten Stock. Das Zimmer ist sehr bequem und hat einen herrlichen Blick auf die Müritz. Im Zimmer befinden sich drei Betten, ein großer Schrank, ein Nachttisch° und ein Tisch mit Stühlen. Frau Singer und Tanja sind etwas müde und machen nach dem Mittagessen immer ein Schläfchen. Herr Singer bleibt unten°. Zuerst sieht er im Brieffach nach, ob er Post bekommen hat. Heute hat er kein Glück. Er möchte seine Familie jetzt nicht stören und geht aus diesem Grunde° in den Lesesaal. Dort setzt er sich hin und liest die heutige Zeitung. Manchmal sitzt er hier und liest ein Buch. Gegen halb drei geht er auf sein Zimmer. Seine Frau und Tanja haben jetzt Lust, *Mensch ärgere dich nicht!*° zu spielen. Tanja zeigt ihren Eltern, daß sie in diesem Spiel sehr gut ist und ab und zu auch gewinnt.

Später am Nachmittag macht Herr Singer einen Vorschlag: „Wie wär's, wenn wir morgen nachmittag zur Freilichtbühne° gingen." Beim Vorverkauf° wird ihnen gesagt, daß *Aschenbrödel*° aufgeführt° wird. „Oh, wie schön!" sagt Tanja. Herr und Frau Singer entschließen sich sofort, Karten für die Vorstellung am nächsten Tag zu kaufen.

moves forward
move/prepare

schiebt…ab pushes off
rudert…herum rows around
shy

already

pea soup

previous

veal fricassee
bites

night stand

downstairs

for this reason

German version of the game Sorry

open-air theater
advance booking/ Cinderella performed

Fragen über das Lesestück

1. Wo liegt die Müritz?
2. Wie wissen Singers, welche Veranstaltungen im Erholungsheim stattfinden?
3. Was kann man alles in dem kleinen Laden im Erholungsheim kaufen?
4. Warum kaufen Singers ihrer Tochter einen Eimer und eine Schaufel?

5. Warum gehen Singers schon früh an den Strand?
6. Warum haben sich Singers einen Strandkorb gemietet?
7. Was macht Tanja am Strand?
8. An wen schreibt Frau Singer?
9. Was spielt Herr Singer zuerst? Und danach?
10. Was machen Singers um elf Uhr?
11. Woran hat Tanja besonders viel Freude?
12. Warum müssen sich Singers gegen zwölf Uhr beeilen?
13. Was essen sie heute zum Mittagessen?
14. Beschreib das Zimmer, in dem Singers während ihres Urlaubs wohnen!
15. Was machen Frau Singer und ihre Tochter nach dem Mittagessen? Und Herr Singer?
16. Wie heißt das Spiel, das Singers am Nachmittag spielen?
17. Wohin gehen sie am nächsten Tag?
18. Wo bekommen sie dafür Karten?

Erweiterung

25. Beendet die folgenden Sätze! Have students read their different sentences to the class.

1. Wenn ich Geld hätte, _____ .
2. Hätte ich viel Zeit, dann _____ .
3. Wenn ich zu euch gekommen wäre, _____ .
4. Peter sagt, er _____ .
5. Sabine meinte, wir _____ .
6. Wenn ich dir geschrieben hätte, _____ .
7. Wäre es warm gewesen, dann _____ .
8. Ich wünschte, ich _____ .
9. Der Ansager erklärt, die Polizei _____ .
10. Wenn ich gute Noten bekommen hätte, _____ .

26. Wie heißt das auf deutsch?

1. If we had known that, we wouldn't have come.
2. I have had enough to eat.
3. Who has to make the choice?
4. Could you take dictation, Ms. Wiegand?
5. She is really clever.
6. I would like to challenge her.
7. Will it work out?
8. What's wrong?
9. Did you join a group?

27. Beantwortet diese Fragen mit einem ganzen Satz!

1. Kannst du tippen? Wie viele Wörter pro Minute?
2. Was muß man alles auf einen Briefumschlag schreiben?
3. In welches Urlaubsgebiet fährst du am liebsten?
4. Wie verbringst du meistens deinen Urlaub?
5. An wen schreibst du gern einen Brief oder ein Karte?
6. Was spielst du leidenschaftlich gern?

28. Beschreibt die folgenden Wörter mit einem ganzen Satz!

1. der Urlaub
2. die Schreibmaschine
3. der Briefumschlag
4. die Anschrift
5. das Erholungsheim
6. der Strand
7. der Schrank
8. die Freilichtbühne

29. Beantwortet diese Fragen!

1. Um wieviel Uhr kommt meistens die Post?
2. Wann nimmst du gewöhnlich deinen Urlaub?
3. Was macht dir viel Freude?
4. Welches Programm siehst du gern im Fernsehen?
5. Wie beendet man einen persönlichen Brief?
6. Nenne drei Sachen, die man in einem Büro findet!

Rückblick
If students should have difficulties completing any of these exercises, you may wish to go back to the lesson in which the particular grammar point was discussed.

I. Change the following sentences from active to passive. Do not change the tense.

Beispiel: *Hast du ihn gefragt?*
Ist er von dir gefragt worden?

1. Ich hatte meine Eltern zum Zug gebracht.
2. Wann holt er sein neues Fahrrad?
3. Die Schüler besuchten ihren neuen Lehrer.
4. Die Kinder haben die Tür aufgemacht.
5. Wir lesen dieses deutsche Buch.
6. Haben Sie das Haus schon gekauft?
7. Die Kapelle spielte moderne Musik.
8. Hattest du den Chef gesehen?

II. Form questions, asking for the italicized words.

Beispiel: *Herr Schmidt ist schnell **nach Hause** gegangen.*
Wohin ist Herr Schmidt schnell gegangen?

1. Sie fahren *auf der Autobahn*.
2. Am Eingang steht *eine Tafel*.
3. *Die Zuschauer* gehen schon früh zum Stadion.
4. Die Touristen fahren *am nächsten Montag* ab.
5. Wir schicken ein Paket *an meine Eltern*.
6. Er hat ein *grünes* Hemd an.
7. Die Kinder glauben *dem Mann* nicht.
8. Dort drüben steht der Wagen *meines Onkels*.
9. Die Schüler haben *ihre Lehrerin* gefragt.
10. Er kann nicht mit mir sprechen, *weil er keine Zeit hat*.

III. Complete each of the following sentences by using the words in parentheses and making the necessary changes.

Peter Tietz hat sich mit (sein Freund) _____ Werner Braun in (die Stadt) _____ verabredet. Sie treffen sich vor (ein Restaurant/bekannt) _____ . Peter kommt etwas spät und entschuldigt sich bei Werner damit, daß er (ein Telefongespräch/lang) _____ führen mußte.

Beide gehen in (die Gaststätte/klein) _____ und setzen sich an (ein Tisch/braun) _____ direkt vor (das Fenster/groß) _____ . Dort sprechen sie über (die Reise/zweiwöchig) _____ , die sie geplant haben. Während sie (die Einzelheiten/genau) _____ besprechen, bringt der Kellner die Speisekarte. Sie bestellen (eine Zwiebelsuppe/französisch) _____ und (das Essen/best-) _____ auf (die Speisekarte/elegant) _____ . Außerdem trinken beide (ein Bier/hell) _____ .

Nach dem Essen fahren Peter und Werner zur Werkstatt, um Werners (Auto/neu) _____ abzuholen. Werner hat es erst gestern gekauft und will mit (sein Wagen/toll) _____ in den Urlaub fahren.

Warum sind hier so viele Menschen? (Augsburg)

Was machen diese Jugendlichen? (Füssen)

Lesestück 2

Weinbau an der Deutschen Weinstraße

Es gibt mehr als zehn deutsche Weinbaugebiete°, die hauptsächlich im westlichen und südwestlichen Teil der Bundesrepublik zu finden sind. Die größten und bekanntesten dieser Weinbaugebiete erstrecken° sich südlich von Koblenz längs° der Mosel und des Rheins. Wer im September und Oktober am Rhein oder an der Mosel entlangfährt, wird sicherlich oftmals anhalten, um die Gegend zu bestaunen. Es bietet sich dem Reisenden ein märchenhaftes Bild von kleinen Dörfern, die von zahlreichen Weinbergen umgeben° sind. Soweit das Auge reicht°, sieht man ein Meer° von Reben°. Während auf dem Rhein immer ein reger° Verkehr herrscht, schlängelt sich die Mosel — auch „die Tochter des Rheins" genannt — friedlich° am Fuße der Weinberge an den kleinen Ortschaften° vorbei°.

Wie heißt diese unvergeßliche Straße, die sich 80 Kilometer lang (von Schweigen nach Bockenheim) durch zahlreiche Weinbauorte schlängelt? Es ist die weltberühmte *Deutsche Weinstraße*. Diese Straße liegt im sonnigsten Teil der Pfalz. Aus diesem Grunde zieht es viele Besucher hierher°. Manche kommen sogar in Sonderzügen°, besonders während der Zeit der Weinfeste, die im September und Oktober stattfinden. Über 25% der deutschen Weinernte° wächst° in der Pfalz. Die Reben gedeihen hier besonders gut. Alle paar Jahre werden neue Reben angepflanzt. Man kann genau sehen, wie die jungen Pflanzen° vorsichtig an den Rebstöcken° festgemacht sind. Es wird zwei oder drei Jahre dauern, bis diese Reben Früchte tragen.

Die Weinlese° beginnt meistens im September und endet im November. Während dieser Zeit arbeiten viele Leute in den Weingärten°. Die Arbeiter schneiden alle Weintrauben ab°, die an den Rebstöcken hängen, und sammeln sie in Eimern. Sobald ein Eimer voll ist, werden die Trauben in einen großen Behälter gekippt°, der von einem kleinen Traktor zum Lastwagen° gefahren wird. Manchmal kippen sie aber die Reben in einen Kübel°, den ein Arbeiter zum Lastwagen trägt, und dann in einen großen Behälter kippt.

Wenn die Behälter auf dem Lastwagen voll sind, werden sie zum Weingut° ins Dorf oder in die Kleinstadt gefahren. Alle Trauben kommen in eine Presse°. Während die Trauben gepresst werden, stellt ein Arbeiter sicher°, daß keine Trauben in der Presse bleiben, bevor die nächste Ladung° ankommt. Ab und zu kostet man den Saft°, um sich von der Qualität zu überzeugen°. Der Saft wird später in riesigen° Tanks gesammelt. Der Saft muß acht Tage lang fermentieren. Nach dieser kurzen Zeit nennt man den Wein *Neuen Wein*. Viele Leute trinken diesen Wein im gleichen Jahr, in dem er

wine-growing areas

extend/along

surrounded
reaches/sea/vines
lively

schlängelt sich...vorbei winds past/peacefully/villages

zieht...hierher attracts here
special trains
harvest of grapes
grow

plants/vines

gathering of grapes

vineyards/schneiden ...ab cut off

dumped
truck
bucket

winery
press
stellt...sicher makes sure
load
juice/satisfied
gigantic

Weinberge bei Bacharach
am Rhein

Im Herbst arbeiten viele
Leute in den Weingärten.
(Stetten, Remstal)

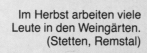

Weinbau an
der Deutschen
Weinstraße

Er trägt seinen Kübel
zum Lastwagen.
(Stetten, Remstal)

Ein Arbeiter kippt die
Reben in einen großen
Behälter. (Kaiserstuhl)

Die Arbeiter
schneiden die
Reben ab.

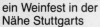

ein Weinfest in der
Nähe Stuttgarts

Die Einwohner und
Besucher kommen gern
zu den Weinlokalen.

geerntet° wurde. Der größte Teil des Weines wird aber mindestens ein Jahr lang oder länger in Holzfässern° gelagert°.

harvested
wooden barrels/
stored

Sobald der Wein sein richtiges Alter° erreicht hat, wird er zur Abfüllerei° gebracht. Dort wird er in Flaschen° gefüllt, verpackt° und gelagert. Jedes Weingut bietet Weine verschiedener Qualität an, von denen viele in andere Länder exportiert werden. Alle Weine, die für den Verkauf bestimmt sind°, erhalten° nach der Weinprobe° der Prüfer° eine Qualitätsbezeichnung°.

age
bottling company/
bottles/packed

are specified/
receive/wine test
tester/quality
designation

Eine bekannte Stadt an der Deutschen Weinstraße ist Neustadt. Nachdem man die Gegend bestaunt hat, sollte man natürlich auch einen Besuch in einem Weinbauort wie Neustadt machen. Im September und Oktober ist hier immer viel Betrieb. Eine Anzahl von Weinständen befindet sich in der Innenstadt. Die Einwohner und Besucher kommen gern hierher, um die verschiedenen Weine aus dieser Gegend zu kosten. Der Höhepunkt während eines Besuches an der Deutschen Weinstraße sind die Weinfeste. Am Anfang eines Weinfestes wird eine Weinkönigin° gekrönt°, die dann an allen Festlichkeiten teilnimmt°.

wine queen/crowned

participates

Fragen über das Lesestück

1. Wo liegen die meisten Weinbaugebiete in Deutschland?
2. Warum ist es besonders interessant, während des Septembers oder Oktobers zu den Weinbaugebieten zu fahren?
3. An welchen beiden Flüssen findet man viele Weinberge?
4. Wo befindet sich die *Deutsche Weinstraße?*
5. Warum wachsen die Reben so gut in der Pfalz?
6. Was machen die Arbeiter in den Weingärten während der Weinernte?
7. Was passiert mit dem Lastwagen, wenn er voll ist?
8. Wie wird der Saft gemacht?
9. Was ist *Neuer Wein?*
10. Wo wird der Wein längere Zeit gelagert?
11. Wohin kommt er dann?
12. Was passiert mit dem Wein, der verkauft wird?
13. Was machen die Leute gern, wenn sie im September und Oktober nach Neustadt kommen?
14. Was muß die Weinkönigin während dieser Zeit tun?

Sprachspiegel

After your students have completed this assignment, have them read their essays to the class. Others should ask questions about the material read.

I. *Schreibe einen Aufsatz über das Thema „Wir fahren in den Urlaub"!* Your description should include such details as preparation, day of departure, arrival, various events while on vacation and return home.

II. *Was passiert alles im Büro?* Develop an imaginary situational dialog of what happens during a typical day at an office. Be as creative as possible.

Du bist dran!

. . . .
Nein, ich habe den Brief noch nicht getippt.
. . . .
So bald wie möglich.
. . . .

Unterschreiben Sie bitte diesen Brief!
. . . .
Der geht an die Autofirma.
. . . .
Leider nicht.

Im Juli machen wir endlich Urlaub.
. . . .
Wahrscheinlich in die Berge.
. . . .
Wir haben uns ein Häuschen gemietet.

. . . .
Morgen soll das Wetter sehr bewölkt sein.
. . . .
Gehen wir doch spazieren. Das Wasser ist bestimmt zu kalt.
. . . .
Gegen zehn.

Haben Sie den Brief an die Firma Müller schon abgeschickt?
. . . .
Gut. Ich möchte ihn nämlich noch einmal durchlesen.
. . . .

Ruderst du gern auf dem See herum?
. . . .
Das strengt doch so sehr an.
. . . .

Das strengt doch so sehr an.

Kulturecke

Famous Castles in Germany

Traveling in Germany can be quite a unique experience, particularly for those who like to relive bygone days. Many castles scattered throughout the country vividly portray the splendor and grandeur in which the nobility lived in those days. The princes, dukes and other nobility had their castles along the Rhine; they controlled the waterway and required river boats to pay heavy duties for the privilege of passing through their principalities. Most of the rulers along the Rhine built their castles on top of hills so that they would be well protected from possible attack. Some castles like *Schloß Mespelbrunn,* located in the Spessart, were erected right in the water to make it difficult for neighboring rival princes to approach their fortress without being detected.

Heidelberg, situated along the Neckar River, is one of the most romantic German cities. Its university, the oldest in Germany (founded in 1386), and the student life connected with it have long been famous for their poignant charm. Equally famous is the 17th century castle that is noted for its lavish interior and the gigantic barrel that holds about 60,000 gallons of wine. The individual buildings of the castle, which have deteriorated over the years, are constantly undergoing renovation so that the structure can be preserved for generations to come.

Perhaps the most famous German castles are located in Bavaria and were built by King Ludwig II (1845-1886). Although King Ludwig II is known primarily for building the castles at *Neuschwanstein, Linderhof* and *Herrenchiemsee,* he spent most of his time at *Schloß Hohenschwangau.* This castle dates back to the 12th century but was completely renovated by King Maximilian II, Ludwig's father. It was here at Hohenschwangau that King Ludwig II spent a great deal of his time during his reign — from 1864 until his death in 1886.

Schloß Neuschwanstein, in the Bavarian Alps, was built by King Ludwig II between 1869 and 1886. This castle, which has been a model for fairy-tale movies and travel posters throughout the world, is an architectural expression of the Romantic period that dominated German art and literature during much of the 19th century. The elaborate thronehall *(Thronsaal)* reflects the king's eccentric nature in the ornamental and extremely plush interior. The marble stairs were planned to lead to a throne built of gold and ivory, but because of the king's untimely death, the work on the throne was cancelled. The huge chandelier, located in the center, is made of gilded brass and can be lowered for cleaning or replacing the 96 candles that it holds.

During the king's life, the hall of the singers *(Sängersaal)* was never used. It was only in 1933 that musical concerts were given in honor of Richard Wagner, who had died 50 years earlier. Richard Wagner's close friendship with the king becomes evident in this as well as other rooms. Various paintings here reflect one of Wagner's musical dramas, *Parsifal.* Additional paintings of another Wagner opera, *Tannhäuser,* are found in the king's study *(Arbeitszimmer).* This room, built in Romanesque style, shows a distinct resemblance to the study in the Wartburg castle, where Luther translated the Bible.

King Ludwig's eccentric nature becomes especially evident in the bedroom *(Schlafzimmer),* which took fourteen sculptors four and a half years to complete. The room shows an abundance of sumptuous and symbolic features reflecting the king's emotional state of mind. Another room deserves mention — the living room *(Wohnzimmer).* The swan was Ludwig's favorite animal and, therefore, is seen not only on the embroidered curtains, but also in paintings, as well as in the big flower vase that has the form of a swan. And, of course, the German word "swan" *(Schwan)* is part of the name of the castle — *Neunschwanstein.*

Whereas *Schloß Neuschwanstein* reminds one of a castle from the Middle Ages and strongly draws on King Ludwig's friendship with Richard Wagner, *Schloß Linderhof* was the king's first attempt to imitate features of the palace of *Versailles,* thus expressing his enthusiasm about the royal French family. The castle, located 30 kilometers from Neuschwanstein, was built within a period of four years (1874-1878). The hall of mirrors *(Spiegelsaal)* was designed by French architects and painters. The various mirrors around this room magnify and reflect the lavishly ornamental and decorative chandeliers, gilded walls and ceiling edges.

The king began to enlarge the bedroom after the castle was completed. Eventually, the bedroom became the largest room in the castle. Most of the paintings were completed before the king's death. The dining room *(Speisezimmer)* is evidence of Ludwig's loneliness. The dining table in the center could be lowered so that the kitchen staff was able to serve him from below. In this manner, the king, who many times ate by himself or with other royal guests, could remain undisturbed.

The blue grotto *(Blaue Grotte)* is located within a few hundred yards of the castle. It was created for the purpose of staging the Wagner operas, which were presented with a full array of colorful lights and with other special effects, such as a machine that produced rainbows. The king created various spots, including a shell-shaped throne from which he could view the spectacle that took place.

Schloß Herrenchiemsee is the third most famous castle built by King Ludwig II between 1878 and 1886. Since the king greatly admired Louis XIV of France, he patterned his castle after the palace of Versailles. This imitation is obvious when going through the beautifully landscaped palace gardens. Although Ludwig could not completely match the interior of the castle with that of Versailles, his castle nevertheless reveals a strong influence, particularly as you view the immense staircase *(Treppenhaus).*

Similar to the bedrooms in the other castles built by Ludwig II, the bedroom here is most lavishly decorated with golden ornaments, displayed on the walls and ceilings, and blue tapestries, reflecting the king's favorite color. The dining room *(Speisezimmer)* also shows a strong French influence. Here again, as at Linderhof, the king could lower the table through the floor to be served from the kitchen below.

Perhaps the most spectacular room at Herrenchiemsee is the gallery of mirrors *(Spiegelsaal).* King Ludwig II requested a matching but scaled-down version of the famous hall of mirrors at Versailles from his architect. The end result is seen in the illustrious hall that displays numerous candelabra and chandeliers reminiscent of the era of Louis XIV.

Schloß Neuschwanstein   das Heidelberger Schloß   Schloß Linderhof

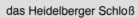

Die Leute wollen zum Schloß Herrenchiemsee fahren.

Um wieviel Uhr kann man zur Herreninsel fahren?

Die Besucher fahren gleich ab.

Schloß Herrenchiemsee

das Treppenhaus (Herrenchiemsee)

der Spiegelsaal (Herrenchiemsee)

Droste-Schloß (Meersburg, Bodensee)

das Schlafzimmer (Linderhof)

Schloß Hohenschwangau

Vokabeln

abschieben *(schob ab, abgeschoben)* to push off

die **Akte,-n** file

aktiv active

sich **anschließen** *(schloß an, angeschlossen)* to join

anstrengen to strain, tire out

Aschenbrödel Cinderella

aufführen to perform

aufstellen to organize, plan

bereits already

sich **beschäftigen mit** to be busy/occupied with

sich **bewegen** to move

bewölkt cloudy

leicht bewölkt slightly overcast

der **Binnensee,-n** inland lake

der **Bissen,-** bite

der **Chef,-s** boss

dagegen on the other hand, however

das **Diktat,-e** dictation

ein Diktat aufnehmen to take dictation

diktieren to dictate

das **Diktiergerät,-e** dictating machine

das **Dokument,-e** document

herankommen *(kam heran, ist herangekommen)* to come close to

herausfordern to challenge

herumrudern to row around

herumspielen to play around

heutig today's

irgendetwas something

das **Kalbsfrikassee** veal fricassee

der **Katalog,-e** catalog

klappen to clap

Das klappt prima. That works out well.

das **Klettergerät,-e** climbing equipment

körperlich physical

die **Langeweile** boredom

leidenschaftlich enthusiastic, passionate

leidenschaftlich gern spielen to love to play

mieten to rent

mittlerweile in the meantime

die **Mutti,-s** mom

der **Nachttisch,-e** night stand, bedside table

nervös nervous

patent clever, ingenious

der **Picknickplatz,-̈e** picnic area

das **Problem,-e** problem

das **Quadrat,-e** square

der **Rechner,-** calculator

der **Reis** rice

der **Sand** sand

satt full

satt sein to have had enough (to eat)

die **Schachfigur,-en** chess figur

das **Schachspiel,-e** game of chess

die **Schaufel,-n** shovel

scheu shy, timid

das **Schläfchen** nap

ein Schläfchen machen to take a nap

das **Schreiben** correspondence, letter

die **Schreibmaschine,-n** typewriter

der **Schwan,-̈e** swan

der **Strandkorb,-̈e** beach chair

der **Tagesplan,-̈e** daily schedule

die **Textverarbeitungsanlage,-n** word processor

tippen to type

überlassen to leave up to

Das ist dir überlassen. That's up to you.

die **Überprüfung,** review, examination

unten downstairs

unterrichten to instruct

jemanden davon unterrichten to let someone know about it

der **Urlaub** vacation

Urlaub nehmen to take vacation

Urlaub machen to go on vacation

der **Urlauber,-** vacationer

der **Urlaubsgast,-̈e** vacationer

das **Urlaubsgebiet,-e** vacation area

der **Vati,-s** dad

Verflixt! Darn it!

das **Vergnügen** enjoyment

sich **vergnügen** to enjoy oneself

der **Volleyball** volleyball (game)

der **Volleyballspieler,-** volleyball player

vorbereiten to prepare

vorhergehend previous

vorschieben *(schob vor, vorgeschoben)* to move forward

der **Vorverkauf** advance booking

der **Wunsch,-̈e** wish

zögern to hesitate

der **Zug,-̈e** move (chess)

zugehen lassen to forward

Lesestück 1

Hoffmanns fahren in die Ferien

Hoffmanns haben schon lange eine Ferienreise nach Bad Orb geplant. Auf einer Karte sehen die Eltern und ihre Kinder nach, wie sie am besten dorthin kommen. Bad Orb liegt im Spessart, ungefähr drei Stunden mit dem Auto von Deggendorf entfernt. An einem Samstag geht's endlich los. Vor der Abreise wird der Wagen noch gründlich nachgesehen. Hoffmanns wollen sicher sein, daß auch alles in Ordnung ist. Frau Hoffmann hilft den Kindern, besonders den kleinen, die richtigen Kleidungsstücke auszusuchen. Für die Reise packt Frau Hoffmann genug Verpflegung° für ihre ganze Familie ein, die Eltern und fünf Kinder. Alles muß gut vorbereitet werden. *food*

Am späten Morgen verläßt die Familie das Haus. Die Haustür wird abgeschlossen. Alle tragen ihr Gepäck zum Wagen. Die Koffer und Taschen müssen in den Kofferraum passen, denn im Wagen selbst ist kein Platz mehr für Gepäck. Sie verabschieden sich von einer Nachbarin° und steigen ein. Sie winkt ihnen zu und wünscht der Familie schöne Ferien. Unterwegs hält Herr Hoffmann vor einer Kirche an. Er möchte seiner Familie diese einzigartige° Kirche zeigen. Sie ist in den letzten zehn Jahren völlig° renoviert worden. In der Kirche ist alles mit Marmor° oder Gold verziert°. Herr Hoffmann erklärt der Familie die Geschichte dieser Kirche. *neighbor / unique / completely / marble/decorated*

Dann geht's weiter. Ab und zu halten Hoffmanns an, wenn es etwas Interessantes zu sehen gibt. An der Donaubrücke° steht ein Denkmal. Die Donau fließt hier vorbei° und dann weiter durch Passau nach Österreich. Dieser Fluß entspringt in Deutschland und ist hier auf dem Weg nach Passau schon ziemlich breit°. Die Kinder schauen von der Brücke auf den Fluß hinab° und sind erstaunt, wie stark die Strömung° ist. *bridge crossing the Danube / runs by / wide / schauen...hinab look down / current*

Am Nachmittag kommen Hoffmanns in Bad Orb an. Sie sind froh, endlich am Ferienort zu sein, denn die Reise ist für alle doch etwas anstrengend° gewesen. Gleich nach der Ankunft wird die Familie von der Besitzerin° der Pension begrüßt. Sie sind schon lange erwartet° worden. Sie besichtigen die einzelnen Zimmer, in denen sie während der nächsten Tage wohnen werden. Besonders gut gefällt den Kindern ihr Zimmer. Es ist schön bunt dekoriert. Die Besitzerin lädt die ganze Familie in ihr Haus nebenan ein und bietet allen etwas zu trinken an. *strenuous / owner / expected*

Während der Ferien lernen Hoffmanns die Umgebung kennen. Neben dem Wohnhaus ist ein kleiner Spielplatz. Dort haben die Kinder viel Spaß beim Spielen. Jeden Tag wandern Hoffmanns eine oder zwei Stunden in der Umgebung. Ein großer Wald ist gleich in der Nähe, wo die Eltern und die Kinder gern ihre Zeit verbringen.

You may want to select only particular sections of this unit for review. The few new words introduced are listed in the margin of the line in which they appear. If your students have some difficulties in completing the exercises, you may want to go back to the lesson in which the particular grammar point or topic was discussed.

Wie in den meisten deutschen Wäldern kann man hier stundenlang° *for hours*
spazierengehen.

Die schönen Ferientage gehen leider schnell zu Ende. Hoffmanns verabschieden sich und bedanken sich bei der Besitzerin für
die gute Unterkunft°. Sie haben vor, im nächsten Jahr wiederzukom- *accommodation*
men. Die Besitzerin freut es auch, daß es ihnen gefallen hat, und sie
wünscht ihnen eine gute Rückfahrt°. Obwohl Hoffmanns schöne *return trip*
Tage verbracht haben, sind sie doch froh, wieder zu Hause zu sein.

Fragen über das Lesestück

1. Wohin wollen Hoffmanns fahren? Wo liegt dieser Ort?
2. Was machen sie noch vor der Abfahrt?
3. Wem hilft Frau Hoffmann?
4. Was packt sie?
5. Wer trägt das Gepäck zum Wagen?
6. Warum müssen alle Sachen in den Kofferraum passen?
7. Warum halten Hoffmanns vor einer Kirche an?
8. Wo halten sie später noch einmal an?
9. Wo entspringt die Donau und wohin fließt sie?
10. Von wem werden Hoffmanns begrüßt?
11. Was besichtigen sie zuerst?
12. Wozu lädt die Besitzerin alle ein?
13. Was ist neben dem Wohnhaus?
14. Was machen Hoffmanns jeden Tag?
15. Wann wollen sie wieder nach Bad Orb zurückkommen?

Am späten Morgen verläßt die Familie das Haus.

Übungen

I. **Determine where you would be most likely to find each of the items listed below. Also, identify each item with a short sentence in German. Are these items related to a *Post, Zoo, Geschäft, Restaurant, Apotheke, Werkstatt* or a *Büro*?**

1. Ersatzteillager
2. Tablette
3. Telefonzelle
4. Schlange
5. Auspuffrohr
6. Schweinebraten
7. Paketkarte
8. Tiere
9. Kellnerin
10. Lebensmittel
11. Gemüsesuppe
12. Diktiergerät
13. Mechaniker
14. Portogebühr
15. Medizin
16. Käse
17. Rechner
18. Speisekarte
19. Robben
20. Briefkasten
21. Koffer
22. Löwe
23. Apfelkuchen
24. Rezept
25. Esel
26. Schreibmaschine
27. Früchte
28. Ferngespräch
29. Auto
30. Wurstwaren

II. **Beantwortet die folgenden Fragen mit einem ganzen Satz!**

1. Was möchtest du in einem Restaurant essen?
2. Was machst du, wenn dein Auto auf der Landstraße streikt und nicht weiterfährt?
3. Was lernst du im Fahrunterricht?
4. Was kauft man in einem Kaufhaus ein?
5. Welche Früchte kann man auf dem Markt bekommen?
6. Was nimmst du mit, wenn du in die Ferien fährst?
7. Was kann man alles in einer Apotheke kaufen?
8. Was für eine Sportart hast du gern? Warum?

III. **Change the following sentences to the past and present perfect tense.**

Beispiel: *Kommt ihr zu uns?*
Kamt ihr zu uns?
Seid ihr zu uns gekommen?

1. Sie bringen das Paket zur Post.
2. Um wieviel Uhr kommt das Flugzeug an?
3. Hoffmanns fahren im Sommer in die Ferien.
4. Trägt er das Gepäck zum Wagen?
5. Der Arzt verschreibt mir ein Rezept.
6. Könnt ihr das gut?
7. Ist alles in Ordnung?
8. Es geht heute leider nicht.
9. Wann rufen Sie an?

IV. Complete each sentence by using the words provided in parentheses. Watch the endings!

1. Die Touristen fahren zu (diese Stadt/mittelalterlich) _____ .
2. Kannst du (ein Paket/groß) _____ mit der Post schicken?
3. Haben Sie schon von (das Gasthaus/beliebt) _____ gehört?
4. Stellen Sie bitte (die Tasche/braun) _____ auf (der Stuhl/klein) _____ !
5. Die Studenten besuchen (dieses Museum/neu) _____ .
6. Ich arbeite für (eine Firma/international) _____ .
7. Viele (Besucher/amerikanisch) _____ kommen jedes Jahr hierher.
8. Welche (die Hose/teuer) _____ haben Sie in (das Kaufhaus/alt) _____ gekauft?
9. Wir lesen ein paar (Bücher/deutsch) _____ .
10. Kennst du die Geschichte (diese Kirche/berühmt) _____?

V. Form a complete sentence, using the information given.

1. Er sagte, _____ .
2. Hätte ich etwas Geld, _____ .
3. Wenn wir Zeit gehabt hätten, _____ .
4. Wenn du doch _____ !
5. Ich würde froh sein, wenn _____ .
6. Sie sieht aus, als ob sie _____ .
7. Wenn es nicht so teuer wäre, _____ .
8. Wenn ich gestern gefahren wäre, _____ .

VI. The sentences below are either in the active or the passive. If a sentence is in the active, change it to the passive. If it is in the passive, change it to the active. Keep each sentence in the same tense.

1. Der Briefträger bringt mir ein Telegramm.
2. Das Geschäft wird von den Verkäufern um sechs geschlossen.
3. Dieser Satz ist von den Studenten gut verstanden worden.
4. Hast du gute Aufnahmen gemacht?
5. Meine Eltern bezahlten die Karten.
6. Warum habt ihr den Lehrer gefragt.
7. Du bist von ihnen eingeladen worden.
8. Das Paket wurde von ihr geschickt.

VII. Supply the proper relative pronouns.

1. Der Briefträger, _____ jeden Morgen die Post bringt, kommt immer pünktlich.
2. Kennst du die Dame, _____ mit dem Bus zur Arbeit fährt?
3. Mein Onkel, von _____ wir gestern ein Telegramm bekommen haben, wohnt in Süddeutschland.
4. Wo sind die Kinder, _____ wir geholfen haben?
5. Ist das der Zaun, an _____ du dein Fahrrad gestellt hattest?
6. Dort steht der Zug, mit _____ wir fahren können.
7. Meine Freundin, _____ ich oft besuche, wohnt in einem Vorort.
8. Der Brief, _____ ich bekommen habe, ist sehr interessant.

Lesestück 2

In der Tankstelle

Jeden Morgen geht Herr Bäumler um acht Uhr zur Arbeit. Seine Arbeitsstelle ist ungefähr 10 Kilometer von seinem Haus entfernt. Mit dem Auto dauert es meistens nur 15 Minuten, bis er dort ankommt.

Auf dem Weg stellt Herr Bäumler fest, daß er noch schnell zur Tankstelle muß. Eine Tankstelle, wo er ein guter Kunde ist, befindet sich direkt an der Landstraße in Richtung Innenstadt. Er fährt seinen Wagen zu einer freien Zapfsäule°. Dort kann er „Normal" oder „Super" Benzin° tanken°. Meistens tankt Herr Bäumler „Normal". Es ist etwas preiswerter. Heute braucht der Wagen fast 50 Liter, der Tank ist fast leer. Sobald er voll ist, hängt er den Schlauch° wieder an die Zapfsäule.

pump
gas/fill up

hose

Herr Bäumler merkt, daß ein Reifen etwas Luft braucht. Er mißt den Luftdruck° und pumpt°, bis der Reifen genug Luft hat. Herr Brauer, der Tankwart°, kennt Herrn Bäumler gut. Er ist immer so hilfsbereit. Herr Brauer sagt ihm, daß der Ölstand° zu niedrig° ist. Herr Bäumler füllt Öl auf und gießt° auch noch etwas Wasser in die Batterie. Frau Brauer ist an der Kasse und liest den Benzinbetrag° ab. Dann bezahlt Herr Bäumler und fährt seinen Wagen noch schnell in die Waschanlage°. Dort spritzt Herr Brauer den Wagen mit einem Schlauch. Herr Bäumler bedankt sich für die gute Bedienung und verläßt die Tankstelle.

air pressure/pumps
service station attendant
oil level/low
pours
amount for gas

car wash

Herr Bäumler füllt Öl auf.

Er hängt den Schlauch an die Zapfsäule.

Was macht Herr Bäumler?

Fragen über das Lesestück

1. Wie lange fährt Herr Bäumler zu seiner Arbeitsstelle?
2. Wo tankt er meistens?
3. Warum tankt Herr Bäumler „Normal"-Benzin?
4. Wieviel Benzin kauft er heute?
5. Was macht Herr Bäumler mit einem Reifen?
6. Was sagt der Tankwart Herrn Bäumler?
7. Was macht er dann?
8. Wie weiß Frau Brauer, wieviel Herr Bäumler bezahlen muß?
9. Warum fährt Herr Bäumler seinen Wagen in die Waschanlage?

Interview

Freizeitgestaltung der Deutschen

The following interview was recorded in Germany. Read it and/or listen to the material on tape and see how much you can understand. Write a short summary of this interview in German.

Ich sitze im Wohnzimmer von Herrn Theodor Schröder. Herr Schröder hat sich liebenswürdigerweise dazu bereit erklärt, einige Fragen über das Thema „Freizeitgestaltung der Deutschen" zu beantworten.

INTERVIEWER: Herr Schröder, unsere Hörer wären Ihnen dankbar, wenn Sie uns etwas über die allgemeine Freizeitgestaltung der Deutschen erzählen könnten.

SCHRÖDER: Da haben Sie mir eigentlich eine große Frage gestellt, die ich wohl kaum in ein paar Minuten beantworten kann. Auf jeden Fall werde ich versuchen, mich kurz zu fassen.

Zunächst sollten wir erst einmal vom Sport reden. Da die wöchentliche Arbeitszeit im letzten Jahrzehnt abgenommen hat, ist natürlich die Bedeutung des Sports wesentlich gestiegen.

Das große Interesse manifestiert sich nicht nur in den Zuschauerzahlen bei Wettkämpfen, sondern auch in den Millionen von Hörern und Zuschauern, die an Rundfunk- und Fernsehapparaten Fußballspiele von internationalem Rang oder andere wichtige Sportereignisse miterleben.

INTERVIEWER:	Sicherlich haben die Olympischen Spiele in München beträchtlich dazu beigetragen, das Interesse der Deutschen für die verschiedenen Sportarten zu verstärken.
SCHRÖDER:	Das stimmt. Aber auch die Fußballweltmeisterschaft in Deutschland ist eines der größten deutschen Sportereignisse in den letzten Jahrzehnten.
INTERVIEWER:	Welche andere Sportarten außer Fußball sind in Deutschland beliebt?
SCHRÖDER:	Turnen steht sicherlich an zweiter Stelle. Die Leichtathletik hat auch viele Anhänger und steht mehrere Male im Jahr im Mittelpunkt des Geschehens. Dasselbe gilt vom Wintersport, der in jedem Jahr viele Tausende Frauen und Männer aller Altersklassen ins Gebirge lockt.
INTERVIEWER:	Skifahren scheint fast nur in den Alpen möglich zu sein. Oder gibt es noch andere Skimöglichkeiten?
SCHRÖDER:	Skilaufen kann man in günstigen Wintern bis in die Täler der Mittelgebirge hinein. Skilifts haben diesem Sport viel von seiner Beschwerlichkeit genommen.
INTERVIEWER:	Wie steht es mit Tennis? Ist dieser Sport auch beliebt?
SCHRÖDER:	In den letzten Jahren ist Tennis zu einer der beliebtesten deutschen Sportarten geworden. Das ist besonders bei internationalen Turnieren zu erkennen, bei denen die Deutschen eine bessere Position im internationalen Turnier eingenommen haben.
INTERVIEWER:	Außer dem Sport gibt es natürlich noch zahlreiche andere Möglichkeiten zur Freizeitgestaltung. Können Sie uns vielleicht einige Beispiele geben?
SCHRÖDER:	Wandern ist für viele Deutsche eine Erholung. Gut markierte Wanderwege laden die Wanderfreunde ein. Die schnelleren Wanderer finden ihre Campingplätze, die im Sommer bei Sonne wie bei Regen aufgesucht werden.

Diejenigen, die noch schneller vorwärtskommen wollen, setzen sich eben in ihr Auto und — obwohl sie mit dem zunehmenden Autobahnverkehr kämpfen müssen — fahren meistens in Richtung Süden. Das ist besonders am Wochenende der Fall.

INTERVIEWER: Ja, es ist unglaublich, wie sich am Wochenende ein Wagen nach dem anderen im Schneckentempo auf den Autobahnen und Bundesstraßen vorwärtsbewegt.

SCHRÖDER: Leider ist dadurch auch die Zahl der Unfälle enorm angestiegen. Außer den Wochenendreisen nach Süddeutschland fahren die Deutschen in den Ferien besonders gern nach Italien, Jugoslawien und Spanien. Deutsche, die den Kampf auf den Verkehrsstraßen aufgegeben haben, fahren entweder zu einem naheliegenden See oder Schwimmbad.

INTERVIEWER: Haben Sie vielen Dank für Ihre Auskunft, Herr Schröder. Sie wird unseren Hörern sicherlich von Nutzen sein.

SCHRÖDER: Nichts zu danken.

Cultural Notes

Dialects

Many Americans going to certain parts of Germany, with what they think is a good command of German, get the shock of their lives when a native starts to speak. Not understanding a word, the American traveler may wonder what kind of language he/she actually learned at school. This could well be the case if the American came to a small town in Bavaria (Bayern), Swabia (Schwaben), the Palatinate (Pfalz) or Hesse (Hessen). In these southern and central parts of Germany, local dialects are often especially difficult for foreigners to understand — even for North Germans, by the way! *Plattdeutsch,* still spoken in rural areas of Lower Saxony (Niedersachsen), Westphalia (Westfalen) and Schleswig-Holstein and in the ports (Hamburg, Bremen), is very similar to the Dutch language and closer to English; but chances are it too will throw most strangers.

The German spoken in Hanover generally is considered to be the best "High-German" (Hochdeutsch) the standard pronunciation. Educated people all over the country are able to speak High-German (although often with a shade of the local dialect), and it will be readily understood by Americans aquainted with the language. But the regional dialects are colorful, and they can be learned if one has patience and a good ear.

Eating Manners

One of the things that startles most Americans arriving in Germany is the way the Germans eat. Whenever they eat something that requires cutting, they hold the fork in the left hand and the knife in the right, keeping them this way throughout the meal. The knife is also used to push the food onto the fork. If a knife is not needed, the left hand is placed on the table beside the plate, not in the lap. Meat is cut with a knife similar to the one commonly used in this country. Fish, however, will be cut with either a special fish knife or a fork.

Seldom will you see a German drink plain water with meals. The most common table drinks for lunch or dinner will be beer or wine for adults and milk or fruit juice for young people.

Visiting Germans

When it comes to visiting each other, Germans tend to be more formal than Americans. Casual visits are rare. Therefore, if you are invited to a private German home, you may consider it as a special gesture of friendship. You may well expect that your visit has been carefully prepared for: the house will be spick and span, *Kuchen* (cake) will have been baked or bought to be eaten with coffee, and the family will be dressed up for the occasion. When invited for a meal, it is quite customary to bring along a little bouquet of flowers for the hostess and candy for small children in the family.

Was steht auf diesem
Schild? (Hamburg)

Was verkauft diese Firma? (München)

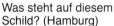

Was bedeutet dieses
Schild? (Bremen)

Personal Pronouns

Singular	Nominative	Accusative	Dative
1st person	ich	mich	mir
2nd person	du	dich	dir
3rd person	er sie es	ihn sie es	ihm ihr ihm

Plural			
1st person	wir	uns	uns
2nd person	ihr	euch	euch
3rd person	sie	sie	ihnen
formal form (plural or singular)	Sie	Sie	Ihnen

Reflexive Pronouns

Singular		Accusative	Dative
1st person	*(ich)*	mich	mir
2nd person	*(du)*	dich	dir
3rd person	*(er)* *(sie)* *(es)*	sich	sich

Plural			
1st person	*(wir)*	uns	uns
2nd person	*(ihr)*	euch	euch
3rd person	*(sie)*	sich	sich
formal form *(Sie)* (plural or singular)		sich	sich

Relative Pronouns

	Singular			Plural
	Masculine	*Feminine*	*Neuter*	
Nominative	der	die	das	die
Accusative	den	die	das	die
Dative	dem	der	dem	denen
Genitive	dessen	deren	dessen	deren

Demonstrative Pronouns

	Singular			Plural
	Masculine	*Feminine*	*Neuter*	
Nominative	der	die	das	die
Accusative	den	die	das	die
Dative	dem	der	dem	denen

Definite Article

	Singular			Plural
	Masculine	*Feminine*	*Neuter*	
Nominative	der	die	das	die
Accusative	den	die	das	die
Dative	dem	der	dem	den
Genitive	des	der	des	der

Der-Words

	Singular			Plural
	Masculine	*Feminine*	*Neuter*	
Nominative	dieser	diese	dieses	diese
Accusative	diesen	diese	dieses	diese
Dative	diesem	dieser	diesem	diesen
Genitive	dieses	dieser	dieses	dieser

Other *der*-words introduced are *welcher, jeder, solcher, mancher, derselbe*.

Question Words: *Wer? Was?*

Nominative	wer	was
Accusative	wen	was
Dative	wem	
Genitive	wessen	

Indefinite Article and *Ein*-Words

	Singular			Plural
	Masculine	*Feminine*	*Neuter*	
Nominative	ein	eine	ein	keine
Accusative	einen	eine	ein	keine
Dative	einem	einer	einem	keinen
Genitive	eines	einer	eines	keiner

Ein-words are *ein, kein* and all possessive adjectives (*mein, dein, sein, ihr, sein, unser, euer, ihr, Ihr*).

Adjectives after *Der*-Words

	Singular			Plural
	Masculine	*Feminine*	*Neuter*	
Nominative	-e	-e	-e	-en
Accusative	-en	-e	-e	-en
Dative	-en	-en	-en	-en
Genitive	-en	-en	-en	-en

	Singular			Plural
	Masculine	*Feminine*	*Neuter*	
Nominative	der alt*e* Film	die nett*e* Dame	das neu*e* Haus	die gut*en* Schüler
Accusative	den alt*en* Film	die nett*e* Dame	das neu*e* Haus	die gut*en* Schüler
Dative	dem alt*en* Film	der nett*en* Dame	dem neu*en* Haus	den gut*en* Schüler*n*
Genitive	des alt*en* Film*es*	der nett*en* Dame	des neu*en* Haus*es*	der gut*en* Schüler

The following words expressing quantity can be used only in the plural with their corresponding adjective endings for *der*-words: *alle, beide*.

Adjectives after *Ein*-Words

	Singular			Plural
	Masculine	*Feminine*	*Neuter*	
Nominative	-er	-e	-es	-en
Accusative	-en	-e	-es	-en
Dative	-en	-en	-en	-en
Genitive	-en	-en	-en	-en

	Singular			Plural
	Masculine	*Feminine*	*Neuter*	
Nominative	ein alt*er* Film	eine nett*e* Dame	ein neu*es* Haus	keine gut*en* Schüler
Accusative	einen alt*en* Film	eine nett*e* Dame	ein neu*es* Haus	keine gut*en* Schüler
Dative	einem alt*en* Film	einer nett*en* Dame	einem neu*en* Haus	keinen gut*en* Schüler*n*
Genitive	eines alt*en* Film*es*	einer nett*en* Dame	eines neu*en* Haus*es*	keiner gut*en* Schüler

The following words expressing quantity can be used only in the plural with their corresponding endings for adjectives after *ein*-words: *andere, ein paar, einige, viele, wenige.*

Adjective Endings for Adjectives Not Preceded by Articles

	Singular			Plural
	Masculine	*Feminine*	*Neuter*	
Nominative	alt*er* Freund	rot*e* Bluse	neu*es* Auto	klein*e* Kinder
Accusative	alt*en* Freund	rot*e* Bluse	neu*es* Auto	klein*e* Kinder
Dative	alt*em* Freund	rot*er* Bluse	neu*em* Auto	klein*en* Kinder*n*
Genitive	alt*en* Freund*es*	rot*er* Bluse	neu*en* Auto	klein*er* Kinder

Comparison of Adjectives and Adverbs

Adjective/Adverb	schnell	warm	gut	hoch	gern
Comparative	schneller	wärmer	besser	höher	lieber
Superlative	schnellst-	wärmst-	best-	höchst-	liebst-

Plural of Nouns

	Singular	Plural
no change or add umlaut	das Zimmer die Mutter	die Zimmer die Mütter
add -n, -en or -nen	die Ecke der Automat die Freundin	die Ecken die Automaten die Freundinnen
add -e or -̈e	der Tag die Stadt	die Tage die Städte
Add -̈er	das Buch	die Bücher
add -s	das Café das Büro	die Cafés die Büros

Prepositions

Dative	Accusative	Dative or Accusative	Genitive
aus außer bei mit nach seit von zu	durch für gegen ohne um	an auf hinter in neben über unter vor zwischen	anstatt trotz während wegen

Inverted Word Order

1. Formation of questions beginning with verb
   Spielst du heute Fußball?
2. Formation of questions beginning with question word
   Wohin gehen Sie heute nachmittag?
3. Command forms
   Hab keine Angst!
   Lauft schnell!
   Passen Sie auf!
   Gehen wir!
4. Sentence beginning with word other than subject
   Am Sonntag fahren wir zu meiner Tante.

Word Order of Dative and Accusative Case (Objects and Pronouns)

Er gibt	dem Fluggast	eine Bordkarte.
Er gibt	ihm	eine Bordkarte.
Er gibt	sie	dem Fluggast.
Er gibt	sie	ihm.

Word Order When Using Relative Pronouns and Conjunctions

1. Relative pronouns
   Der Mann, der ins Auto einsteigt, ist mein Vater.
   Wer ist der Mann, den du getroffen hast?
2. Coordinating conjunctions
   Ich möchte bleiben, aber ich habe keine Zeit.
3. Subordinating conjunctions
   Wir gehen ins Restaurant, weil wir hungrig sind.
   Weil wir hungrig sind, gehen wir ins Restaurant.

Verbs Followed by Dative Case

antworten   danken   folgen   gefallen   gehören   glauben   gratulieren   helfen   passen

   Gabi hilft ihrer Mutter.
   Der Ball gehört mir.

The verb *glauben* may take either the dative or accusative case. If used with a person, the dative follows *(Ich glaube ihm)*. If used with an object, the accusative is used *(Ich glaube das nicht)*.

Verbs with Prepositions Followed by Accusative Case

bitten um	to ask for
denken an	to think of
sich erinnern an	to remember
sich freuen auf	to look forward to
grenzen an	to border on
sich interessieren für	to be interested in
schreiben über	to write about
sehen auf	to look at
sprechen über	to talk about
warten auf	to wait for
zeigen auf	to point to

Verbs with Prepositions Followed by Dative Case

bestehen aus	to consist of
sich beteiligen an	to participate in
erzählen von	to tell about
fragen nach	to ask for
stammen aus	to come from (place of birth, residence)
teilnehmen an	to participate in

Verb Forms — Present Tense

	gehen	**heißen**	**finden**	**arbeiten**
ich	gehe	heiße	finde	arbeite
du	gehst	heißt	findest	arbeitest
er, sie, es	geht	heißt	findet	arbeitet
wir	gehen	heißen	finden	arbeiten
ihr	geht	heißt	findet	arbeitet
sie, Sie	gehen	heißen	finden	arbeiten

	haben	**sein**	**wissen**
ich	habe	bin	weiß
du	hast	bist	weißt
er, sie, es	hat	ist	weiß
wir	haben	sind	wissen
ihr	habt	seid	wißt
sie, Sie	haben	sind	wissen

Verbs with Stem Vowel Change — Present Tense

	a to *ä*	*e* to *i*	*e* to *ie*
ich	fahre	spreche	sehe
du	fährst	sprichst	siehst
er, sie, es	fährt	spricht	sieht
wir	fahren	sprechen	sehen
ihr	fahrt	sprecht	seht
sie, Sie	fahren	sprechen	sehen

Command Forms

Familiar (singular)	Geh!	Warte!	Sei!	Hab!
Familiar (plural)	Geht!	Wartet!	Seid!	Habt!
Formal (singular/plural)	Gehen Sie!	Warten Sie!	Seien Sie!	Haben Sie!
***Wir*-form** (Let's...)	Gehen wir!	Warten wir!	Seien wir!	Haben wir!

Modal Auxiliaries

	dürfen	**können**	**mögen**	**müssen**	**sollen**	**wollen**
ich	darf	kann	mag	muß	soll	will
du	darfst	kannst	magst	mußt	sollst	willst
er, sie, es	darf	kann	mag	muß	soll	will
wir	dürfen	können	mögen	müssen	sollen	wollen
ihr	dürft	könnt	mögt	müßt	sollt	wollt
sie, Sie	dürfen	können	mögen	müssen	sollen	wollen

Future Tense (*werden* + infinitive)

ich	werde
du	wirst
er, sie, es	wird
wir	werden
ihr	werdet
sie, Sie	werden

Sie werden nächstes Jahr nach Deutschland fahren. Wirst du morgen ins Kino gehen?

Past Tense (Narrative Past Tense)

	Regular Verbs		Irregular Verbs				
	sagen	**arbeiten**	**kommen**	**gehen**	**fahren**	**haben**	**sein**
ich	sagte	arbeitete	kam	ging	fuhr	hatte	war
du	sagtest	arbeitetest	kamst	gingst	fuhrst	hattest	warst
er, sie, es	sagte	arbeitete	kam	ging	fuhr	hatte	war
wir	sagten	arbeiteten	kamen	gingen	fuhren	hatten	waren
ihr	sagtet	arbeitetet	kamt	gingt	fuhrt	hattet	wart
sie, Sie	sagten	arbeiteten	kamen	gingen	fuhren	hatten	waren

Present Perfect Tense

regular verbs: *haben* + past participle (*ge* + 3rd person singular)
Sie hat gefragt.
Hast du etwas gesagt?

irregular verbs: *haben* or *sein* + past participle
Ich habe das Brot gegessen.
Wir sind dorthin gefahren.

with modal auxiliaries: *Haben Sie in die Stadt gehen müssen?*
Er hat das nicht essen können.

Past Perfect Tense

Past tense of *haben* or *sein* plus past participle
Hattest du den Brief geholt?
Wart ihr zu Hause gewesen?

Passive

present:	Der Lehrer wird gefragt.
past:	Der Lehrer wurde gefragt.
present perfect:	Der Lehrer ist gefragt worden.
past perfect:	Der Lehrer war gefragt worden.
future:	Der Lehrer wird gefragt werden.

Irregular Verbs

The following list contains all the irregular verbs used in *DEUTSCH: AKTUELL 1* and *2*. Verbs with separable or inseparable prefixes are not included when the basic verb form has been introduced (Example: *kommen, ankommen*). If the basic verb has not been introduced, then the verb with its prefix is included. Verbs with stem vowel changes as well as those constructed with a form of *sein* have also been indicated.

Infinitive	Present Tense Stem Vowel Change	Past	Past Participle	Meaning
abheben		hob ab	abgehoben	to lift (receiver)
abreißen		riß ab	abgerissen	to tear down
abschieben		schob ab	abgeschoben	to push off
anfangen	fängt an	fing an	angefangen	to begin
sich anschließen		schloß an	angeschlossen	to join
sich anziehen		zog an	angezogen	to get dressed
ausleihen		lieh aus	ausgeliehen	to check out
beginnen		begann	begonnen	to begin, start
behalten	behält	behielt	behalten	to keep
bekommen		bekam	bekommen	to get, receive
bieten		bot	geboten	to offer
bitten		bat	gebeten	to ask, plead
bleiben		blieb	ist geblieben	to stay, remain
bringen		brachte	gebracht	to bring
denken		dachte	gedacht	to think
dürfen	darf	durfte	gedurft	to be allowed, may
einladen	lädt ein	lud ein	eingeladen	to invite
einschließen		schloß ein	eingeschlossen	to include
empfehlen	empfiehlt	empfahl	empfohlen	to recommend
entscheiden		entschied	entschieden	to decide
sich entschließen		entschloß	entschlossen	to decide
entspringen		entsprang	ist entsprungen	to originate (river)
essen	ißt	aß	gegessen	to eat
fahren	fährt	fuhr	ist gefahren	to drive, go
finden		fand	gefunden	to find
fliegen		flog	ist geflogen	to fly
fließen		floß	ist geflossen	to flow, run
geben	gibt	gab	gegeben	to give
gedeihen		gedieh	gediehen	to grow
gefallen	gefällt	gefiel	gefallen	to like
gehen		ging	ist gegangen	to go, walk
gelingen		gelang	ist gelungen	to succeed
geschehen	geschieht	geschah	ist geschehen	to happen
gewinnen		gewann	gewonnen	to win
gießen		goß	gegossen	to pour
haben	hat	hatte	gehabt	to have
halten	hält	hielt	gehalten	to hold
hängen		hing	gehangen	to hang
heißen		hieß	geheißen	to be called
helfen	hilft	half	geholfen	to help
hochziehen		zog hoch	hochgezogen	to pull up

kennen		kannte	gekannt	to know (person)
klingen		klang	geklungen	to sound
kommen		kam	ist gekommen	to come
können	kann	konnte	gekonnt	to be able to, can
lassen	läßt	ließ	gelassen	to leave, let
laufen	läuft	lief	ist gelaufen	to run, walk
lesen	liest	las	gelesen	to read
liegen		lag	gelegen	to lie
messen	mißt	maß	gemessen	to measure
mögen	mag	mochte	gemocht	to like
müssen	muß	mußte	gemußt	to have to, must
nehmen	nimmt	nahm	genommen	to take
nennen		nannte	genannt	to name, call
raten	rät	riet	geraten	to advise
reiten		ritt	ist geritten	to ride (horseback)
rufen		rief	gerufen	to call
scheinen		schien	geschienen	to shine
schieben		schob	geschoben	to push
schießen		schoß	geschossen	to shoot
schlafen	schläft	schlief	geschlafen	to sleep
schlagen	schlägt	schlug	geschlagen	to hit, beat
schneiden		schnitt	geschnitten	to cut, chop
schreiben		schrieb	geschrieben	to write
schwimmen		schwamm	ist geschwommen	to swim
sehen	sieht	sah	gesehen	to see
sein	ist	war	ist gewesen	to be
singen		sang	gesungen	to sing
sitzen		saß	gesessen	to sit
sollen	soll	sollte	gesollt	to supposed to, should
sprechen	spricht	sprach	gesprochen	to speak, talk
springen		sprang	ist gesprungen	to jump
stehen		stand	gestanden	to stand
steigen		stieg	ist gestiegen	to climb
tragen	trägt	trug	getragen	to carry
treffen	trifft	traf	getroffen	to meet
treiben		trieb	getrieben	to pursue, do
trinken		trank	getrunken	to drink
tun	tut	tat	getan	to do
umziehen		zog um	umgezogen	to change (clothes)
unterbrechen	unterbricht	unterbrach	unterbrochen	to interrupt
unterhalten	unterhält	unterhielt	unterhalten	to converse, talk
verbinden		verband	verbunden	to connect
vergessen	vergißt	vergaß	vergessen	to forget
verlassen	verläßt	verließ	verlassen	to leave
verlieren		verlor	verloren	to lose
verstehen		verstand	verstanden	to understand
wachsen	wächst	wuchs	ist gewachsen	to grow
sich waschen	wäscht	wusch	gewaschen	to wash
werfen	wirft	warf	geworfen	to throw
wiegen		wog	gewogen	to weigh
wissen	weiß	wußte	gewußt	to know
wollen	will	wollte	gewollt	to be able to, can

Subjunctive

Present subjunctive I

	fragen	kommen	haben	sein
ich	frage	komme	habe	sei
du	fragest	kommest	habest	seiest
er, sie, es	frage	komme	habe	sei
wir	fragen	kommen	haben	seien
ihr	fraget	kommet	habet	seiet
sie, Sie	fragen	kommen	haben	seien

Present subjunctive II

	fragen	kommen	haben	sein
ich	fragte	käme	hätte	wäre
du	fragtest	kämest	hättest	wärest
er, sie, es	fragte	käme	hätte	wäre
wir	fragten	kämen	hätten	wären
ihr	fragtet	kämet	hättet	wäret
sie, Sie	fragten	kämen	hätten	wären

Past subjunctive I

Present subjunctive I of *haben* or *sein* plus past participle.
du habest gesucht
er sei gegangen

Past subjunctive II

Present subjunctive II of *haben* or *sein* plus past participle.
du hättest gesucht
er wäre gegangen

The following selected readings are excerpts from EMC's *Easy Readers*, a series of shortened and simplified texts adapted from works of well-known German authors. The individual excerpts appear in sequential order in terms of vocabulary and grammar difficulty. The vocabulary not listed at the end of the book is printed in italics and explained in the margin of the line in which the word or phrase appears. Vocabulary preceded by the symbol (°) is explained by means of illustrations. Cognates (*Wind, Sand,* etc.) and compound nouns — which can be taken apart and identified in the end vocabulary — are not explained. Phrases and expressions containing grammar unfamiliar to the student at the suggested reading level are also explained in marginal notes.

Lesestück I

Es klingelt an der Tür

Die Kinder *waren* noch nicht nach Hause *gekommen*, und   *had come*
Herr Massing *schmückte* den *Weihnachtsbaum*. Es war ein   *decorated/Christmas tree*
kleiner Baum, denn die Wohnung war nicht sehr groß – zwei
Zimmer und Küche. Da klingelte es an der Tür.

    „Machst du auf, Anna?" rief er hinaus.

    „Ich bin schon da."

    Im nächsten *Augenblick* kam seine Frau ins Zimmer.   *moment*
Sie brauchte ein wenig Zeit, bevor sie sprechen konnte.

    „Eduard! Ein Mann mit einem *Weihnachtsgeschenk* ist   *Christmas present*
an der Tür."

    „Ein Weihnachtsgeschenk? Von wem?"

    „Er weiß es nicht."

    „Führ ihn herein!"   *Bring him in.*

    „Er ist nicht *allein*."   *alone*

    „Dann *bitte* beide *herein*", sagte Herr Massing. *Er*   *ask to come in*
hätte es nicht sagen sollen.   *He shouldn't have said it.*

    Ein Mann im Mantel *trat ein*. Mit ihm ein riesiger   *stepped in*
°*Hund*. Wenn er den Kopf *hob*, konnte er aus dem Fenster   *raised*
sehen. Die Tür *ging* kaum hinter ihm *zu*, so groß war er.   *closed*

der Hund

der Schwanz

Excerpt from: Jo Hanns Rösler WOHIN SIND ALL' DIE JAHRE, copyright Stieglitz Verlag, Mühlacker 1973. The *Easy Reader* (an *A*-level book) entitled GÄNSEBRATEN UND ANDERE GESCHICHTEN, containing this simplified excerpt, is published by EMC Publishing.

„Frohe Weihnachten!" sagte der Mann, *der* den Hund   *who*
führte. „Bin ich hier recht bei Herrn Massing?"

Herr Massing sagte: „Ja." Er war *böse auf* den Hund   *mad at*
und *fürchtete* für seinen Weihnachtsbaum.   *feared*

„Ich soll Ihnen ein Weihnachtsgeschenk bringen",
sagte der Mann.

„Danke schön. Aber können Sie den Hund nicht vor
dem Haus lassen?"

„Das geht leider nicht."

„Warum nicht?"

„Er ist das Weihnachtsgeschenk."

„Wie bitte?"

„*Jemand* schickt Ihnen als Weihnachtsgeschenk den   *somebody*
Hund."

„Das nenne ich ein Geschenk", *schimpfte* Herr Mass-   *grumbled*
ing und sah den riesigen Hund böse an. Der Hund verstand es
falsch und bewegte den °*Schwanz hin und her.* Die Vase auf   *back and forth*
dem Tisch und der Weihnachtsbaum *fielen* fast *zu Boden.*   *fell on the floor*

„Mir schickt jemand einen Hund? Wer, ich bitte Sie?"

„Er hat seinen Namen nicht gesagt. Er hat mir nur gesagt, ich soll den Hund mit den besten Wünschen bei Ihnen
abgeben."   *deliver*

Herr Massing schimpfte: „Das kann ja nicht *wahr* sein.   *true*
Ich *nehme* das Geschenk nicht *an.* Was mache ich mit einem   *accept*
so großen Hund in der kleinen Wohnung?"

„Und was er ißt!" sagte die Frau.

Der Mann sah sich um.

„Sie haben doch Kinder. Vielleicht *ist* der Hund *für die*   *is intended for the children*
Kinder gedacht. Ihre Kinder werden sich sicher freuen."

„Die Kinder?" rief Herr Massing. „Sie können gleich
kommen! Und wenn sie den Hund sehen, werden sie ihn nie
mehr *hergeben.*"   *return*

Jetzt mußte schnell etwas geschehen. Herr Massing
ging auf den Mann *zu* und rief: *walk towards*

„Nehmen Sie ihn wieder mit! Ich behalte ihn nicht.
Bringen Sie ihn zurück. So eine Idee, mir einen Hund ins
Haus zu schicken!"

„Ich weiß nicht, wo er wohnt."

„Dann behalten Sie ihn. Ich schenke ihn Ihnen. Das ist
ein schöner Hund. Was soll ich mit dem *Riesenhund* in un-   *gigantic dog*
serer kleinen Wohnung?"

„Meine Wohnung ist auch sehr klein", sagte der Mann.
„Es kostet zu viel, so einen Hund zu halten. Das kann ich
nicht."

„Dann *geben* Sie den Hund *weiter!* Jetzt zu Weihnach-   *pass on*
ten! Ihre Freunde werden froh sein."

„Nein", sagte der andere, „wer nimmt einen so großen
Hund? Das tut doch kein Mensch."

Der Hund, *der sich hingelegt hatte,* stand plötzlich auf. *which had lain down*
Dabei *fiel* der Tisch *um.* *tipped over*

„Lieber, guter Mann!" rief jetzt Herr Massing. „Sie
können von mir haben, was Sie wollen, nur nehmen Sie den
Hund wieder mit. Sie haben ja Ihr Geld vom *Spender* schon *contributor*
bekommen, aber ich gebe Ihnen fünf mal so viel, wenn Sie
den Hund wieder mitnehmen."

Der Mann im Mantel sagte:

„Der Spender hat mir aber viel Geld gegeben."

„Gut. Ich gebe Ihnen noch mehr. Da, sehen Sie, das ist
für Sie –"

Er nahm schnell einen großen *Geldschein* aus der *bill*
Tasche und gab ihn dem Mann. *pocket*

„Nehmen Sie ihn und dann *nichts wie raus,* Sie und der *get out*
Hund!"

„Lieber alter, guter Keschan!" sagte der Mann im Mantel zu dem Hund, als er ihn wieder auf die Straße führte. „Ich
weiß, das ist ein dummes Spiel, aber du weißt ja, wie sehr ich
dich liebe, mein bester Freund. Aber die *einzige* Möglich- *only*
keit, dich zu behalten, ist, dich jedes Weihnachten viele Male
zu verschiedenen Menschen als Weihnachtsgeschenk zu
bringen. Nur so bekommen wir das *Futtergeld* für das ganze *money for food*
Jahr zusammen und können noch lange, lange zusammen
bleiben…"

Fragen

1. Was macht Herr Massing, als es klingelt?
2. Wer ist an der Tür?
3. Warum will Herr Massing den Hund nicht behalten?
4. Will der Herr im Mantel den Hund wirklich weggeben?

Lesestück II

Herr Schulze und Herr Tobler

Es schneite. Vor dem Postamt in der Lietzenburger Straße hielt eine große Limousine. Ein Herr im *Pelz* stieg aus, ging in das Gebäude und suchte den Schalter für *postlagernde Sendungen*.

    „Ist ein Brief für Eduard Schulze da?" fragte er.

    Der Beamte suchte. Dann *reichte* er einen dicken Brief *heraus*. Der Herr im Pelzmantel steckte den Brief in die *Tasche*, dankte und ging.

    Als der Herr aus dem Postamt trat, öffnete der Chauffeur schnell die Wagentür. Der Herr stieg ein, und das Auto *fuhr davon*.

    Das Essen hatte geschmeckt. Johann, der *Diener*, brachte Zigarren, und Fräulein Hilde, Toblers Tochter, stellte *Mokkatassen* auf den Tisch

    Die *Hausdame* und der Diener wollten gehen.

    „Trinken Sie beide eine Tasse Kaffee mit uns. Ich muß euch allen was erzählen. Ich habe mich nämlich am *Preisausschreiben* meiner eigenen *Fabrik beteiligt* und den zweiten Preis gewonnen", sagte Tobler.

    „Unmöglich", sagte Frau Kunkel, „den hat ein Herr Schulze gewonnen. Das hab ich in der Zeitung gelesen. Sie wollen *uns zum Narren halten.*"

    „Ich *könnte mich ja* auch unter dem Namen Schulze *beteiligt haben*", sagte Tobler.

    „Das ist möglich", sagte Frau Kunkel, „Da kann man leicht gewinnen, wenn man der Chef ist."

    „Kunkel, *man sollte Sie mit dem Luftgewehr erschießen*", rief Hilde.

    „Das habe ich nicht *verdient*", sagte die dicke alte Dame mit *Tränen* in den Augen.

    „*Worin besteht* denn der zweite Preis?" fragte Hilde.

    „Zehn Tage *Aufenthalt* im Grandhotel Bruckbeuren. Hin- und Rückfahrt zweiter Klasse", sagte Johann.

    „*Ich ahne Fürchterliches*", sagte Hilde. „Du willst *als* Schulze *auftreten.*"

    Tobler *rieb sich* die Hände. „Richtig! Ich *reise* diesmal nicht als der Millionär Tobler, sondern als ein *armer* Mann *namens* Schulze. Ich will die Menschen sehen, wie sie wirklich sind."

    „Wann fährst du?" fragte Hilde.

(marginal glosses)

- fur (coat)
- mail that has been held
- handed over
- pocket
- drove away
- servant
- small coffee cups
- housekeeper
- contest/factory/participated
- make a fool of us
- could have participated
- one should shoot you with an air rifle
- earned
- tears
- What does…consist of?
- stay
- I fear something terrible./to appear as
- rubbed/travel
- poor
- by the name of

Excerpt from: Erich Kästner DREI MÄNNER IM SCHNEE, copyright Atrium Verlag AG, Zürich 1969. The *Easy Reader* (a C-level book) containing this simplified excerpt, is published by EMC Publishing.

„In fünf Tagen. Morgen kaufe ich ein. Billige Hemden, einen billigen Anzug, und *damit genug.*"   *that's enough*

„Wenn sie dich als *Landstreicher einsperren,* telegra-   *hobo/put behind bars*
phiere", *bat* die Tochter.   *pleaded*

„Keine Angst, mein Kind. Johann fährt mit. Aber wir werden uns nicht kennen."

Johann saß *niedergeschlagen* auf seinem Stuhl.   *depressed*

„Morgen bekommen Sie beim *Schneider* mehrere neue   *tailor*
Anzüge. Sie sollen aussehen wie ein *Großherzog,* Johann",   *grand duke*
sagte Tobler.

„*Wozu?*" fragte Johann. „Ich will doch lieber Ihr   *what for*
Diener sein."

„Wollen Sie lieber hierbleiben?"

„Aber nein," sagte Johann. „Wenn Sie es *wünschen,*   *wish*
reise ich als Großherzog. Darf ich die ganzen zehn Tage nicht mit Ihnen sprechen?"

„*Unter gar keinen Umständen.* Richtig, einen Skian-   *under no circumstances*
zug müssen Sie auch haben."

„Ich kann nicht Skifahren", antwortete Johann.

„Dann werden Sie es lernen."

„Johann *sank in sich zusammen.* „Darf ich wenigstens   *collapsed*
manchmal in Ihr Zimmer kommen und *aufräumen?* Ich   *straighten up*
werde bestimmt nur kommen, wenn niemand auf dem Korridor ist."

„Vielleicht", sagte Tobler.

Johann sah wieder ganz froh aus.

Fragen

1. Was wollte Tobler auf der Post?
2. Was erzählte Tobler nach dem Essen?
3. Warum konnte Frau Kunkel nichts davon verstehen?
4. Was meinte Hilde von der ganzen Geschichte?
5. Wer sollte mitkommen?
6. Warum konnte er nicht als Diener reisen?

Lesestück III

Auf dem Wege zum Zug war mein Koffer viel schwerer als vor drei Tagen, als ich hier ankam. Ich hatte genau dasselbe im Koffer. Aber jeder Weg wird weiter, jeder Koffer schwerer, wenn man ohne *Erfolg* zurückfährt. *success*

Es war ein Nachmittag im Oktober. Das flache Land *mit* *with its wind that smelled like salt* *seinem Wind, der nach Salzwasser roch*, lag unter einem *water* grauen Himmel. Genau so grau sah es auch in mir aus.

Der Zug sollte hier seine Reise beginnen. Ich *konnte* die *could see* Wagen weiter hinten *stehen sehen*. Es war zu kalt, um eine halbe Stunde hier zu warten. Also ging ich in eine Gaststätte. Ich bestellte mir einen großen *Schnaps*. Der Schnaps ist das *liquor* Beste in dieser Gegend. Er ist klar, sauber und schmeckt nach Sommer und grünen Feldern. Nur der Name auf der Flasche gefällt mir nicht. Es ist der Name des Mannes, *bei dem ich* in *with whom I had had no success at* diesen drei Tagen *überhaupt keinen Erfolg gehabt hatte*. Er *all* ist Millionär. Ich war hierher gekommen, um mit ihm ein Geschäft zu machen, ein Geschäft um eine halbe Million.

Der Name auf der *Schnapsflasche* gefällt mir noch aus *liquor bottle* einem anderen Grunde nicht. Es wird mir jedesmal kalt, wenn ich diesen Namen höre oder sehe. Aber das wußte ich noch nicht, als ich in dem Restaurant saß und einen *doppelten* *double* Schnaps bestellte.

Langsam wurde mir warm. Ich freute mich auf mein Zimmer in Hamburg. Ich freute mich sogar darauf, morgen vormittag meinen Chef zu sehen, wenn ich ihm von meinem Besuch bei dem Schnapsmillionär *erzählen würde*. *would tell*

Mein Koffer war nicht mehr ganz so schwer, als ich zum Zug ging, *der* jetzt *bereitstand*. Es waren nur zwei oder drei *which was ready to go* Menschen auf dem Bahnhof. Ich setzte mich in den Zug. Den Mantel *behielt* ich *an*. Es war recht kalt. Ich hörte *Rufe* — *kept on/shouts* dann fuhr der Zug ab.

Ich sah aus dem Fenster. Es blieb kalt. Zwei Stunden in diesem Wagen zu *frieren*, hatte ich keine Lust. Ich nahm *freeze* meinen Koffer und ging *auf die Suche nach* einem *geheizten* *on the lookout for/heated* Wagen.

Das erste, was ich von ihr sah, war die Hand. Das Mädchen schien zu schlafen. Sie sah aus, *als schliefe sie* schon *as if she had been sleeping* seit Stunden. Na, vielleicht war sie schon müde, *als* sie in den Zug stieg. Aber ich *hatte sie nicht einsteigen sehen*. *had not seen her get in*

Die Hand, *die* neben ihr lag, war ganz weiß – die Hand *which* gefiel mir nicht. So schläft doch niemand.

Excerpt from: Hansjörg Martin KEIN SCHNAPS FÜR TAMARA, copyright Rowohlt Taschenbuch Verlag GmbH, Reinbek/Hamburg 1975. The *Easy Reader* (a *B*-level book) with the same title is published by EMC Publishing.

Ich hatte das alles gesehen und gedacht, *als ich vorbei-gegangen war*. Erst zwei Wagen weiter *setzte* ich meinen Koffer *ab* und ging zu ihr zurück. *Das hätte ich nicht tun sollen!*

    when I went by
    put down
    I shouldn't have done that.

    Ich machte die Wagentür auf und sagte: „Hallo!" und noch einmal etwas lauter: „Hallo!"

    Das Mädchen bewegte sich nicht. Ich ging hinein, um das Gesicht zu sehen. Aber das gelang nicht, denn das schwarze Haar hing über ihrem Gesicht. Ich rief, um *irgendetwas* zu tun, noch einmal: „Hallo!" Dann faßte ich den Arm des Mädchens an – nichts. Ich nahm ihre weiße Hand. Die Hand war sehr kalt. Dann *hob* ich ihren Kopf *hoch*. Das Gesicht war noch weißer als die Hand. Die Augen *waren geschlossen*. An dem linken Auge hing eine °*Träne*. Der Mund war offen. Ich öffnete ihr linkes Auge und sah, was ich schon wußte:

    something

    raised
    were closed

    Das Mädchen war *tot*.

    dead

die Träne

Sie war etwa Mitte bis Ende zwanzig. Das Gesicht hatte ich schon einmal gesehen. Aber ich wußte nicht, wo. Ich konnte nicht klar denken. Aber ich hatte dieses Gesicht schon gesehen.

Ich *ließ* den Kopf *fallen*. Die Haare fielen wieder über ihr Gesicht. Kalt war es in dem Zug. Ich setzte mich *der Toten gegenüber*, um in Ruhe *darüber nachzudenken*, was ich tun sollte. Ich *kam nicht dazu*, denn der Zug hielt. Das Mädchen *fiel* noch mehr *in sich zusammen*.

dropped

across from the dead person

think about

didn't get to it

collapsed

Fragen

1. Wann begann die Geschichte?
2. Warum war der Erzähler in diese Stadt gekommen?
3. Was gefiel ihm nicht an der Schnapsflasche?
4. Warum ging er in eine Gaststätte?
5. Warum suchte er sich einen anderen Wagen im Zug?
6. Was fiel ihm zuerst an dem schlafenden Mädchen auf?
7. Wie sah das Mädchen aus?
8. Wie alt war sie?
9. Woran sah er, daß sie tot war?

Lesestück IV

Die Reise nach Deutschland

Bald kam ich *aus der türkischen Gefangenschaft* wieder nach *Rußland* zurück. Ich blieb aber nicht lange in Rußland, sondern reiste nach Deutschland zurück. In ganz Europa war es in diesem Winter sehr kalt.

    Mein *litauisches* Pferd war in der *Türkei* geblieben. So mußte ich *mit der Postkutsche reisen.* Auf dem Weg kamen wir an eine enge Stelle. An der einen Seite waren hohe *Bäume,* und an der anderen Seite war ein *tiefer* Fluß. Gerade an dieser Stelle sahen wir *eine andere Kutsche, die* an uns vorbeifahren mußte.

from Turkish captivity
Russia

Lithuanian/Turkey
travel by carriage

trees/deep
another carriage which

das Horn

    Ich bat meinen *Kutscher,* mit seinem °*Horn* ein *Zeichen* zu geben. Er versuchte es, aber ohne *Erfolg. Trotz größter Mühe* kam kein Ton heraus. Wir konnten es uns nicht erklären. Und es war wirklich ein *Unglück,* denn wir konnten nicht an der anderen Kutsche vorbeikommen.

    Ich sprang aus meiner Kutsche und *spannte* zuerst die Pferde *aus.* Dann nahm ich die Kutsche mit den vier *Rädern* und allen Sachen auf meinen *Rücken* und sprang *damit* über den Fluß. Das Wasser war ungefähr neun Meter tief. Die Kutsche war natürlich sehr schwer, und es war nicht so leicht, auf die andere Seite des Flusses zu kommen. Dann sprang ich wieder auf den Weg zurück. Unter jeden Arm nahm ich ein Pferd und brachte beide Tiere auf die andere Seite. Als die *fremde* Kutsche vorbeigefahren war, brachte ich unsere Kutsche und die Pferde *auf die gleiche Art* zurück. Ich *ließ* die Pferde wieder *anspannen,* und dann konnten wir weiterfahren.

coachman/signal
success/in spite of the highest effort

misfortune

unharnessed
wheels
back/with it

unfamiliar
in the same manner
had harnessed

Excerpt from: MÜNCHHAUSENS ABENTEUER, copyright Grafisk Forlag A/S 1982. The *Easy Reader* (an A-level book) with the same title is published by EMC Publishing.

Ich muß noch erzählen, daß eines von den Pferden *eine große Dummheit* machen wollte. Es war vier Jahre alt. Als ich zum zweiten Mal über den Fluß sprang, machte es eine starke, unruhige *Bewegung* mit seinen Beinen. Ich nahm seine Hinterbeine und *steckte sie in meine Manteltasche*.

Am Abend kamen wir in eine *Schenke*. Der Kutscher hängte sein Horn *in die Nähe des Feuers* und setzte sich an einen Tisch. Ich setzte mich zu ihm.

Nun hört, *Ihr Herren,* was geschah! Plötzlich hörten wir „Tereng! Tereng! Teng, teng!" Wir machten große Augen und *wunderten uns sehr.* Aber *im gleichen Augenblick* sahen wir, warum das Horn auf der Fahrt keine Töne *herausgebracht hatte*. Die Töne waren in dem Horn *festgefroren*. Und nun kamen sie alle *hell und klar* heraus. Wir hörten viele schöne und bekannte *Lieder*. Und der Kutscher setzte nicht einmal seinen Mund an das Horn.

Dies war mein letztes *Abenteuer* auf meiner russischen Reise.

Viele *Reisende* erzählen nicht immer die *volle Wahrheit* von ihren Abenteuern. So ist es kein Wunder, wenn man ihnen nicht glaubt. Sie können aber sicher sein, meine Herren, daß alle meine *Erzählungen wahr* sind. Sollten Sie trotzdem nicht daran glauben, müssen Sie jetzt lieber nach Hause gehen. Meine nächsten Abenteuer sind nämlich noch *merkwürdiger,* aber doch wahr!

a very dumb thing

move

put them into my coat pocket

tavern

near the fire

gentlemen

were quite astonished/at the same time

had produced/frozen completely
bright and clear
songs

adventure

travelers/whole truth

stories/true

stranger

Fragen

1. Warum reiste Münchhausen mit der Kutsche nach Deutschland?
2. Warum mußte der Kutscher die Pferde ausspannen?
3. Was machte Münchhausen mit der Kutsche und den Pferden?
4. Was hörten sie in der Schenke?

Lesestück V

Durch den Zug geht ein Mann im °*Schlafanzug*. Er kommt
aus dem letzten Wagen und geht *nach vorn* durch die langen,
hellen, leeren °*Gänge*. Der °Schlafwagen*schaffner* auf dem
Gang hat es sich bequem gemacht, hat die harte °*Mütze* vom
Kopf genommen und den °*Kragen* geöffnet und *ist* über seiner °*Kaffeekanne eingeschlafen*. Der Herr im Schlafanzug
geht leise an ihm vorbei, liest die Zahlen an den °*Abteil*türen

has fallen asleep

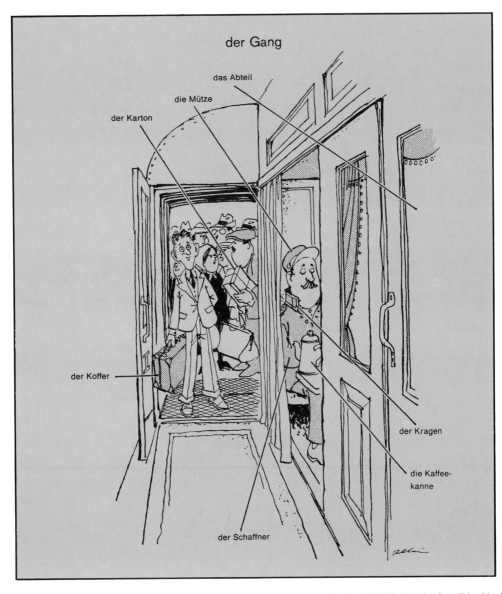

der Gang

das Abteil

die Mütze

der Karton

der Koffer

der Kragen

die Kaffee-
kanne

der Schaffner

Excerpt from: Heinrich Spoerl DER GASMANN, copyright R. Piper & Co. Verlag, München 1962. The *Easy Reader* (a *B*-level book) with the same title is published by EMC Publishing.

der Schlafwagen erster Klasse. Er bleibt vor einer der Türen stehen. Wartet ein paar Minuten, sieht nach rechts und nach links. Es ist nichts zu hören. Dann öffnet er langsam die Tür und *verschwindet ins Dunkel*. Die Tür *geht* hinter ihm *zu* und sieht wieder genau so aus wie die anderen Türen.

disappears into the dark/closes

Dann ist es Morgen. Die Gänge der Schlafwagen werden *lebendig*. Türen öffnen sich. Leute *treten auf* den Gang. Sie *rauchen* ihre erste Zigarette und sehen durch das Fenster. Meistens sind es Herren, *die* nachts fahren. Wenn eine Frau *darunter* ist, dann ist sie meistens schön. Auch der Herr ist wieder da. Er hat noch immer seinen grauen Schlafanzug an. Er sieht *merkwürdig* aus zwischen den anderen Herren, die schon mit Hut und °*Koffer* im Gang stehen und bereit sind, den Zug zu verlassen.

lively/step into
smoke
who
among them

strange

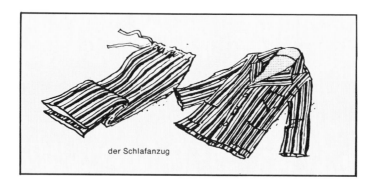

der Schlafanzug

Durch das Fenster kann man schon Berlin sehen. Der Herr im Schlafanzug ist *unruhig* und läuft durch den Gang. Alle Leute *schauen ihn an*. So kommt er an das Ende des Wagens. Hier ist die *reiche* Welt zu Ende. Der internationale Schlafwagen ist *an einen gewöhnlichen Zug angehängt*.

restless
look at him
rich
added to a normal train

In dem Gang der dritten Klasse stehen viele Leute mit Koffern und *Kartons*. Ein Mann im blauen Sonntagsanzug mit einem kleinen Koffer in der Hand ist ein Stück in den Schlafwagen getreten und sieht sich alles an. Er möchte gerne sehen, wie reiche Leute reisen.

Da *tupft* ihm jemand auf die °*Schulter:* „Hören Sie mal!"

taps

die Schulter

„Ich gehe ja schon", sagt der Mann aus der dritten Klasse. Der Herr im Schlafanzug *stellt sich ihm in den Weg*.

blocks his path

„Ich habe Ihnen eine Vorschlag zu machen. Erst eine Frage: Kennen Sie mich?"

Der kleine Mann sieht ihn aus großen Augen an: „Nein, wieso?"   *why*

„Dann ist es gut. Ich möchte Ihren Anzug kaufen."

„Meinen Anzug, den will ich aber gar nicht verkaufen."

„Was wollen Sie dafür haben? Dreihundert Mark – fünfhundert?"

Der Mann im Anzug *rechnet:* dreihundert Mark *wäre* schon viel zu viel; aber fünfhundert Mark…   *counts/would be*

„Wenn Sie wollen, dann können Sie heute Nachmittag mal zu mir kommen. Ich heiße Hermann Knittel, Urbanstraße 163. Soll ich es aufschreiben?"

Der Herr im Schlafanzug sagt *leise:* „Ich brauche den Anzug sofort. Sagen wir achthundert Mark."   *softly*

Er schiebt Knittel in den *Waschraum.* Knittel beginnt, sein Hemd *auszuziehen.* Er ist froh, daß er gestern ein sauberes Hemd angezogen hat. Plötzlich *denkt* er *nach.* Was soll er jetzt anziehen? Er hat gar nichts bei sich. Er kann doch nicht *nackt* in Berlin ankommen.   *lavoratory* / *to take off* / *thinks* / *naked*

„Das ist schlecht", sagt der Herr, „dann müssen Sie meinen Schlafanzug anziehen."

Knittel fragt: „Was! Haben Sie denn keinen Anzug?"

„Nein."

„Sie müssen doch einen Anzug haben? Sie *sind* doch nicht im Schlafanzug *fortgefahren? Ist er gestohlen worden?"*   *have left* / *Has it been stolen?*

Der Herr gibt keine Antwort.

„Ich möchte Ihren Anzug."

„Aber ich kann doch nicht auf dem Bahnsteig im Schlafanzug herumlaufen."

„Einer von uns wird es müssen", sagt der Herr.

„Tun Sie es doch selbst", sagt Knittel, „warum ich?"

„Weil ich *nicht auffallen darf.* Ich bezahle Sie dafür. Wieviel?"   *cannot be conspicuous*

„Die Leute werden doch alle auf mich sehen."

„Das bezahle ich mit", sagt der Herr und fängt an, einen °*Scheck* zu schreiben.

„Und wenn die °*Polizei* kommt?"

der Scheck   die Polizei

„Gut, bezahle ich auch." Der Herr schreibt einen neuen Scheck."

„Und was meinen Sie, was meine Frau dazu sagt, wenn ich ohne Anzug nach Hause komme?"

„Eine Frau haben Sie auch? Dann müssen wir *den Betrag verdoppeln.*" Und er beginnt einen neuen Scheck zu schreiben.

double the amount

„Aber wie heißen Sie denn?" fragt Knittel.

Der Herr gibt keine Antwort; schreibt einen neuen Scheck.

Knittel: „Ja, haben Sie denn kein Geld? Das ist aber *komisch.* Sie laufen hier herum, mit nichts bei sich. Woher kommen Sie?"

odd

Der Herr hat schon Knittels Anzug an. „Hier ist der Scheck", sagt er. Und *ist* schnell *fort.*

is gone

„Meinen Anzug will ich haben!" schreit Knittel und läuft hinter dem Mann her. Der Zug *bremst* schon *ab.* Knittel

applies the brakes

stößt mit einer älteren Dame *zusammen*. Sie sagt: „Oh!" Da denkt er daran, daß er nur *Unterhosen* anhat!

Er geht in den Waschraum zurück. Er ruft durch die Tür nach dem Schaffner. Der Schaffner ist am anderen Ende des Zuges. Schaffner sind das immer. Der Zug fährt langsam in den Bahnhof ein und hält. Knittel sieht gerade noch durch das Fenster, wie der Herr in seinem Anzug aussteigt und *verschwindet*.

Mit seinem schönen blauen Anzug! Zurück liegt der Schlafanzug und *obendrauf* der kleine Scheck. Knittel sieht nicht hin. Er will damit nichts zu tun haben. Aber dann bleibt sein Blick doch daran hängen. Er sieht eine Zahl. Die ist so groß, daß er nicht weiß, wie er das verstehen soll. Er bleibt ganz still und sieht auf den Scheck. Dann steckt er den Scheck *tief* in den °*Strumpf*.

Er weiß, hier kann er nicht bleiben. Langsam zieht er den Schlafanzug an. Das ist besser als nichts! Er geht aus dem Waschraum, verläßt den Zug und geht in dem Schlafanzug, den Koffer in der Hand, den Bahnsteig entlang. Er hat Angst, hat die Augen halb geschlossen. Er sieht niemanden an, geht *geradeaus*.

In Berlin ist man *daran gewöhnt*, Leute in merkwürdiger Kleidung zu sehen.

So kommt es, daß der kleine Mann im Schlafanzug, *der* über den Bahnsteig geht, *ganz und gar niemandem auffällt*. Knittel öffnet die Augen und sieht sich um. Niemand sieht ihn an. Nur eine alte Frau sagt zu einem Schaffner: „Sehen Sie, da geht einer im Schlafanzug!"

„Ja, und?"

Knittel merkt, daß er wieder in seinem lieben Berlin ist. Er fährt mit einem °*Taxi* nach Hause. Er ist etwas *ängstlich*, als sie in die Urbanstraße kommen, wo alle Leute ihn kennen.

Der Wagen hält. Knittel springt aus dem Taxi in das Haus. Auf der Treppe hört er *Stimmen, Er greift sich eine Milchflasche, die* vor einer Tür steht. Bei ihm hat man das

---

collides
boxer shorts

disappears

on top of it

deep

straight ahead
used to that

who
doesn't look conspicuous to anybody

afraid

voices/He grabs a milk bottle which…

der Strumpf   das Taxi

auch schon gemacht. So steigt er froh die Treppe hinauf, mit der Flasche im Arm, sagt „Guten Morgen" und „Danke, gut".

So kommt Knittel in seine schöne Wohnung.
„Erika?"

Er geht durch die ganze Wohnung und sucht seine Frau. In der Küche findet er einen *Zettel:* „Bin mit den Kindern einkaufen." Knittel ist froh darüber. Jetzt hat er Zeit, sich erst einmal anders anzuziehen. *slip of paper*

Als er fertig ist, setzt er sich in die Küche, trinkt Kaffee und *kommt endlich in Ruhe.* Da es niemand sieht, nimmt er drei *Löffelchen* Zucker. *finally calms down* *teaspoons*

Es ist still in der Küche. In der *Tiefe* seines Strumpfes *drückt* ihn der Scheck. Er *holt ihn heraus* und legt ihn neben die Tasse. Er *besieht sich das kostbare Papier* von oben und unten, von hinten nach vorn. Es ist ein bißchen *zerknittert.* *bottom* *presses/gets it out* *examines the valuable paper* *wrinkled*

Er weiß natürlich, was ein Scheck ist. Aber *der Betrag beunruhigt ihn.* Auf dem Tisch liegt mehr, als er in langen Jahren *sparen konnte.* Und leicht *verdient* – viel zu leicht. Viel zu viel Geld für einen dummen Anzug. Und warum wollte der Mann seinen Namen nicht nennen? Auf dem Scheck hat er seinen Namen sogar schreiben müssen, denkt *the amount disturbs him* *could save/earned*

die Unterschrift *H. Böhm*

Knittel und sieht auf die °*Unterschrift* auf dem Scheck. Es ist nicht zu lesen.

Das ist *überhaupt keine Unterschrift,* sieht Knittel, man kann sie überhaupt nicht lesen. — *no signature at all*

Dann kam der *Gedanke:* Der Scheck ist *falsch!* Jetzt ist es ihm klar. Seinen schönen Anzug *ist er los,* und dafür hat er jetzt nichts als ein *wertloses* Stück Papier. Was wird Erika sagen? Der Anzug hat 87 Mark gekostet. Erika wird gar nichts sagen. So dumm ist er nun wieder nicht. Er wird ihr einfach nichts erzählen. Knittel holt den Schlafanzug, legt ihn in seine °*Aktentasche* und schreibt einen Zettel für seine Frau: „Ich mußte ganz eilig zur Arbeit. Gruß Hermann." — *thought/fake* *he's rid of* *worthless*

Knittel geht zur Bank. *Er fühlt sich nicht wohl,* mit einem falschen Scheck zu kommen. Es ist eine sehr feine Bank. Knittel fühlt sich ganz *fremd.* Er geht an den °*Schalter* und fragt dann so leise er kann: — *He doesn't feel well…* *strange*

„Wenn Sie einen Augenblick Zeit haben; ich wollte nur mal hören, wie das mit dem Scheck hier ist."

die Aktentasche

Der Herr hinter dem Schalter sagt: „Bitte, wollen Sie solange Platz nehmen?"

Knittel muß sich in einen der dicken °Sessel setzen. Nach einiger Zeit sagt der Herr hinter dem Schalter: „Bitte", und schiebt ihm ein *Brett* voller Geld hin. „Wollen Sie bitte *nachzählen!*"

tray

check

der Schalter   der Sessel

Ein ganzes Brett voller Geld. Knittel steht davor und *guckt*. Er kann nicht denken. Er sieht nur, daß er Geld bekommt, einen Berg voller Geld, 10 000 Mark. Knittel steht immer noch da und bewegt sich nicht. „Ist etwas nicht in Ordnung?" fragt der Herr hinter dem Schalter.

stares

„Doch, doch", sagt Knittel und beginnt schnell zu *zählen*. Aber er kann gar nicht zählen. Er hat Angst vor dem Geld. Mit *unsicheren* Händen nimmt er endlich das Geld vom Brett. Er weiß nicht, wohin damit. Er steckt es in die *Jackentaschen* und in die Aktentasche.

count

unsteady

coat pockets

Als er draußen ist, sieht er sich noch einmal um. Es kommt niemand hinter ihm her.

Es ist abends gegen zehn. In Knittels Küche ist noch *Licht*. Erika hat die Kinder zu Bett gebracht und einen Kuchen *gebacken*. Knittel sitzt in der Küche. Er trinkt eine flasche Bier, die Jacke hat er ausgezogen. Dann ist Erika mit dem Kuchen fertig. „Hermann, es ist bald elf."

light

baked

Hermann hat noch keine Lust. Hermann liest Zeitung. Dann fragt Erika: „Hermann, bist du noch nicht müde?" Knittel hat keine Zeit, müde zu sein. „Geh nur schon, ich komme nach."

Erika geht ins Schlafzimmer. Die Tür *läßt* sie ein Stück *offen stehen*. Knittel ist allein mit sich und seiner Aktentasche. Er legt sie auf den Tisch und *denkt nach*. Das Geld ist nicht *ehrlich*. So viel Geld kann nicht ehrlich sein. Wohin mit dem Geld? Soll er zur Polizei gehen? Aber er hat ja seinen Anzug dafür verkauft. Er hört, wie Erika ins Bett geht. Sie ist seine liebe kleine Frau. Warum hat er ihr noch nichts davon erzählt? Er wollte es den ganzen Tag tun.

leaves open

thinks about it

honest

„Erika?"

„— —"

„Schläfst du schon?"

„Ja, was hast du denn?"

Knittel beginnt: „Du, soll ich dir mal was erzählen? Heute morgen ist etwas Merkwürdiges geschehen. Im Zug habe ich einen Mann kennengelernt – du wirst es vielleicht nicht glauben, aber sieh selbst."

Knittel hat die Aktentasche mit einem °*Schlüssel* geöffnet. Dann denkt er. Was wird Erika tun, wenn sie das Geld sieht? Er weiß es genau. Sie wird sagen: „Du gehst sofort zur Polizei und gibst das Geld ab." Das weiß er aber auch ohne Erika. Also ist es besser, Erika nichts zu sagen. Morgen will er mit dem Geld zur Polizei gehen.

der Schlüssel

Erika wartet immer noch auf die Geschichte. „Hermann, du wolltest mir doch was erzählen. Was war denn mit dem Mann?"

„– – Ach so – *weiter nichts*. Der hat mir seine Suppe über meinen Anzug *gegossen*."

nothing at all
poured

„Über den guten, blauen Anzug? Du, Hermann, wo ist der überhaupt? Den habe ich noch gar nicht gesehen." Knittel denkt einen Augenblick nach: „Ja, siehst du, den hat dein kluger Mann sofort zur *Reinigung* gebracht. Der wird wie neu, haben sie gesagt."

cleaner

„Darum warst du den ganzen Tag auch so komisch. Komm, denk nicht daran. Komm lieber ins Bett. Ich warte jetzt noch zwei Minuten, und wenn du dann nicht kommst, dann schlafe ich schon." Sie geht und macht die Tür zu.

Jetzt hat Knittel Ruhe. Es ist still um ihn. Er wartet ein paar Minuten, dann steht er auf, nimmt seine Aktentasche und legt sie vor sich auf den Tisch. Die ganze Tasche ist voller grüner 50-Markscheine. Er *befühlt* sie mit den Fingern, ob sie wirklich sind und zählt leise. Er denkt nicht mehr daran, daß hinter der Tür Erika liegt und auf ihn wartet.

feels

Knittel sitzt in der Küche über seinem Geld und *kann sich nicht* von ihm *trennen*. Er spielt mit dem Geld und mit den *Gedanken*.

can't part with it

thoughts

Fragen

1. Was will der Mann im Schlafanzug von Knittel?
2. Wo sind die beiden?
3. Warum will Knittel seinen Anzug nicht sofort verkaufen?
4. Was bekommt Knittel für seinen Anzug?
5. Warum erzählt Knittel Erika nichts von dem Geld?

Lesestück VI

Die Reise nach Berlin kann losgehen

Emil nahm seine *Schülermütze* ab und sagte: „Guten Tag, meine *Herrschaften*. Ist vielleicht noch ein Plätzchen frei?" *student cap / ladies and gentlemen*

Natürlich war noch ein Platz frei. Und eine dicke Dame, *die sich* den linken Schuh *ausgezogen hatte*, weil er *drückte*, sagte zu ihrem Nachbarn, einem Mann: „Solche *höflichen* Kinder sind *heutzutage selten*. Wenn ich da an meine Jugend *zurückdenke. Gott!* Da herrschte ein anderer Ton." *who had taken off / pinched / polite/today/rare / think back/good God!*

Daß es Leute gibt, die immer sagen: Gott, früher war alles besser, das wußte Emil *längst*. Und er *hörte überhaupt nicht mehr hin*, wenn jemand erklärte, *früher sei die Luft gesünder gewesen*, oder die Ochsen hätten größere Köpfe gehabt, denn das war meistens nicht wahr, und die Leute *gehörten bloß zu der Sorte*, die nicht zufrieden sein wollen, weil sie sonst zufrieden *wären*. *for a long time/didn't listen to them any longer / in the past the air was healthier / belonged to the type / would be*

Er *befühlte* seine rechte *Jackentasche* und *war* erst *beruhigt*, als er das *Kuvert knistern* hörte. Die *Mitreisenden* sahen auch nicht gerade wie *Diebe und Mörder* aus. Neben dem Mann und der dicken Frau saß eine andere Frau. Und am Fenster, neben Emil, las ein Herr im *steifen Hut* die Zeitung. *touched/coat pocket / calmed down/envelope/rustle/fellow travelers / thieves and murderers / stiff hat*

Plötzlich *legte er das Blatt weg*, holte aus seiner Tasche eine Ecke Schokolade und sagte: „Na, junger Mann, wie wär's?" *put the paper away*

„Ich bin so frei", antwortete Emil und nahm die Schokolade. Dann nahm er schnell seine Mütze ab, verbeugte sich und meinte: „Emil Tischbein ist mein Name." Die Mitreisenden *lächelten*. Der Herr *lüftete* nun auch ernst den steifen Hut und sagte: *„Sehr angenehm*, ich heiße Grundeis." *smiled/lifted / Pleased to meet you…*

Dann fragte die dicke Dame, die den linken Schuh *ausgezogen hatte:* „Lebt denn in Neustadt der Herr Kurzhals noch?" *had taken off*

„Ja freilich lebt Herr Kurzhals noch", *berichtete* Emil, „kennen Sie ihn?" *reported*

„Ja, grüß ihn schön von Frau Jakob aus Groß-Grünau."

„Ich fahre doch aber nach Berlin."

„Das hat ja auch Zeit, bis du zurückkommst," sagte Frau Jakob.

„So, so, nach Berlin fährst du?" fragte Herr Grundeis.

„Jawohl, und meine Großmutter wartet am Bahnhof Friedrichstraße am *Blumenkiosk*", antwortete Emil und *faßte sich* wieder ans Jackett. Und das Kuvert knisterte, *Gott sei dank,* noch immer. *flower stand/touched / thank God*

„Kennst du Berlin schon?“

„Nein.“

„Na, da *wirst* du aber *staunen!* In Berlin gibt es jetzt Häuser, die sind hundert *Stockwerke* hoch, und die Dächer *hat man* am Himmel *festbinden müssen,* damit sie nicht *wegfliegen*...Und wenn es jemand besonders eilig hat und er will in ein anderes Stadtviertel, so packt man ihn auf dem Postamt in eine Kiste und schießt sie wie einen *Rohrpostbrief* zu dem Postamt, das in dem Viertel liegt, wo er hin möchte...Und wenn man kein Geld hat, geht man auf die Bank und läßt sein *Gehirn* als *Pfand* dort und *kriegt* dafür tausend Mark. Der Mensch kann nämlich nur zwei Tage ohne Gehirn leben; und er kriegt es von der Bank erst wieder, wenn er zwölfhundert Mark *zurückzahlt*...“

will be surprised
stories
they had to tie up
fly away
letter sent through a tube
brain/deposit/get
pays back

„Sie haben wohl Ihr Gehirn auch gerade auf der Bank“, sagte der Mann neben der Frau Jakob zu dem Herrn im steifen Hut und *fügte hinzu: „Lassen Sie doch den Unsinn!“*

added/Don't talk such nonsense.

Emil *lachte gezwungen.* Und die beiden Herren *redeten eine Zeitlang recht unhöflich miteinander.* Emil dachte: *Was geht das mich an!* und packte seine Wurstbrote aus, *obwohl* er eben erst Mittag gegessen hatte. Wenig später hielt der Zug auf einem großen Bahnhof. Emil sah kein Stationsschild, und er verstand auch nicht, was der *Schaffner* vor dem Fenster *brüllte.* Fast alle Fahrgäste stiegen aus, nur der Mann im steifen Hut blieb.

laughed forcefully/talked with each other for a while quite impolitely
What do I care!/although
conductor
shouted

„Also grüße Herrn Kurzhals schön“, sagte Frau Jakob noch. Emil *nickte.*

nodded

Und dann waren er und der Herr mit dem steifen Hut *allein.* Das gefiel Emil nicht sehr. Ein Mann, der Schokolade *verteilt* und *verrückte Geschichten* erzählt, *ist nichts Genaues.* Emil wollte wieder nach dem Kuvert *fassen.* Er *wagte* es aber nicht, sondern ging, als der Zug *weiterfuhr,* auf die Toilette, holte dort das Kuvert aus der Tasche, *zählte* das Geld – es stimmte immer noch – und war *ratlos,* was er machen sollte. Endlich *kam ihm ein Gedanke.* Er nahm eine *Nadel,* die er im *Jackettkragen* fand, *steckte* sie erst *durch* die drei *Scheine,* dann durch das Kuvert und schließlich durch das *Anzugfutter.* Er *nagelte sozusagen* sein Geld *fest.* So, dachte er, nun kann nichts passieren. Und dann ging er wieder ins °*Kupee.*

alone
distributes/crazy stories/is unscrupulous
grab/dared
continued
counted
perplexed
had an idea/needle
jacket's collar/put it through
bills
lining of the suit/nailed, so to speak/tight

Herr Grundeis hatte es sich in einer Ecke gemütlich gemacht und schlief. Emil war froh, daß er sich nicht zu unterhalten brauchte, und *blickte* durchs Fenster. Bäume, *Windmühlen,* Felder, *Fabriken,* Kühe, *winkende Bauern zogen draußen vorbei.* Und *es war* sehr *hübsch anzusehen,* wie sich alles *vorüberdrehte,* fast wie auf einer *Grammophonplatte.* Aber schließlich kann man nicht *stundenlang* durchs Fenster *starren.*

looked
windmills/factories/waving farmers went past outside
it was nice to see
moved by
record player/for hours
stare

das Gepäcknetz · die Notbremse · das Kupee

Herr Grundeis schlief weiter und *schnarchte* ein bißchen. Emil *lehnte* sich in die *entgegengesetzte* Ecke des Kupees und *betrachtete* den *Schläfer.* Warum der Mann nur immer den Hut *aufbehielt?* Und ein *längliches* Gesicht hatte er, einen ganz schmalen schwarzen *Schnurrbart* und hundert *Falten* um den Mund, und die Ohren waren sehr *dünn* und *standen weit ab.*

Wupp! Emil *erschrak. Beinahe wäre er eingeschlafen.* Das durfte er ja nicht. Wenn doch jemand *zugestiegen wäre!* Der Zug hielt ein paar Mal, aber es kam kein Mensch. Dabei war es erst vier Uhr, und Emil hatte noch über zwei Stunden zu fahren. Er *kniff sich* in die Beine. In der Schule half das immer in Herrn Bremsers Geschichtsstunden.

Eine Weile ging's. Und Emil dachte an Pony Hütchen. Aber er konnte sich gar nicht mehr ihr Gesicht vorstellen. Er wußte nur, daß sie – als sie und die Großmutter und Tante Martha in Neustadt gewesen waren – *mit ihm hatte boxen wollen.* Er hatte natürlich nein gesagt, weil sie *Papiergewicht* war und er mindestens *Halbschwergewicht.* Das *wäre* unfair, hatte er damals gesagt. Und wenn er ihr einen Uppercut *ge-*

snored
leaned/opposite
looked over/sleeper
kept on/longish
mustach
wrinkles/thin
stuck out
startled/He had almost fallen asleep.
would have gotten in

pinched

It was O.K. for a while.

had wanted to box with him
paper weight
middle weight/would be

312

ben würde, müsse man sie hinterher von der Wand abkratzen. *would give…you would have had to scrape her off the wall afterwards*
Sie hatte aber erst Ruhe gegeben, als Tante Martha *dazwi-* *between*
schenkam.

Schwupp! Er *fiel* fast von der Bank. Schon wieder ein- *fell*
geschlafen? Er kniff und kniff sich in die Beine. Und trotzdem *wollte es nichts nützen.* *was no use*

Er versuchte es mit *Knopfzählen.* Er zählte von oben *counting buttons*
nach unten und dann noch einmal von unten nach oben. Von
oben nach unten waren es dreiundzwanzig Knöpfe. Und von
unten nach oben vierundzwanzig. Emil *lehnte sich zurück* *leaned back and contemplated why it*
und überlegte, woran das wohl liegen könnte. *was so*

Und dabei schlief er ein.

Fragen

1. Wie viele Personen waren in dem Kupee?
2. Wie hieß der Herr, der Emil Schokolade gab?
3. Was erzählte er Emil von Berlin?
4. Was sagte der andere Mann dazu?
5. Wie sah der Mann aus, der von Berlin erzählte?
6. Was hatte er die ganze Zeit auf dem Kopf?
7. Was machte Emil mit seinem Geld?
8. Wie versuchte Emil, sich wachzuhalten?

Lesestück VII

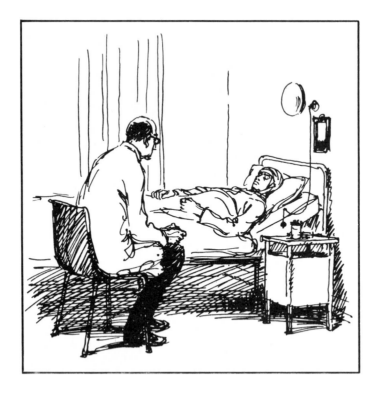

Als die Krankenschwester gegangen war, kam noch einmal der Arzt. Der *Verunglückte* schien ihm jetzt ruhiger zu sein, das Morphium *hatte gewirkt*. Der Arzt wollte ihm noch nicht sagen, daß er sein Bein *verlieren würde*. Das hatte Zeit; erst einmal sehen, wer dieser Mann *überhaupt* war. Das Auto war *völlig ausgebrannt gewesen*, und in der *Brieftasche* hatte man nur ein Foto gefunden, es war so etwas wie eine Katze darauf zu sehen; bißchen wenig, fand der Doktor, um einen *Schwerverletzten* zu identifizieren.

    Er *zog* sich einen Stuhl *heran* und setzte sich ans Bett. Der Verunglückte sah ihn *fragend* an.

    „Hallo", sagte der Doktor, „da sind wir ja wieder."

    „Was ist passiert?" fragte der andere.

    „Sie sind auf freier Strecke gegen eine Brücke gefahren."

    Der Verunglückte schloß die Augen. „Ich sah sie zu spät. Sie saß plötzlich *mitten* auf der Straße. Man sah *im Dunkeln* nur ihre *Pupillen aufleuchten*. Ich *riß* das °Steuer *herum* –"

injured

had taken effect

would lose

actually

completely burned out/wallet

seriously injured

pulled up

inquisitively

in the middle of/in the dark

pupils/light up/swung around

Excerpt from: Wolfdietrich Schnurre DIE TAT, copyright Wolfdietrich Schnurre. The *Easy Reader* (a C-level book) containing this simplified excerpt, is published by EMC Publishing.

die Katze

„Von wem *reden* Sie", unterbrach ihn der Arzt.   *talking*

„Von der Katze", sagte der Mann.

„Ach. Eine Katze war der Grund, daß Sie –?"

Der Verunglückte *nickte schwach*. Er hatte noch immer   *nodded slightly*
die Augen geschlossen. Er *wirkte unruhig*.   *appeared restless*

„Ich *hätte sie überfahren sollen*", sagte er plötzlich,   *should have run over her*
„dann *hätte* ich Ruhe *gehabt*."   *would have had*

„Ruhe –?" fragte der Arzt, „wovor?"

„Na, vor ihr!" Der Mann schrie fast.

„*Beruhigen Sie sich*", sagte der Arzt, „Sie müssen jetzt   *Calm down.*
ruhig liegen." Er *schwieg,* während er den Verunglückten   *was silent*
aufmerksam ansah.   *looked at attentively*

„Ist ja *komisch*", sagte er dann. Er zog seinen Stuhl   *strange*
noch etwas näher heran; der Fall fing an, ihn zu interessieren.

„Wie lange haben Sie das schon?"

„Was?"

„Na, diesen – Katzenkomplex."

das Steuer

„Seit ein paar Wochen. Seit – seit dieser Mensch da zu mir kam."

„Was für ein Mensch?"

„So ein *Spätheimkehrer.*" *person who returned years after the war*

„Ach. Und Sie meinen, der ist die *Ursache* für Ihren Komplex?" *cause*

„Na ja, so ist es nun auch wieder nicht. Ich – ich bin *Anwalt;* er kam, weil er einen *Rat* haben wollte, was er jetzt anfangen sollte." *lawyer/advice*

„Er kannte Sie –?"

„Von – von früher, ja."

„Was nennen Sie früher?"

„Den Krieg", sagte der andere und sah zur *Decke.* *ceiling*

„Sie waren Offizier –?"

„Nur beim *Kriegsgericht.*" *court-martial*

„Nur –"

Der Verunglückte wurde plötzlich *gesprächig.* *talkative*

„Gott, na ja, Sie kennen doch solche Entscheidungen, die da so täglich getroffen wurden."

„Ja, *allerdings*", sagte der Arzt. „Ich hatte einmal den *Tod* eines *Erschossenen* festzustellen. Er war siebzehn Jahre alt und soll *feige* gewesen sein." *of course / death/person who was shot / cowardly*

„Na ja, manchmal *blieb* einem aber auch *nichts anderes übrig,* als hart zu *handeln.*" *had no choice / deal harshly*

„Nein –?" Der Arzt *hatte sich aufgerichtet;* er *mußte sich Mühe geben*, in dem anderen noch den Patienten zu sehen. *„Wie kommen Sie darauf?"* *had set up/had to try hard / What makes you think that?*

„Na, durch diesen da, diesen *Heimkehrer.*" *repatriate (soldier)*

„Ach, Sie hatten im Kriege mal – *beruflich* mit ihm zu tun?" *professionally*

„Nicht mit ihm selbst, es – es war ein Kamerad von ihm, *Unteroffizier* Zabel, Seh'n Sie, das war auch so ein Fall." *corporal*

„Ich denke, Ihr Besucher kam, um zu fragen, was er machen *könnte.*" *could*

„Auch, ja; aber das war nicht der *wahre* Grund, er wollte vor allem mit mir über Zabel sprechen." *real*

„Und was hat der mit Ihrem – Katzenkomplex zu tun?"

„Merkwürdigerweise sehr viel." *Oddly enough, a great deal.*

Jetzt war der Verunglückte wieder Patient.

„Wieso?"

„Ich werd's Ihnen erzählen. Bestimmt hilft es, wenn ich es Ihnen erzähle. *Nicht wahr,* Doktor, so was gibt's doch: daß *man sich leichter fühlt,* wenn man's jemandem gesagt hat?" *isn't that right / one feels better*

„Weiß ich nicht", sagte der Arzt, „die *Beichte* ist ja eigentlich die Aufgabe der Kirche und nicht der Medizin, glaub' ich." *confession*

„Ist mir egal", sagte der Verunglückte *heftig*, „Arzt   *angrily*
oder *Pfarrer – Hauptsache*, Sie hören zu."   *pastor/the main thing*

Der Doktor sah nach der Uhr. „Also gut. Aber bleiben
Sie *um Gottes willen* ruhig."   *for God's sake*

„Ich werde es versuchen", sagte der Verunglückte.

Fragen

1. Wo befindet sich der Verunglückte?
2. Mit wem spricht er?
3. Wie war das Autounglück passiert?
4. Was waren die Folgen dieses Unglücks?
5. Was hatte man in seiner Brieftasche gefunden?
6. Wer hatte ihn in seinem Büro besucht?
7. Was war der Verunglückte im Kriege gewesen?

Lesestück VIII

Die Anhalterin

Es war Freitag, und ich bereitete mich schon auf ein ruhiges Wochenende vor, als man mich anrief: man hatte eine *Tote* gefunden. Als Heines erzählte, wie und wo das geschehen war, wußte ich, daß es mit dem ruhigen Wochenende vorbei war. — *dead woman*

„Chef", sagte Heines, „es muß eine *merkwürdige* Geschichte sein. Ein *Zugführer*, der durch den Wald bei Allershausen fuhr, sah einen Mann, der den Körper einer Frau auf den Armen trug. Er *meldete* am nächsten Bahnhof, was er gesehen hatte. Man schickte von dort einen jungen Mann auf den Weg, und dieser Mann sah plötzlich den Körper einer Frau so auf die °*Schienen* gelegt, daß der nächste Zug die Frau *überfahren* mußte." — *strange* / *train conductor* / *reported* / *run over*

die Schiene

Wir fuhren sofort los. Es war ein kalter Wintertag, kein Tag *zum Sterben*. Und als ich die Tote sah, die man neben die Schienen gelegt hatte, dachte ich: „Und das ist kein Mensch, um zu sterben." Ein junges Mädchen, ein ganz junger Mensch, *getötet*. Das ist so *sinnlos*, so unnatürlich, und ich sagte mir: — *for dying* / *killed/senseless*

„Du wirst den finden, der das getan hat. Und wenn du Tag und Nacht arbeitest, den wirst du finden!"

Es war ein *hübsches* Mädchen, kaum zwanzig Jahre alt. Sie war schon kalt und lag mit geöffnetem Mund da. Ihr Gesicht und ihr helles Haar waren naß. — *pretty*

Excerpt from: Herbert Reinecker DER KOMMISSAR LÄSST BITTEN, copyright Kindler Verlag, München 1976. The *Easy Reader* (a *B*-level book) with the same title is published by EMC Publishing.

Der Arzt war da, hatte die Tote schon untersucht und
sagte:

„Tot durch starkes *Drücken* gegen den Hals." *pressing*

Harry kam aus dem Wald:

„*Spuren,* Chef. Und hier habe ich ihre Handtasche *tracks*
gefunden."

So wußten wir ganz schnell, wer dieses Mädchen war.
Es hieß Irmgard Lenk. Sie war zweiundzwanzig Jahre alt und
wohnte in der Karl-Theodor-Straße. Ich ging den Wald hin-
unter, vorsichtig, um die Spuren nicht zu *zertreten.* Man sah *trample down*
die tiefe Spur von Füßen. Der Mann hatte die Tote ja
getragen.

Harry zeigte auf den Weg.

„Sehen Sie die *Fahrspuren* dort, Chef? Ein °*Lastwa-* *tire tracks*
gen, ganz frische Spuren. Der Wagen hat hier gestanden, und
hier beginnen die *Fußspuren.* Der *Mörder* ist in einem *foot prints/murderer*
Lastwagen gekommen."

Ja, Harry hatte recht. Der Mörder war mit einem
Lastwagen gekommen.

Grabert und ich fuhren zurück nach München und gingen zu dem Haus in der Karl-Theodor-Straße. Im zweiten

der Lastwagen

die Anhalterin

Stock fanden wir die Wohnung: Schultz, Irmgard Lenk, Erika Lenk.

Eine ältere Frau machte uns auf und sah uns *ängstlich* an. Sie *ließ uns eintreten, wandte sich um* und rief: „Fräulein Erika!"

fearful
let us step inside/turned around

Aus einem Zimmer kam ein Mädchen. Die *Ähnlichkeit* mit der Toten war groß. Auch sie hatte lange, helle Haare. Sie sah uns an, sie stand ganz still und sagte sofort:

similarity

„Irmgard? Ist etwas mit Irmgard?"

Ich bringe nicht gern schlechte Nachrichten. Ich finde keine Worte. Meine Leute wissen das und *nehmen mir die Arbeit* meistens *ab*.

take the load off my shoulders

Grabert sagte leise:

„Ist Irmgard Lenk Ihre Schwester? Dann muß ich Ihnen *mitteilen*, daß Ihrer Schwester etwas geschehen ist."

inform

Das Mädchen verstand sofort. Sie war weiß im Gesicht und sagte ganz leise:

„Kommen Sie herein."

Sie *führte* uns in das Zimmer, in dem sie mit ihrer Schwester wohnte und setzte sich. Sie hatte keine *Kraft* mehr und ließ den Kopf hängen. So saß sie eine ganze Zeit, dann *hob* sie den Kopf und antwortete auf unsere Fragen.

led
strength
raised

Wir *erfuhren* folgendes:

found out

Irmgard Lenk fuhr fast jeden Freitag nach Stuttgart hinauf. Dort hatte sie einen Freund, mit dem sie am Wochenende zusammen war. Sie fuhr nicht mit dem Zug, sondern als °*Anhalterin*.

Erika Lenk sagte:

„Ich war dagegen, aber sie war nicht ängstlich. Sie fuhr fast immer mit demselben Mann, mit demselben Wagen. Jeden Tag fährt ein Lastwagen nach Stuttgart hinauf. Der Mann hatte sie einmal mitgenommen und nahm sie nun immer mit, wenn sie um sieben Uhr an der Autobahn wartete."

Das war eine große Hilfe, und ich begann, mich *etwas wohler zu fühlen*. Hier waren Möglichkeiten, *eine Menge* Möglichkeiten.

to feel a bit better
a lot of

Irmgard Lenk fuhr immer mit demselben Mann. Grabert fragte und fragte. Ja, auch diesmal war Irmgard sicher mit demselben Mann gefahren. Sie hatte *allerdings* etwas zu lange geschlafen. Zum Frühstück hatte sie nur ein Glas Milch getrunken.

of course

„Was für ein Wagen war das? Hat sie über den Mann gesprochen? Was für ein Mann war es? Ein älterer Mann? Ein jüngerer Mann?"

Erika Lenk saß da und antwortete auf alle Fragen, so gut sie konnte. Sie konnte nur eins *berichten*: Der Fahrer war jünger, ein jüngerer Mensch. Er war *lustig*, erzählte viel.

report
cheerful

Irmgard hatte gesagt, daß der Mann *sie* immer *zum Lachen brachte. Er habe Kaffee bei sich.* Er habe auch Musik im Wagen. Ein sehr netter Mann, mit dem die Fahrt ganz schnell *verging.*

made her laugh
He had coffee along.

went by

Und noch etwas sagte Erika Lenk. Ihre Schwester wollte gern dem Fahrer etwas geben. Geld hatte er nie angenommen. Deshalb hatte Irmgard einen kleinen Löwen gekauft. Den hatte sie ihm gegeben, für den Wagen.

Grabert schrieb. Er war glücklich. Das war doch eine große Hilfe!

Dann kam noch etwas Wichtiges. Irmgard hatte einmal gesagt, daß der Wagen es bis zur Autobahn nicht weit hatte. Fünf Minuten brauchte er nur bis zur *Auffahrt.*

approach ramp

Grabert sah mich an:

„Na, Chef", sagte er, „den Mann *kriegen* wir. *Den haben wir bald.*"

get/We'll get him soon.

Ich sah das Mädchen an. Erika Lenk hatte acht Jahre mit ihrer Schwester zusammen gelebt. Die Eltern waren tot; die Schwestern hatten niemanden mehr. Ich sah es, ich merkte es bei jedem Wort – die Schwestern hatten sich geliebt.

Nun hatte ich Angst um Erika Lenk, die im Zimmer stand, uns *ernst* ansah. Aus ihren Augen *war alles Lebendige verschwunden.*

serious/all life had disappeared

„Kann ich irgend etwas für Sie tun?" fragte ich, aber das Mädchen sah mich nur an, und ich dachte:

„Komm, geh weg, sie will weinen."

Ich ließ *die Lebende* allein, um der Toten zu helfen.
Wir gingen an die Arbeit.

the living

Das Wichtigste war, daß der Lastwagen, mit dem Irmgard Lenk nach Stuttgart fuhr, nur fünf Minuten bis zur Autobahn brauchte. Wir *rechneten aus,* wie weit ein Lastwagen in fünf Minuten fahren kann und machten einen *Kreis* um die *Autobahnauffahrt.* Dann mußten wir jemand finden, der mehrere Lastwagen laufen hatte und jeden Tag einen Wagen nach Stuttgart schickte.

calculated
circle
freeway approach

Damit arbeiteten wir den ganzen Tag und hatten *dennoch keinen Erfolg.*

still no success

In dieser Nacht schlief ich schlecht. Immer wieder sah ich Bilder vor mir. Die Tote neben den Schienen und Erika Lenk mit ihren leeren Augen.

Sehr müde kam ich ins Büro und wußte nicht, was zur gleichen Zeit geschah. Ich erfuhr es später. Erika Lenk war morgens früh aufgestanden, war zur Autobahnauffahrt hingegangen, hatte sich dort hingestellt.

Sie suchte den Mörder ihrer Schwester *auf ihre Weise.*

in her way

Fragen

1. Was macht eine Anhalterin?
2. Wie weiß man, daß der Mörder in einem Lastwagen gekommen ist?
3. Wo hat man die Tote gefunden?
4. Wie alt war Irmgard Lenk?
5. Was machte Irmgard Lenk fast jeden Freitag?
6. Wer ist Erika Lenk?
7. Warum ist sie zur Autobahn gegangen und hat sich dorthin gestellt?

Lesestück IX

In den letzten Tagen des August 1961 *erwachte* das Mädchen
Rita Seidel in einem kleinen Zimmer im Krankenhaus. Sie
hat nicht geschlafen, sie war *ohnmächtig*. Wie sie die Augen
aufmacht, ist es Abend, und die saubere weiße Wand, auf die
sie zuerst sieht, ist nur noch wenig hell. Hier ist sie zum
ersten Mal, aber sie weiß gleich wieder, was mit ihr, heute
und vorher, geschehen ist. Sie kommt von weit her. Ach ja,
die Stadt. Enger noch: das *Werk*, die °*Montagehalle*. Jener
Punkt auf den °*Schienen*, wo ich *umfiel*. Also hat einer die
beiden °*Waggons* noch angehalten, die da von rechts und
links *auf mich zukamen*. Sie fuhren gerade auf mich zu. Das
war das letzte.

woke up

unconscious

factory
collapsed

came towards me

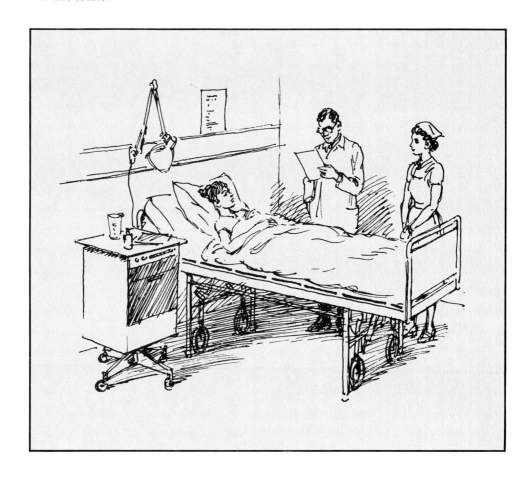

Die Krankenschwester kommt ans Bett, sie hat gesehen, wie das Mädchen *wach geworden ist* und sich mit stillen Augen im Zimmer umsieht. Sie spricht leise und freundlich zu ihr. „Sie sind gesund", sagt sie. Da *dreht* Rita das Gesicht zur Wand und beginnt zu *weinen. Hört* die ganze Nacht *nicht mehr auf.* Als morgens der Arzt nach ihr sieht, kann sie nicht antworten.

woke up

turns
cry/doesn't stop at all

Aber der Arzt braucht nicht zu fragen, er weiß ja alles, es steht ja alles aufgeschrieben. Diese Rita Seidel, eine Studentin, arbeitet nur während der Ferien im *Betrieb.* Sie ist vieles nicht *gewohnt,* zum Beispiel die Hitze in den Waggons nicht, wenn sie aus dem °*Ofen* kommen, wo sie *getrocknet* werden. Es ist *verboten,* bei hohen Temperaturen im Wagen zu arbeiten, aber die Arbeit *drängt.* Die °*Werkzeugkiste* ist schwer, 30-35 kg, sie hat sie noch bis zu den Schienen getragen, und dann fiel sie um.

factory
used to
dried
forbidden
presses

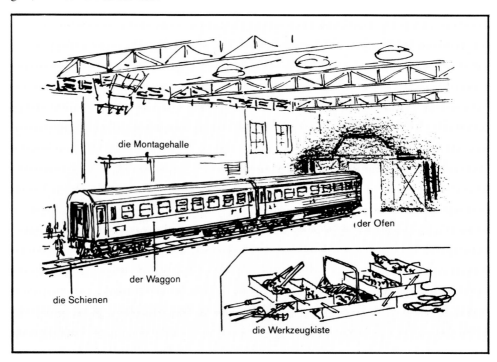

die Montagehalle

der Ofen

der Waggon

die Schienen

die Werkzeugkiste

Nach Tagen, als Rita immer noch *nicht angesprochen werden will,* wird der Arzt *unsicher.* Er denkt, wer dieses hübsche Mädchen nur soweit gebracht hat. *Für ihn steht fest,* daß nur *Liebe* ein Mädchen so krank machen kann.

doesn't want to be spoken to
uncertain
He is sure…
love

Ritas Mutter wird *herbeigerufen.* Auch sie kann nichts dazu sagen. „Das Lernen", sagt sie. „Ich habe mir gleich gedacht, sie *hält es nicht aus."* „Ein Mann? Nicht, daß ich wüßte. Ihr früherer Freund, ein Chemiedoktor, ist doch schon ein halbes Jahr weg." „Weg?" fragt der Arzt. „Nun ja, weggegangen, Sie verstehen."

called in

can't stand it

Das Mädchen Rita bekommt Blumen: *Astern, Dahlien,*   *daisies/dahlias*
Gladiolen, Niemand darf zu ihr, bis eines Abends ein Mann   *gladiolus*
mit Rosen kommt. Der Arzt *gibt nach.* Das kann vielleicht   *gives in*
die ganze Krankheit *bessern.* Ein kurzes Gespräch, der Arzt   *improve*
ist dabei. Aber da kommt nichts von Liebe, nur von einigen
Waggons *wird geredet,* was bestimmt nicht wichtig ist, und   *is discussed*
nach fünf Minuten geht der Mann wieder. Der Arzt *erfährt,*   *finds out*
daß dies der junge *Betriebsleiter* vom Waggonwerk war. Der   *factory manager*
Arzt fühlt, daß dieser junge Mann mehr von Rita Seidel weiß
als die Mutter, mehr als er selbst, der Arzt und als alle die
vielen anderen, die nun kommen: Zuerst die aus der *Brigade*   *brigade (group)*
Ermisch, alle zwölf, dann Ritas Freundin, Studenten aus dem
Lehrerseminar und auch Mädchen aus Ritas Dorf.   *teacher's seminar*

     Die da zu ihr kommen, haben sie alle gern. Sie spre-
chen leise mit ihr. Sie weint jetzt *seltener,* meistens abends.   *more rarely*
Sie sagt niemandem, daß sie Angst hat, die Augen zuzuma-
chen. Sie sieht immer noch die beiden Waggons, grün und
schwarz und sehr groß. Wenn die *angeschoben sind,* laufen   *are pushed*
sie auf den Schienen weiter ohne Halt, dazu sind sie gemacht. Sie rollen weiter. Und wo sie sich treffen werden, da
liegt sie. Da liege ich.

     Dann weint sie wieder.

     Als er damals vor zwei Jahren in unser Dorf kam, *fiel er*   *I recognized him right away*
mir sofort auf. Manfred Herrfurth. Bald wußte ich, daß der
junge Mann Chemie studiert hatte und daß er im Dorf bei
seiner Familie Ferien machen wollte.

     Wenn Rita, die mit Mutter und Tante in einem kleinen
Häuschen am *Waldrand* lebte, früh mit dem Rad die Dorf-   *edge of the forest*
straße *hinauffuhr,* stand er hinter dem Haus und wusch sich   *rode up*
mit kaltem Wasser.

     Wenn er sie kommen sah, *nahm er seine Brille ab* und   *he took his glasses off*
begann sie an seinem Hemd zu putzen. Später sah sie ihn
langsam auf den blauen Wald zugehen, ein großer Mann mit
zu langen Armen und einem schmalen, harten Jungenkopf.

     Aber Sonntag abends im °*Gasthaus* fand sie, daß er äl-
ter und härter aussah, als sie gedacht hatte. Den ganzen

das Gasthaus

Abend sah er zu, wie die Jungen aus dem Dorf mit ihr tanzten. Der *allerletzte* Tanz begann, man öffnete schon die Fenster. Jetzt endlich *trat er zu ihr* und führte sie in die Mitte. Er tanzte gut, aber er *war nicht bei der Sache.* *final* *stepped up to her* *was not attentive*

Sie wußte, am nächsten Tag fuhr er früh in die Stadt zurück. Sie wußte, er *kriegte es fertig,* nichts zu sagen, nichts zu tun, er ist so. Plötzlich sagte sie in seine Augen hinein: „Ist das schwer, so zu werden, wie Sie sind?" *he would be able to*

Er schloß einfach die Augen.

Ohne ein Wort zu sagen, *ergiff* er ihren Arm und führte sie hinaus. *Wortlos* gingen sie die Dorfstraße hinunter. Da standen sie schon am *Gartentor,* langsam ging sie die wenigen Schritte bis zu ihrer Haustür, da sagte er langsam: „Könnten Sie sich in einen wie mich *verlieben?"* *seized* *without a word* *garden gate* *fall in love*

„Ja", *erwiderte* Rita. *replied*

Dann drehte er sich leise um und ging. Rita blieb ganz ruhig an der Tür stehen, bis er nicht mehr zu hören war.

Nachts konnte sie nicht schlafen und am Morgen begann sie auf seinen Brief zu warten. Der erste Brief kam eine Woche nach dem Dorftanz. Der erste Brief ihres ganzen Lebens, nach all den Briefen im Büro, die ja nicht ihre Briefe waren.

Rita, neunzehn Jahre alt, mußte nicht erst lernen, einen solchen Brief zu lesen. Auf einmal zeigte es sich: Die ganzen neunzehn Jahre, Wünsche, *Taten, Gedanken, Träume,* waren zu nichts anderem dagewesen, als sie gerade für diesen Augenblick, gerade auf diesen Brief vorzubereiten. Wie jedes Mädchen war sie sicher, daß vor ihr keine und keine nach ihr *gefühlt hatten* und fühlen konnten, was sie jetzt fühlte. Sie trat vor den °*Spiegel.* Sie war rot bis auf die braunen Augen, *gleichzeitig lächelte sie auf eine neue Weise.* *deeds/thoughts/dreams* *had felt* *at the same time she smiled in a different way*

Sie wußte, es war genug an ihr, was ihm gefiel und immer gefallen würde.

Fragen

1. Warum liegt Rita im Krankenhaus?
2. In welchem Betrieb arbeitete Rita?
3. Wer ist Manfred?
4. Wo hatte Rita Manfred das erste Mal kennengelernt?

All the words introduced in DEUTSCH: AKTUELL 1 and 2 have been summarized in this section. The numbers following the meaning of individual words and phrases indicate the particular lesson in which they appear for the first time. In cases in which there is more than one meaning for a word or phrase and it has appeared in different lessons, both lesson numbers are listed. (Example: die **Frau,-en** Mrs., woman *1;* wife *5*)

Nouns have been listed with their respective articles and plural forms. Verbs with stem vowel change as well as past and present perfect forms of irregular verbs are also presented.

A

ab und zu once in a while *16*

der **Abend,-e** evening *2*

das **Abendbrot** supper *5*

das **Abendessen** supper, dinner *11*

aber but *2*

die **Abfahrt,-en** departure *10*

die **Abfahrtszeit,-en** departure time *10*

abfliegen *(flog ab, ist abgeflogen)* to take off (plane) *11*

der **Abflug,-̈e** departure (flight) *11*

die **Abfüllerei,-en** bottling company *20*

der **Abgeordnete,-n** representative *7*

abheben *(hob ab, abgehoben)* to lift, take off *14; den Hörer abheben* to lift the receiver *14*

das **Abitur,-e** final examination (secondary school) *B*

sich **abkühlen** to cool off *9*

ablesen *(liest ab, las ab, abgelesen)* to read (off) *D*

abräumen to clear *7*

die **Abreise** departure *11*

abreißen *(riß ab, abgerissen)* to tear down *15*

abschieben *(schob ab, abgeschoben)* to push off *20*

abschleppen to tow (away) *19*

abschneiden *(schnitt ab, abgeschnitten)* to cut off *20*

der **Abschnitt,-e** slip (of paper) *6*

der **Absender,-** sender *14*

absperren to block off *9*

der **Abstand,-̈e** gap, distance *19*

die **Abteilung,-en** department *17*

ach oh *18*

acht eight *1*

achtzehn eighteen *2*

der **Adler,-** eagle *15*

der **Affe,-n** ape, monkey *15*

aggressiv aggressive *14*

ähnlich similar *15*

die **Akademie,-n** academy, college *15*

das **Akkordeon,-s** accordion *8*

die **Akte,-n** file *20*

die **Aktentasche,-n** briefcase *11*

aktiv active *20*

alle all *2;* everyone *8*

allerdings at any rate, though *15*

alles everything *3*

die **Alpen** Alps *5*

das **Alpenvorland** Alpine foothills *8*

alphabetisch alphabetical *14*

als than *8*

also O.K. then... *10*

alt old *4*

das **Alter** age *20*

die **Altstadt** old town *12*

Amerika America *5*

der **Amerikaner,-** American (male) *A*

die **Amerikanerin,-nen** American (female) *A*

amerikanisch American *16*

an at *3;* on *8*

anbieten *(bot an, angeboten)* to offer *17*

ander- other, different *4*

andeuten to indicate, suggest *19*

der **Anfang,-̈e** beginning *14*

anfangen *(fängt an, fing an, angefangen)* to begin, start *15*

anfassen to touch *15*

die **Angabe,-n** description, detail *14*

die **Angelegenheit,-en** matter, affair *15*

der **Angestellte,-n** employee (male) *6*

angreifen *(griff an, angegriffen)* to attack *14*

die **Angst,-̈e** fear *2; Hab keine Angst!* Don't worry! Don't be afraid! *2*

anhaben *(hat an, hatte an, angehabt)* to have on *6*

anhalten *(hält an, hielt an, angehalten)* to stop *10*

sich **anhören** to listen to *11*

ankommen *(kam an, ist angekommen)* to arrive *10; Es kommt darauf an.* It depends on it. *16*

die **Ankunft,-̈e** arrival *7*

das **Anmeldeformular,-e** registration form *7*

annehmen *(nimmt an, nahm an, angenommen)* to assume *10*

anordnen to arrange, group *14*

anpflanzen to grow, plant *15*

anprobieren to try on *6*

anrufen *(rief an, angerufen)* to call up *5*

der **Ansager,-** announcer *9*

anschlagen *(schlägt an, schlug an, angeschlagen)* to post, put up *15* sich **anschließen** *(schloß an, angeschlossen)* to join 20

die **Anschrift,-en** address 18

sich **ansehen** *(sieht an, sah an, angesehen)* to look at B

die **Ansichtskarte,-n** picture postcard 13

anstrengen to exert 8; to strain, tire out 20; *Es strengt an.* It is exhausting. 8

anstrengend strenuous, exhausting D

die **Antwort,-en** answer 15

antworten to answer 3

die **Anzahl** number 19

anziehen *(zog an, angezogen)* to put on (clothes), dress 6

sich **anziehen** to get dressed 12; *Er ist angezogen.* He is dressed. 12

der **Anziehungspunkt,-e** attraction 10

der **Anzug,-̈e** suit 6

der **Apfel,-̈** apple 17

der **Apfelkuchen,-** apple cake 16

das **Apfelmus** apple sauce A

der **Apfelsaft,-̈e** apple juice 16

die **Apfelsine,-n** orange 17

die **Apotheke,-n** pharmacy 18

der **Apotheker,-** pharmacist 13

der **Apparat,-e** camera 15

der **Appetit** appetite 16; *Appetit haben auf* to have appetite for 16; *Guten Appetit!* Enjoy your meal! 16

der **April** April 4

die **Arbeit,-en** work 2; *eine Arbeit schreiben* to take a test 2

arbeiten to work 5

der **Arbeiter,-** worker 20

der **Arm,-e** arm 11

das **Armaturenbrett** dashboard 19

der **Arzt,-̈e** doctor 13

das **Arztzimmer,-** doctor's office 18

Aschenbrödel Cinderella 20

Asien Asia 19

das **Aspirin** aspirin 18

astronomisch astronomical 12

die **Atmosphäre,-n** atmosphere 17

auch also, too 1

auf to, on 2; at 14; *auf der Post* at the post office 14

auf und ab up and down C

aufführen to perform 20

auffüllen to fill up D

die **Aufgabe,-n** problem, exercise 4

aufgeben *(gibt auf, gab auf, aufgegeben)* to check (luggage) 11; to send, dispatch 14

auflegen to put on 8

aufmachen to open 11

die **Aufnahme,-n** picture, photo 12; *Aufnahmen machen* to take pictures 12

aufpassen to watch, keep an eye on something 9

der **Aufsatz,-̈e** essay, composition A

aufschreiben *(schrieb auf, aufgeschrieben)* to write down 14

der **Aufseher,-** attendant 9

aufstehen *(stand auf, ist aufgestanden)* to get up A

aufstellen to put up 19; to organize, plan 20

das **Auge,-n** eye 11

der **August** August 4

aus from, out of 2

der **Ausdruck,-̈e** expression 4

der **Ausflug,-̈e** outing, trip C

der **Ausflugsort,-e** excursion area 8

ausfüllen to fill out 7

der **Ausgang,-̈e** exit 11

ausgeben *(gibt aus, gab aus, ausgegeben)* to spend (money) 16

ausgezeichnet excellent 10

aushängen to hang out, display 16

die **Auskunft,-̈e** information 13

das **Ausland** foreign country, foreign countries 16

der **Ausländer,-** foreigner 10

das **Auspuffrohr,-e** exhaust pipe 19

ausleihen *(lieh aus, ausgeliehen)* to check out, borrow 15

ausreichend sufficient 4

ausruhen to rest, relax 14; *zum Ausruhen* for resting 14

aussehen *(sieht aus, sah aus, ausgesehen)* to look, appear 7

der **Außenspiegel,-** outside mirror 19

außer besides, except 6

außerdem besides 18

außerhalb outside 5

aussetzen to sit out 8

die **Aussicht,-en** view 16

aussteigen *(stieg aus, ist ausgestiegen)* to get off 10

aussuchen to select 11

austauschen to exchange 11

die **Auswahl** selection, choice 6

auswählen to choose, select B

auswandern to emigrate 14

der **Ausweis,-e** identification (card) 7

auswendig lernen to memorize, learn by heart 4

der **Auszug,-̈e** excerpt 14

das **Auto,-s** car 5

die **Autobahn,-en** freeway, super highway 11

der **Autofahrer,-** (car) driver 14

der **Automat,-en** automat 3

automatisch automatic(ally) 18

der **Autor,-en** author 15

B

der **Bäcker,-** baker 13

die **Bäckerei,-en** bakery 17

die **Backware,-n** baked goods 17

die **Badesachen** (pl.) swimming stuff 12

das **Badezimmer,-** bathroom 15

die **Bahn,-en** train 10

der **Bahnhof,-̈e** (train) station 3

der **Bahnsteig,-e** platform 8

bald soon 2

der **Ball,-̈e** ball 14

die **Banane,-n** banana 17

die **Bank,-̈e** bench 4

die **Bank,-en** bank 6

der **Bär,-en** bear 12

der **Bärengraben** Bear Pit 12

die **Barkasse,-n** large motor boat, launch 13

der **Barockstil** baroque style 11

der **Basketball,-̈e** basketball 9

die **Batterie,-n** battery D

der **Bau,-ten** structure 12

der **Bauch,-̈e** stomach 18

die **Bauchschmerzen** (pl.) stomachache 18

bauen to build 11

der **Bauernhof,-̈e** farm 10

die **Baustelle,-n** construction site 19

beantworten to answer A; *eine Frage beantworten* to answer a question A

sich **bedanken** to thank 14

der **Bedarf** need, demand, use 15

bedenken to think over, consider 18; *Es gibt ihm zu bedenken.* It makes him think. 18

bedeuten to mean, signify *18*

die **Bedeutung,-en** meaning, significance *4*

bedienen to help, wait on *11*

sich **bedienen** to help oneself *17*

die **Bedienung** service *17*

sich **beeilen** to hurry *3; Beeilen wir uns!* Let's hurry. *3*

beenden to end, finish *10*

sich **befinden** *(befand, befunden)* to be located, be *11*

befriedigend satisfactory *4*

begeistert enthusiastic *11*

beginnen *(begann, begonnen)* to begin *3*

begrüßen to greet *3*

begutachten to look over, evaluate *6*

behalten *(behält, behielt, behalten)* to keep *12*

der **Behälter,-** container *17*

bei at *5;* with *8*

beide both *2*

die **Beilage,-n** addition *16; Beilagen* served with, side dish *16*

das **Bein,-e** leg *11*

beisammensitzen *(saß beisammen, beisammengesessen)* to sit together *11*

das **Beispiel,-e** example *7; zum Beispiel* for example *7*

bekannt well-known *5*

der **Bekannte,-n** friend, acquaintance *12*

der **Bekanntenkreis,-e** (circle of) friends *14*

bekanntgeben *(gibt bekannt, gab bekannt, bekanntgegeben)* to announce *8*

die **Bekanntmachung,-en** announcement *15*

bekommen *(bekam, bekommen)* to get, receive *2*

sich **beklagen über** to complain about *13*

Belgien Belgium *3*

belegt covered *16; belegte Brote* sandwiches *16*

beleuchten to light up, illuminate *14*

beliebt popular *5*

die **Bemühung,-en** trouble, effort *18*

sich **benehmen** *(benimmt, benahm, benommen)* to behave *11*

das **Benzin** gasoline *D*

der **Benzinbetrag** amount for gasoline *D*

beobachten to watch, observe *16*

bequem comfortable *3*

bereiten to prepare *14; anderen Freude bereiten* to please others *14*

bereits already *20*

bereitstehen *(stand bereit, bereitgestanden)* to be ready, stand ready *9*

der **Berg,-e** mountain *5*

die **Bergakademie** mining college *15*

die **Bergbahn,-en** mountain train *12*

der **Beruf,-e** job, profession *15*

berühmt famous *10*

sich **beschäftigen mit** to be busy/ occupied with *20*

beschäftigt busy, occupied *C*

beschreiben *(beschrieb, beschrieben)* to describe *10*

die **Beschreibung,-en** description *4*

die **Beschwerde,-n** complaint, trouble *18; Beschwerden haben* to have trouble *18*

besetzt taken, occupied *C*

besichtigen to view, look over *10*

besitzen *(besaß, besessen)* to own, possess *15*

der **Besitzer,-** owner (male) *16*

die **Besitzerin,-nen** owner (female) *8*

besonder- special, unusual *4*

besonders especially *4*

die **Besorgung,-en** errand *14; Besorgungen machen* to do some shopping *14*

besprechen *(bespricht, besprach, besprochen)* to discuss *4*

die **Besserung,-en** improvement *18; Gute Besserung!* Get well. *18*

bestaunen to marvel at *11*

bestehen aus *(bestand aus, bestanden aus)* to consist of *4*

bestellen to order *B;* to reserve *18*

bestimmt undoubtedly, certainly *6*

bestimmt sein to be specified *20*

der **Bestimmungsort,-e** destination *14*

die **Bestleistung,-en** best performance *9*

der **Besuch,-e** visit *13*

besuchen to visit *5*

der **Besucher,-** visitor *6*

der **Betrag,-̈e** amount *6*

betragen *(beträgt, betrug, betragen)* to amount (come) to *19*

der **Betrieb,-e** business, firm *15;* traffic *17*

das **Bett,-en** bed *5; Er muß ins Bett.* He has to go to bed. *5*

die **Bevölkerung,-en** population *9*

bewahren to preserve *10*

sich **bewegen** to move *20*

der **Bewohner,-** resident, tenant *15*

bewölkt cloudy *20; leicht bewölkt* slightly overcast *20*

bewundern to admire *12*

bezahlen to pay *6*

bezeichnen to label, designate *10*

der **Bezirk,-e** (large) district *15*

die **Bibliothek,-en** library *15*

das **Bier,-e** beer *9*

bieten to offer *7*

das **Bild,-er** picture *11*

bilden to form *9*

sich **bilden** to form *16*

billig cheap *15*

der **Binnensee,-n** inland lake *20*

die **Biologie** biology *4*

die **Birne,-n** pear *17*

bis until *2*

der **Bissen,-** bite *20*

bitte please *6; bitte schön* here you are *13; Bitte sehr?* May I help you? *16*

bitten *(bat, gebeten)* to ask *12*

blau blue *6*

der **Benzinbetrag** amount for gasoline *D*

die **Blaubeermarmelade,-n** blueberry jam *17*

bleiben *(blieb, ist geblieben)* to stay, remain *2*

der **Bleistift,-e** pencil *8*

der **Blick** view *4*

blinken to flash *14*

die **Blockflöte,-n** recorder *9*

blöd dumb, stupid *12*

die **Blume,-n** flower *10*

das **Blumengeschäft,-e** flower shop *15*

der **Blumenstand,-̈e** flower stand *17*

die **Bluse,-n** blouse *6*

der **Blutdruck** blood pressure *18*

der **Bogen,-** sheet *17*

die **Bohne,-n** bean *16*

das **Boot,-e** boat *7*

die **Bordkarte,-n** boarding pass *11*

die **Bordsteinkante,-n** curb *19*

die **Botschaft,-en** embassy *12*

die **Bratkartoffel,-n** fried potato *16*

die **Bratwurst,-̈e** bratwurst, fried sausage *B*

brauchen to need *2*

braun brown *6*

die **Braut,-̈e** bride *12*

der **Bräutigam,-e** groom *12*

brav well-behaved *15*

breit wide *D*

die **Bremer Stadtmusikanten** Bremen Town Musicians *13*

die **Bremse,-n** brake *19*

die **Brezel,-n** pretzel *16*

der **Brief,-e** letter *11*

das **Brieffach,-̈er** postal box *15*

die **Brieffreundin,-nen** pen pal (female) *11*

der **Briefkasten,-̈** mailbox *7*

die **Briefmarke,-n** stamp *13*

der **Briefmarkenautomat,-en** stamp automat *7*

der **Briefträger,-** mail carrier (male) *14*

das **Briefmarkenmuseum** Museum of Stamps *13*

der **Briefumschlag,-̈e** envelope *14*

bringen *(brachte, gebracht)* to bring *A*

die **Brombeere,-n** blackberry *17*

das **Brot,-e** bread *A*

das **Brötchen,-** hard roll *16*

die **Brotkrume,-n** bread crumb *13*

der **Brotstand,-̈e** bread stand *17*

die **Brücke,-n** bridge *8*

der **Bruder,-̈** brother *5*

der **Brunnen,-** fountain, well *10*

das **Buch,-̈er** book *4*

buchen to book *10*

die **Bücherabteilung,-en** book department *6*

das **Bücherregal,-e** bookshelf *15*

das **Bundesland,-̈er** Federal State *5*

die **Bundesliga** Federal League (top league in West Germany) *14*

die **Bundesrepublik Deutschland** Federal Republic of Germany *3*

bunt colorful *6*

der **Bürgermeister,-** mayor *15*

das **Büro,-s** office *4*

sich **bürsten** to brush one's hair *11*

der **Bus,-se** bus *4*

die **Bushaltestelle,-n** bus stop *19*

die **Butter** butter *A*

C

das **Café,-s** café, coffee shop *5*

der **Campingplatz,-̈e** camping ground *18*

der **Cha-Cha-Cha** cha-cha *8*

der **Champignon,-s** mushroom *16*

die **Chance,-n** chance *9*

der **Charakter,-e** character *10*

der **Chef,-s** boss *20*

die **Chemie** chemistry *4*

China China *16*

die **Cola,-s** cola *2*

der **Computer,-** computer *3*

D

da there *1; da drüben* over there *1*

dabei in the process, while doing that *9*

das **Dach,-̈er** roof *19*

dafür for that, for it *4*

dagegen on the other hand, however *20*

damalig of that time, then *19*

die **Dame,-n** lady *6*

die **Damenabteilung,-en** ladies' department *6*

damit so that, in order that *18*

danach after that *15*

daneben next to it *13*

Dänemark Denmark *3*

der **Dank** thanks *10; Vielen Dank.* Many thanks. *10*

danke thanks *1; Danke schön.* Thank you. *5*

danken to thank *16*

dann then *2*

das the, that *1*

daß that *6*

dasselbe the same *7*

das **Datum, Daten** date (calendar) *5*

dauern to last, take (time) *3*

davon of those, of it *11*

dazu with it *A*

decken to cover *A; den Tisch decken* to set the table *A*

defekt defective *19*

dein your *4*

dekorieren to decorate *D*

das **Delikatessengeschäft,-e** delicatessen (store) *17*

denken *(dachte, gedacht)* to think *7*

denken an *(dachte an, gedacht an)* to remember, think about *14*

das **Denkmal,-̈er** monument, memorial *13*

denn used for emphasis *2;* because, for *18; Wieviel Geld brauchst du denn?* Well, how much money do you need? *2*

derselbe the same *18*

deshalb therefore *6*

deuten to point *13*

deutlich clearly *10*

deutsch German *1*

das **Deutsch** German (the language, subject in school) *4*

der **Deutsche,-n** German *14*

die **Deutsche Demokratische Republik** German Democratic Republic *3*

die **Deutsche Lufthansa** German Airlines *19*

Deutschland Germany *3*

der **Dezember** December *4*

dicht close *9*

dick thick, fat *13*

dienen to serve *15*

der **Dienstag** Tuesday *2*

dieser this *3*

diesmal this time *14*

das **Diktat,-e** dictation *20; ein Diktat aufnehmen* to take dictation *20*

diktieren to dictate *20*

das **Diktiergerät,-e** dictating machine *20*

direkt direct, immediate, straight *6*

doch used for emphasis *3*

das **Dock,-s** dock, dockyard *13*

der **Doktor,-en** doctor *18*

das **Dokument,-e** document *20*

der **Dollar,-s** dollar *6*

der **Dom,-e** cathedral *11*

die **Donau** Danube *5*

der **Donnerstag** Thursday *2*

das **Doppelzimmer,-** double room *10*

das **Dorf,-̈er** town, village *15*

dort there *3*

dorthin (to) there *5*

die **Dose,-n** can *17*

dran sein to be one's turn *9; Ich bin dran.* It's my turn. *9*

draußen outside *13*

drei three *1*

dreizehn thirteen *2*

drüben over there *14*

die **Drucksache,-n** printed matter *14*
du you (familiar singular) *1*
durch through *5*
durchfahren (*fährt durch, fuhr durch, ist durchgefahren*) to drive through *13*
durchlesen (*liest durch, las durch, durchgelesen*) to read through *20*
dürfen (*darf, durfte, gedurft*) to be permitted to, may *5*
der **Durst** thirst *14; Durst haben* to be thirsty *14*
durstig thirsty *15*
sich **duschen** to shower, take a shower *11*
das **Düsenflugzeug,-e** jet airplane *19*
das **Dutzend,-e** dozen *17*

E

die **Ebbe,-n** low tide *8*
eben just *4*
die **Ecke,-n** corner *1*
ehe before *18*
die **Ehefrau,-en** wife *12*
der **Ehemann,-̈er** husband *12*
das **Ei,-er** egg *16; ein gekochtes Ei* a boiled egg *16*
eigen own *13*
eigentlich actual(ly), real(ly) *3*
eilig speedy, urgent *16; es eilig haben* to be in a hurry *16*
der **Eimer,-** pail, bucket *20*
ein(e) a, an *2*
einfach simple, one-way (ticket) *3*
die **Einfahrt,-en** entrance *13*
das **Einfamilienhaus,-̈er** single family home *15*
der **Einfluß,-̈sse** influence *16*
einführen to introduce *16*
der **Eingang,-̈e** entrance *6*
die **Einheit** unity *12; Tag der Einheit* Day of Unity *12*
einige a few, several *7*
der **Einkauf,-̈e** purchase *17*
das **Einkaufen** shopping *11*
einkaufen to shop *5; einkaufen gehen* to go shopping *5*
der **Einkaufskorb,-̈e** shopping basket *17*
die **Einkaufstasche,-n** shopping bag *11*
das **Einkaufszentrum,-tren** shopping center *15*

einladen (*lädt ein, lud ein, eingeladen*) to invite *11*
einlegen to put in *19; den Gang einlegen* to put in gear *19*
einlösen to cash (in) *6*
einmal once *3; wieder einmal* once again *3; noch einmal* one more time *5*
eins one *1*
einschließen (*schloß ein, eingeschlossen*) to include *18*
einschließlich including *10*
das **Einschreiben** registered (letter) *14*
einsetzen to put into service *19*
einsteigen (*stieg ein, ist eingestiegen*) to get in(to), board *2*
einstellen to adjust *14*
der **Eintritt** admission *8*
der **Eintrittspreis,-e** admission price *15*
einverstanden sein to agree *12*
einwerfen (*wirft ein, warf ein, eingeworfen*) to mail (letter) *14*
einwickeln to wrap (up) *17*
der **Einwohner,-** inhabitant *3*
die **Einzelheit,-en** detail *14*
einzeln individual, single *14*
einzigartig unique *D*
das **Eis** ice, ice cream *16*
die **Eisdiele,-n** ice cream parlor *2*
der **Elefant,-en** elephant *15*
elegant elegant *7*
der **Elektriker,-** electrician *13*
die **Elektronik** electronics *19*
elf eleven *2*
die **Eltern** (pl.) parents *5*
der **Empfänger,-** receiver, addressee *14*
empfehlen (*empfiehlt, empfahl, empfohlen*) to recommend *17*
das **Ende** end *3*
enden to end *20*
das **Endergebnis,-se** final result *9*
endlich finally *2*
eng narrow *13*
England England *4*
das **Englisch** English (language, subject in school) *4*
englisch English *4*
der **Enkel,-** grandson *5*
die **Enkelin,-nen** granddaughter *5*
die **Ente,-n** duck *15*
entfernt away, distant *4*
die **Entfernung,-en** distance *3*

entgegenlaufen (*läuft entgegen, lief entgegen, ist entgegengelaufen*) to run towards *9*
enthalten (*enthält, enthielt, enthalten*) to contain *16*
entlangfahren (*fährt entlang, fuhr entlang, ist entlanggefahren*) to drive along *20*
entlanggehen (*ging entlang, ist entlanggegangen*) to walk along *16*
sich **entscheiden** (*entschied, entschieden*) to decide *17*
die **Entscheidung,-en** decision *17; eine Entscheidung treffen* to make a decision *17*
sich **entschließen** (*entschloß, entschlossen*) to decide *C*
entspringen (*entsprang, ist entsprungen*) to originate (river) *8*
entweder...oder either...or *13*
entwerten to cancel (tickets) *8*
die **Entwicklung,-en** development *19*
entzündet infected *18*
er he *1*
erbauen to build, construct *10*
die **Erbse,-n** pea *A*
die **Erbsensuppe** pea soup *20*
die **Erdbeere,-n** strawberry *17*
das **Erdbeereis** strawberry ice cream *C*
das **Erdgeschoß,-sse** ground floor, first floor (in America) *15*
die **Erdkunde** geography *4*
die **Erdnuß,-̈sse** peanut *17*
das **Ereignis,-se** event *7*
die **Erfahrung,-en** experience, idea *15*
der **Erforscher,-** explorer *15*
das **Ergebnis,-se** score *14*
erhalten (*erhält, erhielt, erhalten*) to receive, get *20*
die **Erholung,-en** vacation, relaxation *20*
das **Erholungsheim,-e** resort *20*
erinnern an to remind of *10*
sich **erkälten** to catch a cold *18*
die **Erkältung,-en** cold *18*
sich **erkennen** (*erkannte, erkannt*) to recognize each other *11*
erklären to explain *11*
sich **erkundigen nach** to inquire about, ask for/about *18*

erlaubt allowed *19*
das **Erlebnis,-se** experience, event *11*
ernten to harvest *20*
eröffnen to start, inaugurate *19*
erreichen to reach *6*
das **Ersatzteillager,-** parts department *19*
erst only, first *5;* not until *11*
erstaunlich amazing, astonishing *17*
erstaunt astonished, amazed *16*
erstklassig first-class *18*
sich **erstrecken** to extend, stretch *20*
der **Erwachsene,-n** adult *11*
erwähnen to mention *18*
erwarten to expect *D*
erwidern to reply *18*
erwischen to get (hold of) *17*
erzählen to tell *11*
es it *1*
der **Esel,-** donkey *13*
das **Essen** meal *A;* food *8*
essen *(ißt, aß, gegessen)* to eat *5*
die **Essenausgabe,-n** serving counter *7*
etwas some, a little *2*
Europa Europe *5*
europäisch European *8*
der **Experte,-n** expert *8*
exportieren to export *20*

F

das **Fach,-̈er** (school) subject *4*
das **Fachgebiet,-en** subject (area) *15*
das **Fachwerkhaus,-̈er** half-timbered house *10*
die **Fahne,-n** flag *12*
die **Fahrbahn,-en** road *19*
fahren *(fährt, fuhr, ist gefahren)* to drive, go *3*
der **Fahrer,-** driver *19*
die **Fahrkarte,-n** ticket *3*
der **Fahrplan,-̈e** schedule *3*
die **Fahrprüfung,-en** driver's test *8*
das **Fahrrad,-̈er** bicycle *7*
der **Fahrstuhl,-̈e** elevator *7*
die **Fahrt,-en** trip *10*
der **Fahrunterricht** driver's training, driving instruction *19*
das **Fahrzeug,-e** vehicle *14*
der **Fall,-̈e** case *17; auf jeden Fall* in any case *17; auf keinen Fall* by no means *20*
falls in case, if *20*
die **Familie,-n** family *5*

die **Farbe,-n** color *6;* paint *13*
farbig colorful *18*
der **Fasching** carnival *C*
der **Faschismus** fascism *7*
fast almost *5*
der **Februar** February *4*
der **Federball,-̈e** badminton *9*
das **Federbett,-en** feather-bed *15*
fehlen to be missing *18; Was fehlt dir?* What's wrong with you? *18*
feierlich solemn, festive *12*
feiern to celebrate *C*
der **Feiertag,-e** holiday *12*
das **Feld,-er** field *10*
der **Feldweg,-e** field path *4*
das **Fenster,-** window *10*
die **Ferien** (pl.) vacation *9*
das **Ferienland,-̈er** vacation country *5*
der **Ferienort,-e** vacation place *18*
die **Ferienreise,-n** vacation trip *14; auf einer Ferienreise sein* to be on a vacation trip *14*
fermentieren to ferment *20*
das **Ferngespräch,-e** long-distance call *14; ein Ferngespräch führen* to make a long-distance call *14*
der **Fernsehapparat,-e** television set *7*
das **Fernsehen** TV *14; im Fernsehen* on TV *A*
fernsehen *(sieht fern, sah fern, ferngesehen)* to watch TV *5*
der **Fernsehturm,-̈e** television tower *7*
fertig ready, done, finished *5*
fertigstellen to finish, complete *20*
das **Fest,-e** festival *C*
das **Festland,-̈er** mainland *8*
die **Festlichkeit,-en** festivity *15*
festmachen to attach, fasten *12*
feststellen to determine, find out *18*
die **Festung,-en** fortress *10*
der **Festwagen,-** float *C*
das **Fieber** fever *18*
das **Fieberthermometer,-** fever thermometer *18*
die **Figur,-en** figure *10*
der **Film,-e** movie, film *5*
finden *(fand, gefunden)* to find *4*
der **Finger,-** finger *11*
die **Firma,-en** firm, company *20*
der **Fisch,-e** fish *15*
der **Fischmarkt,-̈e** fish market *17*

flach flat *5*
die **Fläche,-n** area, surface *3*
die **Flasche,-n** bottle *20*
das **Fleisch** meat *16*
der **Fleischer,-** butcher *13*
die **Fleischwaren** (pl.) meats *17; Fleisch- und Wurstwaren* meats and sausages *17*
fleißig hard-working, industrious *4*
fliegen *(flog, ist geflogen)* to fly *11*
die **Fliegerei** flying, aviation *19*
fließen *(floß, ist geflossen)* to flow, run *5*
die **Flöte,-n** flute *8*
der **Flug,-̈e** flight *10*
der **Flugbegleiter,-** flight attendant *11*
der **Fluggast,-̈e** flight passenger *11*
die **Fluggesellschaft,-en** airline company *19*
der **Flughafen,-̈** airport *11*
das **Flughafengebäude,-** airport building *11*
der **Flugschein,-e** flight ticket *11*
der **Flugsteig,-e** gate (flight) *11*
der **Flugverkehr** air traffic, air service *19*
die **Flugzeit** flying time, time en route *19*
das **Flugzeug,-e** airplane *7*
der **Flur,-e** hallway, corridor *15*
der **Fluß,-̈sse** river *5*
folgen to follow *7*
folgend following *14*
die **Forelle,-n** trout *8*
die **Form,-en** form, shape *9*
die **Formel,-n** formula *4*
das **Formular,-e** printed form *18*
fortsetzen to continue *10; eine Reise fortsetzen* to continue a trip *10*
das **Foto,-s** photo *11*
das **Fotoalbum,-ben** photo album *B*
fotografieren to photograph, take pictures *B*
foulen to foul *14*
die **Frage,-n** question *A*
fragen to ask *2*
fragen nach to ask for *14*
der **Franken,-** Swiss monetary unit *13*
Frankreich France *3*
Französisch French (language) *6*
die **Frau,-en** Mrs., woman *1;* wife *10*
das **Fräulein,-** Miss *1;* Waitress! *13*

frei free, available *7*

Freie: ins Freie outside *7; im Freien 10*

die **Freilichtbühne,-n** open-air theater *20*

freinehmen *(nimmt frei, nahm frei, freigenommen)* to take (time) off *13*

der **Freitag** Friday *2*

die **Fremdsprache,-n** foreign language *4*

die **Freude** pleasure, joy *20; Es macht mir Freude.* I enjoy it. *20*

sich **freuen auf** to look forward to *11*

sich **freuen über** to be happy about *16*

der **Freund,-e** boyfriend, friend *1*

die **Freundin,-nen** girlfriend *3*

freundlich friendly *17; mit freundlichen Grüßen* sincerely *18*

friedlich peaceful *20*

frisch fresh *12*

der **Friseur,-e** barber, hair stylist (male) *13*

die **Friseuse,-n** ladies' hair stylist, beautician (female) *13*

froh happy, glad *2*

die **Frucht,-e** fruit *17*

die **Fruchtart,-en** kind of fruit *17*

der **Fruchtstand,-e** fruit stand *17*

früh early *9*

früher earlier, in earlier times *11*

der **Frühling,-e** spring *4*

das **Frühstück** breakfast *11*

frühstücken to have breakfast *5*

fühlen to feel *18; sich wohl fühlen* to feel well *18*

führen to lead *10*

der **Führerschein,-e** driver's license *8*

füllen to fill *20*

fünf five *1*

fünfjährig five-year old *20*

fünfzehn fifteen *2*

für for *3*

furchtbar terrible, awful *18*

der **Fürst,-en** prince *10*

das **Fürstentum,-er** principality *13*

der **Fuß,-e** foot *3; Zu Fuß* on foot, walk *3; zu Fuß gehen* to walk *3*

der **Fußball,-e** soccer *7*

der **Fußballfan,-s** soccer fan *14*

der **Fußballplatz,-e** soccer field *14*

das **Fußballspiel,-e** soccer game *14*

der **Fußgänger,-** pedestrian *10*

der **Fußgängerüberweg,-e** pedestrian crossing *19*

die **Fußgängerunterführung,-en** pedestrian underpass *19*

füttern to feed *13*

G

die **Gabel,-n** fork *16*

der **Gabelbaum,-e** boom (surfing) *12*

der **Gang,-e** gear *19*

ganz quite *3;* whole *7*

ganz und gar completely *20*

gar nicht not at all *4*

garantieren to guarantee *20*

das **Gartenlokal,-e** outside restaurant, beer garden *16*

das **Gaspedal,-e** gas pedal *19*

der **Gast,-e** guest *16*

das **Gasthaus,-er** restaurant, inn *11*

die **Gaststätte,-n** restaurant, inn *15*

das **Gebäude,-** building *7*

geben *(gibt, gab, gegeben)* to give *4; es gibt* there is (are) *4*

gebirgig mountainous *13*

gebrauchen to use, apply *4*

die **Gebrüder Grimm** Brothers Grimm (well-known German authors) *13*

die **Gebühr,-en** fee *6*

das **Geburtsdatum,-daten** date of birth *18*

der **Geburtsort,-e** birthplace *18*

die **Geburtsstadt,-e** native town, city of birth *7*

der **Geburtstag,-e** birthday *5*

die **Geburtsurkunde,-n** birth certificate *12*

gedeihen *(gedieh, gediehen)* to grow *20*

die **Geduld** patience *18*

geduldig patient(ly) *12*

geehrt honored *20; Sehr geehrte Damen und Herren!* (Dear) Ladies and Gentlemen! *20*

geeignet sein to be suitable *18*

gefallen *(gefällt, gefiel, gefallen)* to like *6; Es gefällt ihr.* She likes it. *6*

die **Gegend,-en** area *5*

gegenüber across *7*

der **Gegner,-** opponent *14*

Gehacktes ground meat *17*

gehen *(ging, ist gegangen)* to go *1; Wie geht's?* How are you? (familiar) *1; zu Fuß gehen* to walk *3; Das geht.* That's possible. *7; Wohin geht's denn?* Where are you going? *11; Das geht schon.* That's O.K. *17* **gut gehen** to go well *19*

gehen über to go into, merge with *8*

gehören zu to belong to *8*

die **Geige,-n** violin *8*

geistig mental *20*

gekocht cooked, boiled *17*

gelb yellow *6*

das **Geld** money *2*

gelegen located *18*

gelingen *(gelang, ist gelungen)* to succeed *19*

das **Gemälde,-n** painting *7*

die **Gemäldesammlung,-en** collection of paintings *13*

der **Gemeindeverband,-e** community association *15*

gemeinsam together *15;* common, joint *19*

das **Gemüse** vegetable(s) *12*

die **Gemüseabteilung,-en** vegetable department *17*

die **Gemüseart,-en** kind of vegetable *17*

der **Gemüsestand,-e** vegetable stand *17*

die **Gemüsesuppe,-n** vegetable soup *16*

gemütlich pleasant *7;* comfortable, cozy *11; es sich gemütlich machen* to get comfortable *11*

genau exact *7;* closely *12*

genauso wie just like/as *4*

genug enough, sufficient *15*

der **Genuß,-sse** pleasure *16*

geöffnet open *B; Das Geschäft ist geöffnet.* The store is open. *B*

das **Gepäck** luggage, baggage *3*

die **Gepäckausgabe,-n** baggage claim *11*

gerade just *10*

das **Gerät,-e** piece of equipment, gadget *19*

gern gladly, with pleasure *4; gern gehen* like (enjoy) to walk *4; gern haben* to like *20*

gesamt total, complete *19*

das **Geschäft,-e** store *6*

der **Geschäftsbrief,-e** business letter
20

geschehen (*geschieht, geschah, ist geschehen*) to happen, occur *18; gern geschehen* you're welcome, don't mention it

das **Geschenk,-e** present *8*

die **Geschichte** history *4*

geschichtlich historical *10*

das **Geschirr** dishes *7*

geschlossen closed *11*

der **Geschmack,-̈e** taste *8*

die **Geschwister** (pl.) siblings *5*

gespannt sein to wonder, be curious *5*

das **Gespräch,-̈e** conversation, talk *14; ein Gespräch führen* to make a call *14*

gestern yesterday *9*

gesund healthy, well *18*

das **Getränk,-̈e** beverage *7*

das **Getreide** grain *15*

getrennt separate *20; mit getrennter Post* under separate cover *20*

gewähren to yield, grant *19; Vorfahrt gewähren!* Yield the right of way! *19*

das **Gewicht,-e** weight *19*

gewinnen (*gewann, gewonnen*) to win *5*

gewöhnlich usually *14*

gießen (*goß, gegossen*) to pour *D*

die **Gitarre,-n** guitar *A*

das **Glas,-̈er** glass *9*

glauben to believe, think *3*

gleich immediately, right away *1; gleich um die Ecke* right around the corner *1*

das **Gleichgewicht** balance *12; das Gleichgewicht behalten* to keep the balance *12*

das **Gleis,-e** track *3*

das **Glück** luck *2; Glück haben* to be lucky *2*

glücklich happy *12*

der **Glückwunsch,-̈e** congratulations (pl.) *8; Herzlichen Glückwunsch zum Geburtstag!* Happy Birthday! *8; Herzlichen Glückwunsch!* Congratulations! *9*

das **Gold** gold *D*

gold gold *4*

das **Golf** golf *9*

das **Gramm,-e** gram *10*

das **Gras,-̈er** grass *16*

gratulieren to congratulate *9*

grau gray *6*

greifen an to touch *18*

die **Grenze,-n** border *6*

grenzen an to border on *4*

der **Grenzübergang,-̈e** border crossing *13*

die **Grippe,-n** flu *18*

groß big, large *3*

die **Größe,-n** size *17*

die **Großeltern** (pl.) grandparents *5*

der **Großraumjet,-s** Jumbo Jet, B-747 *9*

die **Großmutter,-̈** grandmother *5*

die **Großstadt,-̈e** large city, metropolis *16*

größt- biggest, largest *4*

der **Großvater,-̈** grandfather *5*

grün green *6*

der **Grund,-̈e** reason *20; aus diesem Grund* for this reason *20*

gründen to set up, organize *15*

gründlich thorough, careful *4*

die **Gruppe,-n** group *B*

der **Gruß,-̈e** greeting *18; mit freundlichen Grüßen* sincerely *18*

Grüß dich! Hi! *1; Grüß Gott!* Hello! *1*

die **Gulaschsuppe,-n** goulash soup *16*

günstig favorable, reasonable *10*

der **Gurkensalat,-e** cucumber salad *16*

gut good, well, O.K. *1*

die **Güte** goodness *7; Du meine Güte!* My goodness! *7*

das **Gymnasium,-sien** secondary school *2; Sie geht auf ein Gymnasium.* She goes to a secondary school. *2*

H

das **Haar,-e** hair *11*

haben (*hat, hatte, gehabt*) to have *2*

der **Hafen,-̈** harbor *13*

die **Hafenpolizei** harbor police *13*

die **Hafenrundfahrt,-en** trip around harbor *13*

der **Hahn,-̈e** rooster *13*

häkeln to crochet *5*

halb half *3*

die **Halbzeit,-en** halftime *14*

der **Hals,-̈e** neck *11*

die **Halsschmerzen** (pl.) sore throat *18*

halten (*hält, hielt, gehalten*) to hold *12;* to stop *14*

die **Haltestelle,-n** stop (for bus or streetcar) *2*

die **Hand,-̈e** hand *11*

die **Handbremse,-n** hand brake *19*

der **Handschuh,-e** glove *6*

die **Handtasche,-n** purse *6*

hängen (*hing, gehangen*) to hang *17*

die **Hauptmahlzeit,-en** main meal *16*

hauptsächlich primarily, mainly *14*

die **Hauptstadt,-̈e** capital (city) *3*

die **Hauptstraße,-n** main street *11*

das **Haus,-̈er** house *2; nach Hause gehen* to go home *2; zu Hause* at home *2*

die **Hausaufgabe,-n** homework *5; die Hausaufgaben machen* to do homework *5*

die **Hausnummer,-n** street number *14*

das **Heft,-e** notebook *8*

das **Heftpflaster,-** adhesive tape, Band-Aid *11*

die **Heirat,-en** marriage *12*

die **Heiratsurkunde,-n** marriage certificate *12*

heiß hot *7*

heißen (*hieß, geheißen*) to be called, named *1; Wie heißt du?* What's your name? *1*

helfen (*hilft, half, geholfen*) to help *9*

hell light *16; ein Helles* a light beer *16*

das **Hemd,-en** shirt *6*

herankommen (*kam heran, ist herangekommen*) to come close to *20*

herausfordern to challenge *20*

herauskommen (*kam heraus, ist herausgekommen*) to come out (of) *12*

sich **herausstellen** to turn out, prove *12*

der **Herbergsvater,-̈** youth hostel director *7*

der **Herbst,-e** fall, autumn *4*

der **Herr,-en** Mr., gentleman *1*

herrlich great, splendid *13*

herrschen to be, exist *17*

herumfahren (*fährt herum, fuhr herum, ist herumgefahren*) to drive (ride) around 7

herumlaufen (*läuft herum, lief herum, ist herumgelaufen*) to run around 9

herumrudern to row around 20

herumspielen to play around 20

herzlich sincere, hearty 8; *herzliche Grüße* kind regards, (intimately) love 14

der **Heurige** wine of this year's vintage, new wine 11

heute today 2; *heute abend* this evening, tonight 2

heutig today's 20

hier here 1

hierherkommen (*kam hierher, ist hierhergekommen*) to come here 10

hierherziehen (*zog hierher, ist hierhergezogen*) to attract here 20

die **Hilfe** help, assistance 4

hilfsbereit helpful 17

der **Himmel** sky 10

der **Himmelfahrtstag** Ascension Day 12

hin und zurück round trip 3

hinabschauen to look down D

hineingehen (*ging hinein, ist hineingegangen*) to go inside 7

hineinreichen to reach into 8

hinfallen (*fällt hin, fiel hin, ist hingefallen*) to fall down 14

sich **hinsetzen** to sit down 16

hinter behind 8

der **Hinweis,-e** instruction, hint 18

historisch historical, historic 7

die **Hitze** heat 8; *bei der Hitze* in this heat 8

das **Hobby,-s** hobby 14

hoch high 5

die **Hochschule,-n** college, university 15

höchst- highest 5

die **Hochzeit,-en** wedding 12

der **Hochzeitsgast,-̈e** wedding guest 12

die **Hochzeitskutsche,-n** wedding carriage 12

hochziehen (*zog hoch, hochgezogen*) to pull up 12

das **Hockey** hockey 9

hoffen to hope 6

hoffentlich hopefully 9

die **Höhe,-n** height 6

der **Höhepunkt,-e** highlight 12

die **HO-Kaufhalle,-n** (government-owned) supermarket 5

holen to get, fetch 13

die **Holzschnitzerei,-en** woodcarving 17

das **Holzfaß,-̈sser** wooden barrel 20

hören to listen, hear 4

der **Hörer,-** receiver (phone) 14

die **Hose,-n** pants, slacks 6

das **Hotel,-s** hotel 7

das **Hotelschild,-er** hotel sign 10

das **Hotelzimmer,-** hotel room 18

der **Hügel,-** hill 10

das **Huhn,-̈er** chicken 15

der **Hund,-e** dog 13

der **Hunger** hunger 7; *Hunger haben* to be hungry 7

hungrig hungry A

der **Hustenbonbon,-s** (also: **das Bonbon**) cough drop 18

der **Hustensaft,-̈e** cough syrup 18

I

ich I 1

ideal ideal 14

die **Idee,-n** idea 2

ihn it, him 5

ihr you (familiar plural) 1; their 4; her A

Ihr your (formal) 6

im (or: **in dem**) in the 4

die **Imbißstube,-n** snack bar B

immer always 2; *immer wieder* again and again 7

in in 1

die **Industriestadt,-̈e** industrial city 9

die **Information,-en** information 10

der **Ingenieur,-e** engineer 13

der **Innenspiegel,-** inside mirror 19

die **Innenstadt,-̈e** downtown, center of city 6

innerhalb within 19

ins (or: **in das**) in(to) the 4

die **Insel,-n** island 8

insgesamt altogether, in all 19

inspizieren to inspect 19

installieren to install 19

interessant interesting 7

das **Interesse,-n** interest A

interessieren to interest A

international international 11

irgendetwas something 20

ist is 1

Italien Italy 5

Italienisch Italian (language) 6

J

ja yes 1

das **Jahr,-e** year 2

die **Jahreszeit,-en** season 4

das **Jahrhundert,-e** century 13

der **Januar** January 4

die **Jeans** (pl.) jeans 6

jeder each, every 7

der **Jet,-s** jet airplane 19

jetzt now 1

jubeln to cheer 14

die **Jugend** youth, young people C

die **Jugendherberge,-n** youth hostel 7

der **Jugendherbergsausweis,-e** youth hostel identification (card) 7

der **Jugendliche,-n** youngster, teenager, youth 7

Jugoslawien Yugoslavia 5

der **Juli** July 4

jung young 11

der **Junge,-n** boy 1

der **Juni** June 4

K

die **Kabine,-n** cabin 19

der **Kaffee** coffee A

der **Käfig,-e** cage C

der **Kai,-s** wharf 13

der **Kaiser,-** emperor 11

der **Kakao** hot chocolate, cocoa 9

das **Kalbsfrikassee** veal fricassee 20

kalt cold 7

die **Kalte Platte** cold-cut platter 5

der **Kamerad,-en** buddy 9

sich **kämmen** to comb one's hair 11

die **Kamera,-s** camera 15

der **Kanal,-̈e** canal 9

das **Kanalsystem,-e** canal system 8

die **Kapelle,-n** band 12

Karfreitag Good Friday 12

der **Karneval** carnival C

der **Karnevalszug,-̈e** carnival parade C

die **Karotte,-n** carrot 16

der **Karpfen,-** carp 16

die **Karte,-n** ticket 5; map 6; card B

die **Kartei,-en** card-index 15

die **Kartoffel,-n** potato A

der **Kartoffelsalat** potato salad 8

der **Karton,-s** carton, cardboard box 11

der **Käse** cheese A; *Schweizer Käse* Swiss cheese 17

die **Käsesorte,-n** kind of cheese 17

der **Käsestand,-̈e** cheese stand 17

die **Kasse,-n** cashier's counter 6

die **Kassette,-n** cassette 4

die **Kassiererin,-nen** cashier 17

der **Katalog,-e** catalog 20

die **Katze,-n** cat 13

kaufen to buy 3

das **Kaufhaus,-̈er** department store B

der **Kaufhof** name of department store 6

kaum hardly 9

kein no 2; *keine Zeit* no time 2

der **Keller,-** basement, cellar 15

der **Kellner,-** waiter 16

die **Kellnerin,-nen** waitress 16

kennen *(kannte, gekannt)* to know (someone) 1

kennenlernen to get to know B

das **Kilo,-s** kilogram 17

der **Kilometer,-** kilometer 3

das **Kind,-er** child 11

der **Kindergarten,-̈** kindergarten 15

das **Kinn,-e** chin 11

das **Kino,-s** movie theater 5

der **Kiosk,-e** kiosk 2

kippen to dump, pour 20

die **Kirche,-n** church 7

die **Kirsche,-n** cherry 17

die **Kiste,-n** box, trunk 11

klagen to complain 18

klappen to clap 20; *Das klappt prima.* That works out well. 20

klar clear, O.K. 3

die **Klarinette,-n** clarinet 8

die **Klasse,-n** class 3; *zweiter Klasse* second class 3

klasse sein to be great 5

der **Klassenausflug,-̈e** class trip 7

klassisch classical 12

klatschen to applaud 9

das **Klavier,-e** piano 8

das **Kleid,-er** dress 6

das **Kleidungsstück,-e** article of clothing 6

klein small, little 10

die **Kleinigkeit,-en** small item, thing B

die **Kleinstadt,-̈e** small town 10

das **Klettergerät,-e** climber 20

klettern to climb 16

klingeln to ring 4; *an der Tür klingeln* to ring the doorbell 4

klingen *(klang, geklungen)* to sound 10

klug smart 3

knipsen to take a picture 15

der **Knödel,-** dumpling 16

knusprig crisp, crunchy 17

kochen to cook A

der **Koffer,-** suitcase 3

der **Koffer-Kuli,-s** luggage cart 3

der **Kofferraum,-̈e** trunk 19

der **Kollege,-n** colleague 15

der **Komfort** comfort 18

kommen *(kam, ist gekommen)* to come 1; *Komm doch mit.* Why don't you come along? 1; *Es kommt auf...an.* It depends on... 10

die **Kommode,-n** (chest of) drawers 15

das **Kompliment,-e** compliment 13; *Komplimente machen* to pay compliments 13

das **Kompott,-e** stewed fruit 16

die **Konditorei,-en** café 16

der **König,-̈e** king 14

können *(kann, konnte, gekonnt)* to be able to, can 5

der **Kopf,-̈e** head 11

köpfen to head (the ball) 14

das **Kopfkissen,-** pillow 15

die **Kopfschmerzen** (pl.) headache 18

der **Korb,-̈e** basket 17

der **Korbball,-̈e** basketball 9

körperlich physical 20

der **Körperteil,-e** part of body 11

der **Korridor,-e** corridor, hallway 12

köstlich delicious 13

kosten to cost 4; to taste 11

das **Kostüm,-e** costume C

krank sick, ill 18

das **Krankenhaus,-̈er** hospital 18

der **Krankenpfleger,-** (male) nurse 13

die **Krankenschwester,-n** nurse 13

die **Krawatte,-n** tie 6

der **Kreis,-e** district 15

das **Kreuz,-e** cross 6

die **Kreuzung,-en** intersection 19

krönen to crown 20

der **Kübel,-** tub, big bucket 20

die **Küche,-n** kitchen 5

der **Kuchen,-** cake 13

die **Kuh,-̈e** cow 15

kühl cool 7

der **Kühlraum,-̈e** cooler 17

der **Kuli,-s** (ballpoint) pen 8

kulturell cultural 7

der **Kunde,-n** customer 10

die **Kunst** art 4

künstlerisch artistic 13

der **Kunstschatz,-̈e** art treasure 10

die **Kupplung,-en** clutch 19

der **Kurs,-e** exchange 6

kurz short(ly) A

die **Kutsche,-n** carriage 12

L

der **Laden,-̈** store 17

der **Ladentisch,-e** counter 17

die **Ladung,-en** load 20

lagern to store 20

die **Lampe,-n** lamp 15

das **Land,-̈er** country, land 3; "state" in the *BRD* 4; *auf dem Lande* in the country 16

landen to land 11

das **Landflugzeug,-e** landplane 19

die **Landschaft,-en** landscape 8

die **Landstraße,-n** two-lane highway 10

der **Landungssteg,-e** gangway 13

der **Landwirt,-e** farmer 13

die **Landwirtschaft** agriculture 11

lang long 9

lange long 3

die **Länge,-n** length 5

die **Langeweile** boredom 20

längs along 20

langsam slow(ly) A

längst- longest 5

langweilig boring 2

lassen *(läßt, ließ, gelassen)* to leave 12; let 13

der **Lastwagen,-** truck 20

laufen *(läuft, lief, ist gelaufen)* to run 5; *sich warm laufen* to warm up 14

die **Läufer,-** runner 9

die **Laune,-n** mood 16; *guter Laune sein* to be in a good mood 16

das **Leben** life 15

leben to live 9

lebend living 10

die **Lebensmittel** (pl.) groceries 17

das **Lebensmittelgeschäft,-e** grocery store 17

lecker delicious 8

leer empty 5

leeren to empty 14

legen to place, put 11

der **Lehrer,-** (male) teacher 7

die **Lehrerin,-nen** (female) teacher
   13
der **Lehrling,-e** apprentice *19*
die **Leibesübung,-en** physical
   exercise *14*
leicht easy *3*
leidenschaftlich enthusiastic,
   passionate *20;
   leidenschaftlich gern spielen*
   to love to play *20*
leider unfortunately *B*
die **Leine,-n** rope *12*
der **Leiter,-** head, person in charge *9*
lernen to learn *4; auswendig
   lernen* to memorize, learn by
   heart *4*
lesen *(liest, las, gelesen)* to read
   4
der **Lesesaal,-säle** reading room *15*
letzt- last *8*
die **Leute** (pl.) people *7*
lieben to love *17*
lieber rather *5*
der **Lieblingskuchen,-** favorite cake
   13
der **Lieblingsort,-e** favorite place *10*
Liechtenstein Liechtenstein *5*
liegen *(lag, gelegen)* to lie, be
   located *3*
der **Lienienrichter,-** linesman *14*
die **Limonade,-n** soft drink *9*
das **Lineal,-e** ruler *8*
links left, on(to) the left *7*
die **Lippe,-n** lip *11*
das **Liter,-** liter *10*
loben to praise *16*
locker loose *12*
lokal local *16*
los: was ist los? What's the
   matter? *2; Los!* Come on! *5;
   Los, kommt!* Come on, let's
   go! *5; Es ist viel los.* A lot is
   going on. *12*
lösen to solve *4;* to loosen,
   release (brake) *19*
losfahren *(fährt los, fuhr los, ist
   losgefahren)* to drive off *11*
losgehen *(ging los, ist
   losgegangen)* to start, take
   off *11*
loslaufen *(läuft los, lief los, ist
   losgelaufen)* to start running
   9
loswerden *(wird los, wurde los,
   ist losgeworden)* to get rid of
   18
der **Löwe,-n** lion *15*
die **Luft,-̈e** air *C*

der **Luftdruck** air pressure *D*
die **Luftpost** airmail *14*
der **Luftpostdienst** airmail service
   19
das **Luftschiff,-e** dirigible, blimp *19*
die **Lust** pleasure, joy *2; Sie hat
   Lust…* She would like to… *2*
Luxemburg Luxembourg *3*
der **Luxus** luxury *18*

M

machen to do, make *1; Das
   macht fünf Mark.* That's five
   marks. *3; Das macht nichts.*
   That doesn't matter. *17*
das **Mädchen,-** girl *1*
die **Mahlzeit,-en** meal *10*
das **Mahnmal** memorial *7*
der **Mai** May *4*
mal times *3*
das **Mal,-e** time(s) *9*
man one, they, you, people *3*
manche a few *8*
manchmal sometimes *4*
die **Mandel,-n** tonsil *18*
die **Mandelentzündung** tonsilitis *18*
mangelhaft inadequate *4*
der **Mann,-̈er** man *9;* husband *12*
die **Mannschaft,-en** team *9*
der **Mantel,-̈** coat *6*
der **Marathonlauf,-̈e** marathon run *9*
das **Märchen,-** fairy tale *13*
märchenhaft legendary, fairy
   tale-like *10*
die **Margarine** margarine *17*
die **Mark** mark (German monetary
   unit) *2*
markieren to mark *13; gut
   markiert* well marked *13*
der **Markt,-̈e** market *7*
der **Marktplatz,-̈e** market square *7*
der **Markttag,-e** market day *7*
die **Marmelade** jam *A*
der **Marmor** marble *D*
der **März** March *4*
der **Mast,-en** pole *12*
die **Matheaufgabe** math problem *3*
die **Mathematik** (or: *Mathe*)
   mathematics *4*
der **Mechaniker,-** mechanic *13*
die **Medizin** medicine *18*
das **Meer,-e** sea *20*
mehr als more than *5*
mehrere several *13*
mein my *1*

meinen to mean, think *13;* be of
   the opinion *18*
die **meisten** most *7*
meistens mostly, most of the
   time *5*
die **Melange,-n** Austrian coffee
   (mixed with cream) *13*
die **Mensa** student cafeteria *15*
der **Mensch,-en** person, human
   being *6*
merken to notice *16*
die **Messe,-n** trade fair *9*
messen *(mißt, maß, gemessen)*
   to measure *18*
das **Messer,-** knife *16*
der **Meter,-** meter *10*
der **Metzger,-** butcher *13*
mieten to rent *20*
das **Mietshaus,-̈er** apartment
   building *5*
die **Milch** milk *A*
die **Million,-en** million *3*
mindestens at least *9*
die **Mineralsammlung,-en**
   collection of minerals *15*
das **Mineralwasser** mineral water *16*
minus minus, less *2*
die **Minute,-n** minute *2*
mit with *3*
mitbringen *(brachte mit,
   mitgebracht)* to bring along *7*
miteinander with each other *15*
mithalten *(hält mit, hielt mit,
   mitgehalten)* to keep up *15*
mitkommen *(kam mit, ist
   mitgekommen)* to come along
   5
mitfliegen *(flog mit, ist
   mitgeflogen)* to fly along *19*
mitkommen *Ich komme mit dir
   nicht mit.* I can't keep up
   with you. *15*
mitmachen to participate *9*
mitnehmen *(nimmt mit, nahm
   mit, mitgenommen)* to take
   along *10*
der **Mittag-e** noon *2*
das **Mittagessen** lunch *A*
die **Mittagszeit,-en** noon time,
   lunch time *B*
die **Mitte,-n** middle, center *4*
das **Mittelalter** Middle Ages *10*
mittelalterlich medieval *10*
das **Mittelgebirgsland** central
   highlands *8*
der **Mittelpunkt,-e** focal point *7*
mittlerweile in the meantime *20*
der **Mittwoch** Wednesday *2*

möchten would like to *5*

das **Modell,-e** model *15*

modern modern *B*

mögen *(mag, mochte, gemocht)* to like *5*

möglich possible *2*

die **Möglichkeit,-en** possibility *7*

die **Möhre,-n** carrot *16*

der **Moment,-e** moment *3*

der **Monat,-e** month *2*

der **Montag** Monday *2*

montanwissenschaftlich science of mining *15*

morgen tomorrow *2*

der **Morgen** morning *2; heute morgen* this morning *2*

das **Motorboot,-e** motor boat *13*

die **Motorhaube,-n** hood *19*

das **Motorrad,-̈er** motorcycle *7*

müde tired *A*

der **Mund,-̈er** mouth *10*

das **Münster,-** cathedral *7*

munter awake *A*

die **Münze,-n** coin *13*

das **Museum,-seen** museum *9*

die **Musik** music *4*

der **Musiker,-** musician *11*

das **Musikfest,-e** music festival *5*

die **Musikgruppe,-n** music group *12*

das **Musikinstrument,-e** musical instrument *8*

müssen *(muß, mußte, gemußt)* must, to have to *5*

die **Mutter,-̈** mother *5*

die **Muttersprache,-n** mother tongue *5*

der **Muttertag** Mother's Day *12*

die **Mutti,-s** mom *20*

N

na well *2*

nach to, after *3*

die **Nachbarin,-nen** neighbor (female) *D*

das **Nachbarland,-̈er** neighboring country *3*

die **Nachbarschaft,-en** neighborhood *16*

nachdem after (having) *18*

der **Nachmittag,-e** afternoon *2*

der **Nachname,-n** family name *14*

die **Nachrichten** (pl.) news *A*

nachsehen *(sieht nach, sah nach, nachgesehen)* to check *10*

nächst next *4*

der **Nachtisch,-e** dessert *A*

der **Nachttisch,-e** night stand *20*

die **Nähe** nearness, proximity *2; in der Nähe* nearby *2*

der **Name,-n** name *1*

nämlich namely *8*

die **Nase,-n** nose *11*

naß wet *12*

die **Nationalfahne,-n** national flag *4*

natürlich of course, natural(ly) *4*

neben next to, besides *10*

das **Nebenzimmer,-** adjacent room *18*

nehmen *(nimmt, nahm, genommen)* to take *13*

nein no *1*

nennen *(nannte, genannt)* to name, call *19*

nervös nervous *20*

neu new *4*

das **Neujahr** New Year's Day *12*

neun nine *1*

neunzehn nineteen *2*

nicht not *1*

nichts nothing *12*

die **Niederlande** Netherlands *3*

niedrig low *D*

niemand nobody, none *9*

noch still, yet *2*

nochmal once more *5*

der **Norden** north *3*

nördlich northern, to the north of *11*

die **Nordsee** North Sea *6*

normal normal *18*

die **Note,-n** (school) grade, mark *4*

notieren to jot down, make a note of *9*

der **November** November *4*

null zero *1*

die **Nummer,-** number *9*

das **Nummernschild,-er** license plate *19*

nur only, just *3*

O

ob if, whether *8*

oben on top *10*; above *16*

die **Oberschule,-n** high school *15*

obgleich although *18*

das **Obst** fruit *12*

die **Obstabteilung,-en** fruit department *17; die Obst- und Gemüseabteilung* the fruit and vegetable department *17*

die **Obstschnitte,-n** piece of fruit pie *13*

der **Obststand,-̈e** fruit stand *17; der Obst- und Gemüsestand* fruit and vegetable stand *17*

obwohl although *18*

oder or *5*

offen open *17*

offiziell official *13*

öffnen to open *16*

sich **öffnen** to open *12*

oft often *2*

oftmals often *8*

ohne without *3*

das **Ohr,-en** ear *11*

der **Oktober** October *4*

das **Öl** oil *D*

der **Ölstand** oil level *D*

der **Onkel,-** uncle *5*

das **Opfer,-** victim *7*

orange orange *6*

die **Ordnung,-en** order *10; Es geht in Ordnung.* It will be taken care of. *10; In Ordnung.* O.K. *15*

die **Organisation,-en** organization *16*

der **Organisator,-en** organizer *16*

der **Ort,-e** town, place *10*

die **Ortschaft,-en** village, town *20*

der **Osten** east *3*

Ostern Easter *12; Frohe Ostern!* Happy Easter! *12*

Österreich Austria *3*

die **Ostsee** Baltic Sea *8*

P

das **Paar,-e** pair *6;* couple *12*

paar; ein paar a few, some *3*

das **Päckchen,-** parcel *14;* packet *18*

packen to pack *11*

die **Packung,-en** package *17*

das **Paket,-e** package *11*

die **Paketkarte,-n** package card (form to be filled out when sending a package) *14*

der **Paketschalter,-** package counter *14*

die **Panne,-n** car trouble, breakdown *19*

das **Papier** paper *8*

das **Paradies,-e** paradise *6*

der **Park,-s** park *12*

parken to park *6*

der **Parkplatz,-̈e** parking space, parking lot *6*

die **Parkuhr,-en** parking meter *6*

das **Parlament** Parliament *11*

die **Party,-s** party *8*

der **Paß,-sse** passport *6*

der **Passagier,-e** passenger *19*

   passen to fit *3*

   passend suitable, right *17; das passende Geld* the right change *17*

   passieren to happen *12*

die **Paßkontrolle,-n** passport inspection *11*

   patent ingenious, clever *20*

der **Patient,-en** patient *18*

die **Pause,-n** break *8; eine Pause machen* to take a break *8*

das **Pech** bad luck *12*

die **Pension,-en** boarding house, type of inn *18*

die **Person,-en** person *7*

die **Personenkontrolle,-n** bodily search, security check *11*

   persönlich in person *11;* personal, private *17*

das **Pferd,-e** horse *8*

   Pfingsten Pentecost *12*

der **Pfirsich,-e** peach *17*

die **Pflanze,-n** plant *20*

die **Pflaume,-n** plum *17*

das **Pfund,-e** pound *10*

   phantastisch fantastic, great *9*

die **Physik** physics *4*

die **Physikaufgabe,-n** physics problem *4*

der **Picknickplatz,-e** picnic area *20*

der **Pilot,-en** pilot *11*

   planen to plan *B*

   planmäßig scheduled *19*

der **Plattenspieler,-** record player *15*

der **Platz,-e** seat, place *3*

der **Platzanweiser,-** usher *5*

   plaudern to chat *15*

   plötzlich suddenly *9*

   plus plus *1*

das **Poliermittel,-** polish *17*

   politisch political *7*

die **Polizei** police *9*

der **Polizist,-en** policeman *13*

die **Pommes frites** (pl.) French fries *16*

das **Porto,-s** postage *14*

die **Post** mail, post office *14*

das **Postamt,-er** post office *13*

das **Postfach,-er** post office box *14*

die **Postkarte,-n** postcard *14*

die **Postleitzahl,-en** zip code *14*

   praktisch practical *4*

der **Preis,-e** price *6*

die **Preisklasse,-n** price category *18*

   preiswert reasonable *6*

die **Presse,-n** press *20*

   pressen to press *20*

   prima great, splendid *3*

der **Prinzenwagen,-** prince's float *C*

   pro per *10*

   probieren to try *12*

das **Problem,-e** problem *20*

   produzieren to produce *15*

das **Programm,-e** program *A*

der **Prospekt,-e** brochure *10*

das **Prozent,-e** per cent *9*

der **Prüfer,-** tester *20*

der **Pudding,-e** pudding *16*

der **Pullover,-** pullover *5*

der **Puls,-e** pulse *18*

   pumpen to pump *D*

   pünktlich punctual, on time *2*

sich **putzen** to clean oneself *11; sich die Zähne putzen* to brush one's teeth *11*

Q

das **Quadrat,-e** square *20*

die **Qualität,-en** quality *20*

die **Qualitätsbezeichnung,-en** quality designation *20*

die **Quittung,-en** receipt *14*

R

der **Radfahrer,-** bicycle rider *9*

der **Radiergummi,-s** eraser *8*

das **Radio,-s** radio *15*

der **Rahm** cream *17; saurer Rahm* sour cream *17*

   'ran: 'Ran an die Arbeit! Let's go to work! *8*

   rangehen *(ging ran, ist rangegangen)* to go up *15; Geh näher ran!* Move closer! *15*

sich **rasieren** to shave oneself *11*

die **Rast,-en** rest, break *10; eine Rast machen* to take a rest *10*

   raten *(rät, riet, geraten)* to advise, give advice *18*

das **Rathaus,-er** city hall *7*

   ratsam advisable, wise *18*

der **Ratskeller,-** restaurant (in the basement of the city hall) *16*

der **Raum,-e** room *15*

die **Realschule,-n** secondary school (grades 4-10) *A*

die **Rebe,-n** vine *20*

der **Rebstock,-e** vine *20*

der **Rechner,-** calculator *20*

die **Rechnung,-en** bill, invoice *10;* check *13*

   recht right *1; Das ist mir recht.* That's all right (O.K.) with me. *1; Du hast recht.* You're right. *3*

   rechts on (to) the right *10*

der **Rechtsanwalt,-e** lawyer *13*

das **Regal,-e** shelf *4*

der **Regen** rain *12*

   rege lively *20*

das **Regierungsgebäude,-** government building *7*

   registrieren to register *17*

   regnen to rain *7*

   reichen to reach *20*

   reichlich generous, plentiful *16*

   reif ripe *17*

der **Reifen,-** tire *19*

die **Reihe,-n** row *6; Er ist an der Reihe.* It's his turn. *6; Er kommt an die Reihe.* It's his turn. *14*

   reingehen *(ging rein, ist reingegangen)* to go inside *13*

   reinigen to clean *15*

der **Reis** rice *20*

die **Reise,-n** trip *4*

das **Reisebüro,-s** travel agency *10*

der **Reisende,-n** traveler *18*

der **Reisepaß,-sse** passport *11*

der **Reisescheck,-s** traveler's check *6*

   reiten *(ritt, ist geritten)* to ride (on animal) *C*

die **Reklame,-n** advertising *C; Reklame machen* to advertise *C*

   renovieren to renovate *7*

die **Reparatur,-en** repair *19*

   reparieren to repair *19*

die **Republik,-en** republic *5*

der **Rest,-e** rest *12*

das **Restaurant,-s** restaurant *7*

das **Rezept,-e** prescription *18*

der **Richter,-** judge *9*

   richtig really, correct *10*

die **Richtung,-en** direction *10*

   riesengroß gigantic *13*

das **Riesenrad,-er** Ferris wheel *11*

   riesig gigantic *20*

der **Rinderbraten,-** beef roast *16*

das **Rinderfilet,-s** beef tenderloin *16*

die **Robbe,-n** seal *15*

der **Rock,-̈e** skirt 6
die **Rolle,-n** role, part C
rollen to roll 11
der **Rollstuhlfahrer,-** wheel chair driver 9
die **Rolltreppe,-n** escalator 17
rosa pink 6
der **Rosengarten** Rose Garden 12
der **Rosenmontag** Monday before Lent C
rot red 4
das **Rote Kreuz** Red Cross 9
der **Rotwein,-e** red wine 16
der **Rotweinwanderweg** Red Wine Hiking Path (name) 16
rüberkommen (kam rüber, ist rübergekommen) to come over 2
die **Rückenschmerzen** (pl.) backache 18
die **Rückfahrt,-en** return trip D
der **Rucksack,-̈e** knapsack 11
der **Rücksitz,-e** back seat 19
der **Ruf,-e** cheer, slogan C
rufen (rief, gerufen) to call 14
die **Ruhe** peace, silence 3; Immer mit der Ruhe! Take it easy. 3
ruhig quiet, peaceful 4; Du kannst ruhig… It's all right for you to… 13

S

die **S-Bahn,-en** city train, suburban express train 2
der **S-Bahnhof,-̈e** suburban line station 8
die **Sache,-n** thing, item 17
die **Sachertorte,-n** Sacher torte (famous Viennese torte) 13
der **Saft,-̈e** juice 20
saftig juicy 17
sagen to say, 2
die **Salami,-** salami 17
der **Salat,-e** salad 16; Gemischter Salat mixed salad, tossed salad 16
der **Salatteller,-** salad plate 16
die **Salbe,-n** ointment 18
die **Salzkartoffel,-n** boiled potato 16
sammeln to collect 13
die **Sammlung-en** collection 7
der **Samstag** Saturday 2
der **Sand** sand 20
satt full 20; satt sein to have had enough (to eat) 20
sauber clean 18

die **Sauberkeit** cleanliness, neatness 15
saubermachen to clean 7
sauer angry, annoyed 4; sour 17
der **Sauerbraten,-** sauerbraten (marinated beef) 16
die **Säule,-n** pillar, post 15
das **Schach** chess 7
die **Schachfigur,-en** chess figure 20
das **Schachspiel,-e** game of chess 20
schade too bad 2
das **Schaf,-e** sheep 15
schaffen to manage(it), make(it) 9
die **Schallplatte,-n** record 8
der **Schalter,-** (ticket) counter 3
die **Schaltung,-en** gearshift 19
schauen to look 13; Schau mal! Look! 13
die **Schaufel,-n** shovel 20
das **Schaufenster,-** display window 6
der **Schauspieler,-** actor 13
die **Schauspielerin,-nen** actress 13
die **Scheibe,-n** slice 17
die **Scheibenbremse,-n** disc brake 19
der **Schein,-e** bill, note 17
scheinen (schien, geschienen) to shine 7; to seem, appear 18
der **Scheinwerfer,-** headlight 19
schenken to give (as a gift) 11
scheu shy, timid 20
die **Scheune,-n** barn 15
schicken to send 13
schieben (schob, geschoben) to push 19
der **Schiedsrichter,-** referee 14
schießen (schoß, geschossen) to shoot 14
das **Schiff,-e** ship, boat 7
das **Schild,-er** sign 7
der **Schinken** ham A
die **Schlachterei,-en** butcher shop 17
das **Schläfchen** nap 20; ein Schläfchen machen to take a nap 20
schlafen (schläft, schlief, geschlafen) to sleep 11
die **Schlafkoje,-n** bunkbed 15
das **Schlafzimmer,-** bedroom 5
schlagen (schlägt, schlug, geschlagen) to beat 9
die **Schlagsahne** whipped cream 13
die **Schlange,-n** snake 15
schlängeln to wind, twist 20
der **Schlauch,-̈e** hose D

der **Schlaukopf,-̈e** genius, smartie 4
schlecht bad 1
schleppen to haul, drag 12
schließlich finally C
Schlittschuh laufen to skate 9
das **Schloß,-̈sser** castle 7
schlucken to swallow 18
der **Schlüssel,-** key 15
schmecken to taste B
der **Schmerz,-en** pain 18
schneiden (schnitt, geschnitten) to cut 17
schneien to snow 7
schnell fast, quick(ly) 2
das **Schnitzel,-** cutlet 16; Wiener Schnitzel breaded veal cutlet 16
der **Schnee** snow 14
die **Schnur,-̈e** rope 12
schon already 2; schon wieder again 2
schön beautiful 4; nice 14
der **Schrank,-̈e** closet, wardrobe 15
die **Schraube,-n** propeller (ship) 13
das **Schreiben** letter, correspondence 20
schreiben (schrieb, geschrieben) to write 2
sich **schreiben** to correspond 11
die **Schreibmaschine,-n** typewriter 20
das **Schreibpapier** writing paper 17
der **Schreibtisch,-e** desk 15
die **Schreibwaren** (pl.) stationery 17
schriftlich written 15
der **Schritt,-e** step 11
der **Schuh,-e** shoe 6
der **Schulbereich,-e** school district 15
die **Schuld** fault 5
die **Schule,-n** school 2
der **Schüler,-** pupil, student (at elementary and secondary school) 4
der **Schülerlotse,-n** school patrol 19
die **Schultasche,-n** school bag 8
die **Schulter,-n** shoulder 11
der **Schulweg,-e** way to school 3
der **Schuß,-̈sse** shot 14
die **Schüssel,-n** bowl 16
der **Schwan,-̈e** swan 20
schwarz black 4
das **Schwarze Meer** Black Sea 8
der **Schwarzwald** Black Forest 6
das **Schwein,-e** pig 15
der **Schweinebraten** roast pork 15
das **Schweinefilet,-s** pork tenderloin 16

die **Schweiz** Switzerland *3*
schwer difficult, hard *3*
die **Schwester,-n** sister *5*
schwimmen *(schwamm, ist geschwommen)* to swim *9*
schwindlig dizzy *18; Mir ist schwindlig.* I'm dizzy. *18*
schwingen *(schwang, geschwungen)* to swing, wave *14*
sechs six *1*
sechzehn sixteen *2*
der **See,-n** lake *5*
das **Segel,-** sail *12*
sehen *(sieht, sah, gesehen)* to see, look *3;* to watch *11; Mal sehen...* Let's see... *3; Seht mal!* Look! *4; sehen auf* to look at *4; einen Film sehen* to watch a movie *11*
die **Sehenswürdigkeit,-en** sight(s) *7*
sehr very *3*
die **Seife,-n** soap *15*
die **Seilbahn,-en** cable car *10*
sein *(ist, war, ist gewesen)* to be *3*
sein his *5*
seit since, for *A*
seitdem since *18*
die **Seite,-n** page *4;* side *7*
der **Sekretär,-e** secretary (male) *13*
die **Sekunde,-n** second *2*
selbst in person, myself *16;* itself *D*
selbstverständlich of course *16*
die **Sendung,-en** parcel, shipment *14*
der **September** September *4*
servieren to serve *16*
die **Serviette,-n** napkin *16*
der **Sessel,-** armchair *15*
selbst in person *12;* itself *13; Mach es selbst!* Do it yourself. *12*
sich **setzen** to sit down *11*
setzen to set, put, place *11*
sicher safe, secure *8;* sure *17*
die **Sicherheit** security *19*
der **Sicherheitsgurt,-e** safety belt *19*
die **Sicherheitsüberprüfung,-en** security check *11*
sicherlich surely, certainly *11*
sicherstellen to make sure *20*
sie she, they *1*
Sie you (formal) *1*
sieben seven *1*
siebzehn seventeen *2*

der **Sieger,-** winner *9*
der **Ski,-er** ski *14*
singen *(sang, gesungen)* to sing *B*
sitzen *(saß, gesessen)* to sit *4*
der **Sitzplatz,-̈e** seat *8*
Ski laufen to ski *9*
so so *3*
so...wie as...as *3*
sobald as soon as *9*
die **Socke,-n** sock *6*
das **Sofa,-s** sofa *15*
sofort right away, immediately *6*
sogar even *7*
sogenannt so-called *12*
der **Sohn,-̈e** son *5*
solange as long as *18*
sollen *(soll, sollte, gesollt)* to be supposed to, should *5*
der **Sommer,-** summer *4*
der **Sommermonat,-e** summer month *6*
die **Sommerresidenz** summer residence *11*
das **Sonderangebot,-e** special offer *10*
sondern but *7; nicht nur...sondern auch* not only...but also *7*
der **Sonderzug,-̈e** special train *20*
der **Sonnabend** Saturday *2*
die **Sonne** sun *7*
sonnig sunny *10*
sonst otherwise *17; Sonst noch etwas?* Anything else? *17*
der **Sonntag** Sunday *2*
sonntags on Sundays *8*
sonst besides, otherwise *9*
sorgen für to care for, provide for *11*
die **Soße,-n** gravy *A*
soweit as far as *20*
sowie as well as *10*
sowieso anyhow, anyway *6*
die **Spanische Reitschule** Spanish Riding School in Vienna *11*
spannen to tighten, stretch *12*
sparen to save *B*
der **Spargel,-** asparagus *16*
das **Sparkonto,-ten** savings account *14; ein Sparkonto führen* to keep a savings account *14*
der **Spaß** fun *6; Viel Spaß!* Have fun! *6; Es macht Spaß.* It is fun. *8*
spät late *2; Wie spät ist es?* What time is it? How late is it? *2*

spazierengehen *(ging spazieren, ist spazierengegangen)* to stroll, take a walk *12*
die **Speise,-n** meal, dish *11*
die **Speisekarte,-n** menu *16*
der **Speisesaal,-säle** dining hall *7*
das **Spezialgeschäft,-e** specialty store *13*
sich **spezialisieren auf** to specialize in *17*
die **Spezialität,-en** specialty, special *13*
speziell special *13*
das **Spiel,-e** game *5*
spielen to play *5*
der **Spieler,-** player *14*
der **Spielfilm,-e** feature film *A*
der **Spielplatz,-̈e** playground *12*
die **Spielwaren** (pl.) toys *17*
der **Spinat,-e** spinach *16*
die **Spitze,-n** top *9;* peak *14; an der Spitze sein* to be in front *9;* to be on top *14*
der **Sport** sport *4*
die **Sportabteilung,-en** sports department *17*
die **Sportart,-en** kind of sport *9*
der **Sportler,-** athlete *9*
der **Sportplatz,-̈e** athletic field *B*
die **Sportschau** sport show *14*
der **Sportwettbewerb,-e** sports competition *9*
die **Sprache,-n** language *6*
das **Sprachlabor,-s** language lab *4*
sprechen *(spricht, sprach, gesprochen)* to speak, talk *2; sprechen über* to talk about *2*
die **Sprechstundenhilfe,-n** receptionist, (doctor's) assistant *18*
springen *(sprang, ist gesprungen)* to jump *9*
spritzen to spray *13*
der **Staat,-en** state *3*
die **Staatsangehörigkeit,-en** citizenship *18*
die **Staatsoper** State Opera *7*
das **Staatsratsgebäude** Council of State Building *7*
das **Stadion,-dien** stadium *14*
die **Stadt,-̈e** city *1; in die Stadt gehen* to go downtown *1*
das **Städtische Kunstmuseum** City Art Museum *7*
die **Stadtmauer,-n** city wall *10*
der **Stadtplan,-̈e** city map *10*
der **Stadtrand,-̈er** outskirts of city *18*

die **Stadtrundfahrt,-en** city tour *11;*
eine Stadtrundfahrt machen
to take a city tour *11*

der **Stadtteil,-e** city district *12*

das **Stadttor,-e** city gate *10*

die **Stadtverwaltung,-en** city
administration *13*

das **Stadtwappen,-** city coat of arms
12

der **Stand,-̈e** stand *16*

das **Standesamt,-̈er** marriage
(license) bureau *12*

die **Standesbeamtin,-nen** registrar,
official at marriage bureau *12*

die **Stange,-n** rod *19*

stark strong *16;* severe *18*

der **Start,-s** start *9;* take-off *11*

startbereit ready to take off *12*

starten to start *9*

das **Startsignal,-e** starting signal *9*

die **Station,-en** station *10*

stattfinden *(fand statt,*
stattgefunden) to take place *9*

der **Status** status *4*

stecken to put *14; einen Brief in*
den Briefkasten stecken to
put a letter into the mailbox
14

stehen *(stand, gestanden)* to
stand, be located *4; Es steht*
ihr gut. She looks good in it.
6; Es steht 1:0. The score is
1-0. *14*

der **Stehplatz,-̈e** standing room *14*

steigen *(stieg, ist gestiegen)* to
climb *10*

steigern to increase *14*

der **Stein,-e** stone, rock *16*

die **Stelle,-n** place, spot *9*

stellen to put, place *A*

stempeln to stamp *7*

das **Steuerrad,-̈er** steering wheel *19*

stimmen to be correct *7; Das*
stimmt. That's right. That's
true. *7*

die **Stimmung,-en** atmosphere,
mood *11*

die **Stirn,-en** forehead *11*

der **Stock,-̈e** floor *15; erster Stock*
first floor (America: second
floor) *15*

stolz proud *12*

stören to disturb *15*

straff tight *12*

der **Strand,-̈e** beach *12*

der **Strandkorb,-̈e** beach chair *20*

die **Straße,-n** street *4*

die **Straßenbahn,-en** streetcar *3*

die **Straßenbahnhaltestelle,-n**
streetcar stop *19*

die **Straßenseite,-n** side of street *19*

der **Straßenverkehr** street traffic *16*

die **Strecke,-n** stretch, distance *8;*
auf der Strecke on the track
(road) *9*

streicheln to stroke, pet *15*

streiken to stall (motor) *19*

stricken to knit *A*

die **Strömung,-en** stream, current *D*

der **Strumpf,-̈e** stocking *6*

das **Stück,-e** piece *13*

der **Student,-en** student (at
university) *4*

das **Studentenleben** student life *15*

studieren to study (at university)
4

das **Studium,-dien** studies *4*

das **Stufen- und Bergland** terrace
and highland country *8*

der **Stuhl,-̈e** chair *12*

die **Stunde,-n** hour *2*

stundenlang for hours *D*

suchen to look for, search *4*

südamerikanisch South
American, Latin American *8*

der **Süden** south *3*

südlich southern, southerly *20*

südwestlich south-western *20*

Südamerika South America *19*

der **Südatlantik** South Atlantic
Ocean *19*

die **Suppe,-n** soup *16*

der **Suppenlöffel,-** soupspoon *16*

das **Surfbrett,-er** surfboard *12*

surfen to surf *12; surfen gehen*
to go surfing *12*

die **Süßigkeiten** (pl.) sweets *7*

das **Symbol,-e** symbol *7*

T

die **Tablette,-n** tablet, pill *18*

die **Tafel,-n** board *B*

der **Tag,-e** day *1; Tag!* Hello!
(conversational), Hi! *1;*
Guten Tag! Hello! *1*

der **Tagesausflug,-̈e** one-day
excursion *16*

das **Tagesgericht,-e** daily menu *16*

der **Tagesplan,-̈e** daily schedule *20*

die **Tagessuppe,-n** soup of the day
16

täglich daily *15*

der **Tank,-s** tank *20*

tanken to fill up, tank *D*

die **Tankstelle,-n** service station *D*

der **Tankwart,-e** service station
attendant *D*

die **Tante,-n** aunt *5*

der **Tanz,-̈e** dance *8*

tanzen to dance *8*

die **Tanzgruppe,-n** dance group *11*

der **Tanzpartner,-** dancing partner *8*

die **Tanzschule,-n** dancing school *8*

der **Tanzunterricht** dancing lessons
(pl.) *8*

die **Tasche,-n** bag *3*

die **Tasse,-n** cup *9*

die **Taube,-n** pigeon *13*

tausend thousand *10*

der **Techniker,-** technician, engineer
14

der **Tee** tea *A*

der **Teelöffel,-** teaspoon *16*

der **Teil,-e** part, section *5; zum*
größten Teil for the most
part, mostly *5; zum Teil*
partly, in part *8*

der **Teilnehmer,-** participant *9*

teilnehmen *(nimmt teil, nahm*
teil, teilgenommen) to
participate *20*

das **Telefon,-e** telephone *2*

das **Telefonbuch,-̈er** phone book *14*

das **Telefongespräch,-e** phone call
14; ein Telefongespräch
führen to make a phone call
14

die **Telefonzelle,-n** telephone booth
7

das **Telegramm,-e** telegram *14*

der **Teller,-** plate *16*

die **Temperatur,-en** temperature *18*

das **Tempo,-s** tempo, pace *14*

das **Tennis** tennis *9*

teuer expensive *6*

die **Textverarbeitungsanlage,-n**
word processor *20*

das **Theater,-** theater *7*

die **Theater- und Musiksaison**
theater and music season *11*

die **Theke,-n** counter *8*

das **Tier,-e** animal *13*

das **Tiefland** lowlands *8*

die **Tier- und Pflanzenproduktion**
animal and plant production
15

der **Tiger,-** tiger *15*

tippen to type *20*

der **Tisch,-e** table *5*

das **Tischtennis** table tennis *7*

der **Titel,-** title *15*

die **Tochter,-̈** daughter 5
die **Toilette,-n** toilet 15
der **Toilettenartikel,-** toiletry 15
toll fantastic, wild, terrific 5
die **Tomate,-n** tomato A
der **Tomatensalat,-e** tomato salad 16
die **Tomatensuppe,-n** tomato soup 16
das **Tor,-e** gate 10; goal 14
die **Torte,-n** torte, type of cake 13
der **Torwart,-̈er** goalie, goal keeper 14
der **Tourist,-en** tourist 5
tragen (trägt, trug, getragen) to carry 3
trainieren to train, practice 9
der **Trauring,-e** wedding ring 12
die **Tradition,-en** tradition 16
der **Traktor,-en** tractor 20
die **Traube,-n** bunch of grapes, grapes 20
treffen (trifft, traf, getroffen) to meet 11; die Wahl treffen to make the selection 20
sich **treffen** to meet B
der **Treffpunkt,-e** meeting place 15
treiben (trieb, getrieben) to pursue, do 9; Sport treiben to do sports 9
die **Tribüne,-n** grandstand C
trinken (trank, getrunken) to drink 9
das **Trinkgeld,-er** tip 16
die **Trompete,-n** trumpet 8
trotzdem nevertheless, in spite of it 13
trübe cloudy 14
die **Tschechoslowakei** Czechoslovakia 3
Tschüs! See you! (sometimes spelled Tschüss! or Tschüß!) 2
tun (tut, tat, getan) to do 2
die **Tür,-en** door 4
der **Turm,-̈e** tower 7
die **Turnhalle,-n** gymnasium 15
die **Tüte,-n** bag 17
typisch typical A

U

die **U-Bahn,-en** subway 19
üben to practice 4
über over, above 3; about 10
überall all over, everywhere 12
überblicken to overlook 10

überlassen (überläßt, überließ, überlassen) to leave to 20; Das ist dir überlassen. That's up to you. 20
übernachten to stay overnight 7
die **Übernachtung,-en** (overnight) accommodation 7
überprüfen to check (over), examine 19
die **Überprüfung** review, examination 20
überqueren to cross 19
überreden to persuade 16; Ich überrede ihn dazu. I'm talking him into that. 16
übertreffen (übertrifft, übertraf, übertroffen) to surpass, beat 9
sich **überzeugen von** to convince/ satisfy oneself of 20
üblich usual, customary 16
übereinstimmen mit to agree with 13
überragen to tower above 11
die **Überraschung,-en** surprise 14
überreden to persuade, talk into 16; sich überreden lassen to be talked into 16
die **Überschrift,-en** title 15
übersetzen to translate 11
übrig remaining 19
übrigens by the way 14
die **Übung,-en** exercise, practice 4; Übung macht den Meister! Practice makes perfect. 4
die **Uhr,-en** clock, watch 2; Wieviel Uhr ist es? What time is it? 2; Es ist vier Uhr. It's four o'clock. 2
um at 2; around 1; in order to, to 7; Um wieviel Uhr? At what time? 2
um...herum around 11
umgeben (umgibt, umgab, umgeben) to surround 10; umgeben von surrounded by 20
die **Umgebung,-en** surrounding, vicinity 5
die **Umkleidekabine,-n** fitting room 6
sich **umsehen** (sieht um, sah um, umgesehen) to look around 19
umsteigen (stieg um, umgestiegen) to transfer 10
sich **umziehen** (zog um, umgezogen) to change (clothes) 12
und and 1

undenkbar unthinkable 17
Ungarn Hungary 5
ungeduldig impatient 4
ungefähr approximate(ly) 3
ungenügend unsatisfactory 4
unglaublich unbelievable, incredible 19
unentschieden tied (game) 14
ungeduldig impatient(ly) 18
die **Uni** "U" (abbreviation for Universität) university 4
die **Universität,-en** university 4
unpünktlich not on time 5
uns us 5
unser our 5
unten downstairs 20
unterbrechen (unterbricht, unterbrach, unterbrochen) to interrupt 19
unterbringen (brachte unter, untergebracht) to accommodate 19
unterdessen meanwhile, in the meantime 5
sich **unterhalten** (unterhält, unterhielt, unterhalten) to converse, talk 16
die **Unterhaltung** entertainment 12
die **Unterkunft,-̈e** accommodation D
unterrichten to instruct jemanden davon unterrichten to let someone know about it 20
der **Unterschied,-e** difference 16
unterschreiben (unterschrieb, unterschrieben) to sign 12
untersuchen to examine, inspect 19
die **Untersuchung,-en** medical examination 18
die **Untertasse,-n** saucer 16
unterwegs on the way 10
unvergeßlich unforgettable 12
der **Urlaub,-e** vacation 14; den Urlaub verbringen to spend the vacation 17; Urlaub nehmen to take vacation 20; Urlaub machen to go on vacation 20
der **Urlauber,-** vacationer 20
der **Urlaubsgast,-̈e** vacationer 20
das **Urlaubsgebiet,-e** vacation area 20
die **Ursache,-n** cause, reason 14; Keine Ursache. Don't mention it. 14
urteilen to judge 13

V

der **Vater,-̈** father 5
der **Vatertag** Father's Day 12
der **Vati,-s** dad 20
sich **verabreden** to make an appointment 16; *wie verabredet* as agreed 16
sich **verabschieden** to say good-bye 11
die **Veranstaltung,-en** event 15
verärgert angry 2
der **Verband,-̈e** bandage 18
verbinden (*verband, verbunden*) to connect 8
die **Verbindung,-en** connection 8; link 11
verbringen (*verbrachte, verbracht*) to spend (a vacation) 9
die **Vereinigten Staaten** United States 3
Verflixt! Darn it! 20
vergehen (*verging, ist vergangen*) to pass C; *Die Zeit vergeht.* The time passes. C
vergessen (*vergißt, vergaß, vergessen*) to forget 11
das **Vergnügen** enjoyment 20
sich **vergnügen** to enjoy oneself 20
der **Vergnügungspark** amusement park 11
verheiratet married 12
der **Verkauf,-̈e** sale 20
der **Verkäufer,-** sales clerk 13
die **Verkäuferin,-nen** sales clerk (female) 5
das **Verkaufszentrum,-tren** shopping center 16
der **Verkehr** traffic 4
das **Verkehrsbüro,-s** tourist office 13
das **Verkehrsmittel,-** means of transportation 7
das **Verkehrsschild,-er** traffic sign 10
verlassen (*verläßt, verließ, verlassen*) to leave A
verlieren (*verlor, verloren*) to lose 4; *Verlier keine Worte!* Don't waste any words! 4
vermieten to rent 18
vernünftig sensible, wise 18
verpacken to pack 20
verpassen to miss 11

die **Verpflegung** food D
sich **versammeln** to gather, meet 7
verschieden different, various 7; *verschiedenes* different items 15
verschreiben (*verschrieb, verschrieben*) to write out (a prescription) 18
versorgen to supply, provide 10
versprechen (*verspricht, versprach, versprochen*) to promise 19
der **Verstand** reason, mind 9; *mehr Glück als Verstand haben* to have more luck than brains 9
verstehen (*verstand, verstanden*) to understand 4
versuchen to try 9
verteidigen to defend 14
der **Verwandte,-n** relative 12
verwarnen to caution, warn 14
verzieren to decorate 10
viel much 2
viele many 4
vielleicht perhaps 4
vier four 1
das **Viertel,-** quarter 3; *Es ist Viertel nach acht.* It's a quarter after eight. 3
vierzehn fourteen 2
der **Vogel,-̈** bird 15
die **Vokabel,-n** (vocabulary) word 4
das **Volkslied,-er** folk song 11
der **Volkstanz,-̈e** folk dance 11
Volkstrauertag Day of National Mourning 12
voll full 3
der **Volleyball** volleyball 20
der **Volleyballspieler,-** volleyball player 20
völlig completely D
von from, of 2
vor in front of, before 5
vorbeifahren (*fährt vorbei, fuhr vorbei, ist vorbeigefahren*) to drive by 9
vorbeifließen (*floß vorbei, ist vorbeigeflossen*) to flow (run) by D
vorbeiführen to go past 10
vorbeikommen (*kam vorbei, ist vorbeigekommen*) to come by 9
sich **vorbeischlängeln an** to wind past 20
vorbereiten to prepare 20

der **Vordersitz,-e** front seat 19
die **Vorfahrt** right of way 19
die **Vorfahrtsstraße,-n** main street 19
vorführen to perform, stage 10
vorhaben (*hat vor, hatte vor, vorgehabt*) to plan, intend 6
vorher before, in advance 10
vorhergehend previous 20
vorhin before, earlier 9
der **Vormittag,-e** forenoon 2
der **Vorname,-n** first name 14
vorne in front 11
der **Vorort,-e** suburb 3
vorschieben (*schob vor, vorgeschoben*) to move forward 20
der **Vorschlag,-̈e** suggestion 4
vorschlagen (*schlägt vor, schlug vor, vorgeschlagen*) to suggest 13
vorsichtig careful(ly) 19
sich **vorstellen** to imagine 10
die **Vorstellung,en** performance, show 5
der **Vorverkauf** advance booking 20
die **Vorwahlnummer,-n** area code 14
vorzeigen to show 11
das **Vorzimmer,-** outer office 18

W

die **Waage,-n** scale 14
die **Wachablösung** changing of the guard 7
wachsen (*wächst, wuchs, ist gewachsen*) to grow 16
der **Wagen,-** car 6; cart 17
der **Wagenheber,-** jack 19
die **Wahl,-en** choice, selection 16; *Wer die Wahl hat, hat die Qual.* It's hard to make a choice. 16
während during 5; while 18
die **Währung,-en** currency 13
das **Wahrzeichen,-** landmark 13
der **Wald,-̈er** forest 7
der **Walzer,-** waltz 8
der **Wanderer,-** hiker 16
wandern to hike 6
die **Wanderung,-en** hike 16
der **Wanderweg,-e** hiking path 16
wann when 2

die **Ware,-n** product, goods 6; article, ware 17

warm warm 7

das **Warndreieck,-e** warning sign 19

warnen to warn 8

warten to wait 2; *warten auf* to wait for A

der **Wartesaal,-säle** waiting room 19

warum why 2

was what 1

was für what kind of 4

die **Waschanlage,-n** car wash D

sich **waschen** *(wäscht, wusch, gewaschen)* to wash oneself 11

das **Wasser** water 12

der **Wasserbehälter,-** water container 9

wässerig watery 10

die **Wasserstraße,-n** waterway 8

der **Wasserverkehr** water traffic 8

wechseln to change 19

der **Weg,-e** way 2; *auf dem Weg* on the way 2

weg sein to be gone 13; *weit weg sein* to be far away 15

weh: weh tun to hurt 18; *Es tut mir weh.* It hurts me. 18

Weihnachten (pl.) Christmas 12; *Fröhliche Weihnachten!* Merry Christmas! 12

weil because 18

die **Weile** while 2; *eine Weile* a while 2

der **Wein,-e** wine 9

der **Weinberg,-e** vineyard 16

der **Weinbau** wine-growing 20

das **Weinbaugebiet,-e** wine-growing area 20

der **Weinbauort,-e** wine-growing town 20

das **Weindorf,-̈er** wine-growing village 16

die **Weinernte,-n** harvest of grapes 20

das **Weinfest,-e** wine festival 20

die **Weinflasche,-n** wine bottle 16

der **Weingarten,-̈** vineyard 20

das **Weingut,-̈er** winery 20

die **Weinkönigin,-nen** wine queen 20

die **Weinlese,-n** vintage, gathering of grapes 20

die **Weinprobe,-n** wine test, wine testing 20

der **Weinstand,-̈e** stand offering wine for sale 20

der **Weinstock,-̈e** grape vine stake 16

die **Weintraube,-n** bunch of grapes, grapes 17

die **Weise,-n** manner, way 15; *auf diese Weise* in this way 15

weisen auf to point to 14

weiß white 5

weit far 3

weiter further 4; *Sie gehen weiter.* They keep going. 4

weiterfahren *(fährt weiter, fuhr weiter, ist weitergefahren)* to continue (driving) 10

weitergehen *(ging weiter, ist weitergegangen)* to keep going 17

der **Weitsprung,-̈e** broad jump 9

welcher which 2

die **Welt,-en** world 7

weltberühmt world-famous 10

der **Weltkrieg** world war 19; *der 2. Weltkrieg* World War II 19

die **Weltzeituhr** World Time Clock 7

wenig little 4

wenige few 7

wenigstens at least 6

wenn when 14; if, whenever 18

wer who 2

der **Werkmeister,-** supervisor, foreman 19

die **Werkstatt,-̈en** repair shop, workshop 19

das **Werkzeug,-e** tool 19

wertvoll valuable 13

der **Westen** west 3

westlich western 20

das **Wetter** weather 7

wichtig important 8

wie how 1; like 8; as 14; *Wie geht's?* How are you? (familiar) 1; *wie viele?* how many 3

wieder again 2

wiederholen to repeat A

wiederkommen *(kam wieder, ist wiedergekommen)* to come again 17

wiedersehen *(sieht wieder, sah wieder, wiedergesehen)* to see again 11

wiegen *(wog, gewogen)* to weigh 14

der **Wiener,-** Viennese 13

wieviel how much? 2; *Um wieviel Uhr?* At what time? 2

der **Wind,-e** wind 12

die **Windschutzscheibe,-n** windshield 19

der **Winter,-** winter 4

der **Wintermonat,-e** winter month 6

der **Wintersportler,-** winter sportsman 5

wir we 1

wirken to work, effect 18; *Es wirkt Wunder.* It's working wonders. 18

wirklich really 4

wirtschaftlich economic 11

die **Wirtschaftlichkeit** economy 19

wissen *(weiß, wußte, gewußt)* to know, be familiar with 3

wo where 1

das **Wochenende,-n** weekend 14

woher where from 4

wohin where to 4

wohl indeed, well, used for emphasis 16; *sich wohl fühlen* to feel well 18

Wohl: Zum Wohl! Cheers! To your health! 16

wohnen to live 1

das **Wohnheim,-e** rooming house, dormitory 15

die **Wohnung,-en** apartment 4

das **Wohnviertel,-** residential area 7

der **Wohnwagen,-** camper 18

das **Wohnzimmer,-** living room 5

der **Wolf,-̈e** wolf 15

die **Wolke,-n** cloud 10

wollen *(will, wollte, gewollt)* to want to 5

womit with what 10

das **Wort,-e** word (saying, quotation) 4; *Verlier keine Worte!* Don't waste any words. 4

das **Wort,-̈er** word 4

das **Wörterbuch,-̈er** dictionary 4

wünschen to wish 10

das **Wunder,-** wonder, miracle 18

der **Wunsch,-̈e** wish 20

die **Wurst,-̈e** sausage A

das **Würstchen,-** hot dog 14

das **Wurstschaschlik** sausage kebab 15

Z

zahlen to pay 15

zahlreich numerous 11

der **Zahn,-̈e** tooth 11

der **Zahnarzt,-̈e** dentist 13

die **Zahnbürste,-n** toothbrush *15*

die **Zahnpasta,-sten** toothpaste *15*

die **Zahnradbahn,-en** cog-wheel train *10*

die **Zahnschmerzen** (pl.) toothache *18*

die **Zapfsäule,-n** gas pump *D*

der **Zaun,-̈e** fence *15*

das **Zebra,-s** zebra *15*

zehn ten *1*

das **Zeitalter** age, generation *19*

das **Zeichen,-** signal, sign *9*

zeigen to show *3; zeigen auf* to point to *6*

die **Zeit,-en** time *2*

der **Zeitglockenturm** Clock Tower *12*

zeitlich as to time *19*

die **Zeitschrift,-en** magazine *11*

die **Zeitung,-en** newspaper *5*

die **Zelle,-n** booth *14*

das **Zelt,-e** tent *18*

der **Zentimeter,-** centimeter *9*

das **Zentrum, -tren** center *6*

der **Zettel,-** piece of paper *14*

die **Ziege,-n** goat *15*

das **Ziel,-e** finish (line) *9;* destination *C*

ziemlich rather, quite *11*

das **Zimmer,-** room *2*

der **Zimmernachweis** room referral agency *18*

der **Zimmerschlüssel,-** room key *7*

zögern to hesitate *20*

der **Zoll** customs *11*

der **Zoo,-s** zoo *15*

zu at, too, to *2; zu Hause* at home *2*

zubereiten to prepare (a meal) *7*

züchten to raise (animals) *15*

die **Zuckerrübe,-n** sugar beet *15*

zuerst first *5*

zufrieden satisfied *17*

der **Zug,-̈e** train *3;* parade *C;* move (chess) *20*

zugeben *(gibt zu, gab zu, zugegeben)* to admit *6*

zugehen lassen to forward *20*

zuhören to listen *11*

zuletzt finally, last of all *19*

zumachen to close *B*

zunächst first *19*

die **Zündkerze,-n** spark plug *19*

zurück back *18*

zurückfahren *(fährt zurück, fuhr zurück, ist zurückgefahren)* to drive back *10*

zurückgehen *(ging zurück, ist zurückgegangen)* to go back *6*

zurücksehen *(sieht zurück, sah zurück, zurückgesehen)* to look back *16*

zusammen together *2*

der **Zuschauer,-** spectator *9*

zuschicken to send, mail (to) *10*

zusehen *(sieht zu, sah zu, zugesehen)* to watch *12*

zurückgeben *(gibt zurück, gab zurück, zurückgegeben)* to return, give back *12*

zusammenarbeiten to work together *15*

zusammenkommen *(kam zusammen, ist zusammengekommen)* to come together *15*

sich **zusammenschließen** *(schloß zusammen, zusammengeschlossen)* to merge *15*

zusammensetzen to put together *12*

zusammensitzen *(saß zusammen, zusammengesessen)* to sit together *15*

zusammenzählen to add *17*

zuwinken to wave at *10*

zwanzig twenty *2*

zwei two *1*

der **Zweifel,-** doubt *14*

die **Zwiebel,-n** onion *17*

zwischen between *8*

zwölf twelve *2*

All the words introduced in DEUTSCH: AKTUELL 1 and 2 have been summarized in this section. The numbers following the meaning of individual words and phrases indicate the particular lesson in which they appear for the first time. In cases in which there is more than one meaning for a word or phrase and it has appeared in different lessons, the corresponding lessons numbers are listed.

A

a ein(e) *2*
able: to be able to können
    (kann, konnte, gekonnt) 5
about über *10*
above über *3*
academy die Akademie,-n *15*
to **accommodate** unterbringen
    (brachte unter,
    untergebracht) 19
accommodation die
    Unterkunft,¨e *D*
accommodations (overnight)
    die Übernachtung,-en *7*
accordion das Akkordeon,-s *8*
acquaintance der/die Bekannte,
    -n *12*
across gegenüber *7*
active aktiv *20*
actor der Schauspieler,- *13*
actress die Schauspielerin,-nen
    13
actual(ly) eigentlich *3*
to **add** zusammenzählen *17*
address die Anschrift,-en *18*
addressee der Empfänger,- *14*
adhesive tape das Heftpflaster,-
    18
addition die Beilage,-n *16*
to **adjust** einstellen *14*
to **admire** bewundern *12*
admission der Eintritt *8*
admission price der
    Eintrittspreis,-e *15*
to **admit** zugeben *(gibt zu, gab zu,*
    zugegeben) 6
adult der Erwachsene,-n *11*
to **advertise** Reklame machen *C*
advertising die Reklame,-n *C*
to **advise** raten *(rät, riet, geraten)*
    18

advisable ratsam *18*
affair die Angelegenheit,-en *15*
afraid: to be afraid Angst haben
    2
after nach *3;* nachdem *18*
afternoon der Nachmittag,-e *2*
again wieder *2; again and again*
    immer wieder *7*
age das Alter *20*
aggressive aggressiv *14*
to **agree** einverstanden sein *12*
to **agree with** übereinstimmen mit
    13
agriculture die Landwirtschaft
    11
air die Luft,¨e *C*
airline company die
    Fluggesellschaft,-en *19*
airmail die Luftpost *14*
airmail service der
    Luftpostdienst *19*
airplane das Flugzeug,-e *7*
airport der Flughafen,¨ *11*
airport building das
    Flughafengebäude,- *11*
air pressure der Luftdruck *D*
air traffic der Flugverkehr *19*
all alle *2*
allowed erlaubt *19*
almost fast *5*
along längs *20*
alphabetical alphabetisch *14*
Alps die Alpen *5*
already schon *2;* bereits *20*
also auch *1*
although obgleich, obwohl *18*
altogether insgesamt *19*
always immer *2*
amazed erstaunt *16*
amazing erstaunlich *17*

America Amerika *5*
American der Amerikaner,-
    (male), die Amerikanerin,
    -nen (female) *A*
American amerikanisch *16*
amount der Betrag,¨e *6*
to **amount (come) to** betragen
    (beträgt, betrug, betragen)
    19
amusement park der
    Vergnügungspark *11*
an ein(e) *2*
and und *1*
angry verärgert *2;* sauer *4*
animal das Tier,-e *13*
to **announce** bekanntgeben *(gibt*
    bekannt, gab bekannt,
    bekanntgegeben) 8
announcement die
    Bekanntmachung,-en *15*
announcer der Ansager,- *9*
annoyed sauer *4*
answer die Antwort,-en *15*
to **answer** antworten *3;*
    beantworten *A; to answer a*
    question eine Frage
    beantworten *A*
anyhow sowieso *6*
anyway sowieso *6*
apartment die Wohnung,-en *4*
apartment building das
    Mietshaus,¨er *5*
ape der Affe,-n *15*
appetite der Appetit *16; to have*
    appetite for Appetit haben
    auf *16*
to **applaud** klatschen *9*
apple der Apfel,¨ *17*
apple cake der Apfelkuchen,- *16*
apple juice der Apfelsaft,¨e *16*

apple sauce das Apfelmus *A*

appointment: to make an appointment sich verabreden *16*

apprentice der Lehrling,-e *19*

approximate(ly) ungefähr *3*

April der April *4*

area die Fläche,-n *3;* die Gegend,-en *5*

area code die Vorwahlnummer, -n *14*

arm der Arm,-e *11*

armchair der Sessel,- *15*

around um *1;* um...herum *11*

to **arrange** anordnen *14*

arrival die Ankunft,¨e *7*

to **arrive** ankommen *(kam an, ist angekommen) 10*

art die Kunst *4*

article of clothing das Kleidungsstück,-e *6*

artistic künstlerisch *13*

art treasure der Kunstschatz,¨e *10*

as...as so...wie *3*

Ascension Day der Himmelfahrtstag *12*

Asia Asien *19*

to **ask** fragen *2;* bitten *(bat, gebeten) 12*

to **ask for/about** fragen nach *14;* sich erkundigen nach *18*

asparagus der Spargel,- *16*

aspirin das Aspirin *18*

to **assume** annehmen *(nimmt an, nahm an, angenommen) 10*

astonished erstaunt *16*

astonishing erstaunlich *17*

astronomical astronomisch *12*

at um, an *2;* bei *5; At what time?* Um wieviel Uhr? *2; at home* zu Hause *2*

athlete der Sportler,- *9*

athletic field der Sportplatz,¨e *B*

atmosphere die Stimmung,-en *11;* die Atmosphäre,-n *17*

to **attach** festmachen *12*

to **attack** angreifen *(griff an, angegriffen) 14*

attendant der Aufseher,- *9*

to **attract here** hierherziehen *(zog hierher, hierhergezogen) 20*

attraction der Anziehungspunkt,-e *10*

August der August *4*

aunt die Tante,-n *5*

Austria Österreich *3*

author der Autor,-en *15*

automat der Automat,-en *3*

automatic(ally) automatisch *18*

available frei *7*

aviation die Fliegerei *19*

awake munter *A*

away entfernt *4*

awful furchtbar *18*

B

back zurück *18*

backache die Rückenschmerzen (pl.) *18*

bad schlecht *1; too bad* schade *2*

badminton der Federball,¨e *9*

bag die Tasche,-n *3;* der Beutel,- *11;* die Tüte,-n *17*

baggage das Gepäck *3*

baggage claim die Gepäckausgabe,-n *11*

baked goods die Backware,-n *17*

baker der Bäcker,- *13*

bakery die Bäckerei,-en *17*

balance das Gleichgewicht *12; to keep the balance* das Gleichgewicht behalten *12*

ball der Ball,¨e *14*

ballpoint pen der Kuli,-s *8*

Baltic Sea die Ostsee *8*

banana die Banane,-n *17*

band die Kapelle,-n *12*

bandage der Verband,¨e *18*

Band-Aid das Heftpflaster,- *18*

bank die Bank,-en *6*

barber der Friseur,-e *13*

barn die Scheune,-n *15*

baroque style der Barockstil *11*

barrel: wooden barrel das Holzfaß,¨sser *20*

basement der Keller,- *15*

basket der Korb,¨e *17*

basketball der Basketball,¨e; der Korbball,¨e *9*

bathroom das Badezimmer,- *15*

battery die Batterie,-n *D*

to **be** sein *(ist, war, ist gewesen) 3;* herrschen *17*

beach der Strand,¨e *12*

beach chair der Strandkorb,¨e *20*

bean die Bohne,-n *16*

bear der Bär,-en *12*

to **beat** übertreffen *(übertrifft, übertraf, übertroffen) 9;* schlagen *(schlägt, schlug, geschlagen) 9*

beautician die Friseuse,-n *13*

beautiful schön *4*

because weil *18*

bed das Bett,-en *5*

bedroom das Schlafzimmer,- *5*

beef roast der Rinderbraten,- *16*

beef tenderloin das Rinderfilet, -s *16*

beer das Bier,-e *9; a light beer* ein Helles *16*

before vor *5;* vorhin *9;* vorher *10;* ehe *18*

to **begin** beginnen *(begann, begonnen) 3;* anfangen *(fängt an, fing an, angefangen) 15*

beginning der Anfang,¨e *14*

to **behave** sich benehmen *(benimmt, benahm, benommen) 11*

behind hinter *8*

Belgium Belgien *3*

to **believe** glauben *3*

to **belong to** gehören zu *8*

bench die Bank,¨e *4*

beside neben *10*

besides außer *6;* sonst *9;* außerdem *18*

best best- *7; the best is* am besten *7*

between zwischen *8*

beverage das Getränk,-e *7*

bicycle das Fahrrad,¨er *7*

bicycle rider der Radfahrer,- *9*

big groß *3*

bill die Rechnung,-en *10; bill (money)* der Schein,-e *17*

biology die Biologie *4*

bird der Vogel,¨ *15*

birth: date of birth das Geburtsdatum,-daten *18*

birth certificate die Geburtsurkunde,-n *12*

birthday der Geburtstag,-e *5; Happy Birthday!* Herzlichen Glückwunsch zum Geburtstag! *8*

birthplace der Geburtsort,-e *18*

bite der Bissen,- *20*

black schwarz *4*

blackberry die Brombeere,-n *17*

Black Forest der Schwarzwald *6*

Black Sea das Schwarze Meer *6*

blimp das Luftschiff,-e *19*

to **block off** absperren *9*

blood pressure der Blutdruck *18*

blouse die Bluse,-n *6*

blue blau *6*

blueberry jam die Blaubeermarmelade *17*

board die Tafel,-n *B*

boarding pass die Bordkarte,-n *11*

boat das Boot,-e, das Schiff,-e *7*

body: part of body der Körperteil,-e *11*

boiled gekocht *17*

book das Buch,¨er *4*

to **book** buchen *10*

book department die Bücherabteilung,-en *6*

bookshelf das Bücherregal,-e *15*

boom (surfing) der Gabelbaum, ¨e *12*

booth die Zelle,-n *14*

border die Grenze,-n *6*

border crossing der Grenzübergang,¨e *13*

to **border on** grenzen an *4*

boredom die Langeweile *20*

boring langweilig *2*

to **borrow** ausleihen *(lieh aus, ausgeliehen) 15*

boss der Chef,-s *20*

both beide *2*

bottle die Flasche,-n *20*

bottling company die Abfüllerei,-en *20*

bowl die Schüssel,-n *16*

box die Kiste,-n *11*

boy der Junge,-n *1*

boyfriend der Freund,-e *1*

brake die Bremse,-n *19*

bratwurst die Bratwurst,¨e *B*

bread das Brot,-e *A*

bread crumb die Brotkrume,-n *13*

bread stand der Brotstand,¨e *17*

break die Pause,-n *8; to take a break* eine Pause machen *8*

breakdown (car) die Panne,-n *19*

breakfast das Frühstück *11*

breakfast: to have breakfast frühstücken *5*

Bremen Town Musicians die Bremer Stadtmusikanten *13*

bride die Braut,¨e *12*

bridge die Brücke *8*

briefcase die Aktentasche,-n *11*

to **bring** bringen *(brachte, gebracht) A*

to **bring along** mitbringen *(brachte mit, mitgebracht) 7*

broad jump der Weitsprung,¨e *9*

brochure der Prospekt,-e *10*

brother der Bruder,¨ *5*

brown braun *6*

to **brush (one's hair)** sich bürsten *11*

bucket der Eimer,- *20; big bucket* der Kübel,- *20*

buddy der Kamerad,-en *9*

to **build** erbauen *10;* bauen *11*

building das Gebäude,- *7*

bunkbed die Schlafkoje,-n *15*

bus der Bus,-se *4*

business der Betrieb,-e *15*

business letter der Geschäftsbrief,-e *20*

bus stop die Bushaltestelle,-n *19*

busy beschäftigt *C; to be busy with* sich beschäftigen mit *20*

but aber *2;* sondern *7; not only...but also* nicht nur...sondern auch *7*

butcher der Fleischer,-, der Metzger,- *13*

butcher shop die Schlachterei,-en *17*

butter die Butter *A*

to **buy** kaufen *3*

C

cabin die Kabine,-n *19*

cable car die Seilbahn,-en *10*

café das Café,-s *5;* die Konditorei,-en *16*

cafeteria: student cafeteria die Mensa *15*

cage der Käfig,-e *C*

cake der Kuchen,- *13*

calculator der Rechner,- *20*

call der Ruf,-e *C*

to **call** rufen *(rief, gerufen) 14; to call (name)* nennen *(nannte, genannt) 19*

to **call (up)** anrufen *(rief an, angerufen) 5; to make a call* ein Gespräch führen *14; to be called* heißen *(hieß, geheißen) 1*

camera der Apparat,-e *15;* die Kamera,-s *15*

camper der Wohnwagen,- *18*

camping ground der Campingplatz,¨e *18*

can die Dose,-n *17*

can können *(kann, konnte, gekonnt) 5*

canal der Kanal,¨e *9*

canal system das Kanalsystem, -e *8*

to **cancel (tickets)** entwerten *8*

capital (city) die Hauptstadt,¨e *3*

car das Auto,-s *5;* der Wagen,- *6*

card die Karte,-n *B*

cardboard box der Karton,-s *11*

card-index die Kartei,-en *15*

to **care for** sorgen für *11*

careful(ly) vorsichtig *19*

carnival der Fasching, der Karneval *15*

carnival parade der Karnevalszug,¨e *C*

carp der Karpfen,- *16*

carriage die Kutsche,-n *12*

carrot die Karotte,-n, die Möhre,-n *16*

to **carry** tragen *(trägt, trug, getragen) 3*

carton der Karton,-s *11*

car wash die Waschanlage,-n *D*

case der Fall,¨e *17; in any case* auf jeden Fall *17; in case of* falls *20*

to **cash (in)** einlösen *6*

cashier (female) die Kassiererin,-nen *17*

cashier's counter die Kasse,-n *6*

cassette die Kassette,-n *4*

castle das Schloß,¨sser *7*

cat die Katze,-n *13*

catalog der Katalog,-e *20*

cathedral das Münster,- *7;* der Dom,-e *11*

cause die Ursache,-n *14*

to **caution** verwarnen *14*

to **celebrate** feiern *C*

cellar der Keller,- *15*

center die Mitte,-n *4;* das Zentrum,-tren *6*

centimeter der Zentimeter,- *9*

century das Jahrhundert,-e *13*

certainly bestimmt *6;* sicherlich *11*

chair der Stuhl,¨e *12*

to **challenge** herausfordern *20*

chance die Chance,-n *9*

to **change** wechseln *19*

to **change (clothes)** sich umziehen *(zog um, umgezogen) 12*

character der Charakter,-e *10*

to **chat** plaudern *15*

cheap billig *15*

check die Rechnung,-en *13*

to **check** nachsehen *(sieht nach, sah nach, nachgesehen) 10*

to **check (luggage)** aufgeben *(gibt auf, gab auf, aufgegeben) 11*

to **check out** ausleihen *(lieh aus, ausgeliehen) 15*

to **check (over)** überprüfen *19*

cheer der Ruf,-e *C*

to **cheer** jubeln *14*

Cheers! Zum Wohl! *16*

cheese der Käse *A*

cheese stand der Käsestand,-̈e *17*

chemistry die Chemie *4*

cherry die Kirsche,-n *17*

chess das Schach *7; game of chess* das Schachspiel,-e *20*

chess figure die Schachfigur,-en *20*

chicken das Huhn,-̈er *15*

child das Kind,-er *11*

chin das Kinn,-e *11*

China China *16*

chocolate: hot chocolate der Kakao *9*

choice die Auswahl *6;* die Wahl,-en *16*

to **choose** auswählen *B*

Christmas Weihnachten (pl.) *12; Merry Christmas!* Fröhliche Weihnachten! *12*

church die Kirche,-n *7*

Cinderella Aschenbrödel *20*

citizenship die Staatsangehörigkeit,-en *18*

city die Stadt,-̈e *1*

city administration die Stadtverwaltung,-en *13*

city district der Stadtteil,-e *12*

city gate das Stadttor,-e *10*

city hall das Rathaus,-̈er *7*

city map der Stadtplan,-̈e *10*

city tour die Stadtrundfahrt,-en *11; to take a city tour* eine Stadtrundfahrt machen *11*

city wall die Stadtmauer,-n *10*

clarinet die Klarinette,-n *8*

class die Klasse,-n *3; second class* zweiter Klasse *3*

classical klassisch *12*

class trip der Klassenausflug,-̈e *7*

to **clean** saubermachen *7;* reinigen *15*

to **clean (oneself)** sich putzen *11*

clean sauber *18*

cleanliness die Sauberkeit *15*

clear klar *3*

to **clear** abräumen *7*

clearly deutlich *10*

clever patent *20*

to **climb** steigen *(stieg, ist gestiegen) 10;* klettern *16*

clock die Uhr,-en *2*

close dicht *9*

to **close** zumachen *B*

closed geschlossen *11*

closet der Schrank,-̈e *15*

cloud die Wolke,-n *10*

cloudy trübe *14;* bewölkt *20*

clutch die Kupplung,-en *19*

coat der Mantel,-̈ *6*

cocoa der Kakao *9*

coffee der Kaffee *A*

cog-wheel (train) die Zahnradbahn,-en *10*

coin die Münze,-n *13*

cola die Cola,-s *2*

cold die Erkältung,-en *18*

cold kalt *7*

cold: to catch a cold sich erkälten *18*

cold-cut platter die Kalte Platte *5*

colleague der Kollege,-n *15*

to **collect** sammeln *13*

collection die Sammlung-en *7*

college die Akademie,-n, die Hochschule,-n *15*

color die Farbe,-n *6*

colorful bunt *6;* farbig *18*

to **comb (one's hair)** sich kämmen *11*

to **come** kommen *(kam, ist gekommen) 1; Come on!* Los! *5*

to **come again** wiederkommen *(kam wieder, ist wiedergekommen) 17*

to **come along** mitkommen *(kam mit, ist mitgekommen) 5*

to **come by** vorbeikommen *(kam vorbei, ist vorbeigekommen) 9*

to **come close to** herankommen *(kam heran, ist herangekommen) 20*

to **come here** hierherkommen *(kam hierher, ist hierhergekommen) 10*

to **come out (of)** herauskommen *(kam heraus, ist herausgekommen) 12*

to **come over** rüberkommen *(kam rüber, ist rübergekommen) 2*

to **come together** *(kam zusammen, ist zusammengekommen) 15*

comfort der Komfort *18*

comfortable bequem *3; to get comfortable* sich gemütlich machen *11*

common gemeinsam *19*

company die Firma,-en *20*

competition der Wettbewerb,-e *9; sports competition* der Sportwettbewerb *9*

to **complain** klagen *18; to complain about* sich beklagen über *13*

complaint die Beschwerde,-n *18*

to **complete** fertigstellen *20*

complete gesamt *19*

completely ganz und gar *20;* völlig *D*

compliment das Kompliment,-e *13; to pay compliments* Komplimente machen *13*

composition der Aufsatz,-̈e *A*

computer der Computer,- *3*

to **congratulate** gratuliere *9*

congratulations (pl.) der Glückwunsche,-̈e *8; Congratulations!* Herzlichen Glückwunsch! *9*

to **connect** verbinden *(verband, verbunden) 8*

connection die Verbindung,-en *8*

to **consist of** bestehen aus *(bestand aus, bestanden aus) 4*

to **construct** erbauen *10*

construction site die Baustelle, -n *19*

to **contain** enthalten *(enthält, enthielt, enthalten) 16*

container der Behälter,- *17*

to **continue** fortsetzen *10; to continue a trip* eine Reise fortsetzen *10; to continue (driving)* weiterfahren *10*

to **convince (oneself) of** sich überzeugen *20*

conversation das Gespräche,-̈e *14*

to **converse** sich unterhalten *(unterhält, unterhielt, unterhalten) 16*

to **cook** kochen *A*

cooked gekocht *17*

cool kühl *7*

to **cool off** sich abkühlen *9*

cooler der Kühlraum,-̈e *17*

corner die Ecke,-n *1*

correct richtig *10; to be correct* stimmen *7*

to **correspond** sich schreiben *11*

correspondence das Schreiben *20*

corridor der Korridor,-e *12;* der Flur,-e *15*

to **cost** kosten *4*

costume das Kostüm,-e *C*

cough drop der Hustenbonbon, -s *18*

cough syrup der Hustensaft,⸚e *18*

counter die Theke,-n *8;* der Ladentisch,-e *17; ticket counter* der Schalter,- *3*

country das Land,⸚er *3*

course: of course natürlich *4;* selbstverständlich *16*

to **cover** decken *A*

covered belegt *16*

cow die Kuh,⸚e *15*

cozy gemütlich *11*

cream der Rahm *17; sour cream* saurer Rahm *17*

cream: whipped cream die Schlagsahne *13*

crisp knusprig *17*

to **crochet** häkeln *5*

cross das Kreuz,-e *6*

to **cross** überqueren *19*

to **crown** krönen *20*

crunchy knusprig *17*

cultural kulturell *7*

cup die Tasse,-n *9*

curb die Bordsteinkante,-n *19*

currency die Währung,-en *13*

customary üblich *16*

customer der Kunde,-n *10*

customs der Zoll *11*

to **cut** schneiden *(schnitt, geschnitten) 17*

to **cut off** abschneiden *(schnitt ab, abgeschnitten) 20*

cutlet das Schnitzel,- *16; breaded veal cutlet* Wiener Schnitzel *16*

Czechoslovakia die Tschechoslowakei *3*

D

dad der Vati,-s *20*

daily täglich *15*

dance der Tanz,⸚e *8*

to **dance** tanzen *8*

dance group die Tanzgruppe,-n *11*

dancing lessons (pl.) der Tanzunterricht *8*

dancing partner der Tanzpartner,- *8*

dancing school die Tanzschule, -n *8*

dashboard das Armaturenbrett *19*

date (calendar) das Datum, Daten *5*

daughter die Tochter,⸚ *5*

day der Tag,-e *1*

December der Dezember *4*

to **decide** sich entschließen *(entschloß, entschlossen) C;* sich entscheiden *(entschied, entschieden) 17*

decision die Entscheidung,-en *17; to make a decision* eine Entscheidung treffen *17*

to **decorate** verzieren *10;* dekorieren *D*

defective defekt *19*

to **defend** verteidigen *14*

delicatessen (store) das Delikatessengeschäft,-e *17*

delicious lecker *8;* köstlich *13*

demand der Bedarf *15*

Denmark Dänemark *3*

dentist der Zahnarzt,⸚e *13*

department die Abteilung,-en *17*

department store das Kaufhaus,⸚er *B*

departure die Abfahrt,-en *10;* die Abreise *11*

departure (flight) der Abflug,⸚e *11*

departure time die Abfahrtszeit,-en *10*

to **describe** beschreiben *(beschrieb, beschrieben) 10*

description die Beschreibung, -en *4;* die Angabe,-n *14*

to **designate** bezeichnen *10*

desk der Schreibtisch,-e *15*

dessert der Nachtisch,-e *A*

destination der Bestimmungsort,-e *14*

detail die Einzelheit,-en *14*

to **determine** feststellen *18*

development die Entwicklung, -en *19*

to **dictate** diktieren *20*

dictating machine das Diktiergerät,-e *20*

dictation das Diktat,-e *20; to take dictation* ein Diktat aufnehmen *20*

dictionary das Wörterbuch,⸚er *4*

difference der Unterschied,-e *16*

different verschieden *7*

difficult schwer *3*

dining hall der Speisesaal,-säle *7*

dinner das Abendessen *11*

direct direkt *6*

direction die Richtung,-en *10*

dirigible das Luftschiff,-e *19*

disc brake die Scheibenbremse, -n *19*

to **discuss** besprechen *(bespricht, besprach, besprochen) 4*

dish die Speise,-n *11*

dishes das Geschirr *7*

to **dispatch** aufgeben *(gibt auf, gab auf, aufgegeben) 14*

to **display** aushängen *16*

display window das Schaufenster,- *6*

distance die Entfernung,-en *3;* die Strecke,-n *8;* der Abstand,⸚e *19*

distant entfernt *4*

district der Kreis,-e, der Bezirk,-e *15*

to **disturb** stören *15*

dizzy schwindlig *18; I'm dizzy.* Mir ist schwindlig. *18*

to **do** machen *1;* tun *2*

dock das Dock,-s *13*

dockyard das Dock,-s *13*

doctor der Arzt,⸚e *13;* der Doktor,-en *18*

doctor's office das Arztzimmer,- *18*

document das Dokument,-e *20*

dog der Hund,-e *13*

dollar der Dollar,-s *6*

donkey der Esel,- *13*

door die Tür,-en *4*

dormitory das Wohnheim,-e *15*

doubt der Zweifel,- *14;* das Bedenken *18*

downstairs unten *20*

downtown die Innenstadt,⸚e *6*

dozen das Dutzend,-e *17*

to **drag** schleppen *12*

drawers (chest of) die Kommode,-n *15*

dress das Kleid,-er *6*

to **drink** trinken *(trank, getrunken) 9*

to **drive** fahren *(fährt, fuhr, ist gefahren) 3*

to **drive along** entlangfahren *(fährt entlang, fuhr entlang, ist entlanggefahren) 20*

to **drive around** herumfahren *(fährt herum, fuhr herum, ist herumgefahren) 7*

to **drive back** zurückfahren *(fährt zurück, fuhr zurück, ist zurückgefahren) 10* to **drive by** vorbeifahren (*fährt vorbei, fuhr vorbei, ist vorbeigefahren*) 9

to **drive off** losfahren (*fährt los, fuhr los, ist losgefahren*) 11

to **drive through** durchfahren (*fährt durch, fuhr durch, ist durchgefahren*) 13

driver der Fahrer,- 19

driver (car) der Autofahrer,- 14

driver's license der Führerschein,-e 8

driver's test die Fahrprüfung,-en 8

driver's training der Fahrunterricht 19

duck die Ente,-n 15

dumb blöd 12

to **dump** kippen 20

dumpling der Knödel,- 16

during während 5

E

each jeder 7

eagle der Adler,- 15

ear das Ohr,-en 11

earlier vorhin 9; früher 11

early früh 9

east der Osten 3

Easter Ostern 12; *Happy Easter!* Frohe Ostern! 12

easy leicht 3

to **eat** essen (*ißt, aß, gegessen*) 5

economic wirtschaftlich 11

economy die Wirtschaftlichkeit 19

effort die Bemühung,-en 18

egg das Ei,-er 16; *a boiled egg* ein gekochtes Ei 16

eight acht 1

eighteen achtzehn 2

either...or entweder...oder 13

electrician der Elektriker,- 13

electronics die Elektronik 19

elegant elegant 7

elephant der Elefant,-en 15

elevator der Fahrstuhl,¨e 7

eleven elf 2

embassy die Botschaft,-en 12

to **emigrate** auswandern 14

emperor der Kaiser,- 11

employee der Angestellte,-n 6

empty leer 5

to **empty** leeren 14

end das Ende 3

to **end** beenden 10; enden 20

engineer der Ingenieur,-e 13; der Techniker,- 14

England England 4

English englisch 4; das Englisch 4

to **enjoy** *I enjoy it.* Es macht mir Freude. 20

to **enjoy (oneself)** sich vergnügen 20

enjoyment das Vergnügen 20

enough genug 15

entertainment die Unterhaltung 12

enthusiastic begeistert 11; leidenschaftlich 20

entrance der Eingang,¨e 6

entrance (drive-in) die Einfahrt,-en 13

envelope der Briefumschlag,¨e 14

equipment (piece of) das Gerät,-e 19

eraser der Radiergummi,-s 8

errand die Besorgung,-en 14

escalator die Rolltreppe,-n 17

especially besonders 4

essay der Aufsatz,¨e A

Europe Europa 5

European europäisch 8

evening der Abend,-e 2; *this evening* heute abend 2

even sogar 7

event das Ereignis,-se 7; das Erlebnis,-se 11; die Veranstaltung,-en 15

every jeder 7

everyone alle 8

everything alles 3

everywhere überall 17

exact genau 7

to **examine** untersuchen 19

examination die Überprüfung 20

examination (medical) die Untersuchung,-en 18

example das Beispiel,-e 7; *for example* zum Beispiel 7

excellent ausgezeichnet 10

except außer 6

excerpt der Auszug,¨e 14

exchange (money) der Kurs,-e 6

to **exchange** austauschen 11

excursion der Ausflug,¨e 8

exercise die Übung,-en 4

exercise: physical exercise die Leibesübung,-en 14

exhausting anstrengend 15

exhaust pipe das Auspuffrohr,-e 19

to **exist** herrschen 17

exit der Ausgang,¨e 11

to **expect** erwarten D

expensive teuer 6

experience das Erlebnis,-se 11; die Erfahrung,-en 15

expert der Experte,-n 8

to **explain** erklären 11

explorer der Erforscher,- 15

to **export** exportieren 20

expression der Ausdruck,¨e 4

to **extend** sich erstrecken 20

eye das Auge,-n 11

F

fairy tale das Märchen,- 13

fairy tale-like märchenhaft 10

fall der Herbst,-e 4

to **fall down** hinfallen (*fällt hin, fiel hin, ist hingefallen*) 14

family die Familie,-n 5

family name der Nachname,-n 14

famous berühmt 10

fantastic toll 5; phantastisch 9

farm der Bauernhof,¨e 10

farmer der Landwirt,-e 13

fascism der Faschismus 7

fast schnell 2

to **fasten** festmachen 12

fat dick 13

father der Vater,¨ 5

Father's Day der Vatertag 12

fault die Schuld 5

favorable günstig 10

fear die Angst,¨e 2

feather-bed das Federbett,-en 15

feature film der Spielfilm,-e A

February der Februar 4

Federal Republic of Germany die Bundesrepublik Deutschland 3

fee die Gebühr,-en 6

to **feed** füttern 13

to **feel** fühlen 18; *to feel well* sich wohl fühlen 18

fence der Zaun,¨e 15

to **ferment** fermentieren 20

Ferris wheel das Riesenrad,¨er 11

festival das Fest,-e C

festive feierlich 12

festivity die Festlichkeit,-en 15

to **fetch** holen 13

fever das Fieber 18

fever thermometer das Fieberthermometer,- 18

few wenige 7; einige 7; *a few* ein paar 3; manche 8
field das Feld,-er 10
field path der Feldweg,-e 4
fifteen fünfzehn 2
figure die Figur,-en 10
file die Akte,-n 20
to **fill** füllen 20
to **fill out** ausfüllen 7
to **fill up** auffüllen, tanken *D*
film der Film,-e 5
finally endlich 2; schließlich *C*; zuletzt 19
to **find** finden *(fand, gefunden)* 4
to **find out** feststellen 18
finger der Finger,- 11
finish (line) das Ziel,-e 9
to **finish** beenden 10; fertigstellen 20
firm die Firma,-en 20
first erst, zuerst 5; zunächst 19
first-class erstklassig 18
fish der Fisch,-e 15
fish market der Fischmarkt,¨e 17
to **fit** passen 3
fitting room die Umkleidekabine,-n 6
five fünf 1
flag die Fahne,-n 12
to **flash** blinken 14
flat flach 5
flight der Flug,¨e 10
flight attendant der Flugbegleiter,- 11
flight passenger der Fluggast,¨e 11
flight ticket der Flugschein,-e 11
float der Festwagen,- *C*
floor der Stock 15; *first floor (America: second floor)* erster Stock 15
to **flow** fließen *(floß, ist geflossen)* 5
to **flow by** vorbeifließen *(floß vorbei, ist vorbeigeflossen) D*
flower die Blume,-n 10
flower shop das Blumengeschäft,-e 15
flower stand der Blumenstand,¨e 17
flu die Grippe,-n 18
flute die Flöte,-n 8
to **fly** fliegen *(flog, ist geflogen)* 11
to **fly along** mitfliegen *(flog mit, ist mitgeflogen)* 19
flying die Fliegerei 19
folk dance der Volkstanz,¨e 11

folk song das Volkslied,-er 11
to **follow** folgen 7
following folgend 14
food das Essen 8; die Verpflegung *D*
foot der Fuß,¨e 3; *on foot* zu Fuß 3
for für 3; seit *A*
forehead die Stirn,-en 11
foreign country (foreign countries) das Ausland 16
foreign language die Fremdsprache,-n 4
foreigner der Ausländer,- 10
foreman der Werkmeister,- 19
forenoon der Vormittag,-e 2
forest der Wald,¨er 7
to **forget** vergessen *(vergißt, vergaß, vergessen)* 11
fork die Gabel,-n 16
form die Form,-en 9
to **form** bilden 9; sich bilden 16
form (printed) das Formular,-e 18
formula die Formel,-n 4
fortress die Festung,-en 10
to **foul** foulen 14
fountain der Brunnen,- 10
four vier 1
fourteen vierzehn 2
France Frankreich 3
free frei 7
freeway die Autobahn,-en 11
French (language) Französisch 6
French fries die Pommes frites (pl.) 16
fresh frisch 12
Friday der Freitag,-e 2
friend der Freund,-e 1; der/die Bekannte,-n 12
friendly freundlich 17
friends (circle of) der Bekanntenkreis,-e 14
from von, aus 2
front: in front of vor 5; vorne 11
front seat der Vordersitz,-e 19
fruit das Obst 12; die Frucht,¨e 17
fruit pie die Obstschnitte,-n 13
fruit stand der Obststand,¨e, der Fruchtstand 17
full voll 3; satt (eating) 20
fun der Spaß 6; *Have fun!* Viel Spaß! 6; *It is fun.* Es macht Spaß. 8

further weiter 4

G

game das Spiel,-e 5
gangway der Landungssteg,-e 13
gap der Abstand,¨e 19
gas pedal das Gaspedal,-e 19
gas pump die Zapfsäule,-n *D*
gasoline das Benzin *D*
gate das Tor,-e 10
gate (flight) der Flugsteig,-e 11
to **gather** sich versammeln 7
gear der Gang,¨e 19; *to put in gear* den Gang einlegen 19
gearshift die Schaltung,-en 19
generation das Zeitalter 19
generous reichlich 16
genius der Schlaukopf 4
gentleman der Herr,-en 1
geography die Erdkunde 4
German deutsch 1; Deutsch (language) 4
German der/die Deutsche,-n 14
German Democratic Republic die Deutsche Demokratische Republik 3
Germany Deutschland 3
to **get** bekommen *(bekam, bekommen)* 2; holen 13; erhalten *(erhält, erhielt, erhalten)* 20
to **get dressed** sich anziehen *(zog an angezogen)* 12
to **get (hold of)** erwischen 17
to **get in(to)** einsteigen *(stieg ein, ist eingestiegen)* 2
to **get off** aussteigen *(stieg aus, ist ausgestiegen)* 10
to **get rid of** loswerden *(wird los, wurde los, ist losgeworden)* 18
to **get up** aufstehen *(stand auf, ist aufgestanden) A*
gigantic riesengroß 13; riesig 20
girl das Mädchen,- 1
girlfriend die Freundin,-nen 3
to **give** geben *(gibt, gab, gegeben)* 4
to **give (as a gift)** schenken 11
to **give back** zurückgeben *(gibt zurück, gab zurück, zurückgegeben)* 12
glad froh 2
gladly gern 4
glass das Glas,¨er 9
glove der Handschuh,-e 6

to **go** gehen *(ging, ist gegangen) 1;* fahren *(fährt, fuhr, ist gefahren) 3; to go into* gehen über *8*

to **go back** zurückgehen *(ging zurück, ist zurückgegangen) 6*

to **go inside** hineingehen *(ging hinein, ist hineingegangen) 7;* reingehen *(ging rein, ist reingegangen) 13*

to **go past** vorbeiführen *10*

goalie der Torwart,¨er *14*

goat die Ziege,-n *15*

gold das Gold *D*

gold gold *4*

golf das Golf *9*

good gut *1*

good-bye: to say good-bye sich verabschieden *11*

Good Friday Karfreitag *12*

goodness die Güte *7; My goodness!* Du meine Güte! *7*

goulash soup die Gulaschsuppe,-n *16*

grade (school) die Note,-n *4*

grain das Getreide *15*

gram das Gramm,-e *10*

granddaughter die Enkelin,-nen *5*

grandfather der Großvater,¨ *5*

grandmother die Großmutter,¨ *5*

grandparents die Großeltern (pl.) *5*

grandson der Enkel,- *5*

grandstand die Tribüne,-n *C*

grapes die Weintraube,-n *17;* die Traube,-n *20*

grass das Gras,¨er *16*

gravy die Soße,-n *A*

gray grau *6*

great prima *3;* phantastisch *9;* herrlich *13; to be great* klasse sein *5*

green grün *6*

to **greet** begrüßen *3*

greeting der Gruß,¨e *18*

groceries die Lebensmittel (pl.) *17*

grocery store das Lebensmittelgeschäft,-e *17*

groom der Bräutigam,-e *12*

ground floor das Erdgeschoß, -sse *15*

group die Gruppe,-n *B*

to **group** anordnen *14*

to **grow** anpflanzen *15;* wachsen *(wächst, wuchs, ist gewachsen) 16;* gedeihen *(gedieh, gediehen) 20*

to **guarantee** garantieren *20*

guest der Gast,¨e *16*

guitar die Gitarre,-n *A*

gymnasium die Turnhalle,-n *15*

H

hair das Haar,-e *11*

hair stylist der Friseur,-e; die Friseuse,-n *13*

half halb *3*

halftime die Halbzeit,-en *14*

hallway der Korridor,-e *12;* der Flur,-e *15*

ham der Schinken *A*

hand die Hand,¨e *11*

hand brake die Handbremse,-n *19*

to **hang** hängen *(hing, gehangen) 17*

to **hang out** aushängen *16*

to **happen** passieren *12;* geschehen *(geschieht, geschah, ist geschehen) 18*

happy froh *2;* glücklich *12; to be happy about* sich freuen über *16*

harbor der Hafen,¨ *13*

hard schwer *3*

hardly kaum *9*

to **harvest** ernten *20*

to **haul** schleppen *12*

to **have** haben *(hat, hatte, gehabt) 2*

to **have on** anhaben *(hat an, hatte an, angehabt) 6*

to **have to** müssen *(muß, mußte, gemußt) 5*

he er *1*

head (person) der Leiter,- *9;* **head (body)** der Kopf,¨e *11*

to **head (the ball)** köpfen *14*

headache die Kopfschmerzen (pl.) *18*

headlight der Scheinwerfer,- *19*

health: To your health! Zum Wohl! *16*

healthy gesund *18*

to **hear** hören *4*

hearty herzlich *8*

heat die Hitze *8; in this heat* bei der Hitze *8*

height die Höhe,-n *6*

Hello! Grüß dich!, Guten Tag! *1*

help die Hilfe *4*

to **help** helfen *(hilft, half, geholfen) 9;* bedienen *11; to help oneself* sich bedienen *17*

helpful hilfsbereit *17*

her ihr *A*

here hier *1*

to **hesitate** zögern *20*

Hi! Grüß dich!, Tag! *1*

high hoch *5*

highlight der Höhepunkt,-e *12*

high school die Oberschule,-n *15*

highway die Landstraße,-n *10*

hike die Wanderung,-en *16*

to **hike** wandern *6*

hiker der Wanderer,- *16*

hiking path der Wanderweg,-e *16*

hill der Hügel,- *10*

his sein *5*

hint der Hinweis,-e *18*

historic(al) historisch *7;* geschichtlich *10*

history die Geschichte *4*

hobby das Hobby,-s *14*

hockey das Hockey *9*

to **hold** halten *(hält, hielt, gehalten) 12*

holiday der Feiertag,-e *12*

home: at home zu Hause *2; to go home* nach Hause gehen *2; single family home* das Einfamilienhaus,¨er *15*

homework die Hausaufgabe,-n *5; to do homework* die Hausaufgaben machen *5*

hood die Motorhaube,-n *19*

to **hope** hoffen *6*

hopefully hoffentlich *9*

horse das Pferd,-e *8*

hose der Schlauch,¨e *D*

hospital das Krankenhaus,¨er *18*

hot heiß *7*

hot dog das Würstchen,- *14*

hotel das Hotel,-s *7*

hotel room das Hotelzimmer,- *18*

hotel sign das Hotelschild,-er *10*

hour die Stunde,-n *2*

hour: for hours stundenlang *D*

house das Haus,¨er *2; half-timbered house* das Fachwerkhaus,¨er *10; rooming house* das Wohnheim,-e *15*

how wie *1; How are you?* Wie geht's? *1; how many?* wie viele? *3; how much?* wieviel? *2*

however dagegen *20*

Hungary Ungarn *5*

hunger der Hunger *7*

hungry hungrig *A*

to **hurry** sich beeilen *3; Let's hurry.* Beeilen wir uns! *3; to be in a hurry* es eilig haben *16*

to **hurt** weh tun *18; It hurts me.* Es tut mir weh. *18*

husband der Ehemann,⸚er *12*

I

I ich *1*

ice das Eis *16*

ice cream das Eis *16*

ice cream parlor die Eisdiele,-n *2*

idea die Idee,-n *2*

ideal ideal *14*

identification (card) der Ausweis,-e *7*

if ob *8;* wenn *18;* falls *20*

ill krank *18*

to **illuminate** beleuchten *14*

to **imagine** vorstellen *10*

immediately gleich *1;* sofort *6*

impatient ungeduldig *4*

important wichtig *8*

improvement die Besserung,-en *18*

in in *1*

inadequate mangelhaft *4*

to **inaugurate** eröffnen *19*

to **include** einschließen *(schloß ein, eingeschlossen) 18*

including einschließlich *10*

to **increase** steigern *14*

incredible unglaublich *19*

to **indicate** andeuten *19*

individual einzeln *14*

industrial city die Industriestadt,⸚e *9*

industrious fleißig *4*

infected entzündet *18*

influence der Einfluß,⸚sse *16*

information die Information,-en *10;* die Auskunft,⸚e *13*

ingenious patent *20*

inhabitant der Einwohner,- *3*

inland lake der Binnensee,-n *20*

to **inquire about** sich erkundigen nach *18*

to **inspect** untersuchen, inspizieren *19*

to **install** installieren *19*

to **instruct** unterrichten *20*

instruction der Hinweis,-e *18*

intellectual geistig *20*

interest das Interesse,-n *A*

to **interest** interessieren *A*

interesting interessant *7*

international international *11*

to **interrupt** unterbrechen *(unterbricht, unterbrach, unterbrochen) 19*

intersection die Kreuzung,-en *19*

to **introduce** einführen *16*

to **invite** einladen *(lädt ein, lud ein, eingeladen) 11*

island die Insel,-n *8*

it es *1*

Italian Italienisch (language) *6*

Italy Italien *5*

item die Sache,-n *17*

J

jack der Wagenheber,- *19*

jam die Marmelade *A*

January der Januar *4*

jeans die Jeans (pl.) *6*

jet (airplane) das Düsenflugzeug,-e, der Jet,-s *19*

job der Beruf,-e *15*

to **join** sich anschließen *(schloß an, angeschlossen) 20*

joint gemeinsam *19*

to **jot down** notieren *9*

joy die Freude *20*

judge der Richter,- *9*

to **judge** urteilen *13*

juice der Saft,⸚e *20*

juicy saftig

July der Juli *4*

to **jump** springen *(sprang, ist gesprungen) 9*

June der Juni *4*

just nur *3;* eben *4;* gerade *10; just like/as* genauso wie *4*

K

to **keep** behalten *(behält, behielt, behalten) 12*

to **keep up** mithalten *(hält mit, hielt mit, mitgehalten) 15*

key der Schlüssel,- *15*

kilogram das Kilo,-s *17*

kilometer der Kilometer,- *3*

kindergarten der Kindergarten,⸚ *15*

king der König,-e *14*

kiosk der Kiosk,-e *2*

kitchen die Küche,-n *5*

knapsack der Rucksack,⸚e *11*

knife das Messer,- *16*

to **knit** stricken *A*

to **know (someone)** kennen *(kannte, gekannt) 1;* wissen *(weiß, wußte, gewußt) 3; to get to know* kennenlernen *B*

L

to **label** bezeichnen *10*

ladies' department die Damenabteilung,-en *6*

lady die Dame,-n *6*

lake der See,-n *5*

lamp die Lampe,-n *15*

to **land** landen *11*

landmark das Wahrzeichen,- *13*

landscape die Landschaft,-en *8*

language die Sprache,-n *6*

language lab das Sprachlabor,-s *4*

large groß *3*

last letzt- *8*

to **last** dauern *3*

late spät *2; How late is it?* Wie spät ist es? *2;* unpünktlich *5*

lawyer der Rechtsanwalt,⸚e *13*

to **lead** führen *10*

to **learn** lernen *4; to learn by heart* auswendig lernen *4*

least: at least wenigstens *6;* mindestens *9*

to **leave** verlassen *(verläßt, verließ, verlassen) A;* lassen *(läßt, ließ, gelassen) 12*

to **leave to** überlassen *(überläßt, überließ, überlassen) 20*

left links *7*

leg das Bein,-e *11*

legendary märchenhaft *10*

length die Länge,-n *5*

to **let** lassen *(läßt, ließ, gelassen) 13*

letter der Brief,-e *11;* das Schreiben *20; registered letter* das Einschreiben *14*

library die Bibliothek,-en *15*

license plate das Nummernschild,-er *19*

to **lie** liegen *(lag, gelegen) 3*

Liechtenstein Liechtenstein *5*

life das Leben *15*

to **lift** abheben *(hob ab, abgehoben) 14; to lift the receiver* den Hörer abheben *14*

light hell *16*

to **light up** beleuchten *14*

like wie *8*

to **like** gefallen *(gefällt, gefiel, gefallen) 6;* mögen *(mag, mochte, gemocht) 5; She likes it.* Es gefällt ihr. *6; to like to walk* gern gehen *4; Would you like to…?* Hast du Lust…? *2*

linesman der Linienrichter,- *14*

lion der Löwe,-n *15*

lip die Lippe,-n *11*

to **listen** hören *4;* zuhören *11*

to **listen to** sich anhören *11*

liter das Liter,- *10*

little wenig *4;* klein *10; a little* etwas *2*

to **live** wohnen *1;* leben *9; living* lebend *10*

lively reger *20*

living room das Wohnzimmer,- *5*

load die Ladung,-en *20*

local lokal *16*

located gelegen *18; to be located* liegen *(lag, gelegen) 3;* stehen *(stand, gestanden) 4;* sich befinden *(befand, befunden) 11*

long lange *3;* lang *9*

long-distance call das Ferngespräch,-e *14; to make a long-distance call* ein Ferngespräch führen *14*

to **look** sehen *(sieht, sah, gesehen) 3;* schauen *13; Look!* Seht mal! *4; to look at* sehen auf *4*

to **look around** sich umsehen *(sieht um, sah um, umgesehen) 19*

to **look at** sich ansehen *(sieht an, sah an, angesehen) B*

to **look back** zurücksehen *(sieht zurück, sah zurück, zurückgesehen) 16*

to **look down** hinabschauen *D*

to **look for** suchen *4*

to **look over** begutachten *6;* besichtigen *10*

loose locker *12*

to **loosen** lösen *19*

to **lose** verlieren *(verlor, verloren) 4*

to **love** lieben *17*

low niedrig *D*

luck das Glück *2; to be lucky* Glück haben *2; bad luck* das Pech *12*

luggage das Gepäck *3*

luggage cart der Koffer-Kuli,-s *3*

lunch das Mittagessen *A*

lunch time die Mittagszeit,-en *B*

Luxembourg Luxemburg *3*

luxury der Luxus *18*

M

magazine die Zeitschrift,-en *11*

mail die Post *14*

to **mail (to)** zuschicken *10*

to **mail (letter)** einwerfen *(wirft ein, warf ein, eingeworfen) 14*

mailbox der Briefkasten,- *7*

mail carrier (male) der Briefträger,- *14*

mainland das Festland,-er *8*

mainly hauptsächlich *14*

to **make** machen *1; to make it* es schaffen *9*

man der Mann,-er *9*

manner die Weise *15*

many viele *4*

map die Karte,-n *6*

marathon run der Marathonlauf,-e *9*

marble der Marmor *D*

March der März *4*

margarine die Margarine *17*

mark die Mark *2*

to **mark** markieren *13; well marked* gut markiert *13*

market der Markt,-e *7*

market day der Markttag,-e *7*

market square der Marktplatz,-e *7*

marriage die Heirat,-en *12*

marriage (license) bureau das Standesamt,-er *12*

marriage certificate die Heiratsurkunde,-n *12*

married verheiratet *12*

to **marvel at** bestaunen *11*

mathematics die Mathematik (Mathe) *4*

math problem die Matheaufgabe,-n *3*

matter die Angelegenheit,-en *15; What's the matter?* Was ist los? *2; That doesn't matter.* Das macht nichts. *17*

May der Mai *4*

may dürfen *(darf, durfte, gedurft) 5*

mayor der Bürgermeister,- *15*

meal das Essen *A;* die Mahlzeit, -en *10;* die Speise,-n *11; main meal* die Hauptmahlzeit,-en *16*

to **mean** meinen *13;* bedeuten *18*

meaning die Bedeutung,-en *4*

meantime: in the meantime mittlerweile *20*

meanwhile unterdessen *5*

to **measure** messen *(mißt, maß, gemessen) 18*

meat das Fleisch *16; ground meat* Gehacktes *17; meats* die Fleischwaren *(pl.) 17*

mechanic der Mechaniker,- *13*

medicine die Medizin *18*

medieval mittelalterlich *10*

to **meet** sich treffen *(trifft, traf, getroffen) B;* sich versammeln *7*

meeting place der Treffpunkt,-e *15*

memorial das Mahnmal *7;* das Denkmal,-er *13*

to **memorize** auswendig lernen *4*

mental geistig *20*

to **mention** erwähnen *18*

menu die Speisekarte,-n *16; daily menu* das Tagesgericht, -e *16*

to **merge** sich zusammenschließen *(schloß zusammen, zusammengeschlossen) 15*

meter der Meter,- *10*

metropolis die Großstadt,-e *16*

middle die Mitte,-n *4*

Middle Ages das Mittelalter *10*

milk die Milch *A*

million die Million,-en *3*

mineral water das Mineralwasser *16*

mining college die Bergakademie *15*

minus minus *2*

minute die Minute,-n *2*

mirror: inside mirror der Innenspiegel,- *19*

misgiving das Bedenken *18*

Miss das Fräulein,- *1*

to **miss** verpassen *11*

model das Modell,-e *15*

modern modern *B*

mom die Mutti,-s *20*

moment der Moment,-e *3*

Monday der Montag *2*

money das Geld *2*

monkey der Affe,-n *15*

month der Monat,-e *2*

monument das Denkmal,-̈er *13*

mood die Stimmung,-en *11;* die Laune,-n *16; to be in a good mood* guter Laune sein *16*

more than mehr als *5*

morning der Morgen *2; this morning* heute morgen *2*

most die meisten *7*

mostly meistens *5*

mother die Mutter,-̈ *5*

Mother's Day der Muttertag *12*

mother tongue die Muttersprache,-n *5*

motor boat das Motorboot,-e, die Barkasse,-n *13*

motorcycle das Motorrad,-̈er *7*

mountain der Berg,-e *5*

mountainous gebirgig *13*

mountain train die Bergbahn, -en *12*

mouth der Mund,-̈er *10*

to **move** sich bewegen *20*

to **move forward** vorschieben *(schob vor, vorgeschoben) 20*

movie der Film,-e *5*

movie theater das Kino,-s *5*

Mr. der Herr,-en *1*

Mrs. die Frau,-en *1*

much viel *2*

museum das Museum,-seen *9*

mushroom der Champignon,-s *16*

music die Musik *4*

music festival das Musikfest,-e *5*

music group die Musikgruppe, -n *12*

musical instrument das Musikinstrument,-e *8*

musician der Musiker,- *11*

must müssen *(muß, mußte, gemußt) 5*

my mein *1*

N

name der Name,-n *1; What's your name?* Wie heißt du? *1; first name* der Vorname,-n *14*

to **name** nennen *(nannte, genannt) 19; to be named* heißen *(hieß, geheißen) 1*

namely nämlich *8*

nap das Schläfchen *to take a nap* ein Schläfchen machen *20*

napkin die Serviette,-n *16*

narrow eng *13*

national flag die Nationalfahne, -n *4*

natural(ly) natürlich *4*

nearby in der Nähe *2*

neatness die Sauberkeit *15*

neck der Hals,-̈e *11*

need der Bedarf *15*

to **need** brauchen *2*

neighbor (female) die Nachbarin,-nen *D*

neighborhood die Nachbarschaft,-en *16*

neighboring country Nachbarland,-̈er *3*

nervous nervös *20*

Netherlands die Niederlande *3*

nevertheless trotzdem *13*

new neu *4*

news die Nachrichten (pl.) *A*

newspaper die Zeitung,-en *5*

New Year's Day das Neujahr *12*

next nächst *4; next to* neben *10; next to it* daneben *13*

night stand der Nachttisch,-e *20*

nine neun *1*

nineteen neunzehn *2*

no nein *1;* kein *2; no time* keine Zeit *2*

nobody niemand *9*

noon der Mittag,-e *2*

noon time die Mittagszeit,-en *B*

north der Norden *3*

North Sea die Nordsee *6*

nose die Nase,-n *11*

not nicht *1; not at all* gar nicht *4*

note (money) der Schein,-e *17*

notebook das Heft,-e *8*

normal normal *18*

northern nördlich *11*

nothing nichts *12*

to **notice** merken *16*

November der November *4*

now jetzt *1*

number die Nummer,- *9;* die Anzahl *19*

numerous zahlreich *11*

nurse die Krankenschwester,-, *nurse (male)* der Krankenpfleger,- *13*

O

to **observe** beobachten *16*

occupied besetzt, beschäftigt *C; to be occupied with* sich beschäftigen mit *20*

to **occur** geschehen *(geschieht, geschah, ist geschehen) 18*

October der Oktober *4*

of von *2*

to **offer** bieten *(bot, geboten) 7;* anbieten *(bot an, angeboten) 17*

office das Büro,-s *4*

official offiziell *13*

often oft *2;* oftmals *8*

oh ach *18*

oil das Öl *D*

oil level der Ölstand *D*

ointment die Salbe,-n *18*

O.K. Gut! *1;* klar *3*

old alt *4*

on auf *2;* an *8*

once einmal *3; once again* wieder einmal *3; one more time* noch einmal *5; once more* nochmal *5; once in a while* ab und zu *16*

one eins *1;* man *3*

one-way (ticket) einfach *3*

onion die Zwiebel,-n *17*

only nur *3;* erst *5*

open geöffnet *B;* offen *17; The store is open.* Das Geschäft ist geöffnet. *B*

to **open** aufmachen *11;* öffnen *16*

opponent der Gegner,- *14*

or oder *5*

orange orange *6*

orange die Apfelsine,-n *17*

order die Ordnung,-en *10*

to **order** bestellen *B*

organization die Organisation, -en *16*

to **organize** gründen *15;* aufstellen *20*

organizer der Organisator,-en *16*

to **originate (river)** entspringen *(entsprang, ist entsprungen) 8*

other andere *4*

otherwise sonst *9*

our unser *5*

out of aus *2*

outing der Ausflug,-̈e *C*

outside außerhalb *5;* ins Freie *7;* im Freien *10;* draußen *13*

outside mirror der Außenspiegel,- *19*

over über *3*

to **overlook** überblicken *10*

overnight: to stay overnight übernachten *7*

own eigen *13*

to **own** besitzen *(besaß, besessen)* *15*

owner der Besitzer,- (male), die Besitzerin,-nen (female) *8*

P

pace das Tempo,-s *14*

to **pack** packen *11;* verpacken *20*

package das Paket,-e *11;* die Packung,-en *17*

package counter der Paketschalter,- *14*

packet das Päckchen,- *18*

page die Seite,-n *4*

pail der Eimer,- *20*

pain der Schmerz,-en *18*

painting das Gemälde,-n *7*

pair das Paar,-e *6*

pants die Hose,-n *6*

paper das Papier *8; piece of paper* der Zettel,- *14*

paradise das Paradies,-e *6*

parcel das Päckchen,-, die Sendung,-en *14*

parents die Eltern (pl.) *5*

park der Park,-s *12*

to **park** parken *6*

parking lot der Parkplatz,¨e *6*

parking meter die Parkuhr,-en *6*

part der Teil,-e *5;* die Rolle,-n *C; for the most part* zum größten Teil *5*

participant der Teilnehmer,- *9*

to **participate** mitmachen *9;* teilnehmen *(nimmt teil, nahm teil, teilgenommen) 20*

partly zum Teil *8*

parts department das Ersatzlager,- *19*

party die Party,-s *8*

to **pass (time)** vergehen *(verging, ist vergangen) C; The time passes.* Die Zeit vergeht. *C*

passenger der Passagier,-e *19*

passport der Paß,¨sse *6;* der Reisepaß,¨sse *11*

passport inspection die Paßkontrolle,-n *11*

patience die Geduld *18*

patient der Patient,-en *18*

patient(ly) geduldig *12*

to **pay** bezahlen *6;* zahlen *15*

pea die Erbse,-n *A; pea soup* die Erbsensuppe,-n *20*

peace die Ruhe *3*

peaceful friedlich *20*

peach der Pfirsich,-e *17*

peanut die Erdnuß,¨sse *17*

pear die Birne,-n *17*

pedestrian der Fußgänger,- *10*

pedestrian crossing der Fußgängerüberweg,-e *19*

pedestrian underpass die Fußgängerunterführung,-en *19*

pencil der Bleistift,-e *8*

pen pal der Brieffreund,-e; die Brieffreundin,-nen *11*

Pentecost Pfingsten *12*

people die Leute (pl.) *7*

per pro *10*

per cent das Prozent,-e *9*

to **perform** vorführen *10;* aufführen *20*

performance die Vorstellung,-en *5;* die Leistung,-en *9*

perhaps vielleicht *4*

permitted: to be permitted to dürfen *(darf, durfte, gedurft) 5*

person der Mensch,-en *6;* die Person,-en *7; in person* persönlich

personal persönlich *17*

to **persuade** überreden *16*

to **pet** streicheln *15*

pharmacist der Apotheker,- *13*

pharmacy die Apotheke,-n *18*

phone book das Telefonbuch,¨er *14*

phone call das Telefongespräch,-e *14; to make a phone call* ein Telefongespräch führen *14*

photo das Foto,-s *11;* die Aufnahme,-n *12*

photo album das Fotoalbum,-ben *B*

to **photograph** fotografieren *B*

physical körperlich *20*

physics die Physik *4*

piano das Klavier,-e *8*

picnic area der Picknickplatz,¨e *20*

picture das Bild,-er *11;* die Aufnahme,-n *12; to take pictures* Aufnahmen machen *12;* knipsen *15*

picture postcard die Ansichtskarte,-n *13*

piece das Stück,-e *13*

pig das Schwein,-e *15*

pigeon die Taube,-n *13*

pill die Tablette,-n *18*

pillar die Säule,-n *15*

pillow das Kopfkissen,- *15*

pilot der Pilot,-en *11*

pink rosa *6*

place der Platz,¨e *3;* der Ort,-e *10;* die Stelle,-n *9*

to **place** stellen *A;* setzen, legen *11*

to **plan** vorhaben *(hat vor, hatte vor, vorgehabt) 6;* planen *B;* aufstellen *20*

plant die Pflanze,-n *20*

to **plant** anpflanzen *15*

plate der Teller,- *16*

platform der Bahnsteig,-e *8*

to **play** spielen *5*

to **play around** herumspielen *20*

player der Spieler,- *14*

playground der Spielplatz,¨e *12*

pleasant gemütlich *7*

pleasure die Lust *2;* der Genuß,¨sse *16;* die Freude *20*

plentiful reichlich *16*

plum die Pflaume,-n *17*

plus plus *1*

to **point** deuten *13*

to **point to** weisen auf *14*

pole der Mast,-en *12*

police die Polizei *9*

policeman der Polizist,-en *13*

polish das Poliermittel,- *17*

political politisch *7*

popular beliebt *5*

population die Bevölkerung-en *9*

pork: roast pork der Schweinebraten *15*

pork tenderloin das Schweinefilet,-s *16*

to **possess** besitzen *(besaß, besessen) 15*

possibility die Möglichkeit,-en *7*

possible möglich *2; That's possible.* Das geht. *7*

post die Säule,-n *15*

to **post** anschlagen *(schlägt an, schlug an, angeschlagen) 15*

postage das Porto,-s *14*

postal box das Brieffach,¨er *15*

postcard die Postkarte,-n *14*

post office die Post *14;* das Postamt,¨er *13*

post office box das Postfach,¨er *14*

potato die Kartoffel,-n *A; boiled potato* die Salzkartoffel,-n *fried potato* die Bratkartoffel,-n *16*

potato salad der Kartoffelsalat *8*

pound das Pfund *10*

to **pour** kippen *20;* gießen *(goß, gegossen) D*

practical praktisch *4*

practice die Übung,-en *4; Practice makes perfect.* Übung macht den Meister! *4*

to **practice** üben *4*

to **praise** loben *16*

to **prepare (a meal)** zubereiten *7;* bereiten *14;* vorbereiten *20*

prescription das Rezept,-e *18*

present das Geschenk,-e *8*

to **preserve** bewahren *10*

press die Presse,-n *20*

to **press** pressen *20*

pretzel die Brezel,-n *16*

previous vorhergehend *20*

price der Preis,-e *6*

primarily hauptsächlich *14*

prince der Fürst,-en *10*

principality das Fürstentum,ˮer *13*

printed matter die Drucksache, -n *14*

private persönlich *17*

problem die Aufgabe,-n *4;* das Problem,-e *20*

to **produce** produzieren *15*

product die Ware,-n *6*

profession der Beruf,-e *15*

program das Programm,-e *A*

to **promise** versprechen *(verspricht, versprach, versprochen) 19*

propeller (ship) die Schraube,-n *13*

proud stolz *12*

to **prove** sich herausstellen *12*

to **provide** versorgen *10*

to **provide for** sorgen für *11*

pudding der Pudding *16*

pullover der Pullover,- *5*

to **pull up** hochziehen *(zog hoch, hochgezogen) 12*

pulse der Puls,-e *18*

to **pump** pumpen *D*

punctual pünktlich *2*

pupil der Schüler,- *4*

purchase der Einkauf,ˮe *17*

purse die Handtasche,-n *6*

to **push** schieben *(schob, geschoben) 19*

to **push in** einschieben *(schob ein, eingeschoben) 19*

to **push off** abschieben *(schob ab, abgeschoben) 20*

to **put** stellen *A;* setzen, legen *11*

to **put on (clothes)** anziehen *(zog an, angezogen) 6;* to put on *(records)* auflegen *8*

to **put together** zusammensetzen *12*

to **put up** anschlagen *(schlägt an, schlug an, angeschlagen) 15;* aufstellen *19*

Q

quality die Qualität,-en *20*

quarter das Viertel,- *3; It's a quarter after eight.* Es ist Viertel nach acht. *3*

question die Frage,-n *A*

quick(ly) schnell *2*

quiet ruhig *4*

quite ganz *3;* ziemlich *11*

R

radio das Radio,-s *15*

rain der Regen *12*

to **rain** regnen *7*

to **raise (animals)** züchten *15*

rate: at any rate allerdings *15*

rather lieber *5;* ziemlich *11*

to **reach** erreichen *6;* reichen *20*

to **reach into** hineinreichen *8*

to **read** lesen *(liest, las, gelesen) 4*

to **read (off)** ablesen *(liest ab, las ab, abgelesen) D*

to **read through** durchlesen *(liest durch, las durch, durchgelesen) 20*

reading room der Lesesaal,-säle *15*

ready fertig *5;* startbereit *12*

really wirklich *4;* richtig *10*

reason der Grund,ˮe *20; for this reason* aus diesem Grund *20*

reasonable preiswert *6;* günstig *10*

receipt die Quittung,-en *14*

to **receive** bekommen *(bekam, bekommen) 2;* erhalten *(erhält, erhielt, erhalten) 20*

receiver der Empfänger,- *14; receiver (phone)* der Hörer,- *14*

receptionist die Sprechstundenhilfe,-n *18*

to **recognize (each other)** sich erkennen *(erkannte, erkannt) 11*

to **recommend** empfehlen *(empfiehlt, empfahl, empfohlen) 17*

record die Schallplatte,-n *8*

recorder die Blockflöte,-n *9*

record player der Plattenspieler,- *15*

red rot *4*

Red Cross das Rote Kreuz *9*

referee der Schiedsrichter *14*

to **register** registrieren *17*

registration form das Anmeldeformular,-e *7*

relative der Verwandte,-n *12*

to **relax** ausruhen *14*

relaxation die Erholung,-en *20*

to **release (brake)** lösen *19*

to **remain** bleiben *(blieb, ist geblieben) 2*

remaining übrig *19*

to **remember** denken an *(dachte an, gedacht an) 14*

to **remind of** erinnern an *10*

to **renovate** renovieren *7*

to **rent** vermieten *18;* mieten *20*

repair die Reparatur,-en *19*

to **repair** reparieren *19*

repair shop die Werkstatt,ˮen *19*

to **repeat** wiederholen *A*

to **reply** erwidern *18*

representative der Abgeordnete,-n *7*

republic die Republik,-en *5*

resident der Bewohner,- *15*

resort das Erholungsheim,-e *20*

rest die Rast,-en *10;* der Rest,-e *12; to take a rest* eine Rast machen *10*

to **rest** ausruhen *14*

restaurant das Restaurant,-s *7;* das Gasthaus,ˮer *11;* die Gaststätte,-n *15*

result das Ergebnis,-se *9; final result* das Endergebnis,-se *9*

to **return** zurückgeben *(gibt zurück, gab zurück, zurückgegeben) 12*

review die Überprüfung *20*
rice der Reis *20*
to **ride (on animal)** reiten *(ritt, ist geritten) C*
right rechts *10; That's all right with me.* Das ist mir recht. *1; You're right.* Du hast recht. *3; That's right.* Das stimmt. *7; the right change* das passende Geld *17*
right away gleich *1;* sofort *6*
right of way die Vorfahrt *19*
to **ring (bell)** klingeln *4*
ripe reif *17*
river der Fluß, ̈sse *5*
road die Fahrbahn,-en *19*
rock der Stein,-e *16*
rod die Stange,-n *19*
role die Rolle,-n *C*
roll (hard) das Brötchen,- *16*
to **roll** rollen *11*
roof das Dach, ̈er *19*
room das Zimmer,- *2;* der Raum, ̈e *15*
room key der Zimmerschlüssel,- *7*
rooster der Hahn, ̈e *13*
rope die Leine,-n, die Schur, ̈e *12*
row die Reihe,-n *6; It's his turn.* Er ist an der Reihe. *6*
to **row around** herumrudern *20*
ruler das Lineal,-e *8*
to **run** laufen *(läuft, lief, ist gelaufen) 5*
to **run around** herumlaufen *(läuft herum, lief herum, ist herumgelaufen) 9*
to **run towards** entgegenlaufen *(läuft entgegen, lief entgegen, ist entgegengelaufen) 9*
runner der Läufer,- *9*

S

safe sicher *8*
safety belt der Sicherheitsgurt,-e *19*
sail das Segel,- *12*
salami die Salami,- *17*
salat plate der Salatteller,- *16*
sale der Verkauf, ̈e *20*
sales clerk (female) die Verkäuferin,-nen *5; sales clerk (male)* der Verkäufer,- *13*

the **same** dasselbe *7;* derselbe *18*
sand der Sand *20*
sandwiches belegte Brote *16; a sandwich* ein belegtes Brot *16*
satisfactory befriedigend *4*
satisfied zufrieden *17*
Saturday der Sonnabend *2;* der Samstag *2*
saucer die Untertasse,-n *16*
sauerbraten der Sauerbraten,- *16*
sausage die Wurst, ̈e *A*
to **save** sparen *B*
savings account das Sparkonto, -ten *14*
to **say** sagen *2*
scale die Waage,-n *14*
schedule der Fahrplan, ̈e *3; daily schedule* der Tagesplan, ̈e *20*
scheduled planmäßig *19*
school die Schule,-n *2*
school bag die Schultasche,-n *8*
school patrol der Schülerlotse,-n *19*
score das Ergebnis,-se *14*
sea das Meer,-e *20*
seal die Robbe,-n *15*
season die Jahreszeit,-en *4*
seat der Platz, ̈e *3;* der Sitzplatz, ̈e *8*
second die Sekunde,-n *2*
secretary (male) der Sekretär,-e *13*
security die Sicherheit *19*
security check die Sicherheitsüberprüfung,-en *11*
to **see** sehen *(sieht, sah, gesehen) 3; Let's see…* Mal sehen… *3; See you!* Tschüs! *2*
to **see again** wiedersehen *(sieht wieder, sah wieder, wiedergesehen) 11*
to **select** auswählen *B;* aussuchen *11*
selection die Auswahl *6;* die Wahl,-en *16*
to **send** schicken *13*
sensible vernünftig *18*
separate getrennt *20; under separate cover* mit getrennter Post *20*
September der September *4*
to **serve** dienen *15;* servieren *16*
service die Bedienung *17*
service station die Tankstelle,-n *D*

service station attendant der Tankwarte,-e *D*
to **set** setzen *11*
to **set up** gründen *15*
seven sieben *1*
seventeen siebzehn *2*
several einige *7;* mehrere *13*
severe stark *18*
shape die Form,-en *9*
to **shave (oneself)** sich rasieren *11*
she sie *1*
sheep das Schaf,-e *15*
sheet der Bogen,- *17*
shelf das Regal,-e *15*
shift (gear) die Schaltung,-en *19*
to **shine** scheinen *(schien, geschienen) 7*
ship das Schiff,-e *7*
shipment die Sendung,-en *14*
shirt das Hemd,-en *6*
shoe der Schuh,-e *6*
to **shoot** schießen *(schoß, geschossen) 14*
to **shop** einkaufen *5; to go shopping* einkaufen gehen *5*
shopping das Einkaufen *11; to do some shopping* Besorgungen machen *14*
shopping bag die Einkaufstasche,-n *11*
shopping basket der Einkaufskorb, ̈e *17*
shopping center das Verkaufszentrum,-tren *16*
shopping center das Einkaufszentrum,-tren *15*
short(ly) kurz *A*
shot der Schuß, ̈sse *14*
should sollen *(soll, sollte, gesollt) 5*
shoulder die Schulter,-n *11*
shovel die Schaufel,-n *20*
show die Vorstellung,-en *5*
to **show** zeigen *3;* vorzeigen *11*
to **shower** sich duschen *11*
shy scheu *20*
siblings die Geschwister (pl.) *5*
sick krank *18*
side die Seite,-n *7*
sight(s) die Sehenswürdigkeit, -en *7*
sign das Schild,-er *7;* das Zeichen,- *9*
to **sign** unterschreiben *(unterschrieb, unterschrieben) 12*
signal das Zeichen,- *9*
significance die Bedeutung,-en *4*

to **signify** bedeuten *18*
silence die Ruhe *3*
similar ähnlich *15*
simple einfach *3*
since seit *A;* seitdem *18*
sincere herzlich *8; sincerely* mit
freundlichen Grüßen *18*
to **sing** singen *(sang, gesungen) B*
single einzeln *14*
sister die Schwester,-n *5*
to **sit** sitzen *(saß, gesessen) 4*
to **sit down** sich setzen *11;* sich
hinsetzen *16*
to **sit out** aussetzen *8*
to **sit together** beisammensitzen
*(saß beisammen,
beisammengesessen) 11;*
zusammensitzen *(saß
zusammen,
zusammengesessen) 15*
six sechs *1*
sixteen sechzehn *2*
size die Größe,-n *17*
to **skate** Schlittschuh laufen *9*
ski der Ski,-er *14*
to **ski** Ski laufen *9*
skirt der Rock,¨e *6*
sky der Himmel *10*
to **sleep** schlafen *(schläft, schlief,
geschlafen) 11*
slice die Scheibe,-n *17*
slip (of paper) der Abschnitt,-e
6
slow(ly) langsam *A*
small klein *10*
smart klug *3*
snack bar die Imbißstube,-n *B*
snake die Schlange,-n *15*
snow der Schnee *14*
to **snow** schneien *7*
so so *3*
so-called sogenannt *12*
soccer der Fußball,¨e *7*
soccer fan der Fußballfan,-s *14*
soccer field der Fußballplatz,¨e
14
soccer game das Fußballspiel,-e
14
sock die Socke,-n *6*
sofa das Sofa,-s *15*
soft drink die Limonade,-n *9*
to **solve** lösen *4*
some etwas *2;* ein paar *3*
something irgendetwas *20*
sometimes manchmal *4*
soap die Seife,-n *15*
son der Sohn,¨e *5*
soon bald *2; as soon as* sobald *9*

to **sound** klingen *(klang,
geklungen) 10*
soup die Suppe,-n *16; soup of
the day* die Tagessuppe,-n *16*
soupspoon der Suppenlöffel,- *16*
south der Süden *3*
South America Südamerika *19*
South American
südamerikanisch *8*
southern südlich *20*
spark plug die Zündkerze,-n *19*
to **speak** sprechen *(spricht, sprach,
gesprochen) 2*
to **specialize in** sich spezialisieren
auf *17*
special besonders *4;* speziell *13;*
die Spezialität,-en *13*
special offer das
Sonderangebot,-e *10*
specialty die Spezialität,-en *13*
specialty store das
Spezialgeschäft,-e *13*
specified: to be specified
bestimmt sein *20*
spectator der Zuschauer,- *9*
speedy eilig *16*
to **spend (money)** ausgeben *(gibt
aus, gab aus, ausgegeben)
16*
spinach der Spinat,-e *16*
splendid herrlich *13*
sport der Sport *4; kind of sport*
die Sportart,-en *9*
sports department die
Sportabteilung,-en *17*
sports show die Sportschau *14*
spot die Stelle,-n *9*
to **spray** spritzen *13*
spring der Frühling,-e *4*
square das Quadrat,-e *20*
stadium das Stadion,-dien *14*
to **stall (motor)** streiken *19*
stamp die Briefmarke,-n *13*
to **stamp** stempeln *7*
stamp automat der
Briefmarkenautomat,-en *7*
stand der Stand,¨e *16*
to **stand** stehen *(stand, gestanden)
4*
standing room der Stehplatz,¨e
14
start der Start,-s *9*
to **start** starten *9;* losgehen *(ging
los, ist losgegangen) 11;*
anfangen *(fängt an, fing an,
angefangen) 15; to start an
event* eröffnen *19*
starting signal das Startsignal,-e *9*

to **start running** loslaufen *(läuft
los, lief los, ist losgelaufen) 9*
state der Staat,-en *3*
statement die Angabe,-n *14*
station die Station,-en *10;* der
Bahnhof,¨e *3*
stationary die Schreibwaren
(pl.) *17*
to **stay** bleiben *(blieb, ist
geblieben) 2*
steering wheel das Steuerrad,¨er
19
step der Schritt,-e *11*
stewed fruit das Kompott,-e *16*
still noch *2*
stocking der Strumpf,¨e *6*
stomach der Bauch,¨e *18*
stomachache die
Bauchschmerzen (pl.) *18*
stone der Stein,-e *16*
stop (bus or streetcar) die
Haltestelle,-n *3*
to **stop** anhalten *(hält an, hielt an,
angehalten) 10;* halten *(hält,
gehalten) 14*
store das Geschäft,-e *6;* der
Laden,¨ *17*
to **store** lagern *20*
strawberry die Erdbeere,-n *17;
strawberry ice cream* das
Erdbeereis *C*
stream die Strömung,-en *D*
street die Straße,-n *4; main
street* die Hauptstraße,-n *11;*
die Vorfahrtsstraße,-n *19*
streetcar die Straßenbahn,-en *3*
street number die
Hausnummer,-n *14*
streetcar stop die
Straßenbahnhaltestelle,-n *19*
street traffic der Straßenverkehr
16
strenuous anstrengend *D*
stretch die Strecke,¨n *8*
to **stretch** spannen *12;* sich
erstrecken *20*
string die Schnur,-en *12*
stroke streicheln *15*
to **stroll** spazierengehen *(ging
spazieren, ist
spazierengegangen) 12*
strong stark *16*
structure der Bau,-ten *12*
student der Schüler,- (through
high school) *4;* der Student,
-en (at university) *4*
studies das Studium,-dien *4*
to **study (at university)** studieren *4*

stupid blöd *12*

subject (school) das Fach,⁀er *4; subject (area)* das Fachgebiet,-e *15*

suburb der Vorort,-e *3*

subway die U-Bahn,-en *19*

to **succeed** gelingen *(gelang, ist gelungen) 19*

suddenly plötzlich *9*

sufficient ausreichend *4;* genug *15*

sugar beet die Zuckerrübe,-n *15*

to **suggest** vorschlagen *(schlägt vor, schlug vor, vorgeschlagen) 13;* andeuten *19*

suggestion der Vorschlag,⁀e *4*

suit der Anzug,⁀e *6*

suitable passend *17;* geeignet *18*

suitcase der Koffer,- *3*

summer der Sommer,- *4*

sun die Sonne *7*

Sunday der Sonntag *2; on Sundays* sonntags *8*

sunny sonnig *10*

super highway die Autobahn,-en *11*

supermarket (DDR) die HO-Kaufhalle,-n *11*

supper das Abendbrot *5;* das Abendessen *11*

to **supply** versorgen *10*

supposed: to be supposed to sollen *(soll, sollte, gesollt) 5*

surely sicherlich *11*

to **surf** surfen *12; to go surfing* surfen gehen *12*

surfboard das Surfbrett,-er *12*

to **surpass** übertreffen *(übertrifft, übertraf, übertroffen) 9*

surprise die Überraschung,-en *14*

to **surround** umgeben *(umgibt, umgab, umgeben) 10*

surrounding die Umgebung,-en *5*

to **swallow** schlucken *18*

swan der Schwan,⁀e *20*

sweets die Süßigkeiten (pl.) *7*

to **swim** schwimmen *(schwamm, ist geschwommen) 9*

swimming stuff die Badesachen (pl.) *12*

to **swing** schwingen *(schwang, geschwungen) 14*

Switzerland die Schweiz *3*

symbol das Symbol,-e *7*

T

table der Tisch,-e *5; to set the table* den Tisch decken *A*

tablet die Tablette,-n *18*

table tennis das Tischtennis *7*

to **take** nehmen *(nimmt, nahm, genommen) 13; to take (time)* dauern *3; taken* besetzt *C*

to **take along** mitnehmen *(nimmt mit, nahm mit, mitgenommen) 10*

to **take (time) off** freinehmen *(nimmt frei, nahm frei, freigenommen) 13*

to **take off (plane)** abfliegen *(flog ab, ist abgeflogen) 11*

to **take place** stattfinden *(fand statt, stattgefunden) 9*

talk das Gespräch,⁀e *14*

to **talk** sprechen *(spricht, sprach, gesprochen) 2;* sich unterhalten *(unterhält, unterhielt, unterhalten) 16; to talk about* sprechen über *2*

to **talk into** überreden *16; to be talked into* sich überreden lassen *16; to talk him into that* ihn dazu überreden *16*

tank der Tank,-s *20*

to **tank** tanken *D*

taste der Geschmack,⁀e *8*

to **taste** schmecken *B*

tea der Tee *A*

teacher (male) der Lehrer,- *7; teacher (female)* die Lehrerin,-nen *13*

team die Mannschaft,-en *9*

to **tear down** abreißen *(riß ab, abgerissen) 15*

teaspoon der Teelöffel,- *16*

technician der Techniker,- *14*

telegram das Telegramm,-e *14*

telephone das Telefon,-e *2*

telephone booth die Telefonzelle,-n *7*

television: on television im Fernsehen *A*

television set der Fernsehapparat,-e *7*

television tower der Fernsehturm,⁀e *7*

to **tell** erzählen *11*

temperature die Temparatur,-en *18*

tempo das Tempo,-s *14*

ten zehn *1*

tenant der Bewohner,- *15*

tennis das Tennis *9*

tent das Zelt,-e *18*

terrible furchtbar *18*

terrific toll *5*

test die Arbeit,-en *2; to take a test* eine Arbeit schreiben *2*

tester der Prüfer,- *20*

than als *8*

to **thank** sich bedanken *14;* danken *16*

thanks der Dank *10;* danke *1; Danke schön. Many thanks.* Vielen Dank *10*

that das *1;* daß *6; after that* danach; *so that* damit *18*

the der, die, das *1*

theater das Theater,- *7; open-air theater* die Freilichtbühne,-n *20*

their ihr *4*

then dann *2;* damalig *19*

there da *1;* dort *3;* dorthin *5; over there* da drüben *1; there is (are)* es gibt *4*

therefore deshalb *6*

they sie *1;* man *3*

thick dick *13*

thing die Sache,-n *17*

to **think** denken *7; (dachte, gedacht) 7;* meinen *13*

to **think about** denken an *(dachte an, gedacht an) 14*

thirst der Durst *14; to be thirsty* Durst haben *14*

thirsty durstig *15*

thirteen dreizehn *2*

this dieser *3*

thorough gründlich *4*

though allerdings *15*

thousand tausend *10*

three drei *1*

through durch *5*

Thursday Donnerstag *2*

ticket die Fahrkarte,-n *3;* die Karte,-n *5*

tide: low tide die Ebbe,-n *8*

tie die Krawatte,-n *6*

tied (game) unentschieden *14*

tiger der Tiger,- *15*

tight straff *12*

to **tighten** spannen *12*
time die Zeit,-en *2; time(s)* das Mal,-e *9; What time is it?* Wieviel Uhr ist es? *9;* Wie spät ist es? *2; on time* pünktlich *2; this time* diesmal *14; of that time* damalig *19*
times mal *3*
timid scheu *20*
tip das Trinkgeld,-er *16*
tire der Reifen,- *19*
tired müde *A*
title der Titel,-, die Überschrift, -en *15*
to auf, zu *2;* nach *3;* um *7*
today heute *2; today's* heutig *20*
together zusammen *2;* gemeinsam *15;*
toilet die Toilette,-n *15*
toiletry der Toilettenartikel,- *15*
tomato die Tomate,-n *A*
tomato salad der Tomatensalat, -e *16*
tomato soup die Tomatensuppe, -n *16*
tomorrow morgen *2*
tonight heute abend *2*
tonsil die Mandel,-n *18*
tonsilitis die Mandelentzündung *18*
too auch *1;* zu *2*
tool das Werkzeug,-e.*19*
tooth der Zahn,ʺe *11*
toothache die Zahnschmerzen (pl.) *18*
toothbrush die Zahnbürste,-n *15*
toothpaste die Zahnpasta,-sten *15*
top die Spitze,-n *9; to be on top* an der Spitze sein *9; on top* oben *10*
torte die Torte,-n *13*
total gesamt *19*
to **touch** anfassen *15;* greifen an *18*
tourist der Tourist,-en *5*
tourist office das Verkehrsbüro, -s *13*
to **tow (away)** abschleppen *19*
tower der Turm,ʺe *7*
town der Ort,-e *10;* das Dorf,ʺer *15;* die Ortschaft,-en *20; old town* die Altstadt *12*
toys die Spielwaren (pl.) *17*
track das Gleis,-e *3*
tractor der Traktor,-en *20*

trade fair die Messe,-n *9*
tradition die Tradition,-n *16*
traffic der Verkehr *4;* der Betrieb *17*
traffic sign das Verkehrsschild, -er *10*
train der Zug,ʺe *3; city train* die S-Bahn,-en *2;* die Bahn,-en *10*
to **train** trainieren *9*
to **transfer** umsteigen *(stieg um, ist umgestiegen) 10*
to **translate** übersetzen *11*
travel agency das Reisebüro,-s *10*
traveler der Reisende,-n *18*
traveler's check der Reisescheck,-s *6*
trip die Reise,-n *4;* die Fahrt,-en *10; round trip* hin und zurück *3;* der Ausflug,ʺe *C*
trouble die Beschwerde,-n, die Bemühung,-en *18;* trouble (car) die Panne,-n; *to have trouble* Beschwerden haben *18*
trout die Forelle,-n *16*
truck der Lastwagen,- *20*
trumpet die Trompete,-n *8*
trunk die Kiste,-n *11; trunk (car)* der Kofferraum,ʺe *19*
to **try** versuchen *9;* probieren *12*
to **try on** anprobieren *6*
tub der Kübel,- *20*
Tuesday der Dienstag *2*
to **turn out** sich herausstellen *12*
twelve zwölf *2*
twenty zwanzig *2*
to **twist** schlängeln *20*
two zwei *1*
to **type** tippen *20*
typewriter die Schreibmaschine,-n *20*
typical typisch *A*

U

unbelievable unglaublich *19*
uncle der Onkel,- *5*
to **understand** verstehen *(verstand, verstanden) 4*
unforgetful unvergeßlich *12*
unfortunately leider *B*

unique einzigartig *D*
United States die Vereinigten Staaten *3*
unity die Einheit *12; Day of Unity* Tag der Einheit *12*
university die Universität,-en *4;* die Hochschule,-n *15*
unsatisfactory ungenügend *4*
unthinkable undenkbar *17*
until bis *2; not until* erst *11*
up and down auf und ab *C*
urgent eilig *16*
us uns *5*
to **use** gebrauchen *4*
usher der Platzanweiser,- *5*
usual üblich *16*
usually gewöhnlich *14*

V

vacation die Ferien (pl.) *9;* der Urlaub,-e *14;* die Erholung, -en *20; to spend the vacation* den Urlaub verbringen *17; to take vacation* Urlaub nehmen *20; to go on vacation* Urlaub machen *20*
vacation country das Ferienland,ʺer *5*
vacationer der Urlauber,- *20*
vacation place der Ferienort,-e *18*
vacation trip die Ferienreise,-n *14; to be on a vacation trip* auf einer Ferienreise sein *14*
valuable wertvoll *13*
veal fricassee das Kalbsfrikassee *20*
vegetable das Gemüse *12; kind of vegetable* die Gemüseart, -en *17*
vegetable soup die Gemüsesuppe,-n *16*
vegetable stand der Gemüsestand,ʺe *17*
vehicle das Fahrzeug,-e *14*
very sehr *3*
victim das Opfer,- *7*
Viennese der Wiener,- *13*
view der Blick *4;* die Aussicht, -en *16*
to **view** besichtigen *10*

village das Dorf,⸚er *15;* die Ortschaft,-en *20*
vine die Rebe,-n *20;* der Rebstock,⸚e *20*
vineyard der Weinberg,-e *16;* der Weingarten,⸚ *20*
vintage die Weinlese,-n *20*
violin die Geige,-n *8*
visit der Besuch,-e *13*
to **visit** besuchen *5*
visitor der Besucher,- *6*
vocabulary word die Vokabel,-n *4*
volleyball der Volleyball *20*
volleyball player der Volleyballspieler,- *20*

W

to **wait** warten *2; to wait for* warten auf *A*
to **wait on** bedienen *11*
waiter der Kellner,- *16*
waiting room der Wartesaal, -säle *19*
waitress die Kellnerin,-nen *16*
to **walk** zu Fuß gehen *3*
to **walk along** entlanggehen *(ging entlang, ist entlanggegangen) 16*
waltz der Walzer,- *8*
to **want to** wollen *(will, wollte, gewollt) 5*
wardrobe der Schrank,⸚e *15*
warm warm *7*
to **warn** warnen *8*
to **wash (oneself)** sich waschen *(wäscht, wusch, gewaschen) 11*
watch die Uhr,-en *2*
to **watch** aufpassen *9;* zusehen *(sieht zu, sah zu, zugesehen) 12;* beobachten *16; to watch TV* fernsehen *(sieht fern, sah fern, ferngesehen) 5*
water das Wasser *12*
water container der Wasserbehälter,- *9*
water traffic der Wasserverkehr *8*
waterway die Wasserstraße,-n *8*
watery wässerig *10*
to **wave** wehen *14*

to **wave at** zuwinken *10*
way der Weg,-e *2;* die Weise *15; on the way* auf dem Weg *2;* unterwegs *10; way to school* der Schulweg,-e *3; by the way* übrigens *14; in this way* auf diese Weise *15*
we wir *1*
weather das Wetter *7*
wedding die Hochzeit,-en *12*
wedding carriage die Hochzeitskutsche,-n *12*
wedding guest der Hochzeitsgast,⸚e *12*
wedding ring der Trauring,-e *12*
Wednesday der Mittwoch *2*
weekend das Wochenende,-n *14*
to **weigh** wiegen *(wog, gewogen) 14*
weight das Gewicht,-e *19*
well na *2;* wohl *16;* gesund *18; to feel well* sich wohl fühlen *18*
well-behaved brav *15*
well-known bekannt *5*
west der Westen *3*
western westlich *20*
wet maß *12*
wharf der Kai,-s *13*
what was *1; what kind of* was für *4*
wheel chair der Rollstuhl,⸚e *9; wheel chair driver* der Rollstuhlfahrer,- *9*
when wann *2;* wenn *14*
whenever wenn *18*
where wo *1; where to* wohin *4; where from* woher *4*
whether ob *8*
which welcher *2*
while die Weile *2; a while* eine Weile *2*
white weiß *5*
who wer *2*
whole ganz *7*
why warum *2*
wide breit *D*
wife die Frau,-en *10;* die Ehefrau,-en *12*
to **win** gewinnen *(gewann, gewonnen) 5*
wind der Wind,-e *12*
to **wind** schlängeln *20*
window das Fenster,- *10*

to **wind past** sich vorbeischlängeln an *20*
windshield die Windschutzscheibe,-n *19*
wine der Wein,-e *9*
wine bottle die Weinflasche,-n *16*
wine festival das Weinfest,-e *20*
wine-growing der Weinbau *20*
wine-growing area das Weinbaugebiet,-e *20*
winery das Weingut,⸚er *20*
wine test die Weinprobe,-n *20*
winner der Sieger,- *9*
winter der Winter *4*
wise vernünftig *18*
wish der Wunsch,⸚e *20*
to **wish** wünschen *10*
with mit *3;* bei *8*
within innerhalb *19*
without ohne *3*
wolf der Wolf,⸚e *15*
woman die Frau,-en *1*
wonder das Wunder,- *18*
to **wonder** gespannt sein *5*
woodcarving die Holzschnitzerei,-en *17*
word das Wort,⸚er *4*
word processor die Textverarbeitungsanlage,-n *20*
work die Arbeit,-en *2*
to **work** arbeiten *2;* wirken *18; Let's go to work!* 'Ran an die Arbeit! *8; It's working wonders.* Es wirkt Wunder. *18; That works out well.* Das klappt prima. *20*
worker der Arbeiter,- *20*
workshop die Werkstatt,⸚e *19*
to **work together** zusammenarbeiten *15*
world die Welt,-en *7*
world-famous weltberühmt *10*
would: would like to möchten *5*
to **wrap(up)** einwickeln *17*
to **write** schreiben *(schrieb, geschrieben) 2; to write (out) a prescription* ein Rezept verschreiben *18*
to **write down** aufschreiben *(schrieb auf, aufgeschrieben) 14*
written schriftlich *15*

**wrong: What's wrong with
you?** Was fehlt dir denn? *18*

Y

year das Jahr,-e *2*
yellow gelb *6*
yes ja *1*
yesterday gestern *9*
yet noch *2*
to **yield** gewähren *19; Yield the
right of way!* Vorfahrt
gewähren! *19*
you du *1;* ihr *1;* Sie *1;* man *3*
young jung *11*
youngster der Jugendliche,-n *7*
your dein *4;* Ihr *6*
youth die Jugend *C*
youth hostel die
Jugendherberge,-n *7*
youth hostel director der
Herbergsvater,- *7*
**youth hostel identification
(card)** der
Jugendherbergsausweis,-e *7*
Yugoslavia Jugoslawien *5*

Z

zebra das Zebra,-s *15*
zero null *1*
zip code die Postleitzahl,-en *14*
zoo der Zoo,-s *15*

Abbreviations

Acknowledgements

The author wishes to express his gratitude to the many people in Germany (BRD and DDR), Austria and Switzerland who assisted in the photography scenes for the textbook and the filmstrips. Particularly helpful was Panorama DDR, an organization that set up all the requested photography sessions in the German Democratic Republic. Special thanks should also go to those people who cooperated in setting up photography sessions in the other German-speaking countries: Christoph Arend (Freiburg), Familie Heinz Devrient (Köln), Herr Wolfgang Kaul (Stuttgart), Frau Lotte Löffler (Wien), Herr und Frau Dieter Messner (Lienz), Herr Donatus Moosauer (Deggendorf), Herr und Frau Uwe Schweyer (München), Familie Ingomar Stainer (München), Herr und Frau Helmut Strunk (Essen), Herr Dr. Hartmut Voigt (Düsseldorf).

Furthermore, the author would like to pay tribute to those professionals who contributed in the creative effort beyond the original manuscript: Rosemary J. Barry (Editor), Cyril John Schlosser (Designer) and Chris Wold Dyrud (Illustrator).

Last but not least, the author would like to thank his wife, Rosie, and his two daughters, Heidi and Marci, for showing such tremendous patience during the development of this series and for their valuable contributions before, during and after the extensive trip throughout German-speaking countries.

The following German instructors provided valuable comments for the revision of *Deutsch:Aktuell:*
Norma Ackley, South High School, Milwaukee, Wisconsin; *Sandra K. Benzer,* Urban Junior High School, Sheboygan, Wisconsin; *F. P. Boost,* McNary Senior High School, Salem, Oregon; *Edward H. Bray, Jr.,* Wissachickon Middle School, Ambler, Pennsylvania; *Anita Brückler,* Muskingum College, New Concord, Ohio; *Marge Burk,* Covington Latin School, Covington, Kentucky; *James Caputo,* Wooster High School, Wooster, Ohio; *Lydia Colson,* Cuyahoga Community College, Parma, Ohio; *Fred Covey,* Drake University, Des Moines, Iowa; *Leslie F. Darmek,* University of Arizona, Tucson, Arizona; *William R. Davis,* University of New Hampshire, Durham, New Hampshire; *Craig Deville,* University of Arizona, Tucson, Arizona; *Lucie M. Dilger,* Yorktown High School, Arlington, Virginia; *Lee Dury,* Sauk Prairie High School, Sauk City, Wisconsin; *Wendell Frye,* Hartwick College, Oneonta, New York; *Christa M. Fumea,* Northeast High School, St. Petersburg, Florida; *Karl-Heinz Gabbey,* Buffalo Grove High School, Buffalo Grove, Illinois; *Jacqueline S. Gnagi,* Perry A. Tipler Middle School, Oshkosh, Wisconsin; *Inez Good,* Roanoke College, Salem, Virginia; *Larry Hall,* Sewickley Academy, Sewickley, Pennsylvania; *Jerome P. Harper,* Carson-Newman College, Jefferson City, Tennessee; *Barbara A. Heck,* Arlington High School, Arlington Heights, Illinois; *Richard C. Helt,* University of Arizona, Tucson, Arizona; *Ursula F. Hidebrandt,* Libertyville High School, Libertyville, Illinois; *Frank D. Hirschbach,* University of Minnesota, Minneapolis, Minnesota; *Bradley A. Holtman,* Monroe High School, Monroe, Wisconsin; *Jörg Homberger,* Warwick High School, Lititz, Pennsylvania; *Kim P. Icsman,* Ursuline Academy, Cincinnati, Ohio; *Marie E. Ingram-Helt,* University of Arizona, Tucson, Arizona; *G. F. Jeffries,* North Hills High School, Pittsburgh, Pennsylvania; *Al Johnson,* Austin High School, Austin, Minnesota; *Thomas Kamla,* University of Scranton, Scranton, Pennsylvania; *Guido Kauls,* Minnehaha Academy, Minneapolis, Minnesota; *John Kelly,* Trinity High School, Manchester, New Hampshire; *Nancy M. King,* Parkview High School, Liburn, Georgia; *Peter E. Klose,* Grand Blanc High School, Grand Blanc, Michigan; *George Kopecky,* West Torrance High School, Torrance, California; *Helga Lange,* Cuyahoga Valley Christian Academy, Cuyahoga Falls, Ohio; *Lowell E. Lee,* St. Louis Park Junior High School, St. Louis Park, Minnesota; *Jane Lienau,* Lutheran High School West, Detroit, Michigan; *A. H. Loewenstein,* Scottsdale High School, Scottsdale, Arizona; *Maimu Looke,* Harrison High School, Farmington, Michigan; *Mary Mateer,* DeWitt Middle School, Ithaca, New York; *Reverend J. Anthony Meis,* Bishop McNamara High School, Kankakee, Illinois; *Paul J. Nagy,* North Iowa Area Community College, Mason City, Iowa; *Lisa Oas,* Lakeview Christian Academy, Duluth, Minnesota; *Heinz J. Otto,* The Blake Schools, Minneapolis, Minnesota; *Reverend Ronald V. Perry,* Fairfield Prep School, Fairfield, Connecticut; *Martha Pleggenkuhle,* St. Ansgar Senior High School, St. Ansgar, Iowa; *Patricia Priolo,* Central High School, Scranton, Pennsylvania; *Donald E. Ruhde,* Iowa Falls High School, Iowa Falls, Iowa; *Mary Sexton,* Hamilton High School, Hamilton, Montana; *Gerlinde Sly,* Rockland Community College, Suffern, New York; *William Small,* University of Maine, Orono, Maine; *Debra Starkey,* Mitchell High School, Mitchell, Nebraska; *Michael Still,* De La Salle High School, Concord, California; *Reverend Keven Storek,* Lutheran High School, Rockford, Illinois; *Terry Mitchell Strohm,* West Chicago High School, West Chicago, Illinois; *Elvira Stromberg,* Shorecrest High School, Seattle, Washington; *Ronald Swanson,* Oshkosh North High School, Oshkosh, Wisconsin; *Ingrid von Reitzenstein,* Mundelein High School, Mundelein, Illinois; *Brigitte Wichmann,* Hanover College, Hanover, Indiana; *Hannelore Wilfert,* Russell Sage College, Troy, New York; *Tony Young,* Tokay High School, Lodi, California; *Hans R. Zumpft,* North High School, Sheboygan, Wisconsin.

Photo Credits

All the photos in the *Deutsch: Aktuell 2* (2nd edition) textbook not taken by the author have been provided by the following:

Austrian National Tourist Office: page 19 (center right and bottom left)

Benkert, Christine: cover (flags)

Deidesheim (Tourist Information): page 47 (bottom right)

Devrient, Heinz: pages 47 (top left and top center), 151 (all), 152

Fremdenverkehrsverband Bodensee-Oberschwaben e.V.: page 23 (bottom right)

Fremdenverkehrsverband München-Oberbayern e.V.: pages 24 (right), 72 (bottom right), 72 (left), 263 (right)

Fremdenverkehrsverband Rheinland-Pfalz e.V.: page 259 (top left)

German Information Center: pages 47 (center left and center right), 76, 128, 209 (top right and bottom right)

German Rail: page 23 (top left)

Inter Nationes: pages 259 (bottom right), 264 (bottom left)

Landesbildstelle Berlin: page 23 (bottom left)

Landesfremdenverkehrsverband Baden-Württemberg e.V.: pages 47 (bottom left and bottom center), 95, 155, 182 (top left, top center, top right, center left, center and center right), 210 (right), 211, 259 (top right, center right and center left)

Landeshauptstadt München Fremdenverkehrsamt: page 70 (top left, bottom right and center right)

Landeshauptstadt Stuttgart Verkehrsamt: page 259 (bottom left)

Lufthansa German Airlines: pages 24 (left), 47 (top right and center), 70 (center left), 206 (top right), 230 (all), 263 (center)

Moosauer, Donatus: pages 188 (top and bottom), 212 (top and bottom), 214, 225 (all), 266 (top and bottom), 268, 271 (all)

Panorama DDR: pages 97 (left bottom and bottom right), 98 (left), 126 (left and bottom right)

Schroder, Frank (Tannenblick Studio): pages 156 (top right), 157 (left and right), 187, 206 (center left), 209 (top left and bottom left)

Stokes, Jim: page 137 (center)

Teubner (Studio für Lebensmittelfotografie): pages 160 (left, center and right), 161 (all), 162 (all)